Hermeneutics, Inerrancy, and the Bible

Hermeneutics, Inerrancy, and the Bible

Edited by
Earl D. Radmacher
and
Robert D. Preus

HERMENEUTICS, INERRANCY, AND THE BIBLE

ACADEMIE BOOKS is an imprint of Zondervan Publishing House
1415 Lake Drive, S.E., Grand Rapids, Michigan 49506

Library of Congress Cataloging in Publication Data

Main entry under title:

Hermeneutics, inerrancy, and the Bible.

Includes bibliographical references.
1. Bible—Hermeneutics—Addresses, essays, lectures. 2. Bible—Evidences, authority, etc.—Addresses, essays, lectures. I. Radmacher, Earl D. II. Preus, Robert D., 1924- . III. International Council on Biblical Inerrancy.
BS476.H477 1984 220.6'01 83-21881
ISBN 0-310-37081-7

Designed by Mark Hunt

Printed in the United States of America

84 85 86 87 88 89 / 10 9 8 7 6 5 4 3 2 1

CONTENTS

Publisher's Note

This volume is a record of the ICBI Summit II proceedings; the papers are reproduced essentially in the form in which they were presented at the conference. The reader will therefore find inconsistencies in style and form among the various papers and responses.

General Editor's Introduction

This book is part of a series of scholarly works sponsored by the International Council on Biblical Inerrancy (ICBI). They include the following areas:

GENERAL —*Inerrancy* (Zondervan, 1979), Norman L. Geisler, ed.
PHILOSOPHICAL—*Biblical Errancy: Its Philosophical Roots* (Zondervan, 1981), Norman L. Geisler, ed.
THEOLOGICAL—*Challenges to Inerrancy* (Moody, 1984), Gordon Lewis and Bruce Demarest, eds.
HISTORICAL—*Inerrancy and the Church* (Moody, 1984), John Hanna, ed.
HERMENEUTICS—*Hermeneutics, Inerrancy, and the Bible* (Zondervan, 1984, Earl Radmacher and Robert Preus, eds.

The ICBI is a coalition of Christian scholars who believe that the reaffirmation and defense of biblical inerrancy is crucial to the life and vitality of the Christian church. In addition to these scholarly books, the council has produced two landmark statements: "The Chicago Statement on Inerrancy" (1978), and "The Chicago Statement on Hermeneutics" (1982). These two documents represent a consensus of evangelical scholarship on these fundamental topics.

The ICBI does not endorse every point made by the authors of this book, although all the writers are in agreement with the ICBI stand on inerrancy. Freedom of expression of this commitment was exercised throughout the various books. All wrote with the hope that believers in Christ will become increasingly assured of the firm foundation for our faith in God's inerrant Word.

Norman L. Geisler
General Editor, ICBI

Introduction

"Biblical authority is an empty notion unless we know how to determine what the Bible means." In these words, James Packer, member of the International Council on Biblical Inerrancy, capsulized the challenge that faced ICBI and all others who are committed to the maxim, "What Scripture says, God says." When we have declared, delineated, and defended the Bible's teaching concerning its own inerrancy, however, we have not yet completed the solution to the problem of biblical authority—at least as far as its interpretation and practical application to our lives are concerned. To close this gap, we must answer the question, "How do we know what God means by what He says in His inerrant and infallible Word?" Awareness of this need led ICBI to Summit II in Chicago on November 10–13, 1982.

The chapters of this book give us the papers and responses that were prepared for Summit II which was the culmination of a two-year project of determining the significant issues germane to the problem of interpretation, selecting qualified scholars to research and write on each of the issues, choosing responders of diverse opinions who would evaluate the papers, and, finally, convening panels to discuss the issues with a view to greater understanding and, hopefully, practical and useful solutions—thus allowing the inerrant Word of God to become dynamic in our lives by "handling accurately the word of truth."

It may be helpful for the reader of this work to know how the participants in Summit II operated. Considerably before the time of Summit II, a notebook of all of the papers and responses was sent to each of the participants so that they could be familiar with their content before the Summit. Then a panel of five members (author, two responders, and two others) and a moderator were assigned to each topic for a two-hour discussion of problem areas in the topic. This was culminated with a listing of summary principles considered significant for the drafting committee to include in the final statement of affirmations and denials. Finally, the drafting committee spent major portions of several days and nights producing the Articles of Affirmation and Denial (see Appendix A). One member of the committee, Norm Geisler, was asked to write a brief commentary on the Articles (see Appendix B), and another member, Jim Packer, was asked to present the Exposition on Biblical Hermeneutics (see Appendix C).

The warm appreciation and enthusiastic expressions at the final, plenary session of Summit II made all of the months of preparation worthwhile. Much ground was gained toward the goal. But there is still much more to do by way of refinement of the principles and development of relevant and legitimate application to life. As the reader approaches the papers of this volume, he will find some minor and some major areas of concern. Among the minor concerns will be erroneous phraseology, such as "original autographs," rather than simply "autographs"; "divinely inspired authors," rather than "divinely inspired writings"; etc. No attempt has been made to achieve consistency in such expressions, nor have we sought to create uniformity in outlining, footnoting, transliterating, or Scripture quotation. In like fashion, we have not edited out positions which may be unacceptable to ICBI. In so doing, we have preserved the writings as basic historical documents of the meeting.

Among the major areas of concern that still need further investigation are the following:

1. How can we avoid the tendency to use the term "figurative" as antithetical to "literal" interpretation? Such statements as "We interpret literally *except* . . ." simply do not fit Article XV.
2. Is it really appropriate to speak of "dual authorship" of Scripture? Does the idea of "primary author" and "secondary author" really reflect a biblical view of authorship?
3. Are terms such as "fuller sense" and "canonical process" really compatible with the "single sense meaning" of Scripture as expressed in Article VII? Is meaning determined by subsequent revelation?
4. Is "authorial intention" a poor term to use for expressing the meaning of the author as found in the text? Does it lend itself to the more speculative historical-critical method?
5. Where are the lines to be drawn in the use of cultural accommodation and critical techniques lest God's message to

us in Scripture be evaporated? How can we prevent hermeneutical leakage from the gains we have achieved for biblical authority in the inerrancy debate?

6. How do we relate all of the foregoing to the Scripture's presentation of its own perspicuity? How can we keep from stealing the Scriptures from the common person for whom they were written?
7. Finally, in the process of determining the singular meaning of the text of Scripture, will we be equally aggressive in determining its significance for our own personal lives?

We have learned. We have grown. We are far from having all the answers. But we can all heartily join Dr. Carl Henry in the aspirations expressed in the closing plenary address of Summit II:

> I hope . . . that we have yet to see the best of a movement that holds Spirit and Scripture together as the risen Lord would have us do as He rules His Church through the Spirit by the Scriptures. May these days of fettering Scripture have brought us low before God, without Whose Word our cause is barren; before the risen Jesus, without Whose triumph over death the joy and power of Christian fulfillment would be gone; before the Holy Spirit, Who yearns to fill us daily with virtues that even now sample the age to come; and before the Bible, that we may be even more prone both to defend and to read it.
>
> God said, "Let my people go," meaning free them from bondage and let them take the place in the world that I seek for them. "Let it go" seems now to say to us, "Let my Bible go": go beyond the limitations imposed by critics, beyond the walls of cloisters and churches, beyond even evangelical reticence and timidity; give it free and full scope in the world. Let the earth hear my voice.

Surely, we still do see through a glass darkly. But we are able to see sufficiently of the glory of the Lord in order to keep on being metamorphosed into the image of Christ our Lord.

Earl D. Radmacher, Chairman of Summit II
and Co-Editor with Robert D. Preuss

Truth: Relationship of Theories of Truth to Hermeneutics

John S. Feinberg
Professor of Systematic Theology
Trinity Evangelical Divinity School

1. Truth: Relationship of Theories of Truth to Hermeneutics

John S. Feinberg

As Jesus stood before Pilate, He claimed to testify to the truth, saying that all who were of the truth listened to Him. Pilate responded, "What is truth?" (Jn. 18:38). Pilate did not wait for an answer, but even if he had, it is not clear that there would be an easy answer to the question. Although ordinary language usage seems to presuppose that people know what truth and falsity are, when one begins to analyze the notion of truth, he finds it to be a very elusive concept. Certainly, this has been the case as the notion has come under discussion in contemporary debates over the inerrancy of Scripture. For example, Mickelsen notes that the problem of Scripture's truthfulness is confusing, since the biblical authors seem to use different standards of accuracy in their reporting of material (different from one another and different from modern standards). Moreover, it is claimed that unless those standards can be specified, any discussion about the truth or falsity of Scripture is hopelessly confused.[1] David Hubbard, reflecting on the difficulties involved in the use of the terms 'inerrancy', 'error', and 'infallibility', argues that the words need to be defined in terms of theological usage as determined from Scripture, not on the basis of modern usage of the words or modern standards of truth. According to Hubbard, the problem with many adherents of inerrancy is that their practice is the latter and not the former.[2] From such comments as these it becomes quite clear that if inerrancy is to be defined in terms of truth (as seems the sanest procedure[3]), then participants in the debate over biblical inerrancy need clarification on the meaning of truth.

If the issue of biblical inerrancy is beclouded because of problems surrounding the concept of truth, it is even more confused when taken in conjunction with problems surrounding meaning. Before one can ever determine the truth or falsity of any given statement, he must first determine what it means. But, herein lies the problem, for the notion of meaning is at least as elusive as the notion of truth.

What does it mean to say that a sentence has meaning? How does one determine the meaning of any given sentence? Must one be able to specify a sentence's truth conditions in order for it to have meaning? Unfortunately, there are no easy answers to such questions, but answers are needed in preparation for reflecting on the truth or falsity of any meaningful statement in or out of Scripture.

The issues of the meaning of the concepts of meaning and truth and the relation of the two are at the forefront in contemporary philosophy of language as well as at issue in the contemporary biblical inerrancy debate. Such issues are complex, and one must carefully distinguish what is and is not at issue. When discussing meaning and truth, one could be asking for (1) an analysis of the meaning of the *terms* 'meaning' and 'truth', (2) an analysis of the *concepts* of meaning and truth, or (3) a theory of meaning and a theory of truth. If (1) is the emphasis, then one is asking for an explanation of the various *uses* of the words in different contexts. Such a discussion will not of necessity reflect anything about what truth and meaning *are*; it will only reflect the way the terms are used in ordinary language.[4] On the other hand, if (2) is the emphasis, then one is asking questions about what sorts of things truth and meaning are. Finally, if the focus is (3), then one is asking for an explanation of what it is for a sentence to be true and what it is for a sentence to have meaning. In answering questions about theories of truth and meaning, it seems that one will also wind up answering questions about the concept of truth. Upon reflection it becomes evident that the conceptual and theoretical issues, not the matter of linguistic usage, bring us to the heart of the inerrancy debate. Those issues are the emphasis of this paper.

Once the issues are clarified, the difficult questions concerning them must be addressed. However, it is my contention that there are some fundamental confusions even in the initial understanding of the questions of meaning and truth. Those must be removed before the more substantive issues can be handled. Consequently, in this study I shall be arguing the following six main theses: (1) The questions about *what it means to say* of any sentence that it *has* meaning and of any statement that it *is* true are *ontological*; (2) the questions of *whether* any specific statement is true or false and *whether* any specific sentence has meaning are *epistemological*, and thus, differ from the questions asked under (1); (3) much of the confusion in the debate over the truth and meaning of Scripture comes from looking at the *epistemological* questions, thinking incorrectly that the answering of such questions actually answers the *ontological* questions, and then, upon finding such epistemological questions hard to answer, concluding that we do not know what truth is; (4) some theories of truth are, in fact, more harmful to upholding an inerrant Bible than others, but no genuine theory of truth per se (an ontological matter) confirms or disconfirms whether the Bible is inerrant (an epistemological matter); (5) thus, the ultimate issue of whether Scripture is inerrant cannot be solved solely by getting clear on a proper theory of truth, for such a matter is preliminary to the epistemological issues involved in the actual confirmation or disconfirmation of the Bible's inerrancy; and (6) consequently, failure to resolve the epistemological issues does not indicate any impossibility in resolving the ontological ones, nor can the inerrancy debate legitimately be dropped because of any impossibility of knowing what truth is.

In attempting to support these six theses, my primary concern will be to elucidate the ontological issues, but not to the total exclusion of the epistemological ones. The discussion begins with the matter of truth and then turns to meaning.

I. THE ISSUE OF TRUTH

Many important questions can be asked about truth, but I shall address only three major ones. First, what are the bearers of truth? Second, what does it mean to say of any sentence that it is true, i.e., what sort of thing is truth and what does it mean to say of a sentence that it is true? These are ontological questions. Finally, how does one know whether any statement is true or false? Such questions are epistemological, and are at the heart of the debate on inerrancy.

A. Truth Bearers

In laying the groundwork for the discussion of truth bearers, it is necessary to begin by distinguishing several terms to be used in this study. The first is 'utterance', and Kneale explains that an "utterance is a particular vocal sound or sequence of such sounds. Like other sounds, utterances are common perceptible objects, although of course not material."[5] An utterance may be a sentence, but it need not be, and consequently, "not all utterances even belong to a language."[6] A sentence, on the other hand, is a linguistic formula which has a pattern that might be reduplicated by other examples. Sentences are of varying kinds, e.g., declarative sentences, questions, interjections, and commands. Some philosophers like to distinguish between sentences and statements or assertions,[7] whereas others use the words synonymously, especially when referring to a declarative sentence which asserts something to be the case.[8] Mackie even distinguishes in regard to statements the act of stating something, some kind of performance, and the content of the act, that which is stated.[9] In this study, I shall use 'statement' to refer to declarative sentences, and the focus will be the content of the act, though such content does not designate an abstract entity. 'Sentence' will be used primarily to refer to linguistic units which are questions, commands, or interjections, though, of course, it can also serve for declarative sentences (statements). Finally, some philosophers use the terms 'statement' and 'proposition' synonymously.[10] However, propositions are taken by some to refer to the meanings of sentences, and such meanings are exalted to the ontological status of abstract entities.[11] Because the association of propositions with abstract entities is so notoriously problematic in philosophy, I shall refrain from using the term.[12]

Are utterances, sentences, or statements the bearers of truth? First, an utterance must be ruled out, since it is merely the act of expressing a sound. Such acts and sounds per se are neither true nor false, nor do they bear truth. They are just in the world upon the act of the utterer. Second, sentences are ruled out, for no linguistic formula is true or false simply by being formed, nor does it bear truth or falsity. In fact, some kinds of sentences cannot be the bearers of truth (e.g., questions, commands, interjections), for such sentences are incapable of being either true or false.[13] That leaves statements (declarative sentences) as the only candidate. I agree with Mackie that such are the bearers of truth, for statements enable us to speak of the content of what is said, and it is that content that is either true or false.[14] The *content* of what is stated is the bearer of truth, and the *act* of making a statement is what commits one in some way, as Jager suggests,[15] to the *belief* that the content of the statement is true.

Since only declarative sentences (statements) can be true or false, the scope of the inerrancy debate must be significantly limited, if one defines inerrancy in terms of truth. Nonetheless, there are still plenty of sentences in Scripture that are capable of bearing truth, and thus, the investigation is worthwhile.

B. Theories of Truth

If statements are the bearers of truth, what is truth itself? Is it a property of statements, a relationship involving statements, or what?

Moreover, once one determines what truth is, what does it mean to say a statement is true, i.e., how exactly do statements bear truth? Such questions are addressed by various theories of truth. Many answers have been given historically, but because of the scope of this study, I shall present only the major theories.[16]

Correspondence Theory of Truth

The correspondence theory has historically been the most prevalent theory of truth.[17] According to this theory, truth is not an entity, nor is it a property of statements.[18] On the contrary, central to the correspondence theory is the notion that truth is a *relationship* of some sort between language and world. Specifying the exact nature of that relationship has never been an easy task. Aristotle simply stated, "To say of what is that it is not, or of what is not that it is, is false, while to say of what is that it is, or of what is not that it is not is true."[19] While Aristotle's statement of the theory does not resolve all the problems with correspondence theories, it does convey the central notion that language relates to the world by way of correspondence or non-correspondence. Problems in specifying that relationship arise in three areas: (1) what aspect of *language* is it that corresponds? (2) what is it about the *world* that corresponds to language? and (3) what exactly is this relation of corresponding?

In regard to (1), there are various answers. Some suggest that sentences are what correspond. However, this cannot be the case for many types of sentences such as questions, commands, and interjections. Even declarative sentences simply as linguistic formulae are not the bearers of truth. Instead, the content of what they declare bears truth and is the item which corresponds. Though it seems most likely that statements are what correspond to the world, even here one must carefully distinguish between the act of stating and that which is stated. As Strawson argues, if the correspondence theory is to be usable at all, it must be statements (in the sense of the content that is stated), not the acts of stating, which correspond to the world.[20]

Not only are these items under debate, but there is even greater uncertainty about what in the *world* is the basis for correspondence. To say that the world, reality, corresponds to statements is far too vague, for one wants to know what about the world or reality corresponds to any given statement. An initially attractive view is that facts correspond to statements, but Sommers expresses the problem with using facts when he writes:

> For one primary meaning of 'fact' is "what a statement, when true, states" (Strawson). Another meaning is simply "true statement." Either use presupposes a meaning for 'true'; 'fact' in either of these two senses cannot be used to define truth. It is moreover obvious that what a statement states cannot be the objective relatum responsible for its truth. Those who wish to identify "something in the world" as the correspondence relatum for truth, choose badly if they choose facts.[21]

Though Sommers admits he is using 'fact' in a rather narrow sense, if 'fact' is taken to have such meanings as suggested, a fact cannot be in the world, and thus, cannot be a proper object for correspondence between word and world.[22] In view of such problems, those who hold to a correspondence theory generally claim that words relate to states of affairs that obtain in the world.

If the relata of the correspondence relation are debatable, so is the relationship of correspondence itself. As Pitcher notes, there are at least two major kinds of correspondence. According to the first kind, correspondence-as-correlation, one object or set of objects is correlated to (made to fit) another object or set of objects according to some rule which relates them. The other kind of correspondence, correspondence-as-congruity, is a relation according to which two things agree with or are in harmony with one another.[23] Those who hold a correspondence theory traditionally have opted for correspondence-as-congruity, their point being that in some way the statement agrees with a state of affairs.[24]

In sum, according to the correspondence theory, statements are true or false, and what makes them so is their congruity or incongruity with states of affairs. Truth is a relation between word and world.

Coherence Theory of Truth

Many who reject the correspondence theory opt for this theory. According to this theory, truth is a relation, but it is a relation between statements and statements. The view is that a statement is true if it coheres with or is non-contradictory of a set of other statements which also cohere with one another.[25] Each statement of the set is said to be tied to every other statement by means of logical implication. In fact, some who hold the theory claim that each statement of the system implies every other member of the system, and thus, one cannot know the truth of any given statement apart from the truth of the *whole* system.[26] Such a theory has been held by such philosophers as Leibniz, Spinoza, Hegel, and Bradley.

While the coherence theory seems appropriate for analytic and a priori statements, one wonders why proponents of the theory feel it is also most appropriate for empirical statements. The basic reason given by many who reject the correspondence theory in favor of the coherence theory is that the correspondence theory supposedly relates language and the world, but no one can ever get to the world unmediated by "direct apprehension."[27]

Though the coherence theory is somewhat attractive and has had many an able defender,[28] there are some serious difficulties with it. First, the most frequent complaint is that it is possible to produce several systems which contradict one another but individually are internally consistent. Moreover, a statement may appear in several contradictory systems and cohere with each. The upshot is that it is entirely possible to construct an internally consistent system of error. Dauer, in defending the coherence theory, argues that there is a safeguard against such a problem, viz., only the reports of competent speaker-observers will be incorporated into the system. Dauer explains:

> The coherence theory adopts the maxim of trusting observers until there are reasons to doubt them. Thus, any speaker-observer is competent (at a given moment) unless his observation statement is incompatible with those of others. When such a conflict arises, the minimum requirement is that the observation statements of those eventually judged to be competent are consistent with one another.[29]

According to Dauer, such a method eliminates the possibility of two incompatible but equally internally consistent systems of statements.[30] Dauer's remarks beg the question about who qualifies as a competent speaker-observer, but they also point to a second difficulty with the coherence theory. The observation statement that proves to be incompatible with the other observation statements about the same object is said to be wrong, but why? How does one know that the one statement is wrong and the majority who observe something different are right? If the answer is that this theory of truth demands it, the question is begged. On the other hand, if the coherence theorist rejects the statement that does not cohere *without begging the question* about the accuracy of the majority of cohering statements, it seems that the only justification in so doing is that the observation sentences of the many reflect the world. However, if that is the only justification, then the coherence theory reduces to the correspondence theory.[31]

Pragmatic Theory of Truth

The pragmatic theory of truth is associated with such philosophers as Charles Pierce, William James, and John Dewey. Though each held a different form of the theory, there are some basic conceptions held in common. A pragmatic theory of truth rejects the idea that a thought is true when it conforms to reality, for such a "copy" approach is held to be beyond human ability to attain. The basic notion behind the pragmatic theory is that truth has some social function, some practical value.[32] Statements are true when they prove to be workable, useful, fruitful to one's ends.[33] Given such a view of truth, however, truth becomes relative to the individual at a particular time.[34]

One form of the pragmatic theory which seems to be held by some influential contemporary errantists is labelled by Geisler the intentionality view of truth.[35] According to this theory, a statement is true if it accomplishes its intended function, whereas it is false if it fails to do so.[36] Such a theory is clearly a form of the pragmatic theory of truth, and Berkouwer is one who seems to hold it. When speaking of the time-boundedness of biblical statements, Berkouwer argues that many such statements turn out to be false, if one analyzes truth and falsity according to a correspondence theory.[37] Indeed, such a conception of inerrancy has led many a thinker when confronted with alleged factual inaccuracies to question the very God-breathed nature of Scripture, according to Berkouwer. He claims that this is an erroneous conception of inerrancy (as well as involving a wrong view of truth). The crucial question is not whether the biblical data correspond to what one knows at a given point in history to be true, but rather whether the statements of Scripture fulfill their intended purpose. If they fulfill the author's intention, there is no grounds for debate about the reliability of the biblical witness. Berkouwer summarizes the point as follows:

> This does not imply a dualistic theory of inspiration. For this unmistakable emphasis, as well as the reflection about the nature of faith, corresponds with the intention of Scripture itself. It offers explicit and implicit evidence that it is not a "gnostic" writing but the God-breathed Scripture oriented to the testimony of God's deeds, profitable for teaching, for reproof, for correction, and for training in righteousness (II Tim. 3:16). It is not that Scripture offers us no information but that the nature of this information is unique. It is governed by the *purpose* of God's revelation. The view of inspiration that forms the basis of the misunderstanding of this purpose considers "inerrancy"

> essential as a parallel characterization of reliability; that is a flight of fancy away from this purpose.[38]

In other words, appeal to "inerrancy" according to a correspondence notion of truth is beside the point. Instead, the Bible must fulfill its intended purpose, and that purpose has nothing to do with making statements that correspond to reality.

In response to the pragmatic theory in general and the intentionalist form of it in particular, several comments are appropriate. In regard to the intentionalist form of the theory, there is nothing wrong with focusing on the author's intentions, *so long as the emphasis is the author's intended meaning of a statement, not his intended result when the statement is used.* Focusing on intended results alone creates the following two problems. First, the pragmatic theory is problematic in that it relativizes truth according to what is useful to any given person at any given time. Thus, one can never say of any statement that it is necessarily true. Second, it allows statements which do not accurately reflect the world to be true, anyway, if they turn out to be useful, and it necessitates that statements which are in accord with reality become false if they are useless. For example, the statement 'Jesus Christ rose from the dead for the forgiveness of our sins' becomes false for anyone who finds it useless. Moreover, someone holding the *intentionalist* theory may not be disturbed about supposed scientific and historical inaccuracies in Scripture since they have nothing to do with the intention of Scripture to make men wise unto salvation. However, if he is consistent with the fundamental concepts of his theory of truth, he must admit that statements about the Resurrection are false for the one who finds them unusable, i.e., for anyone not led by them to salvation.[39] A final problem with any form of the pragmatic theory is that it confuses epistemology with ontology. The purpose of a theory of truth is to tell what truth is and what it means for a statement to be true—ontological issues—not to inform how to find or determine truth—an epistemological matter. The problem with pragmatic theories of truth is that they offer an epistemological answer to an ontological question, for they substitute a method of determining truth for an account of truth.

Semantic Theory of Truth

The semantic theory is a very widely accepted theory of truth among philosophers today. It is a form of the correspondence theory originated by Alfred Tarski. Several key concepts are involved in

Tarski's understanding of truth as a semantic conception. First, Tarski states that the basic conception of truth is that a sentence (and for Tarski, it must be a sentence in a particular language, for sentences have truth only within a particular language[40]) is true if it designates an existing state of affairs. Consequently, if a definition of truth is to conform to the basic notion, it must imply an equivalence such as the following: "The sentence 'snow is white' is true if, and only if, snow is white."[41] The sentence in single quotes is the *name* of the sentence, whereas the sentence on the right hand side of the equivalence is the sentence itself. Second, Tarski then moves to generalize the formula as follows:

> Let us consider any arbitrary sentence; we shall replace it by the letter '*p*.' We form the name of the sentence and replace it by another letter, say 'X.' We ask now what is the logical relation between the two sentences "X is true" and '*p*.' It is clear that from the point of view of our basic conception of truth these sentences are equivalent. In other words, the following equivalence holds:
>
> (T) *X is true if, and only if, p.*
>
> We shall call any such equivalence (with '*p*' replaced by any sentence of the language to which the word "*true*" refers, and 'X' replaced by a name of this sentence) an "*equivalence of the form* (T)."[42]

Tarski notes that equivalence (T) is not a definition of truth, but instead, the equivalence, when replaced by specific sentences and their names, explains wherein the truth of the sentence in question lies.

Third, Tarski explains that this conception of truth is a semantic one. He explains:

> *Semantics* is a discipline which, speaking loosely, *deals with certain relations between expressions of a language and the objects* (or "states of affairs") "*referred to*" *by those expressions*. As typical examples of semantic concepts we may mention the concepts of *designation*, *satisfaction*, and *definition* as these occur in the following examples:
>
> *the expression "the father of his country" designates (denotes) George Washington;*
>
> *snow satisfies the sentential function (the condition) "x is white";*
>
> *the equation "2 • x = 1" defines (uniquely determines) the number 1/2.*[43]

For Tarski, the word 'true' also expresses a semantic conception, for it "expresses a property (or denotes a class) of certain expressions, viz., of sentences."[44]

Finally, as for a definition of truth, Tarski opts for another semantic notion, satisfaction. Satisfaction is a relation between arbitrary objects and certain expressions which are called "sentential functions." For example, 'x is greater than y' is one such sentential function, and the numbers 5 for x and 3 for y satisfy the sentential function. Tarski says that to gain a definition of satisfaction "we indicate which objects satisfy the simplest sentential functions; and then we state the conditions under which given objects satisfy a compound function"[45] (such as disjunction or conjunction). The notion of satisfaction is applicable to sentences, sentential functions containing no free variables. Moreover, in regard to a sentence it is either satisfied by all objects or no objects. "Hence we arrive at a definition of truth and falsehood simply by saying that *a sentence is true if it is satisfied by all objects, and false otherwise*."[46] Tarski adds that this definition of truth implies all equivalences of the form (T). Thus, it is both materially adequate (relevant to (T)) and formally correct (relevant to the definition of truth in terms of satisfaction).[47]

The semantic theory, whether in Tarski's form or in a more current form as refined by Donald Davidson[48] has proved to be the most acceptable theory among contemporary philosophers. Equivalence (T) clearly seems to incorporate the key notions of a correspondence theory, viz., that truth is some kind of relation between language and world, and the theory's formal element (defining truth in terms of satisfaction) seems to avoid some problems which more traditional forms of the correspondence theory have encountered.

A Biblical Theory of Truth?

Are any of the theories of truth presented relevant to the Bible, or must one look for a different theory of truth as taught in Scripture? Though the question may initially seem strange, it is of no small import, for some claim that if we are to judge the errancy or inerrancy of Scripture, we must do so on the basis of Scripture's concepts of truth and error. Moreover, it is claimed that a concept of inerrancy defined in terms of formal accuracy (usually presupposing that statements correspond to the world) is foreign to Scripture's understanding of truth and error.

One of the commonly heard objections to the inerrantist's concept of error is that error theologically as defined by Scripture is not to be understood as some variation from formal standards of accuracy, but rather as willful deception. Hubbard explains:

> As used in the delicate theological discussions in which evangelicals are now engaged, error should surely be defined in theological terms derived from and limited to the Bible itself. Yet time and again in the arguments presented by those who purport to follow the Hodge-Warfield position words like *error,* or *inerrancy,* or *infallibility* are defined by secular, twentieth-century standards, sometimes with an appeal to Webster's Dictionary for support.
>
> We can no more define these terms from their use in common parlance, than we can define a biblical word like *love* on the basis of a popular song, or a concept like *covenant* with the use of Anglo-Saxon law. *Error* theologically must mean that which leads us astray from the will of God or the knowledge of this truth. The notion of *error* in Scripture is too important to be trivialized as it is in danger of being in the current discussion.[49]

Berkouwer similarly explains that the biblical writers were time-bounded in their statements, and consequently, they made some statements which are formally inaccurate. The problem with inerrantists, according to Berkouwer, is that they feel obligated to defend the truth of such inaccurate statements, anyway, but in so doing, they have missed the biblical concept of error. That concept involves sin and deception, not divergence from formal accuracy.[50]

Just as errantists argue that error must be defined biblically, so they demand that truth be defined biblically. The problem, of course, is that in Scripture there are various usages of the words for 'true' and 'truth'. As Thiselton notes, it is often argued that a common conception of truth takes its derivation from the Old Testament word *'ᵉmeṯ* which focuses on the faithfulness of God, not on some correspondence to facts. If one applies this notion to all of Scripture, he realizes that the biblical concept of truth is not abstract and theoretical, but grounded in the faithfulness of God.[51]

In view of such claims, can one speak about a biblical concept of truth in terms of the categories established by the philosophers? Such might seem impossible, but I strongly disagree. There seem to be several major difficulties with what Hubbard, Berkouwer, and others of their stripe are suggesting.

First, for the sake of argument grant Hubbard, Berkouwer, *et al.* their notion that the biblical concept of error is willful deception.

Their argument is that, given the time-boundedness of the biblical writer, he is obviously not omniscient. Thus, he may make some factually erroneous statements, even though he has no intention whatsoever to deceive anyone. Since the error is unintentional, the writer is not guilty of any sin, but the text still includes factual errors. While this may seem like an ingenious way to allow mistakes into the biblical text without bringing any condemnation against the biblical text or author, and while I suspect it is meant to safeguard the integrity of the doctrinal and practical sections of Scripture, it will not work. The initial problem is that it does not safeguard the truth of doctrinal and practical sections. If biblical writers were time-bounded as to matters of empirical fact, how much more were they such in regard to doctrinal truth! Thus, a biblical writer could have no intention to deceive anyone in regard to any doctrinal or practical issue and yet still include mistakes in such areas simply by reflecting his time-boundedness. Such mistakes would not count as errors, though, since he does not intend to deceive anyone. Thus, this definition of error does not guard those portions which it was intended to protect. A more fundamental problem, though, with this notion of error is that it sounds plausible if one limits the authorship of Scripture solely to the human writers, but it fares poorly when one recognizes that the Holy Spirit is also the author of Scripture. The Holy Spirit as omniscient is not time-bounded in His knowledge. Moreover, He obviously will not willfully deceive us. Once these facts are admitted along with the fact of the Holy Spirit's superintendence of the biblical authors, the case for errancy falls flat. If the Holy Spirit refuses to deceive us in regard to whatever He knows, and if He knows everything (this also entails that He cannot unintentionally deceive us out of ignorance), then His participation in the production of Scripture as co-author eliminates both willful deception, factual error, and doctrinal error of any kind. Thus, the definition of error proposed accomplishes nothing for the errantist's position.

Second, the notion of truth as faithfulness is also problematic. Those who raise it seem to think it gives a notion of truth that differs from, for example, a correspondence view of truth. Consequently, whether statements in Scripture correspond to the facts becomes unimportant, for the biblical concept of truth is not correspondence.  Though such claims are symptomatic of a much deeper error to which I shall turn shortly, Thiselton points out an initial devastating problem for such theories. He writes in regard to *'ᵉmeṯ* as faithfulness:

> But this particular use of *ʼemet̠* does not lie behind every occurence of the word. The Hebrews recognized the *logical* truth that others also recognized, that a true word can be relied upon because it accords with reality, and that both for a God of truth and for a man of truth, word and deed are one. Thus serving God "in sincerity and truth" (Jos. 24:14) means serving him with honest intention and integrity. Those who call on God "in truth" (Ps. 146:18) do so honestly. God's decrees are enacted with *ʼemet̠* (Ps. 111:8), because, in Calvin's words, there is agreement between the sayings and doings of God. . . . This is the logical point which lies behind the connexion between truth and faithfulness, and it is not to be confused with arguments about "faithfulness" found in most studies of this subject.[52]

The preceding comments indicate problems for errantists' claims about the biblical concepts of truth and error. However, the whole approach of thinkers such as Hubbard and Berkouwer contains even more fundamental errors. The most fundamental error in such discussions of error and truth is a confusion of the meaning of the *terms* 'truth' and 'error' with the meaning of the *concepts* of truth and error. At the outset of this study, the difference was explained. Giving the meaning of a term involves an analysis of its usage. Such a study, however, is not the same as an analysis of a concept. Though the *usage* of a term may suggest something about the concept indicated by the term, nonetheless, the analysis of a term is not the same as the explication of a concept.[53] Moreover, it is also evident that Hubbard and Berkouwer's comments focus on the biblical usage of the *terms* 'err' and 'error'. However, such analyses indicate nothing about concepts or theories of error and truth, nor do they specify anything about biblical criteria and standards of truth and accuracy (the point which led at least Hubbard to his lengthy analysis).

The preceding objection suggests another problem. Hubbard distinguishes error theologically from nontheological error, but what does the distinction mean? From the standpoint of the *concepts* of truth and error (analyzed under theories of truth) there is no distinction to be made. For example, a statement, whether in Scripture or not, either does or does not correspond to reality, cohere with other statements, or satisfy its sentential function. Thus, why must a proper *theory* of truth and error be derived from Scripture rather than from a philosophical discussion? Moreover, there is no reason to assume that a *theory* of truth a biblical writer uses as he writes must be any different from a *theory* a nonbiblical writer would use as he writes.

Hubbard's distinction is neither necessary nor legitimate. In fact, the only distinction possible is a distinction regarding the *usage* of the *terms* 'truth' and 'error' in theological as opposed to nontheological contexts, but again, that has nothing to do with a proper *theory* or *concept* of what truth and error are.

Merely rejecting Hubbard and Berkouwer's analyses does not exhaust what can be said about the biblical notion of truth. However, little progress can be made in this discussion without some key distinctions. First, one must distinguish between the biblical *usage* of terms such as 'truth' and 'error' and the biblical *teaching* concerning the concept or theory of truth. Second, one must distinguish further between the biblical teaching about the concept or theory of truth and the theory of truth *presupposed* by biblical writers as they wrote.

In regard to the former distinction, several things are of import. First, biblical writers do use the *terms* 'truth' and 'error' in various ways. One needs only to peruse Thiselton's excellent discussion of biblical usage of 'truth' to convince himself.[54] However, as already argued, different *uses* of the term do not necessitate that a *theory* of truth is *taught* by the biblical writer when he uses the term in a different way. Moreover, different uses of the term do not prove that biblical writers hold varying *concepts* of truth. There is no necessary connection between a specific use of the *term* 'truth' and a particular *theory* of truth. Thus, variant uses do not indicate variant theories of truth. Second, the biblical writers do *not* seem to *teach* anywhere any concept or theory of truth. Certainly, it is not their intention to give a philosophical treatise on the nature of truth, nor do they do so. Jesus, of course, says that He is the truth, but neither He nor the biblical writer claims that His claim presents a *theory* of truth which explains wherein the truth or falsity of any *statement* lies. The only way one could argue that the biblical writers *teach,* i.e., assert as correct, a particular theory of truth is to say they do so by using such a theory as they composed their work. However, presupposing a theory of truth as one writes is no proof of *intention* to teach such a theory as the correct theory. Thinking that it is proof of such intention is just as wrong as thinking that by using a particular spelling of a word the biblical writer intends to teach that such is the correct spelling of the word. Such considerations leave me very unsympathetic when theologians talk of the biblical teaching on truth as though the writers *assert* some conception or theory of truth as correct.

The second distinction puts us on the right track. Although biblical writers teach no theory of truth, they do presuppose one as they write. Since the biblical writers do this, we need to know which theory it is in order to understand the basis for judging the error or truth of what they wrote. If, for example, as they wrote they were thinking only of coherence of statements, then it is illegitimate to complain if some statements do not correspond to reality, since correspondence would not have been their intention. In fact, though, the correspondence theory in some form seems to be foundational to what they wrote. Even biblical usage of the *terms* 'truth' and 'error' seems to rest on a correspondence notion. As noted, Thiselton made that point in relation to *‘emeṯ*. Furthermore, his discussion of "truth" in the New Testament shows that New Testament usage of terms for true and truth ultimately rests on a correspondence *theory*. Even if one defines error as willful deception, such a definition rests on a correspondence theory. Leaving aside the willful part, how does one know what has been told is a deception? What does deception mean if it does not ultimately rest on the notion that something corresponds to the way things are, its negation does not, and someone intentionally suggests the latter corresponds to reality or that the former does not? Thus, even to elucidate the notion of deception, one must invoke the concept of correspondence. Finally, when one turns from the biblical writers' usage of 'truth' and 'error' to see what they wrote, he finds that they presupposed a correspondence theory. They were not merely presenting views they thought were true because they "worked" better than other ideologies (pragmatic). Nor were they claiming to hold the tenets of the faith and the historicity of the events of Christ's life, for example, only because they thought such concepts cohere with one another. Instead, they claimed that what they reported corresponds to what is the case. For example, when John begins his first Epistle (I Jn. 1:1-3) with an appeal to tangible eyewitness evidence of Jesus' life, when Peter emphasizes repeatedly that he and the other apostles were eyewitnesses of the things they report (Acts 1:22; 2:32; 3:15; 5:32; 10:39; I Pet. 5:1-2; II Pet. 1:16-17), and when Paul emphasizes that Christ actually appeared to many people after His resurrection (I Cor. 15:1-8), it seems obvious that they are marshalling evidence to establish that what they report actually corresponds to what they have seen and what is the case. If the writers of Scripture were trying to write statements which correspond to reality, then the crucial question is whether or not they succeeded. In fairness to the biblical writers, the interpreter should not assess what was said according to some other theory of truth.

Does Scripture, then, teach a theory of truth, and how does such a theory fit the philosophical discussion? The answer to the former question is "no." The biblical writers seem to incorporate some form of the correspondence theory (and at that point the philosophical and theological discussions overlap), but they do not teach (assert as correct) any *theory* of truth.

C. Epistemological Questions

The preceding discussion has clarified various conceptions of what truth is, but, with the exception of the pragmatic theory, nothing said heretofore addresses the actual truth or falsity of any given statement. Though space does not permit the discussion of all questions relevant to that matter, I shall focus on two epistemological matters which are in need of clarification as they have arisen in the contemporary inerrancy debate.[55]

Truth and Certainty

How does one know when he has marshalled enough evidence to verify a statement as certainly true? Such a question raises the issue of truth and certainty. Some might think truth and certainty are the same thing. If a statement is not certainly true, then it is not true at all, some would argue. As for Scripture, some demand that the Bible be more than highly probably true if its teachings are to be trusted for one's eternal destiny.[56]

Is truth equivalent to certainty, though? Albert Menne presents several distinctions which are crucial to making headway in this discussion. First, Menne distinguishes between the meaning of 'true', 'verified', and 'certain'. Too often there is confusion between the meaning of 'true' and 'verified'. If, in a concrete situation, the accused was at the scene of the crime, then a statement accusing him of such is true, regardless of whether anyone did or did not see him. The claim either does or does not correspond to reality (correspondence theory), does or does not cohere with other statements in the system (coherence theory), or does or does not satisfy its sentential function (semantic theory). The truth or falsity of any statement has nothing to do with whether or not it can be verified as such or with the degree of certainty to which it can be proved or disproved. As Tarski aptly states, "All provable sentences are true, but there are true sentences which are not provable."[57] Though his claim refers to certain mathematical disciplines, it seems applicable to other disciplines. Verification of a statement allows for degrees, but not so for the truth of a statement.[58]

Menne further distinguishes between truth, verification, and certainty as follows:

> When a proposition is thrown open to discussion by the question 'Is it so?', then we are asking whether the proposition is true. When the question is whether it has been established that the proposition is true, then we are asking whether it has been verified. When the question is whether it has been recognized as certain that this proposition is true, then we are asking whether it is certain or only probable.[59]

Though I agree with Menne's analysis, it can be further clarified. What Menne calls verification is what many label *objective certainty,* whereas what he terms certainty is often called *subjective certainty.* I shall use 'objective certainty' and 'subjective certainty', because they avoid the ambiguities of using 'certainty' without either qualifying adjective. Furthermore, there could be subjective certainty without objective certainty, but the goal when trying to confirm the truth of a statement is for the former to arise as a result of the latter kind of certainty.

What should be clear from Menne's distinctions is that one need not be in a position to say that a statement is either objectively or subjectively certain in order to assert correctly that it is true, because truth is not determined by certainty (objective or subjective), nor vice versa. In view of the difference between truth and objective certainty, it is safe to say that if errantists question the *truth* of Scripture at various points *because they doubt the objective certainty of the statements in question (or even because no one has yet verified the statements),* they are confusing the terms and the concepts (as well as the issue of inerrancy).

Are scriptural statements certain, though, i.e., are they confirmable to the point of warranting subjective certainty? Many argue that only for analytic statements can one have absolute subjective certainty, for they are deductively verified; synthetic statements warrant less than absolute subjective certainty, because they are inductively verified and thus, only highly probable at best. Of course, since most scriptural statements are synthetic, it seems that though they are true, one cannot marshall evidence to make them more than highly probable, and many find that undesirable. For many, such a Bible is as problematic as an errant one.

The problem of certainty can be resolved by using certain Wittgensteinian notions. In both the *Philosophical Investigations* and *On Certainty* he discusses the issue of certainty (in particular, the relation of objective to subjective certainty). He argues that certain statements (e.g., 'I have a mind') are beyond any question of doubt, because they are so foundational to all we are and do that they could not reasonably be brought into question. As for other statements, they can be meaningfully doubted, but their truth can be verified to such a degree that it no longer makes sense to doubt them.[60] Some such statements are synthetic. The key to this matter seemingly lies in Wittgenstein's statement that "the kind of certainty is the kind of language-game."[61] Note that Wittgenstein did not say the degree of certainty, but the kind of certainty. His point is that one can achieve subjective certainty to the same degree in the language-game of religion, history, or science as in the language-game of mathematics and logic, but the kind of objective certainty on which it is based will differ. Deduction is not induction. Thus, methods of verification in logic and math, as well as the kind of evidence appropriate for so doing, for example, differ from those used in history or science, because the language-games differ. Nonetheless, as Wittgenstein argues, after a certain amount of evidence and explanation is produced, it no longer makes any sense to doubt a statement's truth (i.e., to question whether objective certainty warrants subjective certainty in such a case), regardless of whether the statement comes from the language-game of history, science, mathematics, or whatever.[62]

The upshot of this discussion is that if one can marshall the evidence for a statement's truth, one is warranted in being absolutely subjectively certain of the statement's truth, even if it is synthetic. One need not reject inerrancy either because of confusing truth and certainty or because of fear that Scripture's statements cannot be absolutely certain since so many are synthetic.

Standards of Truth and Precision of Statements

Thinkers such as Berkeley Mickelsen have argued that since various biblical statements lack exact precision, standards of truth and accuracy used by the writers must differ from those of modern times. However, if standards vary, how can one be certain that biblical statements are inerrant? In discussing Lindsell's explanation of inerrancy, Mickelsen notes two key areas, correctness in any particular assertion and avoidance of any deception or deceit. As to the former, he writes:

> In the first of these two areas—correctness or incorrectness in particular assertions—the standard one uses to judge error

> (incorrectness) is crucial. There are a variety of possibilities. We may apply the standards adhered to in biblical times or our modern standards, or a mixture of the two; and we may vary the degree in which we use them, from applying them rigorously, but still carefully, down to applying them only carelessly.[63]

Though Mickelsen (and others such as Hubbard) claim that varying standards of accuracy and inaccuracy are at work in Scripture, they do not explain what those are. They merely assume that everyone can see that the biblical authors used varying standards. Nonetheless, even if one grants that different standards of truth and error were used in ancient times as opposed to modern times, I do not see why that necessarily eliminates inerrancy. If different standards are used in the writings of the ancients, then specify them, and let us test what the ancients wrote to see whether they met their standards. Someone may reply, "But, we can't do that, because we can't be sure that we know what their standards were exactly." However, if one cannot specify what the standards are, how, then, does he know they differ from modern standards? It sounds tremendously astute to say that standards differ, but unless one can explain the difference and set forth the ancient standards, the whole notion must be dropped as vacuous. On the other hand, if the ancients' standards can be specified, then why cannot those standards be used to test the accuracy of the writings of ancient times?[64] In either case, the outlook for inerrancy is hardly hopeless.

In spite of the problems with Mickelsen's analysis, one must admit that for whatever reason, there seems to be some imprecision in biblical statements of facts. This is true in ordinary language as well as in biblical usage. Nonetheless, several items are of crucial import here. First, the imprecise is not *necessarily* false. If there were 10,007 people present in a public auditorium last night but I say 25,342 were present, I am both imprecise and in error. However, if I make an approximation that 10,000 people were present, my statement could be more precise, but it is hardly false, *unless I specify that 10,000 is an exact figure*. Nicole's comments are especially helpful here:

> Similarly, when people are queried about their age, assuming that they wish to convey truthful information, they do not reply: "32 years, 5 months, 4 days, 2 hours, 52 minutes, and 35 seconds"; but they usually provide an approximate figure simply in terms of years. The integrity of truth is not at stake here. God, who knows all figures without approximation, has never-

> theless seen fit to use approximations repeatedly throughout the Scripture. This is undoubtedly the case in all kinds of matters like numbers of people, size of armies, as well as in chronological matters or in measurements. Punctilious accuracy in the scientific sense is obviously not an aim of Scripture. As long as approximations are appropriate, no charge of failure to observe the truth can be leveled.[65]

Second, the imprecise is considered false only when (1) the number is so far off that it could not be an approximation, (2) when the writer intends to give an exact account and imprecisely does not, or (3) when the writer's statement directly contradicts a true statement. In regard to (3), it should be added that approximations cannot appropriately be considered as direct contradictions of precise true statements, nor are contraries necessarily contradictories. Contraries allow for imprecision without necessarily entailing falsehood or contradiction.

Third, the matter of intention is also of crucial import. One must determine the writer's intention in giving his report. If he intends to give an exact report and does not, then there is an error, but if he intends to give an approximation and to use it for some other purpose than science, geography, etc. such as to teach a moral or ethical lesson, there is no reason to assume that imprecision in such a case is falsehood.

Fourth, Scripture is written in ordinary language. It is rather amusing to hear the biblical text contrasted to ordinary language (modern or otherwise) as if the former was produced by some complex computer capable of utmost precision. Dual authorship of Scripture does not entail a Bible written in anything but ordinary language. The reason for raising this point is that ordinary language is notoriously imprecise and ambiguous, but neither qualities are considered marks of falsehood.[66] Standards of formal accuracy and clarity which apply to more technical literature are not required of ordinary language. Since ordinary *speech* is not false because it is imprecise or ambiguous, why should Scripture, *written* in ordinary language, be suspect because of imprecision or ambiguity?

Finally, when a biblical writer is accused of using different standards of precision than do moderns (or his peers), the *accusation* may stem from nothing more than a confusion of literary habits of style with formal standards of accuracy and precision. A particular writer's literary style may be to use approximations when dealing with numbers or to paraphrase when quoting, but such practices do not necessarily entail setting forth any *standards of accuracy and precision* by using such habits of style. Even if all writers of a period use approximations and paraphrase, that does not necessarily suggest standards of precision and accuracy; it may only reflect common habits of style prevalent at the time. Moreover, if two writers differ in regard to paraphrasing or quoting the Old Testament, such practices may indicate only habits of style peculiar to each author, not varying standards of accuracy. Thus, varying habits of style may be attributable to varying standards of precision and accuracy, but they need not be. Such a connection certainly requires proof. Moreover, if variations of style and not variations in standards of accuracy and precision are involved, it must be remembered that such stylistic matters are neither true nor false, accurate or inaccurate, but only typical or atypical of a given writer's style. Matters of poetic license (e.g., grammatical usage, habits of quoting authors, or habits of reporting numbers) are hardly matters for determining truth or error of statements.

II. THE ISSUE OF MEANING

If there is difficulty in understanding truth, there is even greater difficulty in relation to meaning. The basic problem is lack of agreement on what constitutes a correct account of meaning. Nonetheless, progress can be made in areas relevant to the inerrancy debate. In this portion of the study I shall first handle the matter of meaning bearers, and then I shall turn to the major question of an appropriate account of meaning. Both of these are ontological issues, not epistemological. On the other hand, a third issue will be more epistemological in nature, viz., how does one determine the meaning of any specific linguistic unit?

A. Meaning Bearers

In discussing truth it was argued that truth bearers are not words alone but statements. However, such an answer is inappropriate for the question of meaning bearers, for questions, commands, interjections have no truth-value, but they obviously have meaning. Thus, there are only two viable candidates for meaning bearers, viz., individual words or sentences. Some might argue for phrases, but whatever problems beset individual words as meaning bearers also apply to phrases. In relation to words as meaning bearers, common sense suggests such as bearers of meaning. "After all," one might argue, "we do define words, don't we? Therefore, we must know what they mean, and they must be the bearers of meaning." While it is true that words are defined in isolation from one another, it does not follow that they are meaning bearers, if one is talking about *semantic* meaning.[67] The point can be clarified by two distinctions common within philosophy of language. The first is the distinction between the intension and the extension of a word or concept. Church explains:

> The *intension* of a concept consists of the qualities or properties which go to make up the concept. The *extension* of a concept consists of the things which fall under the concept; or, according to another definition, the *extension* of a concept consists of the concepts which are subsumed under it (determine subclasses).[68]

The second distinction (most clearly enunciated by Gottlob Frege) is between the sense and reference of a word. The sense of a word is the meaning or descriptive content of the word. As such, the sense of a word is basically equivalent to its intension. On the other hand, the reference of a word is the specific object which is designated by referring or denoting. Thus, the word 'man' has a particular sense, i.e., one can specify the concept of manhood, but in a given sentence it may refer to or designate Socrates, Plato, or Aristotle.

When speaking of the extension of a term, 'extension' may be used synonymously with 'reference', but as Baylis notes, not necessarily.[69] When speaking of the intension, sense, and extension (where extension is *not* equivalent to reference) of a word, one speaks in total abstraction from reality, i.e., he says nothing about anything in the world. In fact, outside the confines of a sentence, isolated words say nothing about the way things are in the world, for they have no specific reference to objects, states of affairs, or concepts in the world. Moreover, this is precisely why words, taken individually, have no semantic meaning. Thus, while individual words are definable, they do not bear semantic meaning, the kind which does relate to the world.[70]

If isolated words are not meaning bearers, then sentences must be, and on that point many philosophers agree. As Ricoeur argues, individual words are semiotic entities or signs, and such signs are units within a specific linguistic system, but they do not relate to extralinguistic realities such as things or events.[71] He explains:

> . . . the sentence as a whole is the bearer of the meaning. Here we mean to designate something other than and something more than the signified of the individual signs. It is a distinctive

> feature which may be identified as the predicative function. . . . The predicative constitution of the sentence provides it with a meaning. This meaning should be called the intended rather than the signified of the sentence, if we want to preserve the distinction between the semiotic and the semantic order. This intended is what we seek to translate when we transpose a discourse from one language into another. The signified is untranslatable in principle. It cannot be transposed from one system to another since it characterizes one system in opposition to the other. The intended, on the contrary, is fundamentally translatable since it is the same intended unit of thought transposed from one semiotic system into another.[72]

When Ricoeur speaks of the intended, he is not suggesting that meanings are some abstract or mental entities. He is using 'intended' in the sense of reference defined. His point is that semantic meaning involves both sense and reference, that only semantic meaning and not semiotic meaning relates to the extralinguistic world, and that such meaning is found not in individual words or phrases, but in sentences. Sentences are meaning bearers.

B. Theories of Meaning

Sentences bear meaning, but ontologically, what sorts of things are meanings, and how do sentences have meaning? Such questions raise the task of specifying an appropriate theory of meaning. Rather than presenting all available theories of meaning, four broad categories of theories will be treated.[73]

Ideational Theories

According to ideational theories, the meaning of a word or some other linguistic expression is an image, concept, or idea.[74] Thoughts are considered independent of words, and words are used as "marks" of ideas. If no one needed to communicate ideas to others, there would be no need for words. However, since there is a desire to transfer thoughts to others, words become the public vehicles of doing so. As Alston explains, "Communication is successful when my utterance arouses in you the same idea which led, in me, to its issuance. Thus the crucial fact about a word, semantically, is its regular association with a certain idea."[75] Some of the more famous proponents of this theory are John Locke and Aristotle. As Locke stated, "The use, then, of words is to be sensible marks of ideas; and the ideas they stand for are their proper and immediate signification."[76] Interestingly, both Locke and Aristotle state the theory in terms of the meanings of words, not sentences. However, there is nothing in principle against constructing an ideational theory in terms of sentences. Such a theory would probably argue that the one "grand" concept, the sentence, results from the conjunction of all the ideas indicated by the words in the sentence.

Philosophers have objected to the theory on several key grounds. First, the theory rests on the assumption that when two people use the same word, the same mental image is aroused in them, but common experience indicates the contrary. If the theory were correct, ambiguity in language would seemingly be impossible, and no one would ever misunderstand anyone else. Someone might respond that misunderstanding stems not from different images for the same word, but from people having the wrong image because they do not know the meaning of the word in question. However, such an objection begs the question of whether or not every word is associated with one and only one image. Moreover, even if for some words the same mental image is aroused, such would not necessarily be the case in relation to words denoting abstract concepts. Furthermore, as Gyekye argues, Aristotle's point is problematic in relation to those who belong to different linguistic communities. The Englishman who uses 'red', the Frenchman who uses 'rouge', and the German who uses 'rot' do not beyond a shadow of a doubt have the same mental image. If this is so with words denoting colors, how much more will it be so in finding equivalents for words denoting abstract concepts![77]

A second major difficulty with the ideational theory is that it presupposes that for every meaningful linguistic expression there is an idea which is regularly associated with it. As Alston argues:

> Consider a sentence taken at random, "Increases in the standard of living have not been offset by corresponding increases in the income of clerical personnel." Ask yourself whether there was a distinguishable idea in your mind corresponding to each of the meaningful linguistic units of the sentence, "increases," "in," "the," "standard," etc. One can safely predict that most people not only would report no distinctive imagery actually occurring when they spoke or heard the sentence but would not be able to call up an idea distinctive of each of the constituent words.[78]

Finally, ideational theories rest on the faulty assumption that thought and language can be dissociated. In contemporary philosophy of language it is generally agreed that thought without language is impossible. Those who think language is unnecessary to thought need to specify how one can think without language. Those who claim that thought is impossible without language of some sort but such a language can be a private one need to be apprised of Wittgenstein's private language argument. As he argues, the only language which is genuine language is public language. Thought without language is impossible.[79]

Referential Theories

Probably the most prevalent theories of meaning historically have been referential theories. There are many variations of such theories, but a general description will suffice. In its various forms, the key notion of referential theories is that a linguistic expression (word, phrase, sentence) has its meaning in virtue of what it names. Thus, only those expressions have meaning which name, designate, or refer to something other than themselves. On this theory, for example, "the meaning of the words 'the Parthenon' is the Parthenon, that physical object of which 'the Parthenon' is the name, or in other words, the 'bearer' of this name."[80] As Alston explains, there are two broad forms of the theory, viz., those for which an expression's meaning is that to which it refers, and those for which an expression's meaning is the relation between the expression and its referent. In the case of the latter, it is the referential connection which constitutes the meaning. As Alston notes, most serious referential theories are of the second kind, but the first kind does play a role in much popular thinking about meaning.[81]

The theory of Gottlob Frege, though incorporating elements which go beyond the basic referential notion, is nonetheless classifiable as referential in that it relies heavily on the notion of reference.[82] In Frege's theory, each expression which is a component of the sentence names some object, and in fact, the sentence as a whole is a name. However, that cannot be the whole picture, and it is at this point Frege's theory departs from a strictly referential one. The point is that if names have meaning in virtue of their referent alone, then the following dilemma arises: the expression 'the Morning Star' has the same referent as the expression 'the Evening Star'. If the referent of the name is all that constitutes meaning, then there should be no difference in the meaning of 'the Morning Star is the Morning Star' and 'the Morning Star is the Evening Star', but obviously, the latter is much more informative than the former. In order to resolve this dilemma, Frege suggested there is more to meaning than name and referent. There is also the sense of the expression involved, i.e., the descriptive content of the name "in virtue of which and only in virtue of which it refers to its reference."[83] In summarizing this important distinction between sense and reference, Searle writes:

> The reason why 'The Evening Star is the Morning Star' can be more factually informative than 'The Evening Star is the Evening Star', even though the reference is the same, is that the sense of 'The Evening Star' is different from the sense of 'The Morning Star', and the statement conveys that one and the same object has the features specified in the different senses of the two expressions.[84]

Not only did Frege extend this theory to individual words and phrases, but also to sentences. As will be noted in more detail later, Frege's view regarding sentences was that they express a thought or concept as their sense and have a truth condition as their reference.[85] Moreover, he distinguished between the thought expressed by a sentence and the assertion of that thought. Consequently, the sentences 'Snow is white' and 'Is snow white?' express the same thought, but only the former asserts it.

Though referential theories are quite plausible, they are not entirely unobjectionable. An initial problem is the assumption that each term in a sentence stands for one and only one thing, and that such a relation always exists. Even terms such as nouns and pronouns, however, do not always have a fixed referent (though they do have a reference). For example, the phrase 'my friend' has as many different referents as there are people who say 'my' and people who are the referent of the word 'friend'.[86] Second, one of the major reasons Wittgenstein rejected his picture theory of meaning (a referential theory) was his realization that words vary in meaning according to their use in various language-games. There simply is no one meaning for each term which never varies, and thus, there is no single object to which a given word always refers. Moreover, he recognized that there is not even some thing that every use of a given term has in common with all other uses of the term. Usage varies too much to be able to pin a word to a referent in the world.[87] Third, referential theories assume that every term has a referent. However, such words as 'if', 'and', 'or', and 'about' certainly have no such referents.[88] Finally, referential theories claim that the meaning of a certain word is a certain object. In considering the words 'the Parthenon', Parkinson explains the difficulty:

> Certainly, a building is the reference of these words, but it is not what they mean. It makes no sense to say that the meaning of the words 'the Parthenon' is made of marble, and was seriously damaged in the seventeenth century; and if, at some future time, the Parthenon is completely destroyed, it will not be correct to say that after this date the words 'the Parthenon' no longer have meaning.[89]

Meaning as a Function of Truth

Some theories of meaning rely so heavily on the notion of truth that it is fair to say they understand meaning in terms of truth. Referential theories tend in this direction, but other theories do as well. Moreover, there are at least two broad kinds of theories for which meaning is a function of truth. According to the first kind, if one knows the conditions which make a sentence true, he also knows what the sentence means (truth conditional semantics). According to the second variety, if one knows the verification conditions of a sentence, he knows its meaning.

Frege's theory of meaning is an example of the former kind. When his theory was discussed as a referential theory, it was noted that his theory ultimately hinges on truth as well, for he claimed that the reference of a sentence is its truth condition. Frege distinguished between sense and reference in order to resolve such problems as those created by expressions with the same reference but a different sense. Since, according to Frege, a complex expression depends only on the reference of its parts, the referent of a whole sentence could not be a proposition (a whole thought or concept). Moreover, the problem with reference of individual terms has already been noted. It seemed that when a singular term with its sense is substituted for another singular term with a different sense but the same reference only the truth condition of the sentence remained constant. Consequently, Frege argued that the truth condition of the sentence must be the ultimate reference of the sentence, and if one knows the conditions which make a sentence true or false, he must know the meaning of the sentence.[90]

A second truth conditional semantics theory is Donald Davidson's theory. Davidson adopts a Tarskian theory of truth which defines truth in terms of satisfaction, but he makes two major refinements. First, he argues that truth is a relation between sentences, speakers, and dates or times. A given statement is true in virtue of who utters it and the time of uttering, as well as the content of the sentence.[91]

Thus, Tarski's 'X is true if, and only if p' is modified to "Sentence *s* is true (as English) for speaker *u* at time *t* if and only if *p*."[92] Davidson's second and more radical claim is that it is just Tarski's condition (T) which also serves as an adequate basis for an account of meaning. Consequently, in knowing the conditions under which a sentence is true, one also knows its meaning.[93]

The prime example of a theory analyzing meaning in terms of verification conditions is the verification theory of meaning (originally held by the Vienna Circle).[94] Before turning to that theory, however, it would be helpful to distinguish truth conditional semantic theories from verification condition theories. The difference is basically the following: for a truth conditional semanticist, one knows the meaning of a sentence if he knows what conditions make it true. For example, 'snow is white' is true just in case snow *is* white. For a verification condition theorist, one knows the meaning of a sentence if he knows how to establish its truth or falsity. The point is that one could know the conditions for the truth of a statement without having the vaguest idea of a verification procedure for it (cf. Goldbach's conjecture). Moreover, the distinction between the two kinds of theories can also be drawn in terms of my distinction between ontological and epistemological questions in regard to truth and meaning. The truth condition semanticist says that sentences have meaning through relation of component terms of these sentences to objects in the world (ontological perspective in defining meaning). The verificationist says sentences obtain meaning by relation of components of the sentences to known verification procedures (clearly an epistemological matter).

As for the verification theory itself, one must initially distinguish between the verification theory of meaning and the verification criterion. The theory, according to such philosophers as Moritz Schlick, is "the meaning of a proposition is the method of its verification."[95] The basic idea behind the theory is that if one knows how to verify or falsify a statement, he knows what the statement means.[96] Holders of the theory are not saying that a sentence must be verified in actuality before it is meaningful. Instead, it must be verifiable in principle, and it must be possible to specify the method of verification for the sentence to be meaningful.[97] The verification criterion, on the other hand, is not a theory about meaning, but offers a criterion for meaning. A. J. Ayer's classical statement of the criterion, while not unobjectionable, will suffice for our purposes. He writes:

> The criterion which we use to test the genuineness of apparent statements of fact is the criterion of verifiability. We say that a sentence is factually significant to any given person, if and only if, he knows how to verify the proposition which it purports to express—that is, if he knows what observations would lead him, under certain conditions, to accept the proposition as being true, or reject it as being false.[98]

On this account of meaning, proponents of the verification theory claim there are whole categories of statements which are meaningless. For example, it is argued that one cannot even in principle state verification conditions for the claims of metaphysics, ethics, and theology. Thus, such statements are meaningless.[99]

Though theories analyzing meaning in terms of truth have many defenders, they are not unobjectionable. Most of my comments, however, relate to verificationism, for I think there is something fundamentally correct in what Davidson is suggesting. First, for many statements which are considered meaningful, we do not, in fact, know their verification or falsification conditions. Statements about metaphysics, theology, and ethics do have meaning, even if one does not know how to verify or falsify them. Some philosophers claim they express emotions, others that they indicate intention to act a certain way, and others interpret them as statements of fact. Nonetheless, each group considers such statements to be meaningful. The point can be demonstrated by the following utterances: 'Fruit cups growl madly at freedom' and 'Invisible unicorns inhabit invisible planets 8,000,000,000,000 miles from earth'. I do not know the verification or falsification conditions for either sentence, and I doubt anyone else does or could. However, the second statement is meaningful, whereas the first is not. The problem is not lack of grammaticalness, for both are grammatical. Nor is the problem the matter of truth, for the truth of each is inaccessible, but nonetheless, one of the statements has meaning. Given this example, meaningfulness does not seem reducible to verifiability and falsifiability.

Second, verification theories seem to confuse meaning conditions and verification conditions. Admittedly, it would be very difficult to specify conditions for verification of a statement, if one were ignorant of its meaning, but on the other hand, it does not seem that if one knows how a sentence comes to be meaningful and whether it is meaningful, he would necessarily know *thereby* how to verify or falsify it. Once the meaning of a sentence (or even the conditions for determining its meaning) is known, one still must indicate how to determine its truth or falsity.

Third, such theories seem to confuse the concepts of meaning and verification. They confuse ontological questions (what is it for a sentence to have meaning?) with epistemological questions (how does one determine the truth or falsity of a given statement and how does one determine the meaning of a given sentence?). An adequate theory of what meaning is cannot be given in terms of an account of how to determine the meaning or truth of any given sentence. Verification *procedures* cannot serve as an account of what meaning is.

Finally, a word must be said about truth conditional semantics and the debate surrounding them. Initially, one might suspect that such theories cannot be correct, because they only account for sentences in the indicative mood. However, Dummett argues that theories of meaning which take truth as their central notion must contain two parts, one part formed by a theory of sense and a theory of reference, and another part consisting of a theory of force. The former focuses on truth as its central notion, but that alone will not be enough to allow the user or hearer to grasp an utterance's meaning. To grasp the meaning one must also understand the force of an utterance. The theory of force gives the necessary account of the various kinds of linguistic acts that can be performed by a linguistic utterance. In so doing, the problem relating to mood will be handled.[100] If Dummett is correct, the objection against truth conditional semantics which claims that such theories of meaning cannot account for the meaning of sentences not in the indicative mood seems misguided. On the other hand, if one can prove that illocutionary force is essentially related to locutionary meaning of the sentence (truth conditional semanticists deny this), then truth conditional semantics do fall prey to the objection, since their theory of reference and sense is based on truth but would ignore the matter of mood. Moreover, what is equally problematic and moot is the question of whether, in fact, a viable theory of force can be formulated for theories of meaning for which truth is the central notion.[101]

Meaning as a Function of Use

Relying heavily on the later philosophy of Wittgenstein is the concept of meaning as a function of use. Wittgenstein came to hold that the meaning of a word, phrase, or sentence is determined by its use. Various theories have arisen in recent years which incorporate this insight. I shall briefly sketch two.

A first example is Wittgenstein's use theory of meaning. According to Wittgenstein, language is to be understood as a complex of language-games. What he means by a language-game is probably seen best in his statement, "I shall also call the whole, consisting of language and the actions into which it is woven, the 'language-game'."[102] In other words, language is more than mere words, for language is always used in a context, a context which includes behavior. Accordingly, "the term 'language-*game*' is meant to bring into prominence the fact that the *speaking* of language is part of an activity, or of a form of life."[103] Wittgenstein's concept of a form of life is of a complete way of doing something, including both verbal and nonverbal behavior. As to the verbal portion of a language-game, he claims that its meaning is to be explained in terms of use. He argues that "for a *large* class of cases—though not for all—in which we employ the word 'meaning' it can be defined thus: the meaning of a word is its use in the language."[104] The same is also true of a sentence, for Wittgenstein writes that one should "look at the sentence as an instrument, and at its sense as its employment."[105] Sentences have meaning in virtue of their use, and they perform a function in a language-game.[106]

A second theory emphasizing use is the speech act analysis of language. The rudiments of this theory can be seen in Wittgenstein's claim that language is a form of life and in the work of J. L. Austin. The basic point of such theories is that meaning must be analyzed in terms of the whole speech act, i.e., one must ask how the speaker is using language in a given context. The speech act analysis of language relies heavily on the context of the sentence's uttering as well as what the speaker is trying to do by uttering the sentence. In analyzing the meaning of any given sentence, Austin argued that one must distinguish several acts performed by uttering a sentence, viz., a locutionary act, an illocutionary act, and a perlocutionary act. A locutionary act is the act of uttering or saying an utterance. The illocutionary act is the further act the utterer uses the locutionary act to perform. The perlocutionary act is the act the utterer produces (even intends to produce) as a response by the hearer to the locutionary and illocutionary acts.[107] For example, uttering 'I shall be present on campus tomorrow at 10 A.M.' is performing a locutionary act. When I utter that sentence, I also perform the illocutionary act of promising. As a response I intend to elicit from my listener belief and persuasion to be present at the same time at the same place. According to Austin, in analyzing the meaning of a sentence too often the locutionary force is all that is considered, but meaning can only be fully determined in terms of the total set of speech acts.[108] The speech act analysis of language has undergone much revision and development since Austin, but its various forms still rest on the central notion that meaning can only be understood and analyzed completely in terms of the act it is used to perform in a given verbal and nonverbal context.[109]

Though there is much attractive about use theories, something fundamental is still troublesome about such theories. The problem is that there needs to be some kind of referential element in order to tie language to the world. Without it there seems to be no reason other than pure convention as to why a certain utterance and not another is appropriate for performing a given speech act. For example, if meaning is determined in terms of use and convention alone without any ontological tie to the world, then if I want to warn my friend that he is about to be bitten by a snake, I can do so just as easily by saying 'It's a beautiful day for a walk in the park!' (or even 'Glippity glop is glipping!') as I can by saying 'Be careful! There's a snake near your foot!' However, this seems to leave open the possibility, ontologically speaking, that there actually is no snake and no foot. My utterance might be nothing more than a reflection of what is going on in my mind, and it is that lack of necessary relation between language and world which troubles me about use theories.

In summing up this section on theories of meaning, it seems evident that no single theory of meaning is entirely satisfactory. It is beyond the purpose and scope of this study to delineate an appropriate account of meaning. However, I suggest that an appropriate account of meaning ought to include at least the following: the notions of reference, use within a context, the performance of a speech act, and the idea of conventions of language.[110] These items as well as the demand that sentences be grammatical seem to be the basic constituents of a proper theory of meaning.[111]

C. Meaning of Individual Sentences

The preceding sections included nothing specific in regard to determining the meaning of any given sentence. Detailed exposition of such matters is beyond the scope of this study, but a few key items are noteworthy.

First, the matter of determining the meaning of any given sentence is an epistemological and not a metaphysical issue. This is so because giving an exegesis of a sentence requires investigating the definitions of words and their use in the contexts of the sentence and the act of uttering the sentence. Moreover, this is true even for truth conditional semanticists. For such theorists to understand a sentence's truth condition (and thereby its meaning) they need to perform the kinds of investigations mentioned.

Second, just as for truth, the epistemological questions seem to be the most significant for the issue of inerrancy. Before determining whether any statement of Scripture is inerrant, one must know what it means. However, this does not necessitate first determining one's theory of meaning before answering whether a given sentence is in error. Only if a theory of meaning *dictated* the method of determining the meaning of an individual sentence would the theory provide criteria essential to knowing the meaning of a given sentence. Since this is not the case, determining one's concept of meaning and determining the meaning of a particular sentence are two distinct procedures. Determining sentence meaning involves setting forth rules for interpreting sentences and applying those rules. Which principles one chooses and how he applies them will determine what meaning is attributed to the sentence, and that will determine what the specific assertions will be which must be verified or falsified. It is of utmost import in determining principles of interpretation that one does so in isolation from any problem passage (problematic in regard to inerrancy) of Scripture. If one determines his principles *so that* he can wind up giving a problem verse an interpretation he knows will be true or which he knows will be false, such a determination of hermeneutical principles will be question begging in regard to the inerrancy debate.

Finally, though I do not intend to specify all appropriate principles of interpretation, it would be helpful to pause long enough to note the importance of determining in the interpretive process the intended meaning of the author. Some object to such a requirement, for they believe it requires the interpreter to reconstruct a "psychological history" of the author's development of thought. Since it is impossible to do so, it is argued that any attempt to appeal to authorial intention when interpreting is illegitimate. Others argue that while one cannot know the author's intention if such means entering his private mental states, one can know his intention, if he tells us what he intended. Though this sounds appealing, it is not altogether unobjectionable. In reflecting on an author telling his intentions, Wittgenstein explains that the listener may still not know the author's intentions. Even if the author states his intentions, that does not guarantee that anyone knows his intentions, for he may be lying when he states them.[112] Considerations such as these have led such literary critics as Wimsatt and Beardsley to conclude that any attempt to specify a writer's intention is totally illegitimate. They label attempts to discern authorial intention the intentional fallacy.[113]

Is there a way out of this dilemma? On the one hand, the author's intentions seem inaccessible to the reader, but on the other hand, the interpreter must try to interpret according to what the *author* intended to say. Within the later philosophy of Wittgenstein there is an answer to this dilemma. Wittgenstein argues that intentions are embedded in the public situation. He writes:

> But didn't I already intend the whole construction of the sentence (for example) at its beginning? So surely it already existed in my mind before I said it out loud!—If it was in my mind, still it would not normally be there in some different word order. But here we are constructing a misleading picture of 'intending', that is, of the use of this word. An intention is embedded in its situation, in human customs and institutions. If the technique of the game of chess did not exist, I could not intend to play a game of chess. In so far as I do intend the construction of a sentence in advance, that is made possible by the fact that I can speak the language in question.[114]

This emphasis on knowing the author's intention through the public situation (specifically the public document he has written with its dependence on human customs and institutions) is just the answer to the problem. In fact, what Wittgenstein suggests fits precisely with the interpreter's claim that if there is proper application of literal, grammatical, historical hermeneutics to the text, one will understand what the author intended to say. Such a hermeneutic demands that the interpreter note the historical and cultural institutions and situations that confronted the author as he wrote. In so doing he will find the author's intended meaning in the text. Without such analysis, it will be difficult, if not impossible to determine the author's meaning.

The upshot of this discussion on intention as it relates to inerrancy is that the interpretive process can and must take into account the intended meaning of the author. Attempts to uphold the inerrancy of any portion of Scripture on the basis of the author's intended meaning are not illegitimate.

III. TRUTH AND MEANING

Having set forth an understanding of truth and meaning, it is now necessary to relate the two to one another and to the inerrancy issue. Some of the relationships have already been noted, but most will be suggested now. I shall first speak of the relation of meaning to truth, and then conclude with several comments about inerrancy.

Perhaps the most obvious point from the preceding discussion is that some theories of meaning directly relate truth to meaning by defining meaning in terms of truth. The theories of Frege, Davidson, and the verification theory all incorporate the notion of truth. Problems with such approaches to meaning have been noted, but the point here is that such theories of meaning directly incorporate the concept of truth. Furthermore, all three of those theories seem to include the notion of reference in relation to their concept of meaning, and all incorporate some form of the correspondence theory of truth (in the following discussion, I am considering the semantic theory as a form of the correspondence theory). It does not seem impossible to define meaning in terms of truth without using some form of the correspondence theory, but I suspect that any such theory of meaning which incorporates the notion of reference as essential to the determination of truth will, most likely, also incorporate some form of the correspondence theory of truth. The referential element in language involves indicating what objects, etc. in the world the word or sentence names or designates, and such an approach to meaning most naturally fits some form of the correspondence theory.

Second, from the analysis of theories of meaning and theories of truth, it becomes obvious that with the exception of theories of meaning which define meaning in terms of truth, there seems to be no intrinsic link between *meaning* and *truth*. That is, the concept of what sort of thing meaning is does not have to include any concept about what sort of thing truth is. Moreover, by specifying the *meaning* of a particular sentence, one has not thereby indicated truth conditions or verification conditions of the sentence or even if the sentence is true or false or has a truth-value (commands, interjections, and questions have no truth-value to be demonstrated or not demonstrated).

Third, after reflecting on theories of meaning and theories of truth, it seems as well that there is nothing inherent in a *theory* of meaning or a *theory* of truth which logically necessitates that certain *theories* of truth attach to certain *theories* of meaning. It seems possible to construct theories of meaning which define meaning in terms of truth and yet are open as to the particular *theory* of truth they adopt. Of course, certain theories of meaning generally seem to *fit* better with certain theories of truth, but there seems to be no necessary connection. For example, a correspondence theory seems to fit best with a referential theory of meaning or one with the notion of reference incorporated in it, but in principle it seems that, for example, a correspondence theory could be made to fit with a use theory or an ideational theory. As for the coherence theory, it seems to fit best with some nonreferential theory of meaning, but one could structure his theories of meaning and truth so as to fit a referential theory with a coherence theory of truth. After determining the referent of the sentence in order to know its meaning, rather than asking if the sentence corresponds to the way the world is, one could simply ask if the statement coheres with other statements or sets of statements. It is possible to link a referential theory with a coherence theory of truth even when a referentially interpreted statement turns out, on a correspondence theory, to be false. For example, consider the sentences 'the present king of France is totally bald' and 'the present queen of France kissed the bald head of the present king of France'. These statements are both false on a correspondence theory of truth, since France presently has no king or queen. However, if the *meaning* of these sentences is analyzed on a referential theory of meaning, the statements do have meaning, and if one adds a coherence theory of truth, one would probably say both are true. On the other hand, if to the set is added 'the present king of France's royal barber gave the king a haircut', then on a referential theory of meaning, the sentence has meaning, but with a coherence theory of truth, one or more of the sentences (but not all three as in the case of a correspondence analysis) must be false, for the third sentence contradicts the preceding two. Finally, a pragmatic theory is incorporative with any of the major types of theories of meaning. In sum, then, by choosing one's theory of truth one does not thereby lock himself automatically into any theory of meaning and vice versa.

Finally, from the discussion of theories of meaning, one can conclude that the relation between truth and meaning in regard to specific sentences is asymmetrical. While it seems impossible to specify a statement that has a truth-value but no meaning, not every sentence that has a meaning must have a truth-value, for only sentences which assert something or make statements have truth-values.

In the previous paragraphs I have related meaning and truth, but how does the whole discussion relate to the inerrancy debate? I shall first plot the relationship of theories of meaning to inerrancy, and then note the relation of theories of truth to inerrancy. Since theories of meaning and theories of truth (and, in most cases, meaning and truth) are not intrinsically linked to one another, one should not assume that comments about meaning and inerrancy will automatically determine what will be said about theories of truth and inerrancy.

As for theories of meaning and inerrancy, in general no theory of meaning is inherently harmful or beneficial to inerrancy. This is so, because theories of meaning on the whole are not about truth; no theory of meaning necessitates any particular theory of truth, and inerrancy is a matter that deals with truth. The only exceptions are theories of meaning which interpret meaning in terms of truth, since such do incorporate the notion (truth) which is of crucial import for the inerrancy debate. Since such theories of meaning can be made to fit with more than one theory of truth, whatever is determined about the relation of theories of truth to inerrancy will determine how detrimental or beneficial a specific theory of meaning defined in terms of truth will be for inerrancy.

While, with the exception noted, no *theory* of meaning is intrinsically more or less harmful to inerrancy, certain *methods of hermeneutics* are more harmful to inerrancy than others. In particular, methods such as spiritualizing hermeneutics or existentially oriented hermeneutics (which first analyzes the human situation and then interprets the biblical text to fit the exegete's perception of the human condition) do not emphasize the author's intended meaning as expressed in the written text. Of course, if the literal, grammatical, historical meaning of the sentence is not the focus, the interpreter tends to wind up not with the biblical author's thoughts but with the product of the *uninspired* exegete's eisegesis, and the latter is much more likely to contain error than the former.

As to theories of truth and inerrancy, three basic points are noteworthy. First, only one basic theory of truth seems to be presupposed by biblical writers as they wrote. Some version of the correspondence theory underlies the writing of Scripture, just as it does ordinary language.

Second, if inerrancy is to be defined in terms of truth, how should truth be understood? It was argued that the most appropriate account of truth is some form of the correspondence theory (in particular, the semantic theory). In addition to arguments already presented, another consideration is that the correspondence theory most adequately accomplishes what a theory of truth should do. What anyone wants to know is whether his thoughts as expressed in language reflect the way things are in reality, and only the correspondence theory makes reflecting the way the world is by language the main point. If someone's thoughts are consistent but do not reflect the way things are, such thoughts are of little value for living in the actual world. Certainly, one would want biblical statements to correspond to reality, for few, if any, would rest their eternal destiny on notions that have nothing to do with the world and universe in which they live.

Finally, if biblical writers presupposed the correspondence theory in their writings, if some form of the theory is the correct theory of truth (as seems the best conclusion), and if the correspondence theory tells us about truth what we most need to know, then the correspondence theory is obviously the least harmful to inerrancy while others are detrimental to it. The problem with the coherence theory is that it allows one to construct an internally consistent system of error, i.e., the set of statements may be noncontradictory (true on this theory) and yet in whole or in part not reflect the external world. According to the coherence theory, the Bible's statements could be self-consistent and still tell the reader nothing relevant to his life and eternal destiny because of reflecting nothing about reality. As for the pragmatic theory of truth, it is detrimental to inerrancy, because it determines truth or error in Scripture in terms of a statement's effect. On this theory, no statement is guaranteed to state the way things are, but nonetheless, any statement in Scripture may turn out to be true solely because it has positive results for someone. Moreover, such a theory also necessitates that whatever is true in Scripture is so in a totally person-relative way. Absolute truth is an impossibility. Neither the errantist nor the inerrantist should be satisfied with a theory that offers a Bible whose truth varies in relation to the readers' experiences.

IV. CONCLUSION

At the conclusion of a study such as this, one cannot help thinking that much still remains for further study. Such areas as the relation of truth and meaning to metaphor[115] and the relation of truth and meaning to time-designating statements[116] could not be handled, but should be pursued. Nonetheless, much headway has been made. If nothing else, hopefully this study has clarified the genuine issues between errantists and inerrantists as epistemological, not ontological. Since the key issues are not about what truth and meaning are, objections that the debate should be dropped because no one has a clear understanding of what truth and meaning are should themselves be dropped. Jesus said, "Thy Word is truth" (Jn. 17:17). What must be done is to get on with everything involved in confirming or disconfirming that statement, rather than stagnating over whether anyone knows what truth is. One's theory of truth *does* make a difference to biblical inerrancy, but the larger issues in regard to truth which separate errantists and inerrantists need yet to be debated in the epistemological arena.

NOTES

[1]Berkeley Mickelsen, "The Bible's Own Approach to Authority," *Biblical Authority,* ed. Jack Rogers (Waco, Tex.: Word, 1977), 86. For a discussion of the whole problem, see Mickelsen's comments on pp. 84-87. See also J. Ramsey Michaels, "Inerrancy or Verbal Inspiration? An Evangelical Dilemma," *Inerrancy and Common Sense,* ed. Roger Nicole and J. Ramsey Michaels (Grand Rapids: Baker 1980), 59 for the same point.

[2]David Hubbard, "The Current Tensions: Is There a Way Out?," *Biblical Authority,* ed. Jack Rogers (Waco, Tex.: Word, 1977), 167-68.

[3]See Paul D. Feinberg, "The Meaning of Inerrancy," *Inerrancy,* ed. Norman Geisler (Grand Rapids: Zondervan, 1980) and Roger Nicole, "The Nature of Inerrancy," *Inerrancy and Common Sense,* ed. Roger Nicole and J. Ramsey Michaels (Grand Rapids: Baker, 1980).

[4]For discussions of the use of the terms 'meaning', 'true', and 'truth' see Avrum Stroll and Henry Alexander, " 'True' and Truth," *Philosophy of Science,* 42 (1975): 384-410; J. R. Lucas, "True," *Philosophy,* 44 (July 1969): passim; Albert Menne, "What Is Truth?" *Ratio*, 16 (June 1974): 68-75; *The New International Dictionary of New Testament Theology,* s.v. "Truth," by Anthony Thiselton, 3: 874-94; and Dennis W. Stampe, "Toward a Grammar of Meaning," *Philosophical Review,* 77 (April 1968): 137-74.

[5]William Kneale, "Propositions and Truth in Natural Languages," *Mind,* 81 (April 1972): 231. Compare Douglas Browning, "Creativity, Correspondence, and Statements About the Future," *Philosophy and Phenomenological Research,* 28 (June 1968): 517.

[6]Kneale, "Propositions and Truth," 231.

[7]J. L. Mackie, *Truth Probability and Paradox* (London: Oxford University Press, 1973), 18ff. See also J. L. Austin, "Truth," *Truth,* ed. George Pitcher (Englewood Cliffs: Prentice-Hall, 1964), 20, who says "A sentence is made *up of* words, a statement is made *in* words."

[8]Alfred Tarski, "The Semantic Conception of Truth," *Semantics and the Philosophy of Language,* ed. Leonard Linsky (Chicago: University of Illinois Press, 1952), 14. See also W. V. Quine, *Philosophy of Logic* (Englewood Cliffs: Prentice-Hall, 1970), chapter 1, passim.

[9]Mackie, *Truth Probability,* 19. At this point Austin's distinction between a locutionary act and an illocutionary act is important. A locutionary act is the act of saying something. What is said has meaning. An illocutionary act is the performance of an act (e.g., warning, promising) *in* saying something. Illocutionary acts presuppose and incorporate locutionary acts with the locutionary meaning of the utterance. See J. L. Austin, *How To Do Things With Words* (Cambridge, Mass.: Harvard University Press, 1962), 94, 98-100, 121 for such distinctions.

Similarities between Mackie's and Austin's views are evident upon minimal reflection.

[10]Mackie, *Truth Probability,* 21. Mackie refers to the two synonymously.

[11]Quine, *Philosophy of Logic,* 2.

[12]See Quine, *Philosophy of Logic,* chapter 1, for example, and James F. Thomson, "Truth-bearers and the Trouble About Propositions," *Journal of Philosophy,* 66 (November 1969): 737-47 for some of the problems with propositions. In this study, I shall use 'statement' instead of 'proposition'. However, some authors I quote use 'proposition'. The reader should assume they mean the same basic thing I do when I use 'statement'.

[13]Austin, "Truth," 29.

[14]Mackie, *Truth Probability,* 21.

[15]Ronald Jager, "Truth and Assertion," *Mind,* 79 (April 1970): 161.

[16]It is clear that Scripture calls Christ the truth. However, theories of truth are about the truth of propositions, not about personal truth. Thus, refusal to discuss Christ as truth does not disparage Him as such but only recognizes what subjects are relevant to the matter of theories of truth. Further, two theories which will not be handled are worthy of note. They are the performative theory and the redundancy theory. For discussion of the theories see P. F. Strawson, "Truth," *Truth,* ed. George Pitcher (Englewood Cliffs: Prentice-Hall, 1964); *Encyclopedia of Philosophy* s.v. "Performative Theory of Truth," by Gertrude Ezorsky, 6; F. P. Ramsey, "Facts and Propositions," *Truth,* ed. by George Pitcher (Englewood Cliffs: Prentice-Hall, 1964); A. J. Ayer, *Language, Truth and Logic* (New York: Dover, 1952); and Donald Davidson, "True to the Facts," *Journal of Philosophy,* 66 (November 1969).

[17]Such a view has been held by such as Aristotle, Frege, and the Wittgenstein of the *Tractatus.* For a summary of the main proponents of the correspondence view, along with arguments for and against their position, see *Encyclopedia of Philosophy,* s.v. "Correspondence Theory of Truth," by A. N. Prior, 2.

[18]See George Pitcher, "Introduction," *Truth,* ed. George Pitcher (Englewood Cliffs: Prentice-Hall, 1964), 4-5 for problems with viewing truth as a property of statements (or even of sentences). As he shows, the concept of truth as a property is foreign to the correspondence theory.

[19]Aristotle, "Metaphysics," *The Basic Works of Aristotle,* ed. Richard McKeon (New York: Random House, 1941), Bk. 1, Chap. 7, 1011b26ff., p. 749.

[20]Strawson responds in "Truth," *Truth,* ed. George Pitcher (Englewood Cliffs: Prentice-Hall, 1964), 33-35 to Austin's analysis that appears in Austin, "Truth," 18-31. For further discussions of the Austin-Strawson debate see Mackie, *Truth Probability,* 45-51; G. J. Warnock, "A Problem About Truth," in *Truth,* ed. George Pitcher (Englewood Cliffs: Prentice-Hall, 1964), 54-67; and J. L. Mackie, "Simple Truth," *Philosophical Quarterly,* 20 (October 1970): 323.

[21]Fred Sommers, "On Concepts of Truth in Natural Languages," *Review of Metaphysics,* 23 (December 1969): 275-76.

[22]Some do not take 'fact' in so narrow a sense. For example, see Ludwig Wittgenstein, *Tractatus Logico-Philosophicus.*

[23]Pitcher, "Introduction," 10. See Austin, "Truth," 22 for a much more intricate notion of correspondence.

[24]Pitcher, "Introduction," 11. For further discussions of the correspondence theory see Norman Geisler, "The Concept of Truth in the Inerrancy Debate," *Bibliotheca Sacra,* 137 (October-December 1980); Lawrence A. Bonjour, "Sellars

on Truth and Picturing," *International Philosophical Quarterly,* 13 (June 1973); and Wonfilio Resendiz, "Truth," *Diogenes* (Fall 1972).

[25]Wonfilio Resendiz, "Truth," *Diogenes* (Fall 1972): 137. See also Thiselton, "Truth," 896.

[26]*Encyclopedia of Philosophy,* s.v. "Coherence Theory of Truth," by Alan R. White, 2:130.

[27]For a discussion of this matter as it appears in the philosophy of Wilfrid Sellars, see Lawrence A. Bonjour, "Sellars on Truth and Picturing," *International Philosophical Quarterly,* 13 (June 1973): 245.

[28]See for example, Francis W. Dauer, "In Defense of the Coherence Theory of Truth," *Journal of Philosophy,* 71 (December 1974).

[29]Dauer, "Coherence Theory," 796.

[30]Dauer, "Coherence Theory," 797.

[31]See Thiselton, "Truth," 896 for further objections to the theory.

[32]Resendiz, "Truth," 140-41. See also Thiselton, "Truth," 896.

[33]*Encyclopedia of Philosophy,* s.v. "Pragmatic Theory of Truth," by Gertrude Ezorsky, 6: 428. See also Mackie, *Truth Probability*, 23-24.

[34]Resendiz, "Truth," 141.

[35]See Norman L. Geisler, "The Concept of Truth in the Inerrancy Debate," *Bibliotheca Sacra,* 137 (October-December 1980) and Rex A. Koivisto, "Clark Pinnock and Inerrancy: A Change in Truth Theory?" *Journal of Evangelical Theological Society,* 24 (June 1981).

[36]Geisler, "Concept of Truth," 328 and 338, n. 18. See also 337, n. 8-11.

[37]G. C. Berkouwer, *Holy Scriptures:* Studies in Dogmatics, trans. Jack Rogers (Grand Rapids: Eerdmans, 1975), 182-83. I am interpreting what Berkouwer means by "false," but it seems clear that the interpretation given is correct.

[38]Berkouwer, *Holy Scriptures*, 183-84.

[39]Someone might respond, "But, these are all consequences of a pragmatic theory. Until you indicate why such consequences are problematic, you have not presented arguments against the validity of the theory." Indeed, these are consequences, but they also point to problems with the theory. The reason one does not want a theory of truth which relativizes truth is that we expect of truth that it will be constant and dependable. Without such consistency it becomes very difficult to live in a world where one cannot depend on any idea to be true from one moment to the next. Even the dictum of doing what has proved to have positive results is undependable, for one does not know that he will get the same results each time. Thus, if truth were actually what the pragmatic theory indicates it is, it would be very hard to live in the world—nothing would be dependable. But, in fact, the world is dependable. Statements that accord with reality consistently give us reliable information about what to expect in the world, regardless of how things turn out in regard to our personal interests when we follow such statements. So, it seems appropriate to reject the pragmatic theory, because it is a pragmatically deficient theory.

[40]Tarski, "Conception of Truth," 14. Tarski and Davidson use the word 'sentence' rather than 'statement,' but they seem to mean the same thing I do when I use "statement." Certainly, Tarski is not claiming that questions, commands, and interjections have truth-values. Davidson is harder to interpret, since he offers a theory of meaning in terms of truth and since he intends to give an account of meaning for *all* sentences in a language, not just statements. He tackles the problem

of bringing nondeclarative sentences under the purview of truth theory in such papers as "What Metaphors Mean," *Reference, Truth and Reality: Essays on the Philosophy of Language,* ed. Mark Platts (Boston: Routledge and Kegan Paul, 1980). Nevertheless, Davidson's main focus is the content of the sentence, regardless of the mood, and that is my basic focus.

[41]Tarski, "Conception of Truth," 15.

[42]Tarski, "Conception of Truth," 16.

[43]Tarski, "Conception of Truth," 17.

[44]Tarski, "Conception of Truth," 17.

[45]Tarski, "Conception of Truth," 25. Tarski calls this a recursive definition of satisfaction. It leads to his recursive definition of truth.

[46]Tarski, "Conception of Truth," 25.

[47]Tarski, "Conception of Truth," 25. An important variation of Tarski's insights is Quine's position. Quine defines satisfaction in terms of the relation of expressions to sequences of objects, not merely to objects simpliciter. See W. V. Quine, *Philosophy of Logic,* chapter 3. Also, for further discussions of Tarski's theory see Sommers, "On Concepts of Truth in Natural Languages"; Mackie, *Truth Probability;* Mackie, "Simple Truth"; Kneale, "Propositions and Truth in Natural Languages"; Saul Kripke, "Outline of a Theory of Truth," *Journal of Philosophy,* 72 (November 1975): 694-699; and especially the penetrating analysis by Hartry Field in Hartry Field, "Tarski's Theory of Truth," *Journal of Philosophy,* 69 (July 1972).

[48]For Davidson's theory see Davidson, "True to the Facts," Donald Davidson, "Truth and Meaning," *Synthese,* 17 (1967), and Donald Davidson, "Belief and the Basis of Meaning," *Synthese,* 27 (1974). Helpful discussions of Davidson's views appear in J. A. Foster, "Meaning and Truth Theory," *Truth and Meaning: Essays in Semantics,* ed. Gareth Evans and John McDowell (Oxford: Oxford University Press, 1976); Stephen P. Stich, "Davidson's Semantic Program," *Canadian Journal of Philosophy,* 6 (June 1976); Neil Tennant, "Truth, Meaning and Decidability," *Mind,* 86 (July 1977); and Edward Martin, Jr., "Truth and Translation," *Philosophical Studies,* 23 (1972).

[49]Hubbard, "Current Tensions," 167-68.

[50]Berkouwer, *Holy Scripture,* 181. See also Jack Rogers and Donald McKim, *The Authority and Interpretation of the Bible: An Historical Approach* (New York: Harper and Row, 1979).

[51]Thiselton, "Truth," 877, shows that some use this claim to dichotomize Old Testament and New Testament concepts of truth.

[52]Thiselton, "Truth," 882.

[53]Even Thiselton, though, does not seem to have caught this point, for he speaks of the New Testament *concept* of truth and then essentially offers a word study of the *term* 'truth'. See Thiselton, "Truth," and Anthony C. Thiselton, *The Two Horizons: New Testament Hermeneutics and Philosophical Description* (Grand Rapids: Eerdmans, 1980), 411-15.

[54]See Thiselton, "Truth," and *The Two Horizons,* 411-15.

[55]An earlier draft of this chapter included comments on truth and confirmation. However, due to space limitations and the abbreviated nature of my comments, it was decided to remove the section. One can, however, get some flavor of the comments by seeing my discussion of Wittgenstein's comments on confirmation as it relates to particular language-games in my "Noncognitivism: Wittgenstein,"

Biblical Errancy: An Analysis of Its Philosophical Roots, ed. Norman L. Geisler (Grand Rapids: Zondervan, 1981).

[56]See, for example, Michaels, "Inerrancy or Verbal Inspiration?" 67 and Cornelius Van Til, *Apologetics* (Nutley, N.J.: Presbyterian and Reformed) as they relate the matter to apologetic methodology.

[57]Tarski, "Conception of Truth," 26.

[58]Menne "What Is Truth?" 72.

[59]Menne, "What Is Truth?" 72.

[60]See Ludwig Wittgenstein, *On Certainty*, ed. G. E. M. Anscombe and G. H. von Wright (New York: Harper & Row, 1972), sect. 559, p. 73[e], sect. 370, p. 48[e], sect. 257, p. 34[e], sect. 519, p. 68[e], as well as secs. 111-112, 234-235, 337, 446, 512, and 514.

[61]Ludwig Wittgenstein, *Philosophical Investigations* (New York: Macmillan, 1968), p. 224[e]. For explanation of the concept of a language-game, see page 34 of my text.

[62]For example, see Wittgenstein, *On Certainty*, sect. 257, p. 34[e] and Wittgenstein, *Investigations*, sect. 87, pp. 40[e]-41[e], and p. 180[e]. At this point, one might ask how one knows whether there is appropriate evidence to establish a statement's truth. Actually, there is an appropriate kind of evidence and an appropriate amount. As to the former, evidence is proper if it is relevant to the issue under discussion, if it is true, and if it is properly used in structuring one's argument, i.e., the argument contains no errors in reasoning, for even truthful information structured into an illogical argument will not help prove one's case. As to the latter, that issue is in part under discussion in the text, but also, one has enough evidence when the evidence of the kind mentioned is so rationally convincing that one cannot reasonably maintain a doubt. To maintain doubt under such circumstances indicates that the doubter is looking for some "final explanation" (which, in fact, he may already have), and yet does not know what it would look like if offered. Thus, there is no set number of arguments or pieces of evidence that must be reached to remove doubt. More important than the number of pieces of evidence and of arguments is the quality of the evidence and arguments.

[63]Mickelsen, "The Bible's Own Approach," 84; cf. p. 86.

[64]I suspect there are actually few differences in standards. It seems that many alleged variations arise from variations in style or from variations in language-games, i.e., in a given language-game (which language-game needs to be determined from the author's intent) the goal may not be exact precision, whereas in others it may be.

[65]Nicole, "Nature of Inerrancy," 84.

[66]Is ambiguity falsehood? Normally, this issue is not raised, but as long as one is talking about exact precision, it should be raised. Minimal reflection will assure one that ambiguity is not falsehood, nor is it considered as such.

[67]*Dictionary of Philosophy*, s.v. "Semantics," by Alonzo Church, 288.

[68]*Dictionary of Philosophy*, s.v. "Intension and Extension," by Alonzo Church, 147-148.

[69]*Dictionary of Philosophy*, s.v. "Denotation," by Charles A. Baylis, 76.

[70]What is said of individual words is also true of phrases. Outside the context of the sentence, they have no reference to the world. See also Paul Ricoeur, "Creativity in Language," *Philosophy Today*, 17 (Summer 1973): 98 for the concept that words in isolation have no relation to reality. Frege was one of the pioneers

of this idea. John Wallace is especially helpful in making this point as he discusses Frege's position in "Only in the Context of a Sentence Do Words Have Any Meaning," *Contemporary Perspectives in the Philosophy of Language,* ed. Peter A. French, Theodore E. Uehling, Jr., and Howard K. Wettstein (Minneapolis: University of Minnesota Press, 1979), 305-311.

[71]Ricoeur, "Creativity in Language," 98.

[72]Ricoeur, "Creativity in Language," 99. See also *Encyclopedia of Philosophy,* s.v. "Meaning," by William P. Alston, 5:238 and J. C. Nyiri, "No Place for Semantics," *Foundations of Language,* 7 (1971): 57.

[73]Another interesting theory which space does not permit to discuss is the stimulus-response theory. For explanation and discussion of the theory see Alston, "Meaning," 236, William P. Alston, *Philosophy of Language* (Englewood Cliffs: Prentice-Hall, 1964), 28ff.; G. H. R. Parkinson, "Introduction," *The Theory of Meaning,* ed. G. H. R. Parkinson (London: Oxford University Press, 1968), 6-7; and W. V. O. Quine, *Word and Object* (Cambridge, Mass.: The M.I.T. Press, 1960), 220-21.

[74]Parkinson, "Introduction," 4-5.

[75]Alston, "Meaning," 235. See also Alston, *Philosophy of Language,* 22-23.

[76]John Locke, "Essay Concerning Human Understanding," *From Descartes to Locke,* ed. T. V. Smith and Marjorie Grene (Chicago: University of Chicago Press, 1970), Book 3, Chap. 2, p. 406. See also Aristotle's statement of the theory in Aristotle, "On Interpretation," *The Basic Works of Aristotle,* ed. Richard McKeon (New York: Random House, 1941), Chap. 1, 16a3-9, 40.

[77]Kwame Gyekye, "Aristotle on Language and Meaning," *International Philosophical Quarterly,* 14 (March 1974): 74.

[78]Alston, "Meaning," 235.

[79]Wittgenstein, *Investigations,* secs. 243-246, 256-263, 272, for example. For further discussion of difficulties with this kind of theory see Hilary Putnam, "Meaning and Reference," *Journal of Philosophy,* 70 (November 1973) and Eddy M. Zemach, "Putnam's Theory on the Reference of Substance Terms," *Journal of Philosophy,* 73 (March 1976). For a clear statement of the opposite position, however, see Jerry A. Fodor, *The Language of Thought* (Cambridge, Mass.: Harvard University Press, 1979).

[80]Parkinson, "Introduction," 3. See also Alston, *Philosophy of Language,* 12-13 and Alston, "Meaning," 234.

[81]Alston, *Philosophy of Language,* 12-13. Some argue that the category of referential theories is no longer a useful one, since so few theories fit a precise definition of a referential theory. However, although there are problems with the category, it is still a useful one for philosophy of language. Some outstanding contemporary philosophers of language such as Alston and Parkinson have certainly thought so.

[82]Gottlob Frege, "Sense and Reference," *Philosophical Writings,* translated by P. T. Geach and M. Black (Oxford: Blackwell, 1952). Wittgenstein's picture theory is also a referential one. For explanation of the theory see Ludwig Wittgenstein, *Tractatus Logico-Philosophicus* (London: Routledge & Kegan Paul Ltd., 1971) and my "Noncognitivism: Wittgenstein." Two other noteworthy referential theories are those of Bertrand Russell and the structuralist theory of Fodor and Katz. For details of Russell's theory see Bertrand Russell, "On Denoting," *Readings in Philosophical Analysis,* ed. H. Feigl and W. Sellars (New York: Appleton-

Century-Crofts, 1949) and J. R. Searle, "Introduction," *The Philosophy of Language*, ed. J. R. Searle (London: Oxford University Press, 1971). For details of the structuralist theory see J. J. Katz and J. A. Fodor, "The Structure of a Semantic Theory," *The Structure of Language*, ed. J. J. Katz and J. A. Fodor (Englewood Cliffs: Prentice-Hall, 1964) and J. J. Katz, "The Philosophical Relevance of Linguistic Theory," *The Philosophy of Language*, ed. J. R. Searle (London: Oxford University Press, 1971). For an interesting discussion of the structuralist theory see Souren Teghrarian, "Linguistic Rules and Semantic Interpretation," *American Philosophical Quarterly*, 11 (October 1974).

[83]Searle, "Introduction," 2.

[84]Searle, "Introduction," 2-3. See also Thiselton's helpful footnote in Thiselton, *The Two Horizons*, 122, n. 28.

[85]Searle, "Introduction," 3. See also Michael Dummett, "What is a Theory of Meaning? (II)," *Truth and Meaning: Essays in Semantics*, ed. Gareth Evans and John McDowell (Oxford: Oxford University Press, 1976), 72-74.

[86]Parkinson, "Introduction," 3. This objection does not respond to Frege's theory. Frege was dealing only with semantics of a formalized language, since he believed that natural languages are so vague and so dependent on circumstances that one could not give a semantics for such languages. However, in Frege's formalized language the element of indexicality drops out, so the objection misses his theory.

[87]See Wittgenstein, *Investigations*, secs. 27, 39, 41, and 47 for these ideas. For further comment that meanings are not entities but a use, see Thomas D. Sullivan, "Between Thoughts and Things: The Status of Meanings," *New Scholasticism*, 50 (Winter 1976): 89.

[88]Alston, "Meaning," 234. This objection does not apply to Wittgenstein's picture theory, for whereas referential theories generally claim that each expression in language names some object, Wittgenstein claimed that logical constants (such as 'or', 'and', 'if') do not represent or refer (See *Tractatus*, 4.0312, p. 69 and 4.0621, p. 73).

[89]Parkinson, "Introduction," 3. For a detailed discussion of referential theories see Alston, *Philosophy of Language*, 12-22.

[90]Michael Dummett, "Truth," *Truth*, ed. George Pitcher (Englewood Cliffs: Prentice-Hall, 1964), 93. In Dummett, "What is a Theory of Meaning? (II)," 74, Dummett generalizes from Frege's theory to describe the main characteristics of any theory of meaning based on truth.

[91]Davidson, "Truth and Meaning," 319. See also Davidson, "True to the Facts," 754.

[92]Davidson, "True to the Facts," 756.

[93]Davidson, "Truth and Meaning," 310. See also Davidson, "Belief and the Basis of Meaning," 317ff.

[94]Wittgenstein's picture theory of meaning also relies on the notion of truth. It has certain affinities with early forms of the verification theory. Logical positivists expressed a great debt to the *Tractatus*, though Wittgenstein claimed they never really understood him. Michael Dummett is also a proponent of the view that meaning is to be understood in terms of verification conditions; see Dummett, "What is a Theory of Meaning? (II)".

[95]M. Schlick, "Meaning and Verification," *Readings in Philosophical Anal-*

ysis, ed. H. Feigl and W. Sellars (New York: Appleton-Century-Crofts, 1949), 148.

[96]Parkinson, "Introduction," 11.

[97]Alston, *Philosophy of Language*, 70.

[98]Ayer, *Truth and Logic*, 35.

[99]See Ayer, *Truth and Logic*, chapters 1 and 6.

[100]Dummett, "What is a Theory of Meaning? (II)," 74-75. See also pp. 76 and 117 in the same article.

[101]Davidson also discusses the problem in "What Metaphors Mean."

[102]Wittgenstein, *Investigations*, sect. 7, p. 5^e.

[103]Wittgenstein, *Investigations*, sect. 23, p. 11^e.

[104]Wittgenstein, *Investigations*, sect. 43, p. 20^e.

[105]Wittgenstein, *Investigations*, sect. 23, pp. 11^e-12^e.

[106]Wittgenstein, *Investigations*, sect. 11, p. 6^e.

[107]Austin, *How To Do Things With Words*, 94, 99-108.

[108]Austin, *How To Do Things With Words*, 100.

[109]For further development of the speech act analysis of language see J. R. Searle, "What is a Speech Act?", *The Philosophy of Language*, ed. J. R. Searle (London: Oxford University Press, 1971); H. P. Grice, "Utterer's Meaning, Sentence-Meaning, and Word-Meaning," *The Philosophy of Language*, ed. J. R. Searle (London: Oxford University Press, 1971); Alston, "Meaning," 238; Peter A. Facione, "Meaning and Communication," *New Scholasticism*, 49 (Winter 1975); and David Welker, "Locutionary Acts and Meaning," *Philosophical Forum*, 3 (Fall 1972). For further studies in general on the notion of meaning as use see Maurice Charlesworth, "Meaning and Use," *Australasian Journal of Philosophy*, 44 (December 1966); D. M. Taylor, "Meaning and the Use of Words," *Philosophical Quarterly*, 17 (January 1967); and J. F. M. Hunter, "Wittgenstein and Knowing the Meaning of a Word," *Dialogue*, 10 (1971).

[110]For discussions relevant to the conventional aspect of language, see Alston, *Philosophy of Language*, 56-61; Hilary Putnam, "Meaning and Reference," Eike von Savigny, "Meaning By Means of Meaning? By No Means!," *Erkenntnis*, 9 (1975): 139-42; and David Haight, "The Source of Linguistic Meaning," *Philosophy and Phenomenological Research*, 37 (December 1976): 244-47. All the above agree with the claim I hold that the particular words chosen to refer to specific objects is a matter of convention. Others, however, argue that there are determinant reference relations established between terms in a language and objects in the world and that such relationships persist despite any changes in convention. See, for example, Saul A. Kripke, *Naming and Necessity* (Cambridge, Mass.: Harvard University Press, 1980).

[111]Garth Gillan, "Language, Meaning, and Symbolic Presence," *International Philosophical Quarterly*, 9 (1969): 440.

[112]Wittgenstein, *Investigations*, sect. 641, pp. 164^e-165^e.

[113]William K. Wimsatt, Jr. and M. C. Beardsley, "The Intentional Fallacy," *An Introduction to Literary Criticism*, Marlies K. Danziger and W. Stacy Johnson (Boston: D. C. Heath, 1967).

[114]Wittgenstein, *Investigations*, sect. 337, p. 108^e.

[115]For interesting discussions on metaphor, see Ricoeur, "Creativity in Language"; Alston, *Philosophy of Language*, 96-106; Paul Olscamp, "How Some Metaphors May Be True or False," *Journal of Aesthetics and Art Criticism*, 29

(Fall 1970); and Earl R. MacCormac, "Scientific and Religious Metaphors," *Religious Studies*, 11 (1975).

[116]For interesting discussions of this issue, see Quine, *Philosophy of Logic*, 13-14; Thiselton, *The Two Horizons*, 95-97; Douglas Browning, "Creativity, Correspondence, and Statements About the Future," 514-36; and Jaakko Hintikka, "Time, Truth, and Knowledge in Ancient Greek Philosophy," *American Philosophical Quarterly*, 4 (January 1967).

A Response to Truth: Relationship of Theories of Truth to Hermeneutics

Norman L. Geisler
Professor of Systematic Theology
Dallas Theological Seminary

A Response to Truth: Relationship of Theories of Truth to Hermeneutics*

Norman L. Geisler

This is a crucial topic. In many respects it is the most basic in the inerrancy debate. Most points made by the author are helpful and some are essential.

I. AREAS OF AGREEMENT

First, let me mention some areas of broad agreement with Professor Feinberg.

1. How one views truth is crucial to the whole inerrancy debate.
2. The errantists (Rogers, Hubbard, Mickelsen) have a faulty (intentionalists) concept of truth.
3. The basic problem in this area is not theological, it is epistemological.
4. The correct theory of truth is a correspondence theory of truth.
5. The bearer of truth is not a word as such but a sentence.
6. We must distinguish between the intended *meaning* of an author expressed in the text and the intended *result*. (The former is the correct one.)
7. The *definition* of truth (e.g., as correspondence) is to be distinguished from the *confirmation* (or justification) of truth.
8. Intention is imbedded in the context of the verbal expression.
9. The so-called intention of the author behind the text is wrongheaded and unbiblical. Beauty is not *behind* a painting

*Publisher's note: This response is based on the paper originally presented by John Feinberg at the ICBI Conference. Prior to the publication of this volume, Feinberg revised his paper. Page references given in this response direct the reader to the section of the revised paper under discussion, and because of the revision some phrases that are referred to have been clarified or deleted.

but *in* it. Likewise, meaning is not *behind* the words of Scripture but is expressed *in* them.

This list is not intended to be exhaustive, but merely illustrative of some of the more important points with which we are in hearty agreement.

II. SOME AREAS NEEDING FURTHER EMPHASIS

First, I would like to have seen more emphasis placed on the *objectivity* of truth as versus the subjective view. This would have included more on the propositional as versus the purely personal view of truth (*a la* Brunner).

Second, only passing reference was made to the *absolute* nature of truth. This is an important oversight. The concept of absolute truth needs more emphasis, especially vis-a-vis the process view of truth.

Third, further clarification needs to be made on the word "intention" of the author. It is ambiguous. It can mean (1) intention *behind* the words (as Jack Rogers implies); (2) *purpose* of the author, which is not at all the same as the meaning of the author; (3) intended *meaning* of the author as expressed in the text. The latter is the usage consistent with an evangelical view of Scripture. To avoid the ambiguity of the word "intention" (especially in view of the common usage by errantists of numbers 1 and 2), I suggest we discard the word "intention" and speak of the *meaning* of the author expressed in the text.

Fourth, greater emphasis could be placed on the falsity of a conventionalist theory of meaning. This should begin by stressing that *words* (or symbols) are conventionally chosen, but the *meaning* of a statement is not conventional or arbitrary. Meaning is objective and essential. This could be done by showing that the "essence" of a statement is a "whole" or gestalt made of parts which may be arbitrary as individual parts, but they need not convey an arbitrary meaning when put together into a whole.

III. SOME AREAS NEEDING FURTHER CLARIFICATION

First, Professor Feinberg speaks of "inspired authors" (p. 40). Actually, the Bible refers only to inspired *writings* (2 Tim. 3:16). Inspired authors can lead to some deviant theological positions we must take care to avoid. Second Peter 1:20-21 speaks of Spirit-moved *writers*, but we have only God-breathed *writings*.

Second, there is a reference to "dual-authorship" of Scripture. This is moot. The early fathers, as many have pointed out, spoke of God as the *source* (ablative) and the prophets as the *instrument*. This fits with the prophetic model as used in Scripture (Heb. 1:1, 2; 2 Peter 1:20, 21; Isa. 59:21; Matt. 22:43; Acts 4:24, 25: 1 Cor. 2:13).

Third, Dr. Feinberg's view of meaning looks eclectic (p. 26). He could have avoided this if he had made the distinction between a conventionalist theory of *symbols* which we both agree is wrong) and a conventionalist theory of *meaning* (see "II, third" above).

Fourth, there is at least an apparent inconsistency in the author's refutation of the pragmatic view of truth. Feinberg seems to reject it because it doesn't *work*! (p. 33) That is a strange (pragmatic) refutation of pragmatism, especially for one who holds a correspondence view of truth. Why not reject it simply because it does not correspond with reality?

Fifth, there is a real problem in claiming that there is no necessary connection between epistemology and ontology (p. 34), especially for one who holds to a correspondence view of truth. Is this not precisely what a correspondence view means—that the epistemological is speaking of the ontological?

Sixth, the author needs to explain why he would disjoin meaning and truth (p. 29). Is it not so that every statement must be meaningful in order to be true? That is, are not only meaningful statements either true or false? If so, then it seems wrongheaded to argue that "no *theory* of meaning . . . is inherently harmful . . . to inerrancy" (p. 39). I take it that Feinberg's critique of some of the theories of meaning (such as conventionalism) showed that he really believed they are inconsistent with inerrancy.

Seventh, Feinberg weakens his case for a correspondence view of truth when he claims it is not taught in the Bible. It may not be *directly* taught, but then again neither is the Trinity. Surely, however, both the Trinity and a correspondence view of truth are *indirectly* taught.

These limitations notwithstanding, Feinberg's suggestions are generally helpful and the major points are absolutely essential to defending an evangelical view of inerrancy.

A Response to Truth: Relationship of Theories of Truth to Hermeneutics

W. David Beck
Associate Professor and
Department Chairman of
Philosophy
Liberty Baptist College and
Seminary

A Response to Truth: Relationship of Theories of Truth to Hermeneutics*

W. David Beck

A. THE NATURE OF THE PROBLEM

The topic that was posed for this exchange of papers was to clarify the relationship between theories of truth and hermeneutics in light of the question of inerrancy. Feinberg's answer, I take it, is that in the end there is no direct relationship between theories of truth and theories of meaning. At least, there is no logical dependence. There might of course, be historical or even traditional connections. The only exception to this is, naturally, any theory which defines meaning in any way that uses the notion of truth. In addition, Feinberg argues that theories of meaning do vary in their compatibility with the concept of inerrancy. Some, indeed, make it outright impossible.

Let me begin my response by trying to get clear as to just what the problem here is. Let us suppose that in some possible world, W_1, everyone confessionally subscribes to inerrancy. All hands in all quarters hold that the Bible is true in all that it teaches—biology, geography, history, ethics, and theology alike.

W_1 could of course, be the millennial kingdom. Otherwise, there appears to be at least three reasons not to accept the statements of certain W_1 seminary professors at face value.[1] First, it might be the case that they, and perhaps everyone, have a definition of "true" and its cognates that differs from what we expected. It could, for example, refer to the color of the words and translate roughly as "inky black." Or it might mean something like "practical," or "awe-inspiring," or "purpose-attaining," or even some concept with no English equiva-

*Publisher's note: This response is based on the paper originally presented by John Feinberg at the ICBI Conference. Prior to the publication of this volume, Feinberg revised his paper. Page references given in this response direct the reader to the section of the revised paper under discussion, and because of the revision some phrases that are referred to have been clarified or deleted.

lent whatsoever. In addition, we must suppose that W_1 does have a word equivalent in meaning to "true" in our actual world.

There is a second possibility. Suppose that in W_1 "true" has come to mean "observational," "existentially fulfilling," or what have you, and no equivalent to "adequately describes the real world" exists. Perhaps Kuhn and Rorty[2] have been successful in W_1 and epistemology has been relativized into hermeneutics. "True" thus refers to those propositions that are accepted and affirmed by all rational members of the society.

Thirdly, it might be the case that the semantics of W_1 are completely identical to our actual world's. "True" means just what it does to us. However, the residents of W_1 hold that the meanings of statements of other societies and times (perhaps even five minutes ago) are no longer ascertainable. They have grounds for holding all of the propositions of the Bible to be true, but they are valueless since no one can ever know what they mean.

Note that I have concerned myself only with problems that might arise when inerrancy is *affirmed*. The point is simply that such an affirmation is not enough, either in W_1 or in our actual world. What all three of the above situations have in common is that there is a hermeneutical issue that must be settled before the value of the affirmation can be settled.

In the first case the hermeneutical problem is the trivial one of knowing the meaning of another's words. The second case involves us in what is frequently called the *hermeneutical circle*: that is, our problem is not one of finding out which word means "true," but of finding out what "true" means. In the third case we have a problem of procedure. How, if at all, can we determine the meaning of another's words? The first problem is practical hermeneutics, the second is theoretical, the third is methodological. But in each case knowing and communicating are related.

The importance of this little fable about W_1 is to illustrate some connections between aspects of a theory of truth and some respective aspects of hermeneutical theories in order to get clear about Feinberg's thesis. I want first to say something about what a theory of truth is designed to accomplish.

B. THE COMPONENTS OF A THEORY OF TRUTH

Just what is a theory of truth? It is at this point that Feinberg's use of terms seems confusing to me. In one place we are told that the "issue" of truth comprises many questions (5). He identifies three major ones as the question of truth-bearers, the question of what sort of thing truth is, and the question of how one knows which statements are true. The second of these is said to be ontological, the third epistemological. Further on, however, we find that the "theory" of truth refers only to the ontological problem (11).

In fact, the pragmatic theory of truth is criticized for not being a *theory* of truth at all, but answering only the epistemological question (11). We are also told that there is no necessary connection between theories of truth and criteria (14). Finally, we must remember that it is in light of this usage that Feinberg concludes that *theories* of truth do not determine theories of meaning.

Now the reason this terminology seems unfortunate to me can be seen from the "theories" Feinberg discusses. *Correspondence,* for example, is primarily a criterion for truth. In fact, it does not even necessarily imply a relational definition of truth. John Austin explicitly absolves himself from any definitional implications of correspondence and treats it as purely conventional in nature.[3]

Coherence, too, is a criterion. That it is not a logically distinct view of truth is shown by the fact that some incorporate it with a correspondence criterion.[4] Feinberg is certainly correct that the *pragmatic* theory refers to a criterion, but we should not ignore the fact that it also involves a definition of truth. James, for example, said that "the true is the name of whatever proves itself to be good in the way of belief."[5] Thus truth is a property of (constantly changing) beliefs.

The *performative* theory of truth—which we need to carefully distinguish from the important general theory of performatives—tells us something about the use of "true," to be more specific, the purpose of its use. The *semantic* theory gives us the conditions for its use.

The important point is that none of these theories are total theories of truth. They are all answers to more than one question. What is more, many of them, with a little imagination all of them, could coexist in one overall view of truth. And there is a reason for that: all of these components, and many more, are used or eliminated by different larger theories of truth as dictated by another factor, namely the question of how we know the truth.

The issue of the method of knowing is, in fact, the component which supplies the logical connections to other components of a total view of truth. By this I do not mean that knowing is always the chronological starting point of any system. In Plato, for example, it clearly is not. But nevertheless, without the dialectic there is no connection between the forms and linguistic expressions.

Pragmatic criteria are simply the inevitable result of a strict empirical method of knowing. It must follow that "true" is to be defined as a conventional property of beliefs (James) or statements within systems of beliefs (Quine). In the extreme view it becomes a matter of simple consensus (Rorty). In addition one can expect such a system to use some version of correspondence, usually in a causal or stimulus-response version, to explain the foundation or primitive level of knowing.

One more example must do. In recent process epistemologies it is the view of knowing as an internal relation, both causal and mental, that conditions the whole theory of truth. This dipolar knowing results for Whitehead in a distinction between the objective form of the prehension of knowing into a proposition and the resulting intellectual prehension whose subjective form is judgement. Whitehead continues:

> We shall say that a proposition can be *true* or *false*, and that judgement can be *correct,* or *incorrect,* or *suspended.* With this distinction we see that there is a 'correspondence' theory of the truth and falsehood of propositions and a 'coherence' theory of the correctness, incorrectness, and suspension, of judgements.[6]

The question, then, of how we know the truth is not only important, but it is crucial in determining the whole structure of a theory of truth. Now we must turn to what this means for hermeneutics, and we can then give a final evaluation of Feinberg's main thesis.

C. THE IMPLICATIONS OF A THEORY OF TRUTH

Feinberg divides the issue of meaning again into three components: the questions of the bearers of meaning, of what meaning is, and of the determination of meaning. Again as well, the second of these is referred to as ontological, the third as epistemological. I would only suggest that here, as well as in the discussion of truth, we ought to avoid this kind of reifying of terms. The question is really not what meaning is, but what the meaning is, and it is not at all clear to me that that is an ontological question, that is, a question about what there is. But perhaps this is only semantic preference.

We must now note that in this section "theory of meaning" refers only to answers to a specific question, namely to what the meaning of a linguistic unit is. Since theories of meaning as truth are really referential and since behavioral theories are in fact, denials of meaningfulness as such, we are left with three choices: that the meaning of language is the idea to which it belongs, or the real-world counterpart to which it refers, or the use to which it is put.

Feinberg now concludes that answers to the question of what truth is have no implications for answers to the question of what meaning is, except, of course, when the latter is explicitly defined by the former (36). This is, we must remember, a very narrow thesis, but I think a correct one. It ought to be obvious from the very fact that there are many meaningful statements to which the notion of true or false does not even apply. It is just here, of course, that verificationist views go wrong.

This conclusion does have an important implication for inerrancy. Namely, that if inerrancy is construed simply as a doctrine regarding the *truth* of Scripture, then it does not apply to many of Scripture's statements. This is precisely one of Ramsey Michael's objections to the general use of the word.[7] But this is only to say that "inerrant" cannot be an extensionally adequate replacement for "inspired."

Feinberg also concludes, and I agree that a final theory of meaning must in fact be composite. This is certainly part of the fallout of Wittgenstein's "toolbox" view of language. Language is used for many purposes and there is no good reason to think that meaning can function in only one way or always in the same way. Scripture contains performatives, descriptions, poetry, ethical commands, non-ethical commands, questions, analogies, and many other types of sentences.

Here is where the matter gets difficult. We want to be able to give a clear solution to the kinds of problems I posed at the beginning of this paper as occurring in some possible world W_1. Some think that this can be brought about by insisting on an universal element of referentiality in all occurrences of meaning. That seems hopeless to me.

On the other hand, we cannot leave the problem here. Inerrancy of descriptive language is of course impossible if we cannot provide some link between truth and communication. That is no argument for such a link, and here is not the place for one, except to note that all factual communication depends on it. But I must at least locate the argument.

I have already argued that the connections within the theory of truth are formed by answers to the question of knowledge. Now it seems to me that there is also an additional factor to be included in an overall theory of meaning, namely, the matter of preserving meaning which is simply the hermeneutical question. That is, can the same meaning, including that of true descriptions, be communicated from one person to another? Here, I would argue is the connection to the crucial issue of how we know.

A few examples must do. Probably the best study of this connection between truth theories and specifically biblical hermeneutics in the modern period is Hans Frei's *The Eclipse of Biblical Narrative*.[8] Here we have a detailed analysis of how the shift from realist to rationalist and empiricist epistemologies transformed hermeneutical theory and practice in the eighteenth century, the results of which still shape our thinking.

If what we know is the real world, then it is possible to speak accurately of the real world. There is a real connection, and an immediate one, between language and events. In particular, Frei notes, what the realist does not place between the word and the event is "the meaning." The account "referred to and described actual historical occurrences."[9]

Modern epistemologies, culminating in Kant, invent a new entity that comes between word and event. For Locke it was the idea to which words refer. Inevitably, what becomes important to the student of the Bible, then, is not the described event but the detachable meaning, the concepts, images, symbols, the way-they-were-saying, which is not, of course, what they said.

Kant thought that he had bridged the chasm between knowledge and object by the transcendental deduction. Few enough of us have understood that argument and very few have judged it adequate. Certainly the nineteenth century did not, and thus we get Hegel and Schleiermacher. In neither of them is understanding bound to the fixed object and thus hermeneutics becomes concretized into twentieth-century theology as the search for the meaning-for-me.[10]

A second helpful example can be found in contemporary process hermeneutics. Surely one of its best proponents is Russell Pregeant, a disciple of Schubert Ogden. In his *Christology Beyond Dogma*[11] Whiteheadian epistemology is applied to Matthew's view of Christ. One chapter, however, is devoted to hermeneutical theory.

The key in Whitehead's view of apprehending truth is that in each knowing event the object acts always as a lure. Pregeant puts it thus:

> The dichotomy between subject and object has been relativized, but not obliterated. . . . We perceive the datum, always and only, in relation to a particular significance it has for us. Whitehead's epistemology, then, involves a concept of participatory knowledge, which represents one aspect of his broader metaphysical doctrine of internal relations.[12]

Consequently, our language about events must always be inexact, analogical, value-laden, luring, and only secondarily true.[13] Hermeneutics, then, is the art of following those "lures to feeling." We seek the meaning, but always relativized by the meaning to us.

These examples must suffice to show the connection between truth, specifically the method of knowing truth, and hermeneutics. This was just the point of the little fable about W_1: without a stated epistemology and interpretive method any affirmation of inerrancy is of no value.

I should note that this discussion has dealt only with propositional language. This leaves many questions about the meaning of language unanswered. I want only to caution against following a solution that has become extremely popular since Wittgenstein's language-game concept of the *Philosophical Investigations*. Feinberg's criticisms are quite to the point. The problem will not be solved by creating a *religious* language-game which contains all of Scripture's statements and has its own notion of truth. This is simply a way of holding on to the Kantian dilemma while finding some worthwhile use for religion.

D. TRUTH, HERMENEUTICS AND INERRANCY

There is one last issue which must be touched on now that I have stated that a connection between truth and hermeneutics does exist. That is, why is this important to the present inerrancy debate?

The reason, I think, is this: inevitably our systems of thought are formed by our epistemology. That does not mean that our definitions of knowledge and truth are not specified, modified or even made possible by other pieces of the pie—be it metaphysics or revelation, or whatever. Say what you will, we all start with the "thereness" of reason, system, knowing, logic, or Logos.

Now the next point will, at first, seem to contradict the last one, but I beg for patience until I finish it. I want to hold further that the real issue in the inerrancy debate is not inerrancy. We really are not quibbling about the extent of biblical truth at all. The best evidence for that is that nonevangelicals do not, in fact, disagree with us: they do not even make sense of what we are saying. This has to strike one whenever one reads of us as misguided, anarchronistic fundamentalists (still "swinging from the trees" as Gore Vidal recently remarked), who think that every word of the Bible has to be interpreted literally. Inerrancy is a security blanket some have yet to outgrow. The Bible is eternal, religious truth known only to faith.

What one sees repeatedly in such statements is the view that inerrancy is not false, it is inconceivable. That is, there could be no such thing as true propositions about the factual world spoken by God to an individual man, because God is not that sort of being with that sort of relationship to the scientific world. In other words, there is a metaphysical commitment that obstructs any theology in which God is a real, but nonmaterial person who is an agent in ordinary history. This point is not new, but perhaps it needs to be emphasized that the issue is the very conceivability of inerrancy not its facticity. Given another view of God, inerrancy is obvious. The very nature of religion as such is at stake here.

This metaphysical commitment, however, does have epistemological roots. Those roots are primarily Kantian. This is not the place to continue this point, but it is crucial to see the dependence of inerrancy on hermeneutics, and hermeneutics ultimately on a view of knowledge and truth. Knowing that, we must concentrate on dealing with the Kantian framework, not only of contemporary theology but of our society as a whole.

We have now come full circle. Let me conclude with an agenda. What is central in a Kantian framework is not the empirical methodology and its application to biblical interpretation (Locke had given us that a century earlier), but the placing of God, values and religion in a separate, noumenal, category. From this we get the distinction between science and religion (read: evolution and creation), knowledge and belief, fact and faith, and so on, that is so central to the contemporary mindset.

This problem is philosophical at root, but it touches every science, and it will need to be countered at every point. We need historians who will show that "secular" history is just bad history, psychologists who will demonstrate that behaviorism is just bad psychology, and so on. Especially in theology, it seems to me, we must again make a case for the facticity of God and his actions, especially the Resurrection. We must at this point not allow a theological fideism—which itself has Kantian roots—to prevent us from defining truth. Yes, God is infinitely truth. But we are persons in his image, capable of knowing and determining truth, however hampered by sin.

If what I have said above is correct, the most urgent task is to show that the Kantian starting points are unwarranted and do not accord with our experience.[14] Once we have made inerrancy credible, it is far easier to show its truth. To do so will mean to start with some hermeneutical clarifications, but these will lead inevitably to epistemological foundations.

NOTES

[1]It is difficult not to think here of Jack Rogers' reported statement: "If inerrancy means that the Bible is true, trustworthy, and authoritative, I believe in the full inerrancy of the Bible." Quoted by Leslie Tarr, "Group Voices Alternative to Verbal Inspiration," *Christianity Today* XXV 14 (August 7, 1981): 34.

[2]I refer to the thesis argued in Thomas Kuhn's *The Structure of Scientific Revolutions* (Chicago: University of Chicago Press, 1962) and recently in Richard Rorty's *Philosophy and the Mirror of Nature* (Princeton: Princeton University Press, 1979).

[3]See John Austin, "Truth" in *Truth,* ed. G. Pitcher (Englewood Cliffs: Prentice-Hall, 1964). My reference is particularly to p. 18.

[4]See for example Gilbert Harman, *Thought* (Princeton: Princeton University Press, 1973); Keith Lerner, *Knowledge* (Oxford: Clarendon Press, 1974); and also Michael Williams, "Coherence, Justification, and Truth" in *Review of Metaphysics* XXXIV, 2 (Dec. 1980): 243.

[5]William James, *Pragmatism* (New York: Longmans, Green, and Co., 1908), 76.

[6]Alfred N. Whitehead, *Process and Reality* (New York: MacMillan, 1929), 290.

[7]I refer here to his essay "Inerrancy or Verbal Inspiration? An Evangelical Dilemma" in *Inerrancy and Common Sense*, ed. R. Nicole and R. Michaels (Grand Rapids: Baker, 1980), 58.

[8]Hans Frei, *The Eclipse of Biblical Narrative*, (New Haven: Yale University Press, 1974).

[9]Frei, *Biblical Narrative*, 2.

[10]On this point see especially Frei, *Biblical Narrative*, chap. 15.

[11]Russell Pregeant, *Christology Beyond Dogma*, (Philadelphia: Fortress Press, 1978).

[12]Pregeant, *Christology*, 35. See A. N. Whitehead, *Process and Reality*, 471.

[13]I remind the reader that this and what follows is Pregeant, not Whitehead.

[14]This is also not an original thesis. I remember it being pounded into me by my respected seminary professor John Gerstner.

Historical Grammatical Problems

Bruce K. Waltke
Professor of Old
Testament
Regent College

2. Historical Grammatical Problems

Bruce Waltke

The importance of more clearly identifying and analyzing problems in the historical grammatical method of exegesis ought to be obvious. By articulating the problems we will be in a better position to remedy them and thereby be able both to hear God's Word more clearly and to remove some of the theological barriers separating those communities of faith based on the inerrancy of God's Word.

The need for accurate rules in interpreting the Bible also ought to be obvious. If misinterpretations take place with frustrating regularity between people speaking the same language, living in the same community and even under the same roof, and who have the advantage of accompanying gestures, facial expressions, and tonal inflection, how much greater must the difficulty be when we are reaching across a gap of centuries to people speaking "dead" languages, living in a culture in which some of the common objects of daily life are unfamiliar to us, and whose minds have not been shaped by about two millennia of Western Civilization.[1] Just as Odysseus found on his visit to Hades that the dead seer Teiresias could not speak to him until his inarticulate ghost had been brought to life by the blood of a sacrifice,[2] so also the ancient, inspired spokesman and scribes of Holy Scripture cannot become articulate to succeeding generations of the faithful without accurate and judicious rules of interpretation.[3]

The need for accurate interpretation of the Bible far exceeds the importance of a correct rendering of other ancient writers. The Bible is the Word of the sublime God; the others are merely the words of fallen man. In the spirit of St. Augustine, Evangelicals affirm: "What Scriptures says, God says." The canon of Scripture, inspired by the Holy Spirit yet without negating the distinctive personality of its human contributors, is the authoritative Word of God, making us wise unto salvation and profitable for doctrine, reproof, correction, and instruction in righteousness (2 Tim. 3:16). But as James Packer frankly states, "Biblical authority is an empty notion unless we know how to determine what the Bible means."[4] The community faithful to the Bible universally concedes that the Bible, when rightly interpreted will not mislead us. But the catch here is the phrase, "when rightly interpreted."

Not only does the Bible's divine authority and sublime intention call for accredited rules of interpretation, but the Church's yearning for unity also demands our diligent establishment of them. Don Carson noted:

> Every debate in the history of the church is conditioned in part by hermeneutical considerations; and those happy souls who naively think they can without loss avoid such considerations and 'just believe the Bible' in fact adopt all sorts of hermeneutical stances unawares. Although hermeneutical positions *alone* do not *necessarily* determine one's theological conclusions in advance, the role they play is much larger than is often allowed.[5]

Four and a half centuries of Christendom divided into denominations and other ecclesiastical bodies, all of which appeal to the authority of Scripture in support of their divergent doctrines and practices, empirically validates the observation of the Westminster divines: "all things in Scripture are not alike plain in themselves, nor alike clear unto all" (Westminster Confession. 1. vii.).

Now to make the importance of our subject, "Historical Grammatical Problems," even more acute, we need to observe that many of these divided ecclesiastical bodies affirm the historico-grammatical method of exegesis as the most appropriate method of exegeting text. The signers of the Chicago Statement on Biblical Inerrancy represent denominations divided in part by doctrinal differences, and yet affirm not only the inerrancy and authority of Scriptures but also "that the text of Scripture is to be interpreted by grammatico-historical exegesis,"[6] an affirmation assumed in this paper.

Concerning the history of the use of the nomenclature "grammatico-historical" Kaiser, basing himself on Milton S. Terry, wrote:

> Every since Karl A. G. Keil's Latin treatise on historical interpretation (1788) and German textbook on New Testament hermeneutics (1810), exegetes have generally adopted his term as being descriptive of their own approach to the exegetical task: the 'grammatico-historical' method of exegesis. The aim of the grammatico-historical method is to determine the sense required by the laws of grammar and the facts of history.
>
> The term *grammatico-*, however, is somewhat misleading since we usually mean by "grammatical" the arrangement of words

> and construction of sentences. But Keil had in mind the Greek word *gramma,* and his use of the term *grammatico,* approximates what we would understand by the term *literal* (to use a synonym derived from the Latin). Thus the grammatical sense, in Keil's understanding, is the simple, direct, plain, ordinary and literal sense of the phrases, clauses and sentences.[7]

This method, as normally understood, attempts to recover the author's meaning and intention[8] by carefully establishing the context—the meaning of his words, the grammar of his language and the historical and cultural circumstances, etc.—in which he wrote. But this is easier said then done. Commenting on speakers sharing the same language, history and culture, Ogden and Richards said:

> Normally, when ever we hear anything said we spring spontaneously to an immediate conclusion, namely, that the speaker is referring to what we should be referring to were we speaking the words ourselves. In some cases this interpretation may be correct: this will prove to be what he has referred to. But in most discussions which attempt greater subtleties than could be handled in a gesture language this will not be so."[9]

From what has been said thus far it follows that for the Bible to speak more clearly, for its authority over our beliefs and practices to be realized more perfectly, and for our unity to be more complete we need to be more precise in the application of the grammatico-historical method. The divisions between those within the church employing this method of exegesis bears mute testimony to the fact that the method has problems, and we may be sure that these problems will not be solved until we can first uncover and analyze them. To that end we direct our paper. In my judgment the crucial and broad problem areas in the application of the historico-grammatical method are: (1) prejudgment; (2) biblical criticism; and (3) context.

I. PREJUDGMENT

Traditionally the historico-grammatical method has focused its attention on the context of the biblical writers in order to control their meaning and neglected the context of the interpreter. This one-sided approach to interpretation was further exacerbated by Descartes' theory of knowledge, in which man as active subject looks out on the world as passive object.[10] Olthuis wrote:

> The Cartesian subject-object split ('I am' and the sense-perceivable world) has denatured the interpretative process. One

> does not begin from a desire to bring self in the proper mode of relation to a text with the purpose of dialogue, sharing and communion. Rather, we begin with the observing consciousness as the supreme arbiter of reality to which all things must give account, including Scripture; the text is simply a passive object to be mastered. Mastery, control, exploitation, is the basic form of human engagement with the world. The subject-subject dialogue between an interpreter and an author who has objectified his meaning in a text is denatured into an operation of a presupposition-less, body-less, a-historical mind who determines the meaning of a passive object through rigorous application of procedures in accordance with the rules of exegesis. The movement is one way: from subject to object.[11]

But modern hermeneutics has turned attention from the text to the interpreter and underscored that it is impossible for him to be neutral or presuppositionless; rather his prejudgment *(Vorurteile)* decisively influences his understanding of the text before him. Schleiermacher, the father of modern hermeneutics, pointed out that our critical tools have led to misunderstandings and not to consensus; Gadamer exposed the naivete of the historian who assumes he can abandon his own concepts and think only in those of the epoch to be researched;[12] Dilthey shattered the illusion that understanding a text could be purely "scientific";[13] R. Bultmann argued "there cannot be any such thing as presuppositionless exegesis";[14] Heidegger theorized that the interpreter stands with a "world" decisively shaped by his own historicality.[15] Bernard Lonegran asserted:

> The principle of the empty head rests on a naive intuitionism. . . . The principle . . . bids the interpreter forget his own views, look at what is out there, and let the author interpret himself. In fact, what is out there? There is just a series of signs. Anything over and above a reissue of the same signs in the same order will be mediated by the experience, intelligence and judgment of the interpreter. The less that experience, the less cultivated that intelligence, the less formed that judgment, the greater will be the likelihood that the interpreter will impute to the author an opinion that the author never entertained.[16]

The new hermeneutic has made it painfully apparent that it is much too simplistic to speak of interpreting the Bible by granting the texts its normal meaning. For many interpreters "normal" unwittingly means "according to my prejudgments, preconceptions and preunderstanding."

Before considering the problem of how we shall overcome this problem of prejudgment, let me first say that I agree with I. Howard Marshall[17] that some new hermeneuts overemphasize the differences between the context of the original authors and their audiences, on the one hand, and the context of the modern reader, on the other hand. Their argument that our situation is so different from that of the biblical world that we can not do a straight reinterpretation of the meaning of the biblical text in order to gain teaching for ourselves overlooks the fact all men are made in the image of God so that God can speak to all men, however, accommodating that language must be, as Packer stressed.[18] But in spite of this important caveat, it seems to me that Evangelicals need to look afresh at Bultmann's and his students' hermeneutic circle for its epistemological, philological and spiritual value. In this circle the interpreter must bring his preunderstandings, his prejudgment to conscious awareness. According to Bultmann, preunderstanding "must be raised to consciousness to be critically examined in the course of understanding a text, to be gambled with; in short, this is required: to allow oneself to be questioned during one's inquiry of the text and to listen to its claims."[19] To use Wink's term, the interpreter must allow critical inquiry to *distance* him from the way in which the text has become embedded in the church's tradition and/or in his own culture. Nicholls complained:

> Throughout the history of Western Christian theology the truth of the gospel has suffered from an unconscious assimilation of conflicting tenets and practices. Augustine was unable to completely free himself from neo-platonism. Aquinas synthesized biblical faith and Aristotelian philosophy. Modern liberal theology in the West has been deeply influenced by the philosophies of the Enlightenment, evolutionary science and existentialism, and in the East by the philosophies of Hinduism and Buddhism. . . . A contemporary example of cultural syncretism is the unconscious identification of biblical Christianity with 'the American way of life.'[20]

Olthuis cogently stated the need for consciously and critically distancing our culture and preconceptions from the authoritative text:

> The existential surrender to the God of the Scriptures is always embedded in the historical process: it happened here, at this time, in this community, through this particular vision of biblical authority. It is in terms of the language and symbolism of a certain tradition that the submission to God and the Word of God takes place. . . .

> At the same time, the fact that our confession of biblical authority takes place in terms of a particular tradition ought to remind us that the particular way we confess submission to the Scriptures is not simply the aggress of faith, but the articulation of faith in interaction with and filtered through the kind of persons we are, with the conceptual frameworks we work, in the kind of communities we live in, in the historical times that we live. That reality once accepted brings a necessary distinction to the fore and with the distinction a relativity. We need to distinguish our faith surrender to the Scriptures and their authority from the way we conceptualize and articulate it.
>
> Recognizing this and acknowledging that both our conceptualizations and the tradition in terms of which we articulate are not without shortcomings, we are able to be open to other confessions of biblical authority. We will be able to relativize our own view of biblical authority without relativizing our surrender to the Scriptures. If we can resist the temptation to canonize our views about the canon, we will be able to honor the sincere conviction of others that they submit to the Scriptures even though we are convinced that their view of Scriptural authority is inadequate.[21]

That we cannot assume that the interpreter comes to the text *tabula rasa* is graphically illustrated by the paintings of the Madonna given as gifts by artists from many countries around the world and hanging in the sanctuary of the Church of the Annunciation in Nazareth. Each artist of the same subject has either consciously or unconsciously portrayed Mary according to his own culture. For the Japanese artist she is an Oriental; for the Mexican a Latin; for the African a Negress, etc. None represents her as a Jewess. All represent her subjectively and inaccurately. So also each interpreter "colors" the Bible with his own world, and until he consciously separates his own culture from that of the Bible he will misinterpret it. The emphasis on distancing oneself from one's own prejudgment is not unique to the new hermeneutic; it is totally consistent with the historico-grammatical method.

In addition to distancing himself from the text by critical study and reflection the interpreter within the hermeneutical circle must also consciously allow the distinctive message of the text to reshape progressively his own questions and concepts. As developed by Bultmann's students, especially Fuchs and Ebeling, the interpreter finds that in dialogue with the text, the text progressively changes his historical, cultural, psychological and ideological world. In this circle, the hermeneut becomes involved in a two-way process of encounter between himself and the Word of God, on the one hand, and his own culture, on the other hand. In this dialogue, according to Gadamer, "the interpreter is free to move beyond his own original horizons, or better, to *enlarge* his own horizons until they come to *merge* or *fuse* with those of the text. His goal is to reach the place at which a merging of horizons *(Horizontverschmelzung)*, or fusion of 'worlds,' occurs."[22] Thiselton noted: "in Gadamer's notion of the merging of horizons we find a parallel to Wink's ideas about 'fusion' and 'communion,' and Fuchs' central category of Einverstandnis" (= "common understanding," "mutual agreement," "empathy").[23] Thiselton further added: "This is achieved . . . only when, firstly, the interpreter's subjectivity is fully engaged at a more than cognitive level; and when the text, and the truth of the text, *actively* grasps *him* as its object."[24]

To be sure evangelicals must avoid the pitfalls of the new hermeneutics—that the recognition of the author's meaning is an impossibility, that what the text once meant can no longer be authoritative theological statement in the modern era, that the text and one's experience of it enter into a relationship of mutuality, that the interpreter and text are necessarily swallowed up in a sea of historical relativity, that the objective meaning of the text is no longer the interpreter's goal, that meaning takes place in the existential encounter between text and interpreter.[25] Nevertheless, the practitioner of the historico-grammatical exegesis should pick up the strengths of the new hermeneutics; namely, of letting the text correct his own preunderstanding and of entering into the Bible's own culture—its facts, its "world" of ideas and values and above all its supra-historical and supra-cultural factor of conversion to the God of Israel and his Christ along with the acceptance of his Lordship over creation and history, in contrast, for example, to secularism, humanism and Marxist atheism.

By submitting in faith to these cultural dimensions of the text, conversion takes place and spiritual understanding ensues. The hermeneut is now spiritually prepared to translate the text in addition to being cognitively prepared for its historico-grammatical translation. This spiritual transformation, brought about by an encounter with the text and a decision on the part of the interpreter to surrender fully to its claims, also removes emotional blockages, political allegiances, socio-economic and other conscious or unconscious prejudices.[26]

To be sure the so-called new hermeneutic is not altogether new. Jesus accused his critics of erring in their interpretation of Scripture for spiritual reasons (Matt. 22:29). Lady Wisdom rebuked the fools of her day: "If you had responded to my rebuke, I would have poured out my heart to you and made my thoughts known to you" (Prov. 1:23). Paul likewise emphasized spiritual understanding (1 Cor. 2:10-3:4). Although the principle of commitment to that which is being looked into has always been understood by both Evangelicals, especially by those within the pietistic tradition, and by philosophers who stressed associating knowing with experience, to my knowledge it has never been consciously linked as part of the historico-grammatical method of interpretation. This positive and abiding value of the new hermeneutic is in keeping with the method of the Reformers, who proposed a hermeneutical circle that sought to allow the Scriptures to correct the church's traditions. What is new is the stress upon correcting one's unconscious prejudices regarding the Scripture's meaning. Unfortunately, Bultmann himself never overcame his own prejudgment. Nicholls rightly observed: "Bultmann's acceptance of a mechanistic, scientific world view precludes any meaningful recognition of the supra-cultural elements in the biblical story."[27]

II. BIBLICAL CRITICISM

A. Textual Criticism

The starting point in the historico-grammatical method is that of establishing the correct text of the "original autographa" from the witness of the Hebrew manuscripts and ancient versions. Through the canons of textual criticism the exegete seeks to restore this text, and for both scientific and theological reasons we have good reason to think that the text is well-preserved and that no essential doctrine stands in doubt. But in spite of these convictions we must admit that the practice is fraught with problems. Here we address ourselves to four problems: (1) What do we mean by "original autograph?" (2) Is the Masoretic vocalization inspired and what weight do we grant it? (3) What weight should be accorded the varying witnesses to the text? (4) What is the boundary of the text?

First of all, then, what do we mean by original autograph? The Chicago Statement on Biblical Inerrancy states: "We affirm that inspiration, strictly speaking, applies only to the autographic text of Scripture."[28] Our problem is occasioned by the phenomenon that books of the Bible seem to have gone through an editorial revision after coming from the mouth of an inspired spokesman. For example, an editor of the Second Book of the Psalter almost certainly revised the original psalm in his collection by systematically substituting Elohim for YHWH. The name YHWH occurs in the other four books of the Psalter 642 times in contrast to 29 occurrences of Elohim, but in Book II YHWH occurs 30 times and Elohim 164 times. Furthermore, Elohim sometimes occurs as the parallel for YHWH in the "b line" in the other four books, and vice-versa in Book II (cf. Ps. 70:1). Then, too, in synoptic psalms Book I uses YHWH where Book II has Elohim (cf. Ps. 14:2 with 53:2; 40:13; with 70:1). To judge from the rules of the Qumran community, where a member was to be expelled for uttering the divine name (1Qs 6:27-7:2), Book II represents a very early piece of evidence for the reverential evasion of the divine name and ought to be regarded as the product of editorial activity. Differences in other synoptic passages of the Old Testament are also probably due to intentional editorial activity as well as to unintentional scribal error. Editorial activity almost certainly took place in other books of the Bible as well. If this be so, then the notion of an original autograph should also take account of later inspired editorial activity. From this perspective it is important to distinguish inspired scribal activity from noninspired scribal changes introduced into the text. But in practice such a distinction may prove difficult to establish. Brevard Childs relieves the difficulty by suggesting that even scribal "error" became part of the canon,[29] but I cannot accept his resolution because he does not reason from a well-defined doctrine of revelation and inspiration.

Then too, there ought to be a debate among Evangelicals concerning the inspiration of the text's vocalization. Matthias Flacius defended the vowel signs by the "domino theory" that if these are not dependent on God as the primary cause, but on human writers themselves, then the authority of all of Scripture must be called into question.[30] His conviction regarding the inspiration and authority of the vowel points found credal formulation in the Helvetic Confession. But today it is customary to scoff at this position because later research established beyond reasonable doubt that the vowel points were added to the consonantal text at a relatively late date and therefore, it is thought, they have less authoritative weight than the consonantal text. The difference in weight granted the consonantal text over the Masoretic vocalization is reflected in the practice of the NIV translators. When they departed from the consonantal text of the Masoretes they felt obliged to indicate that fact in the footnotes of their translation, but when they emended the vowels they felt no constraint to inform their reader of their departure from the received text.

But the fact that the vowels indicators were added later does not preclude the possibility that the vowels are indeed inspired. J. I. Packer noted: "It makes no difference to inspiration (how could it?) whether its product is oral or written. When in the past evangelical theologians defined God's work of inspiration as the producing of God-breathed Scriptures, they were not denying that God inspired words uttered orally as well."[31] God said to Jeremiah: "I will put my words in your mouth." Now words consist of both consonants and vowels. It makes a great deal of difference, for example, what vowel is inserted between the consonants "f-r" ("for," "fir," "fear, "fire"). When God's words were placed on manuscripts the consonants alone were written, but surely they were "read" with the intended vowels. The consonants were passed down via writing, the vowels via voce, but together they constitute the inspired "word." It ought to be obvious that both are inspired even though they were represented and transmitted in different ways. Why should differences in their manner of transmission make any difference in our evaluation of their authority? Even the consonantal text underwent a serious revision when it was transposed from the paleo-Hebrew script to the Aramaic script. But who would wish to argue that because it has been represented differently in the course of its transmission that the consonants we have in hand were not inspired? It seems wrongheaded then to disparage the vowel points because they were put into writing at a late date.

Admittedly the vocalized portion of the inspired text is probably more vulnerable to corruption than the written text. But we have good reason to think, as I have argued elsewhere, that the text's vocalization was conservatively transmitted until the time of the Masoretes and accurately represented by them.[32]

Another textual problem relates to the weight to be given to varying text types. The debate in New Testament studies between those favoring the majority text type versus those favoring an editorially reconstructed text along the lines of arguments advanced by Westcott-Hort are well-known. In Old Testament studies inerrantists disagree regarding the degree to which priority should be given to the Masoretic text type over that represented in the *Vorlage* of the Septuagint. A comparison of the NASB with NIV will show that the former stands much closer to the Jewish text than the latter (cf., for example, their rendering of Ps. 73:7).[33]

Finally, there is a problem regarding the establishment of the text's boundaries. Some inerrantists proceed on the assumption that the "original text" can be restored from the witness of the Hebrew manuscripts and ancient version and that the method of conjectural emendation should be set aside. Others accept the possibility that on occasion the text is so badly corrupted that the original reading must be conjectured. The argument now has been tilted in favor of allowing by conjecture a larger boundary than that attested in the traditional witnesses to the text with the discovery and establishment of an original *paragraph* in 4QSam[a], a reading heretofore attested only in Josephus.[34]

B. Historical Criticism

I. H. Marshall defined "historical criticism" as the study of any narrative which purports to convey historical information in order to determine what actually happened and is described or alluded to in the passage in question."[35] The term is sometimes employed more broadly for the aim to elucidate an obscure text by throwing light on it from its historical setting, but we shall limit ourselves here to its more narrow aim to test the historical accuracy of the text.

Before considering the positive contribution this criticism may have to the historico-grammatical method, we must admit that there are good historical, philosophical and theological reasons for excluding it. In the first place, most of its practitioners drink from the philosophical fountains that sprang up in English deism, French skepticism, and the German Enlightenment, which made human reason the touchstone and yardstick for whatever truth may be found in Scripture and finished off transcendence by confining the universe within a closed system of earthly cause-effect relationships. Furthermore, its practitioners often insist on handling the Bible as a book little different from any other book. Johann Salomo Semler (late eighteenth century) is usually designated as the father of this technique which revolted against miracles, the supernatural and heaven itself, and Ernst Troeltsch may be regarded as its great systematizer. Peter Stuhlmacher summarizes his unexcelled explanation of the structure of historical criticism:

> According to Troeltsch, historical criticism operates with three indissolubly connected principles. He calls them criticism, analogy, and correlation. Criticism denotes a systematic skepticism which the historian applies without partiality to all historical tradition. This criticism is made possible by analogy,

> that is, the assumption of an intrinsic similarity in all historical occurrence. Troeltsch speaks emphatically of the 'omnipotence' and 'all leveling purport' of analogy, because it embraces all present and past historical occurrence in a single context of events, allows no arbitrary establishment of occurrences or revelatory texts without analogy, and enables the interpreter to make contemporary historical phenomena which are directly known and familiar to him the interpretative framework and criterion for comparable events in the past. The third principle, of correlation, that is, of the coherence and reciprocal action of historical events, is indeed already given with the concept of analogy, but now where (sic!) expressly named, it prevents arbitrary criticism or use of the scheme of analogy.[36]

Practiced with these three principles, the Old and New Testament were pitted against each other in a manner unlike that experienced in the church since Marcion, the clarity and sufficiency of Scripture to make one wise to salvation were destroyed, and the theologian was compelled to establish a canon within a canon, based on his subjective tastes and experiences. In sum, it eroded and destroyed the foundation of the Christian faith.

Gerhard Maier and Peter Stuhlmacher have for some time been involved in an important debate over the validity of the historical-critical method. Maier calls for the end of it. He argues that the method is invalid: "The statement that we must inquire into a theological subject with methods independent of theology, i.e., with 'atheological' methods, is a contradiction in itself and just the opposite of what is needed."[37] He also argues that the method is contrary to good historiography: "To be sure, as long as one makes analogous classification a precondition for acceptance, much in the Bible remains without foundation. But how can the *pure* historian without further ado reject something just because it happens only once? What can be experienced and what has analogies can certainly not be declared synonymous."[38] In addition, it rests on a prejudgment contrary to Scripture, and those prejudgments determine the result beforehand. Then too, it leads inevitably to the conclusion that we must find a canon with the canon: "The bold program of finding a 'canon in the canon' demands nothing else than this: to be more biblical than the Bible, more New Testamently than the New Testament, more evangelical than the Gospel, and even more Pauline than Paul. Radical earnestness is the intention, radical dissolution is the result."[39]

Peter Stuhlmacher also rejects historical criticism as practiced on Troeltsch's assumptions, but he comes at the problem differently. Rather than calling for the end of the historical-critical method he appeals instead for a "theology of consent," an approach that shows his indebtedness to the new hermeneutic. The historic critic, he argues, should give up his pretext of scientific detachment and recognize that his preunderstanding is decisively influencing his work: "The expectation . . . that the scholar was able in some way to hold himself aloof from the object of his research and thus allow them to speak for themselves has lain unfulfilled." He acknowledges the indispensability of historical criticism but adds the principle of "hearing," from which will result a dialogue between interpreter and text. In other words, he urges the historic critic to operate with a view of history and reality that is open to "transcendence." Against Baur he wrote:

> If the concept of history here is too narrow to allow a disclosure by way of revelation (of whatever kind) historical-critical results must of necessity oppose the gospel's revelatory claim. Conversely, if historical criticism operates with a view of history and reality which is open to transcendence, it can glean essential data for the orientation of church and preaching.[40]

Both men reject the practice of historical criticism based on presuppositions that preclude transcendence and divine intervention. But whereas Maier, building his case on cognitive arguments, represents traditional orthodoxy, Stuhlmacher, appealing to subjective experience, represents neo-orthodoxy. Both of their attacks against normative historical criticism are cogent. In addition to rejecting false premises of normative historical criticism, I also consider it illegitimate to call into question the Bible's accuracy either because the events it relates are not otherwise well attested or because they are contradicted in nonbiblical sources. We have sufficient historiographic and theological reasons to trust the Bible's accuracy. Caird helpfully commented: "It is well to recall that the ancient Israelite had in his legal system ample acquaintance with the notion of sufficient attestation."[41]

But is there a "legitimate" form of historical criticism, a legitimate way of calling into question whether the historical referents, persons and objects in Scripture actually existed and events really happened as presented in them, while at the same time accepting God's transcendence and activity in *Heilsgeschichte* and in the Scripture's inerrancy. In my judgment such historical criticism is possible in six connections.

In the first place, we must reckon with the possibility that the biblical writers may employ conventional language. The past is not accessible to us by direct scrutiny but only interrogation of biblical witnesses and the possibility of conversation with them depends on the interpreter's ability to speak their language. Goldingay put it this way:

> At this point we need to recall that God's written Word was given to us through human means, according to human conventions of particular historical situations. We may not write this way, but we must not treat our literary conventions as if they were absolutes. They are just a different set of conventions. These conventions must be understood and allowed for if we are to identify the assertions being made through them, which have their reliability that comes through inspiration.[42]

As an example of the way in which conventional biblical language may mislead us about what actually happened we may consider the biblical notices about the authorship of books. Jude, for example, says that Enoch, the seventh from Adam, prophesied certain things (vv. 14-15), but Goldingay commented that the book of Enoch which Jude is quoting "unquestionably belongs to the intertestamental period, and doubtless, in aspiring to antediluvian authorship, never aimed to mislead anyone."[43] Matthew cites Jeremiah for a quotation taken from Zechariah (Matt. 27:9); Mark cites Isaiah as the prophet of a passage taken from Malachi (Mark 1:2); the Book of Proverbs commences with the editorial heading, "The proverbs of Solomon, son of David," but includes material that is neither proverbial (contrast 10:1 with the economiums to wisdom in 1:8-9:18) or Solomonic (cf. 30:1 and 31:1). In the light of these facts, is it not possible to call into question the historical accuracy of references to Moses and Isaiah in the New Testament and to think of them instead as conventional ways of locating a passage? On the other hand, when Jesus builds his case for Messianic identity on the fact that Psalm 110 claims Davidic authorship, we should accept the Psalm's claim at face value.[44] In sum, we need to determine authorship of a book on other grounds than merely an appeal to the biblical notices regarding authorship. It seems to me that Article XVIII of the Chicago Statement on Biblical Inerrancy contains a built-in tension. On the one hand, it affirms that "the text of Scripture is to be interpreted by grammatico-historical exegesis, taking account of its . . . devices," and, on the other hand, it denies the legitimacy of "rejecting its claims to authorship." But

Scripture's "devices" may not necessarily lead to an historically accurate representation of its authorship.

Second, in deciding this matter of what actually happened, we need to reckon with the reality that biblical writers believed in dual causation of events; at one level events could be explained as the effects of earthly causes, while at another level they could be viewed as the work of heaven. But whereas, the modern historian is more likely to look to earthly causes in the chain of historical events, the biblical writers normally pointed to the Playwriter who wrote history's script. In the case of David's deliverance from Absalom, we have the advantage of both perspectives from two different authors. In Psalm 3 David praises the LORD for delivering him from his son, but the historian who wrote 2 Samuel attributes a large measure of the success to Hushai's wit. Both are historically accurate; both inform us about what actually happened, but without the historical record, we might have erred in our judgment about what actually happened by excluding the earthly factor in favor of restricting our explanation of the event exclusively in terms of the divine intervention. In Psalm 139:13 David attributes his birth to God's creative activity, but we all know that it would be mischievous to pit this heavenly explanation of birth against the genetic processes involved in conception and birth. Similarly, Genesis 1 explains the creation of the cosmos exclusively as the work of God, but an interpreter might err in his historical judgment of what actually happened by excluding the possibility of "natural," earthly causes. What actually happened from the earthly perspective is not always given in the Bible, and we might err when we pit the heavenly view against earthly factors at work in the event, or when we exclude the possibility of such factors in our interpretation. In the matter of dual causation, historical criticism has a legitimate role to play in the historico-grammatical method of interpretation.

Third, it is legitimate to consider in this matter of deciding historical accuracy the literary genre in which events, persons or objects are reported to have occurred and existed. None would assume a historical referent for persons, objects or events in fables (Judg. 9), parables (Matt. 13) and allegories (Isa. 12). Since the Bible contains such fictitious pieces of literature we are left with the problem of determining the extent of such writing in the Bible. It is possible, for example, that the rich man and Lazarus in hell and Abraham's bosom (Luke 16) are not historical figures. On the other hand, we ought not to argue in a circle in deciding a text's historical credibility by labelling it as a saga, legend or myth on the basis of a bias against transcendence, and then turn around and appeal to this classification as evidence that the referents in the literature are nonfactual.

Fourth, we need to take account of the fact that numbers in the Bible are notoriously difficult to accept on face value, especially as given in the received text of Chronicles, and are legitimately the subject of historical criticism. Some ascribe the large numbers in Chronicles to textual corruption, whereas others think they are used symbolically. Goldingay opts for accommodation as the explanation:

> When Chronicles says a million fought against Asa, what it means is that the odds against him were huge (and thus the victory given him by God was the more glorious), or more specifically that the army was of such a size that it would be the equivalent of a million in the military conditions of the writer's day (the Persian period, in which he wrote, was an age of great armies). To speak of thousands (the likely actual number) would make it seem a rather small-scale occasion. The Chronicler's infallibility consists in his giving the right impression of the magnitude of the occasion for the people of his age.[45]

Fifth, most will agree the speeches in Acts and elsewhere are abbreviated versions of what was actually said and to that extent do not precisely represent the historical situation.

Finally, we need to take account of the aim or intention of the writer. I have in mind here the point well-established in New Testament studies that the gospels do not give us a day-by-day chronological account of Jesus' ministry. The differences between the gospels demonstrate that they cannot all have followed a chronological order but must have rearranged events according to their purposes.

It has not been my aim in this discussion of historical criticism to solve the problems I have raised. I merely aimed to underscore that historical criticism may play an illegitimate or legitimate role in the historico-grammatical method of exegesis. It is illegitimate when it is undertaken in the prejudgment that rules out transcendence and divine intervention, or when it demands extra-biblical confirmation. On the other hand it may be both legitimately and profitably pursued as part of the historico-grammatical method when it is a matter of taking note of the biblical writers' conventions, heavenly perspective, use of nonhistorical literary forms, tendency to abbreviate and to present material according to his aim in writing about divine matters.

C. Source Criticism

Practitioners of the historico-grammatical method of exegesis rightly insist that an author's meaning must be determined in part by his historical situation. But who are the authors of the Bible and under what historical situations did they write? Kaiser wrote:

> Lest it be said that we are advocating the abandoment of all introductory studies, let it be announced in bold relief that it is exceedingly important that the interpreter complete a thorough investigation of the biblical book's author, date, cultural and historical background. It is virtually impossible to locate the book's message in space and time without this essential material.[46]

But this question of authorship raises several thorny problems. Many of the books of the Bible are anonymous, and we have already seen that references to authorship do not necessarily have to be taken at face value. In addition, if we accept the notion of editorial activity and redaction criticism we open the door to the problem of multiple authorial intentions in the literature. And finally, in narrative texts we need to recognize three levels of authorship; the characters in the narrative, the human author presenting their statements, and God.

With regard to this last concern let it be noted simply that we are concerned with the human author's intention in using the characters in his story. In addition it is wrongheaded to contrast the human author's intention with that of God's. Caird rightly noted regarding the first two levels of authorship that we are "not to assume that the authors of the Old Testament approve all that is said or done by the characters in their story." But he erred when he attempted to drive a wedge between the Author's meaning and the human authors' intention. He suggested: "The Bible contains many instances in which the intention of God differs from that of his agent or messenger."[47] In support of this conviction he calls attention to Genesis 50:20; Isaiah 10:5-11; Isaiah 45:1-4, but in all these instances he confounds agents *within* the books with the author of the book itself. In no case does he undermine Augustine's contention: "What Scripture says, God says."

We shall address the second problem regarding discontinuity and continuity in authorial intentions as the texts were edited and became part of a larger canon of literature in another connection.[48] Here, then, we confine ourselves to the first problem: who authored the books of the Bible, especially the anonymous books.

Some younger scholars with a "high view" of inspiration and

the Bible's infallibility are finding it more and more difficult to accept traditional "conservative" answers to this question. Goldingay, for example, wrote:

> I suggest that it is in fact possible to combine an acceptance of the Bible's authority, inspiration and infallibility; a conviction that the Bible is God's Book, that His Spirit inspired it, that it is exactly what He wanted it to be, that it is the only sure source of the Gospel; . . . with a refusal to accept that a corrollary to this commitment is a commitment to traditional approaches to critical questions.[49]

In place of tradition these scholars employ critical source tools such as literary criticism, form criticism, tradition criticism, redaction criticism, canonical criticism, etc., and these tools not only serve them in deciding the matter of authorship, date and unity, but also as exegetical tools in their own right. Carson wrote:

> 'Source criticism,' 'form criticism,' 'tradition criticism,' 'redaction criticism,' 'audience criticism,' and the like . . . when these literary tools were first introduced, they did not make their appearance as hermeneutical principles but as ways of getting behind the Gospels as we have them in order to illumine the 'tunnel' period and perhaps know something more about the historical Jesus. To use these tools at that stage usually meant buying into a larger conceptual framework concerning the descent of the tradition—a framework which evangelicals (and many others for the matter) were bound to differ.
>
> Yet in the case of the Synoptic Gospels, at least, we have enough comparative material to be certain that there are literary borrowings; identifiable forms whose history can be traced, however, tentatively; and demonstrable rearranging and shaping of the pericope to support certain theological ends. The literary criticisms were not necessarily evil after all; they became increasingly acceptable as exegetical tools, devices to enable us better to understand the text.[50]

According to David Wenham the decisive evidence for the use of sources in the New Testament lies in the New Testament documents themselves:

> Not only are there dislocations and apparent duplications in the documents which suggest that the gospels, for example, have undergone a more complex editorial process than is often imagined; but much more important and much less ambiguous evi-

> dence is provided by the striking phenomenon of agreement between the synoptic gospels in certain passages. The agreement is too close to be explained as the accidental convergence of independent accounts, and the only adequate explanation is either in terms of a common source lying behind the different accounts or in terms of mutual dependence.[51]

With respect to source criticism I propose in this paper to consider more specifically the two-fold problem vis-à-vis the validity and value of employing various types of literary critical tools as part of the historico-grammatical method of exegesis. Because of my own competence and because of limited space I shall confine my attention to the Pentateuch.

D. Literary Source Criticism

"Orthodox" literary critics, to use Child's label, employ the four criteria of varying divine names, doublets, linguistic differences and diverse theologies to facilitate their efforts in isolating literary strands in the Pentateuch, and when these four criteria are brought to bear on Genesis 1:1-2:25 they work together consistently in dividing this passage into two distinct creation stories. Putative "P" (1:1-2:3), among other features, uses the divine name Elohim, but "J" (2:4-25) has YHWH: "P" presents a distinct account of the creation climaxing with the creation of man; "J" begins with man; "P" uses *'adam* as a generic term for "mankind," "J" as a proper name, "Adam;" "P" presents God as transcendent, "J" as immanent.

Not only does the coincidence of these four criteria lend support to the contention of orthodox critics, who approach the text with a dissecting knife, that Genesis 1:1-2:25 consists of two originally separate literary accounts of creation, but it finds further corroboration in the research of "classic" literary critics, who assume that a work is a unity and direct every effort to understand the whole of what they read. From their perspective one notes that the two accounts, isolated by orthodox literary critics, present the reader with two distinct plots, which Aristotle defined as a series of events having a beginning, middle, and end. Their analysis reveals two distinct introductions (1:1-2 and 2:4-6), which are syntactically similar containing a summary statement followed by a circumstantial clause describing the negative state at the time of creation using the construction *w* noun + *hyh,* (1:2 and 2:5-6), followed by the main creation account introduced by *waw consecutive* (1:3 and 2:7). Moreover, the middle sections of the two accounts differ in their unifying principle—P develops the progress of creation according a very orderly plan marked off by a strict repetitive structure, whereas J develops it by means of dramatic plot. P's style is formal and straight forward, J's is that of a storyteller. P's theme presents God as the transcendent ruler over creation, J as the immanent God within it. Finally both accounts end with an epilogue—P explains the origin of the Sabbath, J explains the origin of marriage.

On the basis of the independent research of both types of literary criticism I think it is most reasonable to conclude that Genesis 1 and 2 consists of two accounts of creation which were probably originally isolated sources, and that these sources were later fused together to constitute complementary accounts about the creation. Moreover, I think it is fair to conclude that the analysis of literary critics contributes significantly to a more accurate exegesis of these chapters and also toward more profound reflection on divine matters. They have helped the exegete to see more clearly the structure of these two accounts, their styles and themes and to define words such as *'Adam* more precisely. In addition to these exegetical gains their analyses has heuristically placed us in the position to perceive more clearly theological truths that must be held in dialectical tension: in P God is transcendent, in J He is immanent; in P God is sovereign over the cosmos giving names to its life supportive systems—"Day," "Night," "Sky," "Earth," "Sea"—in J man, as God's responsible vice-regent over the earth, names all the animals. In P we feel comfortable, assured that God is in control, but uncomfortable because he seems remote. But in J we feel uncomfortable because we are uncertain about what man will do but reassured that God is with us. In P God calls upon man to subdue the earth, in J He places man in the Garden to tend it.

But there are features of orthodox literary criticism that are invalid. First, we should stoutly deny that the sources contradict one another. Second, we should jettison their posture of approaching the text primarily to isolate earlier sources. This approach should be rejected in the first place because it is often impossible. Although distinct literary units with the final text form can sometimes be clearly observed because all the knives of the literary critics cut the text at the same place, the fact of the matter is that often they do not. For example, Alan Jenks in his doctoral dissertation defended at Harvard contradicted the German scholars Fohrer and Eissfeldt by denying that the following portions of Genesis belong to putative "E": portions of Genesis 15, all of 21:1-7; portions of 22, all of 24 and 25; portions of 28, all of 29 and 30; portions of el, all of 32 and 34; portions of 35 and all of 36 and would radically alter their views regarding the Joseph story (Genesis 37:50.)[52] The reason for his difference with the German scholars is not hard to find: Jenks gave priority to the theological criteria; the Germans to the linguistic. In spite of Eissfeldt's claim to the contrary, the criteria often work against each other. The Canadian scholar, Van Seter, against the Germans and Jenks allows only Genesis 20:1-17 to E in the Abraham pericope. The Joseph story, formerly regarded as a sure mine for discovery E material, has now been set aside by Coats and Whybray as a possible text for source criticism.[53]

In contrast to this uncertainty about the isolation of sources in the Pentateuch is the certainty, newly won by rhetorical critics, that the Book of Genesis displays a unity and integrity that transcends its sources. Although one can sometimes with some confidence isolate distinct literary blocks in Genesis, he cannot separate these blocks from one another and still make sense of the story from any one of them by itself. For example, the so-called J account of the Flood commences: "The LORD said to Noah, 'Go into the ark,' " but without the preceding P material the audience is unprepared for the reference to the ark. Childs stated: "When this P material is joined to the earlier material the relationship is not redactional. The essential basis of this assertion is particularly clear in the fusion of strands within the flood story."[54]

In addition, we ought to reject the orthodox critical emphasis on dissecting the Bible into sources not only because it is often impossible and because the work in hand constitutes a unique and unified literary achievement, but also because this emphasis rests on a faulty theology. Most orthodox literary critics minimize the doctrines of revelation and inspiration, and with this prejudice they err against God and man. The canon of Scripture that resulted from the two-fold divine and human activity consists not of unattested and incomplete J and P documents and of a dubious E, but of the books of Genesis, Exodus, etc. These sacred books, and not the sources contained in them, constitute the Scriptures that bear witness to our Lord Jesus Christ and are endorsed by Him and His apostles as the authority for our faith and practice.

Furthermore, in addition to discarding both the orthodox critical chaff that the sources contain contradictions in alleged doublets and their preoccupation with isolating sources and writing theologies based on them, we ought also to reject the notion that the date and fusion of these sources are necessarily late. In contrast to the orthodox critical consensus of fifty years ago, today most orthodox critics recognize that the sources in the Pentateuch contain early and reliable historical remembrances. The Albright school during the course of the past half century through indefatigable labor in field archaeology and through brilliant and numerous publications turned the weight of scholarly opinion away from the entrenched Wellhausian idea that the ancient history portrayed in these sources was nothing more than a mirage projected into the distant past by the imagination of the sources' writers, to the conviction that these sources contain accurate memories of the Patriarchal and Mosaic age. On the other hand, these later orthodox critics also concur in the view that the sources also contain later materials. But when one tries to pin down this allegedly later material he quickly discovers that the critics do not agree about its content or date. Childs speaks boldly and authoritatively to the point. Regarding the dating of P, he concluded: "a tentative enterprise at best."[55] Regarding the recent effort of Winett and his students, N. Wagner and J. Van Seters, to redate J and to separate into an earlier and post-exilic strand: "In my judgment, the major significance of these monographs has been to call into question many of the unexamined assumptions of the 'orthodox' literary critical method rather than to establish a convincing new hypothesis regarding sources."[56] After surveying the attempt to trace the traditio-historical development of D he concluded: "Needless to say, the very fluid state of research shows no signs of moving toward a consensus in respect to this set of issues."[57] In sum, scholars have identified, established and defended ancient, historical notices in the alleged Pentateuchal sources, but they have been unable to demonstrate either late materials in these sources of their date of composition beyond reasonable doubt.

Finally, we need to recognize that we cannot date scientifically the time when these sources were fused because we have evidence of redaction over at least two millennia, from 1800 B.C. to A.D. 200 Donald J. Wiseman wrote:

> Tigay has shown that redactors completed the remoulding of the earlier Sumerian poems into one 'Gilgamesh' tradition (ca. 1800 B.C.), about the same time as the Hittites made a summary of 5 tablets of Gilgamesh into one; and about the same time as the Kassite period of Babylonia (1540-1250) when scribes began copying the Gilgamesh, and other epics, in a traditional

> way which was to hand them on virtually unchanged for more than a thousand years.[58]

In 1975 Tigay reemphasized the point made by George Foot Moore in 1889 that Tatian in his Diatessaron, wove the four gospels into a single running narrative in Syriac or Greek around the year A.D. 170.[59] The same type of redaction took place in the Samaritan Pentateuch dated by James Purvis to about 110 B.C.. In a number of passages in Exodus the scribes within this tradition conflated the text by adding to it passages from Deuteronomy.[60] Furthermore, we know from the manuscripts at Qumran that these plusses were added to the text sometime between 400 B.C. and 100 B.C. in the earlier proto-Samaritan text on which the Samaritan sectarian recension was based.[61]

Now if we can establish ancient material in the sources and cannot establish later material in them, and if the fusion could have taken place at a very early period we have no reason to reject out of hand the notion that Moses authored the essential core of the Pentateuchal material.[62]

E. The Problem of Oral Tradition

Form criticism, tradition criticism and canonical criticism are all based on the conviction that the materials contained in the Pentateuch were reformulated, reworked, represented, and supplemented until they were finally written down and granted canonical status in the post-Exilic community. These modern source critics think that these stories were transmitted orally at local sanctuaries by tradents, that is, by circles or centers of traditionalists who preserved, reinterpreted and added to Israel's diverse traditions and theological heritage. To the older "orthodox" critics' redactor and literary sources, the modern critics have added tradents and oral traditions. These critics uncritically accept the notion that oral communication was the chief mode of transmitting sacred materials through successive generations. Nyberg stated the conviction in this famous quote:

> Transmission in the East is seldom exclusively written, it is chiefly oral in character. The living speech plays in the East from ancient times to the present a greater role than the written presentations. Almost every written work in the Orient went through a longer or shorter oral transmission in its earliest history, and also even after it is written down the oral transmission remains the normal form for the preservation and use of the work.[63]

But what is the evidence for the conviction that oral tradition was the chief form of transmission of sacred materials in the East and for tradents that reshaped these traditions? The answer to this question is crucial for the historico-grammatical method of exegesis. The notion that Israel's sacred heritage was handed down in a fluid oral form raises a whole complex of problems about the Bible's historical accuracy and authorial intentions and meanings. On the other hand, if it can be established that they were written down at an early period and transmitted conservatively these problems are minimized. To answer that question I will direct my attention to the cultures and literatures surrounding ancient Israel. We will turn first to Ebla in Northern Syria (ca. 2350 B.C.), then to Mesopotamia whose coherent culture can be traced with confidence for over two millennia, until it was dealt what proved to be a fatal blow by Alexander the Great at about 330 B.C., then to the Hittites (1450 to 1250 B.C., then to the later Old Arameans of Northern Syria (900 to 800 B.C.), to ancient Ugarit (1400 B.C.), then to the united Egyptian culture and literatures from about 2500 to 500 B.C., then to the Northwest Semites, including the Hebrews, and finally to the earliest stages of Islam. In this wide-ranging survey I have but one question: "Did these peoples represent and preserve their cultural heritage through oral tradition easily subject to alteration or through written texts precisely with a view that their heritage not be corrupted?"

1. Ebla

According to Pettinato[64] the Ebla tablets contain economic-administrative texts, lexical (onomastica) lists, historical-juridical matters (royal ordinances and edicts, state letters, lists of cities subject to Ebla), true literature (myths, hymns, incantations, collections of proverbs), and syllabaries (for learning Sumerian, grammars of Eblaite, and bilingual grammars). This ancient city, which antedates Moses by a millennium was highly literate and preserved that part of its heritage and culture which it considered important in writing, and these tablets do not allude to tradents or oral tradition, at least to my knowledge and to the extent to which they have been published thus far.

2. Mesopotamia

In Mesopotamia we find collections of Sumerian proverbs copied as schoolboy texts that achieved canonical status as early as about 1500 B.C. Moreover, by comparing these collections of proverbs with later collections dated to the Neo-Babylonian period (ca. 600 B.C.) we discover that they were transmitted in writing with relatively little modification.[65] Their great creation epic, the *Enuma Elish,* was probably composed during the time of Hammurabi (ca. 1700 B.C.), and its earliest extant copy is dated only 100 years later, and this is clearly a copy. The law codes of Lipit Ishtar, Eshmunna, Hammurabi, etc. antedate Moses by centuries. Moreover, in the Akkadian culture, according to O. Weber,[66] it was the rule that only an agreement that was fixed in writing was juridically valid. The Code of Hammurabi, with striking similarities to the Book of the Covenant concluded: "Observe all these laws with care." Here, too, we find hymns from the early Sumerian period (ca. 1900 B.C.), but what arrests our attention about thse hymns is the fact that though they were intended to be sung at cultic centers they were written down. In fact these hymns contain technical terms probably related to their liturgical use that Sumeriologists cannot decipher, precisely as in the case of the biblical hymns which contain notices that Hebraists cannot interpret.[67] Letters, too, were read from written texts. One letter from Mari (1750 B.C.) reads: "Your tablet which you did send forth, I have heard."[68] Representing the historical literary genre we have the famous Sumerian king lists and the later and equally famous Assyrian annals. Representatives of the religious genre include rituals, incantations, and descriptions of festivals. In all this literature there is no mention of tradents or oral tradition.

What then is the evidence for oral tradition in Mesopotamia? There is one text that shows it was copied from oral recitations. Its colophon reads: "written from the scholars' dictation, the old edition I have not seen." But this exception actually proves the rule. Commenting on this text Laessoe wrote: "It would seem to appear that oral tradition was only reluctantly relied upon, and in this particular case only because for some reason or other an original written document was not available."[69] The situation represented by this colophon differs *toto caelo* from that supposed by form critics. The scribe is a faithful copyist and not a tradent who feels free to reformulate and supplement the tradition.

With regard to the Mesopotamian epics, one may theorize that oral traditions in smaller units existed behind the epic complexes, but this notion rests on pure speculation, not on evidence. We have already noted that these larger epics were on occasion redactions of earlier written sources and that they were composed at a very early period.

3. Hittites

From the Hittites we have not only their law codes that were granted canonical authority so that they could not be tampered with, but also their international treaties, and according to George Mendenhall[70] and Klaus Baltzer[71] they present us with striking similarities to the Book of Deuteronomy. These treaties could not be changed; e.g., to cite but one typical statement: "whoever changes but one word of this tablet, may the weather god . . . root that man's descendants out of the land of Hatti."

4. The Arameans

For lack of space let me cite from the Arameans only the Sefire treaty, which was written in triplicate in rock: "Whoever . . . says, 'I will efface some of its words, 'may the gods overthrow that man.' " To my knowledge in all the literature of the Hittites and Arameans there is no mention of tradents such as are envisioned by modern source critics.

5. Ugarit

The peoples of ancient Ugarit wrote down their hymns and myths celebrating their nature deities and recited them at their sanctuaries, and there is no evidence to suggest that oral recitation ever existed without the written text we have in hand or that it had priority over the written witnesses to their beliefs.

6. Egypt

From Egypt we have numerous texts of many of the literary genres represented in the Bible, and once again the evidence shows that the scribes attempted to preserve their heritage in writing as accurately as possible. One colophon reads: "The book is completed from its beginning to its end, having been copied, revised, compared and verified sign by sign."

But is there any evidence for oral tradition among the Egyptians? Volten in his *Studien zum Weisheitsbuch des Anii* and van de Walle, in *La transmission des texts litteraires Egyptiens* compared identical texts from earlier and later periods in Egypt's history and showed three types of variants: (1) entirely graphic error; (2) auricular error; and (3) slips of memory. These scholars suggest that the slips of memory may have been due to the fact that the teacher was dictating from memory, or that the scribe copied from memory, or that the pupil copying from dictation forgot what the teacher had said. But scribal error due to faulty hearing or from copying from memory is certainly not sufficient evidence upon which to rest a case that the Egyptians transmitted their sacred heritage in a fluid oral form. Both Volten and van de Walle describe these changes as errors. But the hypothetical tradents imagined by modern source critics do not accidentally change the text through faulty hearing or memory, but intentionally alter it, sometimes drastically, to keep the traditions contemporary with changing historical conditions.

7. Northwest Semitic

When we turn to the evidence from Northwest Semitic civilizations and cultures we have less literary evidence, apart from the Old Testament itself, which may be due to both the perishable nature of the materials on which they wrote and to their climate which was so inimical to their preservation. But the evidence we do have suggests widespread literacy in this part of the ancient Near East, even at the time of Moses. If scholars accurately interpret the Proto-Sinaitic inscriptions, these inscriptions represent the *written* prayers of Semites enslaved by the Egyptians at about 1475 B.C., and this gives us strong reason to believe that the descendants of Abraham, though lowly slaves in Egypt, were also literate. The witness of the Old Testament comports favorably with that of its neighbors. It, too, appeals to literary sources, not oral ones. Its authors cite "The Book of Songs (LXX 3 Kings 8:53); "The Book of the Upright" (8:13), "The Book of the Wars of Yahweh" (Josh. 10:13; 2 Sam. 1:18), "The Diaries of the Kings" (Kings and Chronicles, passim). Not once do they cite an oral source on which they rest their work. A man must write a bill of divorce (Deut. 24:3), and kings had secretaries to assist them in their writing (2 Sam. 8:14). According to Judges 8:14 a young man wrote down for Gideon "the names of the seventy-seven officials of Succoth." This text assumes the literacy of Israel's youth. Its legal literature was written down (Deut. 31:9; Josh. 24:25-26; 1 Sam. 10:25), and it must not be altered (Deut. 4:2; 12:32). The prophets refer to the Law as a written document. Hosea 8:12 reads "I wrote for them the many things of my law" and speaks of "the lying pen of scribes has handled the law falsely." To judge from Isaiah 8:16 and Jeremiah 36 the originally oral messages of the prophets were written down shortly after their delivery, exactly the same as happened in the case of Mohammed, as we shall shortly see. To be sure, the Law was to be memorized, as were the Proverbs, and to be recited orally (Exod. 12:24-26; Deut. 6:6, 20-25; Josh. 1:8; Ps. 1:2), but we must not suppose that these exhortations to memorize the Law contradict the notices that it had to be written. Ringgren[72] demonstrated by comparing synoptic passages in the Bible that many variants are graphic errors and that others are due to mistakes of hearing or faulty memory, but like Volten and van de Walle, he describes the situation in terms of "mistakes," which assumes that the copyists intended not to be innovators but preservers of Israel's sacred heritage. I argued above that some of the changes were intentional, but the quality and quantity of these changes suggested by the texts themselves do not compare with the changes envisioned by source critics. The minor changes introduced into Israel's written traditions are qualitatively and quantitatively different from changes due to hypothetical tradents who deliberately reinterpreted and reformulated the nation's spiritual heritage being transmitted in a fluid oral form.

8. Arabic

South Arabic inscriptions, which are notoriously difficult to date, do show that even bedouins were literate. From a much later period, Widengren demonstrated that Mohammed not only contributed directly or indirectly to putting the Qurân into writing, but even made some interpolations into the text.[73] In one of his essays on oral tradition Widengren wrote: "Written tradition was written down early in order to fix the oral tradition and to preserve it." And again: "We are confronted with the fact that in the earliest Islamic period the first generation were the collectors of traditions."[74] The situation in Islam seems very similar to that of Christianity—within a generation or two the witnesses to Christ were written down.

The only evidence for an oral tradition such as source critics envision to have happened in the transmission of the materials contained in the Old Testament comes from Indo-European peoples of a much later time, especially from Old Icelandic (ca. A.D. 1300). Here one finds a mighty priesthood trained in the oral transmission of their religious heritage. A somewhat similar situation can also be attested in the modern Serbo-Croatian heritage. But the objections to founding a theory for the development of the biblical sources on this sort of evidence is surely apparent. Widengren wrote:

> Is it not queer to observe that in order to prove the predominant role of oral tradition among such a Semitic people in antiquity as the Hebrews all real evidence from their closely related

> neighbors, the Arabs, has been left out of consideration . . . whereas evidence from all kinds of Indo-European peoples was adduced, so that even the old Icelanders were called upon to render their service in which case neither the 'great interval of time' nor that of space seems to have exercised any discouraging effect?![75]

In all of the Eastern literatures we have considered there is not one reference to the hypothetical tradent, the key to tradition criticism. This central figure in the source critical theories that Israel transmitted their precious spiritual cargo in the leaky boat of oral tradition turns out to be a nonexistent ghost.

III. THE CONTEXT

The first and weightiest rule of speech is that context determines meaning. But what precisely do we mean by context? In the broadest analysis of the notion of context we need to distinguish the audience's context from that of the speaker's. The audience context may be further analyzed into that of the original hearers and that of successive generations up to the present. We have already considered problems connected with the later audience contexts in our discussion of "understanding our preunderstanding," or to put it another way, the need to take off our spectacles through which we view the text. In this section, however, I will restrict my attention to problems pertaining to the speaker's context. The words of the biblical writers occur in at least six contexts—linguistic, literary, cultural, situational, scriptural, and theological. Each of these has its own problems.

A. The Linguistic Context

Melanchthon truly said: "The Scripture cannot be understood theologically, until it is understood grammatically."[76] The first problem to be resolved in grammatical analysis is that of distinguishing linguistic structure from the speaker's referential or intended sense. F. de Saussure distinguished *la langue* (language) and *la parole* (speech), which marked the birth of the modern science of linguistics. Caird commented: "By language Saussure meant the whole stock of words, idioms and syntax available, the potential, the common property of all users. By speech he meant any particular and actual use of language by a speaker or writer."[77] "Language" offers what Otto Jespersen has called "a latitude of correctness."[78] Marshall noted: "We need to know about the world of language to which our text belongs, so that we may know what individual words can mean, and how words can be connected together syntactically."[79] The possible and public meaning of words is the business of the lexicographer and the limits of their possible connections is the work of the grammarian. In this section we will first concern ourselves with the language of the community—their "rules" or conventions of communication—and then we shall address ourselves to the meaning of the individual.

It is not my intention here to consider problems that the standard lexicographers and grammarians address themselves to. Rather, I hope to raise linguistic issues that lie behind and beyond these tools.

1. Problems in Lexicography

Change in meaning, polysemy or multiple meanings, bivocals and the use of different words for the same referent belong to the conventions of a language and present problems for the exegete, along with the well-known problem of deciding the meaning of hapax legomena.

The first problem pertains to the recognition that a word which originally meant one thing by constant repetition may change its referent. Most words can be traced back to roots denoting originally something that can be grasped by the senses. Some words came to be used with a double referent, a material reality and a related mental idea, and at that stage were metaphors. Eventually, through constant use, the material reference was lost and only the intellectual idea remained. For this reason, for example, Hebrew expresses psychological states by words indicating the organs of the body, such as "kidney" and "heart." In a similar way, language appropriate for the tangible expressions of the Canaanite religion came to be filled with new meaning when referred to the LORD, who did not have physical form. Many scholars at the time when the theory of the progressive evolution of religion was chic made the mistake of thinking that expressions such as "food of God," or "to see the face of God" represented a more primitive stage of Israelite belief. But these "Canaanisms" meant in Hebrew religion "offering" and "to be received into God's audience" respectively. Regarding the latter idiom Caird noted: "a regular Hebrew idiom for being received in audience by someone of consequence (Gen. 43:3, 5; 2 Sam. 14: 24)."[80] The texts of the latter convention, however, were changed consistently from the active stem to the passive stem, from "see the face of God" to "appear at the face of God" on account of pious pedantry on the part of later scribes.

Words may change meanings through constant repetition either gradually (e.g. the English word "exception") or suddenly (e.g. "gay"). First Samuel 9:9 offers a good example of the Hebrew writer's awareness that a word has changed its meaning.

Two practical conclusions ought to become apparent from this study. First, while it may be interesting to study a word's etymology, etymology cannot decide an author's meaning. The English word "bead," for example, originally meant "prayer," but by constant association with the object accompanying the prayer it came to denote the rosary and similar objects. Here, however, is an example of an intellectual notion being transferred to a physical object.

Secondly, when deciding an author's use of a word out of its many possible meanings offered in a lexicon, the exegete must decide the date of his material. NIV, for example, erred in rendering *ysd* in Psalm 8:2 by "ordain," a meaning attested only in postexilic Hebrew but never in preexilic Hebrew, where it always means "to lay a foundation" (cf. RSV).

It ought to be obvious that if a word's meaning is decided in part on the date of its usage then lexical studies are inextricably meshed together with introductory studies. Unfortunately, no consensus has been reached on the date of much of the biblical literature and some lexicographers have injudiciously spoken too prematurely and dogmatically on the subject. BDB, for example, presumed that Aramaisms were late, but later research into the Aramaic inscriptions proved them wrong.

In addition to changing meaning diachronically words came to pick up several references synchronically. Polysemy, "more than one meaning," offered the connection between David's intention to build God a "house" and God's intention to build David's "house." However, we must reject with Augustine the ancient "game" of assigning many meanings to the same word at the same time and in the same place. Augustine concluded: "a principle of this nature . . . must introduce very great uncertainty in exegesis, than which nothing can be more pernicious."[81]

But some words are truly bivocals, i.e., they connote what are at least two ideas in another language. The Hebrew term, for example, "fear of the LORD" in English always denotes "God's revealed will," its objective reality, and "man's unconditional surrender to it," its subjective reality. *Toda* denotes both the sacrificial animal and the spoken word accompanying it to express the worshiper's "confession" that God had intervened in his life. Bivocals bring translators to grief because normally another language does not have a bivocal to express the same two references.

But when confronted with polysemy, how does the exegete decide which meaning the speaker had in mind? Several factors, none of which is free from its own problems, come to his aid: the literary form and the situation in which the word occurs, a speaker's idiosyncracies, and logic. In English "ball" means one thing on the social page and quite another in the sport's section of the newspaper. It makes a difference whether "table" is used in a furniture store, in a geology class dealing with underground water, or in a business meeting. So also it makes a difference whether *mašal* is used in wisdom literature, in which case it means "a proverb" or in prophetic literature, where it normally means "burden, oracle." We have already noted that *'adam* means "mankind" in P, but a proper name, "Adam," in J. Yet in Genesis 5:1, traditionally P, it also functions as a proper name showing once again that the alleged sources have not been redacted but fused. But above all the exegete employs logic in deciding meaning, more specifically the test of coherence. Just as music has a code and semiphore is a code and mathematics has a code, so also language is a code, a logically coherent entity, and when something does not fit, our computer-like minds "kick it out." When an unintelligible code becomes logically coherent, we say we have deciphered the code. So also in the case of words, the meaning must "fit" the logic of the text. If more than one meaning "fits" we can only speak in terms of plausibility or decide that the writer himself was ambiguous or punning for either intentional or unintentional reasons.

Words that occur only once, hapax legomena, or so rarely that we cannot induce its meaning with conviction, confront the exegete with their own set of problems. In these cases he must rely on cognate languages, ancient versions or rabbinic tradition. The problem occasioned by a word's propensity to change meaning diachronically or develop several meanings synchronically become exacerbated when we shift to its development and use in another language. Ancient translators confronted the same problems as moderns as Ben Sirach's Prologue makes us painfully aware. But in spite of his humble confession he was probably less aware of his own limitations and prejudgments than we are, less sophisticated in linguistics, and had poorer tools than we with which to work. Rabbinic traditions are at best uncertain. James Barr has brilliantly addressed himself to these problems and offered helpful rules for the use of the cognate languages and ancient versions; there is no need to rehearse them here.[82]

In some cases the exegete must reach certainty about his uncertainty and say so. For example, *selah,* at present cannot be known because the ancient versions disagree, Kimchi and Rashi disagree and modern scholars have proposed up to sixty different meanings for it largely on the basis of cognate studies. In a case like this the translator can put dots, which is intellectually the most honest, or guess at a translation and footnote his uncertainty, which is psychologically most satisfying, or transliterate the Hebrew, which mocks the uneducated.

In the case of Hebrew grammar the exegete confronts problems similar to those encountered in lexicography: change of form and meaning, polysemy, uncertainty and varying surface structures for the same idea.

A good historical grammar will trace the evolution of the phonemes, morphemes and syntax of a language. Our problem here is that we have no good historical grammars of the Hebrew language written in English.

First-year students in Hebrew and Greek become aware all too soon that the genitive case can convey many different ideas and that the exegete's decision in this matter can radically effect one's understanding of the author's intention. It takes several more years of study, however, to come to the realization with Caird that "the only grammatical form which appears to be wholly unequivocal is the vocative case." But Caird can not resist adding:

> We may of course be left in doubt about the referent of a word in a vocative (are the people addressed in Gal. 3:1 north Galatians living in Ancyra and Pessinus, or south Galatians living in Antioch, Iconium, Lystra and Derbe?), or about the degree of emotional intensity involved (John 2:4).[83]

The grammarian assumes the task of establishing and setting forth the morphemic and syntactic boundaries of a language, and it is the exegete's task of deciding a writer's specific use by the same critieria employed in the case of lexical polysemy.

In addition to morphemic polysemy we also confront morphemic uncertainty. To date grammarians still have not reached agreement about the significance of the Hebrew "tenses," the so-called perfect and imperfect. Moscati, et al. said: "the 'tense' system presents one of the most complicated and disputed problems of the Semitic languages."[84] He thereupon proceeded to dub the term "tense" as "improper" because he argued that they denoted not the time of the action but the kind of action. Joüon complained:

> Certain exegetes or translators, especially the more ancient ones, seem to have had only some vague idea concerning this matter. When translating, they were guided more by instinct than by a precise knowledge of the value of forms.[85]

But in contrast to Moscati, et al. he thereupon argued that time, not aspect, constituted the principal idea of the forms in question. A. Sperber disallowed any semantic difference between the so-called tenses but contended instead that the perfect and imperfect are used interchangeably and suggested for the word tenses "a neutral, timeless terminology, which is based on morphological characteristics . . .; suffix tense (instead of perfect) and prefix tense (for imperfect)."[86]

But to put this discussion about uncertainty into perspective it is reassuring to note that most modern scholarship is leaning toward the idea that aspect is the essential notion of the Hebrew "tense," and that the problem is narrowing itself to defining aspect more precisely. O'Connor wrote:

> Aspect, as is clear from two recent studies of Semitic aspect, McCarus (1976) on Arabic and Kurylowicz (1973) on Semitic in general, is a problematic area even when the system is fairly obvious. Kurylowicz observes that in a system with two finite verb forms, the opposition must be between simultaneity and anteriority (Latin *imperfectum* and *perfectum*). This is the basic structure of the Arabic system, and it is distinct from the three-way opposition in Slavic and Classical Greek which opposes both imperfective and perfective, and linear and punctual categories. Kurylowicz reserves the term aspect for systems with both these oppositions; McCarus uses it in the distinct sense of the type of action predicated by the verb. In Arabic there is no aspectual (in Kurylowicz' sense) or temporal marking of verb forms; the relevant information is conveyed on the syntactic level.[87]

In contrast to polysemy we need to reckon with Chomsky's well-known hypothesis that the surface structure of language needs to be contrasted with the deeper structure in a speaker's mind. Because of this difference, a speaker may refer to the same reality by more than one expression. For example, a writer may have in mind a "god" qualified by the notion of being "foreign." In Hebrew this notion may be expressed in several ways: by an adjective, "foreign gods"; by a construct, "gods of foreignness"; by a clause, "gods which are foreign'; by a phrase, "gods belonging to foreigners"; by apposition, "gods, the foreigners"; by hendiadys, "gods and foreigners"; by an accusative, "gods in foreignness." The referent alluded to by these varying constructions is identical and the speaker chooses any of these options for either conscious stylistic reasons or unconscious linguistic factors at work in the language.

We now turn our attention from the rules governing communication within a community, and which the exegete must master to prevent him from false interpretations beyond the limits which the language will allow, to the speaker's intended meaning.

First, we need to ask ourselves whether or not it is possible to speak of the Word of God when it comes to us in translation. The answer here depends on the meaning we invest in the word "Word." If we mean the symbols on the page, then the answer is obviously "no," but if we mean the sense the author intended by them the answer is just as obviously "yes." Packer made the point well:

> (Verbal plenary inspiration) does not imply a Koranic view of inspiration, whereby translations of the original are precisely *not* the Holy Book. As Reformation theology used to say, it is the sense of Scripture that is Scripture, and all translations are in truth the Bible, at least to the extent that they are accurate.[88]

Olthuis similarly stated:

> For, although meaning is mediated by words, it is not contained in their form. Words are symbols through which we open up (or obscure, as the case may be) the universe and our place in it. In their lingual meaning they refer beyond themselves to (non-semantic) reality.[89]

Thiselton rightly declared that understanding the author's sense is an *art*.[90] We have already noted the problems occasioned by changed meanings, polysemy, uncertainty, etc., and we have suggested ways of approaching them, but we have not yet observed that the speaker's intention may also be opaque because he expressed himself elliptically. Caird noted:

> In one of his most tantalizing sentences Paul uses no fewer than five opaque terms—'the rebellion,' 'the man of lawlessness,' 'the mystery of lawlessness,' 'the restraining power,' 'the restraining person'—and adds the comment that he explained all this to the readers last time he was with them (2 Thess. 2:3-7).

We shall return to this matter of elliptical opaqueness in connection with our discussion of the literary context.

The theologian should also be aware that words and morphemes do not necessarily coincide with the speaker's concepts. For example, almost all Hebrew nouns belong to one of two genders, masculine and feminine, but this does not mean that the Hebrews were unconscious of what we would call the neuter gender. We can infer from other languages also deficient in the grammatical distinction of genders that the grammatical expression does not precisely correlate with the speaker's thought. Turkish, for example, nowhere—not even in its pronouns—grammatically distinguishes gender, whereas French moulds all its nouns into either the masculine or feminine genders. But as James Barr pointed out, no one would suppose that the Turks were unaware of sexual differences, or that this proves the legendary erotic interests of the French.[91] To enter the speaker's world of thought we need to integrate linguistic studies with anthropology.

Another problem we need to address ourselves to is whether an utterance can have a meaning beyond what the original speaker intended. Kaiser answered this question with an emphatic "No,"[92] but I would prefer a qualified "Yes." To be sure there are numerous statements in which the speaker has a particular person, thing or event in view. When, for example, the psalmists referred to the Law (Pss. 1, 19, 119) they probably had the Deuteronomic Code in mind.[93] The gospel writers had in view a particular high priest that condemned Jesus to death. On the other hand, however, there are some statements that are deliberately open-ended without a particular referent in the speaker's mind. For example, the wit of the proverb is meant for the wisdom of all in many diverse situations. The "wise son" in Proverbs 10:1 is not one particular wise son, and the foolish son refers to every foolish child. Each one in the audience will color the meaning of the proverb according to his own experience, an experience that lies beyond the experience of the author. A parable such as the prodigal son is also intended to have as many interpretations as there are hearers. Each listener, according to his own experience, will interpret somewhat differently the younger brother's folly and repentance and the older brother's self-righteousness. Obviously there is an ambiguity built into our original question. In some instances the speaker intended his statement to have a meaning beyond his own particular meaning.

Generic prophecies are also intended to have an open-ended meaning. I am indebted to Kaiser for alerting me to Beecher's identification of this important type of prophetic utterance. Beecher defined generic prophecy as:

> One which regards an event as occurring in a series of parts, separated by intervals, and expresses itself in language that may apply indifferently to the nearest part, or to the remoter parts, or to the whole—in other words, a predication which, in applying to the whole of a complex event also applies to . . . its parts.[94]

Caird compares this kind of utterance to a "Situation Vacant" advertisement. The famous prophecy regarding the woman's seed that would destroy the Serpent (Gen. 3:16) finds its fulfillment in all whom God elects to put enmity against Satan (cf. Rom. 16:20). It finds a unique fulfillment in Christ, but it also has reference to all who share faith with Him and in Him. Eve mistakenly applied it to Cain and likewise Abraham to Ishmael. In this kind of prophecy the speaker deliberately leaves his words open-ended to be filled in particularly according to the course of history.

The question of single meaning becomes more complex when a later biblical writer used an earlier canonical text in a way unintended by the original speaker. We shall discuss that problem in connection with the scriptural context.

In deciding this matter of what a speaker meant and of whether or not a speaker had more than one meaning in view, it will prove helpful to recognize that speakers use language in various ways. Linguists distinguish at least four functions of language: informative, which aims to clarify and convey an idea (e.g. the creation narratives); performative, which does not report an action but affects it (e.g. God's spoken Word that brought about the creation); expressive, which aims to capture and communicate an experience (e.g. "sabbath" in the epilogue to the creation account which evoked feelings of gratitude, joy and patriotism in Israel); and cohesive language, designed primarily to denote rapport (e.g. "greet one another with a holy kiss"). These categories often overlap and the same utterance may be designed to serve more than one purpose. In fact, all of Scripture according to Paul serves a dual purpose: it is profitable for doctrine—the informative use of language, and for reproof, correction and instruction—the performative use of language. With respect to the informative use of language one may profitably speak of single meaning but with respect to its performative function the term is less useful because the text's meaning is relative to the experience of each one in its audience.

Expressive and cohesive language raises the problem of its appropriate translation. Emotive terms such as "Sabbath," "circumcision," and "blood" do not create the same emotions in us as they did in ancient Israel. In fact, these emotive and cohesive expressions may have just the opposite effect in a later audience than that intended by the author. Shall we retranslate this kind of language into the dynamic equivalents of another culture? For example, shall we substitute "handshake" for "holy kiss" or "Sunday" for "Sabbath," or "baptism" for "circumcision?" The Wycliffe Bible translators[95] utilize language theory strikingly similar to Wittgenstein's concept of "language-game" vis-à-vis the speaking of language is a "form of life."[96] I think it best not to translate these emotive expressions by the dynamic equivalents in another language because they are not precise enough. Rather, I suggest, it is better to let the exegete explain this phenomena of language and meaning in a commentary.

B. The Literary Context

By literary context we mean the forms of literature at the speaker's command for presenting his thought (the form critic's object of study), the devices employed in these literary forms, his own unique structuring of the material (the rhetorical critic's object of study) and other literary devices writers employ, such as figurative language.

A major problem confronting the practitioner of the grammatico-historical method is that of deciding the literary genre of his text. As we shall see, his decision in this matter significantly modifies the way in which he interprets the text. For example, what shall we label the literary genres of Genesis 1:1-2:3 and 2:4-25? In the case of the former, it will not do to label it as a scientific document because its subject is God (an "object" of study not possible for scientific inquiry) and not hydrogen gas, quarks, or molecules, the proper object of scientific inquiry. But many Evangelicals err egregiously against the text by reading it as a scientific treatise. Then, too, it is not history in the proper sense of that term because no man was present to record the events at the time of creation. We could label it as "myth" if we define that debated term to mean a lens through which we can better understand the world we live in, a story to explain the present and the future. But we must reject this term because for many it also denotes the notion that the story lacks historical credibility and the lens for interpreting life was ground in human imagination. Then, too, it is not theology because truths about divine matters are presented in narrative form and not in systematized abstractions. We could define it as *Torah,* teaching about divine matters to make us wise unto salvation, but this nomenclature lacks precision, for Deuteronomy, which is very different from Genesis 1, is *Torah* par excellence. Perhaps the best we can do is to call it a Creation Story in Torah.

But even that label is not without its problems for it does not distinguish the literary genres of the two creation accounts in Gen. 1:1-2:3 and 2:4-25. In contrast to the first account, the second story presents us with both historical and suprahistorical events. To be sure, the latter story as we have it in the Bible, is intended to be understood as an account of factual persons and events, at least to judge from the genealogies that take us back to Adam and from the way in which the Garden of Eden is so precisely located. But the story is also intended to be read as suprahistorical, that is, the persons and events in the story represent every man and woman and their experience in divine matters. None has ever suggested that God sentenced only the historical Eve to painful labor in childbearing or only the historical Adam to frustrating work and death. Every reader understands that Adam and Eve represent every man and every woman. Gerhardus Vos has shown convincingly that the Tree of Life, the Tree of Knowledge of Good and Evil, the Garden of Eden, etc., all serve as representations of eternal truths.[97] Shall we label the second account then as a Suprahistorical Creation Story in Torah? How ever we might label these accounts, it is essential that the exegete wrestle with the problem if he aspires to understand the meaning and intention of the author.

We have already raised the question regarding the appropriateness of labelling the biblical accounts according to their historical credibility. The writer of Genesis gives his reader no indications that he intended his narrative to be read as saga or legend. Those labels stem more from the prejudgment of the interpreter than from the text itself.

Having identified and labelled the writer's selection of literary genre, the exegete must then consider the literary devices of the genre. In *narrative literature* the writer allows the words and actions of the people in his story, rather than didactic statements on his part, to convey his teaching, though in the case of Genesis he peppered his stories with direct theological statements (cf. 2:2-3, 25; 15:6; 25:26; etc.). In this sort of literature the exegete must consider such factors as the selection and arrangement of the material, statements in the story by God or His obvious spokesman, the climax of the story or how it turns out, and the larger context which may include clear didactic teaching. Genesis, as part of the Pentateuch, ought to be interpreted in the light of the clear teaching of Deuteronomy. When we speak of the larger literary context, however, we have entered the arena of the scriptural context.

But is the storyteller's intention so unambiguous that we can speak authoritatively regarding the doctrine or moral values he aims to instill in his readers? For example, can we be certain about the propriety or impropriety of Abraham's sojourn in Egypt or Paul's visit to Jerusalem? Perhaps in cases like these the writer is deliberately ambiguous.

In the case of the interpretation of *prophetic literature* it is a well-recognized fact that the prophet often presents future events synchronically. Although Peter makes it clear that they knew that the glories of Christ would follow his sufferings, the prophets did not fully understand the sequence of all future events nor the extent of time separating them. They looked to the future with a bifocal vision. With their nearsightedness they foresaw immanent, historical events and with their farsightedness they foresaw the near event merging with the day of the Lord. Evidently their audience was able to discern the distinction between the two because while they recognized the prophet's gift in predicting the circumstances attending the immediate historical event, they did not stone him when all his predictions about the future did not come to pass. Presumably the immediate fulfillments of some prophecies proved he was not a false prophet, and therefore they were willing to accept the validity of unfulfilled predictions and assured they awaited fulfillment in succeeding generations. This dual prophetic vision confronts the interpreter with the problem of deciding the time when the prophecy was or will be fulfilled.

It is also clear that the prophets presented their utterance of judgment absolutely, though they knew that through these predictions God intended the recipient of the death sentence to repent. Jonah predicted: "Within forty days Nineveh will be destroyed," but he later admits that the reason why he fled to Tarshish was that he knew God would relent if the Ninevites repented (Jonah 3:4; 4:1-3). The episode recounted in Jeremiah 26:18-19 makes it perfectly clear that the prophet's original audience understood that though the message of doom was stated absolutely, the unstated divine intention was that they relent. The prophetic literary device of presenting prophecy absolutely, however, makes the prophet appear false to the modern reader.

Another literary device employed by the prophet that the hermeneut must take into consideration is the principle that the prophets predicted the future in terms of their present. This principle is generally conceded by all exegetes, but they disagree on the extent of its application. Premillennialists, who employ the principle charingly, might allow that the prophets predicted the day of the Lord or of Israel's future kingdom in terms of his own culture. For example, few premillennialists would insist that Israel's still future attackers from Gog will come riding on horses and be armed with the small and large shield, the bow and arrow, and the war club and spear—the weapons of warfare in Ezekiel's time—or that at that time Israel will disarm itself by removing its walls along with its gates and bars (cf. Ezek. 38). But he will deny the amillennialist's extension of this principle to his claim that the prophets predicted the present, spiritual form of the kingdom in language appropriate to its geo-political form as the prophet experienced it. When the principle is stretched to this extent the premillennialist accuses the amillennialist of "spiritualizing" the text, which for him is an illegitimate principle. In favor of the premillennialist's caution against the "spiritualizing" of the text, one notes that prophecies pertaining to Christ's first advent were physically and not "spiritually" fulfilled. He was born in Bethlehem of a virgin, physical fulfillments of the prophetic predictions. The premillennialists argue on this basis that since these prophecies which we can test by historical experience were fulfilled exactly as predicted, we have no right to spiritualize other prophecies not historically fulfilled exactly as predicted. Rather, he argues these prophecies should be understood as referring to Israel's future kingdom. But the amillennialist might answer that during the course of His ministry Jesus sought to open Israel's eyes to the spiritual intention of these prophecies. In one incident after another Jesus moved His audience from an earthly interpretation of an Old Testament reference to a heavenly one. He transferred the "temple" from a physical building to His Body (John 2:19-21) and the water of Jacob's well to inner springs of spiritual water (John 4:1-15). He brought these two images together in His invitation: "If a man is thirsty, let him come to Me and drink. Whoever believes in Me, as the Scripture has said, streams of living water will flow from within him" (John 7:37-38). In this statement "water" means the Spirit of God, and the Scripture He had in mind was Ezekiel's vision of a temple with water coming out from under the threshold of the temple, water that grew ever more abundant as its course progressed (Ezek. 47:1-12).[98]

If it is legitimate to stretch the principle that the prophets predicted the future in terms of their own experience to that of spiritualizing the text, it might be helpful to supplement it with the principle of embellishment.[99] If Ezekiel's vision of a river emanating from the temple is to be interpreted spiritually as a reference to the Holy Spirit's welling up within the temple of the believer's body, then his vision of fruit trees that never failed growing along its banks and of swarms of living creatures and fish in the sea when the river reached its fullest dimensions might be best understood as embellishments to evoke the feeling of full satisfaction, delight, and life in this river.

When we turn from prophetic literature to *legal literature* we must reckon among its devices the use of synecdoche and the demand for spiritual interpretation. When the Law instructs one to put a parapet around the roof of a new house so as not to bring guilt of bloodshed on its builders (Deut. 22:8), it offers its subjects an explicit example of the meaning of the commandment "You shall not take innocent life either intentionally ('murder') or unintentionally ('manslaughter')" (Deut. 5:17). The law in Deut. 22:8 serves merely as an illustration of the principle. It would be most unfortunate if one interpreted the legal literature in such a way as to argue that because something was not forbidden, therefore it was permitted. No, just the opposite. Its precise laws serve an exemplary function and are meant to be extended to include similar practical measures. The law to build a parapet around the roof of the house also means to put a fence around an open well. In sum, the laws are not exhaustive but synecdochic.

Jesus and Paul explicitly teach the law is to be interpreted according to its spirit and not according to its letter, and the Old Testament application of the law in narrative demonstrates the same truth. Though the law forbad the marriage of the Canaanite, we find in the narrative of the book of Joshua that God approved the marriage with the Canaanite prostitute Rahab, and though the law excluded a Moabite from the congregation of Israel for ten generations, God smiled with favor on the faithful Moabitess, Ruth. In sum, though the Lawgiver presented His commands absolutely and concretely, He intended them to be interpreted according to the Spirit of a personal relationship with God (Deut. 6:5) rather than as a binding, legal, impersonal contract.

The *apocalyptics' literary device* of presenting his thoughts through symbolism presents the interpreter with one of the greatest challenges in interpreting the Bible. This device is difficult both because we are not always sure when the apocalyptics' material is symbolical, but also because we are sometimes uncertain about the symbol's referent. For example, are we to take the one thousand years in Revelation 20 as actual years, or as a symbol of an indefinite and prolonged period of time? I am inclined to take it as the latter. But what about the division of the tribulation into three and a half years, or forty-two months, or 1260 days? Here I am inclined to take them as actual, but my procedure is more instinctive than founded on principle.

A literary device of both the prophets and apocalyptics is that of picturing judgment in terms of cosmic collapse. Jeremiah writhes in anguish at his vision of the cosmos returning to chaos (Jer. 4:23ff), but the immediate referent of his vision is the coming devastation of Israel. Isaiah's oracle against Babylon pictures God as putting out the lights of the sun, moon, and stars and pitching the whole cosmos into darkness (Isa. 13:9-13). Later he envisions the fall of Edom and the other nations in connection with the Lord's sword cutting the stars loose to fall on their heads (Isa. 34:1-5). These texts challenge the hermeneut to decide whether he will employ the principle of generic prophecy or hyperbolic embellishment.

The didactic saying is the most difficult literary device to interpret in the *wisdom literature*. The sage's intention is perfectly clear when he employs precepts, for he expresses his aim in the imperatival mood. But in the didactic saying he describes something as it is without disclosing his intended meaning, or to put the matter another way, its performative function. For example, in the didactic saying: "The wealth of the rich is their fortified city, but poverty is the ruin of the poor" (Prov. 10:15), does he aim to instruct his audience to accumulate wealth in order to have security in times of crises? Or does he intend to say that both riches and poverty are undesirable financial postures because the rich has a false security in his money and the poor has no financial security. The didactic saying is obviously vulnerable to misinterpretation. These ambiguous sayings must be interpreted within the sage's broader literary context where, by precept and by other clear forms, he makes his intention known. In the light of his other sayings it becomes clear, for example, that in Proverbs 10:15 he aims to warn us against accumulating wealth for it will prove a snare in leading us into a false sense of security. Elsewhere he admonishes his readers to "Trust in the LORD" (Prov. 3:5; passim) who gives those who trust in him a proper balance in the possession of property. Agur prayed: "Give me neither poverty nor riches, but give me only my daily bread. Otherwise, I may have too much and disown you and say, 'Who is the LORD?' Or I may become poor and steal, and so dishonor the name of my God" (Prov. 30:8-9). The sage admonished: "Do not wear yourself out to get rich; have the wisdom to show restraint. Cast but a glance at riches, and they are gone, for they will surely sprout wings and fly off to the sky like an eagle" (Prov. 23:4-5). In sum, the didactic saying must be interpreted by other more clear sayings.

In his study of the literary context the hermeneut ought now to familiarize himself with the new discipline of rhetorical criticism. This discipline is traced back to Muilenberg's presidential address to the Society of Biblical Literature in 1968.[100] Muilenberg argued that form criticism had reached the limits of usefulness. Because form criticism emphasized typical features of literary units, its unique features were being disregarded. He advocated, therefore, that form criticism be supplemented by rhetorical criticism "to supplement . . . form critical analysis with careful inspection of the literary unit in its precise and unique formulation." This concern accords well with the historico-grammatical method of exegesis. The main problem with it is that the exegete lacks adequate tools for employing the new discipline. Parunak,[101] who himself has made a notable contribution, stated the need: "a 'grammar' describing the functions of various structural features is still very much needed." He sought to remedy the need in part by positing that the "essential element in biblical structure is correspondence." Space fails me, however, to develop his rhetorical grammar further.

A most significant tool for analyzing Hebrew poetry is that of M. O'Connor, *Hebrew Verse Structure* (1980). His work makes R. Lowth's classic analysis of Hebrew parallelism seem like "child's play." The same can be said of works based on D. Müller with his attention to strophic and larger structures. From now on all studies of Hebrew poetry will have to build on and interact with O'Connor's emphasis on construction in contrast to meter and on syntactical parallelism and tropes based on linguistic awareness in place of roughly defined semantic parallelisms.

Literate men employ figures of speech as a stock-in-trade device for disclosing reality. Poets, especially the hymn writers, the sages and the prophets who authored the Scriptures, skillfully employ them in order to give their audiences another way of looking at and beyond the phenomenological world of sight. But how can the audience be sure that the author intended a certain locution to be understood as a figure? And how can he validate the author's intended meaning through this elliptical speech?

According to St. Augustine: "Whatever there is in the Word of God that cannot, when taken literally, be referred to either purity of life or soundness of doctrine, you may set down as figurative."[102] "Purity of life," according to him, "has reference to love of God and one's neighbor, and soundness of doctrine to the knowledge of God and one's neighbor." With that imprecise and theologically-oriented criterion for identifying figurative language, Augustine opened the door to allegorizing the text. He undoubtedly would have defended himself against this charge by arguing that the authors of Scripture intended their stories as allegories. Most exegetes today, however, following the historico-grammatical method of exegesis, concur that instead of exposing the author's hidden meanings he, in fact, imposed on the text hidden meanings not derived from the text itself.

Figurative language can be identified by two criteria: juxtaposition and ellipsis. By juxtaposition I mean that the poet transferred a word or a larger piece of literature from its normal linguistic environment into a literary environment where it is not at home. For example, in the sentence "The LORD is my shepherd" (Ps. 23:1) the word "shepherd," which is at home with words which have reference to animal husbandry, is here transferrred and juxtaposed with the LORD, a word pertaining to a transcendent, spiritual being. Furthermore, the author has elided his full thought in the transference. When David prayed, "Cause me to hear joy and gladness," he juxtaposed objects that refer to an emotional state with a verb that refers to a physical activity. Elsewhere the poet says, "the trees clapped," whereby he transferred a verb that normally describes a human activity to that of an inanimate subject. A juxtaposition of semantic realms also takes place when Elijah taunts the prophets of Baal, "Cry louder, for he is a god," for the statement grants existence to Baal in the very context where he is proving he does not exist. In all these examples—metaphor, metonomy, personification, and irony respectively—the poets artfully and evocatively communicated their thought by transference and in none of them did they fully explicate their meaning.

Having identified a locution as figurative and having labelled it appropriately, the exegete now confronts the problem of deciphering the author's meaning in this elliptical speech. Here he must rely on clues within the literary discourse itself. For example, in the case of metaphor, he looks for a descriptive term such as a defining word, a qualifying adjective, etc.

A problem that arises in the case of metaphor is that of deciding when one is dealing with a dead metaphor. A metaphor is the transference of a term from its normal referent to a second referent in order that the second referent might be illuminated by the first. The first serves as a lens through which the second can be seen and frequently evokes powerful emotions along with it. As long as the speaker and his audience are aware of the double reference it is a living metaphor, but when, through overuse, the first referent is lost sight of it fades and eventually dies. Dead metaphors in English include "eye of a needle" and "mouth of a river." "Heart," "kidneys" and "bowels," are dead metaphors in the Bible and may be better rendered by their second referents. When the language itself is "dead," as is the case with the biblical languages, it is difficult to decide this matter.

Metaphor and metonymy can fail for one of two reasons. They may fail because the first referent is unknown to the audience. Caird cites Geothe's couplet: "Wer den Dichter will verstehen, Muss in Dichters Lande gehen"[103] ("Whoever wishes to understand the poet must go to the poet's land"). "Circumcision" of the heart is a case in point. Only an elite caste of priests and warriors dedicated to the service of the Egyptian deity were circumcised.[104] This primary referent was picked up and applied in Israel to all males to describe and evoke feelings of Israel's honor and unique privilege in becoming God's kingdom of priests. Without an understanding of the significance of the custom in ancient Israel, however, the significance of the figure is almost unintelligible. Biblical metaphors based on ancient Near Eastern pagan myths often not only do not communicate to the modern reader but may actually mislead him. Lucifer, referred to only in Isaiah 14, is a case in point here. Lucifer probably has as its primary referent the morning star Venus and the role it played in an ancient Near Eastern myth. The second referent is not Satan, as it so often is erroneously interpreted, but Sennacherib, king of Babylon.[105] Sometimes figurative comparisons (metaphor) and associations (metonymy) fail because the audience overextends the point of similarity between the two referents. Caird points out that the "neck" of a bottle has nothing to do with a head of beer.[106] The audience must discern through clues, such as those suggested above, the point of comparison. Sometimes the first referent shows many similarities with the second; e.g., the use of "body" to describe the church. Other times, however, the comparison is restricted to only one point as is the case of likening the sun's rise to that of a bridegroom coming out of his nuptial chamber.

Just as we have polysemy in lexicography and grammar, so also an author or authors may use the first referent as a vehicle or lens of understanding with diverse second referents. For example, "water" may refer secondarily to "cleansing" or "life producing." Sometimes "firstfruits" has as its second referent giving God the best or the first to rise from the dead. But sometimes the second referent is so constant that the metaphor becomes a symbol, as is the case with "light" which consistently has "moral illumination" as its second referent, and with "break the jaw" which refers to abject humiliation. Sometimes it is debatable whether a vehicle has more than one second referent as is the case with "leaven."

Another feature of the Bible's literary style is that of absolute, categorical statements. We already noted the absolute way in which the prophets delivered their message of impending judgment. The proverbs also present truth without qualification. The sages promise the righteous life, property, favor with God and man, a smooth path, mental and physical well-being, and material prosperity (Prov. 3:1-10), but our Lord on the cross experienced none of these. The sage in the Book of Proverbs is looking to a future that outlasts death and his focus in his sayings is on the righteous' final state of bliss. His focus becomes very apparent in his admonition: "Do not lie in wait like an outlaw against a righteous man's house . . . for though a righteous man falls seven times he rises again" (Prov. 24:15-16). Job and Koheleth by contrast directed their attention at the righteous man when he appeared to be counted out. Confronted with this Semitic predilection for paratactic constructions, hyperbolic language and unqualified, categorical, absolute statements the exegete must set the paradoxical statements side by side and attempt to infer the logic of their relationship. This need to allow categorical statements to qualify each other and to suggest their own logical connection is absolutely essential in such theological antinomies as God's election and man's responsibility, God's repenting and the fact He does not repent, the fact the Son of Man will come without heraldry and yet only after a series of warning, the fact that the Kingdom of God has arrived and yet is to come; etc.

C. The Cultural Context

G. Linwood Barney has given a helpful model for analyzing the structure of a culture. He suggested that each culture is a series of layers, the deepest of which consists of ideology, cosmology and world view. A second layer which probably derives from the first is that of values. Stemming from both of these layers is a third containing a culture's institutions such as marriage, law, and education. These institutions constitute a bridge to the fourth and surface layers of material artifacts and observable customs.[107] Barney's analysis is not only helpful in bringing more precision to a discussion about the cultural context of a writer, but it also assists us in deciding those features of the biblical cultures which are of abiding value and authority on succeeding generations of the faithful. The first two layers are eternally normative; the fourth is historically relative; the third is more debatable. We will say more about this.

We will discuss the first two layers of the biblical writers' culture in connection with their theological context. Their cosmology, however, might profitably be considered here. Israel's cosmology has two aspects: a heavenly, revelatory aspect and an earthly, phenomenological aspect. The revelatory dimension of their cosmology, namely that God created the world, belongs to their theology and presents us with eternal, unchanging truth. Their earthly observation of it, however, as a three-tiered universe consisting of heavens above, earth beneath and waters below the earth is phenomenologically conditioned and has no abiding theological significance. If the biblical writers aimed to teach a geocentric view of the universe in opposition to a heliocentric view of it, then that view of the cosmos would have eternal theological significance. But this is not the case. The exegete, however, must understand the earthly cosmology in order to interpret accurately their references to it.

With regard to the upper two levels of their culture we need to distinguish between precept and practice as well as the situations in which directions regarding their institutions, customs and artifacts are given. We shall discuss the latter concern in connection with the situational context. New Testament precepts such as the command to observe the Lord's Supper and baptism ought to be observed in the Church, but the practices associated with them, such as the hour of their meeting, the exact shape of their services, which may be found in James, we need not keep.

The similarity of Israel's outward religious garb in its institutions, customs and artifacts to its pagan counterparts often present a problem to the beginning student of Israel's religion. But the problem largely disappears when one realizes that in God's desire to disclose his nature, mind and will for his subjects he humbled himself and became incarnate, taking on human dress. That which distinguishes biblical religion from other religions is not so much on the upper two cultural levels but on the bottom two. While Jesus appeared like any other man, no other man spoke as he did, and while Israel's cultus and literary forms resemble those of its pagan neighbors, none of the latter knew Israel's ethical monotheism.

But this similarity between Israel's religion and their pagan neighbors raises another problem. To what extent did Israel adopt the forms of pagan religions? Armerding said: "Comparative religions research (religions-geschichtliche methode) begins with an assumption that the religion of the Old Testament is best understood by analogy to ancient religions in general.[108] More specifically, to what extent did Israel model its great Fall Festival after the pagan festivals such as the Mesopotamiam Akitu Festival or the Egyptian Sed Festival? And to what extent is such a festival assumed in Israel's hymnic literature? I suggest that future generations of evangelical scholars will have to address themselves to the problem of how to apply comparative religions research to biblical studies.

There is also a problem in deciding the extent to which Israel's literature and practices aimed to correct pagan practices. Israel's religion was both a sponge and a repellent. Leah Bronner[109] has argued persuasively that the miracles in the Elijah-Elisha pericopae had a polemical intention against the Canaanite worship of Baal, which nearly eradicated the worship of the LORD from Northern Israel. But does Genesis 1 also serve a polemic intention against worshiping the creation rather than its Creator?

D. The Situational Context

By the situational context we mean the occasion of the utterance and the factors that prompted it. Dispensationalists have made a contribution of inestimable value to hermeneutics by their insistence on considering the situation or occasion in which a performative or commissive utterance is given. The problem of many apparent contradictions in Scripture would readily disappear if this context were allowed to play its legitimate role in the historico-grammatical method. Failing to note the diverse situations in which discourse is carried on in the Bible, Kueng found the New Testament a *complexio oppositorum*, a collection of various testimonies which he regarded as contradictory and as having varying degrees of validity.[110] Ernest Käsemann spoke of "irreconcilable theological contradictions" and James Barr emphasized the multiplex nature of the Old Testament tradition. We do not argue that many of these alleged contradictions must be harmonized because a high view of inspiration demands that we do so. Quite the contrary; we argue that careful attention to the situation in which words are spoken demands that we not pit many of these statements against one another.

Isaiah said the LORD has determined not to destroy Jerusalem; Jeremiah said that he is determined to destroy it. These statements, which on the surface seem so contradictory, are in fact uttered in diverse circumstances. Isaiah's is made at the time of Hezekiah's prayer and before the atrocious reign of Manasseh; Jeremiah's is given after Manasseh's wicked reign and a superficial revival. Moses allowed divorce, Jesus disallowed it; Moses established dietary laws, Jesus and the apostles abrogated them. In fact the early church essentially did away with the specific commands of the Mosaic law which were meant for people living in the land and were not intended for a universal, spiritual kingdom composed of Jews and Gentiles and in which the Aaronic priesthood was superseded by the heavenly high priesthood of Jesus Christ (cf. Acts 15; Deut. 12:1; Hebrews).

But of what value then are the specific commands of the Mosaic Law which are either superseded by the heavenly reality in the high priesthood of Jesus Christ or abrogated? Their eternal and abiding value which will never pass away is found in the eternal, spiritual law stemming from the character of God that stands behind them. More specifically, each command in the Mosaic Code gives expression to the ideal of either loving God or loving man, and the modern reader needs to extrapolate from the specific commands of the ancient code its eternal truth and give it concrete expression in his own situation.

Taking note of the speaker's situation will also help to explain why the Psalmist found the Law an instrument to life while Paul found it an instrument of death (Ps. 1:1-3; Romans 7:1-11). In fact, one finds in Paul himself opposing statements about the Law. In some passages he commends it as spiritual, holy, good and profitable (cf. Rom. 7:12, 16; 2 Tim. 3:16), but in others he says it provokes to sin; sometimes he speaks of the Church as free from the Law, yet in others he implies that we are to fulfill it (Rom. 7:5-11 and 13:28). Paul's disparaging statements about the Law must be read out of his own background in legalistic Judaism where he attempted to keep the Law while uncircumcised in his heart and dead in his sins (Col. 2:13ff) and his situation in which he is attempting to debunk incipient Gnosticism and full-blown legalism. Marshall aptly noted:

> Reading a New Testament letter has often been likened to listening in to one end of a telephone conversation, and realizing that in order to understand what we can hear we also need to hear what is being said at the other end of the line.[111]

Then, too, it must be borne in mind that the Law was addressed to a situation where all things are equal. For example, the Law not to intermarry with the Canaanite had in view the normal situation in which the Canaanite would remain a loyal devotée of the pagan cult (cf. Deut. 7:3-4); it did not have in view the situation of a proselyte from Baal worship to the worship of the LORD, such as occurred in the case of Rahab. Then, too, it did not have in view those situations where the faithful were confronted with tragic moral choice. The Law categorically proscribed profaning the shewbread, but evidently it was always understood that when confronted with starvation or eating the shewbread the law was not applicable.

E. The Scriptural Context

By scriptural context I mean other portions of the Bible outside of the biblical book in which an utterance is found. Practitioners of the historico-grammatical approach concur that any statement must be interpreted in light of the entire book in which it occurs, its broader linguistc context. But should this literary context be expanded to include the total canon of Scripture? In raising this question, however, we have moved from a purely linguistic concern to the concern of the biblical theologian, who assumes as his work the task of observing, analyzing, and classifying progressive themes of Scripture. The biblical theologian locates a text not only in its immediate linguistic context but also in the progress of revelation.

Few exegetes would care to deny that a text ought to be interpreted in the light of antecedent revelation pertaining to that theme with which it is connected, assuming that the author was conscious of the earlier revelation. But the question arises whether or not a text should be interpreted in the light of later revelation related to it. Admittedly, the New Testament should be interpreted in the light of the Old Testament, but should the Old Testament be interpreted in the light of the New Testament?

Kaiser answered our question with an emphatic. "No!" He argued: "In no case must . . . *later* teaching be used exegetically (or in any other way) to unpack the meaning or to enhance the usability of the individual text which is the object of study."[112] He proposed:

"comparisons with similar (sometimes rudimentary) affirmations found in passages that have *preceded* in time the passage under study" and thought "surely most interpreters will see the wisdom and good sense in limiting our theological observations to conclusions drawn from the text being exegeted and from the texts which preceded it in time."[113] He allowed, however, that the exegete ought to make summaries in which the target passage is related to later texts: "After we have finished our exegetical work of establishing what, indeed, the author of the paragraph or text under consideration was trying to say, *then* we must go on to set this teaching in its total biblical context by way of gathering together what God has continued to say on the topic. . . . But mind this point well: canonical context must appear only as part of our summation and not as part of our exegesis."[114]

Now undoubtedly there is an important sense in which an earlier writer was unaware of what would happen to his text after it left his pen, but I would argue that in addition to exegeting a text's original sense, the exegetical process is incomplete until it is exegeted in the light of the entire canon. The Old Testament ought to be exegeted in the light of the New Testament. In support of this contention I advance the following arguments.

In the first place, the doctrine of inspiration demands that we consider a text within its canonical context. All who hold to the inerrancy of Scripture agree that the Scriptures have a dual authorship: God and man. In a very real sense there is one Author along with many human authors, and because there is one Author we ought to consider his entire unified corpus of inspired literature in the interpretation of any one piece of it. Students of Aristotle and other literate men exegete their individual compositions in the light of all their works. Why should we do less when considering the works of the Holy Spirit? Heidegger says: "Every poet composed from only a single poem. . . . None of the individual poems, not even the total of them, says it all. Nevertheless, each poem speaks from the whole of the one poem and each time speaks it."[115]

Closely related to this recognition of a common divine authorship of all the Scriptures is the realization that the canon constitutes a unified linguistic context. We understand the parts of a linguistic stretch in terms of its larger unities. The words of Scripture are understood with its sentences, its sentences within its paragraphs, its paragraphs within its chapters, its chapters within its books and its books within its canon, and this understanding of the whole work qualifies and modifies our understanding of the smaller parts right down to the individual words. The linguistic unity of Scripture calls for an interpretation of its parts within the total canon containing both testaments. Thiselton rightly remarked: "The *total* of any theological utterance is hardly less than Scripture. . . . In Heinrich Ott's words on the subject, 'Scripture as a whole constitutes the "linguistic room" the universe of discourse, the linguistic net of coordinates in which the Church has always resided. . . .' "[116]

The doctrine of progressive revelation also calls for exegeting earlier texts in the light of later ones. It will help here to recognize that revelation takes place on several levels. On the primary level God reveals Himself to the characters in the literature. On the second level He further explicates that revelation through the inspired writers who recorded it and incorporated it in their written works. But after the text has left their hands God may continue to clarify the original revelation through other inspired writers. There are then at least three loci of any revelation: that of the original event, that of the inspired writer of the book reporting it, and that of the canon containing it. Each level must be kept distinct, but the exegete has not completed his work until he has exegeted the revelation in the light of all three levels. Let me illustrate the point. God originally gave a covenant through Nathan to David that he would give David an eternal dynasty and that though he would discipline the house of David for sin, he would never negate his commitment to that house. On the second level of revelation the inspired writer juxtaposes this covenant with David's sin with Bathsheba, and by this juxtaposition he confirms and clarifies the covenant—even David's murder of the innocent Uriah and his defilement of the pure Bathsheba do not negate God's promise never to dispose of the house of David. On the canonical level the same truth is reaffirmed, but on this level it becomes clear that God's covenant continues in effect over centuries filled with all sorts of scandals and finds its fulfillment in Jesus, the greater Son of David. Within the New Testament it becomes clear also that the eternal dynasty finds fulfillment in the eternal Son of God, that the eternal throne exists in heaven at God's right hand, while the earthly one on Mount Zion is only a replica of the heavenly one, and that the eternal kingdom is spiritual composed of Israel's physical seed and Abraham's spiritual seed, and that while the present age fulfills the original charter, it will be consummated in the eternal state. How much richer is our understanding of the original revelation in the light of the total revelation.

Finally, Marshall pointed out the practical need of interpreting the Old Testament in the light of the New Testament by noting that the Jews without the New Testament interpret the Old Testament very differently from Christians:

> It has sometimes been observed that the Old Testament leads up to both the Christian religion and also to the Jewish religion: both Christians and Jews would claim that they are holding fast to the essential message of the Old Testament, and it is at this point that one may see that two different total interpretations of the Old Testament are possible; how do we decide which is the correct one, and what effect does adoption of it have on our detailed understanding of the Old Testament?[117]

In connection with the scriptural context we also need to consider the principle of the analogy of faith. This principle springs from the conviction that any given text of Scripture should be interpreted in the light of the canonical context. But this principle can easily slide into the rule of faith. The principle of the analogy of faith calls for the interpretation of unclear texts in the light of clear ones, but the rule of faith demands that Scripture be interpreted in such a way that it conforms with the church's traditions, creeds and confessions. In theory practitioners of the historico-grammatic method of exegesis decry the rule of faith, but all too often in practice they allow their creeds to usurp the place of the author's intended meaning. The problem then comes down to preventing the valid principle of the analogy of faith from degenerating into the mischievous rule of faith. I suggest that this can be prevented by limiting the role of the principle of the analogy of faith to the negative function of restricting the interpreter from interpreting an unclear passage in such a way that it contradicts a clear passage. We must not, however, domesticate difficult texts by facile harmonizations with familiar ones.

F. The Theological Context

By theological context I do not have in mind that progress of revelation as analyzed, classified, and systematized by the biblical theologian, but rather that model or paradigm of divine matters that the systematic theologians create through imagination and logic for understanding the Scriptures. Jack Rogers has helpfully defined paradigms and our need for them:

> Ian Barbour, a physicist and theologian, says that a model is 'a symbolic representation of selected aspects of the behavior of a complex system for particular purposes' (*Myths, Models*

> *and Paradigms: A Comparative Study in Science and Religion* (San Francisco: Harper and Row, 1974), p. 6). A model can be physical, like a model airplane. Or it can be mental, like the concept of an atom. A model is a tool for cutting complex things down to a manageable size and organizing them so that we can get a hold of them. It is not the same as the data we seek to describe. But it helps us enormously to understand data which would otherwise be beyond our grasp. Once we have a model, then we can perhaps learn some new things about the data it represents.[118]

In sum, the model proposed by the systematic theologian provides the exegete with the final and decisive move in the interpretation of Scripture.

Now, while the paradigms proposed by the systematic theologian is essential for exegesis, we should be fully conscious of the problems associated with them. One problem with paradigms is that they restrict our view of divine matters to that data accounted for by the paradigm, but rarely do they represent the totality of Scripture. While they assist us in understanding certain aspects of Scripture we must be careful not to absolutize them in such a way that we rule out of our thinking data that does not fit them. A second problem is that we get attached to them. For psychological reasons once we commit ourselves to a paradigm we are reluctant to give it up. A third problem is that even when we have a paradigm that has problems in it we will not let go of it until we are sure we have a better one. Then too, we absolutize them so that they become authoritative as the text itself, though in theory we deny this. Finally, we find it difficult to believe that our paradigms are relative to our understanding and that with more maturity we should let them go for better ones. In short, the problem with paradigms is that we absolutize them. We fail to understand what they really are: human models to advance our understanding of the text.

NOTES

[1]G. B. Caird, *The Language and Imagery of the Bible* (Philadelphia: Westminster, 1980), 10.

[2]I am indebted to Caird, *Language of the Bible*, 202f. for this allusion.

[3]See Walter Kaiser, Jr., *Toward an Exegetical Theology* (Grand Rapids: Baker, 1981), 25-28 for a sample of some of Ernesti's key affirmations in his *Elements of Interpretation*.

[4]James Packer, "Hermeneutics and Biblical Authority," *Themelios* (1975): 3.

[5]D. A. Carson, "Hermeneutics: A Brief Assessment of Some Recent Trends," *Themelios* 5 (1980): 12.

[6]Article XVIII.

[7]Kaiser, *Exegetical Theology*, 87f.

[8]Bruce J. Nicholls in *Contextualization: A Theology of Gospel and Culture* (Downers Grove: InterVarsity, 1979), 49 strangely contrasts meaning and intention: "The purpose of this method is to discover what the biblical writer said, and it must be distinguished from the more speculative historical-critical method which aims to discover the author's intention."

[9]C. K. Ogden and I. A. Richards, *The Meaning of Meaning*, (New York: Harcourt Brace Jovanovich, 1959), 15, cited by Caird, *Language of the Bible*, p. 10.

[10]A. C. Thiselton, "The New Hermeneutic," in *New Testament Interpretation*, ed. I. Howard Marshall (Grand Rapids: Eerdmans, 1978), 317.

[11]James H. Olthuis, "On Interpreting an Authoritative Scripture: A Proposal for a Certitudinal Hermeneutic," in Conference Papers for *Interpreting an Authoritative Scripture*, held June 22-26, 1981, pp. 22f.

[12]Hans Georg Gadamer, *Truth and Method*, translation ed. Garrett Barden and John Cumming (New York: Continuum, 1975), 357f.

[13]Cited by Thiselton, "New Hermeneutic," 314.

[14]Thiselton, "New Hermeneutic," 313.

[15]Thiselton, "New Hermeneutic," 318.

[16]B. J. F. Lonegran, *Method in Theology* (New York: Seabury, 1972), 157, cited by Thiselton, "New Hermeneutic," p. 313.

[17]I. Howard Marshall, "How Do We Interpret the Bible Today?" *Themelios*, 5 (1980): 9.

[18]J. I. Packer, "Hermeneutics and Biblical Authority," *The Churchman*, 81 (1967): 7-21.

[19]R. Bultmann, "Das Problem der Hermeneutik," *Zeitschrift für Philosophie und Kirche*, 47 (1950): 63, cited by Olthuis, "Interpreting Scripture," 25f.

[20]Nicholls, *Contextualization*, 30.

[21]Olthuis, "Interpreting Scripture," 2f.

[22]Cited by Thiselton, "New Hermeneutic," 317.

[23]Thiselton, "New Hermeneutic," 317.

[24]Thiselton, "New Hermeneutic," 317f.

[25]For incisive criticisms of the new hermeneutics see Anthony C. Thiselton, *The Two Horizons* (Grand Rapids: Eerdmans, 1980); Carson, "Hermeneutics," 15; Kaiser, *Exegetical Theology*, 30; J. W. Montgomery, "An Exhortation to Exhorters," in *Christianity Today*, 17 (1973): 606.

[26]Cf. Olthuis, "Interpreting Scripture," 32f.

[27]Nicholls, *Contextualization*, 42.

[28]Article X.

[29]Brevard S. Childs, *Introduction to the Old Testament as Scripture* (Philadelphia: Fortress, 1979), 105.

[30]Cited by Gerhard Maier, *The End of the Historical-Critical Method* (St. Louis: Concordia, 1977), 68.

[31]J. I. Packer, "The Adequacy of Human Language," in *Inerrancy*, ed. Norman L. Geisler (Grand Rapids: Zondervan, 1979), 198.

[32]Bruce K. Waltke, "The Textual Criticism of the Old Testament," in *The Bible Expositor's Commentary*, ed. Frank E. Gaebelein (Grand Rapids: Zondervan, 1979), I: 211-30.

[33]Waltke, "Textual Criticism," 211-30.

[34]F. M. Cross, Lecture at Vancouver School of Theology, April, 1980.

[35]I. H. Marshall, "Historical Criticism," in *New Testament Interpretation*, 126.

[36]Peter Stuhlmacher, *Historical Criticism and Theological Interpretation of Scripture*, trans. and intro. Roy A. Harrisville (Philadelphia: Fortress, 1975), 45.

[37]Gerhard Maier, *The End of the Historical-Critical Method* (St. Louis: Concordia, 1977), 53.

[38]Maier, *End of Historical-Critical Method*, 16.

[39]Maier, *End of Historical-Critical Method*, 45.

[40]Stuhlmacher, *Criticism and Interpretation*, 42.

[41]Caird, *Language of the Bible*, 201.

[42]John Goldingay, "Inspiration, Infallibility, and Criticism," *The Churchman*, 90 (1976): 12.

[43]Goldingay, "Inspiration," 12.

[44]Goldingay, "Inspiration," 13.

[45]Goldingay, "Inspiration," 12.

[46]Kaiser, *Exegetical Theology*, 50.

[47]Caird, *Language of the Bible*, 60.

[48]Cf. below.

[49]Goldingay, "Inspiration."

[50]Carson, "Hermeneutics," p. 13.

[51]David Wenham, "Source Criticism," in *New Testament Interpretation*, p. 139.

[52]Alan Jenks, *The Elohist and North Israelite Traditions* (Chico, Calif.: Scholars Press, 1977).

[53]G. W. Coats, *From Canaan to Egypt* (1976) and R. N. Whybray, "The Joseph Story and Pentateuchal Criticism," *Vetus Testamentum* (1968): 522-528.

[54]Childs, *Introdüction to the Old Testament*, 147.

[55]Childs, *Introduction to the Old Testament*, 124.

[56]Childs, *Introduction to the Old Testament*, 121.

[57]Childs, *Introduction to the Old Testament*, 208.

[58]D. J. Wiseman, "Israel's Literary Neighbours in the 13th Century, B.C., *Journal of Northwest Semitic Languages*, 5 (1977): 82.

[59]Jeffrey H. Tigay, "An Empirical Basis for the Documentary Hypothesis," *Journal of Biblical Literature* (1975): 329.

[60]Bruce K. Waltke, "The Samaritan Pentateuch and the Text of the Old Testament," in *New Perspective in the Old Testament*, ed. J. Barton Payne (Waco: Word, 1970), 212-39.

[61]Waltke, "Samaritan Pentateuch," 212-39.

[62]Barton Payne, "Higher Criticism and Biblical Inerrancy," in *Inerrancy*, 102.

[63]Nyberg, *Studien zum Hoseabuche* (1935), 7.

[64]Giovanni Pettinato, *Biblical Archaeologist* (1976): 45.

[65]Bruce K. Waltke, "The Book of Proverbs and Ancient Wisdom Literature," *Bibliotheca Sacra*, 136 (1979): 221-38.

[66]O. Weber, *Die Literatur der Babylonia und Assyrer* (1970), 249.

[67]S. N. Kramer, *Sumer.*

[68]*Archives Royales de Mari:* I:6, 5; 9:5; 10,4; 20,5; 22,4: passim.

[69]Laessoe, *Literary and Oral Tradition in Ancient Mesopotamia* (1953), p. 205.

[70]George E. Mendenhall, *Law and Covenant in Israel and the Ancient Near East* (1955).

[71]Klaus Baltzer, *The Covenant Formulary* (Philadelphia: Fortress, 1971).

[72]Helmer Ringgren, "Oral and Written Transmission in the Old Testament," *Studia Theologica*, 3 (1950-1951): 34-59.

[73]George Widengren, *Literary and Psychological Aspects of Hebrew Prophets* (1945), p. 49.

[74]Widengren, "Oral Tradition and Written Literature Among the Hebrews in Light of Arabic Evidence, with Special Regard to Prose Narratives," *Acta Orientali*, 23 (1959): 201-62.

[75]Widengren, "Oral Tradition," 201-62.

[76]Cited by Kaiser, *Toward Theology*, 27.

[77]Caird, *Language of the Bible*, 38.

[78]Caird, *Language of the Bible*, 40.

[79]I. Howard Marshall, *Themelios*, 5 (1980): 6.

[80]Caird, *Language of the Bible*, 64.

[81]Kaiser, *Toward Theology*, 26.

[82]James Barr, *Comparative Semitic Philology and the Text of the Old Testament* (New York: Oxford University Press, 1968).

[84]Sabatina Moscato, *An Introduction to the Comparative Grammar of the Semitic Languages* (New York: International Publication Services, 1969), 131.

[85]P. Paul Joüon, S. J., *Grammaire de l'hebreu biblique* (Rome: Pontifical Books, 1923), 289.

[86]A. Sperber, *A Historical Grammar of Biblical Hebrew* (1966), 591.

[87]M. O'Connor, *Hebrew Verse Structure* (Winona Lake, Ind.: Eisenbrauns, 1980), 146.

[88]Packer, *Inerrancy*, 211.

[89]Olthuis, "Interpreting Scripture," 17.

[90]Thiselton, "New Hermeneutic," 314.

[91]James Barr, *Semantics of Biblical Language* (New York: Oxford University Press, 1961), 39.

[92]Kaiser, *Toward Theology*, 24ff, *passim*.

[93]Barnabas Lindars, "Torah in Deuteronomy," *Words and Meanings*, eds. Peter R. Ackroyd and Barnabas Lindars (New York: Cambridge University Press, 1968), 131f.

[94]Willis J. Beecher, *The Prophets and the Promise* (Grand Rapids: Baker, 1963), 130. See Walter C. Kaiser, Jr., "Legitimate Hermeneutics," in *Inerrancy*, 137.

[95]Wycliffe Bible Translators.

[96]Wittgenstein.

[97]Gerhardus Vos, *Biblical Theology* (Grand Rapids: Eerdmans, 1948), 27-40.

[98]Zane C. Hodges, "Rivers of Living Water—John 7:37-49," *Bibliotheca Sacra*, 136 (1979): 239ff.

[99]Henry Van Dyke Parunak, *Structural Studies in Ezekiel* (University Microfilms, 1979).

[100]James Muilenburg, *Journal of Biblical Literature*, 88 (1968): 7-18.

[101]Muilenburg, *Journal of Biblical Literature*.

[102]Stuhlmacher, *Criticism and Interpretation*, 30.

[103]Caird, *Language of the Bible*, 145.

[104]Clarence J. Vos, *Women in Old Testament Worship* (Delft: Judels and Brinkman, 1968), 56ff.

[105]Seth Erlandson.

[106]Caird, *Language of the Bible*, 16.

[107]G. Linwood Barney, A revised unpublished edition of "The SupraCulture and the Cultural: Implications for Frontier Missions" in *The Gospel and Frontier Peoples*, ed. R. Pierce Beaver (South Pasadena: William Carey Library, 1973), cited by Nicholls, 11.

[108]Carl Armerding, "An Evangelical Old Testament Criticism?", in *Conference Papers for Interpreting an Authoritiative Scripture*, 21.

[109]Leah Bronner, *The Stories of Elijah and Elisha as Plemics Against Baal Worship* (1968).

[110]Cited by Maier, *End of Historical-Critical Method*, 46.

[111]Marshall, *Themelios*, 5 (1980): 7.

[112]Kaiser, *Exegetical Theology*, 140.

[113]Kaiser, *Exegetical Theology*, 136.

[114]Kaiser, *Exegetical Theology*, 136.

[115]Heidigger.

[116]Thiselton, "New Hermeneutic," 315.

[117]Marshall, *Themelios*, 7.

[118]Jack Rogers, "Mixed Metaphors, Misunderstood Models, and Puzzling Paradigms," in *Interpreting an Authoritative Scripture*, 9.

A Response to Historical Grammatical Problems

Kenneth L. Barker
Executive Secretary of the NIV Committee on Bible Translation and Director of the Bible Translation Department for the New York International Bible Society.

A Response to Historical Grammatical Problems

Kenneth L. Barker

First, by way of preliminary comment, I wish to state that I count it a great honor and privilege to respond to a paper by my dear friend and esteemed former colleague, Bruce Waltke. His work manifests the usual scholarship and erudition that we have come to expect of him. I find myself in agreement with probably at least 90 percent of his presentation. In fact, I will not comment on most of his paper precisely because I agree with it and can add nothing significant to it. If I differ in a minor way here and there, I do so to reflect my own viewpoint in the spirit of constructive criticism. My approach, then, is intended to be positive, not negative.

My remarks correspond to specific points in the outline to Waltke's paper.

I. PREJUDGMENT

In his discussion of the "new hermeneutic," Waltke notes, "What is new is the stress upon correcting one's unconscious prejudices regarding the Scripture's meaning" (p. 78). Goldingay underscores the importance of being open to such correction:

> It is actually impossible to study without having one's own beliefs and framework of thinking, and being influenced by them. Indeed, we need some such framework if we are to make coherent sense of the data we examine. What is important is to be open to recognizing our presuppositions, and then to be prepared for the material we are studying to challenge them and to modify the perspective with which we approached it.
>
> It is, of course, always easier to see someone else's perspective vitiate his interpretation than to see the same process at work in one's own efforts.[1]

II. BIBLICAL CRITICISM

A. Textual Criticism

Waltke believes that an editor of Book II of the Psalter "almost certainly revised the original psalms in his collection by systematically substituting Elohim for YHWH" (p. 78-79). He states: "To judge from the rules of the Qumran community, where a member was to be expelled for uttering the divine name (IQs 6:27-7:2), Book II represents a very early piece of evidence for the reverential evasion of the divine name and ought to be regarded as the product of editorial activity" (ibid.).

However, this is an oversimplification of complex literary traditions. Boling's analysis of and conclusions regarding the use of YHWH and Elohim in the Psalter have always seemed to me to be the preferred solution to this problem:

> It is highly improbable that the frequence of *'ɛlôhîm* in E, where it is A-word in parallelism, could result from editorial adjustments of a pattern in which it was predominantly B-word, since this would presuppose a highly sophisticated approach to editorial problems. These distributions thus reflect preferences for sharply contrasted stylistic forms in which divine names are used in a fixed traditional order. . . . Psalms which are preserved in a double recension and further indication that it was neither an aversion to one name nor a perference for the other *per se* which produced the contrasts in J and E,[2] but consistent preference for a given order in parallelism, which involves avoidance of the divine name in the first member of "Elohistic" bicola and pairs of bicola.[3]

He continues:

> . . . the names for God are genuine variants and not the result of editorial adjustments in the text.
>
> There is not a single clear example in these doublets where *yahwêh* as B-word has been replaced by *'ɛlôhîm* in the "Elohistic" passage. There are two clear examples in which *yahwêh* is the "Elohistic" B-word with variant parallels in the first position. In "Elohistic" psalms the Tetragrammaton is frequently avoided in the first colon, perfectly acceptable in the second.[4]

He concludes:

> The frequences of *yahwêh* and 'ɛlôhîm in J and E thus represent opposing stylistic preferences. The distributions of the

> two in parallelism show that the basis of the opposition is a fixed traditional sequence in poetic construction. . . . The common "Yahwistic" sequence, *yahwêh* (A) - 'ɛ*lôhîm* (B), is merely reversed in E. These contrasts were also carefully preserved in Psalms with double J and E recensions.
>
> These conclusions pose an entirely new literary and historical problem. Both traditions must be extremely ancient in order to be so firmly established, so flatly opposed to one another, and so faithfully perpetuated in double recensions. A "late" redaction of Pss. 42-83, in which the Tetragrammaton was more or less systematically replaced by 'ɛ*lôhîm*, becomes extremely improbable.[5]

This is a much more likely explanation of the phenomena. Or so it seems to me.

Later in this same section Waltke indicates that "the vocalized portion of the inspired text is probably more vulnerable to corruption that the written text" (p. 80). I fully concur with this judgment. However, he goes on to say, "A comparison of the NASB with NIV will show that the former stands much closer to the Jewish text than the latter" (p. 80). Because of my position, I trust that I will be pardoned if I suggest that "much closer" be toned down to "a little closer."

B. Historical Criticism

Waltke asserts that "Matthew cites Jeremiah for a quotation taken from Zechariah (Matt. 27:9); Mark cites Isaiah as the prophet of a passage taken from Malachi (Mark 1:2)" (p. 84). But according to Hendriksen, this too is an oversimplification:

> What Matthew does . . . is this: he combines two prophecies, one from Zechariah and one from Jeremiah [19]. Then he mentions not the minor prophet but the major prophet as the source of the reference. This mentioning of only one source when the allusion is to two is not peculiar to Matthew. Mark does this also. Mark 1:2, 3 refers first to Malachi, then to Isaiah. Nevertheless Mark ascribes both prophecies to "Isaiah," the major prophet.[6]

Waltke also mentions the problem of large numbers and asserts that they "are notoriously difficult to accept on face value, especially as given in the received text of Chronicles" (p. 86). This rather negative view of the Chronicler's accuracy in using numbers needs to be balanced by Payne's more positive evaluation.[7]

C. Literary Source Criticism

Although Waltke later appears to retract or at least qualify some of his earlier statements in this area, he nevertheless seems to make certain concessions that I personally am not willing to make (pp. 87–93). For example, it is just as reasonable to me that Genesis 1 and 2 (which I do not regard as two accounts of creation[8]) were composed originally by one and the same author (why not Moses?). After presenting in *summary* form a *general* account of creation (which included man and woman), the author next focuses on Adam and Eve in Eden in order to furnish more *specific* details about them in *particular.* According to Kitchen,[9] such an approach is quite common in the world of ancient Near Eastern literature. The whole narrative makes more sense to me when conceived of as a single literary unit. So-called "P" and "J" are simply structural parts of a unified whole. Waltke himself acknowledges the overall unity of the final form of Genesis. I prefer to attribute this unity to a single author (Moses, in my view) who organized his work around the literary device of the *tōleḏōṯ* formula.

But perhaps I have partially misunderstood my friend, since he himself concludes, "Now if we can establish ancient material in the sources and cannot establish later material in them, and if the fusion could have taken place at a very early period, we have no reason to reject out of hand the notion that Moses authored the essential core of the Pentateuchal material" (p. 93).

D. The Problem of Oral Tradition

Here his treatment and conclusion are excellent. I heartily agree with his final statement: "that Israel transmitted their precious spiritual cargo in the leaky boat of oral tradition turns out to be a nonexistent ghost" (pp. 99).

III. THE CONTEXT

A. The Linguistic Context

1. Problems in Lexicography

Waltke makes the rather bold pronouncement that the NIV "erred in rendering *ysd* in Ps. 8:2 by 'ordain', a meaning attested only in postexilic Hebrew but never in preexilic Hebrew, where it always means 'to lay a foundation' " (p. 101). This may be another oversimplification, since one must always be open to the possibility that later research will prove the conclusion about *ysd* wrong—particularly in the light of the Septuagint and New Testament rendering (Matt. 21:16).

Shortly after this, one encounters a very helpful definition of "the fear of the LORD": it is " 'God's revealed will,' its objective reality, and 'man's unconditional surrender to it,' its subjective reality" (p. 101).

I have hermeneutical problems with the statement, "A parable such as the prodigal son is also intended to have as many interpretations as there are hearers" (p. 106). Probably most of us would agree with Ramm that we should "look for the one central thesis of the parable."[10]

B. The Literary Context

It is my judgment that in his advocacy of a "spiritualizing" approach to much of the prophetic literature (pp. 110-12) Waltke goes too far, the discussion is too subjective, and there are not enough hermeneutical controls over the exegetical or interpretative process.

Waltke's claim that O'Connor's method of analyzing Hebrew poetry replaces "roughly defined semantic parallelism" (p. 114) is an overstatement of the case. O'Connor's principles *supplement* thought parallelism, but they do not supplant it. Thought parallelism—particularly synonymous parallelism—is simply too transparent in Hebrew (and Ugaritic) poetry to be discounted.

C. The Cultural Context

Some Old Testament scholars challenge the view that Israel's cosmology conceived of a "a three-tiered universe consisting of heavens above, earth beneath and waters below the earth" (p. 118).[11]

Later the question is raised: "Does Genesis 1 also serve a polemic intention against worshiping the creation rather than its Creator?" (p. 117). My answer is "Yes." Indeed, I would add that Genesis 1 is a polemic against competing views of creation, as I have attempted to demonstrate elsewhere.[12]

D. The Situational Context

To the discussion of what I would call the false dichotomy between the letter of the law and the spirit of the law (pp. 119–21) I would add the Pharisaic view of the Sabbath in the New Testament. Jesus made it clear that it is *always* lawful and right to do good and to save life (Matt. 12:12; Luke 6:9; 13:15-16; 14:5). In my opinion, such an understanding had always been God's intention for the *spirit* of the law of the Sabbath.[13] He had never intended that the Sabbath law prohibit doing good and saving life.

E. The Scriptural Context

I agree wholeheartedly with Waltke's contention (against Kaiser) that "in addition to exegeting a text's original sense, the exegetical process is incomplete until it is exegeted in the light of the entire canon. The Old Testament ought to be exegeted in the light of the New Testament." (p. 122).[14] Similarly, Johnson argues, "Thus the work of the biblical interpreter is not necessarily finished when he has come to the meaning intended by the original human author."[15] He continues, "The total context of a passage is necessary for its correct understanding and, therefore, the intention of the secondary author must be subordinated to the intention of the primary author, God Himself."[16] Saphir illustrates the point:

> Supposing that there is a little plant before me. I can examine it. But supposing that I have a powerful microscope. I look at it, and now I can see a number of things which before were entirely non-existent to me. Have I put anything into that plant that was not there before? Have I changed the plant? Have I introduced my pet ideas into that plant? So, when we read Leviticus with the light of the epistle to the Hebrews; when we read the whole Old Testament with the light of the evangelists and the epistles, that is exposition, not imposition. We do not put anything into it. The Holy Spirit enlarges our vision to see what is there.[17]

Goldingay likewise addresses this issue:

> Finally, are OT and NT theology to be studied in isolation from each other? . . . theologically it seems questionable. The Bible as a whole is the normative context for interpreting any one of its parts; therefore to fence off one area (Old or New) and generalize about it in isolation seems likely to lead (and has led) to imbalance. Christian theology needs a biblical theology, rather than an OT theology which has difficulty in referring to Christ, or a NT theology which omits the NT's normative but unspoken theological background and context.[18]

As Waltke astutely observes, "Students of Aristotle and other literate men exegete their individual compositions in the light of all their works. Why should we do less when considering the works of the Holy Spirit?" (p. 122).

Unfortunately, there are occasional differences of opinion among us as to how the New Testament is interpreting the Old Testament in specific instances. For example, Waltke claims that "the present age fulfills" the Davidic Covenant and that "it will be consummated in the eternal state" (p. 123). This depends on what one means by "present age." In my view, the New Covenant era includes the present church period and a future literal form of the Messianic kingdom on this earth in time-space history, as I have argued elsewhere.[19]

To Waltke's discussion of the analogy of faith and the rule of faith (p. 124) I would add a reference to the treatment by Ramm.[20] Waltke declares that all too often practitioners of the historico-grammatical method of exegesis "allow their creeds to usurp the place of the author's intended meaning" (p. 124). I concur. Indeed, in my opinion, the rule-of-faith procedure should not be part of our exegetical method. Even the church must be prepared, if necessary, to modify its traditions, creeds and confessions if biblical exegesis and biblical theology clearly dictate that it should. I personally do not believe that this will ever need to happen in the case of commonly accepted cardinal doctrines of the Christian faith, but it could easily happen in the case of the church's understanding of other doctrines and specific passages of Holy Scripture.

F. The Theological Context

Similarly, we must be willing to revise and refine our systematic theology if biblical exegesis and biblical theology indicate that we should do so. If this means that systematic theology (other than in the areas of universally acknowledged cardinal doctrines of historic Christianity) must, at least to some extent, be always in a state of flux, so be it. As Waltke points out, probably the chief problem with systematic theology paradigms "is that we absolutize them. We fail to understand what they really are: human models to advance our understanding of the text" (p. 125). But if "our understanding of the text" requires us, in turn, to revise our systematic theology paradigms, we must be prepared to do precisely that. Otherwise, inerrancy no longer attaches to the text of Scripture but to our understanding of it. After all, this is the International Council on *Biblical* Inerrancy, not the International Council on *Ecclesiastical* Inerrancy. Therefore, in the final analysis, Scripture itself, when interpreted properly through the process of biblical exegesis and when synthesized legitimately through the process of biblical theology, must stand in judgment on all our humanly devised systems of dogmatic theology. For Goldingay's assertion is valid: "Dogmatic theology has often imposed its own concerns on biblical study and hindered the Bible's own concerns and categories from emerging."[21]

NOTES

[1]John Goldingay, *Approaches to Old Testament Interpretation* (Downers Grover: InterVarsity, 1981), 18.

[2]Boling uses J and E merely as a means of convenient classification of the psalms in which Yahweh (or Jahweh) and Elohim predominate, respectively, not in reference to Pentateuchal documents or sources.

[3]Robert G. Boling, " 'Synonymous' Parallelism in the Psalms," *Journal of Semitic Studies* 5 (July 1960): 248.

[4]Boling, " 'Synonymous' Parallelism," 250.

[5]Boling, " 'Synonymous' Parallelism," 254-55.

[6]William Hendriksen, *Exposition of the Gospel According to Matthew*, New Testament Commentary (Grand Rapids: Baker 1973), 948.

[7]J. Barton Payne, "Part 1: The Validity of the Numbers in Chronicles," *Bibliotheca Sacra* 136 (April-June 1979): 109-28; idem, "The Validity of the Numbers in Chronicles: Part 2," *Bibliotheca Sacra* 136 (July-September 1979): 206-20.

[8]Nor does Aalders so regard them. He writes: "The revelation about the creation of the world is followed by a description of the history of that created world. The first scene portrayed in that history is Paradise and the events associated with it, primarily the Fall into Sin." G. Ch. Aalders, *Genesis: Bible Student's Commentary*, 2 vols. trans. William Heynen (Grand Rapids: Zondervan 1981), 1:78. He further states that "it is certainly incorrect to call Genesis 2:4b-3:24 a second creation narrative. The contents of this section clearly belie such a designation." Ibid., 79.

[9]K. A. Kitchen, *Ancient Orient and Old Testament* (Chicago: Inter-Varsity 1966), 116-19.

[10]Bernard Ramm, *Protestant Biblical Interpretation* (Boston: Wilde, 1956), 261.

[11]See, for example, Walter C. Kaiser's discussion in *Theological Wordbook of the Old Testament*, ed. R. Laird Harris et al. (Chicago: Moody, 1980), 1:501.

[12]Kenneth L. Barker, "The Value of Ugaritic for Old Testament Studies," *Bibliotheca Sacra* 133 (April-June 1976): 120-21.

[13]Cf. Kenneth L. Barker, "False Dichotomies between the Testaments," *Journal of the Evangelical Theological Society* 25 (March 1982).

[14]Barker, "False Dichotomies."

[15]S. Lewis Johnson, *The Old Testament in the New* (Grand Rapids: Zondervan, 1980), 51.

[16]Ibid. Johnson, *Old Testament in the New*, 51.

[17]Adolph Saphir, *The Divine Unity of Scripture* (New York: Hodder, 1895), 64; cited by Johnson, *Old Testament in the New,* 108.

[18]Goldingay, *Approaches*, p. 36.

[19]Barker, "False Dichotomies."

[20]Ramm, *Protestant Biblical Interpretation*, 125-28.

[21]Goldingay, *Approaches*, 21.

A Response to Historical Grammatical Problems

Allan A. MacRae
President of Biblical
Theological Seminary and
Professor of Old
Testament

A Response to Historical Grammatical Problems

Allan A. MacRae

After being asked to respond to a paper on "Historical Grammatical Problems" I was surprised to find that very few of its twenty sections deal with either grammar or history. Perhaps the content of the paper could be better represented by such a title as "Problems confronting those who attempt grammatico-historical interpretation of the Bible."

Much of the paper deals with matters of great importance, many of them subjects to which I have devoted years of research and thought. My views regarding some of them differ substantially from those in the paper to which I am responding. I trust that this will not be considered as in any way a reflection against the author personally.

I read the paper by Dr. Waltke with great interest. There are many statements in it with which I wholeheartedly agree. There are others with which I feel a strong disagreement. One matter is so basic that I would like to respond to it at length before dealing with the sections of the paper in order. I refer to material on pages 22-25 and elsewhere that speaks approvingly of the division of Genesis 1-2 into documents that it designates as P and J, and thus endorses the foundation stone of what has been called the Higher Criticism, the Graf-Kuenen-Wellhausen theory, and, more recently, "Orthodox Literary Criticism of the Pentateuch." (It should be noted that in this connection "orthodox" does not mean "in line with generally accepted Christian ideas" but "in line with the views that were held by most biblical critics between 1880 and 1920.")

There are several reasons why I am disturbed by the use of the terms P and J and by statements in support of the ideas that they represent:

1. There has been no movement more effective in destroying Christian faith than the "Higher Criticism." A century ago most of the so-called evangelical denominations in Europe and America accepted the Bible as inerrant and proclaimed its great central doctrines.

Today there are leaders in most of those denominations who strongly oppose belief in the inerrancy of Scripture and many of them deny the cardinal doctrines of the Christian faith. No force has been more effective in producing this change than the spread of the Wellhausen theories, which introduced the terms P and J.

2. The terms P and J originated from the Wellhausen theory and represent a denial of the Pentateuch as containing historical truth. The symbol P stands for "Priestly Document" and implies Wellhausen's claim that many parts of the Pentateuch are taken from a long document composed by the Jerusalem priests centuries after the time of Moses in order to enhance their own authority and income. The symbol J is derived from the German representation of YHWH, the personal name of God that is used preeminently in connection with God's dealings with mankind, and particularly in connection with those who would be the special objects of His love and care. This name, represented in the KJV by LORD, occurs frequently in the book of Genesis and almost universally in the other four books of the Pentateuch, which particularly involve God's dealings with His covenant people. The symbol J represents an alleged document, written before P, but still long after the events that it claimed to describe. The name represented by YHWH actually occurs far more often in the so-called P document than in the J document.

To many readers, use of Wellhausen's symbols would seem to imply that his antichristian reconstruction of Bible history is true. Wellhausen declared that we can learn nothing from the Pentateuch about the time with which it deals, but only about the evolutionary development of the religion of Israel, many centuries after the supposed time of Moses.

3. These terms reflect the continuing use of concepts and attitudes that most secular literary scholars abandoned nearly half a century ago. In fact, many of them have forgotten that their discipline ever wandered in these erroneous bypaths.

The history of science is filled with movements that have flourished for a time and then have been abandoned. For centuries it was held that one of the best ways of treating most diseases was to remove blood from one's body. This was done by either making a cut or attaching leeches that would suck out some of the blood. Some historians believe that George Washington's death was due to well-intentioned efforts to relieve him of a minor malady by bleeding him. As recently as fifty years ago advertisements in Philadelphia offered leeches for sale for medical purposes. Today the exact opposite is universally held and blood banks and transfusions are commonplace.

Use of the terms J and P, as well as a number of related statements in the paper, reflect a blind alley in which general literary study wandered for over a century. Although most students of general literature abandoned such efforts nearly fifty years ago, these attempts to divide biblical documents into alleged but otherwise undocumented sources are still taught as valid procedure in many university departments of religion and in nearly every theological seminary that is over sixty years old, even though no ancient copy of a J document or a P document has come to light, and there is no reference to any such document in any ancient writing.

Early in the present century it was often said by those who espoused the theories of source criticism that we must treat the Bible the same way we would treat any other book. Unfortunately most Bible students, whether conservative, liberal, or radical, are quite unaware of an important fact: the idea that great literary works have been composed by the interweaving of various sources and can be reasonably separated into original component parts was strongly attacked by prominent literary critics during the first third of the present century, and was so completely demolished that it has not only been abandoned by most students of literature but has almost been forgotten.

When source criticism was introduced into the Pentateuch its proponents declared that anyone familiar with literary study would know exactly what was meant by the term "Higher Criticism" because of its use in connection with general literature. About twenty years ago I looked at all the standard works on literary criticism in the University of Pennsylvania library and found that few even listed the term "Higher Criticism" in the index. In the rare cases where it appeared it proved to be only a reference to biblical criticism, and not related to general literary criticism at all.

This trend in literary studies began in Germany during the eighteenth century and was first applied to such great classics as the writings of Homer, which F. A. Wolf declared to have been formed by the combining of several previous writings. Goethe was so impressed by Wolf's genius that he asked Wolf's daughter to hide him in the closet in Wolf's classroom so that he could hear the professor lecture without embarrassing him by his presence. Yet later, as Goethe continued to study the *Iliad* he publicly repudiated his former stand, declaring that the essential unity of the work proved that it could only have been produced by one man, though of course the author might have drawn many of his ideas from stories that were already in circulation.

The famous literary scholar, Karl Lachmann, devoted much time to detecting sources in Homer, and declared that the newly-discovered *Nibelungenlied* had been composed by the fusion of twenty different lays.

Scherer claimed that diversities of style and inner contradictions in the Prologue of *Faust* showed that certain lines had been written in the enthusiasm of Goethe's youth and others inserted in the disillusionment of his old age. Long after Goethe's death a manuscript copy of *Faust* was found, that had been copied while he was comparatively young, and it proved to include the lines that had been labeled as later insertions.

Many followed J. M. Manly in declaring that *Piers Plowman,* the great English poem from the fourteenth century, was really the work of five men. Others thought it was formed by the joining of three sources. The process of dividing ancient and medieval writings into alleged original sources was carried to great extremes.

Yet as scholars continued their search for sources it came to be recognized that most good writers use several different styles and that even in the writings that are known to be composite it is extremely difficult to identify the parts written by various individuals. Richard Altick says: "Though we know that half a dozen men (Swift, Arbuthnot, Pope, Gay, Parnell, and the Earl of Oxford) composed the *Memoirs of Martinus Scriblerus,* we cannot positively isolate the contributions of any one of them."[1] Professor René Wellek of Yale University wrote: "Even in the case of Beaumont and Fletcher, in which we have the advantage of having work definitely only by Fletcher written after the death of Beaumont, the division between their shares is not established beyond controversy; and the case is completely lost with *The Revenger's Tragedy* which has been assigned to Webster, Tourneur, Middleton, and Marston alternatively or in various combinations."[2]

Early in the present century a reaction against the whole divisive criticism appeared among literary scholars, who began to insist that a great work of art must have a single author, though, of course, this author may draw ideas from many sources. Professor R. W. Chambers of the University of London scoffed at the idea that "those lost lays" were of such a character that an epic could be made by fitting them together. He said: "Half a dozen motor-bikes cannot be combined to make a Rolls-Royce car."[3]

Most literary scholars now are willing to accept the claim of Sir Arthur Quiller-Couch of Cambridge University that *Piers Plowman* is a single work, written by William Langland.[4]

In his *Preface to World Literature* (1940) Professor Albert Guerard of Standord University gave his evaluation of the Homeric controversy, saying: "Internal evidence, of a convincing nature, reveals a commanding artistic personality. To dissolve Homer into a myth or a committee, much stronger acid would be needed than the Wolfian school has been able to supply."[5]

In 1962 George Steiner described the changed attitude toward the divisive theories. He wrote:

> In the late 19th century dismemberment was all the rage. . . . The plays attributed to that illiterate actor Shakespeare appeared to have been compiled by a committee which included Bacon, the Earl of Oxford, Marlowe, recusant Catholics, and printers' devils of extraordinary ingenuity. This fine fury of decomposition lasted well into the 1930's. As late as 1934 Gilbert Murray could discover no reputable scholar ready to defend the view that a single poet had written either or both the *Iliad* and the *Odyssey*. Today the wheel has come full turn. . . . To Professor Whitman of Harvard, the central personal vision and "ineradicable unity" of the *Iliad* are beyond doubt.[6]

In 1963 Robert Gordis wrote:

> We may note the growing disfavor in which the atomization of ancient literary documents is viewed by contemporary scholarship. Increasingly, the study of ancient literature, like that of the Homeric epics, has been focusing attention on the unity and meaning of the whole work rather than upon the disparity of the constituent elements. That the indiscriminate (and even accidental) lumping together of scattered literary fragments by an obtuse redactor, who often did not understand the material he was working with, could produce a masterpiece—that naive faith of 19th century literary critics is no longer widely held today.[7]

Professor H. Gardner of Oxford has said:

> The modern scholar or critic concentrates in the first place on making what he can of his text as it has come down to him. There has been a strong reaction against the study of even extant and known sources, much more against the discussion of hypothetical ones. . . . The importance of the single author and

> the single work dominates literary studies, as can be seen if the plan and treatment of the new *Oxford History of English Literature*, now in progress, is compared with that of the old Cambridge History.[8]

My fourth reason for wishing that no trace of the method so generally abandoned in literary studies were retained among believers in biblical authority is the fact that source-hunting, as now practiced in Bible departments, no longer can be said to possess what was formerly its most effective argument, the claim that it was a system agreed upon in its major positions by all critical scholars. It is true that during the first fifth of this century most of the various scholarly presentations of the higher criticism agreed very closely. But this unanimity has been completely shattered. To understand this we should briefly examine the history of the criticism of the Pentateuch.

Starting at about A.D. 1800 various theories of the division of the Pentateuch into alleged sources were presented by a number of scholars in Germany and other countries. For some time one theory after another of the alleged origin of various parts of the Pentateuch came into favor. By 1878 the so-called supplement hypothesis was held by most of the believers in source criticism. Then Julius Wellhausen, a brilliant German scholar who possessed unusual ability to write in a very clear style, wrote his "Prolegomena to the History of Israel" in which he presented a theory that completely reversed the previous ideas of the nature and sources of the Pentateuch. The theory that he advanced was so startlingly different from previous views that it was called a Copernican revolution. It claimed to show the evolution of the Israelite religion from very primitive ideas to a very complicated system of ritual.

At that time evolution was sweeping much of the scholarly world and Wellhausen's theory appealed greatly to the younger scholars though most of the older scholars continued to hold the supplement theory to the end of their lives. Wellhausen's ideas were introduced into England by W. Robertson Smith, S. R. Driver, and T. K. Cheyne, and in the course of a few years they came to be accepted as certain in the religion departments of most British and American universities as well as in many theological seminaries.

The process of disintegration was soon extended to other parts of the Old and New Testaments and there is hardly an Old Testament book that critics have not claimed to analyze into a series of separate sources, most of which could not be proven to have ever had a separate existence.

For nearly fifty years Wellhausen's complete system was taught as established fact in most university departments of religion and in an increasing number of theological seminaries. Wellhausen himself was so sure that his ideas were correct that he paid no attention to the developing science of archaeology. However, others did, and they found that at point after point the findings of archaeology were proving statements in the Pentateuch to fit the background of the time at which they claimed to be written and not to fit the background of the time of writing required by the Wellhausen theory. As a result, scholars began revising the theory at one point after another, and soon a great diversity of opinion developed. In 1929 Dr. William F. Albright said to me: "In Germany there are now only two orthodox Wellhausenists left, and even they are not orthodox." In succeeding years more and more variety was introduced into the theory with hardly any two scholars agreeing.

About twenty years ago I examined a number of standard detailed books about the Pentateuch, written by leading supporters of the Wellhausen theory. When a chart was made with various colors to indicate their views of the alleged J, E, and P documents it showed more differences than agreements among them. In his commentary on the book of Genesis in the *Anchor Bible,* E. A. Speiser pointed out that all previous critics had agreed in assigning Gen. 29:24 and 29 to P, as they were "the type of statistical detail that is customary with P," but declared on the basis of the Nuzi tablets that "it is precisely these two verses that are most likely to constitute direct transcripts from some old and authentic document."[9]

Today the alleged consensus can no longer be claimed. Every critic has his own theory of sources, though most try to preserve the Wellhausenist terminology.

We shall look at other aspects of this matter later on, when we look at Literary Source Criticism as we go through the paper in order. Now we shall begin to respond to its successive parts, as far as time and space permit.

The introduction makes the following statement about "grammatico-historical exegesis": "The divisions between those within the church employing this method of exegesis bears mute testimony to the fact that the method has problems" (p. 73).

Personally I incline strongly to the opinion that most of the divisions among Christians are not the result of problems in using the grammatico-historical method, but rather of failure to use it. All too often we go to the Bible to find proof texts to support views that we already hold instead of carefully examining the Bible to see what each sentence actually says. I believe that the principal need in hermeneutics is unbiased lexical and grammatical study of the Bible, comparing passage with passage to see what God has said, rather than spending much time in consideration of the ideas of those who reject our basic view that the Bible is God's inerrant word through which He desires to tell His people what He wants them to know.

I. PREJUDGMENT

An especially common form of this danger is present when one approaches a verse with an idea of a definite truth taught elsewhere in the Scripture and assumes that this is the subject of the particular verse. When I was still a seminary student I was sometimes shocked at hearing a verse that seemed at first sight to contradict a particular theological truth so treated by the professor as to rob the verse of all meaning whatever. I felt that the Lord must have had a reason for placing the verse in the Scripture and that we should seek to discover that reason rather than to try to explain it away.

One of the greatest needs for interpreting Scripture is to make every possible effort to avoid allowing prejudgments or presuppositions to influence one's interpretation. It might be helpful to begin by trying to interpret each verse in as many ways as possible, even including those that might seem to contradict what had already been learned from other passages, and then carefully to weigh each suggested interpretation. What God expresses in one place will not contradict what he has stated elsewhere, but the words would not be there unless God intended to convey a definite idea and it would be worth a substantial effort to discover the meaning of the particular verse. It might alter some detail of our understanding of something taught elsewhere, or perhaps add a new fact or angle.

At the moment I am busily preparing a study of the prophecies of Daniel. Apart from a few main facts clearly taught in the New Testament I am trying very hard to avoid bringing in anything that is not specifically contained in the statements in the book of Daniel, and when studying its earlier prophecies I am carefully refraining from reading into them anything gained from later prophecies, although I feel it altogether right in interpreting his later prophecies to take into account material gleaned from his earlier ones. I am looking at every reasonable interpretation, but excluding from my conclusions everything that would be at all questionable, not because I do not believe that great progress can be made by study of the Scripture as a whole, but because I feel that one of the great needs, particularly in the area of prophecy, is to study each section very carefully, avoiding prejudgment as much as possible, in order: (1) to see exactly what the section definitely teaches; (2) to see what it may possibly teach; and (3) to determine what ideas should be definitely excluded from the particular passage.

Dr. Waltke deserves credit for beginning the paper with this emphasis on the danger of prejudgment. Yet I see no reason why it should be necessary to give credit to any so-called new hermeneutics for something that should have been recognized throughout the history of interpretation, nor do I feel that the importance of the matter is strengthened by quotations from men whose vision is clouded by their failure to accept the Bible's claim to inerrancy. His remarks about "the pitfalls of the new hermeneutics" in the first half of the middle paragraph on page 8 would seem to give sufficient reason for Bible believers to avoid this particular movement.

II. BIBLICAL CRITICISM

A. Textual Criticism

God has enabled us to possess far more manuscript copies of the Old Testament and of the New Testament than of any other ancient writing. Many a text of an ancient Greek or Roman classic has been preserved to us in only one copy—sometimes in one written as late as the twelfth century A.D.; yet material from such a copy may be used to try to contradict a statement in all the manuscript copies of the Bible. The amount of material available to us for textual criticism of the Bible is so great that there are very few questions of real significance about the actual wording of either Testament.

God has stated and emphasized in Scripture the important truths He wishes His people to have. I know of no variation attested by any substantial number of manuscripts that affects any important teaching. I know of no place where the deletion of a word, phrase, or verse that is said not to be in the earliest manuscripts of the New Testament would remove any thought from the Scripture.

The question whether the last sixteen verses of the Gospel of Mark were original or not is of no real importance, though I am very sure that Mark did not end with the statement "and they were afraid." There must have been an original ending, whether by these words or by others. These verses contain hardly anything that is not already present in the parallel passage in Luke. About the only thing in them that is unique is the statement that "they will take up serpents and not be hurt," and properly interpreted this gives no basis for making public displays or taking foolish risks. It was spoken to the disciples and was literally fulfilled at Malta when Paul accidentally took up the viper and suffered no injury from it, though the bystanders expected him to die.

In both Testaments textual criticism is a very interesting study, but for interpretation its importance is minimal, though the exegete should be aware of textual problems in order that he may avoid building any conclusion on a verse in which there is a serious textual problem. Every important idea in Scripture is clearly presented in verses on which there is no such problem.

When a textual difference causes real uncertainty the exegete should see what the two renderings have in common and stop there. The purpose of Scripture is to give us the thoughts God wishes us to have, and I believe we have ample material for discovering them.

B. Historical Criticism

Under this head Dr. Waltke has made some excellent statements about the dangers of illegitimate historical criticism and then has mentioned six connections in which historical criticism is said to be legitimate. Under the first of these he points out that the biblical writers, like ourselves, sometimes use conventional language. Thus when we say "the sun set," the Hebrew would say, "the sun went in."

It seems strange to place under "conventional language" a discussion of the authorship of biblical books. The paper says that we should accept the claim of Psalm 110 to Davidic authorship at face value, but seems to question the validity of all other biblical statements about authorship when it says that "we need to determine authorship of a book on other grounds than merely an appeal to the biblical notices regarding authorship."

I agree that we need to interpret carefully on this point, and to determine in each case whether a statement refers specifically to a writer or speaker, or whether it is merely a conventional way to indicate a book or perhaps to refer to a group of books that might begin with the one mentioned. All these methods are in common use today in referring to sources.

When the New Testament says that Moses made a certain statement, belief in inerrancy would require that we accept it as a fact that Moses actually did make such a statement. In Romans 9:27,29;

10:16,20; and 15:12, Paul specifically quotes from Isaiah the man and thus the Holy Spirit placed His seal upon the authenticity of the first, second, and third sections of Isaiah, and denied in advance the modern critical theory of three Isaiahs.

I do not agree with the inference on page 84 that Jude quoted from the rambling apocryphal book of Enoch. When Jude says that Enoch made a certain statement, we who believe in inerrancy have no doubt that Enoch did so, though we do not know whether God revealed this fact to Jude or whether his statement was based on an ancient tradition that the Holy Spirit authenticated. In either case the statement gives us no warrant for saying that Jude considered the apocryphal book of Enoch to be inspired.

The second suggestion is that we should reckon with the reality that "the biblical writers believed in dual causation of events." This merely points to the fact that while God controls all things and is the prime mover behind everything that happens, the liberty of lesser beings is also a fact and we are responsible for what we do. Thus it is true to say that God tempted David and equally true to say that Satan tempted David.

The third point discussed here is that of deciding what literary genre is involved. Here I would say that parables and allegories are usually designated as such in Scripture. When there is no clear designation we should go slow about being dogmatic.

In the fourth area mentioned I find myself in strong disagreement. I do not believe "that numbers in the Bible are notoriously difficult to accept on face value." The first response includes a good treatment of this point, but I would like to add two remarks: (1) except for foreign proper names, numbers are the most difficult materials to transmit accurately; (2) in dealing with numbers there is always the possibility that some factor with which we are not familiar is involved. Thus until recently the numbers given for the reigns of the kings of Israel and Judah were considered quite impossible to harmonize. We are grateful to E. R. Thiele for having brought to the interpretation of these numbers some previously unrecognized principles of chronology. In his introduction to Thiele's book, Professor William A. Irwin of the University of Chicago, who is certainly no conservative on biblical matters, said, "It is a matter of first-rate importance to learn now that the books of Kings are reliable in precisely that feature which formerly excited only derision." While the possibility of an occasional textual error must be admitted, particularly in the case of numbers, Professor Irwin mentions the fact that even in pre-Christian times these numbers were thought to be quite corrupt, but says, "The vast bulk of them are precise to the point of astonishment."[10]

The fifth point mentioned is that "the speeches in Acts and elsewhere are abbreviated versions of what was actually said and to that extent do not precisely represent the situation." It should be pointed out that it is never possible to "precisely" represent a historical situation since there are always innumerable facts involved. One has to make a selection and can be precise only to a certain point. We can trust what the Bible says, but should not read into it a degree of precision beyond what is intended. If it says an event follows another event, that makes the order clear. If it simply mentions two events without indicating which came first, we have no right to be sure, without further evidence, as to the order in which they occurred, or whether one followed the other immediately or with an interval between. Thus 2 Kings 19:36-37 mentions Sennacherib's return to Nineveh and immediately tells of his assassination, with no mention of the twenty years between these two events. Scriptural accounts may be arranged in chronological or logical order and we have no right to assume a particular order unless it is so stated in the narrative.

C. The Problem of Oral Tradition

Since these three subjects are closely related I shall discuss them together. Dr. Waltke has done a very excellent job of demolishing the idea, so strongly presented by the Scandinavian school of critics, that much of the content of the Pentateuch was passed on by oral tradition for centuries with many changes, and that in the course of this oral tradition various segments were brought together and interwoven until finally the present form was reached. I believe he summarizes it very well when he says, "In all of the Eastern literatures we have considered there is not one reference to the hypothetical tradent, the key to traditional criticism. This central figure in the source critical theories that Israel transmitted their precious cargo in the leaky boat of oral tradition turns out to be a non-existent ghost." (p. 99). I thoroughly concur with this conclusion regarding the views of the Upsala school of critics, but feel that the same words ought to be applied to "source criticism" and "literary source criticism." While these sections contain some very excellent statements they also include some that impress me as being based on unwarranted assumptions.

The first sentence in the section on "Literary Source Criticism" includes the words, "when these four criteria are brought to bear on Gen. 1:1-2:25, they work together consistently in dividing this passage into two distinct creation stories."

I find it necessary to differ sharply with this statement which supports the foundation stone of the Wellhausen theory, and I am grieved by the presence of similar statements in the following pages. I do not believe that the four criteria mentioned prove that these are "two distinct creation stories."

The criteria named are, "varying divine names, doublets, linguistic differences, and diverse theologies." We shall briefly look at each of them.

The alternation of various names may seem strange to the American or English reader, because it is different from our usual custom. Yet many writers in other languages frequently use various names for an individual and even oscillate back and forth between them. The name of the patriarch Jacob was changed to Israel, but both names continued to be used in combination with the two names for God as a means of producing two consistent documents.

All of us at times use different names for an individual in different connections, depending on the particular relationship. Thus a woman may speak of her husband to her close friends as "Henry," to her chilren as "Dad," and to strangers as "Dr. Smith." Having begun with one usage it is natural to continue it until there is reason to switch to another.

In Gen. 1:1-2:4, which tells of the creation of the universe, the general name which stresses God's power is most appropriate. In the next few chapters, which give details of the creation of human beings and describe God's dealings with them, the most appropriate name is the one represented in the KJV by "the LORD," which shows God in an intimate relation with His people.

The second criterion is called "doublets." This can hardly mean that the stories are doublets in their entirety. Genesis 1 tells of the creation of the heavens and the earth; of light; of the sun, moon, and stars; of plants; and of animals. None of these acts of creation are described in Genesis 2. The only real point of overlapping is the creation of mankind, which is briefly portrayed in its proper place in the course of chapter 1, and described in more detail in chapter 2. (Some critics say that God's planting a garden is a doublet to God's creation of vegetation and that God's bringing the animals to Adam to see what he would name them is a doublet to God's creating the animals, but these alleged doublets are obviously far-fetched.) There is really only a slight amount of overlapping.[11]

As an analogy to the relation of these two chapters we might suggest an account of a trip around the world before air travel became common. The first chapter might contain a short survey of the voyage across the Atlantic from New York, the cities visited in Europe and Asia and the boat trip across the Pacific to San Francisco, and a brief statement of having driven across the United States and been joyfully welcomed home. The second chapter might begin at San Francisco and tell of the problems involved in selecting and buying a car, the difficulties and disappointments experienced while roads were still unpaved and cross-country travel still uncommon, the visit with relatives along the way, and the changes that had occurred at home while the writer was making his journey.

There would be doublets: both chapters would describe trips and both would tell that America was crossed by automobile. Further doublets could be found by noting the similarity of one or two incidents in Europe with some of the same experiences in America. Doublets would not prove different sources unless there were unexplainable contradictions.

The third criterion is "linguistic differences." It is hard to see how this term would apply unless the material were in a different dialect. Probably what is meant is differences in style. The next page says the "P's style is formal and straightforward, J's is that of a storyteller." I am sure that many writers use both of these styles, depending on the subject matter. In the analogy of the trip around the world, the first chapter could easily be "formal and straightforward," briefly listing places visited and expenses at each; the second could be developed "by means of a dramatic plot" as it described interesting experiences while motoring across America. It would be at least as easy to find linguistic differences as in Genesis 1 and 2, perhaps easier since an occasional word in a foreign tongue might occur in the first part.

The fourth criterion is called "diverse theologies." This can hardly mean that the theological view of the two chapters contradict each other, for it is said on page 90, "We should stoutly deny that the sources contradict one another." If it means only that one chapter stresses the transcendence of God and the other His immanence, it is my feeling that either of these thoughts about God is incomplete without the other, though I do not feel distressed when emphasis is put on one of them without the other being immediately mentioned.

We can hardly expect every chapter of the Bible to cover every aspect of theology. I see no reason on this account to say that these two chapters must originally have been separate accounts of creation.

On pages 90-92 enough errors and weaknesses of literary source criticism are mentioned to seem in my opinion to prove the whole procedure unworthy of confidence. Since the method has been abandoned in general literary studies and does not work out consistently in biblical studies, and since no copies of manuscripts P and J have ever been found it is my opinion it is better to jettison the method altogether.

Personally I would feel much happier if the section ended on a more positive note than the one that is sounded in its concluding sentence: "we have no reason to reject out of hand the notion that Moses authored the essential core of the Pentateuchal material.

III. THE CONTEXT

A. The Linguistic Context

Of the six contexts listed, this is by far the most important. Dr. Waltke's discussion includes many important suggestions for which we should be grateful.

I do not think he is right in saying that before deciding on the author's use of a word it is necessary to decide the date of his material. On page 103 he laments the lack of a good historical grammar of the Hebrew language in English, but I am quite sure that there is not enough material available for anyone to make a trustworthy historical grammar of Hebrew. If this knowledge were necessary to understand the Bible, God would have provided us with such material.

On page 104 he points out the difficulty of exact understanding of the meaning of Hebrew tenses. English has a very extensive set of tenses while Hebrew has very few. I do not feel that H. Sperber is right in suggesting that we do away with the terms "perfect" and "imperfect." In spite of occasional difficulties we can say that as a general rule the perfect tense refers to an event in past time, while the imperfect generally points to future time or to something that is future to the event or situation that immediately precedes its use. It is all too easy for a careless exegete to ignore the differences in the tenses. Thus Isaiah 53 ends with four verbs, three of which are in the perfect and the last in the imperfect, but most translations completely ignore this difference. They translate the last phrase as if it were merely a repetition of the general thought included in the first three. Yet if the verbs are translated literally, the meaning becomes immediately apparent. While the first three very aptly describe the atoning work of Christ at Calvary, God enabled Isaiah, by the fourth verb, to look forward to the later activity of Christ, as He sits at the right hand of God making intercession for us.

The listing of functions of language as informative, performative, etc. seems to me to raise more questions than it solves. Dr. Waltke has well said that it is "best not to translate these emotive expressions by the dynamic equivalent and in another language because they are not precise enough."

B. The Literary Context

This section begins with a somewhat confusing attempt to label the genres of various parts of the Bible. To say that Genesis 1 is not history because no man was present to record the events may be only a quibble about words. After all, God is a person, and He was there. Since the events really happened, I prefer to call it history.

To say that a chapter is both an account of an important event in the life of the first human beings and also a picture of every man and woman opens the door to all sorts of allegorizing. It would be better to restrict exegesis to determination of the actual event and its effects and to consider lessons drawn from it as application rather than exegesis. Use of the term "suprahistorical" adds nothing to understanding.

C. The Cultural Context

As the first response has suggested, the statement that writers of the Bible believed in a three-tiered universe rests on an arbitrary translation of certain biblical statements that was colored by the misunderstanding of the translators.

There is an interesting question on page 119: "To what extent does Israel adopt the forms of pagan religions?" The history in the Bible shows them doing this repeatedly, and the prophets constantly rebuked them for it. The conflict between what God had ordered and what neighboring peoples did was unending. People then, as today, were always faced with the decision between God and Baal.

It seems strange to give Bronner credit for trying to prove the obvious—that the immediate purpose of the work of Elijah and Elisha was to lead the Israelites to follow God rather than Baal. But to go on from this obvious fact to the question about the intention of Genesis 1 is rather fanciful. Any writing may accomplish many results. But the purpose of Genesis 1 is clear: to tell how it all began.

D. The Situational Context

This chapter presents the question of which laws are intended to be temporary and which permanent. It is not always easy to distinguish the moral law, which is of permanent duration and validity, from civil law, which is an application of the moral law to specific situations. Careful study of the relevant passages is needed.

E. The Scriptural Context

Next to *A. The Linguistic Context,* this is the most important part of this section of the paper. Study of the interrelation of the parts of the Bible is vital, but this study should be preceded by careful examination of each part.

All the teaching of Scripture is interrelated. The more we learn about any part of Scripture the easier it becomes to understand every other part. Yet there is great danger here. It is easy, by reading into a sentence something derived from another part of Scripture, to miss God's purpose in giving us the particular sentence. I strongly advocate that each chapter, each section, each book be first studied by itself, seeking to list all possible meanings and interpretations and then comparing them and determining which best fits the context in each case.

F. The Theological Context

As Dr. Waltke points out, theology should be the result of Bible exegesis, not its basis. If proper exegesis and synthesis are first performed, correct theology will result. We should not approach the Bible merely as a set of proof texts and a collection of illustrations, but rather as an inexhaustible source of truth. The faith of John Robinson that God would yet cause more truth to be found in his Word is still valid.

Important as it is that we do not allow our theology to have too great an effect on our interpretation of individual verses, still greater caution needs to be exercised in deriving ideas of Bible interpretation from writers who hold views opposed to Bible truth. We would laugh at the idea of a gardener making suggestions for improved production of airplane motors. One who does not take the Bible as God's Word may gather material on history or archaeology that can be helpful in understanding something of the background of the Bible, but when suggestions about Bible interpretation are made by unbelievers they should be examined with great skepticism. Aside from the apologetic purpose of preparing to answer attacks upon Christianity the study of books on hermeneutics written by men who deny biblical inerrancy is more apt to be misleading than helpful. At times it seemed that the paper was too ready to take as fact ideas or suggestions presented by writers whose presuppositions are quite different from ours, and to show far less skepticism toward their statements than toward the ideas of men who believe the Bible. Unless the Holy Spirit is helping a student, how can he be expected to interpret God's Word correctly?

It has been a stimulating experience to go through the paper and I hope that my suggestions will prove to be of some value. Since I am grateful for the many statements of confidence in God's Word that it contains, I was sorry indeed that it was necessary to devote so much of my response to pointing out statements with which I have to disagree.

NOTES

[1]Richard D. Altick, *The Art of Literary Research* (New York: 1963), 71.

[2]René Wellek and Austin Warren, *Theory of Literature* (New York: Harcourt, Brace, 1949, 1956), 60.

[3]R. W. Chambers, *Man's Unconquerable Mind* (London: Cape, 1939), 63-64.

[4]Ibid., Chambers, *Man's Mind,* 85.

[5]Albert Guerard, *Preface to World Literature* (New York: Holt, 1940), 72.

[6]George Steiner, "Introduction: Homer and the Scholars," in *Homer, A Collection of Critical Essays,* ed. George Steiner and Robert Fagles (Englewood Cliffs: Prentice-Hall, 1962), 2.

[7]Robert Gordis, "Elihu the Intruder: A Study of the Authenticity of Job," in *Biblical and Other Studies,* ed. Alexander Altmann (Cambridge: Harvard University Press, 1963), 66.

[8]Helen Gardner, *The Business of Criticism* (London: Oxford University Press, 1959), 97.

[9]E. A. Speiser, *Genesis: The Anchor Bible,* 2 vol. (New York: Doubleday, 1964), 1:226.

[10]Edwin R. Thiele, *The Mysterious Numbers of the Hebrew Kings* (Chicago: University of Chicago Press, 1951), p. xvii.

[11]For a fuller discussion of this question see A. A. MacRae, "The Principles of Interpreting Genesis 1 and 2, *Bulletin of the Evangelical Theological Society,* 2, 4 (1959): 1-9.

Genre Criticism—Sensus Literalis

Grant R. Osborne
Associate Professor of New Testament
Trinity Evangelical Divinity School

3. Genre Criticism—Sensus Literalis[1]

Grant R. Osborne

Genre criticism concerns the application of principles derived from the "type" of literature which describes a certain text to the "sensus literalis" or intended meaning of that text. As such, it can be an important tool in the inerrancy debate, since it stands or falls on the basis of individual textual interpretations. However, the very concept of genre, so central to hermeneutical theory in recent years, is an elusive one. Webster's Third International Dictionary defines genre as "a category of artistic composition characterized by a particular style, form, or content." However, this definition is an outgrowth of the traditional view of genre as a device for classifying types of literature. The modern debate asks whether genre regulates or merely describes a literary work. This issue is the focus of our study. If the former, genre may provide a major hermeneutical tool for uncovering the original meaning of a work, because as Hirsch argues (see below) the "intrinsic genre" of a work will provide interpretive laws for determining its intended message. If the latter, however, the genre may differ from work to work and aid the task of interpretation only peripherally.

Plato and Aristotle were the precursors of modern genre theory. Plato took a descriptive approach while Aristotle developed a theory of mimesis or imitation.[2] In ensuing centuries the Platonic approach prevailed and distinctions between genre types were all but forgotten. However, the neoclassical period of the seventeenth and eighteenth centuries rediscovered Aristotle, and genre as mimesis became the foundation of literary theory. Prescriptive laws demanded conformity to the classical literary types like lyric, epic, or drama, but there was "little consistency or even awareness of the need for a rationale" for such genre "laws."[3]

The Romantic movement provided a revolt against such arbitrary distinctions of genre classification. Romantists believed that every work is autonomous, a genre in itself. Literature was viewed as in process of development, a "becoming"-ness which never finds completion,[4] and genres formed "a single, comprehensive poetic" whole. Some advocated the complete abolition of all generic classifications.[5]

This multiplicity of approaches has continued unabated to the present. Today the Romantics are paralleled by the "deconstructionists," who argue that genres, since they intermix, are no longer "pure" and therefore cannot be classified.[6] Paul Ricoeur states that hermeneutics (which we might link with concepts of genre) has developed in three stages: 1) a classificatory system (the classical period); 2) an epistemological base in Schleiermacher and Dilthey, characterized by a diachronic interest in history; 3) an ontological approach beginning with Heidegger and extending through Gadamer to the present, centering on the synchronic problem of being.[7]

As one can surmise from this brief perusal of approaches to genre, any attempt to grasp easily this complex topic is indeed doomed to disappointment. For one thing, one must ask whether genre relates to the whole or to the parts as well. This is crucial, for many of the arguments addressed against the value of genre are based upon the so-called mixture of genres (e.g. Derrida's article above). If genre relates to smaller units, the arguments are less effective. Furthermore, one's evaluation of the place of genre in various critical schools depends upon this aspect of the definition. For instance, James Muilenberg has said that one of the lasting benefits of form criticism was "that it addressed itself to the question of the literary genre represented by a pericope,"[8] while Vernon K. Robbins recently stated that form criticism has "turned scholarship away from genre analysis."[9] The difference, of course, is one of definition. Muilenberg looks at genre as dealing with small units of tradition; Robbins is concerned with the whole of a work. We will argue below that both aspects are valid. In fact, Michael Beajour has gone so far as to claim that the Bible by its very nature as divine revelation transcends "all actual genres, since divine revelation could not be generic in a logical sense of the word."[10] This, of course, is to ignore the analogical nature of God-talk as well as its human accommodation. However, it does illustrate the importance of a proper definition of genre.

There are so many aspects of genre theory to consider that the task of definition becomes even more difficult. Adrian Marino has discussed various methods for defining literary genre, arguing that the best method for determining literary genre is structure, which consider the internal cohesion of the genres which together make the whole. Marino defines genre as types of creativity based on self-reflection and participation in the creative act, arguing that only this can produce unity or solidarity between genres.[11] While much of the article is quite insightful, we believe that he has negated many of the methods too cavalierly (e.g. content, practical usage, imitation, language, form) and that in actuality a proper consideration of genre must make use of each of these approaches. They are not mutually exclusive but rather interdependent.

The modern debate asks whether genre is a literary form[12] or a mode, dependent upon the historical dimension of semantics which constantly changes.[13] The issue is important: does genre help to determine formal meaning or is it determined itself by the contingencies of history? These are certainly the two poles of the debate; yet one might question whether they are as dichotomous as some would intimate. We will argue below for a "both-and" situation; our working definition is the classical statement in Wellek and Warren:[14]

> Genre should be conceived, we think, as a grouping of literary works based, theoretically, upon both outer form (specific meter or structure) and also upon inner form (attitude, tone, purpose—more crudely, subject and audience).

GENRE AND CLASSIFICATION

Most works on genre in a biblical perspective assume that classification is the thrust of the concept. For instance, C. H. Talbert's *What is a Gospel*? never discusses or defines "genre," but works entirely from a classificatory perspective. John J. Collins, in his introductory essay in Semeia 14, *Apocalypse: The Morphology of a Genre*, says, "By 'literary genre' we mean a group of written texts marked by distinctive recurring characteristics which constitute a recognizable and coherent type of writing."[15] The essays in that volume attempt to isolate the morphological traits which distinguish the apocalyptic genre.

There is an intimate connection between the reformation principle of "sensus literalis" and genre criticism as a classificatory device. Martin Luther formulated this principle in antithesis to the *regula fidei* of the Catholic Church. However, he linked this with the historical-grammatical method and thus with a hermeneutical approach to the original context. Several recent scholars recognize the close connection between a literal hermeneutic and a generic approach to the biblical text. For instance, R. C. Sproul says, "The study of such things as literary forms, figures of speech and style . . . is crucial to accurate interpretation," using as an example the

Balaam's ass incident, which he calls historical narrative rather than poetic personification.[16] Many, of course, would disagree with his assessment of the genre behind the Balaam story and use this as an example of the difficulty of genre analysis.

Among literary critics one of the first topics for discussion concerns the basic generic types. Due to the complete lack of consensus regarding basic types, we must note two realities: 1) the distinction of literary types will differ from period to period, for such generic classifications are history-bound; 2) before one can classify literature into types, it is crucial to establish the criteria for doing so.

A growing consensus in genre criticism recognizes that generic categories shift with periods of literary interest. Johannes A. Huismann in his study of medieval literature concludes that genres are bound to particular epochs and that therefore generic categories are meaningful only if one recognizes they are history-bound and relate mainly to one's own period.[17] Champigny argues that since genre classification is historically controlled, descriptive categories must be semantically chosen to fit the period. Otherwise they will remain unclear and lack import.[18] For biblical study it is vital to establish generic connections with ancient works of the same periods. A good example is Semeia 14 (see footnote 15), which attempts to do this for apocalyptic. The volume studies successively Jewish, early Christian, gnostic, Greek and Latin, rabbinic and then Persian apocalypses in order to establish a literary/morphological pattern for that ancient genre. There are many attempts to identify the basic genre found within the Bible. Hermeneutic textbooks discuss the most important in their sections on "special hermeneutics."[19] The main point of debate here centers upon the mixture of genres within each category, e.g., the use of poetry as well as prose within apocalyptic and the presence of all four types in both the Gospels and the epistles. This leads to the next topic.

The second reality, criteria for distinguishing generic categories, is very debated, in terms of both identification and validity. As we stated above, both external and internal characteristics must be considered in establishing proper criteria. Horst develops three criteria: 1) internal considerations, i.e., "fable, plot and action, narrative perspective and stance, uniqueness and interrelationship of compositional elements";[20] 2) detail, which determines its internal cohesion and the type of literature it represents; and 3) silhouette, which enables the reader to pause and identify with the text in a new way.[21]

An exceedingly worthwhile study of the value of such from the standpoint of practical hermeneutics is provided by Gordon Fee, who tries to determine hermeneutical principles for interpreting passages within diverse biblical genre like epistles, Gospels and apocalyptic.[22] While many of his principles do not develop from generic considerations but rather from general hermeneutical theory, they well illustrate the necessity of approaching each type of genre with a separate set of hermeneutical criteria.

A couple of biblical examples will illustrate the validity of genre as classification. Judges 4-5 provides an interesting story on the deliverance of Israel from the Canaanites and the death of Sisera at the hands of Jael, a Kenite woman. One of the so-called contradictions concerns the manner of his death: 4:21 says Jael drove the peg into Sisera's temple while he was asleep, while 5:25-27 seems to place it in the midst of the hospitality (i.e. giving him milk to drink) and has him falling at her feet. Many attempts at harmonization have Jael waking Sisera up and then killing him with the spike. However, the answer is almost certainly to be found in the two genres employed. Chapter 5 is a poetic celebration of the events in the previous chapter and the differences are certainly due to poetic compression of the event (vv. 25-26) and a poetic celebration of the victory employing hyperbole (v. 27). In similar fashion the interpretation of such peripheral details as the compartmentalized Hades in the parable of the rich man and Lazarus (Luke 16) or the meaning of the symbols in Revelation 13 must depend on the interpretive principles derived from a study of parable and apocalyptic forms, respectively.

However, we must also note the growing disenchantment with any classificatory system whatsoever. In fact, the whole of the seventh volume in the Glyph series reflects this mood. Philippe Lacoue-Labarthe and Jean-Luc Nancy in the opening essay present the basic thesis when they state that every form contains all genres and so is "non-genre" because each type actually comprises a mixture of genres. Genre is therefore characterized by interpenetration and confusion.[23] Perhaps the best statement in the volume is provided by Dennis Kambouchner, who doubts whether any unifying criteria exist, since no telos or "achieved configuration" of any text can be said to achieve a synthesizing/systematizing function which alone can provide a "provisional generality" for the text. The overlapping of genre boundaries means that no unifying criteria exist by which a literary corpus can be classified as possessing common characteristics; the genre laws adduced are too precarious and unstable.[24] Jacques Derrida argues from a deconstructionist perspective, declaring that those who form genre theory presuppose a natural order between literary works. However, the intermixing of genres means that no genre-class can have unrestricted access to any single generic trait. The law of non-closure is in control; the text never closes and so declasses genre.[25]

While the arguments of the above critics possess a certain validity, we do not believe that they compel one to surrender the classificatory side of genre. There are several reasons why a broader definition of genre, encompassing epistemology and ontology, will obviate the criticism. When one recognizes the internal as well as external side of genre (as we mentioned above and will argue further below) the problem of the formal intermixing of generic substance is not as conclusive as many believe. Kambouchner himself admits, "It is not necessary, to speak succinctly, for the genre qua unity to have an absolute form and position; it is only necessary that genre exist, as a frame of reference and as a guarantee of generalization."[26]

Let us consider Derrida's argument as a case in point. He focuses upon one of the "new novels" (Maurice Blanchot's *LaFolie du jour*) as a paradigm of genre mixture in order to prove his position. The problem partially lies in his selection, for the French new novel deliberately seeks to upset all the conventional modes and thereby only demonstrates that one can intermix genres. In fact, the "new novel" as a genre itself demonstrates our thesis, for one interprets it on the basis of its own internal criteria. The major difficulty is the isolation of any genre at all if they mix freely; we believe that there are two answers: First, genres can be identified in small as well as large units; the Gospel is a genre in itself yet contains parable and apocalyptic as well as straight prose.[27] Second, a deliberate choice on the part of any author to mingle genres does not destroy the validity of those he chooses to employ; in fact, the very possibility of discussing the combination of novel, drama and poetry within a single work demonstrates the validity of those generic categories.

GENRE AS EPISTEMOLOGY AND ONTOLOGY

The movement today in genre criticism is away from classification. Baird speaks about the value of a new method. Because form and content provide an ambiguous approach to genre, he prefers the internal concept of "mode" (see above), an inductive approach which begins with the text itself and does not impose characteristics upon it from outside.[28] Baird's approach has epistemological overtones. Mary Gerhart discusses the necessity of critiquing the "reader" in as rigorous a fashion as the "text" in hermeneutics. She argues that the reader can only come to understanding at the epistemological level. Therefore, genre criticism must take into cognizance the reader as well as the text, for the former determines the interpretation and is "informed" by generic considerations.[29] Kambouchner stresses the act of reading, which is generically informed by literary theory. Reading deals only with small units and is functional. As a result, the event-centered moment of reading is infinite in its effects, leading to multiple meanings.[30] For both scholars, the reader becomes an epistemological dimension which interacts with genre to produce meaning.

A proper understanding of this theory is crucial at this stage. These critics argue that the epistemological dimension of reader and the resultant act of reading replaces the "intention" of the text with "polyvalence" or "multiple meanings." This demands two further considerations—1) Gadamer's theory of historical distance and the fusion of horizons; and 2) the new emphasis on "polyvalence" in biblical criticism. Hans-Georg Gadamer views interpretation as an historical act, a "placing of oneself within a process of tradition in which past and present are constantly fused."[31] This "tradition" forms our pre-understanding, for it is the present set of ideals which our experiences and culture have shaped. Therefore, the "temporal distance" between ourselves and the text becomes a means of sifting our pre-understanding so as to select only those aspects which will prove meaningful in interpreting the text, thus avoiding pure subjectivity. In this way Gadamer merges the "horizon of text" with the "horizon of the interpreter," i.e., merging past with present.[32]

If the text and interpreter fuse in a blend of horizons, and if the text is autonomous from the moment of its inception, it is a logical corollary to move on to discuss polyvalence or multiple meanings. Semeia 9 is devoted to a discussion of "Polyvalent Narration." Biblical scholars have approached this topic from the Perspective of semiotics or structuralism. Here then we move directly into ontology. Structuralism presupposes that the human mind organizes thought and meaning via symbols or codes, which must be deciphered to determine the meaning behind the symbols. All the elements in the work as a whole form the clue or "code" which leads to the deeper structure behind the writer's surface words. The words do not produce that structure but presuppose it. Because of this, one cannot utilize a "diachronic" approach to the text in order to discover what it "meant" (which lies in the past) but can only take a "synchronic" approach in order to decipher what it "means." Structuralism is unconcerned with the author's intended meaning; the "deep structure" determines the created product at the sub-conscious level, i.e., the "common world" of the author. Therefore, structural analysis studies the whole rather than the parts, i.e., plot, genre and the "plurality of meanings" behind the text.[33]

Genre is very important to this school, determining the synchrony of the whole. The narrative itself is divided along generic lines and charted for its literary relationships and characteristics then is compared to an external grid of generic counterparts and interpreted to discover the subconscious structure which unifies the surface messages. Erhardt Güttgemanns' "generative poetics" adds the form-critical construct of "forms" or "genres" to the semiotic concept of compositional structure. Genre is a "text type" or "universe of discourse" which generates a certain "performative sense" in the text. It is within this field that the symbols may be delineated according to the "games rules" or alternatives applied by text and interpreter to the hermeneutical task.[34]

Polyvalence occurs when various contemporary patterns are utilized to interpret the resultant grid. In Semeia 9 the parable of the prodigal son is examined from three such perspectives: psychoanalysis, Jungian categories, and strict structuralism. The results, needless to say, point to "A Theory of Multiple Meanings," the following essay by Susan Wittig. Her basic premise is that the situation as it is (i.e. different readings of a text like a parable by different people produce differing meanings) demands a theory which explains the phenomenon. The answer is found in a semiotic approach to both reader and text: the critical perspective of the interpreter is just as determinative as the structure of the text in producing meaning. The mind of the perceiver may be more determinative of unstated meaning (signified) than the analytic system employed, for it "generates" or reshapes the interplay of text and interpreter.[35] In other words, the text and the reader have ontological significance in reshaping meaning, which is removed from the author's intention at the moment of reading. This current interplay may produce any number of valid "meanings" depending upon the context of the reader.

We could hardly conclude our discussion of the ontic level of genre without considering Paul Ricoeur, certainly the most influential hermeneutical logician on the scene today. Ricoeur reworks the classical distinction between "sense" as the objective content of the text and "reference" as the interpreter's response to the text. Metaphor bridges the gap and is a living entity, a "semantic event." Ricoeur thus redefines the hermeneutical circle. It is not a subjective interpenetration of author and reader but rather is an ontological "dialectic between disclosing a world and understanding one's self in front of this world."[36]

Within this system it is understandable that for Ricoeur genre performs a generative function as praxis. In his discussion of "distanciation" he argues that writing as discourse becomes an "event" and a "work" which immediately becomes distanced from the author. Since a text is "open to an unlimited series of readings," it "decontextualizes" itself in new situations; in this way "distanciation" from the author is inherent both in the text as written and as interpreted. Genres deal not with classification but with production.

> To master a genre is to master a "competence" which offers practical guidelines for "performing" an individual work. . . . The same competence in the reader helps him perform the corresponding operations of interpretation. . . . The function of literary genres is to mediate between speaker and hearer by establishing a *common dynamics* (his italics) capable of ruling both the production of discourse as a work of a certain kind and its interpretation according to the rules provided by the "genre."[37]

To encapsulate the presentation in this section, many literary critics believe that a proper consideration of the reader/perceiver/interpreter in the hermeneutical task introduces an epistemological and ontological aspect which makes any classificatory understanding of genre impossible to uphold. The epistemological dimension of the reader's understanding removes one from the historical genre employed by the original writer, and the hermeneutical circle thus established involves the constant intrusion of the interpreter's own perspective as well as the autonomous nature of the text itself. This "distanciation" grounds genre in the ontological nature of language itself, which removes one even further from any systematic generalities. Genre is no longer a closed system but the system which the interpreter reads into the text.

However, while we agree that the epistemic and ontic functions of genre are crucial, we wonder whether the critics above have actually proven their point. Does the factor of the reader and the problem of historical distance actually make final generic classification an impossibility? Is the author's perspective lost in the hermeneutical circle of text and interpreter? Is it possible to isolate the "literal meaning" of the text or are we caught in a hermeneutical circle which makes objective interpretation impossible? We wonder whether the fusion of the horizons is as necessary as Gadamer and other phenomenologists claim.

We are troubled by the semantic negation of any distinction between meaning and significance and, in fact, the disappearance of original meaning from the hermeneutic horizon (see below for further discussion). Interpretation is not nearly as open-minded as the New Literary Critics posit, and genre is much more than praxis or performance. Further, their dynamic view of language is too narrow, for we would argue that there may be both "dead" (static) and "live" (dynamic) metaphors in the linguistic endeavor. For instance, God-talk has both an analogical (picturing God in finite terms) and a univocal (an objective revelation about the nature of God) function. The Bible contains both language event and propositional truth. It is unnecessary and inadequate to stress the one and negate the other. The preoccupation of these scholars with linguistic encounter becomes subjective, and without an absolute referent interpretation drowns in a sea of irrelevance. We will argue below that the original intent of the author may be discovered in the hermeneutical task; here we argue philosophically that it is an epistemological necessity as the control whereby the hearer is confronted with an absolute truth outside his "common world," a truth which leads him into an understanding which goes beyond himself. Thiselton argues correctly that it is one thing to "understand the text . . . more deeply and more creatively" and another to "understand it correctly".[38]

The same must be said about the theories of polyvalence. Three papers in a recent SBL seminar examine J. D. Crossan's *Cliff's of Fall,* which argues that "play" between text and interpreter demands a theory of multiple meaning. Howard Clark Kee deplores the negativism of Crossan's philosophy of absence and the lack of any historical reference points in his view of metaphor/allegory. This "ontological chasm," Kee asserts, is a methodological failure because it assumes that the whole process of identity exists only in the individual human mind. Tremendous theological difficulties result, since Crossan replaces any doctrine of creation, incarnation or redemption with "the endlessly repeated game" of play, an ontological priority of mind over theology.[39] Mary Ann Tolbert takes issue with Crossan's view that all language is metaphorical; she argues that language thereby will become "unrecognizable and meaningless." She finds "problems of arbitrariness, collapsing of distinctions, and expansion to universals," especially in the choice of "play" as the metamodel. Further, in Crossan's biblical examples, his diachronic approach and "canonical" interpretations mitigate against the basic thesis of plurality.[40] Finally, David Tracy notes the ambiguity of Crossan's attempt: he seems to differentiate "religious" parables (which are polyvalent) from non-religious or theological parables (which are not), yet at the same time hints that all "live" texts are polyvalent. Tracy finds the deconstructionist approach of Crossan and Derrida unnecessary and prefers Wayne Booth's criteria of "relative adequacy" in determining a "critical pluralism of readings" seen within "articulated critical understandings of the text." The result then is an understanding informed by various methods (formalist, semiotic, etc.).[41]

I, for one, am much happier with Tracy's approach to pluralism. None of us, I think, would deny the many instances in which we must "agree to disagree" on an especially tricky exegetical or theological point. Yet we believe that understanding and meaning are possible and legitimate goals of the hermeneutical task. Polyvalence is not the sole conclusion or necessary result of the interpretive act, nor are we required to denigrate the possibility of discovering the "original" meaning of a text on the basis of its so-called ontological autonomy.[42] With respect to the aspect of genre, Longman follows Wellek and Warren when he asserts:[43]

> While it is true that the individuality of many compositions must be maintained, the similarities between the form and content of texts must not be denied. That there are similarities between texts which can serve as a rationale for studying them as a group is especially true for ancient literature where literary innovations were not valued highly as they are today.

GENRE AND HERMENEUTICS

Before we can modify any of the approaches above, we must present our own philosophical view of genre and the semantic enterprise, then defend that position against the criticisms of its opponents. A good bridge from Ricoeur to Wittgenstein and Hirsch would be an illuminating article on Ricoeur's "diagnostics" by Mary Gerhart. Diagnostics as a concept occurs primarily in Ricoeur's early and middle writings and denotes the means by which empirical (or object) language and common sense (or subject) language inform one another in the pursuit of knowledge. Objective knowledge must always be attained through subjective experience, yet at the same time it provides the information by which that experience is interpreted. The reality which results is a "diagnosed reality," primarily influenced by the "primordiality of subjectivity."[44]

On the basis of this, Gerhart reconciles poetics and empirics via her concept of verification. The reader, on the basis of critical awareness of the text, sifts the possible multiple meanings of a text and "verifies" probable interpretations. Thus the "self" encounters the "world" of the text, which becomes a model not behind but "in front of" the reader (Ricoeur).[45] Interestingly, she sets Ricoeur and Hirsch side by side in her discussion. In fact, it may be that her construction presents a blend of the two which would be unsatisfactory to both. This paper sides more with Hirsch in his separation of meaning from significance, a step which neither Gerhart nor Ricoeur would countenance. Before we can discuss Hirsch, however, we must consider the important contribution of Wittgenstein to this discussion.

The later Wittgenstein of the *Investigations* is best known for his view of "language games," which stresses the priority of particular descriptions over general observations: language is multi-faceted and speaks differently in differing semantic situations. It cannot be expanded to abstract principles or universals but can only be applied to specific contexts. For example, he writes, "Think of the tools in a tool-box: there is a hammer, pliers, a saw, a screw-driver, a rule, a glue-pot, glue, nails and screws.—The functions of words are as diverse as the functions of these objects. (And in both cases there are similarities.)"[46] Language is dynamic and takes its meaning from its situation in life. Thiselton notes two aspects of this: 1) Language games take place within a dynamic, developing context subject to historical and temporal change; as a result there is no fixed form but "new types of language, new language-games . . . come into existence, and others become obsolete and get forgotten."[47] 2) The concept of language games is grounded in "human practice, use, application, or training"; so it is not the definition of a term but its utilization in specific contexts which determines its meaning.[48]

E. D. Hirsch links his concept of "intrinsic genre" with Wittgenstein's "family resemblances" between language games. Hirsch defines genre in ontological categories as the "type of utterance" which narrows down the "rules" that apply to a particular speech. When one discovers the literary type behind the whole, the interpretation of the details are greatly facilitated.[49] Although one's preunderstanding plays a major role in interpretation, further details can and should alter the generic stance with which he begins. This is especially true since "understanding" is itself genre-bound, i.e., the verbal meaning depends upon isolating the genre which is intrinsic to the passage. The problem is whether there is a "stable generic concept" or whether it disappears when the interpreter interacts with the text and thereby alters the writer's original generic intention (Gadamer's position). However, Hirsch argues, intrinsic genre is "that sense of the whole by means of which an interpreter can correctly understand any part of its determinacy."[50] The interpreter examines the potential extrinsic genre-types (i.e. those imposed from outside the passage) to determine the intrinsic, originally intended genre. In summation, the intrinsic genre helps one to delineate the proper hermeneutical principles to employ in seeking the meaning of a passage. Through it one can discover the allusions to other ancient ideas which the writer and his readers presupposed, but we cannot. Further, it forces one to move behind his/her own background to the writer's intention.

Within this, however, one must ask whether "intended meaning" can be discovered at all. Hirsch separates between "meaning," the act of comprehending the intended message of a text and "significance," the act of inserting that meaning into a present context or structure, for instance one's own value-system. The relativists (he calls them "cognitive atheists") deny any such distinction. Hirsch believes that Heidegger's teacher, Husserl, provides an alternative. Rather than a hermeneutical "circle," Husserl posited a different metaphor, "brackets," which refers to the ability of the mind to "bracket" certain alien information (i.e. previously unknown) and therefore to work back to the original intent behind it. Both metaphors serve as conceptual models for differing types of learning experiences.[51] This is crucial for the phenomenological view of meaning, for it relates to the possibility of moving behind preunderstanding to the text. If the text is totally autonomous from the author[52] and the reader cannot move from significance to meaning, then the intention of the author can never be determined. However, we believe that the above arguments invalidate the thesis regarding the complete autonomy of the text.

Against this, let us note the critique of R. E. Palmer, who presents three objections (from Gadamer's school) to Hirsch's position:[53]

1) It is founded upon an Aristotelian view of meaning which assumes the possibility of objectively founded knowledge and ignores the interaction of the subject. Yet Palmer himself notes that the answer may be a "both-and" rather than an "either-or" but then fails to follow his own logic to the possibility of recovering the author's intention. If one can detect the "probable" intention of the author, this in itself makes it important to do so.[54]

2) Palmer argues further that it is wrong to link hermeneutics only to the philological aspect and not to the significance for the reader, since the very rules by which we interpret philologically come from our own experience and are filtered through our modern worldview. Palmer is correct regarding an overly rigid dichotomy between fact/value or meaning/significance. I agree that hermeneutics properly done must bridge the gap from the author's intent to its significance for the reader's own situation. However, Hirsch clarifies himself in his later *The Aims of Interpretation*. His actual polemic is against the replacement of knowledge by value, not the connection between them. His major premise, the possibility of recovering that intended meaning, still stands.

3) Palmer believes that Hirsch has oversimplified the problem of verifying knowledge and has avoided modern linguistic analysis,[55] which notes the importance of determining the meaning behind the author (semiotics) and the impossibility of removing modern conceptions of reality. However, it seems that he has somewhat misunderstood Hirsch's proposal. It is not so much "removing" modern conceptions as "bracketing" the author's conceptions and allowing the interpretive options to be sifted and challenged in order to discover that "intent," then returning to those modern perspectives in the task of discovering value or significance.

In the Bible, there is a clear statement of authorial intent in passage after passage regarding the normativeness of the propositional truth content. Of course, here we encounter the debate regarding inspiration and biblical authority: is that authority instrumental or propositional?[56] However, let us look again at Thiselton, this time at his discussion of "Wittgenstein and the Debate about Biblical Authority." He argues that propositional truth in Scripture is experienced in "dynamic and concrete speech-acts of particular language games." Moreover, propositional truth is not obviated but upheld by such experience language, for it is the "scaffolding" upon which such statements are made.[57] On this basis, then,we have the internal evidence in Scripture which demands that we seek the author's intent as "indispensable" to biblical hermeneutics.

Finally, let us consider one other linguist whose position parallels that of Wittgenstein and Hirsch. Eugene A. Nida has been a pioneer in the field of practical linguistics, and his own approach is summarized in his co-authored (with C. R. Taber) *The Theory and Practice of Translation*.[58] Similar to Wittgenstein's "language games" and Hirsch's "intrinsic genre" is Nida and Taber's "semotaxis," which also provides an ontological perspective for semantic analysis. They look at communication as an organic whole and posit that every term in a discourse draws its meaning from the congruence of the other terms which surround it. All the given elements in a surface structure interact with each other. The critical aspect is the modifiers, which provide an ever-narrowing field of possibilities and for our purpose become a key to the generic identification of the rules to be applied to the "game" played in the act of communication.

The hermeneutical rules provided by Nida and Taber help one to see how Hirsch's claim regarding the viability of identifying the author's intended meaning might be accomplished. They posit three stages to translation/interpretation: 1) analysis, in which the surface structure is studied as to grammatical relationships and word meaning; 2) transfer, in which the material from stage one is transferred to another language/culture; 3) restructuring, in which the material is now reworked to be understandable for the new culture. We would note that "meaning" applies to step one and "significance" to steps two and three. Once again we see how Wittgenstein, Hirsch and Nida speak to the same problem of fact and value in the interpretive process.

The place of genre in this hermeneutical process is crucial. It provides the linguistic framework for the semantic verification which the interpreter attempts. As such it is: 1) classificatory, identifying and describing the basic literary categories and sub-categories as a means of defining the mimetic background(s) to any single text; 2) epistemological, describing the way in which the human mind both states and interprets messages which it seeks to communicate; and 3) ontological, the very categories in the mind which enable it to communicate "meaning" or "significance," "fact" or "value." Therefore, we disagree with Michael Beajour's deconstructionist statement: "The ontological situation demands the overcoming of genres, which trivialize the Essence of writing and desacralize its End."[59] Nor can we accept Thomas Winner's structuralist solution, that the abstract idealizations which govern traditional genre theory are so rigid and unlike any single work that they must be replaced by an aesthetic approach. This views genre as dependent on synchronic and diachronic elements, with both sender and receiver (and thus the game) establishing "certain parameters of expectations" in the interpretive process.[60] Both are too narrow and fail to recognize the dynamic nature of genre, which has classificatory as well as epistemological/ontological aspects.

In conclusion, we have attempted to demonstrate that genre as a dynamic tool makes it possible to discover the "literal sense" of a passage, especially a biblical passage. The negative conclusions of the deconstructionist critics are due to the application on their part of a false "language game," which extends partial truths, i.e., the mixing of genres and the preunderstanding of the reader, to a wholistic misstatement about meaning in particular and genre as a whole. We would uphold the classificatory function of genre so long as one both avoids overgeneralizing it and understands that genre also functions from an epistemological and ontological perspective. The individual genre (e.g. parable) properly applied (i.e. in its first century development) helps the interpreter to narrow down the hermeneutical "rules" and thereby to approach the individual text with the correct tools to get behind preunderstanding to the probable intent of the author. The key is to be comprehensive in one's usage of generic parallels and background information and to sift through and verify each of the possible interpretations on the basis of the "intrinsic genre" or "semotactic" relationships. In short, we agree that genre is more descriptive than prescriptive but disagree that this function necessarily restricts its value as a hermeneutical tool. Tremper Longman uses several metaphors to describe the process: genre is an "institution" which provides rules and regulations but may be changed by author or reader; a "contract" which is agreed upon by author and reader as part of the communication process; a "game" whose rules govern the success of the endeavor; a "generative language" which governs the text; and "patterns of expression" to which authors conform.[61]

GENRE AND ACCOMMODATION

While this topic will be discussed in full in another paper of this colloquy[62] we would be remiss if we failed to note that aspect of accommodation which relates to our interpretation of genre as a dynamic hermeneutical tool. To peruse briefly the historical dimension of the issue, the principle of accommodation appeared quite early in the history of the church as a means of explaining such scriptural phenomena as the anthropomorphic terms for God. It was the means of explaining how the infinitely wise God had bridged the unfathomable gulf between himself and mankind.[63] Calvin used it to explain seeming contradictions such as the question of God's "repenting" (answer: Scripture speaks of God's purposed action in terms that we can understand, namely, changing his mind).[64] In recent years, however, the principle has been given another hue, i.e., accommodation to human *error*. Since the true revelation of God is seen in concepts rather than words, human finiteness has crept into the vehicle by which God decided to reveal himself. One therefore finds infallibility in the salvific message but error in peripheral details, either scientific or historical.[65]

We would posit a return to the traditional view of accommodation which concerns the adequacy of human language[66] rather than the fallibility of the divinely inspired writings. While Rogers and McKim (previous footnote) believe they have followed the classical perspective, we agree with the extensive critique by John Woodbridge that they have read their own views back into the theologians of the past.[67] Within this traditional understanding of accommodation, genre plays an important role. Indeed, this entire essay has been an exercise in linguistic and semantic theory and as such has prepared for a renewal of the issue of accommodation and God-talk. Genre in this light becomes a basic statement of the means by which God has revealed himself to man.

In fact, genre as accommodation helps to clear up many of the so-called discrepancies of Scripture. In addition to the examples cited in the first section ("Genre and Classification"), we might note the problem of the empty tomb narratives. The differences between them are well known and need not be enumerated here; especially significant would be the great difference betweeen John and the Synoptics. Numerous attempts have been made to harmonize them, and elaborate theses attempt to illustrate how multiple journeys to the tomb could have been undertaken without crossing paths.[68] While nuanced harmonization is indeed viable, detailed attempts at a Tatian-like salvation are too complex to be probable. It seems rather that a proper understanding of the historical genre will provide a better solution.

First of all, we must recognize that differences between accounts do not mean that there is not a historically verifiable event behind them. G. B. Caird studies the ten different ways by which the death of Christ is described in the New Testament and declares, "We cannot say that where there is more interpretation there is less history, because the referent is in each case the same. . . . With this list before us we may firmly rebut the facile depreciation of the historical element in Christianity by those who have argued that the evangelists and those who before them transmitted the gospel tradition were preachers, not historians."[69] With this in mind we would note certain tendencies in the Gospel genre which have a bearing on the problem at hand, realizing that we do not have the space for a full-fledged discussion. First, a basic principle is the law of selection and coloring, which means that each evangelist has selected both episodes and details (within the episodes chosen) in order to provide a certain "color" or message. Second, one must look at the whole before judging the parts; that is, each Gospel is a unified whole and one cannot simply isolate sections without looking at the influence of the broader purposes.[70]

When this is applied to John's account, for instance, we discern several points: 1) A stylistic peculiarity of the fourth evangelist is his selection of a single individual out of a group, upon whom he will center his basic message. 2) Chapter 20 presents four types of faith, leading up to the conclusion in verse 29; this is very much a part of John's soteriological stress throughout his Gospel. 3) Certain language in John's account may show an awareness of the synoptic tradition.[71] Therefore it is our belief that John has abbreviated and highlighted,[72] then expanded[73] the synoptic tradition. Neither is "more" historical than the other, and both present their own basic message. The discrepancy disappears when one applies the rules of the proper "language game" to the problem.

Accommodation is seen in the very necessity of four Gospels. Any single narration of the significance of Jesus the Christ would be insufficient. If one accepts any of the proposed solutions to the "synoptic problem," it seems that the later evangelists felt a necessity to write another account, incorporating and sublimating the data in the earlier to their own message. God knows that finite man could not find any single version sufficient in itself, and so each version provides a different vista of meaning. The differences between the Gospels do not relate to history so much as theology.[74]

CONCLUSION

The task of interpretation and the place of genre within that enterprise is indeed a complex process. However, we feel justified in taking a positive stance with respect to the possibility of fusing the horizons of both text and reader while maintaining the integrity of both. Moreover, genre plays a positive rule as a hermeneutical device for determining the "sensus literalis" or intended meaning of the text. Genre is more than a means of classifying literary types; it is an epistemological tool for unlocking meaning in individual texts. As a result genre plays an active role in debates on inerrancy, which inevitably depend upon the consideration of specific texts.

Yet one must ask how genre functions in this role. We have already discussed the internal criteria for determining generic parallels: form, content, plot, structure. However, to these synchronic elements we must add diachronic considerations. We are engaged in a historical as well as literary study, and therefore must provide a comprehensive delineation of ancient generic categories as they apply to biblical literature. Longman attempts to do this for Akkadian literature as background to certain Old Testament passages, and we need more studies of that ilk. Unless we can provide a wide-ranging list of control samples for elucidating generic counterparts, we will tend to draw erroneous conclusions. Here we must build upon general hermeneutics, in which the misuse of parallels is a major consideration. Robert Kysar has shown in an illuminating article how Bultmann's and Dodd's commentaries selectively utilized parallels to build their case, while ignoring those parallels which did not fit their thesis.[75] Such a narrow proof-texting from seeming generic facsimiles is quite common among scholars.

The generic identification of a text-type impacts upon every aspect of Gospel study, including questions of historicity as well as meaning. For instance, Robert Gundry's recent commentary on Matthew identifies the peculiarly Matthean pericopes as "creative midrash" rather than historical narrative, building upon haggadic parallels within the fictive genre. He posits that Matthew reworked tradition (e.g. the Markan shepherd incident into the Magi's story) and Old Testament narrative (e.g. the suffering of the elect at the exile into the slaughter of the innocents) in order to present a theological portrait of Christ. As many have shown, the basic problem lies in his misuse of genre. The parallels are lacking, and he neither defines "midrash" nor shows sufficient criteria for distinguishing such stories from historical narratives in Matthew.[76] In short, one must be extremely careful when utilizing genre to determine broad issues of historicity rather than specific questions of interpretation. Without massive evidence, it is a mistake to give it such a function.

The work which most wholistically tackles the issue of biblical genre is Fee and Stuart's *How to Read the Bible for All It's Worth,* which consciously organizes itself around the necessity of interpreting each biblical genre by the rules of its own language game. Successive chapters on the Epistles, Old Testament narratives, Acts, the Gospels, the parables, the Law(s), the prophets, the Psalms, Wisdom, and the Revelation demonstrate the importance of genre criticism as an interpretive tool. While I certainly cannot agree with all their conclusions (e.g. the differences between the genre of the Gospels and Acts), the entire work is a step forward in the growing consensus that genre helps to unlock the "sensus literalis" of the text.

Genre dare not be misused to go beyond an interpretive function and determine the "authenticity" of a text such as a Gospel pericope. The movement today is away from such rigid characterizations as "myth" vs. history. For instance, Gerald O'Collins critiques James Mackey's *Jesus The Man and the Myth* (1979) at exactly this point. While Mackey recognizes that myth and history are not mutually exclusive, he uses the term "myth" in such a way that it differs not at all from the genre "story." The identification of genre leads Mackey to stress the ministry and death of Jesus over his resurrection. He denigrates the special salvation-historical events which are at the core of Christianity.[77]

The Gospel genre combines history and theology, and inerrancy as a doctrine demands both. We are seeking the "single intent" of the original authors, i.e., the message which they sought to portray by omitting or highlighting different nuances from the original historical narrative (e.g. compare the healing of the demon possessed/epileptic child in Mk. 9:14-29 and Matt. 17:14-19). The stress on "story" in recent approaches to Old Testament and New Testament historical narrative tries to recognize this component.

Genre as a whole comes into play at the focal point between the author and the text and then again between the text and the reader. As such it brings together all three elements of the interpretation process: writer, text, reader. The key is for the reader to align himself/herself with the originally intended genre, and as argued above this is both a possible and a necessary enterprise. Genre participates in the culture within which it originated and is clarified by that historical context. While some genres may be unique, such as the Gospels, none are completely without antecedent. Even the Gospels borrowed from Jewish and Hellenistic biography or apocalyptic genres, among others.[78]

Genre is particularly useful the further the contemporary situation is removed from the ancient culture. Historically considered, it forces one to recognize the proper language game. As such the primary purpose of genre is literary/aesthetic, i.e., it is an epistemological tool for discovering the intended meaning of a text. The apologetic result, i.e., the resolution of seeming discrepancies, is a secondary biproduct of this major goal. Nevertheless, genre is both valid and valuable in this latter enterprise. Genre, as an inherent part of all language, has a transcultural dimension; as an initial part of the hermeneutical task, it is foundational to exegetical theology and thereby to apologetics. We deny that genre criticism may legitimately have priority over Scripture or introduce categories which *a priori* negate the internal evidence in the historical record of Scripture. Genre cannot be studied in isolation from the other theological-exegetical disciplines. It is one among many tools in the historical-grammatical enterprise, purposing to unlock the rules of the proper language-game in order to trace the text back to its original, intended meaning.

Therefore, we must note the important connection between genre, the literal sense and the doctrine of inerrancy. One who has read carefully this article will note that we have never attempted a definition of inerrancy or a philosophical argument on behalf of inerrancy on the basis of our study of genre. However, we have studied practical problems which concern the doctrine, and it is no accident that most of our illustrations have dealt with critical issues more than exegetical problems. Genre as a tool for discovering the "literal intent" can note the different ways one will interpret poetry, apocalyptic, parabolic passages, etc., and will thereby keep one from seeing "surface" discrepancies in the text. On the pragmatic side of the issue, genre criticism[79] is crucial for any doctrine of inerrancy, for in the final sense it rises or falls not from philosophical argumentation but from the internal evidence of the text itself. As I have argued elsewhere, the doctrine must flow out of Scripture's own self-understanding, and this is done both for the inherent sense of authority/inspiration and for a consideration of what constitutes "error."[80] It is my belief that the literary approach (from a proper understanding of genre) will not only discover the true "literary sense" but will also provide the strongest possible apology for the doctrine of inerrancy by resolving many so-called contradictions or errors in Scripture.

NOTES

[1]See also the more detailed version of this article in *Trinity Journal* 19 (1983).

[2]For good general discussions, see A. N. A. Orsini, "Genres," *Princeton Encyclopedia of Poetry and Poetics*, A. Preminger, ed. (Princeton: University Press 1974[2]), p. 307; and Gerard Genette, "Genres, 'Types,' Modes," *Poetique* 8 (1977), pp. 389-421 (especially 389-92). Both argue that the classic differentiation of three "basic genres"—lyric, epic, and drama—developed as a result of a later misunderstanding of Plato and Aristotle.

[3]Rene Wellek and Austin Warren, *Theory of Literature* (New York: Harcourt, Brace & World, 1956), p. 219.

[4]Phillipe Lacoue-Labarthe and Jean-Luc Nancy, "Genre," *Glyph* 7 (1980): 1-2.

[5]Orsini, p. 308. Genette, pp. 415-18, argues that the romantics confused modes with genres, failing to realize that only the former is a natural, formal device while the latter is historical and aesthetic. Therefore, their true revolt was against mode rather than genre.

[6]See Jacques Derrida, "The Law of Genre," *Glyph* 7 (1980): 207-9; also Geoffrey Hartman, "Preface," *Deconstruction and Criticism,* Harold Bloom, et. al. (New York: Seabury Press, 1979), pp. vii-ix, who discusses the primacy of language over meaning and of metaphor over "positive and exploitative truth."

[7]Paul Ricoeur, "The Task of Hermeneutics," *Ph Tod* 17 (1973): 112-28.

[8]James Muilenberg, "Form Criticism and Beyond," *JBL* 88 (1969): 2.

[9]Vernon K. Robbins, "Mark as Genre," *SBL 1980 Seminar Papers,* p. 376. He adds, p. 380, "In the ensuing years of energetic form critical analysis, genre criticism lay at rest as an unimportant issue." See also Robert Guelich, "The Gospel Genre," *Das Evangelium und die Evangelien,* ed. M. Hengel and O. Hofius (Tubingen: Mohr, 1983), who discussed the mistaken use of "form" and "genre" interchangeably by form critics.

[10]Beajour, "Genus Universum," pp. 18-19.

[11]Adrian Marino, "Toward a Definition of Literary Genres," *Theories of Literary Genre,* Strelka, ed., pp. 47-48.

[12]Ernest L. Stahl, "Literary Genres: Some Idiosyncratic Concepts," *Theories of Literary Genres,* Strelka, ed., pp. 80-83.

[13]Robert Champigny, "Semantic Modes and Literary Genres," *Theories of Literary Genres,* Strelka, ed., pp. 94-110.

[14]Wellek and Warren, p. 221.

[15]John J. Collins, "Introduction: Towards the Morphology of a Genre." *Apocalypse: The Morphology of a Genre, Semeia* 14 (1979): 1. See also Robbins, pp. 373-85, who traces genre approaches to Mark.

[16]R. C. Sproul, *Knowing Scripture* (Downers Grove: InterVarsity Press, 1977), p. 49 (cf. pp. 49-53). See also Walter Kaiser, *Toward an Exegetial Theology* (Grand Rapids: Baker Book House, 1981), ch. 4. The standard hermeneutical texts such as Terry or Michelson do not discuss genre but assume it in their sections on "special hermeneutics." Ramm has a short discussion but is inconclusive in his comments.

[17]Johannes A. Huismann, "Generative Classifications in Medieval Literature," *Theories of Literary Genres,* Strelka, ed., pp. 143-49.

[18]Champigny, pp. 105-107. Doty p. 440, states, "Hence it is vital to comprehend generic exemplars in their total literary contexts, which especially include works upon which the exemplar has had influence (positively or negatively)."

[19]Kaiser, pp. 5-7, mentions four: prose, poetry, wisdom, and apocalyptic. A more complete list is discussed in the excellent volume by Gordon Fee and Douglas Stuart, *How to Read the Bible For All It's Worth* (Grand Rapids: Zondervan, 1982). They take a genre-based approach to Bible study, noting how to interpret the diverse types of literature in the Bible.

[20]Horst, p. 112. D. E. Aune, "The Problem of the Genre of the Gospels: A Critique of C. H. Talbert's *What is a Gospel?,*" *Gospel Perspectives II,* R. T.

France and David Wenham, ed. (Sheffield: JSOT Press, 1981), p. 9, speaks of "the necessity of a diachronic, or historical, study of generic types in addition to a consideration of their internatl or external form."

[21]Horst, pp. 112-22. See also J. Arthur Baird, "Genre Analysis as a Method of Historical Criticism," *SBL Proceedings, 1972,* vol. 2, pp. 386-87.

[22]Gordon Fee, "The Genre of NT Literature and Biblical Hermeneutics," *Interpreting the Word of God,* S. J. Schultz and M. A. Inch, ed. (Chicago: Moody Press, 1976), pp. 105-27. See also Fee and Stuart, *How to Read the Bible for All It's Worth.*

[23]Lacoue-Labarthe and Nancy, pp. 1-10.

[24]Dennis Kambouchner, "The Theory of Accidents," *Glyph* 7 (1980): 156-61.

[25]Derrida, pp. 210-13.

[26]Kambouchner, p. 157.

[28]Baird, pp. 389-91.

[29]Mary Gerhart, "Generic Studies: Their Renewed Importance in Religious and Literary Interpretation," *JAAR* 45/3 (1977): 309-25.

[30]Kambouchner, pp. 161-75. See also Champigny, pp. 94-107, who states that genre as "modes must be defined as "styles" or "logics" which relate to semantics and involve both text and interpreter, who through different perceptions may change the genre of a single text and via a different comprehension may alter its meaning or value.

[31]Hans-Georg Gadamer, *Truth and Method,* tr. G. Barden and J. Cumming (New York: Seabury Press, 1975), p. 258.

[32]Ibid., pp. 258-78.

[33]See Daniel Patte, *What is Structural Exegesis?* (Philadelphia: Fortress Press, 1976), for a good description of the system. For evangelical critique, see Carl Armerding, "Structural Analysis," *Themelio* 4/3 (1979): 96-104 and Vern S. Poythress, "Structuralism and Biblical Studies," *JETS* 21/3 (1978): 221-37.

[34]*Erhardt Güttgemanns, "What is 'Generative Poetics'?"* *Semeia* 6 (1976): 7-8; and "Narrative Analysis of Synoptic Texts," *Semeia* 6 (1976): 131, 171.

[35]Susan Wittig, "A Theory of Multiple Meanings," *Semeia* 9 (1977): 75-101, especially 84-92.

[36]Paul Ricoeur, "Metaphor and the Main Problem of Hermeneutics," *New Literary History* 6, No. 1 (1974): 107-108 (c.f. 103-110), as discussed in Robert Detweiler, *Story, Sign and Self* (Philadelphia: Fortress Press, 1978), pp. 46-48. See also Paul Ricoeur, "Biblical Hermeneutics: The Metaphorical Process," *Semeia* 4 (1975): 81-88, where he compares metaphor to the verb "to be" as that function of poetic language within which reality is redescribed and restructured along the lines of heuristic fiction.

[37]Paul Ricoeur, "The Hermemeutical Function of Distanciation," *Philosophy Today* 17 (1973): 135-36 (cf. 129-41).

[38]A. C. Thiselton, "The New Hermeneutic," *New Testament Interpretation,* p. 323. See also my review of McKnight, Detweiler and Peterson in *Trinity Journal* n.s. 1/1 (1980): 100-105.

[39]Howard Clark Kee, "Polyvalence and Parables: Anyone Can Play," *Seminar Papers: SBL 1980* (Chico, California: Scholars Press, 1980), pp. 57-61.

[40]Mary Ann Tolbert, "Polyvalence and the Parables: A Consideration of J. D. Crossan's *Cliffs of Fall,"* *Seminar Papers: SBL 1980,* pp. 63-67.

[41]David Tracy, "Reflections on John Dominic Crossan's *Cliffs of Fall:* Paradox and Polyvalence in the Parables of Jesus," *Seminar Papers: SBL 1980,* pp. 69-74.

[42]I particularly appreciate Doty's statement (p. 427) on this point: "A great deal of confusion in literary criticism has been caused by focus upon the nature of the genre (its ontology, as it were) rather than upon the actor who *uses* the genre according to his own *intentions*" (italics his).

[43]Longman, pp. 3-4.

[44]Mary Gerhart, "Paul Ricoeur's Notion of 'Diagnostics': Its Function in Literary Interpretation," *J REL* 56 (1976): 137-44.

[45]Ibid., p. 145-53. While we agree with much of her thesis, we disagree with her acceptance of Ricoeur's view that the text is "closed" or autonomous with respect to both author and reader.

[46]Ludwig Wittgenstein, *Philosophical Investigations,* tr. G. E. M. Anscombe (New York: Macmillan, 1953), 6a (sect. 11).

[47]Thiselton, *Two Horizons,* p. 376. Quote from *Investigations,* sect. 23.

[48]Thiselton, pp. 376-78.

[49]E. D. Hirsch, *Validity in Interpretation* (New Haven: Yale University Press, 1967), pp. 69-71.

[50]Ibid., p. 86 (cf. 72-88).

[51]E. D. Hirsch, *The Aims of Interpretation* (Chicago: University of Chicago Press, 1976). One could argue that the "bracket" describes that aspect called "meaning" and the "circle" that aspect called "significance."

[52]This is the basis of Champigny's (p. 110, footnote 1) critique of Hirsch. The writer's interpretation of the text cannot produce the most coherent result, because one is "author" only so long as the text is unfinished. Once done, the text's meaning transcends the author's intention.

[53]R. E. Palmer, *Hermeneutics: Interpretation Theory in Schleiermacher, Dilthey, Heidegger and Gadamer* (Evanston: Northwestern University Press, 1969), pp. 60-65.

[54]Several articles have appeared in recent years on the importance of probability theory over the quest for necessary knowledge, e.g., J. L. Pollock, "Criteria and Our Knowledge of the Material World," *PH REV* 76 (1967): 55-60; R. Firth, "The Anatomy of Certainty," *PH REV* 76 (1967): 3-27.

[55]See also Frank, pp. 73-74, who asserts that Hirsch errs when he regards the text as a self-contained entity centering upon the author's intention. "The history of widely different semantic relativations, even the every day experience of the non-identity of two readings of one and the same text," makes any such isolation of authorial intent an impossible task.

[56]For a good recent discussion upholding the instrumental side, see Paul J. Achtemeier, *The Inspiration of Scripture* (Philadelphia: Westminster Press, 1980), pp. 57-75 (against the conservative position), pp. 137-61 (implications of Scripture as proclamation).

[57]Thiselton, *Two Horizons,* pp. 432-37.

[58]E. A. Nida and C. R. Taber, *The Theory and Practice of Translation* especially Ch. 3 on "Grammatical Analysis." The paragraphs below summarize their thought. While their discussion proceeds from a translational perspective more than an interpretive viewpoint, each step applies to both. From their standpoint, translation proceeds from interpretation.

[59]Beaujour, *Glyph* 7, p. 17. Frank, *Glyph* 7, pp. 77-78, agrees, arguing that

any intended meaning is undiscoverable since it is "infinite"; when meaning is absolutized, the signs themselves become unstable and genre becomes questionable. The disappearance of limits removes any possibility of deciphering the "original" meaning.

[60]Winner, *Theories of Literary Genre*, ed. Strelka, pp. 262-331 (cf. 254-68).

[61]Longman, pp. 5-7.

[62]Vern S. Poythress, "Adequacy of Language and Accommodation."

[63]See, for example, Clement of Alexandria (Strom 2.16.72) Origen (C. Cels. 4.71 and especially *On First Principles*); Tertullian; John Chrysostom, etc.

[64]See Calvin's *Institutes*, 1.17.12-13.

[65]In addition to the dialectical theologians and logical positivists, see Jack B. Rogers and Donald K. McKim, *The Authority and Interpretation of the Bible* (New York: Harper and Row, 1979), pp. 430-33 (drawing especially from Berkouwer) and *passim*; and also Ford Lewis Battles, "God was Accommodating Himself to Human Capacity," *Int* 3 (1977): 19-38, where he discusses Calvin's view and draws conclusions similar to that of Rogers and McKim.

[66]For excellent discussion of this parallel topic, see John Frame, "God and Biblical Language: Transcendence and Immanence," *God's Inerrant Word*, ed. J. W. Montgomery (Minneapolis: Bethany, 1974), 159-77; and Packer, "Adequacy," 197-226. Both answer the normal arguments by logical positivists, dialectical theologians and analytical linguists against the possibility of propositional truth and God-talk. For the contrary view, which seeks to blend Roman Catholic views on inspiration with Gadamer's theory, see Prosper Greech, "The Language of Scripture and its Interpretation: An Essay," *BTB* 6 (1976): 161-76.

[67]John Woodbridge, "Biblical Authority: Towards an Evaluation of the Rogers and McKim Proposal," *Trinity Journal* n.s. 1/2 (1980): 165-236. See also his *Biblical Authority: A Critique of the Rogers/McKim Proposal* (Grand Rapids: Zondervan, 1982). Because of this usage of the term "accommodation," Norman Geisler, *Christian Apologetics* (Grand Rapids: Baker, 1976), pp. 357-60, argues for the term "adaptation" rather than "accommodation." While I applaud the purpose, however, I disagree with the solution; I would rather argue for a proper understanding of the term than surrender it to those who would redefine it.

[68]See, for example, Zane Hodges, "The Women and the Empty Tomb," *Bib Sac* 123 (1966): 301-309; and John W. Wenham, "The First Easter Morning," Unpublished paper read at the Tyndale Conference, Cambridge, July 1972, as well as the bibliography therein. For my own approach, see ch. 6 of my *The Resurrection Narratives; A Redactional Study* (Grand Rapids: Baker Book House, forthcoming).

[69]G. B. Caird, *The Language and Imagery of the Bible* (Philadelphia: Westminster, 1980), 212. His entire chapter, "Language and History" (pp. 201-218), helps to blend linguistic theory with historical narrative. For a more evangelical defense of historicity, see Colin Brown, ed. *History Criticism and Faith* (Downers Grove: InterVarsity Press, 1977), Section II.

[70]For a more detailed account, see my articles, "The Evangelical and *Traditionsgeschichte*," *JETS* 21/2 (1978): 117-30; and "The Evangelical and Redaction Criticisms: Critique and Methodology," *JETS* 22/4 (1979): 305-22. For the viability of this within a doctrine of inerrancy, see Feinberg, "Meaning of Inerrancy," *passim*.

[71]See C. K. Barrett, *The Gospel According to John* (Philadelphia: Westmins-

ter, 1978[2]), pp. 15-17; J. A. Bailey, *The Traditions Common to the Gospels of Luke and John* (Leiden: Brill, 1963).

[72]He has abbreviated the journey of the women to the tomb by centering upon Mary, then highlighted her part in the event.

[73]If we accept Luke 24:12 (which I do), then John has expanded that story in 20:2-10.

[74]For good discussions of the relationship between history and theology, see I. H. Marshall, *Luke: Historian and Theologian* (Grand Rapids: Zondervan 1970), Ch. 2; R. P. Martin, *Mark—Evangelist and Theologian* (Exeter: Paternoster, 1972), Chs. 2-4; and S. S. Smalley, *John: Evangelist and Interpreter* (Exeter: Paternoster, 1978), Ch. 5.

[75]Robert Kysar, "The Background of the Prologue of the Fourth Gospel: A Critique of Historical Methods," *Canadian Journal of Theology* 16 (1970): 250-55.

[76]See the extensive review of D. A. Carson, "Gundry on Matthew: A Critical Review," *Trinity Journal* 3/1 (1982): 71-91, especially pp. 81-85.

[77]Gerald O'Collins, *What Are They Saying About Jesus?* (New York: Paulist Press, 1983[2]), pp. 40-51, cf. John Mackey, *Jesus the Man and the Myth* (New York: Paulist Press, 1979).

[78]See the conclusion of the version in the *Trinity Journal* (fn. 1) for a discussion of this, especially the articles by David Aune and Robert Guelich.

[79]Reichert, "Limits of Genre Theory," pp. 57-58, asserts that one must separate "genre criticism" (which classifies literary works on the basis of similarities) from "genre theory" (using the tools of the former to develop a comprehensive theory of literature and methods for studying it). We are using this term, however, in a more wholistic sense, i.e., the tools which derive from the theory.

[80]G. R. Osborne, "Redaction Criticism and the Great Commission: A Case Study Toward a Biblical Understanding of Inerrancy," *JETS* 19/2 (1976): 73-85 (especially pp. 83-85).

A Response to Genre Criticism—Sensus Literalis

Ronald B. Allen
Professor of Old Testament
and Exegesis
Western Conservative
Baptist Seminary

A Response to Genre Criticism—Sensus Literalis

Ronald B. Allen

In earlier studies, Dr. Grant R. Osborne has been something of a pace-setter for an evangelical scholar in the understanding of and appreciation for Redaction Criticism.[1] In his present paper, a work of considerable erudition, Dr. Osborne has set the stage for a new investigation of the issue of genre in evangelical hermeneutics and the relationship of genre criticism to the issue of inerrancy.

The concept of genre is so germane to the stuff of life that it should be an axiomatic part of our thinking. Genre and form are constant elements in the matrix of discourse and interaction.

Think for a moment of music and the role that genre and form play there. Levels of expectation, appreciation, initiation, concentration—even exasperation!—reflect our awareness of and involvement in differing genre of music. From the Muzak in an elevator to the orchestra in a symphony hall, we are keenly aware of differing responses we may have to differing genre and forms. We simply listen differently to different kinds of music. We do not give the same attention to nor expect the same rewards from all types of music. These responses on our part are learned responses within one's culture, but they function on the intuitive level. We do not sit back and reason concerning genre, we *respond* to it.

In our reading we are also conditioned to respond in a variety of ways to differing genre-induced stimuli. We do so without thinking about it. We read differently and expect different rewards when we move from the *T.V. Guide* to the poems of T. S. Eliot, from the latest Ludlum thriller to a devotional classic.

Why then—why in the world then!—do we need to *stop and think* when it comes to the issue of differing genre in the Bible? Perhaps we have so insisted on the monolithic nature of the Bible as revelation, or have so stressed the authoritative thrust of the Bible, or have been wrongly prompted by the sameness of verse paragraphs with justified margins of the Authorized Version, or have listened to too many sermons which were prepared without a thought given to literary issues, or . . . ? But for whatever the reason, many Christian people have not learned to think on an intuitive level of differing genre when it comes to their reading of the Bible.

I recall a scene in a film where the matriarch of a Southern family was reading from 1 Chronicles 1 for devotions before dinner. She introduced each verse in turn as she solemnly intoned: "Verse 21: Hadoram, Uzal, Diklah." (Pause.) "Verse 22: Ebal, Abimael, Sheba." (Pause.) I imagine she heard the flutter of angels' wings and smelled the smoke of Sinai with each portentous sound. Had we world enough and time, I would have loved to have heard her recite the Song of Solomon—but only briefly; it would have lost all of its music.

Popular devotional books and well-known seminar speakers often cite passages from disparate literary contexts as one might slice so many chunks of cheese from a huge wheel. All the texts are used to prove some point or another, proverb joining hands with injunction, poetic fragment married to incidental in parable, each assumed to be speaking on the same level of directness to the crises of bedroom and pocketbook of frustrated white, middle-class, North American women (who are the ones who buy the books and who drag their husbands along with them to the latest conference: "Biblical Insights on Diet and Rebellious Daughters"—all enjoyed on a luxury cruise liner).

We simply must learn to appreciate differences in genre in the Bible the way we have learned to do in all other areas of culture. Gordon Fee begins his essay on genre in New Testament study by saying:

> It should be an axiom of biblical hermeneutics that, as part of valid contextual exegesis, the interpreter must take into account the literary genre of the text he is interpreting as well as the questions of text, philology, grammar, and history. Such a principle would appear to be so self-evident as not to need belaboring. Yet, except for the Apocalypse, this principle is seldom applied in the interpretation of the New Testament.[2]

What is done by readers of one Testament is done by readers of the Old Testament as well. If possible, this latter is a more serious offense if only because there are more varieties of literary genre in the Older Testament that become confused. James I. Packer observes that many present-day readers of the Old Testament texts treat these Scriptures as though they were contemporary literary forms:

> So, for example, Genesis 1 is read as if it were answering the same questions as today's scientific textbooks aim to answer, and Genesis 2 and 3 are read as if they were at every point prosaic eyewitness narratives of what we would have seen if we had been there, ignoring the reasons for thinking that in these chapters "real events may be recorded in a highly symbolic manner," and books like Daniel, Zechariah, and Revelation are expounded in total disregard of the imaginative conventions of apocalyptic. But it does not follow that because Scripture records matters of fact, therefore it does so in what we should call matter-of-fact language.[3]

For these reasons I wish to state my congratulations to Osborne for his serious inquiry into the nature of genre in biblical studies, my appreciation to him for his work in tracing the history of the idea through time and in analyzing the issues proffered by contemporary theorists of Structuralism,[4] semiotics,[5] polyvalence,[6] the New Hermeneutic,[7] and the like, and my concurrence with his basic conclusions:

> The relationship between genre and sensus literalis is direct and crucial. Genre is more than a means of classifying literary types; it is an epistemological tool for unlocking meaning in individual texts and an indispensable aid to the interpretive task.[8]

I am also pleased with Osborne's emphasis upon the relationship genre has to the doctrine of inerrancy:

> It is my belief that the literary approach (from a proper understanding of genre) will not only discover the true "literary sense" but will also provide the strongest possible apology for the doctrine of inerrancy by resolving many so-called contradictions or errors in Scripture.[9]

Having stated my indebtedness to Dr. Osborne along these lines, I desire now to offer a few observations and recommendations for our further work in genre criticism.

1. *The beginning point for an evangelical appraisal of the issue of genre is in its divine choice and selection.* In the accompanying response by Dr. David P. Scaer there is the facetious (I trust!) comment: "It would have been convenient for the church, if the Holy Spirit had given us only a Marcionite type canon."[10] He then speaks of an appropriately catalogued collection of proof texts in a canon of convenience. Given the tendency of man to pervert even the most transparent verses of Scripture, the convenience of such a canon

would likely not last long. The canon we have (and Dr. Scaer surely agrees!) is God's rich gift to us, commensurate with his character and suggestive of his mystery.

When we begin to think of the richness of genre in canon we are impressed not only with the variety of genre that does occur; we also observe that not every type of genre possible is to be found. There is, for example, nothing that is puerile or prurient. Whereas some of the writers of the Bible may not have had the ancient equivalents of the finest schools, there is nothing about their writings that is childish. The writers of the Bible were not prudish, but neither did they follow the scatological models that were not lacking in the ancient world. The variety of genre in the Bible is a measured variety, whose ultimate origin is in God. Carl F. H. Henry observes: "From start to finish, the forms, no less than the actuality, content, and recipients of God's disclosure, are solely a matter of divine determination."[11]

2. *The recognition of different genre in the Bible may lead to false identifications based on critical prejudgments.* When the *New English Bible* begins the narrative of the tower of Babel with the words, "Once upon a time all the world spoke a single language" (Genesis 11:a), there has already been a decided prejudgment as to the genre of that text. Certainly the translation "Once upon a time" does not spring directly from the Hebrew word *way(y)*^{e}*hî!* Similarly, the speaking donkey in the Balaam narrative has caused more than one critic to speak of the genre of fairy-tale, legend or *Märchen* in the Bible.[12]

I am not unaware that the manner in which I have phrased this issue betrays my own prejudgment. The major point I wish to make concerns not the issue of the fairy-tale as a genre of biblical literature, so much as the predisposition of some readers to assume certain genre are present.

3. *The study of genre should take precedence over questions of origins, the so-called higher criticism.* By a strange word game of biblical studies we usually use the phrase "literary criticism" of a decidedly nonliterary activity. Wellhausen and his heirs were meticulous, ingenious, novel, imaginative, combative—indeed, any number of words may be used to describe their work. But the term "literary" is the least felicitous adjective one might imagine. A literary approach to the Bible looks at the literature that is there present. It would seem from the results of their study that the literature there present was the least of the concerns of the literary critics. Tolkien once said, "We should be satisfied with the soup which we are served

and not desire to see immediately the bones of the ox in which it was boiled."[13]

I find that I am fully in agreement with Leonard Thompson in concept, if not fully with his methodology, when he insists on the priority of a literary study of the Scripture to the atomizing approach of most modern scholars. He writes:

> Literary criticism, with its focus upon the language of the Bible and the world created through that language, is the foundation upon which all historical and theological criticisms build. Literary criticism should be at the center of all biblical interpretation.[14]

4. *Genre speaks of the how of literature*. I sometimes introduce a lecture on the nature of the poetry in the Psalms by showing the approach and results of coming to these passages with the same questions, methods, interests, and approaches conventionally used in the study of the New Testament epistles. I term this "the Ephesians treatment" (with no animus to be attached to the Book of Ephesians in this description; I do not believe "the Ephesians treatment" does justice even to the Book of Ephesians!).

In such a trans-genre approach the stated desire of the interpreter is to understand *what* the text meant and means. An equally important question is *how* a text means. If the communication of information were the sole or even the most important concern of the biblical writers (and the Spirit), it is hard to justify the use of poetry, the language of experience. Indeed it is hard to justify literature in the Bible, for literature is the language of the imagination. Our concern for *meaning* is misdirected if we ignore the clear implications of genre, that *how* is as important as *what* of the Scripture.[15]

5. *A study of genre should proceed along the lines of literary inquiry*. (The seeming tautology in these several points is in fact a good element of Hebrew style—repetition and restatement for emphasis.) Dr. Osborne has excelled in presenting the philosophical issues relating to the concept of genre. Nevertheless, the issue of genre is finally one of literature, not philosophy. The literary demands of the literary sections of the Word of God need to be met along truly literary lines. Leland Ryken, in an article that seems to be touched a bit by a sense of discouragement at really being heard by biblical scholars, writes:

> Biblical scholars tend not to ask the questions that a literary critic asks. Their tendency is to fragmentize the text and to move away from the text to the process of composition behind

> it. Verse by verse commentary is the staple. A literary critic also looks closely at the details, but not without first discovering the elements of structure and unity in a work. A literary critic approaches a story, for example, by asking, How is the story structure? What are the unifying narrative principles by which the story teller has selected his material? How do the individual episodes relate to these overriding narrative principles? How does the story unfold sequentially, and what is important about this ordering of events? What are the plot conflicts, and how are they resolved? How does the protagonist develop as the story progresses? What archetypal plot motifs are important in the story? How is the thematic meaning of the story embodied in narrative form? It is these narrative questions that biblical scholars seem to find unimportant, yet it is the task of the literary critic to ask them.[16]

6. *Genre studies should recognize particulars and universals of literature*. Maintaining balance in this area seems to me to be particularly difficult. But we must maintain this balance to be true to the text of Scripture on a literary level. We wish to see the genre of biblical texts on their own grounds, of course. Dr. Osborne has stated: "In summation, the intrinsic genre helps one to delineate the proper hermeneutical principles to employ in seeking the meaning of a passage."[17] Well and good. He also speaks of the importance of seeking comparable genre from the ancient world for comparative purposes.[18] Again, we agree. But in my reading of his essay I did not sense an equal stress made on the importance of seeking how a particular biblical genre relates to trans-cultural and universal aspects of genre in literature.

Have you ever watched the expressions on the faces of North American Baptist or free church tourists as they enter for the first time in their lives an Eastern Orthodox Church building in the Holy Land? They are often so baffled by the trappings and ornamentation of an alien aesthetic style, that they fail to see the larger and more important structural affinities with Western Catholic buildings with which they are more familiar.

The Old Testament is an Eastern book in the same way that a church building may be an Eastern church. There is a tone and a color, nearly the smell of the East on its pages. But these elements are ornamentation and trappings. The major types of genre of the Bible are universal types. One of the most important interests of the interpreter of the genre of Scripture should be the conventions of world literature. The haiku and the Petrarchan sonnet are quite distinct; both may aid the interpreter of the Psalms of David![19]

6. *A study of genre in the Bible should not omit the sense of mystery, wonder and music.* Not all of the Bible is literary in the usual sense of that word. But a great deal of the Bible is literature, and some sections of the Bible are "world class" literature by any standard of excellence. Again we ask, Why literature? Certainly literature is not to aid in precision or detail. Literature is simply not that pragmatic. May we not regard the literary sections of the Bible and the genre they employ to be designed to call for a response in the reader of mystery, wonder and music? Think again along the lines of music, as we began these notes. As we develop skills in listening and appreciating music, do we not develop further our capacity to respond? Is it not the bore who falls asleep at the opera? Is it not the oaf who snores at the concert? Is it not the Philistine who yawns in the reading of a Psalm of David?

Ryken defines literature as experiential rather than abstract, and artistic, manifesting elements of artistic form.[20] Then he says, "from a literary point of view, the transcendental stance of biblical literature and its theme of the two worlds make it preeminently the literature of mystery, or the literature of wonder."[21] This latter is what non-Evangelical Thompson describes as "a more fantastic country."[22] Call it what you will, such an emphasis is lacking in approaches to the literary sections of the Bible that do not proceed along literary lines.

May I pursue this just a bit further? Even a detailed study of a Hebrew poem may still lead the interpreter to a short-changed result. It is not enough to classify types of parallelism, deal with rhetorical devices, work with metrical issues, parse obscure verbals, solve textual difficulties, and the like. Unless the interpreter is caught up finally with the music of the text, unless he or she is brought to a level of response, this is just another example of "The Ephesians approach."[23]

7. *A study of genre will lead to the solution of many difficulties in the Bible.* Dr. Osborne brings his study of genre criticism to a head when he relates this discipline to the area of inerrancy. Issues of concern here include surface discrepancies in the text and internal evidence of the Scripture's own self understanding.[24]

We may comment briefly on two examples that Osborne presents. The first concerns the report of the death of Sisera as described in the prose of Judges 4 and the poetry of Judges 5. Osborne seems certainly to be correct in seeing the solution of these discordant data to be in the respective genre used.[25]

Less convincing to the present reader is Osborne's solution of the problems of the narratives of the empty tomb, particularly between John and the Synoptics. While he rightly notes the logical difficulty of a highly complex solution based on traditional attempts at harmonization,[26] his own approach does not appear to be "simple." What is the relationship between genre and the purpose of the writer? Does the different purpose of John mean that he used a different form of the Gospel genre than did the Synoptic writers? Or is the genre of Gospel broad enough to allow for both concerns? If so, is this really an issue of genre or of authorial intent? The issue of theology and history is most complex.[27]

This is not to say that I reject Osborne's solution here out of hand, but to say that it is not without its difficulties. Further, in defense of Hodges, I observe that in his paper there are two elements of good literary principle: (1) the first is an analysis of character—the sense of surprise, shock and trauma on the part of the original witnesses of the Resurrection, accounting for some of the difficulty we have in reading these accounts as a consistent whole, and (2) an awareness of the point of view of the author—the technique of the gospel writers of moulding "scattered incidents into a connected story in which the absence of unmentioned details is not allowed to mar the flow of the narrative."[28] Is not this second principle similar to Osborne's observations of the style of the fourth evangelist of abbreviating, expanding and highlighting the synoptic tradition?[29]

In any event, I am confident that the study of genre will serve the evangelical scholar well in being at least a part of the solution to these and other difficulties in the Bible. My hope is that the utilitarian desire to use research in genre for the solution of difficulties will not obscure the aesthetic function of genre in biblical hermeneutics.

NOTES

[1]See, e.g., Grant R. Osborne, "Redaction Criticism and the Great Commission: A Case Study Toward a Biblical Understanding of Inerrancy," *JETS*, 19/2 (1976): 73-85.

[2]Gordon Fee, "The Genre of New Testament Literature and Biblical Hermeneutics," *Interpreting the Word of God*, ed. Samuel J. Schultz and Morris A. Inch (Chicago: Moody, 1976), 105.

[3]James I. Packer, "Encountering Present-Day Views of Scripture," *The Foun-*

dation of Biblical Authority, ed. James Montgomery Boice (Grand Rapids: Zondervan, 1978), 78. The quoted words are from the same author's *"Fundamentalism" and the Word of God* (London: Inter-Varsity; Grand Rapids: Eerdmans, 1958), 99.

[4]See Grant R. Osborne, "Genre Criticism-Sensus Literalis," p. 170ff., for a brief description of Structuralism and its emphasis on an underlying "structure" beneath the surface of culture/text. Alain Blancy describes Structuralism not so much as a method of interpretation "but a method of reading. It does not extricate the only or final meaning, but it sets forth all the possible meanings. It does not choose between interpretations according to the lines of (in-)coherence, but it establishes the system of significative differences. The meaning is always plural. It is always an interplay of reflections between signifiers without a final signified who worked it out (except for God). The meaning grows richer by never becoming fixed. The structural method never ends. It is aesthetic, not ethical." Alain Blancy, "Supplemental Theses," *Structuralism and Biblical Hermeneutics*, ed. and trans. by Alfred M. Johnson, Jr. (Pittsburgh: The Pickwick Press, 1979), 180.

[5]Osborne speaks of semiotics and biblical interpretation on a number of occasions. I have found Susan Wittig's essay a suitable beginning discussion on "the study of the sign and sign system, within the context of its production, its performance, and its reception." "A Theory of Multiple Meanings," *Semeia*, 9 (1977): 79.

[6]Polyvalence, or plurisignification, stands, of course, strongly at odds with traditional ideals of Protestant biblical interpretation to seek *the* meaning of a given Scripture. Blancy says that "the text is not a screen to be penetrated but a fabric to be unfolded." "Supplemental Theses," p. 179. Wittig concludes her study on the parable of the Prodigal Son with these words: "If the parable has any single, dependable meaning, it is that the human mind creates significance, and can understand itself completely only when it can comprehend itself in the act of making meaning. The nature of the parabolic sign—its indeterminate semantic structure—makes polyvalency, multiple significations, inevitable. The only danger is that we will too easily accept our understandings as truly residing in and springing from the text itself, rather than deriving from our own vision." "Multiple Meanings," pp. 97-98.

[7]In these approaches, "The critical perspective of the interpreter is just as determinative as the structure of the text in producing meaning." Osborne, "Genre Criticism," p. 172. Jacques Derrida, mentioned frequently by Osborne, is the subject of the most recent issue of *Semeia* (Vol. 23, 1982): "Derrida and Biblical Studies," ed. Robert Detweiler.

[8]Osborne, "Genre Criticism," 182. (The differences in wording reflect changes made by the author in revising his original paper for inclusion in this publication. The responders' papers are printed here as they were originally given.)

[9]Osborne, "Genre Criticism," 185.

[10]David P. Scaer, "A Response to Genre Criticism-Sensus Literalis," 210.

[11]Carl F. H. Henry, *God, Revelation and Authority*, vol. 2, *God Who Speaks and Shows, Fifteen Theses, Part One* (Waco, TX: Word, 1976), 77.

[12]So, e.g., Sigmund Mowinckel, "Der Ursprung der Bil'āmsage," *ZAW*, Vol. 48 (1930), p. 237. I have discussed this in my essay, "The Theology of the Balaam Oracles," *Tradition and Testament: Essays in Honor of Charles Lee Feinberg*, ed. John S. Feinberg and Paul D. Feinberg (Chicago: Moody, 1981), 79-119.

[13]So observed by Leonard L. Thompson, *Introducing Biblical Literature: A More Fantastic Country* (New Jersey: Prentice-Hall, 1978), xv.

[14]Thompson, *Introducing Biblical Literature*, 9. Some of the terminology and categories of Thompson spring from the very literary criticism that he eschews in his definition. Nevertheless, he does present many literary categories well along with the dynamics they manifest. A splendid evangelical work along the same lines is that by Leland Ryken, *The Literature of the Bible* (Grand Rapids: Zondervan, 1974).

[15]I have attempted to develop these ideas in my book on the Psalms, *Praise! A Matter of Life and Breath* (Nashville: Thomas Nelson, 1980), chapter 3, "How is a Psalm," and chapter 4, "Poetry—The Language of the Psalms." In the words of W. H. Auden, a fundamental part of the poetic process is "to hang around words and overhear them talking to one another" (*Praise!*, p. 45)—a most appropriate activity for the reader of Hebrew poetry!

[16]Leland Ryken, "Literary Criticism of the Bible: Some Fallacies," *Literary Interpretations of Biblical Narratives*, ed. Kenneth R. R. Gros-Louis, et al. (Nashville: Abingdon Press, 1974), 27-28. He concludes this essay in these words: "Biblical literature constitutes a literary achievement of unavoidable importance and indisputable value. Any literary study of the Bible will succeed best if it is based on an adequate theory of literature and literary criticism." Ibid., 40. I encourage my students in Hebrew exegesis to have Dr. Ryken's book, *The Literature of the Bible*, on the same shelf as their Brown, Driver and Briggs *Lexicon* and their *Macmillan Bible Atlas*.

[17]Osborne, "Genre Criticism," 177.

[18]Osborne, "Genre Criticism," 183. (The differences in wording reflect changes made by the author in revising his original paper for inclusion in this publication. The responders' papers are printed here as they were originally given.)

[19]My experience in teaching the Hebrew Scriptures in South Asian countries in 1978 confirmed for me in a personal way my conviction that the Old Testament is an Eastern book. Oriental students in my classes in this country are often too Westernized to sense the point that I make here. But, as Ryken insists, biblical scholars need to know more about the archetypes of literature before pressing so strongly their claims about the uniqueness of the literature of the ancient Near East. See Ryken, "Literary Criticism," 31. Calvin D. Linton has some splendid suggestions to aid one in the appreciation of the form of narration in the Bible and of the mood of drama. He judges that drama in its general sense "is the term that best hints at the literary majesty of the entire Book." "The Bible as Literature," *The Expositor's Bible Commentary*, ed. Frank E. Gaebelein (Grand Rapids: Zondervan, 1979), 1:133.

[20]Ryken, *Literature of the Bible*, 13-14.

[21]Ryken, *Literature of the Bible*, 17.

[22]Thompson, *Introducing Biblical Literature*, especially Chapter 1 "Language and the Biblical World," where he develops a metaphor from an analysis of Robert Penn Warren's *All the King's Men*.

[23]I regard the following words as a high complement, although misstated, when someone says to me concerning a sermon, "You have really made the Bible live for me." What they mean is that the preaching of the text has been done in such a way as they were brought to see the life that the text does have. But this happens when both preacher and people are brought to the level of response, when together we hear mystery, wonder and music.

[24]Osborne, "Genre Criticism," 185.

[25]Osborne, "Genre Criticism," 169.

[26]Osborne, "Genre Criticism," 182. On traditional attempts to demonstrate harmonization of difficulties, Carl F. H. Henry has stated: "Evangelical scholars do not insist that historical realities conform to all their proposals for harmonization; their intent, rather, is to show that their promises do not cancel the logical possibility of reconciling apparently divergent reports. . . . Evangelicals do not claim inerrant harmonization." *God, Revelation and Authority,* Vol. IV. *God Who Speaks and Shows; Fifteen Theses, Part Three* (Waco, TX: Word, 1979), pp. 364-65.

[27]To the excellent references Osborne gives in his note 68, I should like to add the studies by Leon Morris, "The Relationship of the Fourth Gospel to the Synoptics," especially pp. 62-63, and "History and Theology in the Fourth Gospel," especially pp. 104-105, *Studies in the Fourth Gospel* (Grand Rapids: Eerdmans, 1969). These references were noted for me by my colleague Dr. W. Robert Cook.

[28]Osborne speaks of Zane C. Hodges in his note 74, "The Women and the Empty Tomb," *Bibliotheca Sacra* 123 (1966): 301-9; the quotation I have made is from pp. 301-2.

[29]Osborne, "Genre Criticism," 181.

A Response to Genre Criticism—Sensus Literalis

David P. Scaer
Professor of Systematic Theology and New Testament
Concordia Theological Seminary, Fort Wayne, Indiana

A Response to Genre Criticism—Sensus Literalis

David P. Scaer

The International Council on Biblical Inerrancy would naturally have an interest in any topic that would make biblical inerrancy a more credible doctrine among that great majority of Christian scholars for whom the concept is no longer operative. The concept of biblical inerrancy belongs to the apologetic task of the church, since the concept involves attempts of answering those who discredit the biblical documents by locating discrepancies within the texts themselves. Any person or document which can be shown to have obvious contradictions is less than reputable or at least less than reliable. Such a concern is especially applicable to any documents claiming to be God's Word or having His authority behind them. Genre criticism promises direct relief.

Dr. Osborne has pointed out in his highly detailed essay on the history and analysis of genre criticism that failure to recognize and, more important, to identify the variety of genre within the biblical texts could have the unfortunate results of having to deal with discrepancies, apparent or real, when in fact the entire discussion about resolving such alleged discrepancies, would be inappropriate. Dr. Osborne calls these " 'surface' discrepancies."[1] The death of Sisera is an example of how genre criticism can be helpful.[2] The advantages of literary criticism are summarized by Dr. Osborne's concluding sentence:

> It is my belief that the literary approach (from a proper understanding of genre) will not only discover the true "literary sense" but will also provide the strongest possible apology for the doctrine of inerrancy by resolving so-called "contradictions" or "errors" in Scripture.[3]

The church previously confronted with discrepancies in the biblical text that proved embarrassing to its message and integrity now can resolve these difficulties simply by recognizing that the biblical authors have used the "facts" according to the already established patterns of a generally recognized genre.

Genre criticism in biblical studies is not really a new discipline, as even a superficial reading of the Bible will indicate that various types of literature are easily identifiable. The same is also true of all literature. Communication between individuals is only possible because the listener is able to recognize the genre being used by the speaker. Though genre criticism appears complex, it should be considered completely esoteric. I would endeavor to say that the ability to use and recognize genre is intuitive, even though it can be further shaped by one's environment. The basis of much humor is telling a story that is capable of being understood according to several genre. In-house humor can only be enjoyed by those who are privy to a particular understanding of certain words and phrases not known to the outsider. The outsider hearing or reading such humor sees absolutely nothing amusing in the apparent meaning of the words, but those aware of the higher or lower meaning are roaring in the aisles.

The comic strip *Doonesbury* by Gary Trudeau is a sophisticated spoof on American political and cultural life and can only be appreciated by those who have lived through conservative and liberal conflicts of the sixties and seventies. While the comic strip has absolute political truth, in no way does it attempt to preserve the historical truth that some Americans are in training for sunbathing contests.

The human mind is so geared to recognizing genre that those persons who cannot recognize the use of literary genre by the speaker are downright dull. They are operating only on one literary level. Lively and intelligent conversation and writing depends on the speaker's and the writer's ability to change horses in midstream—without in any way suggesting that we are really all now standing in the water looking for the banks of the river so that we can really exchange steeds more safely. Dr. Osborne speaks about mingling genre.[4]

Failure to recognize the biblical genre can also be highly amusing, though at the time the failure of the scholars to recognize them was quite serious and highly respected. German Rationalism used the Christmas story to lecture on animal husbandry and John 21 might have been used to demonstrate the point that if you have fished in one place for too long that perhaps you should try the middle of the lake.

In a more serious vein is whether the actions and commands given to the early church are necessarily mandates for the church today.[5] For if they were, even the command for world evangelism might mean that we would have to make our first mission calls in the environs of Jerusalem. This would be a boon for the economy of the state of Israel to have all mission boards headquartered in their capital city, but we might find ourselves in direct opposition to Christ's commands. As will be indicated below, the failure to agree on the identification of genre and the further failure to agree on the binding character of genre, even where there is agreement of the identification of the genre is one cause of schism within Christendom.

Genre recognition and the subsequent controversy in the church are not really new. Without some type of genre conflict, the church might have easily been spared all of its doctrinal division. What is new is the greater precision in identifying the biblical genre. The biblical scholars are applying principles and terminology developed in connection with secular literature and applying them to the sacred texts. As Dr. Osborne points out certain procedures, e.g., the New Hermeneutic, presents a problem because the meaning is no longer solely determined by the author but later audiences.[6] While genre criticism may be called a science because there are certain static principles, it may better be called an art since a certain creativity is required in recognizing the genre.

We can agree with Dr. Osborne's verdict on those who are looking for something absolutely definite in all respects in genre research. "As one can surmise from this brief perusal of approaches to genre, any attempt to grasp easily this complex topic is indeed doomed to disappointment."[7] The challenge in genre criticism in biblical studies is not acknowledging that the Bible uses genre—if it did not, obviously no one would understand its message and it could hardly serve as a vehicle for divine revelation—but identifying the particular genre.

At first there was every reason for those committed to traditional Christianity to be opposed to genre criticism, because it seemed to threaten the historical moorings of the faith. Incarnation and resurrection could be dissolved into parables and fables. Any genre which from the outset would permit several contradictory interpretations could hardly serve as the foundation and pillar of the truth. At second glance, conservative Christians have more to gain than any other group in Christendom not because it opens to them a new horizon, but rather because it puts the authoritatively accepted biblical data in a different perspective. Simply because we are agreed in that God through the Holy Spirit is responsible for the biblical texts in their final form, does not mean that we have correctly identified or recognized the genre or that our understandings have exhausted the particular pericopes. Recognizing the Bible as the Word of God means that the Holy Spirit is responsible for its final form not that all of the Bible is binding in the same way on everyone.[8] Here of course lies also the cause of divisions within Christendom. Today conservative Christians sharing a common attitude to biblical inerrancy seems to be increasingly divided over women in the pastoral role.[9]

It would have been convenient for the church, if the Holy Spirit had given us only a Marcionite type canon. Theology could have been constructed on the somewhat more transparent passages of the Pauline corpus and the Jesus stories could have taken from the less offensive and more graceful Gospel of Luke. Gordon Fee aptly notes, "Traditionally for most Christians the epistles seem to be the easier portions of the New Testament to interpret."[10]

Paul's writings have in fact become the lodestone for the New Testament canon. Conservative Protestants may in fact be Marcionites without being aware of it. For many conservative Protestants, an ideal book for canonization would be one in which the various proof texts would be catalogued under the appropriate dogmatical headings.

For whatever reason the Holy Spirit preserved His revelation not in theorems but in writings that share in the wide spectrum of human literary genre. In time the divine use of human genre developed in their own right into types of genre themselves and became standards or examples for other writings.

At the risk of oversimplification, my reaction to Dr. Osborne's quite sufficient essay will be in the form of theses with commentary.

(1) *The genre must flow from the intersecting point of the speaker with his audience.* The genre, whether used for secular or religious purposes, cannot be totally new if it is to be understood by the intended audience. In choosing the genre, a process of which the speaker may not be totally conscious,[11] the speaker selects a form which does justice to the content of the message which he intends to convey and which will be grasped immediately by his audience. Our task today is to identify those original genre. As Dr. Osborne says, "For biblical study it is vital to establish generic connections with ancient works from the same period."[12]

(2) *The genre must be immediately recognizable by the first intended audience, but may in the passing of time not be understood by subsequent generations.* Protestant theology operates under the principle of Scriptural perspicuity, especially in connection with its

concept of the principle of the universal priesthood of all believers. Scriptural perspicuity may have been overstated if this means that all parts of the Scriptures are directly accessible to the reader in regard to its original meaning. The original audience has to be in a position to grasp the meaning. In addition, if the Scriptures' purpose is to bring about a recognition of who Jesus is, i.e., the Law and Gospel principle, first the sinner's condemnation and then the message of his salvation, the genre cannot be so alien to the original hearer that he can have no idea of what is being said to him. Gordon Fee cautions that frequently the nonexpert today can more readily recognize the intended meaning than the expert.[13]

If speaking in tongues is a genre, then such a genre, cannot serve God's saving purposes because it was unintelligible to the first audience and subsequent audiences.[14] Other genres used for biblical revelation may for subsequent audiences tend to lose their usefulness in communication. The science of hermeneutics attempts to create the original situation and identify the genre.

(3) *A genre may undergo a certain readjustment recognizable and traceable within the biblical texts themselves.* Without questioning that Jesus uniquely and creatively used the genre of parable in addressing the message of salvation to his audience, the evangelists may further adjust the genre to address their audiences. Later evangelists may even further rework that of the earlier one.[15] Apparently the more complex material of Matthew is simplified by Luke. This genre readjustment is not limited to the parables, but may also include the use of the historical and biographical data about Jesus.

(4) *Certain genre may be considered inappropriate for his audience and hence not used.* It is significant that Paul does not adopt the preaching methods of Jesus in addressing his audiences in parables. As noted, the simplification of the material from Matthew to Luke may have been necessitated by the Gentile mind for whom the Jewish parables may have been somewhat confusing. This is handled by Osborne.[16]

(5) *Every genre is in a very real sense an accommodation of the speaker to his audience.* The speaker who does not accommodate his message to his audience is simply incomprehensible and hence useless. The speaker first 'reads' his audience and selects the appropriate genre for his message.[17]

(6) *The genre in its original secular form before its incorporation in revelation has certain divine characteristics, since the man in whom the genre first took form was made in God's image. On that*

account the accomodation of divine revelation to the human genre should not be overstressed. The raw data for all genre is the human situation, which, though now perverted by sin, inherently bears certain divine characteristics. The concern over an infinite transcendent God bridging the "unfathomable gulf between Himself and mankind"[18] should be replaced by incarnational view of God who finds himself perfectly at home in the human situation with its genres because he is its creator. Incarnation is not for God an uncomfortable embarrassing interlude. Fundamental to biblical genre criticism is the Word's becoming flesh. As Dr. Osborne says: "Genre in this light might become a basic statement of the means by which God has revealed himself to man."[19] Consider the use of agricultural figures for the purpose of divine revelation. Behind the parable in which Jesus is the sower is God who once planted a garden of Eden. God does not condescend to appear to us as a farmer, but rather the agricultural imagery finds its prototype in him.

(7) *The Word of God is not a genre.* God's words are those human words that God takes into his service for the purpose of revelation. The phrase "the Word of God" is adjectival or descriptive in that it explains that attribute of those words which appear at first to be human words, but which make the claim of being authorized by God. God does not superimpose a uniquely divine genre on men, as it would be unrecognizable to them; but he uses human genres for his own purposes and thus they become his own words. There is no revelation of salvation apart from incarnation.

(8) *Though in classifying genre, we use secular norms, ultimately a particular genre classification must be determined by how it fits the biblical data and not any outside rigid secular norms.* Osborne speaks of how the norms for literature must be derived from that literature itself.[20]

(9) *Some genre by their use in revelation and Scriptures become so associated and freighted with theological meaning that the genre's primary sense may become theological.* The association of a genre with its use in Scripture may through ordinary use replace memory of the origin of the genre in the secular literature. The interpreter is obligated to determine the original setting of the genre; however, the genre for all practical purposes becomes a religiously connected genre. This is especially true of the Western world in which the English King James Version of the Bible has so influenced speech. Such genre may now be used for secular purposes but the audience has a general recognition that they have originated in the Bible.

(10) *The same genre may be used for different but not opposing purposes from its original use.* This issue Dr. Osborne addresses when he says that a monolithic view of metaphor should not replace a multi-faceted one.[21] A multi-faceted view of metaphor does not relieve the interpreter of "determin(ing) the intrinsic, originally intended genre."[22]

No dogmatic principle of *sensus literalis unus est* can be so superimposed upon the biblical texts so that the multiple use of the same genre in different situations for a different purpose is per se heretical. The meaning of a genre can develop the biblical texts. The same parable can serve different but not opposing purposes. Paul's quotation of the prohibition from Deuteronomy 25:4 against muzzling the ox is used in a different but not opposing way in 1 Timothy 5:8 in regard to salaries of pastors.

(11) *That theory of polyvalence that permits the listener to address his concerns to the genre irrespective of the original situation and to consider his reaction as "canonical" is destructive of any meaningful concept of biblical revelation.* Dr. Osborne speaks of that type of genre scholarship, that also embraces the New Hermeneutic, that gives a contributing or equal value to the interpreter as to the original sense. "The critical perspective of the interpreter is just as determinitive as the structure of the text in producing meaning."[23] What a text means to the hearer now replaces what was meant.[24] Such an approach to biblical genre becomes impossible for those who understand biblical authority as providing a definitive word of God for his church and who do not understand that authority merely as producing a reaction in the church today. Any negative word spoken against this polyvalence theory of genre interpretation which lets every listener in any time put his interpretation of the genre on the same level as the original speaker must also be directed against alleged devotional use of the Bible. Such devotional use of the Bible permits the reader to consider his initial and most frequently uninformed reaction as an expression of the divine truth.

(12) *The readjustment or reapplication of the biblical genre to the current audience belongs to the church's homiletical and not hermeneutical task.* Just as a readjustment of genera within the biblical texts can be noted, so the preacher must adjust those genera in his preaching for his audience today. Just as the biblical genera cannot be superimposed upon the church today as in some cases they may be inappropriate, so our readjustment of the genera for preaching may not be understood as part of the hermeneutical task. This is,

however, the method of the New Hermeneutic. The hermeneutical and homiletical tasks cannot be confused or the one replaced by the other. The church's reaction to the original genre presented in a homiletical context may not be considered as canonical or normative.

The presentation of the biblical genre without interpretation can produce worthless or even destructive results among the people. Before the preacher preaches, he must first be a qualified interpreter of the biblical genre. After determining the original intent of the biblical genre, the preacher will then adjust that genre to fit his audience or choose other genera which will more adequately convey that message. If the original biblical genre would have been adequate in all situations, only the reading of the Scriptures and no sermons would have even been necessary. Jesus would have quoted only the Old Testament and not preached and Paul would have quoted Jesus and not written the epistles. The homiletical reuse, reconstruction, and in certain cases, replacement of the original biblical genre, are not normative in determining that original intent.

(13) *The classification of the genre by the church in the past is open to reexamination and critique*. The church since the beginning has been engaged in genre classification, even though the techniques as a science had not been developed. Traditional classifications and understandings should not be considered above criticism and hence readjustment. For example, the church's understandings of the parables, other preachings of Jesus, the Epistle of James, just to mention a few, may have to be reevaluated on the basis of genre criticism. Without depreciating the historical character of certain incidents in the Bible especially, the Gospels, understanding some literature as chiefly historical and not theological in character may have been detrimental in exhausting the full meaning of certain pericopes.[25]

(15) *The misapplication or misunderstanding of a genre makes impossible the task of receiving the full, original, or intended meaning of a pericope*. The church must never canonize its own past hermeneutical procedures or conclusions. New opportunities can be opened with the application of more precise procedures of genre criticism.

(16) *Divisions within Christendom result frequently from disagreement on the genre of specific pericopes*. Genre criticism can possibly be used to reenforce a priori theological opinions. Past differences have arisen because of disagreement over the binding nature of particular genre. Participants in genre critique must proceed from previously agreed upon principles of procedure in examining controverted sections. Procedures should not be determined by dogmatic

conclusions determined before the text itself is examined. Such traditionalism is an inherent denial of the *sola scriptura*.

(17) *Genre criticism promises to be most productive in the study of the Synoptic Gospels*. Conservative theology has tended to be dominated by Pauline and Johannine theology. This has resulted from the comparative ease with which these writings may be read. Much can be said for recognizing the 'Gospel' itself as genre created by the church in which Jesus is portrayed as both the teacher of his message and the object of faith. This might mean that addressing historical questions to each point in the Gospels may be less than fully appropriate.[26]

If the 'Gospel' is itself a genre, then it might be time to resurrect the ancient church view that held that Matthew is the first gospel and hence that evangelist is the creator of the 'Gospel' genre. Dr. Osborne addresses this specifically though I might have a little difficulty with his statements: "Any single narration of the significance of the Jesus the Christ would be insufficient." "God knows that finite man could not find any single version sufficient in itself, and so each version provides a different vista of meaning."[27] Each version may provide "a different vista of meaning," but I am not so sure that one Gospel could not have met the needs of finite man.

Should Matthew be understood as the first gospel, then in the other three gospels there is a readjustment of that genre addressed to specific church and theological needs. But such a view would not suggest that one Gospel, especially Matthew, would not meet the needs of finite man. I can wholeheartedly agree with Dr. Osborne's conclusion that, "The difference between the Gospels do not relate to history so much as theology."[28]

Osborne suggests that instead of addressing historical questions to the passion and resurrection narratives of the Gospels, we begin addressing theological ones. Within the general genre of 'Gospel,' each evangelist can be recognized as using, readapting, and constructing his material according to genre which he finds most appropriate for his audience.

Genre criticism is a complex art, but it promises the rewards of further refining the church's concept of biblical inerrancy and opening the biblical theology to even greater depths.

NOTES

[1]Grant R. Osborne, "Genre Criticism—Sensus Literalis," 185.
[2]Osborne, "Genre," 169.
[3]Osborne, "Genre," 185.
[4]Osborne, "Genre," 166.
[5]Gordon Fee, "The Genre of New Testament Literature and Biblical Hermeneutics," *Interpreting the Word of God,* ed. S. J. Schultz and M. A. Inch (Chicago: Moody, 1976), 117.
[6]Osborne, "Genre," 170.
[7]Osborne, "Genre," 166.
[8]Fee, "The Genre," 108-9.
[9]Fee, "The Genre," 113.
[10]Fee, "The Genre," 106.
[11]Osborne, "Genre," 177.
[12]Osborne, "Genre," 168.
[13]Fee, "The Genre," 127.
[14]I Corinthians 14:20-23.
[15]Osborne, "Genre," 182.
[16]Osborne, "Genre," 182.
[17]Osborne, "Genre," 182.
[18]Osborne, "Genre," 182.
[19]Osborne, "Genre," 181.
[20]Osborne, "Genre," 169.
[21]Osborne, "Genre," 176. (The differences in wording reflect changes made by the author in revising his original paper for inclusion in this publication. The responders' papers are printed here as they were originally given.)
[22]Osborne, "Genre," 176. (The differences in wording reflect changes made by the author in revising his original paper for inclusion in this publication. The responders' papers are printed here as they were originally given.)
[23]Osborne, "Genre," 172.
[24]Osborne, "Genre," 171.
[25]Fee, "The Genre," 120.
[26]Fee, "The Genre," 119-23.
[27]Osborne, "Genre," 182.
[28]Osborne, "Genre," 182.

Problems of Normativeness in Scripture: Cultural Versus Permanent

J. Robertson McQuilkin
President of Columbia Bible College

4. Problems of Normativeness in Scripture: Cultural Versus Permanent

J. Robertson McQuilkin

Only recently Bible scholars and theologians have begun to realize that interpreting Scripture is not their private preserve. The behavioral scientists have moved in and soon may take over. Theologians gather in small groups and discuss with one another the meaning of difficult and disputed texts while the psychologists gather thousands of pastors to tell them how it is done and anthropologists show missionaries the way. It is worse than that for the former "queen of the sciences." As a leading anthropologist recently told me, theologians are not qualified to do theology anyway. They may have a few valid insights for people in their own highly select academic culture, but to understand God's truth for ordinary people requires tools the theologian does not even have, the tools of cultural anthropology.

What are we to do? Scoff at the accusation and continue to talk profoundly to ourselves while the new, "meaningful" and "relevant" approaches move in? My concern is not that the "in" crowd may be squeezed out. Actually, we are committed to the thesis that the Bible does not belong to the elite anyway—not pope, nor theologian, nor behavioral scientist. But a great deal is at stake. My contention in this paper will be that the authority of Scripture is at stake.

If this evaluation is true, how did we get into this precarious position? Is the drift in the way Evangelicals understand Scripture merely part of the larger popular shift of authority to the new high-priestly cult of the psychologist and his blood brothers, the sociologist and the anthropologist? Perhaps this popular shift has conditioned the Christian public to look in the direction of the behavioral scientist for a word of authority, but I believe a more important cause can be found in our own backyard.

From of old, the task of the Bible scholar has been defined as determining the meaning intended by the original authors of Scripture. It was felt not only possible but imperative to determine this meaning, for it is God's word of revelation to man. Gregg Bahnsen put it this way:

> Because of their respect for Scripture's objective authority and saving purpose, the Reformers were motivated to delineate carefully the rudimentary principles for correctly interpreting the Bible. It was thought important to approach biblical interpretation in a manner which would comport with submission to Scripture as possessing a unique status as the infallible word of the eternal, self-sufficient, completely sovereign God. Scripture revelation was necessary for men in their creaturely and sinful state, as well as being completely sufficient to accomplish God's designed ends. Accordingly, given this view of God and His verbal revelation, the Reformation insisted that God's written word was perspicuous in its basic message to the ordinary reader and that Scripture alone could serve as the source and final norm of Christian belief and practice—thereby assuming an efficacious clarity and authoritative supremacy over all extra-biblical sources of knowledge available to reason. With this in mind, the Reformers laid down the principle that it is Scripture which interprets Scripture as the necessary, sufficient, and clear authority in communicating God's Word successfully to its hearers. Respect for the Scripture as the rule of its own interpretation meant that readers should give a biblical passage its normal sense, consistent with the rest of the Bible, according to its literary genre and its historical-grammatical context.[1]

The inerrant words of Scripture were so important that we developed a whole discipline for establishing the text and called it textual criticism. The task of exegesis or determining the meaning of the original author was so important that we developed rules for correct exegesis and called the discipline "hermeneutics." We trained budding pastors diligently in these disciplines. And then we sent them out to proclaim the truth of Scripture, to apply it to contemporary faith and life. But we did not develop the guidelines for doing so. There was no discipline to bridge the gap between exegesis and application. It was every man for himself and the devil seemed to take not only "the hind-most" but some of the foremost as well!

Into this gap stepped the behavioral scientist. Whether he was preceded or followed by some of the more contemporary biblical scholars does not matter. The gap had to be filled. The aim of biblical study must be not only to know what the original author meant, but what God means today. How can the Bible be made existentially viable for the contemporary context? We did not work hard at answering the questions of how to determine the recipient of any given Bible passage, or how to know for sure what response God intends today. If someone else has moved in with influential answers to these questions, answers with which we are unhappy, we have ourselves to thank. We failed to develop principles for applying Scripture the way we developed principles for interpreting its meaning, principles that would safeguard the authority of Scripture. What can we do about it at this late date? Before offering a suggested approach, let me review my presuppositions.

Any word derives its authority from its source. Tell me who said it and I will tell you what authority the word has. If God says something, that word is absolutely trustworthy and it is authoritative. How much of the Bible is true and authoritative? Well, how much of it is from God? I hold that all of it is from God. I do so for two reasons. First of all I hold that all of it is from God and, therefore, trustworthy because that is the way Jesus Christ treated the Bible he had and he is my Lord. There is also a philosophical reason. If I select from among the teachings of Scripture those that are true and those that are in error, Scripture is no longer an independent authority. The person who makes that judgment is the final authority.

Furthermore, my presupposition is that God's activity in inspiring men to write Scripture resulted in a document that was without error in its verbal expression of the truth God desires to reveal to men. Therefore, the Bible and only the Bible is trustworthy in every statement, and absolute in its authority for faith and life. What does this presupposition mean?

I believe God's activity in revealing His truth to biblical writers safeguarded not only general concepts from error, but safeguarded the words themselves. It is difficult for me to conceive of true meaning being communicated apart from true words. If the words themselves are in error, how much more the meaning for which they serve as a vehicle! Thus, to me inerrancy is the predictable result of divine inspiration.

Therefore, because of the Bible's ultimate authority, to understand the meaning God intended is of first importance. And this meaning cannot be discovered apart from the verbal form in which it was given, nor can it be in conflict with that form.

The contemporary emphases on deriving principles from Scripture and emphasizing the function of Scripture are certainly legitimate. But if some deduced principle or contemporary function is used to disallow the verbal form and its original meaning, Scripture is no longer the authority. I hold, then, that both the form and meaning of Scripture are permanent revelation and normative. That is, the words of Scripture, inspired to convey the meaning God intended, constitute the permanent revelation of God's truth. But the function of Scripture is also important. Without authentic application of God's Word, its purpose remains unfulfilled.

We did right, therefore, to emphasize sound principles for interpreting the meaning of Scripture. We did not do well in failing to develop guidelines that would identify the recipient of any given passage and apply the teaching for contemporary faith and life. We must articulate guidelines for identifying the contemporary recipient and clarifying the response God intends. But such guidelines must be based wholly on a fully trustworthy and authoritative Scripture, not imposed from some external source.

In the light of these presuppositions, how does an understanding of the cultural context fit the task of interpretation and application?

It is helpful in establishing the meaning of a passage to see it in the cultural context of the author and his original audience. Furthermore, it is helpful in making an authentic application of biblical truth, to see it in the cultural context of the contemporary audience. But if an understanding of some biblical cultural context or some contemporary cultural form is used to contravene the plain meaning of the text, Scripture itself is no longer the authority. Thus, the meaning, recipient, and application must be established within the limits set by the data of Scripture.

Several approaches have been proposed for discerning between the permanent, universal, normative teaching of Scripture on the one hand and, on the other hand, that which is transient, not applicable to every people in every culture, not intended to function as a mandate for normative behavior. Consider these approaches.

I

A. How is God at Work Today?

For some, the answer to the question about the meaning of Scripture does not begin with Scripture at all, but with the contemporary context. Liberation theology is the most notable example of this approach. For the more moderate liberation theologians it is simply that the contemporary context sets the agenda, it asks the questions for Scripture to answer. However, for many God at work in the revolutionary events of our day is actually "the word of God" and the Bible becomes a paradigm or example of this. One of the leading spokesmen, Hugo Assman, puts it this way:

> The word of God is no longer a fixed absolute, an eternal proposition we receive before analyzing social conflicts and before committing ourselves to the transformation of historical reality. God's summons to us, God's word today grows from the collective process of historical awareness, analysis and involvement, that is, from praxis.
>
> The Bible and the whole Christian tradition do not speak directly to us in our situation. But they remain as a basic reference about how God spoke in quite a different context, which must illuminate His speaking in our context.
>
> It is true that this kind of historical hermeneutics may destroy the false security of the word of God given once for all, the absolute of the word of God in itself. The word doesn't exist for us in that sense.[2]

As Harvey Conn says, "the Bible functions not as the given revelation of God, but as a pattern for liberation. The exodus of Israel from bondage in Egypt and the resurrection of Christ are viewed no longer as history."[3]

If it is argued that this is an extreme view, note the more moderate position of Emilio Castro, a liberation theologian, now director of the Commission on World Mission and Evangelism of the World Council of Churches:

> Throughout the Gospel, Jesus is given complete freedom to deal with situations according to specific needs, demonstrating the love of God the Father through words of love, reproach, explanation, or through acts of healing . . .
>
> Thus, as with Jesus Christ, mission leaves the church and every individual Christian completely free to choose options; it leaves us free to use our own judgment as to the words or deeds best suited to the circumstances at a given time, provided they are always aligned on Jesus Christ.[4]

The form of contextualization called liberation theology is thus frankly committed to improvise freely on biblical teaching at the least, or, more typically, viewing the Bible merely as an historic example of the way God worked at one time and place in history. The revelation of His will comes from the events He is shaping in the world today. Clearly, in this approach for making the Bible culturally relevant, the Bible itself is not viewed as the final authority.

B. What Response Does God Desire?

This approach takes the words of Scripture (the form) seriously in order to get at meaning. And it is interested in meaning in order to get behind the meaning and discern what response the author desired from his original audience. When this response is identified, through a process called dynamic equivalence interpretation, the present-day interpreter asks, "How can I produce that response in my audience today?" The answer to this question will be God's revelation of His will.

Charles Kraft is a leading spokesman for this position. To him the words of Scripture are not accurate.[5] Even the concepts of Scripture are culture-bound. The task of the interpreter, therefore, is to discern the cultural universal in the biblical data and to reproduce in contemporary society the impact, not the form, God intended in that society.

> An anthropologically informed approach . . . identifies as the constants of Christianity the functions and meanings behind such forms, rather than any given set of doctrinal or behavioral forms. It would leave the cultural forms in which these constant functions are expressed largely negotiable in terms of the cultural matrix of those with whom God is dealing at the time. In what follows, then, I will argue that it is the *meaning conveyed* by a particular doctrine . . . that is of primary concern to God. There is, I believe, no absoluteness to the human formulation of the doctrine, the historical accuracy of the way in which the ritual is performed, or the rigidity with which one abides by one's behavioral rules . . .
>
> . . . godliness lies in the motives behind the meanings conveyed by the forms of belief and behavior, not simply in adherence to the beliefs and practices as traditionally observed. The beliefs and practices are simply the cultural vehicles (the forms) through which God-motivated concern, interest, and acceptance are to be expressed. And these forms must be continually watched and altered to make sure that they are fulfilling their proper function—the transmission of the eternal message of God. As culture changes, these forms of belief and behavior must be updated in order to preserve the eternal message.[6]

The end result of this approach for Kraft is not merely that the church is free to baptize or not, as the culture may demand, or that one may arrange church government in accordance with local cultural norms. Far more basic theological teaching is modified through cultural understanding. For example, people are saved without a knowledge of Christ[7] and, in fact, the direction one is headed makes a person a Christian, not his position. People are saved through faith in what they know and which their culture will permit them to receive. Cultural norms such as polygamy and infanticide may be left for believers in such cultures to work out[8] and, in fact, polygamy may be required as a prerequisite for holding church office in some societies.

Kraft has many brilliant insights of value for cross-cultural communication. But the basic approach is relativistic and the end effect is to make not only the application of Scripture but its interpretation as well, relative to some contemporary culture. Words point to meaning and the meaning intended by the original author illuminates the response God desired. When the anthropologist-theologian has that desired response in mind, through a process of contemporary revelation just like the original process of revelation[9] he can discern the word of God necessary to produce the same results today.

Note the difference between this position and that of the liberation theologian. The liberation theologian begins with the contemporary context and uses Scripture only as certain elements in it are useful as models. On one occasion I asked Dr. Kraft what would prevent the liberation theologian from using Kraft's approach and coming to the conclusions of the liberation theologians. He responded that they could do so, but should not. In other words, there is a close affinity between the two approaches. The ethno-linguistic or dynamic equivalence approach to biblical interpretation could be used to produce liberation theology though the spokesman for that approach would not approve of such a result. But the two approaches are nevertheless different. The dynamic equivalence approach uses the Bible as a starting point, not as an ending point when convenient as do the leading liberation theologians. In this way, for the dynamic equivalence interpreter, biblical revelation is unique. But the Scripture itself, and particularly its verbal form and original meaning, are not authoritative.

C. Does This Biblical Teaching Reflect a Universal Cultural Norm?

An increasing number of biblical scholars who consider themselves evangelical accept as normative only those teachings in Scripture that reflect universal cultural formulations, such as "thou shalt not steal." The rest of biblical teaching is culture-bound, speaking to cultural specifics. The task of the interpreter is to set the teaching free from its cultural bondage to speak a universal truth or principle. Depending on the interpreter, Christ's teaching against divorce, Paul's teaching against homosexuality, biblical norms for the role of the woman in marriage are all culture-specific teachings and are not normative, demanding obedience in every culture of every age.

This approach has much in common with Kraft's approach, but some who use it do not look beyond the meaning for a cultural universal in the intended impact, but rather seek the enduring principle in the meaning itself. For them the meaning itself is valid, but is normative only when teaching a culturally universal truth. The criteria for authoritative application are extra-biblical cultural norms.

I was seated across the luncheon table from a leading biblical linguist. We were discussing the question of what teaching in Scripture is normative.

"What do you think," I asked, "should be required of all people in every tribe and culture?"

"Why," he responded immediately, "those teachings that are culturally universal."

"For example?"

"Well," he hesitated, "I'm not altogether sure."

I suggested, "Something like murder?"

"Why yes," he said, "that would be a cultural universal."

"I'm surprised to hear that. I would have thought that killing and perhaps even eating the victim would be considered a virtue in some societies."

"Well, I guess you're right. . . ."

The conversation continued in the same vein with considerable uncertainty as to whether there were any universally valid cultural norms. I felt that the situation was becoming socially indelicate and probed in my mind for ways to extricate myself from the conversation when my new acquaintance burst out, "I don't know about these things. I'm no theologian. I'm just a linguist and anthropologist." Nevertheless, as a leading authority, his responsibilities give him a voice in the approach used in hundreds of translations.

Yet I understand his frustration. Since the Bible itself makes no distinction between cultural universals and cultural specifics, for us to seek to make this distinction and to undertake the enormous task of certainly identifying any cultural universals at all is well-nigh impossible, even if we are professional anthropologists. And to attempt the distinction will result in making culturally relative teaching out of most Scripture. Thus the independent authority of Scripture is set aside.

D. What Is the Normative Principle That Lies Behind This Specific Bible Teaching?

One writer puts it this way:

> New Testament ethics should be defined as: prescriptive principles stemming from the essence of the gospel and usually embodied in the example and teachings of Jesus, which are meant to be applied to particular situations by the direction and enablement of the Holy Spirit, being always motivated and conditioned by love.
>
> Its principles, I argue, are to be taken as normative. The way those principles were put into practice in the first century, however, should be understood as signposts at the beginning of a journey pointing out the proper path to be taken if we are to reapply those same principles in our day. It will not do simply to ask: Does the New Testament say anything explicit concerning this or that social issue?, with the intent being to repeat that answer if it does and to remain silent if it doesn't. Such an approach assumes the record to be a static codification of ethical maxims. What we need to do, rather, is to ask the following two questions: What principles deprived from the Gospel does the New Testament declare to be important for the area of social morality?, and What practices in application of those principles does the New Testament describe as setting a paradigm for our reapplication of those same principles today?[10]

With this question concerning principles in Scripture we have reached an approach that takes seriously the authority of Scripture. In fact, this approach is very appealing, not only because it makes life easier, in a sense, but because there is a strong element in the approach that is true to an authoritative Scripture. The approach of limiting normative teaching to principles derived from biblical specifics need not be an attempt to subvert or get around Scripture, but rather to implement the authority of Scripture.

My problem with the approach is simply that I find it nowhere enunciated in the Bible. Where in Scripture are we told that the specific declarations of God's truth and God's will for men are not normative, but only the principles that lie behind them? It seems to me that the explicit declarations (the "maxims") are treated as normative both in the Old Testament and the New Testament. To disallow the authority of explicit statements on this ground is not to permit Scripture to make the choice. The Bible gives both maxims or specifics, and generic principles. Furthermore, it is quite legitimate to derive generic principles from these specifics so long as the principle is not turned on the specific to abrogate the specific teaching itself. To set aside any specific teaching of Scripture, allowing only the principle deduced for the particular(s) to be normative, is to impose an extra-biblical notion and violate the authority of Scripture.

E. Is This Teaching of Scripture Based On the Nature of God or the Order of Creation?

Now we are getting much closer to the treatment of Scripture as an independent authority. We are not establishing principles of any kind as the sole abiding norm. In addition to principles, specific teachings which are based on the nature of God or the order of creation are considered normative.

Walter Kaiser enunciates this position:

> Therefore, there is an absolute loyalty in Scripture to the principles founded in the nature of God or the ordinances of creation; yet, there is more flexibility in applying those other commands such as sanitary laws, dietary laws . . . ceremonial regulations. . . .[11]

A parallel approach is taken by Gordon Fee:

> Similarly, one should note whether the matter in hand is inherently moral or nonmoral, theological or nontheological. Although some may differ with my judgment here, it would appear that eating food offered to idols, head covering for women when they pray or prophecy, women teaching in the church, and Paul's preference for celibacy, are examples of issues not inherently moral; they may become so only by their use or abuse in given contexts.[12]

I am confident that neither of these biblical scholars would use this approach to set aside any basic biblical teaching. However, I am uncomfortable with the principle. Where did it come from? If Scripture itself does not identify which teaching is founded upon the nature of God or the ordinances of creation and which teaching is purely culturally based, on what grounds do I make such a distinction? It seems to me that those grounds become my authority.

Furthermore, I have a problem in applying the principle suggested. Is the fall of man based on the nature of God or the order of creation? Certainly it is inherently theological. Or is it? Is teaching concerning the Lord's Supper and its observance grounded in anything other than the authoritative word of Christ? It does not seem to be inherently grounded in the nature of God nor the order of creation. It was a cultural form that He made normative. What of the command that the wife should be in subjection to the authority of her husband or that homosexual behavior is wrong? If all explicit teaching of Scripture, not limited by Scripture itself, is taken as normative, these teachings are normative. However, if only those teachings that can be demonstrated to be theological in nature or to be certainly grounded in the nature of God or in the order of creation are considered normative, these teachings along with many others become legitimate questions for debate.

It seems to me that seeking for the theological basis of any teaching or searching for its foundation in the nature of God or the order of creation is very helpful in several ways. To demonstrate this kind of foundation may reinforce or clarify specific teaching. It helps in discerning general principles lying behind specifics. This approach may be used along with other indicators in the text itself to ferret out that which Scripture did not intend as a universal norm. But to set aside any specific teaching simply because its theological nature cannot be proved is to introduce an extra-biblical hermeneutical principle that violates the independent authority of Scripture.

F. Is This Behavior Directly Commanded or Forbidden in Scripture?

Although this approach is no longer as popular as it once was, there are those who make normative only the direct commands of the Bible. However, this is certainly not the way Scripture treats itself. More than a book of maxims, Scripture is certainly a book of principles. If all principles which are not directly commanded are classified as having less authority, if only the specifics are normative, we are indeed greatly impoverished. The abolition of slavery and the establishment of a monogamist society are two examples of what we now consider normative biblical behavior that would fall as casualties if this approach were adopted. Since Scripture itself makes no such distinction, I find it illegitimate so to do.

G. Is the Old Testament Teaching Repeated in the New?

This is an approach to disallow all Old Testament teaching as normative unless it is reaffirmed in the New Testament. My problem with this approach is the same as in each of the earlier approaches: Where does Scripture make this distinction? Both Christ and the apostles treated the Old Testament as the Word of God, their final authority. I freely grant that there are many interpretive problems relating to Old Testament teaching, but to handle these problems by disallowing the normative nature of the Old Testament is certainly an attack on the authority of the majority of Scripture.

Furthermore, there are some interesting practical results. Many Old Testament commands such as those against bestiality and rape are not repeated in the New Testament. Are they, therefore, no longer normative?

In the scope of this presentation it has not been possible to exhaustively treat these various approaches, but I feel that it is important to identify them. And to treat them in this brief way may not be wholly illegitimate since they have one thing in common. They make distinctions between normative teaching and that which need not be considered normative on premises not enunciated in Scripture itself. If the Bible is our final authority, it must define what are permanent, universal requirements and what teaching is limited.

II

My thesis is that a fully authoritative Bible means that every teaching in Scripture is universal unless Scripture itself treats it as limited. If this is true, in what ways does Scripture limit the applications of its teaching? Are there ways of identifying that which is not normative while safeguarding the full, independent authority of Scripture? I believe there are.

A. Does the Context Limit the Recipient or Application?

In 1 Corinthians 7, Paul advocates a life of singleness. But he limits this teaching in several ways. He says this advice is for those who are so gifted. He says that this advice is "in view of the present distress." Twice in the chapter he says that at least some of the teaching is from himself rather than from the Lord, and in another section qualifies the teaching with the statement, "according to my judgment." Although his intention in these limitations is disputed, it must be granted that the teaching is in some sense limited in its application.

When the context limits the recipient of a particular teaching or the application of that teaching, it is a violation of the authority of Scripture to make it universal. To insist on celibacy as normative, for example, even for those with vocational "holy orders" is to violate biblical authority.

B. Does Subsequent Revelation Limit the Recipient or the Application?

Christ told his disciples not to take certain amenities for their journey, but he later lifted this ban. The Old Testament law of divorce was modified by Christ (Matt. 5:31, 32; 19:8–9).

If subsequent revelation limits the intended recipient or application of a teaching, we must consider that limitation authoritative.

Furthermore, a whole class of Old Testament teaching may be set aside. When a class of commandments or instructions is set aside, it is not necessary to seek for the abrogation of specific commands—all norms within that class must be evaluated in the light of later revelation.

For example, when the sacrificial system was done away in Christ, according to the author of the letter to the Hebrews, the entire ceremonial function of the law as pointing to the coming Messiah was done away and is no longer applicable. In Galatians, Paul not only disallows circumcision as a necessary sign of a covenant relationship with God, but along with circumcision the entire system is in some sense set aside. When Christ says that he will build his church (Matt. 16:18) and that his kingdom is not of this world (Matt. 26:52; John 18:36), he is setting aside as normative the entire structure of a civil government for his people, at least in the church era. All foods are reclassified as legitimate for Christians (Mark 7:13; Acts 10:15), so the dietary laws, though perhaps instructive, are no longer normative for God's people.

C. Is This Specific Teaching in Conflict With Other Biblical Teaching?

Because we hold that all Scripture is inspired and therefore true, we seek to discern the harmonious unity that lies behind any apparent conflict. There are a number of ways in which this apparent conflict may be resolved, but one of the legitimate ways is to research the cultural background. If the stronger, clearer, more enduring teaching of Scripture would seem to be contrary to that of a specific passage, insight into the cultural pattern of the day may provide a reason for that conflict.

For example, though there are passages in Scripture that speak of women remaining quiet in church, there are other passages that seem to speak approvingly of women prophets (Acts 2:17; 21:9; 1 Cor. 11:5). An understanding of cultural patterns may help to explain this apparent discrepancy. Research into the role of a woman in the Jewish synagogue, the seating arrangement there, and other cultural factors may alert us to greater sensitivity for cues in the passage itself which would indicate a limitation of the teaching to a specific circumstance. For some men long hair was symbolic of holiness (Num. 6:5) whereas for others it was shameful (1 Cor. 11:14). How is the conflict resolved? Cultural insight should help.

But is this guideline legitimate? Is it not importing into the text extrabiblical data to set aside what the author seems to intend as normative? I am suggesting that the cultural factor be introduced only as part of other hermeneutical guidelines in order to resolve apparent conflicts. If cultural factors are introduced to avoid application of an uncontested meaning, the authority of Scripture itself is under attack. But if the factor is introduced to resolve an apparent conflict of Scripture with Scripture, the purpose is to defend the authority of Scripture and is therefore compatible with the way Scripture views itself.

D. Is the Reason for a Norm Given in Scripture and Is That Reason Treated as Normative?

Many of the teachings, commands, promises of Scripture are given without the benefit of an explanation as to why they are given. No theological ground is provided. For one committed to the authority of Scripture, the only response is faith and obedience. But when a reason is given for the teaching, it may be assumed that the teaching is normative only when the reason itself is treated as universal and permanent.

For example, the people in Thessalonica were told to comfort one another with the teaching concerning Christ's return (1 Thess. 4:18). We rightly assume that this is normative and applicable to all Christians in all ages until the return of Christ. In the same letter, however, Paul tells the people to work with their hands (1 Thess. 4:11). Is this normative? In this case Paul gave a reason: so that you may have a good reputation among the people among whom you live. In other words, the reason given has to do with the culture that valued this kind of labor. That reason is nowhere in Scripture made normative and so we can assume that manual labor itself is not made a universal norm. Paul here in the context and elsewhere explains the basic principle that Christians are not to be idle but to work, to earn their own livelihood. This is indeed a norm of permanent and universal application.

But what of the argument that women were to keep silent in the churches because women did not have an education in that society? Therefore, it is held this command is not normative in societies where women are educated. Here a reason is introduced from outside of Scripture and sets aside the teaching of Scripture. Actually, in 1 Corinthians 11, a number of cultural reasons are urged in support of the teaching (traditions, dishonor, shame, you all judge, seemly, the natural thing, honor, custom). I suppose it is a matter for negotiation how these stated reasons are to be related to the theological reasons that are intertwined in the same argument. If the cultural factors are introduced simply to reinforce the theological reasons for the regulation, surely it must be considered normative. On the other hand, if it can be demonstrated that the theological base is here being applied to a clearly enunciated specific cultural setting, then it should be permissible to reapply the same theological truth differently to a different cultural setting. Hair length and head covering would then be viewed as the way in that culture the universally normative roles of women and men were to be fulfilled. But if a cultural factor not alluded to in Scripture itself is introduced, the potential is almost limitless for setting aside biblical teaching which we do not like on the basis of some cultural reason that would make it dispensable.

E. Is the Specific Teaching Normative as well as the Principle Behind It?

I suppose all would agree that the principle behind a specific teaching is normative. One should not only refrain from saying "raca" but any other derogatory term as well. But the specific teaching itself is normative as well, unless the condition of the teaching is not mandated in Scripture and it does not exist in the situation at hand. Pray for the king (the specific). Pray also for the Governor and President (the principle applied). You do not have to anoint a king to obey the command—just obey the principle. But if you do have a king, obey the specific command and pray for him. Do not shoot him!

But if the condition implied by a command is not mandated in Scripture, only the principle, not the specific command is normative. Wash your brother's feet if they are dirty and someone ought to. But serve him in other ways if he does not need your help with his feet at the moment. Treat oxen kindly if there are any around, but you do not have to move to a farm. Just do not kick your dog.

Does not this open the door to loosening the demands of what we have assumed to be normative? Homosexual behavior was sinful because it was promiscuous, they tell us. That was the condition to which Paul spoke. The principle is that any relationship should be in love and faithfulness. But this interpretation introduces a condition not given in the context or elsewhere in Scripture. To be set aside as normative, the command should have prohibited *promiscuous* homosexual behavior. Then other varieties would have been legitimate. But the condition of the command *in Scripture* is straightforward and prohibits any sexual relations between people of the same sex.

In this way, both the specific teaching and the principle inherent in it are normative unless the concomitant condition for obedience indicated in Scripture itself is not treated as normative. Only then are we free to ignore the specific teaching and follow only the principle.

F. Does the Bible Treat the Historic Context as Normative?

Whatever the Bible records is true; history took place the way it is reported. But to be authoritative as a model for behavior, a God-given norm for all people of all time, any historic event must be so designated by an authorized spokesman for God. Just through being reported as truly happening, no event becomes the revelation of God's universal will.

Many teachings of the Bible are historic-specific and the Bible nowhere teaches that by inclusion in holy writ, behavior is thereby intended as normative. It is certainly recorded on purpose and often that purpose is clear. The Scripture in the context may commend or condemn the behavior; similar behavior may elsewhere be evaluated by Scripture. Certainly the actions of good men, and especially authorized spokesmen for God such as prophets or apostles, should be considered seriously as to whether they are intended as model behavior. Furthermore, if the behavior is not only evaluated but the reason for that commendation or condemnation is given, that historic incident becomes normative to the extent it is illustrative of the truth enunciated.

However, if Scripture does not give the reason for its approval or disapproval or if no value judgment is passed on a particular record of human behavior, we may not make it normative. This is very obvious in passages such as the record of Lot's sexual relationship with his daughters. The daughters' activity is simply reported. But no one has held that this is therefore normative behavior. That which is very apparent in such an extreme case seems to be less apparent in many other historical passages for they are taken as normative by many interpreters. But this is not legitimate.

Consider two varieties of historic-specific teaching.

1. The historic occasion itself

The fact that Job was tempted by Satan does not mean therefore that all temptation is a result of the direct activity of Satan. It does mean that some testing may in fact be the result of Satanic activity. Elihu's speech to Job may make sense or it may not make sense, but it does not have authority as revealed truth. The inspiration of the book of Job only means that the record of his speech is accurate.

Why do interpreters disallow any normative role for the story of Lot's daughters, but insist on the normative place of Pentecost or early Christian "communism?" We do not like to think of the speeches of Job's friends, and particularly of Satan's speeches, as normative but we would very much like to think that Mary's Magnificat is inerrant. Perhaps it is, but that will need to be proved by some other evidence than the fact of its inclusion in the record. We consistently make normative Paul's response to the jailer, "Believe on the Lord Jesus Christ and thou shalt be saved," but we consistently refuse to make normative Christ's response to a similar question of the rich young ruler, "Go, sell what you have, and give to the poor, and come follow me." We resist this even though Christ repeats it elsewhere as a normative statement (Luke 12:33)! Why is it that we tend to feel Paul's behavior is always exemplary and that Peter's behavior is (almost) always the opposite?

An event or specific behavior should not be considered normative on the sole basis that it is recorded in the Bible. It must be evaluated in the light of direct biblical teaching.

2. Teaching directed to a specific individual or group

There are many passages in Scripture addressed to an individual or group. When these injunctions to a specified individual or group parallel general teaching found elsewhere, they may be viewed as normative, but not on their own strength.

When God said to Moses, "Take off your sandals, for the place where you are standing is holy ground" (Exod. 3:5); or when Christ said, "Untie (the donkey and her colt) and bring them to me" (Matt. 21:2-3) all will agree that the command is historic-specific.

It applies only to the individual involved. But this principle can be abused so that all the teachings of the epistles or of Christ are made historic-specific rather than normative. Rather, we must take the teaching of Christ or of the epistles as normative, because that is the way the early apostles took these teachings, unless the context indicates an obvious historical limitation to the person or people addressed.

In cases where this distinction is difficult to make, in the interest of maintaining the independent authority of Scripture, I hold that we should err on the side of assuming the normative nature of the teaching rather than dispensing with it too facilely. To broaden the scope of this principle would be far too costly for the independent authority of Scripture.

G. Does the Bible Treat the Cultural Context as Limited?

Note that I have suggested a principle of interpretation for dealing with teaching that is limited to a specific historic setting. I have not spoken of culture-specific teaching. But is there a legitimate distinction between history and culture? Is not history the record of behavior as well as of events? Is not a culture part of history? Indeed there is a great deal of overlap and interplay so that they are sometimes hard to distinguish. But I believe the distinction is crucial for biblical interpretation.

What is culture?

> Culture in its broadest sense is cultivated behavior, that is, the totality of man's learned, accumulated experience which is socially transmitted, or more briefly, behavior acquired through social learning.[13]
>
> All the culturally created designs for living, explicit and implicit, rational, irrational and nonrational which exist at any given time as potential guides for the behavior of men.[14]
>
> Now the mass of learned and transmitted motor reactions, habits, techniques, ideas, and values—and the behavior they induce—is what constitutes culture. Culture is the special and exclusive product of men, and is their distinctive quality in the cosmos.[15]

As a matter of fact, Kluckhohn and Kroeber have uncovered over 160 different definitions of the term "culture." However, all of these center in the idea of human behavior, morals, values, the way of doing things.

Unevaluated and uninterpreted cultural elements in Scripture may be no more normative than unevaluated and uninterpreted historic events. But the difference is vast. Much of history in Scripture is unevaluated and uninterpreted while virtually all teaching of Scripture is cultural—human behavior, morals, values, ways of doing things are constantly evaluated, prohibited, enjoined. It is not too much to say that the purpose of divine revelation is to create a culture, a special people of God. He is out to change culture, though at the same time He uses human culture as the vehicle for revealing Himself and His truth. The teachings of Scripture are not often "aimed at" history. True, historical events are often demonstrated to be the acts of God but revelation simply records this setting. Whereas most of biblical teaching is directly "aimed at" culture—human behavior is the object of revelation.

My contention is that the historic context of a teaching is normative only if Scripture treats it that way, whereas the cultural context is normative unless Scripture treats it as limited.

As we have seen, history is often recorded without an evaluation as to whether the human behavior is good or bad. God must take the initiative through revelation to make it normative. David's polygamy, uncondemned in Scripture, should not be taken as a normative model, nor should Paul's taking a Jewish religious vow. But the apostles' response, "We must obey God rather than man," though unevaluated in the immediate context, is obviously viewed as a model to follow because of abundant corroborating teaching in Scripture.

It is true that culture, or human behavior as the way of life of a people may also be recorded without an evaluation as to whether it is to be taken as normative. Then "culture" is no more normative than an historical record. Was the behavior of the slaveowner in making his slave serve tables after working in the field all day—and then giving him no thanks—a normative model to be followed in labor-management relations (Luke 17)? But unevaluated cultural behavior is far less common than unevaluated historical events, because the purpose of revelation is to create a way of behavior (culture).

Therefore, value-free or culturally relative records of human behavior are not typical. Rather, cultural change is the point of revelation. Therefore, God must take the initiative through revelation to make cultural teaching not normative.

I hold, therefore, that the teachings of God concerning human behavior are final in authority and to be set aside only when Scripture itself limits the audience intended or the response God desires. If anyone else sets such "cultural" teaching aside he has become the authority sitting in judgment on Scripture.

When I speak of cultural factors I am not speaking of elements traditionally considered by biblical scholars in interpreting Scripture. Incidental and transient Eastern customs that illuminate the meaning of the biblical text are not at issue. The behavioral definition of culture which includes all the thought and behavior patterns of a people is the issue before us. Are such cultural norms all relative to the specific culture in which they are found or does the Bible speak of absolute and universal cultural norms, standards of human behavior?

Most of us may agree that washing another's feet at meal time, leaving ladies hair uncut and other such commands are "culturally specific" and therefore do not apply universally. Specifically, they do not apply to us! However, in recent years we have discovered that this same principle can apply to virtually any teaching of Scripture. But to set aside any of Scripture simply on the basis that it is cultural and therefore valid only for one specific cultural setting is to establish a principle that can be used to set aside any or even all biblical teaching. The interpreter thus becomes the authority over Scripture, establishing as normative for human belief or behavior only those elements of Bible teaching or those principles deduced from Bible teaching which prove universally valid relative to some cultural criteria.

Because of this difference between historical records and culture-based teaching, it is legitimate to say of a historical event that Scripture does not evaluate, "This should not be made normative." But of teaching concerning human behavior (what should happen as distinct from what did happen) it must be said, "This is normative unless Scripture itself limits the intended recipient or application."

A teaching about human behavior may be culture-specific and not normative, but Scripture itself must so designate it or we open the door to total cultural relativism. If the basis for setting aside a teaching as authoritative is simply evidence that it is compatible with one culture and not another, external criteria are used to evaluate Scripture and the intent of the original author is no longer the independent, authoritative word from God.

No, Scripture is not a prisoner of culture. Rather, culture, in the language of biblical authors and the context in which they wrote, is the vehicle of Scripture and at the same time, that very culture is the object of change demanded by Scripture. To disallow any teaching of Scripture because it is "cultural" is actually to make all Scripture vulnerable to this relativistic approach.

Of what value, then, is cultural understanding? Much in many ways.

The chief element in human culture is human language. Words not only *can* convey truth, *only* words can convey abstract truth and broad generalizations. And God chose to safeguard this truth by safeguarding the words through verbal inspiration. These words, reflecting the culture of the writers and the original recipients are the vehicles of propositional truth. Words are not given merely to carry us beyond themselves to meaning and beyond the meaning to the intended impact. No, they are words that in themselves are true and the permanent embodiment of God's revelation. God chose to reveal His truth in the form of words bearing meaning. This form and this meaning are permanent. To study diligently this cultural factor—the language—is of utmost importance, and understanding the entire cultural setting can often clarify the meaning of those words. Of course, we must be modest. We must recognize that our understanding of the culture of that day is limited. And in any event cultural understanding may not be used to set aside the plain meaning of the text itself, for Scripture must be its own authority. But cultural understanding is legitimate to clarify the meaning. It becomes illegitimate when it changes or imposes meaning on the text.

But God's intent was never simply to give us a static deposit of propositional truth. He intended for this truth to function as a living and vital authority in our lives. In order for this to take place we must not only do the task of exegesis to clarify the meaning, we must identify the recipient God intended for each passage and clarify the response He desires. In this task of discerning the present-day significance of the meaning, the task of application, it is essential to understand the contemporary culture. It is essential in enabling us to ask the questions of Scripture that must be asked. It is essential in making application of the principles of Scripture so that the response God desires will be found in our faith and obedience today.

It has been well said that one's understanding of the biblical setting and his understanding of the contemporary setting cannot be isolated from one another. They are so intertwined in our mental process as to make the task of exegesis and application interdependent. Nevertheless, if the Bible is to be the authority for contemporary faith and life, application must be built on exegesis and not the other way around.

Authority is the crucial issue of our times. Perhaps it is the crucial issue of any time. And biblical authority is the crucial issue in Christianity. Central in the issue of biblical authority is the question of error in Scripture. We do well to focus our attention, therefore, on the doctrine of inspiration. But what we gain for the authority of Scripture in the ongoing debate concerning inspiration may well be lost through hermeneutical leakage. It is very well to affirm a Bible without error, but to treat it in interpretation as culturally relative will undermine its independent authority just as certainly as affirming error in Scripture. Against this subtle yet fatal erosion from within, we must hold that all of Scripture is normative for contemporary faith and life except that which Scripture itself limits to other people or times.

What, then, in Scripture is permanent? The words, the concepts, the principles of Scripture are the eternal Word of God. What teaching of Scripture is not permanent or universal? That which Scripture itself treats as limited in its scope must be so treated today.

NOTES

[1]Gregg L. Bahnsen, "Pannenberg and the Hermeneutical Problem of Modern Theology," paper given at the 1979 annual meeting of the Evangelical Theological Society at Bethel Theological Seminary, 1.

[2]Torres and Eagleson, *Theology in America* (Maryknoll, NY: Orbis, 1975), 299.

[3]Harvey Conn, *The Presbyterian Journal* (July 23, 1975): 8.

[4]Emilio Castro, *Occasional Bulletin* (July 1978): 88.

[5]Charles Kraft, *Christianity and Culture, A Study in Dynamic Biblical Theologizing in Cross-Cultural Perspective* (Maryknoll, NY: Orbis, 1979), 204, 208, 211.

[6]Kraft, *Christianity and Culture*, 118-19.

[7]Kraft, *Christianity and Culture*, 231, 250, 254-56.

[8]Kraft, *Christianity and Culture*, 364.

[9]Kraft, *Christianity and Culture*, 178ff., 192, 206, 207, 212, 237.

[10]Richard N. Longnecker, "The Hermeneutics of New Testament of Social Ethics," a paper without a date, pp. 13, 15.

[11]Walter C. Kaiser, Jr., "Legitimate Hermeneutics," *International Council on Biblical Inerrancy Summit Papers* (Oakland, CA: 1978), pp. 6.23-6.25.

[12]Gordon Fee, *Inerrancy and Common Sense*, ed. Roger R. Nicole and J. Ramsey Michaels (Grand Rapids: Baker, 1980), 174.

[13]Felix M. Keesing, *Cultural Anthropology, The Science of Custom* (New York: Holt, Rinehart & Winston, 1965), 18.

[14]C. Kluckhohn and W. H. Kelly, "The Concept of Culture," *The Science of Man in the World Crises*, ed. R. Linton (New York: 1945).

[15]A. L. Kroeber, *Anthropology* (New York: Harcourt, Brace and World, 1948), 8.

A Response to Problems of Normativeness in Scripture: Cultural Versus Permanent

George W. Knight
Professor of New Testament
Covenant Theological
Seminary

A Response to Problems of Normativeness in Scripture: Cultural Versus Permanent

George W. Knight, III

I. HERMENEUTICAL THESIS

The well-ordered presentation of Dr. McQuilkin with its incisive analysis of problems and solutions deftly charts the course for interpreting Scripture in reference to its normativity. His thesis is "that a fully authoritative Bible means that every teaching in Scripture is universal [normative] unless Scripture itself treats it as limited" (pp. 4-14). In positing such a thesis, he is articulating the same absolute and universal language that the apostle Paul has used in asserting the Scripture's comprehensive didactic significance ("All Scripture is inspired by God and profitable for teaching, for reproof, for correction, for training in righteousness; that the man of God may be adequate, equipped for every good work," 2 Tim. 3:16). Since Christ's apostle indicates that this is true of *all* Scripture, then only it itself can teach us what it regards as limited and not universally normative. Even Scripture's teaching of the limited significance of a certain statement is part of its profitability and normativity (cf. the apostle's "But this I say by way of concession, not of command" and his "I wish" followed by the recognition of divergent gifts given by God, 1 Cor. 7:6, 7). In short, the thesis is a self-conscious and exceedingly important application of the recognized hermeneutical principle that Scripture is its own interpreter (modeled for us by our Lord Jesus in a striking way in his response with Scripture to the devil's misuse of Scripture, Matt. 4:5-7; Luke 4:9-12).

II. INADEQUATE APPROACHES

McQuilkin demonstrates the need for reaffirming this basic hermeneutical principle in our day by passing in review seven other contemporary approaches, which, in effect, make something other than the Scriptures the standard for judging the normativity of a

Scriptural teaching. The controlling factor in each approach is summarized by means of the basic question which each asks:

A. How is God at Work Today?
B. What Response Does God Desire?
C. Does This Biblical Teaching Reflect a Universal Cultural Norm?
D. What Is the Normative Principle Which Lies Behind This Specific Bible Teaching?
E. Is This Teaching of Scripture Based on the Nature of God or the Order of Creation?
F. Is This Behavior Directly Commanded or Forbidden in Scripture?
G. Is the Old Testament Teaching Repeated in the New?

The wisdom of McQuilkin's approach highlighting the tendency to allow or make an a priori govern one's evaluation of Scripture is illustrated by the writing of another on the problem of cultural relativity. That author asks the question, "How does one determine what is cultural and therefore belongs only to the first century, and what is transcultural and therefore belongs to every age?"[1] In a footnote to this question, he admits "in all candor" "that this last question is usually answered by our own cultural predispositions." He even seems to illustrate, almost without realizing it, his own cultural predisposition by describing those who think 1 Timothy 2:9-15 is transcultural and applicable today as those whose context is "more strictly patriarchal" and describes those who think otherwise without any such pejorative categorization.

Alerted as this author has made us to the need to beware of "our own cultural predispositions" as the a priori that will govern the way we begin to appraise a passage before we have even studied its content and argument, it is important for us to alert one another when we see that happening even in the statement of our proposed solutions. Again we see this illustrated in the same author.[2] Fee presents six "guidelines for determining that which is culturally relative."[3] Two of the guidelines indicate how the Scripture is to be followed in interpreting itself. Another is not really a guideline but an appeal for Christian charity. It is the remaining three guidelines that illustrate the need for being aware of "our own cultural predispositions."

One of the guidelines is to "note whether the matter in hand is inherently moral or nonmoral, theological or nontheological." The problem with this approach is that it virtually encourages the interpreter to make an a priori judgment on the issue before letting the Scriptures speak on the subject. Fee illustrates this problem by going on to give his "judgment" and declares among other things that "women teaching in the church" is an example "of issues not inherently moral."[4]

Another guideline is to "keep alert to possible cultural differences between the first and twentieth centuries that are sometimes not immediately obvious."[5] Fee illustrates this guideline by saying in effect that the difference in educational opportunities for women in the first and twentieth centuries "may affect our understanding of such texts as 1 Timothy 2:9-15" and the determination of "the role of women in the twentieth-century church."[6] But this cultural difference is not the reason the apostle gives for women not exercising authority over and teaching men in the church in 1 Timothy 2:9-15. The seriousness of this approach may be seen in Kenneth Kantzer's editorial in *Christianity Today* in which he argues that this educational factor, which is not presented as a reason or argument in the text of 1 Timothy 2:9-15, may in effect set aside Paul's appeal to the creation order and thus may allow Kantzer to declare that this passage is not normative today for the question of women's ordination to the teaching or ruling offices in the church.[7] Kantzer does the very thing McQuilkin has indicated in principle is contrary to Scripture's own unique authority ("Here a reason is introduced from outside Scripture and sets aside the teaching of Scripture" p. 233). The havoc of this position is not only what it does to the principle of Scripture interpreting Scripture and to Scripture's normativeness for all time in regard to this question, but also that it by logical implication must concede that the apostle erred in this teaching even in his own day by asserting a universal ("I do not allow a women to teach or exercise authority over a man") which this position must logically and consistently insist is not universal in his own day in reference to women such as Priscilla who, by being adequately educated, could and should be allowed to teach men publicly in the church.

As a last illustration of the need to be more self-critical, we will take one more guideline from Fee, namely, "One should first determine what is the central core of the message of the Bible and distinguish between that central core and what is dependent upon and/or peripheral to it."[8] Fee himself is sensitive to the dangers to which this may lead by adding immediately his caution, "this is not to argue for a canon within the canon."[9] The problem is that this very approach, especially as the first guidelines of determining that which is culturally relative, has, in the very area Fee has used to apply these questions, women's role in the leadership of the church, been used to set Scripture over against Scripture and to choose for a canon within the canon. Galatians 3:28 is surely part of the central core of the message of the Bible and it teaches that there is no ethnic or religious, social, or sexual distinction among humans in reference to believers being "all one" in the one seed, Jesus Christ. But unfortunately it is presumed by some that this central core passage and its teaching on soteriological standing rules out the possibility of any role distinctions being made by the apostles for men and women in marriage and in the leadership of the church. The distinctions that the apostles do make are then regarded as contrary to the central core, peripheral to it, and thus expendable as either erroneous or culturally relative. This position unwittingly manifests an arrogance that says in effect that our theological deduction and application is superior to the inferior, inconsistent, and possibly erroneous theological correlation and application on the part of Christ's apostles as Christ's appointed and Spirit directed spokesmen (cf. "the things which I write to you are the Lord's commandment," 1 Cor. 14:37).

This last guideline may only ask us to ascertain the Scripture's own distinctives; or it may be misused, as I have sought to demonstrate. We must therefore use it with great care, letting the Scriptures judge us even in the way we are handling its teachings in relation to ourselves and others.

III. GUIDELINES FOR THE APPLICATION OF THE HERMENEUTICAL THESIS

When McQuilkin comes to demonstrating and applying his hermeneutical thesis "that a fully authoritative Bible means that every teaching in Scripture is universal [normative] unless Scripture itself treats it as limited" (p. 230), he does so by posing and answering seven questions:

A. Does the Context Limit the Recipient or Application?
B. Does Subsequent Revelation Limit the Recipient or the Application?
C. Is This Specific Teaching in Conflict With Other Biblical Teaching?
D. Is the Reason for a Norm Given in Scripture and Is That Reason Treated as Normative?
E. Is the Specific Teaching Normative as well as the Principle Behind It?

F. Does the Bible Treat the Historic Context as Normative?
G. Does the Bible Treat the Cultural Context as Limited?

The genius and propriety of these questions is that they each require the interpreter to look to the Scripture and to the Scripture alone for the answers and for any indications of limitations of its teaching. Just as his list of inadequate questions highlighted the inappropriate approach to the Scripture and its normativity, so these questions highlight the appropriate approach to the Scripture and its normativity and give specific examples from the Scripture itself. The only caveat that I would bring to the form of the questions is to suggest that question C, the third question, might better be phrased by adding the words underlined so that it reads: "Is *My Understanding of* This Specific Teaching in Conflict with Other Biblical Teaching?"

IV. 1 CORINTHIANS 11:14—A TEST CASE

In McQuilkin's desire to be fair and irenic in maintaining his undoubtedly sound hermeneutical thesis, he may concede more to cultural relativity and thereby import into rather than derive from the Scripture his appraisal of certain arguments of the Apostle Paul. I refer to his list of what he calls "cultural reasons" urged in support of Paul's teaching in 1 Corinthians 11 - (p. 233). It is not my intention to analyze nor argue the entirety of 1 Corinthians 11:1-16; time and space do not permit. It seems to me that McQuilkin wisely recognizes that this passage contains permanent principles; i.e., the teaching on headship (11:3) based on theological considerations (the Trinity [11:3], man being created in God's image and thereby his glory, and the creation order of how woman is made from man [11:7-9]), and a cultural application in terms of a "covering" for woman while praying or prophesying (11:5,6,10,13) as expressive of this permanent teaching or principle. In effect the apostle ends his appeal for not abandoning or throwing off the culturally significant "covering," which would be tantamount to repudiating the headship principle which it signified, by saying that in the final analysis God has really already provided women with a covering in the hair he has given her ("For her hair is given to her for a covering," 1 Cor. 11:15). Thus, in cultures where the presence or absence of an added covering has no cultural significance in connection with the headship question, the apostle's argument resolves itself into an insistence on a differentiation in terms of the cover provided by the hair itself. Most translations, commentators, and lexicographers have understood his reference to "hair" in verses 14 and 15 to be to "long hair" and since this is also demanded by this context, we will regard it as an accepted given. The conclusion is then that men must not cover their heads with long hair and to do so is a "dishonor" and that it is appropriate for women to utilize long hair as a covering and gift from God and to do so is a "glory."

As a paradigm for this question of cultural versus permanent, I am going to focus on just this question of hair and the arguments used in connection with it. I do so not because I regard this question as the most important in the Bible or for the church today in and of itself, but just because it is so often treated as purely cultural and thus it proves to be a good paradigm because it is one of the most difficult and controverted passages. Fee may again serve as a typical example. "Many of the same Christians insist that men today should not have long hair, because 'nature itself teaches us' this (although it is seldom recognized that short hair is 'natural' only as the result of a *non*-natural means—a haircut!)"[10] But is Paul only arguing from the "haircut practice" of his day? Is that the "nature" to which he appeals? Is he just saying that their own cultural practices bear out what he is saying? If this is true, then it was a kind of *ad hominem* argument for that day and age which has indeed no permanent significance for our age and for Christians today. But if he is arguing from something that is really part of the natural reality as God has ordered it and if he means that this natural order itself teaches us this lesson about men and women, then we may not treat it so cavalierly but must heed it today as well.

Again, we must let the Scripture provide its own answer by ascertaining from it the meaning and significance of the key words and concepts as they are used in this statement. *The* key term around which the whole question turns is that translated "nature" by most English translations. The Greek term which it renders is *phusis*. This term occurs in all thirteen times in the New Testament, of which eleven are in Paul. Within the scope of its basic and central meaning of "nature," these eleven occurrences in Paul reflect a degree of diversity of usage and meaning found in the Greek language of the day. In 1 Corinthians 11:14, the emphasis is on *phusis* as being itself (*autē*) that which teaches or instructs those at Corinth and with a value judgment ("it is a dishonor [*atimia*] to him"). Although 1 Corinthians 11:14 is the only place where Paul uses *phusis* in the nominative and as the subject of the sentence, it is used similarly in

Romans 1:26,[11] along with the related *phusikos* (Rom. 1:16, 17), to denote, as Cranfield has put it, "that order which is manifest in God's creation and which man has no excuse for failing to recognize and respect."[12] Epictetus uses *phusis* in virtually the same way as Paul does in 1 Corinthians 11:14, arguing that nature has distinguished men and women as such by differences in facial hair and voice and this provides a clear indication of the use of *phusis* in this sense.[13] For Paul, of course, *phusis* teaches because nature is God's creation which reveals to man made in God's image certain aspects concerning God and God's ethical order (cf. Rom. 1:16-20, 26, 27, 32; 2:14, 15). It is in this sense that Paul the apostle uses *phusis* in 1 Corinthians 11:14.

How does *phusis* teach the dishonorableness of men having long hair?[14] Either by providing inherently a relative difference in hair length for the sexes and/or by providing ("by nature") a self-consciousness that this difference should be maintained. Lietzmann in his commentary on 1 Corinthians has indicated that it is correct to say, although relatively not absolutely, that nature does provide men with shorter and women with longer hair.[15] A similar indication is given in the article on Hair in the *Encyclopedia Britannica*.[16] Although we may not rule out this consideration from Paul's perspective on how nature functions and thus teaches, it seems however that he is appealing more to the sense of propriety or impropriety in how men and women respectively handle long hair. Verses 14 and 15 speak of nature itself teaching that it is a "dishonor" "*if*" a man has long hair and that it is a "glory" "*if*" a woman has long hair. The indication for both men and women is that they should heed this teaching and act accordingly; i.e., men not do the dishonorable thing and wear long hair. Earlier Paul has spoken of the shame for a woman's hair to be completely shorn or shaved (verse 6).

The conclusion to our study finds that the key term "nature" is used here by Paul to refer to the order of "God's creation" and the teaching that it gives is to indicate within men and women how they should respond intuitively and naturally to this question. The implication for the hermeneutics question of cultural versus permanent is to indicate the absolute necessity and importance of letting the Scripture speak for itself without coming with "our own cultural predispositions" or with our own prior evaluation as to whether the issue is inherently moral or theological, or not.

Even when the study of Scripture itself has brought us to this understanding, questions may still be raised which deserve an answer, even when they are raised almost as objections. For example, one may hear or read the quotation "for God sees not as man sees, for man looks at the outward appearance, but the Lord looks at the heart" (1 Sam. 16:7) with the implication implied or assertion added that since this verse says what it does God couldn't possibly have taught what Paul said or at least any understanding of 1 Corinthians 11:14 that seeks to apply it is in error. But is that what 1 Samuel 16:7 teaches as a general truth, that God never has any regard for conduct? Not at all. Rather the passage says in its own setting that man only regards the outward while God goes beyond the outward and is not taken in by or only concerned about the outward. But there is abundant evidence in the Old Testament that God prescribed and proscribed outward appearance and conduct so that even in its Old Testament setting this understanding is in error. To oppose 1 Corinthians 7:14 with 1 Samuel 16:7 is to place in opposition two passages that are speaking about different questions. To do so is to misuse Scripture and to confuse issues.

But again appeal is made to the Nazarite vow (Num. 6:1-21; Judg. 13:5; 16:17; 1 Sam. 1:11), one aspect of which was to allow the hair to grow long so that it might be presented to God (Num. 6:18; Acts 18:18; 21:23-24). The appeal is that what the Nazarite vow allows must be as allowable for any man anywhere, and that the teaching of 1 Corinthians 11:14 or the understanding of it is erroneous or not generally applicable. The Scriptures show, however, that the Nazarite vow in requiring men to let their hair grow long is by that very requirement an indication that this itself is the exception that proves the rule. The Nazarite vow implies that all believing men who are not taking this vow should not be growing their hair long and then it states that when the period of the vow ends the long hair shall be cut off (Num. 6:18–19). God may mandate or allow, contrary to a natural order of things, special actions for religious purposes without that special action nullifying God's normal order for things (cf. 1 Cor. 7:5). Paul certainly sees no conflict between his and others participating in a Nazarite type situation and his teaching in 1 Corinthians 11:14 (cf. Acts 18:18, 21:23-26). So 1 Cor. 11:14 stands as God's normal order for men.

V. CONCLUSION

This test case has demonstrated both the need of checking "our own cultural predispositions" and the need to let Scripture interpret Scripture. It has also demonstrated that unless we observe the two above-mentioned items we are in danger principally and pastorally of mishandling the Word of God and in treating it or regarding it as if it were in error in that which it teaches.

Take this passage as an example. On the face of the text it asserts that nature teaches that long hair is a dishonor to man. When we handle this text as a culturally relative teaching, we end up saying, and Christians end up hearing us say, that "nature" does not teach anything about hair for men and women. We may not mean to give that impression, but we appear to embrace and to communicate that Paul and the Scripture in 1 Corinthians 11:14 is in error or at best only wrote something that first-century, not twentieth-century, people would accept. We have communicated, albeit unintentionally, that the Christian can't really accept at face value what the Scripture says or he can only understand it after the expert has explained it.

Finally, consider the pastoral opportunities the church has for knitting parents and children together, and bridging the gap between the older and younger generations by bringing them all in submission to this Word of God through opening it up and teaching it, rather then dismissing it as cultural. Think of the moment of truth when Christians, and even some non-Christians, said that it seemed unnatural to them for men to wear their hair as long as women, some but not all reaching out from their inner sensibilities to 1 Corinthians 11:14. It is true that the sensitivity sometimes came in a culturally relative and stereotyped crew-cut type reaction. It is also true that some men were only following the styles of their generation naively and without thinking, even though for some of their generation and for some of them the long hair was a situation in which they more or less consciously sought to express their rebellion and their opposition to authority.

What were some of the failures of the church in that moment of truth? May we not learn by reviewing that history? Some properly appealed to 1 Corinthians 11:14 but failed to explain it and to encourage an understanding and willing response. Some in properly appealing to the text failed to recognize that Paul speaks about a principle which is bounded by two extremes and which has leeway in the middle. To summarize those extremes, we may say that the apostle opposes women going to the extreme of having their hair shorn or shaved and he opposes men wearing their hair as long as is possible and glorious for a woman. Within those parameters lies the principle of differentiation between men and women.

Some sided with the young men either because they thought the person was more important than even the Scripture's teaching, or because they had some appreciation for the breaking out of or away from tradition, or because they thought there was no issue at all either because they had not thought of 1 Corinthians 11:14 or because they regarded it as culturally relative. Some sided with neither or thought they could best bridge the gap by assuring both that it wasn't an issue. Some berated and belittled Christians and non-Christians who felt such long hair for men was unnatural and laughed at their naive appeal to 1 Corinthians 11:14. The tragedy of much of this, and we can learn from our mistakes and involvement, was that rather than going through the trauma and agony of the moment of truth by fully struggling with this Scripture passage and coming out stronger Christians more sure of the transcultural truth of God's inerrant Word, many came out less sure and less trustful of the reliability of the Bible as the Word of God for the real life situation and became more dependent on the wisdom of themselves and the world, "our own cultural predispositions."

Each action, each decision has the potential of setting in motion or becoming part of and carrying on a trend or direction. The trend today is to regard a larger and larger segment of the Scripture as culturally relative, a priori, because of course it was given in and through a different culture than that of today. But all revelation from God has been given and only given through a culture and in a cultural form usually different in some way from that of today. This gives no a priori for cultural relativity over against permanence. Rather, since the message of the Scripture is addressed primarily to man as man, to man as sinner, to man as saved, to man as the one who must be obedient to the God who is the same yesterday, today, and forever, and not to man primarily because of or in a culturally distinct or unique situation, we may appropriately expect that its message will apply to man in the cultures of this day and age and in the cultures of tomorrow.

It is the Scripture itself that should lead us to join McQuilkin in offering his thesis "that every teaching in Scripture is universal unless Scripture itself treats it as limited."

NOTES

[1]Gordon D. Fee, "Hermeneutics and Common Sense: An Exploratory Essay on the Hermeneutics of the Epistles," *Inerrancy and Common Sense*, ed. Roger R. Nicole and J. Ramsey Michaels (Grand Rapids: Baker, 1980), 173.

[2]Fee, "Hermeneutics and Common Sense," This author is *not* being singled out for criticism. Rather his work is only being used to illustrate how even when we are most concerned for the Scripture's authority and proper interpretation, as he is, we must be most critical of ourselves, our own cultural predispositions, the biases we unconsciously bring in interpreting. Fee is incisively critical of Lindsell, almost ruthlessly so, as if to distance himself from Lindsell (p. 161) and is equally so to others' inconsistency as he perceives it (p. 163f.) but seems to be quite a bit less incisive, as we all unfortunately are, in being self-critical.

[3]Fee, "Hermeneutics and Common Sense," 174.

[4]Fee, "Hermeneutics and Common Sense," 174.

[5]Fee, "Hermeneutics and Common Sense," 175.

[6]Fee, "Hermeneutics and Common Sense," 175f.

[7]Kenneth S. Kantzer, "Women's Role in Church and Family," *Christianity Today* 25 (1981): 254.

[8]Fee, "Hermeneutics and Common Sense," 174.

[9]Fee, "Hermeneutics and Common Sense," 174.

[10]Fee, "Hermeneutics and Common Sense," 164, underlining, quotation marks, and exclamation point are his.

[11]So Walter Bauer, William F. Arndt, F. Wilbur Gingrich, and Fredrich W. Danker, *A Greek-English Lexicon of the New Testament and Other Early Christian Literature*, 2d ed. (Chicago: University of Chicago Press, 1979), 869, who give the specific meaning for these two places as "nature as the regular natural order."

[12]C. E. B. Cranfield, *A Critical and Exegetical Commentary on the Epistle to the Romans, the International Critical Commentary*, 2 vols. (Edinburgh: T. & T. Clark, 1975), 1:126.

[13]Epictetus, I, 16, 9ff.; text and English translation made available by W. A. Oldfather, *Epictetus, The Loeb Classical Library*, (Cambridge: Harvard University Press, 1961), 1:110-11. Epictetus ends this section by saying "Wherefore, we ought to preserve the signs which God has given; we ought not to throw them away; we ought not, so far as in us lies, to confuse the sexes which have been distinguished in this fashion."

[14]Note the citation in BADG, *Greek Lexicon*, p. 869, as the last item under 1 Corinthians 11:14, "*phusis* as well as *nomos* prescribes long hair for women, short hair for men." See also Helmut Koester, *Theological Dictionary of the New Testament* edited by Gerhard Friedrich (Grand Rapids: Eerdmans, 1974), 9:272, who says that *phusis* in 1 Corinthians 11:14 "represents the general order of nature and its only task is to remind us of what is seemly and becoming."

[15]Hans Lietzmann and Werner Georg Kummel, *An die Korinther I-II, Handbuch zum Neuen Testament 9* (Tubingen: J. C. B. Mohr, 5th ed., 1969), p. 55.

[16]"Hair," *The Encyclopaedia Britannica* (New York: Encyclopaedia Britannica, 11th ed., 1910 and 13th ed., 1926), 9:823. The article gives as an example the following: "Among European men the length rarely exceeds twelve to sixteen inches, while with women the mean length is between twenty-five and thirty inches. . . ." It indicates that among other racial groups and types of hair, differences are not noticeable.

A Response to Problems of Normativeness in Scripture: Cultural Versus Permanent

Alan F. Johnson
Professor of New Testament
and Christian Ethics
Wheaton College

A Response to Problems of Normativeness in Scripture: Cultural Versus Permanent

Alan F. Johnson

In the first place many good things can be said about McQuilkin's paper. He has tackled with courage a very difficult and little researched but highly important area of contemporary hermeneutics. His thesis is clearly presented, amply illustrated, and passionately pleaded. He is rightly concerned over any encroaching relativism in biblical authority introduced through the door of cultural hermeneutics. McQuilkin not only affirms the absolute and final authority of the Bible so that what Scripture teaches God teaches, but he wants to bring the discipline of the interpretation and application of Scripture under this same biblical authority. This approach will eliminate a type of cultural relativity that destroys the full authority of Scripture. The author calls attention to the dearth of discussion on the matter of how Scripture is to be applied correctly. The paper also amply demonstrates that some scriptural teaching is culturally limited and not universal. With all these matters I am in wholehearted agreement.

Furthermore, McQuilkin has rightly emphasized the need to seek the original meaning of the text in its cultural form through grammatical-historical exegesis, as well as to identify the recipient intended for each passage, and to understand the specific response God desires. Finally, in order to apply the text faithfully, he sees the need to understand our own contemporary culture. He has called for the priority of exegesis over the application of the text. While these matters are not new, McQuilkin has correctly chosen to re-emphasize them in the present discussion.

The author has impressively identified and described the various positions held today on the question of the cultural limitations of biblical teaching. To my knowledge these various contemporary views have not been brought together in any previous Evangelical discussions of this issue. We are indebted to McQuilkin for this service.

However, my primary assignment is not to elaborate on all the good things that are said in his paper, but to offer some response and critique of the ideas and content of the proposal. My response will first trace briefly the thesis and main flow of the paper, then offer several broad points of critique followed by an evaluation of the content, and finally close with some proposals for further directions in the light of the critique I have offered.

I. THESIS AND FLOW OF THE PAPER

If I have understood McQuilkin correctly, his main thrust is that any information, concept or principle that is not part of an explicitly biblical statement cannot be introduced either to explain the original meaning of a text or to separate its meaning from its cultural form as the text is applied to the contemporary Church. The thesis of the author is that "a fully authoritative Bible means that every teaching in Scripture is universal unless Scripture itself treats it as limited." (p. 230). This means that not only the principle that lies behind the specific cultural teaching, but both the principle and the cultural form are normative unless the Bible itself states some limitation. Only if we follow this approach, argues McQuilkin, can we preserve the full biblical authority against cultural relativism due to the modern incursions of the social sciences into the field of biblical hermeneutics.

The first major section of the paper identifies and describes seven different contemporary approaches to the problem of what is universal and what is local in biblical teaching. Each of these views are deemed to contribute more or less to the erosion of full biblical authority since they introduce principles for distinguishing the permanent from the limited which the Bible itself does not state.

In the second and final section of the paper McQuilkin enumerates seven questions that he suggests we ask any text under examination in order to ascertain its normativity for the church today. These questions are designed to query the biblical text itself to see if there is anything in the passage that would directly indicate that the teaching is limited. If no such indicators are found, then the teaching and the cultural form in which it is expressed is to be understood as universally binding on the church for all ages. Again, only by adhering to the thesis that the Bible is always universal in both message (principle) and cultural form unless the Scripture itself limits itself can we be preserved from undermining the permanent teaching authority of God's Word.

II. CRITIQUE

Because of space, I must limit my remarks considerably, and focus on the chief problems which in my opinion render the main thesis of the proposal unacceptable. Certainly any word in this area cannot be the last, since Evangelicals are just beginning to say the first words. Hopefully, a fruitful dialogue is now commencing.

Broader Issues

There are several more fundamental issues which the paper raises. Before looking at a critique and evaluation of both the seven contemporary views cited and the seven guiding questions advanced as McQuilkin's own thesis, these more basic matters should be addressed.

1. In the first place, the controlling thesis of the paper is suspect on two counts. Let us repeat McQuilkin's thesis in his own words: "My thesis is that a fully authoritative Bible means that every teaching in Scripture is universal unless Scripture itself treats it as limited" (p. 230). Thus, each of the seven contemporary views that the paper analyzes (p. 230) is judged unacceptable because the principle advocated in each case is "nowhere enunciated in the Bible" (p. 227).

The first obvious problem with this thesis is that it is self-defeating. Where does the Bible itself teach us that every teaching in the Scripture is universal unless the Scripture itself treats it as limited? McQuilkin's thesis, while it attempts to rely more heavily on the independent authority of the Bible, is itself also an inference based on reason, since the Bible nowhere teaches McQuilkin's thesis. This proposal is self-defeating, and therefore should not be taken as the only way to develop a fully God honoring and biblical approach to the question of the normativeness of Scripture. To raise a fatal objection to another view by saying, "Where does the Bible teach it?" is irrelevant since McQuilkin's own view is nowhere taught in the Bible. In fact, the Bible does not explicitly teach any theory about the relationship of the normative to the culturally relative in God's revelation. McQuilkin's view might be right (though I think not), but not on the grounds that the Bible teaches it. It would stand or fall on the basis that the whole Scriptural phenomena points in the direction of his thesis. Once it is clear that the Bible does not directly teach any specific approach to this issue, we can then look at different views more openly, to assess strengths and weaknesses of each, and to formulate guidelines for the interpreter in this important area.

The second problem with the thesis is that the converse could be equally true. There is as much warrant biblically to hold just the opposite of McQuilkin's thesis. Instead of assuming that every teaching of the Bible is universal unless limited by Scripture, why not assume that every teaching of the Bible is a specific Word of God, and thus limited to its historical-cultural context unless the Scripture teaches us that it is universal? As far as I can see, this could be argued from the Bible with a full view of Biblical authority in just the same manner as McQuilkin has done. Yet, I would not want to defend this thesis anymore than I would the author's since either view is too reductive, and hence inadequate in the light of the full biblical phenomena. I will try to demonstrate this in the following pages.

2. Second, one could have wished for McQuilkin to have delineated some theory as to the relationship of divine revelation to human language. The impression we receive from the paper is that God reveals his truth in "words" or in "statements" in the form of propositions. The author states:

> Words not only *can* convey truth, *only* words can convey abstract truth and broad generalizations. And God chose to safeguard this truth by safeguarding the words through verbal inspiration. These words, reflecting the culture of the writers and the original recipients are the vehicles of propositional truth. Words are not given merely to carry us beyond themselves to meaning and beyond the meaning to intended import. No, they are words which in themselves are true, and the permanent embodiment of God's revelation. (p. 239)

While it is important to insist that God's truth is expressed reliably in human language, the overemphasis on "words" in McQuilkin's view of revelation tends to restrict God's truth disclosure to propositional "statements." But can we limit the rich way that God discloses his Word to merely propositional statements? What becomes then of the diverse literary genres in the Bible as poetry, parable, story, and symbolic-apocalyptic? In such forms it is scarcely possible to find mere "words" that are true. God's truth is not conveyed alone in any of the specific "words" which go to make up the account. Rather, revelation takes place in whole semantic units of language or speech-acts.[1] As far as I can see, *words* are not true or false in themselves. Words are symbols that point to concepts, to *meanings*. The meaning of a word is conditioned decisively by the total context in which it occurs. Included in this larger context that shapes the meaning of the language is not only the immediate grammatical and literary units of phrases, sentences, paragraphs, sections, accounts, books, but in fact *the whole conceptual framework of the Bible itself.* Furthermore, the meaning is clearly also related to *the specific historical and cultural setting which occasioned and conditioned* the writing.

Now, since the meaning of these words is always culturally

related, as the culture changes the meaning of the same words will also change. For example, today the word "man," whether for good or ill, is gradually coming to mean "male," whereas formerly it usually bore the sense of male and female, or man and woman. Therefore, to quote the old translation of Deuteronomy 8:3, "Man shall not live by bread alone, . . ." is to risk misunderstanding in today's larger culture. To wed permanently the meaning of God's truth to its ancient particular cultural form is to eliminate the possibility of expressing that same precise meaning in any other historical or cultural situation. On the other hand, to reformulate the words need not necessitate abandoning the original form (a view with which McQuilkin charges Kraft, p. 225). The two forms ought to coexist in the church's vocabulary, because the original form (when correctly understood) is the inerrant mode that always serves to judge the accuracy of the multiple cultural reformulations. Our task, then, can never be merely to conserve and transmit the ancient cultural forms of revelation, as necessary as that is. We must also find contemporary cultural forms and language that allow the biblical message to be heard in meaningful terms that correspond as closely as possible with the understanding the original hearers would have received.

McQuilkin correctly concludes that God's revelation transforms culture especially in the area of human behavior. But he is less correct, in my opinion, when he insists that the particular cultural form the revelation originally takes is always frozen, fixed, static from that point onward unless God specifically states that it is local (p. 237). It simply does not follow that if the point of revelation is to create a way of cultural behavior, that "therefore God must take the initiative through revelation to make cultural teaching not normative" (p. 237). There are good reasons for questioning this logic.

In the first place, God's revelation has different effects on the culture into which it comes. In some instances the revelation of God's will calls for very little perceivable change in the behavior in some areas so that it might be said that God's truth *affirmed* certain values, norms, and actions within the non-Christian culture. For example, Jesus apparently kept the Jewish lifestyle of his day in many particulars including synagogue worship (Luke 4:16). Likewise, Paul admonished the Philippians to think on whatsoever is honorable, just, pure, lovely, etc. regardless of the source (Phil. 4:8). He also exhorted the Asians to observe the pagan "house-table" rules of his society (cf. Eph. 5:21-6:9). In other cases, revelation sharply *challenged* the behavior style. Thus Jesus condemned the practice of Corban among the Jews (Mark 7:11); the early Church dropped the practice of circumcision for Gentile converts (Acts 15); and John commands believers to "love not the world" (1 John 2:15). In yet other instances, God's truth *transformed* the cultural forms without either affirming existing behavior patterns or condemning them, but instead, altering them to conform to the Lordship of Christ. Thus the practice of holding slaves was altered so that the Christian slave rendered his service to Christ, and the believing master treated the Christian slave as a brother-beloved (Eph. 6; Philem. 16).[2] Thus, because of God's general revelation, not all pagan culture is devoid of expressions of God's will on the behavioral level (Rom. 2:14–15). Neither does revelational transformation of culture mean that the particular cultural form in which the truth is conveyed must be permanent.

In this regard, it would have been helpful for McQuilkin to distinguish *levels of cultural particularity* in the behavior teaching of Scripture.[3] Yet, he is reluctant to do this because the Bible doesn't tell us to do it. Nevertheless, it is obvious that some biblical behavior teaching is quite general, such as "love your neighbor as yourself" or "be kind to one another, tenderhearted, forgiving one another, as God in Christ forgave you." While these injunctions must still be understood in the literary, cultural, and historical situation in which they occur, the exhortation is sufficiently general to be obeyed in any culture. On the other hand, there are other commands that are so highly particular to a given historical situation or specific cultural expression that for the modern reader the injunction is either irrelevant, there being no current cultural parallel (such as eating food sacrificed to idols), or if it is followed literally, it conveys no meaning in modern cultures, or it conveys a different meaning than originally understood (such as women being veiled [covered] in worship services).[4]

Additionally there are areas that lie between these poles where some ambiguity exists as to how much is culturally local and how much is to be taken as universal or general, such as the injunction calling for wives to be silent in the churches. To acknowledge such ambiguity does not necessarily threaten hermeneutics with relativism provided adequate guidelines are developed, and these are consistently applied to the biblical text.

Contrary to McQuilkin's thesis, the cases where Scripture tells us that a specific behavior is limited are not designed to be exhaustive (where does the Bible tell us this?), but rather these instances serve as clues to alert us that other portions of Scripture that are particular in their symbolic cultural form may also be limited, and thus require reformulation into corresponding cultural equivalents. What is required of us as obedient servants of the Word is to study and analyze the biblical phenomena as widely as possible, then to formulate principles, and to apply these principles consistently to the particular cases under consideration. What we seem to learn from the total biblical phenomena, if I may risk a prejudgment, is that form and meaning are intrinsically related but not in an absolute sense that would prohibit the divine revelation from being expressed in different cultural forms especially at the symbolic level. As Marshall's study has shown that "although the message is necessarily expressed in the categories of particular cultures, it can break through the limits of existing cultural categories of expression, and can be re-expressed in terms of fresh cultural categories which may lead to its enrichment."[5]

Perhaps one further remark may be made under this general category of the relationship of divine revelation to human language. McQuilkin draws no distinction between doctrinal teaching and categories of behavioral teaching in the Scriptures. While a strict separation is not justified, it seems reasonable and scriptural to point out that when God reveals theological truth about himself, about man, or the world that this truth, though expressed in culturally laden human language, is not relative to any particular culture. Neither are the moral universals and general moral principles found in Scripture. Here I would put such condemned practices as homosexual sexual acts, extramarital sexual relations, hatred, lying, incest, love of the world, idolatry, racism, the neglect of the poor, revenge, and a host of other biblical teaching. However, when we look at the category of culturally particular expressions of these universals and general principles, we encounter numerous symbols relative to the culture in which they were first expressed. Were McQuilkin to recognize such a distinction, the area of potential cultural relativity in the Bible would be greatly reduced.

3. Thirdly, I fail to find any significant evidence in McQuilkin's paper that he brings the doctrine of creation to bear on his concept of revelation and hermeneutics. Repeatedly the author refers to the "independent authority" of Scripture (pp. 236, 240). Should we gather from this that there is no other expression of divine authority than in the Bible? McQuilkin paints a quite negative picture of the social scientific disciplines of psychology, anthropology, and sociology as they may correlate with and complement the biblical exegete and theologian's task. These disciplines are described as having

"moved in and may soon take over" (p. 219). We gain the impression that Evangelicals who utilize the insights of the human science disciplines in hermeneutics are suspect of undermining the "independent authority of the Bible" (p. 227). But what does the author mean by the expression "independent authority" of the Bible? If it means an autonomous, sole authority over the Christian faith and life, this can scarcely be an adequate Evangelical view. On the other hand, if it means that the Scriptures are the supreme and final authority among other authorities, well and good. This latter view would be compatible with both a high view of biblical authority and a positive view of the role of behavioral sciences in hermeneutics and theologizing. Should we not recognize that creation itself is a continual source of God's truth? Augustine and Luther, among many others, recognized that wherever truth is discovered, whether in the Bible or without, it is to be owned as God's Truth.[6]

It seems impossible any longer to ignore the fact that hermeneutics is both a cross-cultural and a cross-disciplinary enterprise.[7] While knowledge from all the sciences must be viewed critically, ideally the biblical exegete and theologian works in dialogue with the social scientist. Each aids and complements the other in his or her special contribution to understanding God's total revelation. I fault Kraft as an anthropologist for his meager dialogue with the biblical exegetes and theologians as well for overexaggerating the role of the behavioral scientist in hermeneutics and theology. They could have helped him in understanding the biblical text and biblical world, and saved him from a number of exegetical and theological weaknesses. On the other hand, I fault McQuilkin for his meager dialogue with Evangelical scientists like Kraft who could have spared him numerous inaccurate generalizations about modern understandings of culture, linguistics, and anthropology as well as his underemphasis of the significance of these disciplines to hermeneutics and theology.

4. Finally, there appears throughout the paper the assumption that there is a "plain meaning" to Scripture that is clear and unambiguous. This plain meaning, that is ascertained simply by examining the Bible itself, cannot be set aside by any cultural understanding (p. 239). McQuilkin argues that an understanding of ancient cultural factors may legitimately "clarify" the meaning of a passage of Scripture (p. 239), and contemporary cultural perceptions may aid in the application of the message to modern audiences. But he denies that any cultural understanding, ancient or modern, may be allowed to challenge the *plain meaning* of the text. McQuilkin states, "If an

understanding of some biblical cultural context or some contemporary cultural form is used to contravene the plain meaning of the text, Scripture itself is no longer the authority" (p. 222). Apparently for McQuilkin, the only time when extra-biblical cultural features can be legitimately admitted into the interpretive process is when a conflict in biblical teaching occurs, such as when Paul speaks on the one hand approvingly of women prophets in the church at Corinth (1 Cor. 11:5), but also gives the exhortation for wives to remain silent (1 Cor. 14:34). Here the author allows nonbiblical cultural features to be introduced to solve the difficulty (p. 232). But, again, this can only be done if the cultural features do not subvert some "uncontested meaning" the text already conveys (p. 232).

Here I think is a major difficulty with McQuilkin's whole understanding of culture and hermeneutics. The biblical text, on the one hand, already possesses intrinsically a clear, plain, uncontested meaning that is derived by simply comparing one passage of Scripture with another. Cultural or historical understandings of the biblical author's world or insights into our own pre-understanding cannot alter this plain meaning. At best it can only *clarify* the text or resolve conflicts in the biblical teaching. Yet, on the other hand, McQuilkin urges us to see the text "in the cultural context of the author and his original audience as helpful in establishing the meaning of a passage" (p. 222). Are these two assertions compatible? I think not, at least in the way McQuilkin presents his case. In his zeal to protect the biblical teaching from all relativism, the author has produced the classic argument where he is right in what he affirms, but wrong in what he denies. A few comments along this line may sketch the direction of my objections.

In the first place, the doctrine of the *perspicuity* or clarity of Scripture which has its roots at least in the Reformers had to do, I am told, with the *Bible's basic message of salvation* by grace through faith and the basic outline of Christian obedience. Such themes are repeated so often under a variety of literary, cultural, and historical situations that the person with little or no education, who simply reads or hears a reliable translation of the Scriptures, can understand the Bible's main teaching on these matters. The early churches' Rules of Faith including the Apostle's Creed provide a helpful reference for this understanding of the perspicuity of Scripture. They are worthy attempts to state what all Christians believe is the *plain meaning* of the Bible. In such matters it is perfectly appropriate to affirm that no ancient or modern cultural information can contravene these basic affirmations. But to extend this clarity of the basic themes to embrace whole systems of doctrine and practice including specific matters such as male-female role relations, the form of church government, the meaning of the parable of the good Samaritan, or many other biblical texts and themes seems to savor more of a rationalistic and enlightenment mentality (truth is "clear and distinct ideas") than a biblical and historically Christian mind-set.

To offset the idea that Scripture could be interpreted only by the elite church clergy, who at times imposed on the biblical texts their own views and extraneous philosophical systems with excessive allegorizations, the Reformers insisted that the Bible in its message of salvation can be understood by all Christians (priesthood of all believers), and is self-interpreting. However, they also insisted that the message of the Scriptures as the Word of God was tied up with the meaning of the biblical author's language in its ancient cultural and historical sense.

To use the principle of the clarity of the Bible to deny that the sense and meaning of the ancient writers is inseparable from the whole literary, cultural and historical context in which they wrote is to risk losing the true Word of God for our own supposed "plain meaning" of the text. What often happens *defacto* is that we impose our own theological system or cultural perspective on the text, and call this the "plain meaning" of the text. As Padilla points out, the task of the interpreter is to "let Scripture speak without imposing on it a ready-made interpretation. This does not mean, of course, that total objectivity is possible." But he is quick to add that "unless objectivity is set as a goal, the whole interpretive process is condemned to failure."[8] Thus the interpreter strives to understand the objective meaning of the text by bringing the full ancient context to bear on the passage. Not until I as an interpreter have brought all the resources available to the text, can I indicate the probable more objective sense. Until the last stage is reached, the interpreter must be willing to have his/her understanding corrected, or even reversed by the evidence.

Secondly, modern hermeneutics has rightly emphasized the role the modern interpreter himself/herself plays in the way the text is read. At this point I find Kraft's discussion of "plain meaning and interpretational reflexes" quite helpful and convincing. Kraft points out that since the Scriptures were not written for our culture, but for the ancient culture, they assume a number of cultural matters which are not mentioned in the text. These assumed items are necessary for the sense of what is being communicated. But in another cultural context, these same features may not be assumed. Think, for example, of a modern newspaper description of a local wedding. Elaborate remarks are made concerning the bride's attire, but nothing is usually said about the groom's clothing, and nothing is stated about the congregation. We simply assume that the groom and others present were clothed appropriately. Yet, in an entirely different culture than our own, someone reading the same account may conclude that no one else was dressed! When someone reads the Bible, which was written from an Eastern more Oriental perspective, from a Western cultural set of assumptions the so-called plain meanings that arise are often misleading unless the statements in Scripture are very general.[9]

Other interpreters have emphasized this same point by using terms such as "pre-understanding" or the interpreter's "horizon" in contrast to the biblical writers' horizon or culture. Thisleton, for example, points out how the modern interpreter's cultural biases both help and hinder in assessing the ancient writers' "intended meaning."[10] Thisleton, Packer, Padilla and other Evangelicals have wisely suggested that we use what amounts to a hermeneutical circle consisting of a continual dialogue between (1) the interpreter's own historical situation, (2) the interpreter's world-view, (3) Scripture itself understood from the biblical authors' viewpoint, and (4) our theological formulations.[11] Packer has rightly argued that basic to the Evangelicals' pre-understanding is his understanding of the inerrant nature of the Bible's inspiration.[12]

What seems, then, to be called for is first of all the distancing of ourselves from the biblical text by a thorough examination of the Bible's literary, cultural, historical, and theological context. This is to be followed by a serious reflection on our own contemporary cultural predispositions, values, practices, etc. Only then can we fuse the two horizons, the biblical and ours.

In any event, exegesis in the fullest sense including insights from both ancient and modern cultural concerns must be able to do more than *clarify* the text; it must be able also to modify and even *change* our understanding of certain biblical teachings. Otherwise, we are bound to human ecclesiastical traditions and our own provincial view of Scripture. It is not the use of sound exegesis that includes extra-biblical cultural understanding that leads to the weakening of biblical authority and to relativism. The problem stems, rather, from the misuse of the discipline in the hands of those who bring to it either faulty assumptions about the nature of Scripture or incompetence in the process of hermeneutics.

FURTHER OBSERVATIONS AND CRITIQUE

We may now briefly examine McQuilkin's analysis of seven contemporary positions on the problem of the normativeness of Scripture vis-a-vis cultural particularity. His *first analysis* (A) focuses on the liberation theologians' view of praxis as a starting point for biblical interpretation (pp. 222-24). Here I am in agreement with the author. While I think we have much to learn from certain of the Latin American theologians, such as Segundo, Sobrino, Boff and others, I feel that their uncritical adoption of the Marxist analysis of society as a starting point for reading the Bible is not acceptable. On the other hand, neither do I find an uncritical adoption of the free enterprise system or Western individualism as an acceptable starting point. Harvey Conn's penetrating appraisal of liberation theology and the need for Evangelical self-criticism should be pondered carefully by every thinking Evangelical.[13]

McQuilkin's *second view* (B) involves the recent contributions of Charles Kraft, Professor of Anthropology and African Studies, School of World Mission, Fuller Theological Seminary (pp. 224-26). Kraft is viewed as one who has "many brilliant insights of value for cross-cultural communication, but whose basic approach is relativistic, and the end effect is to make not only the application of Scripture, but its interpretation as well relative to some contemporary culture" (p. 225). Kraft is concerned to discover the response in the receptor that the original form of the revelation would have evoked, and to find the dynamic equivalent of this response in modern cultural forms. McQuilkin charges Kraft with not only relativizing minor biblical forms, such as the form of church government (does McQuilkin have the truth on this?), but also with major doctrines such as whether people can be saved without the knowledge of Jesus Christ, or whether infanticide and even polygamy may be allowed today among the church leaders in certain cultures.

While I have many problems with Kraft's exegesis and theology, as to the matter of salvation without the knowledge of Christ, it seems to me this has been a theological position held by Christians since earliest times, and advocated by staunch Evangelicals in our own day.[14] On the issue of infanticide and polygamy, McQuilkin misunderstands Kraft's point. Kraft does not approve of these practices. Instead, he argues that they are peripheral matters, and should be first understood from the point of view of the worldview of the people who are newly receiving Christianity. When their worldview changes under the impact of Christian faith, these matters can gradually be changed.[15]

The only substantial critique of Kraft's approach that is offered is that Kraft does not hold that the original verbal form and meaning of the text is authoritative for us today (p. 225). But while I find many points of disagreement with Kraft, I cannot fault him for his view that all language including the language of revelation is culture-related for its meaning.[16] As cultures change, the language signification also changes, and if we are concerned to preserve the original meaning for different cultures, this requires finding new formulations of the language. As one reads Kraft, it is possible to dismiss him too quickly by focusing primarily on his concept of receptor response rather than on the significance of his discussion for understanding the meaning intended by the biblical author. What Kraft calls the "eternal message" is precisely what McQuilkin is after in his emphasis on the normative authority of Scripture. Where the two differ is over whether the *form* the message takes is also "eternal" (unless God designates its limitation).

The *third view* discussed (C) involves certain unidentified Christians who find only those teachings normative which reflect "universal cultural formulations" (pp. 225-26). But since the Bible does not distinguish between the cultural universal and the culturally specific, McQuilkin feels it would be well-nigh impossible to identify any cultural universals. To attempt to do so would render most of the Bible culturally relative, and thus would annul the independent authority of Scripture.

But I fail to see why it follows that to seek to identify cultural universals descriptively, as an anthropologist might do, and to relate them to revealed cultural universals would jeopardize biblical authority. Why are the two incompatible? If the God of Scripture is also the God of creation who reveals his norms to all people through the witness of creation (Rom. 1:20, 21, 32; 2:14-16), then certain fundamental norms should be describable among the human family. I am not competent to say how wide spread is the consensus, but David Little cites Ralph Linton (1952) and Marshall Sahlins (1959) as two competent contemporary anthropologists who have isolated a number of universal moral principles found among all human communities from which specific local norms are derived.[17] Certainly such information, though subject to revision, cannot be totally ignored by Evangelicals who seek to integrate their Christian faith with God's creation order and his revelation through that creation. We have nothing to fear from the truth regardless of where it may appear or from whose lips. The Scripture remains for Evangelicals the final authority. But, because of the doctrine of creation, as I have indicated earlier, the Bible is not our only point of reference for the knowledge of God's will. In fact, we find in Scripture itself more general principles out of which more particular injunctions are formed. For example, Paul admonishes the "strong" Christian at Rome to stop eating meat or drinking wine (particular injunctions) if it creates a stumbling block to another believer. He then states that to do so under the circumstance he outlines would not be to "walk in love" (general principle) toward the "weak" believer (Rom. 14:13, 15, 21). Jesus also summarizes our many obligations to God and neighbor by saying "you shall love the Lord your God . . . You shall love your neighbor as yourself" (Matt. 22:37-39, cf. Rom. 13:9).

A *fourth view* (D) which McQuilkin concedes does take seriously the authority of Scripture is Richard Longenecker's position that attempts to derive principles from the biblical particulars and to make these principles normative (pp. 227-28). McQuilkin objects to this approach because he says that "I find it nowhere enunciated in the Bible. Where in Scripture are we told that the specific declarations of God's truth and God's will for man are not normative, but only the principles which lie behind them?" (p. 228). I have already pointed out the fallacy of this kind of objection since the Bible never tells us either that the specifics are normative. Longenecker's approach has a twofold merit. First, it seeks to allow the whole biblical phenomena to instruct us on this matter. Secondly, it includes the necessary recognition that language and practice are culturally related and are *not* universal at certain levels of expression. I believe that Longenecker's approach contains very fruitful insights for Evangelicals as they seek to honor Scripture, and also to grapple with this complex area of hermeneutics. However, caution is needed. For example, what would the general principle be that lies behind the specific teaching about "baptism for the dead?"

A *fifth view* (E) identified with two Evangelicals, Walter Kaiser and Gordon Fee, distinguishes between theological principles rooted in the nature of God and non-theological matters, and between moral principles rooted in the ordinances of creation and non-moral matters. It would seem that this is both a necessary and valid distinction to make in assessing the normativeness of a matter in Scripture, but

McQuilkin objects along the same line offered to Longenecker's approach: "Where did it come from? . . . on what grounds do I make such a distinction?" The answer to McQuilkin is that the distinction is made on the grounds of the *whole biblical viewpoint,* not merely on the basis of some *statement* in Scripture. Scripture informs us in many different ways as we consider the whole sweep of biblical revelation.

In a further objection to this view, McQuilkin asks whether the fall of man is on their basis theological or nontheological? In the first place, Kaiser and Fee are not talking about all biblical teaching, but at this point only about "commands," "principles for behavior," etc. It is very important to distinguish these matters. The fall of man is a doctrinal teaching of Scripture, and while man's fallen condition may find different cultural expressions, the reality of man's broken relation to God is universally true. When, however, behavioral norms are under consideration, it is appropriate to ask whether these norms are related to God's revealed character or to his purposes for the creation. The ordinance of the Lord's Supper is unquestionably related to the theological significance of Christ's death and resurrection and the reality of the Church's participation in this grace. The *form* of the ceremony (bread and wine) is explicitly linked by Christ to the salvation-history events rooted in the Passover and Exodus events. Its continuing significance is kept alive by a select community of people who continue to embue the cultural symbols with meaning. The Protestant Church has recognized only two such ordinances commanded to be perpetually observed by Christians—Baptism and the Lord's Supper. It would be quite unacceptable to build a whole principle of normativeness on these two cases, especially when they are not inherently moral matters of universal significance to all people. The command that wives should be subject to their husbands is a borderline case (as present Evangelical opinion testifies), but not homosexual practice which is regularly condemned as sin in both Old and New Testaments ("those who do such things shall not inherit the kingdom"). Homosexual behavior is contrary to the creation purpose of male-female sexuality. Paul says as much in Romans 1:26.

McQuilkin's failure to bring an adequate doctrine of creation to bear on specific texts is evidenced when he states, "But to set aside any specific teaching simply because its theological nature cannot be proved is to introduce an extra-biblical hermeneutical principle that violates the independent authority of Scripture" (p. 229). On the contrary it is Scripture itself which teaches us, for example, that creation is "good." Therefore when we find prohibitions in Scripture linked to material substances we should ask, "In this particular situation why has God restricted the free use of his good creation?" Being a vegetarian, for example, is *not* morally wrong (except as one condemns a nonvegetarian) and Paul makes this very clear (Rom. 14). A woman's speaking in church cannot be a moral issue (again, except in a given context) because it is *not* a matter of one's ultimate relationship to God—and because, as McQuilkin admits, the New Testament is ambiguous on this matter. The injunction in the Old Testament against wearing a garment of mixed fabrics (Deut. 22:11) cries out for some explanation that would relate this culturally specific prohibition to some larger principle that would connect it to the worship of God or to man's universal obligations to his fellowman. The whole context of the passage and the larger context of the biblical worldview would correctly lead us in this instance to search for some extra-biblical culturally specific situation which would help us to understand, for example, that the wearing of mixed clothing was associated with some pagan idolatrous practice. When the culture changed, the specific teaching lost its significant connection to idolatry. To insist that God's people of every age wear single fabric outfits because "to set aside any specific teaching unless we are told to do so is to introduce a foreign hermeneutical principle that violates the independent authority of Scripture" would seem to lead to an extreme cultural fundamentalism in the name of preserving us from cultural relativism.

A *sixth view* (F.) that makes only what is directly commanded or forbidden the normative is rightly rejected by McQuilkin as too restrictive (p. 229).

Finally, a *seventh view* is presented (G.) whose proponents argue that only that part of the Old Testament is normative which is reaffirmed in the New Testament (pp. 229-30). This view is likewise correctly rejected as excluding the authority of the Old Testament. McQuilkin, however, is not arguing for the normative nature of everything in the Old Testament as he later explains (pp. 230-31).

McQuilkin now turns to seven principles or questions that from his viewpoint we may legitimately ask the biblical text in order to ascertain whether the teaching is limited. A "no" to any of these seven questions will indicate that the scriptural matter under examination is normative both in meaning and form (general and specific). The seven questions are:

A. Does the context limit the recipient or application?
B. Does subsequent revelation limit the recipient or the application?
C. Is this specific teaching in conflict with other biblical teaching?
D. Is the reason for a norm given in Scripture and is that reason treated as normative?
E. Is the specific teaching normative as well as the principle behind it?
F. Does the Bible treat the historic context as normative?
G. Does the Bible treat the cultural context as limited?

A few comments on these proposed questions will complete our critique of McQuilkin's paper.

A. Does the context limit the recipient or application? (p. 230)

This is a good principle. McQuilkin recognizes that the historical situation of Paul's instruction on marriage and singleness affects the normativeness of the teaching (1 Cor. 7). What the author, however, needs to see is that all the literature of the New Testament is occasional. Therefore, the larger context including the historical, cultural, and theological situation must be brought to bear on questions of meaning and normativeness even when the text itself does not explicitly mention all these factors. Incidently, while McQuilkin rightly does not make celibacy normative, he fails, however, to emphasize that singleness is a valid option for today's Christian.

B. Does subsequent revelation limit the recipient or the application? (p. 231)

This is also a valid principle. Yet, we may raise some questions about McQuilkin's exegesis. Has Christ really changed Moses on the law of divorce? Does Paul argue for the abrogation of the whole law *system* in Galatians? How much of the teaching of the Pentateuch is linked to the civil government of the people? Would McQuilkin abrogate all these injunctions including capital punishment? Nevertheless, differences of exegesis do not invalidate this good principle.

C. Is this specific teaching in conflict with other biblical teaching? (pp. 231-32)

Again, I find this a helpful principle that throws us back into the cultural, historical and larger theological context for the meaning of the language used. Yet McQuilkin's restrictions upon introducing cultural factors *only* when there is a conflict and *only* if some alleged "plain meaning" is not set aside is far too restrictive. When carefully exegeted conflicts arise, they serve as clues that indicate that every word from God comes in ordinary human language and addresses itself to specific historical situations. Furthermore, would McQuilkin see a conflict between Galatians 3:20 ". . . there is neither male nor female . . ." and 1 Timothy 2:12 "I permit no woman to teach or to have authority over men! She is to keep silent"? If so, would he permit cultural features to resolve the difficulty?

D. Is the reason for a norm given in Scripture and is that reason treated as normative? (p. 232).

While this principle sounds safe enough, McQuilkin's own criteria may render it suspect since where does the Bible tell us which reasons are cultural and which reasons are universal? He is unable to decide in 1 Corinthians 11 (p. 233). Furthermore, why should we expect the biblical writers to give us reasons for their injunctions even when they are culturally relative except where there is a need to call some special attention to why the behavior is important in this instance. I believe McQuilkin is right in what he affirms but wrong in what he denies. He will not allow the careful study of the full context of the statement including extra-biblical material from the first century cultural, historical and theological occasion to determine the meaning of the text and its consequent normativeness. What should control our exegesis of Scripture is the full evidence in any given case.

Relativism ought to be controlled not by some preconceived theory as to what the text already means but by the full biblical, cultural, historical and theological context in which the truth is given. The interpreter is not licensed, as McQuilkin alleges, to manufacture unlimited cultural reasons "for setting aside biblical teaching." The alternative to thorough and reasonable historical and cultural study is real cultural-bondedness (our own), provincialism and traditionalism in interpretation (shades of the Pharisees?). For example, in 1 Corinthians 11 McQuilkin sees "universally normative roles for women and men" to which hair length and head covering were local expressions. But rather than distinguishing roles could not Paul be distinguishing the sexes in the worship of the church because women were impersonating men in pagan worship practices in the first century? Hair length and head covering were ways in Paul's culture of distinguishing men from women. Women wearing dresses would be a suficient sign in our culture. Without careful and responsible full context concerns, including extra-biblical understanding, we may be in greater danger of relativising the biblical teaching by reading into the text our own preconceived notions as to what the Bible means. In either extreme the Word of God is potentially lost.

E. Is the specific teaching normative as well as the principle behind it? (p. 233)

McQuilkin argues that not only the principle but the specific teaching is normative "unless the condition of the teaching is not mandated in Scripture and it does not exist in the situation at hand" (p. 233). This seems like a good principle for distinguishing the culturally relative from the normative. But what exactly is meant by "unless the condition of the teaching is not mandated in Scripture?" I am in full agreement that every expression of homosexual practice is sinful, and not merely *promiscuous* homosexual activity or homosexual practice by heterosexuals. Homosexual acts under any conditions ought to be be rejected but on different grounds than McQuilkin offers. These acts are not acceptable because the full biblical conceptual and exegetical context under various cultural conditions uniformly condemns the practice as *sinful*. Furthermore, the *evidence* adduced to support the view that certain homosexual acts were not in Paul's mind is not convincing.

As I have pointed out earlier, the larger problem I see in the strict limitation in this principle is that it does not sufficiently take into account the real implicit cultural assumptions in the mind of the biblical writers. We cannot assume that when we read the texts that those same ingredients are present in our minds unless we can know something of the larger biblical context both from the study of Scripture and the study of the world in which the writings occurred.

Finally, is there not another condition beyond the two McQuilkin suggests? Is it only when the condition no longer exists that the principle only may be normative? Or is it not also when the condition though still in existence, has undergone cultural semantic change from the biblical times to the present cultures? For example, "Greet the brothers and sisters with a holy kiss" teaches us that Christians should greet one another with physical contact using the lips. Under McQuilkin's rule the implied conditions are (1) other Christians, (2) occasions of meeting each other, (3) the ability to kiss and (4) the need of Christians to express love to one another. This seems to meet all of McQuilkin's conditions for a normative *form* (kiss) as well as a normative principle (show warm affection to each other when you meet). Does he advocate this or practice it (he did not do this to me the last time we met!)? However, under my suggestion the changed social-cultural meaning attached to expressions of kissing (especially homosexual) within the present American culture would lead us to forego kissing and instead to exchange vigorous handshakes. More seriously, my point is that the form can only be required where the cultural meaning is approximate to the early biblical culture. The same principle may be applied to social institutions and authority structures. As institutions change, the way people relate to one another and the way authority is mediated changes. In a democratic society to protest government or even Supreme Court decisions is not a sign of insubordination to government but a part of the way we relate to this form of societal institution. I would also apply this principle to the family, church, and societal governance structure with regard to the male-female questions of today's culture.[18]

F. Does the Bible treat the historic context as normative?

(p. 234)

McQuilkin argues that if a particular historical episode is evaluated or reasons given for that evaluation, we may treat the instance as normative. Again, McQuilkin is right in what he affirms (evaluated behavior is normative) but wrong in what he denies (unevaluated incidents are not normative). As I have argued earlier this view of revelation is truncated. God reveals his truth through the total context of a passage and not merely by propositional statements. McQuilkin ignores or misunderstands that in Scripture all historical narrative is revelatory and thus theological and ethical in its intent; it is kerygmatic history whether in the book of Chronicles or in Luke-Acts. As Gorden Fee has argued, historical precedent can be normative if it is related to the author's intent to establish precedent. Furthermore, even when the primary intent is not to establish precedent, narrative can have illustrative and pattern value (cf. 1 Cor. 10:1-3).[19]

McQuilkin concludes that we should "take the teaching of Christ or of the epistles as normative, because that is the way the early apostles took these teachings" (p. 236). What does this mean? Where do the apostles make this distinction? Certainly the teaching of Christ as recorded in the historical-theological narrative of the Gospels is normative. But where does the idea come from that the epistles are more normative than "Mary's Magnificat" simply because the latter has a historical frame and is not evaluated in any direct statement?

There are fallacies to this type of thinking. First, it creates an artificial distinction at the practical level between so-called didactic passages and descriptive passages where the former are normative while the latter are historic-specific. Actually much of the so-called didactic is occasional and much of the historical is designed to teach. Secondly, it limits the normative to only one type of literary genre thus ignoring that God teaches us through many different forms. For example, some of Paul's most effective teaching is given by personal testimony that is a *description* of his own experiences.

The *seventh* and final question (G.) asks whether *the Bible treats the cultural context as limited* (p. 236). McQuilkin's contention here to use his own words is that "the historic context of a teaching is normative only if Scripture treats it that way, whereas the cultural context is normative unless Scripture treats it as limited" (p. 237). Under the previous point I offered a critique of the first part of this statement. As to the second part, the following may be said in addition to what was presented earlier in this paper. McQuilkin's distinction between history and culture is fuzzy and in my opinion not convincing. Is not all historical writing cultural and all culture historically structured? History is an act the same as biography, and no person is acultural.

In my opinion, the way to avoid an unjustified cultural relativism is not to advance a rigid wedding of the meaning and culturally particular form of revelation (p. 238). Relativism in hermeneutics ought to be checked when the interpreter develops and applies consistently careful guidelines designed to honor the evidence of the full biblical context including an understanding of the historical occasion and the cultural language. To treat as culturally absolute what God never intended to be universal will just as certainly undermine the full authority of the Bible as an approach that fosters uncontrolled relativism. It will do this by creating a nonbiblical fundamentalism that ultimately imprisons portions of the Word of God within ancient cultural forms irrelevant to the contemporary world.

As far as I can determine, the following cases meet all McQuilkin's requirements for normativeness in today's church.

1. The "holy kiss" in greeting (1 Thess. 5:26; I Peter 5:14)
2. Men lifting up holy hands in prayer (1 Tim. 2:8)
3. OT prohibition against usury (Lev. 25:36)
4. Levirate marriage law (Deut. 25:5-10)

5. Prohibition against boiling a kid in its mother's milk (Exod. 23:19)
6. Speaking in tongues in the church (1 Cor. 14:39)
7. Drinking wine (moderately) for stomach upset and other ailments (1 Tim. 5:23)
8. "Bitter water" test for the adulteress (Num. 6:16-22)
9. Selecting church leaders by throwing dice (Acts 1:26)
10. Anointing the sick with oil (James 5:14)
11. Wives should call their husbands, "lord" (sir) (1 Peter 3:6)
12. Wives should not braid the hair, wear gold, or costly dresses (1 Peter 3:3)
13. Every married couple must bear children (Gen. 1:28)
14. No widow may be eligible for Church relief unless she has raised children (1 Tim. 5:10)
15. Limiting church offices to *men* who are married (1 Tim. 3:1-13)

Many other particular cultural exhortations also would fit McQuilkin's requirements.

CONCLUSIONS AND PROPOSALS

Finally, where does all this leave us? McQuilkin and I both share the concern to maintain the full authority of Scripture. We both recognize that hermeneutics is a crucial area that can lead to compromise and inconsistency in the use of the Bible as the final norm for the life and thought of God's people. We disagree as to the method the church should follow as it seeks to correctly interpret and relate the biblical teaching to our own situation. McQuilkin's approach, I have argued, unduly restricts the use of cultural factors in understanding the biblical message to the narrow context of words and statements made in the immediate context of the biblical texts. This approach may eliminate some of the relativism attached to certain modern interpretations of Scripture. It does so at a twin risk. The intended message of the biblical authors may be misunderstood and God's message to our own age may be obscured as we insist without any biblical warrant that the message and its culturally particular form cannot be separated without destroying the independent authority of Scripture. The result in both cases is a failure to hear the true Word of God and a consequent loss of a more complete obedience to God.

I have argued that there is another alternative, an approach which honors the full authority of Scripture and at the same time takes into account the total language context in which the message is given including the larger biblical, cultural, historical and theological context. Its strict adherence to well-defined guidelines and actual evidence provides the needed corrective to extremes in cultural interpretations. This method, I believe, is more adequate than arbitrarily limiting cultural dimensions brought to the text to those mentioned only in the text. What I believe would further the discussion at this point is a full investigation of the following areas:

1. History of the church's views on the question of the normativeness of Scripture
2. The places and ways in which the Bible itself limits, modifies or abrogates its own teaching as a clue to instruct us as to how we should approach all Scripture.
3. All the various commands of Scripture—to classify and study their nature, levels of cultural particularities and interrelation
4. Identify the various classes of grammatical utterances in the Bible and contexts in which they occur such as Thisleton has begun to do[20]
5. Continue the in-depth examination of the biblical world of both testaments with dialogue as to how these matters aid our understanding of Scripture
6. A critical but positive assessment of the relationship of theology to anthropology as Harvey Conn has recently begun[21]
7. The modern culture *since the Reformation* in an effort to understand how these cultural concerns affect the pre-understanding of the twentieth-century interpreter of Scripture

If these interchanges will stimulate others to go beyond what has been said in these papers, the effort will have been worthwhile and the Church ultimately enriched in its encounter with the living and abiding Word of God.

Let me conclude with an attempt to state (without elaboration) a number of principles which I believe the interpreter might use to determine the normativeness of any biblical behavioral teaching. I have included a number of McQuilkin's suggestions.

PRINCIPLES

1. How does my specific social-cultural and psychological background aid and distort my reading of the scriptural matter?

2. Is the matter theological (affecting our relationship to God) or moral (affecting our relationship to others)?
3. Does the immediate context limit the recipient or the application?
4. Does subsequent revelation limit the recipient or the application?
5. Is the specific teaching in conflict with other biblical teaching?
6. Is the exhortation a general moral principle, or is it a particular cultural directive?
7. If the exhortation is a particular cultural directive, does the immediate context or the larger biblical context or the biblical author's cultural context help to identify the author's intent or the general moral principle behind the particular directive?
8. Are there cultural conditions mentioned in the biblical context or assumed in the author's larger cultural context?
9. Is the particular cultural *form* present today? If so, does it have the same semantic symbol value as in the ancient culture? Is a more appropriate form available to express the same symbol value of the form in the ancient culture?
10. If the teaching is found in poetry, story, apocalyptic symbolism or historical narrative, what is the author's intent in the material? The matter *may* be normative if the larger biblical context affirms it.
11. Is the exhortation related to a social institution? Has subsequent cultural changes affected the way people relate to each other in the institution?

NOTES

[1]Anthony C. Thiselton, "The Semantics of Biblical Language As An Aspect of Hermeneutics," *Faith and Thought* 103 (1976): 115. I believe Carl F. H. Henry contributes to this same problem by limiting truth to propositional statements when he says that "the word truth can only be used metaphorically or incorrectly when applied to anything other than a proposition" (*God, Revelation and Authority*, III p. 429). Thiselton has shown the polymorphorous character of the word "truth" (ἀληθεια) in the New Testament. Only one usage out of six relates to what might be termed truth statements or propositions (*The Two Horizons: New Testament Hermeneutics and Philosophical Description*.) (Grand Rapids: Eerdmans, 1980), 411-15. See note 16.

[2]cf. I. H. Marshall, "Culture and the New Testament," Chapter 2 in John R. W. Stott and Robert Coote, eds. *Down to Earth: Studies in Christianity and Culture* (Grand Rapids: Eerdmans, 1980).

[3]As Kraft has attempted to do in *Christianity in Culture, A Study In Dynamic Biblical Theologizing in Cross-Cultural Perspective* (Maryknoll, New York: Orbis, 1979), 139-43; also his earlier "Interpreting in Cultural Context" *Journal of the Evangelical Theological Society* 20 (1978): 363-67.

[4]Some today distinguish three levels of abstraction or degrees of universality in biblical commands: (1) Universals or Absolutes—applicable in any area of human relations such as love and justice; (2) General principles or area rules which express more specifically the universals applicable in most circumstances; (3) Specific cultural forms or cases (symbolic level), as "males" lifting up their hands in worship or the prohibition against boiling a kid in its mother's milk or the obligation to raise up children with a dead brother's widow. Behavior which is enjoined upon us at the first two levels will apply to all believers in every culture, whereas at the symbolic level the behavior form is relative (not optional) and must be translated into its appropriate cultural equivalent.

[5]I. H. Marshall "Culture and the NT", 26.

[6]See Augustine On Christian Doctrine, 2.18.28: "every good and true Christian should understand that wherever he may find truth, it is the Lord's." Luther observed: "Verily the Decalog is lodged in the conscience. If God had never given the Law by Moses yet the mind of man naturally has this knowledge that God is to be worshipped and our neighbor to be loved," in *Die erste Disputation gegen die Antinomer* (1537), *Werke (Weimer Ausgabe)* 39, Part I, 374.

[7]See William A Dryness, "Putting the Truth in Human Terms" a review of Charles H. Kraft, *Christianity in Culture,* CT (April 18, 1980):40.

[8]C. Rene Padilla, "Hermeneutics and Culture—A Theological Perspective" in Stott and Coote (see note 2), 72.

[9]Kraft, "Interpreting in Cultural Context," 360-63; also *Christianity In Culture,* 131-34.

[10]Anthony Thiselton, "Understanding God's Word Today" Chapter 4 in *Obeying Christ in a Changing World: Vol. I The Lord Christ,* ed. John Stott (Glasgow: Collins, 1977), p. 102f.; idem, *The Two Horizons* (Grand Rapids: Eerdmans, 1980), 107-14; Bruce J. Nicholls attempts to identify these factors under two general categories: (1) supra-cultural factor and (2) cultural factors, *Contextualization: A Theology of Gospel and Culture* (Downers Grove; InterVarsity, 1979), 40-45.

[11]Padilla, "Hermeneutics," 67-77.

[12]James I. Packer, "Hermeneutics and Biblical Authority" *Themelios* 1 (1975): 4. This is an excellent article which unfortunately is little known.

[13]Harvey Conn, "Theologies of Liberation: An Overview" and "Theologies of Liberation: Toward a Common View" Chapters 8, 9 in *Tensions In Contemporary Theology,* ed. Stanley Gundry and Alan Johnson rev. ed (Chicago: Moody, 1979).

[14]See J. N. D. Anderson *Christianity and Comparative Religion* (Downers Grove. Ill: InterVarsity, 1970), chapter 5.

[15]Kraft, *Christianity In Culture,* 360-64.

[16]Kraft's attempt to work with anthropology and biblical interpretation-theology is a relatively new discipline. It will require a long process of critical dialogue

to revise and sharpen the insights of the discipline as they may relate to biblical studies. Kraft is often exegetically and theologically weak, but I find this same fault among some evangelicals who attempt to do philosophical-theology or historical-biblical theology or missiological-theology, etc. The paradigmatic models Kraft uses in his understanding of cultural anthropology are subject to constant revision within the scientific community itself as Harvey Conn has recently pointed out. Not only are McQuilkin's anthropological sources of twenty to thirty years ago near obsolete but the "new anthropology" may also date some of Kraft's working assumptions (Harvey Conn "Theology and Anthropology: The New Dialogue" Unpublished, Annual Church Growth Lectures, School of World Mission, Fuller Theological Seminary, 1981). Kraft's labels such as "closed conservatives" are unfortunate. His work, then, takes a reactionary stance and leads to an overstatement of the functional, relational side of divine revelation. However, I see the same reactionary trend in McQuilkin and Henry (see Henry's review and strong critique of Kraft's book in "The Cultural Relativizing of Revelation" in *Trinity Journal* INS (1980): 153-64). In my opinion they have swung too far in the opposite direction and have overstated the propositional view of truth with its corollary of truth as "objectivity", "plain meaning," or "clear and distinct ideas" with a consequent undervaluing of Scripture's culturalness and relational nature. Kraft's work (as most anthropologists) contains no theory of how meaning is related to form (see William Dryness, "Putting the Truth in Human Terms," 40).

[17]David Little, "Calvin and the Prospects for a Christian Theory of Natural Law," Chapter 6 in *Norm and Context in Christian Ethics*, ed. Gene Outka and Paul Ramsey (New York: Scribner's), 186-190; cf. also Kraft, *Christianity In Culture*, 86-88; see also note 4.

[18]For two slightly different approaches to the hermeneutical questions and male-female role relations but similar to McQuilkin's vein see John Jefferson Davis "Some Reflections on Galatians 3:28, Sexual Roles, and Biblical Hermeneutics" *Journal of the Evangelical Theological Society* (1976): 201-16; Grant Osborne, "Hermeneutics and Women in the Church" *Journal of the Evangelical Theological Society* 20 (1977):337-52; my colleague, Arthur Holmes, suggests that we identify within every institutional structure three ingredients: (1) the divine purpose for the existence of the institution, (2) the basic relational values willed by God between the people within the institution, and (3) the cultural expression or form in which these previous two entities may be embodied at any time or place. The form may change from age to age and from culture to culture or in a pluralistic culture within the culture itself.

[19]Gorden D. Fee, "Hermeneutics and Historical Precedent—A Major Problem in Pentecostal Hermeneutics," chapter 8 in *Perspectives on the New Pentecostalism*, ed. Russell P. Spittler (Grand Rapids: Baker, 1976); idem, "Hermeneutics and Common Sense: An Exploratory Essay on the Hermeneutics of the Epistles," chapter 7 in *Inerrancy and Common Sense*, ed., Roger R. Nicole and J. Ramsey Michaels (Grand Rapids: Baker, 1980); idem, "The Genre of New Testament Literature and Biblical Hermeneutics" chapter 6 in *Interpreting the Word of God*, ed., Samuel Schultz and Morris Inch (Chicago: Moody, 1976).

[20]Anthony Thiselton, *Two Horizons*, 389-407.

[21]Harvey Conn, *Theology and Anthropology*.

The Trustworthiness of Scripture in Areas Relating to Natural Sciences

Walter L. Bradley
Professor of Mechanical Engineering
Texas A & M

Roger Olsen
Ph.D. Geochemistry
Colorado School of Mines

5. The Trustworthiness of Scripture in Areas Relating to Natural Science

Walter L. Bradley and Roger Olsen

I. INTRODUCTION

A. The "Yom" and the "Bara/Asah" of Genesis 1

For the past one hundred plus years, the principal tension point between orthodox Christianity and modern science has been the question of origins. The Bible addresses this question specifically in Genesis 1-3 with only a few additional references found in other portions of Scripture. How does one properly interpret these passages in light of developments in geology and biology that suggest the universe and the earth are quite old and that life began and developed to its current forms including man by completely natural means? The Roman Catholic Church historically made a serious mistake when it refused to reconsider its interpretation of certain passages of Scripture in light of the theory of Copernicus which was strongly supported by the observations of Galileo. We dare not diminish the significance of this lesson by simply noting that the church was led astray by Aquinas's incorporation of early Greek thought into the exegesis of certain Scriptures. We should seek to avoid similar mistakes today where the possibility of the exegetical error may be for a quite different reason.

In this paper we would like to focus on the interpretation of the Hebrew words "yom" and "bara/asah" as they are used in the early chapters of Genesis to describe the time frame and mechanism of creation. A careful examination of both biblical and scientific data will be summarized. A critique of the current models based on this data will be made leading to our summary of how at present we think one may best harmonize all of the available information.

Before considering the biblical and scientific particulars, a general overview will be presented to clearly show the distinctive frames of reference used to interpret the data by various evangelical Christians today.

B. Naturalism and Supernaturalism

It is common today to pit naturalism against supernaturalism. This is a result of the fact that many naturalists assume the universe to be a closed system of cause and effect. Nature is implicitly assumed to be autonomous and God is considered to be either an absentee or nonexistent "landlord." A biblical view of nature by contrast assumes the existence of a system of cause and effect that depends moment by moment on God's will and reflects His providential care for His creatures in His customary way. He may minister to the needs of His creatures in some extraordinary way occasionally, and we call these phenomena miracles. Thus, nature is seen as being neither a closed system nor an autonomous one.

Scientists may study only God's customary way of caring for His creatures. The laws of nature so called are in fact descriptions of this regular pattern. The law of gravitational attraction describes in the language of mathematics the attraction of mass for mass but gives no explanation for why such an attraction should exist. Sir Isaac Newton who first formulated the laws of motion as well as the law of gravity felt that the common cause of nature is the result of God's immediate, sustaining activity (cf. Col. 1:17).[1] John Donne has cautioned us against allowing a preoccupation with miracles to blind us to God's direct hand in the everyday physical reality in which we presently exist. He says, "There is nothing that God has established in the course of nature, and which therefore is done everyday, but would seem a miracle and exercise our admiration if it were done but once, and only the daily doing takes off the admiration."[2]

In summary a proper Christian view of nature sees God as the immediate cause for both the natural and the supernatural. Application of this concept to the question of origins suggests that God could have used his customary means (process), some extraordinary means (miracle), or both in bringing plant and animal life, and ultimately, man into existence. We will next examine the three most common Christian views of origins and see that they suggest God's use of miracle exclusively, process exclusively, or a combination of miracle plus process.

C. Christian Views of Origins

We believe that all Christian views of origins may be divided into three categories as shown in Table I. Mature creationists see God working only through fiat miracle, therefore needing no significant amount of time.[3] Thus, they interpret the yom of Genesis 1 as successive twenty-four hour days and the "bara and asah" as being fiat miracle. The progressive creationist sees God working ("bara and asah") through a combination of miracle plus process.[4, 5] Because a part of God's work involves process (laws of nature, God's customary way of acting), the six yoms of Genesis 1 are assumed to encompass a much longer time span. The theistic evolutionist would have God's work accomplished almost exclusively[6] through process, and therefore, requiring again long time periods for the "yom" of Genesis.[7, 8, 9] It is clear that the various Christian views of origins as summarized in Table I can be simply classified by the interpretations of the Hebrew words "bara and asah" and "yom." The remainder of this paper will be concerned with examining the biblical and scientific evidence pertinent to interpreting these Hebrew words.

Before looking at the evidence in detail, a few comments about the significance of the evidence are in order. God has revealed Himself in His Word (the Bible) as well as in his creation (the world). We believe these revelations are equally valid and essentially complementary. Properly understood, they should give a consistent account of origins. It is sometimes argued that our exegesis should not be influenced by scientific observations. We believe this view is mistaken. While the Bible clearly gives more specific information about our relationship to God then one can possibly deduce from natural revelation, it does not necessarily follow that our understanding of the physical world, its origin, etc. will also be more clearly deduced from God's revelation in His Word than His revelation in His world. Since both are revelations from God, and therefore, give a unified story, it seems quite permissible to consider all of the evidence (scientific as well as biblical) to be significant to the degree that each revelation can be clearly interpreted. Herein is the rub. The theologian may feel His interpretation of the biblical data is unequivocal whereas the scientist may have a different but also unequivocal view of the scientific data. At this point both must be willing to give serious consideration to the other data or else assume, as some do, that the Bible deals only allegorically with origins while science deals with what actually happened, and thus, a harmony of the two accounts is not expected anyway.

In the sections that follow, we shall assume Genesis 1 deals with real time-space events and seek to interpret the Genesis 1 account of origins in the most general way possible. The goal is to first define the latitude of permissible interpretation of the biblical account of origins. Then God's revelation of his world as perceived through the eyes of science will be used to identify the best possible interpretation of origins within the previously prescribed boundary. This methodology allows the authoritative position of Scripture to be maintained while taking advantage of insights from scientific studies to supplement our understanding where the Genesis 1 account is ambiguous.

We will consider the "bara" and "asah" of Genesis 1, evaluating both the biblical and scientific data to determine God's mechanism in creating the universe, earth, plant, and animal life, and most recently man. Then we will consider the biblical and scientific evidence for the time frame of this creative activity.

II. GOD'S MECHANISM(S) IN CREATION

The question to be considered in this section is God's mechanism in creation; i.e., miracle, process, or a combination of the two. We will consider first the biblical data and then the scientific data pertinent to this question.

A. Biblical Data

The active verbs used in Genesis 1 to describe God's activity in creation are "bara" (1:1, 21, 27) and "asah" (1:7, 16, 25, and 31), usually translated "created"[10] and "made"[11] respectively. "Bara" is used only thirty-three times in the Old Testament with essentially all implying some degree of supernatural activity on the part of God. A few imply God working through a combination of miracle and process; e.g., the creation of the nation of Israel or the blacksmith in Isa. 54:16. Many of the usages of "bara" have the sense of a radical newness, something distinctively different.[12]

"Asah" is used 624 times in the Old Testament and quite often refers to the normal activity of people making or forming something.[13] Where God's "asah" is mentioned, the implication is occasionally one of miracle, but quite often God's providential care for His creatures in His customary way is implied, such as when He makes the storm clouds which bring rain (Zech. 10:1). Most Old Testament references to God's creating the heavens and the earth use the verb "asah." "Bara" and "asah" are sometimes used interchangeably (Gen. 1:26, 27, 31).

The implication is that the use of "bara" and "asah" suggest God's mechanism in creation probably involved miracle plus process rather than fiat miracle, except for Genesis 1:1, where essentially all evangelicals seem to agree that fiat miracle is implied. It is interesting to note that Dr. Robert Jastrow, head of the Goddard Space Center, has interpreted recent developments in astrophysics and astronomy as implying a miraculous birth to the universe in the generally accepted "Big Bang Theory" of the origin of the universe.[14]

Arguments for a mechanism of creation that utilizes *only* fiat miracle cannot be based on the common usage of "bara and asah" as previously noted. Rather such arguments are inferred from the interpretation of "yom" as a twenty-four hour day, which leaves insufficient time for process to play a significant role in God's creation activity. The validity of this argument will be considered later.

Arguments for process only after Genesis 1:1 are offered by theistic evolutionists who generally assume the intent of Genesis 1 is to establish God as Creator apart from the communication of any meaningful scientific detail as to mechanism or time frame.[15] God is assumed to have used the process of evolution as His mechanism to bring life to an appropriately high level at which time He imparted to man a soul. Genesis 2:7 is sometime cited to support such a claim. However, the same Hebrew words translated living soul (or being) in Genesis 2:7 are translated living creature in Genesis 1:21 and 1:24. The idea in all three verses therefore seems to be God animating with life previously lifeless matter rather than infusing a soul in a highly evolved primate.

Some theistic evolutionists go even further and suggest that Adam is a symbolic rather than historical figure who represents fallen mankind.[16] Jesus (Matt. 19:4-6), Paul, (1 Cor. 11:8-9, Rom. 5:12-14, 1 Tim. 2:12-13), Luke (Acts 17:25, Luke 3) and Moses (Gen. 5) all made reference to Adam and Eve as actual people. References by Jesus, Peter, and the author of Hebrews to Noah further support the idea that Gen. 1-11 is dealing with real history rather than allegory or poetry. Furthermore, the detail of Gen. 2:10-25 would seem quite inappropriate for an allegory of creation. The repeated references in Genesis 1 to animals and plants reproducing after their own kind (1:11, 12, 21, 24, 25) as well as Paul's reference in 1 Cor. 15:39 to men, animals, birds and fish having different flesh would also seem to preclude a common ancestry and genetic relationship between all animals and all plants in their respective kingdoms. Thus, the general theory of evolution seems incompatible with a literal interpretation of Genesis 1 and 2. An allegorical interpretation of Genesis 1-3 seems to be precluded by the numerous references made by later authors to a historical Adam and Eve.

In summary, the "bara" and "asah" of Genesis 1 seem to suggest God working through a combination of fiat miracle and process (microevolution) wherein God created the major types of animal and plant life and then used process to develop the tremendous variety of life forms we observe today. Adam is seen to be a historical figure who originated as a special creation of God.

B. Scientific Data

The scientific data with respect to orgins may now be evaluated to see what is implied about God's mechanism(s) in creation; i.e., miracle, process, or a combination of the two. The development of current biological systems is assumed to have begun with the formation of the various elements, some of which reacted to form simple gaseous compounds such as methane, ammonia, and carbon dioxide. The compounds in turn reacted under the influence of solar energy or electrical discharge (lightning) to form more complex molecular "building blocks" such as amino acids, phosphates, bases, and sugars. These compounds then combined under the influence of energy to form quite complex macromolecules such as protein and deoxyribonucleic acid. The organization of these and other macromolecules with the development of permeable membranes to protect the system resulted in the first living organism. From this first living cell subsequently developed simple plants and animals, and in time, the more complex plant and animal forms we see today.[17]

The distinguishing feature in this scenario of the origin of life is a monotonic increase in complexity. Nobel laureate I. Prigogine[18] has recently noted commenting on biological complexity:

> All these features bring the scientist a wealth of new problems. In the first place, one has systems that have evolved spontaneously to extremely organized and complex forms. Coherent (orderly) behavior is really the characteristic feature of biological systems.

May this increasing complexity be achieved within the framework of God's customary ways of superintending creation (natural processes; i.e., the laws of nature) or is an extraordinary work of God (fiat miracle) required? Is a completely naturalistic (God working in His customary way) explanation of origins possible today? Is it reasonable to expect that such a complete naturalistic explanation will be forthcoming in the future? Is it safe to place God's supernatural activity in some of the current "gaps" in our scientific explanation, realizing that these gaps may be filled later by new insights in our scientific understanding? We will consider these questions as we examine the scientific evidence concerning origins. This will be done in two sections: first, the development of simple living systems, usually called prebiotic evolution and second, the progression of such systems to more complex forms, usually called macroevolution.

1. Prebiotic Evolution

Increasing chemical complexity is the most distinctive feature of prebiotic evolution and also represents the single biggest challenge to explain by natural processes. The Second Law of Thermodynamics asserts that the universe or any isolated system therein is tending toward maximum entropy, where entropy can be thought of as a measure of the disorder of the system.[19] Thus, the Second Law suggests a progression from order to disorder, from complexity to simplicity in the physical universe. Yet biological evolution involves a hierarchical progression to increasingly complex forms of living systems, seemingly in contradiction to the Second Law of Thermodynamics. Whether this discrepancy between the theories of thermodynamics and evolution is apparent or real is the question to be considered in this section. The recent controversy evident in an article in *The American Scientist* along with the replies it provoked demonstrates that the question is still a timely one.[20]

Harold Morowitz[21] and others have suggested that the solution to the "apparent" contradiction is found in recognizing that the earth is not an isolated system, since it is open to energy flow from the sun. One cannot, however, simply dismiss the problem of the creation of order in biological systems by some vague appeal to open system thermodynamics. One must specify how the energy flow through the system may be converted into the necessary chemical and coding "work" required. Nicolis and Prigogine[22] have succinctly commented on this problem as follows:

> Needless to say, these simple remarks cannot suffice to solve the problem of biological order. One would like not only to establish that the second law is compatible with a decrease in overall entropy (via energy flow through the system), but also to indicate the mechanisms responsible for the emergence and maintenance of coherent states.

In the formation of the basic macromolecules essential for the biochemical function of living systems (e.g., DNA, protein, etc.), two types of "work" must be done. First the chemical energy of the macromolecules must be increased over that of the simple building blocks from which they are constructed. Second, the building blocks must be arranged in a very specific sequence to achieve proper function in the system much the same way letters must be arranged in certain specific sequences on a page to give a useful function, i.e., communicating information. We will call the first type of work chemical work and the second type of work coding work.

One of the authors has recently surveyed the literature on attempts to synthesize DNA and protein in the laboratory under simulated prebiotic conditions.[23] The conclusions from this survey were, first, that no successful experimental results have yet been achieved, and second, that the coding work is far more difficult to do than the chemical work. This is intuitively what one might expect. Miller and Orgel[24] summarized their chapter on prebiotic condensation reactions in *The Origin of Life on Earth* with:

> We believe that very limited progress has been made in the study of prebiotic condensation reactions. Many interesting scraps of information are available, but no correct pathways have yet been discovered.

One may gain insight into the problem by considering the analogous problem of converting chemical energy in gasoline into transportation. One might simply pour the gasoline into a modest size bucket, ignite it with a match and be off on one's trip if a single trip to an unspecified destination is acceptable. By contrast, if one puts the gasoline into an automobile, the same energy is released. However, the energy released is converted into mechanical work which is then converted into torque on the rear wheels of your automobile. Thus, the design of the automobile allows chemical energy to be converted into torque, making possible transportation. In a similar way, photosynthesis allows conversion of solar energy into chemical energy which may then be "burned" in living plants and animals to allow them to grow to maturity and maintain themselves in this condition. A "metabolic motor" is involved in the initial conversion of solar energy into chemical energy and a second "metabolic motor" is required to allow the combustion of these chemicals in such a way that the associated energy released may be coupled to the specific chemical and coding work required by the organism. While the details of the "metabolic motors" in various plants and animals vary, they have certain common components such as DNA (acting as a template) and proteins (acting as catalyses) that channel the flow of the energy through the system and regulate the rate at which it is released. Apart from such a metabolic motor, coupling of energy flow through the system to do the necessary ordering work would not be possible.

This is precisely why prebiotic[25] synthesis experiments fail. "Raw" energy does not seem to be capable of doing the ordering work necessary to construct the complex macromolecules of living systems. In fact the uniform failure of literally thousands of experimental attempts to synthesize protein or DNA under prebiotic conditions is a monument to the difficulty in achieving a high degree of information content, or order from the undirected flow of energy through a system.

It is sometimes argued that there are self-ordering tendencies in nature that may account for the observed order in living systems. Crystal formation as well as vortices (as in your bathtub when it is nearly empty) or convective heat currents are offered as examples of the self-ordering tendencies in nature. Such analogies fail to recognize that the ordering in vortices, crystals, etc. is very redundant compared to the observed ordering in living systems which is quite diverse and information intensive. The three sequences of letters below illustrate a random arrangement, a highly ordered but redundant arrangement, and a highly ordered, information intensive arrangement:

(a) random:
ACDBGEF ADGEBFC CBFGEAD
(b) ordered but redundant (like a crystal):
ABCDEFG ABCDEFG ABCDEFG
(c) ordered and information intensive (like DNA or protein):
THIS SEQUENCE OF LETTERS CONTAINS A MESSAGE!

A few investigators have claimed a degree of ordering (nonrandomness) in their attempts to synthesize protein. However, Miller and Orgel[26] have evaluated this work as follows:

> The degree of nonrandomness in thermal polypeptides so far demonstrated is minute compared to the nonrandomness of protein. It is deceptive, then, to suggest that thermal polypeptides are similar to protein in their nonrandomness.

The problem in obtaining a plausible chemical pathway from living systems has recently caused Nobel laureate, Sir Francis Crick,[27] who discovered the structure of DNA, to postulate that life may have come to this planet from another planet. While recognizing that this does not solve the problem but only transfers it to another location, he argues that maybe the conditions for the origin of life were somehow more favorable there than they are here. He comments later in the same paper:

> Unfortunately we know next to nothing about the probability that life evolves within a few billion years in a rich prebiotic soup, either on our own Earth, or still less on other earthlike plants.

Polyani[28] has correctly noted that the laws of chemistry and physics as presently understood cannot explain the existence of machines or living systems. Though the operation of living systems may be described in terms of the laws of chemistry and physics, it is in the fixing of the boundary conditions (e.g., making the first metabolic motor) that the necessary function (coupling the energy flow through the system to do specific work) becomes possible. Man designing and building an internal combustion engine constitutes such a fixing of the boundary conditions for the chemical energy in gasoline to be converted into useful work. In a similar way the metabolic motor common to all living systems allows maintenance of the living systems in their highly ordered conditions.

In summarizing this section, we should like to reemphasize that one *cannot* dismiss the possibility of ordering simple chemicals into complex living organisms by an appeal to the Second Law of Thermodynamics since the earth is an open system. However, an open system without some mechanism to couple the energy flow through the system to the required ordering work is equally unacceptable as a model for the origin of life. Either there is some as yet undiscovered energy coupling mechanism or self-ordering mechanism, or else, God accomplished this part of His creation in a supernatural way.

2. *Macroevolution*

We begin this section by making a distinction between microevolution and macroevolution since it is only the latter that is of possible concern to us as we seek to better understand God's mechanism(s) in creation. Evolution seeks to explain changes in living organisms. Microevolution would limit itself to consideration of smaller changes occurring in given levels of complexity; i.e., increasing diversity including speciation. Macroevolution would attempt to show the relationship between all living organisms, which is more difficult to do. We shall consider the "historical" evidence for evolution as it is preserved in the fossil record. Then we shall consider possible mechanisms to account for this increasing complexity observed in living systems.

It has always been assumed that change occurs slowly in living organisms. Thus, it is assumed that long periods of time are involved and that there are many minute steps along the way. If this is so, then one would reasonably expect to find in the fossil record a continuous increase in complexity with time. Initially when the fossil record was found to show numerous gaps, it was assumed that these gaps would eventually be filled by subsequent finds. Today it is widely recognized that the major gaps still persist. Professor Kitts[29] has commented with reference to this problem:

> Despite the bright promise that paleontology provides a means of seeing evolution, it has presented some nasty difficulties for the evolutionists the most notorious of which is the presence of 'gaps' in the fossil record. Evolution requires intermediate forms between species and paleontology does not provide them. The gaps must therefore be a contingent feature of the record. Darwin was concerned enough about this problem to devote a chapter of the 'Origin' to it. He accounts for the 'imperfections of the geological record' largely on the basis of the lack of continuous deposition of sediments and by erosion. Darwin also holds out the hope that some of the gaps would be filled as the result of subsequent collecting. But most of the gaps were still there a century later and some paleontologists were no longer willing to explain them away geologically.

Dr. Gould[30] of Harvard has recently commented on the same problem as follows:

> The extreme rarity of transitional forms in the fossil record persists as the trade secret of paleontology. We fancy ourselves as the only true students of life's history; yet to preserve our favored account of evolution by natural selection, we view our data as so bad that we never see the very process we profess to study.

Dr. Pierre-Paul Grasse, past president of the French Academy of Science and editor of the thirty-five volume "Traite de Zoologie" makes the following statements in his recent book *Review of Evolution of Living Organisms*:[31]

> There is almost total absence of fossil evidence relative to the origin of the phyla. . . . The lack of direct evidence leads to

> the formation of pure conjectures as to the genesis of the phyla. We do not even have a basis to determine the extent to which these opinions are correct.

Dr. E. L. Core in his textbook *General Biology*[32] succinctly notes:

> We do not actually know the phylogenetic history of any group of plants or animals.

Coffin and Anderson[33] have detailed in laymen's terms the current gaps in the fossil record in their monogram *Fossils in Focus*. A recent article in *Life* magazine discusses the problem of gaps in the fossil record.[34]

The problem of gaps in the fossil record was one of the main topics considered at an international conference on Macroevolution in Chicago in the fall of 1980.[35] At this conference the clear absence of transitional forms and the persistence of gaps in the fossil record were openly discussed and the significance of same were roundly debated. Gould of Harvard and others are now advocating a new model to account for the many discontinuities in the fossil record. This model called "punctuated equilibrium" assumes change is not gradual after all. Rather, species remain unchanged for long periods of time and then experience a very rapid series of changes that make any fossil record of the transition unlikely. That such a model should be proposed and have so many distinguished advocates tends to confirm the validity of the previous quotations. It should be recognized that such a model has no mechanism at present and would predict a fossil record indistinguishable from that expected if God simply created the major types of plant and animal life. Thus, it may prove to be impossible to scientifically demonstrate "punctuated equilibrium" to have any unique features to distinguish it from "special creation."

Having noted the lack of clear support for macroevolution in the fossil record, we turn our attention next to the proposed mechanism for evolution: namely, mutation/natural selection. Mutations are the result of replicating mistakes along the DNA chain. Such alterations change the information coding implicit in the base sequence along the chain. Usually such mutations are harmful, sometimes lethal, and quite infrequently advantageous (it is debated by some creationists whether mutations are ever beneficial). Natural selection acts to filter out the change that is not desirable so that over a period of time even very occasionally beneficial mutations can give rise to species more adapted to their respective environments.

The important question, however, is not whether mutations can give rise to change but whether they can give rise to increasing information content along the DNA chain resulting in increasing complexity of the organism. Professor Eden[36] of MIT has allegorically pictured the problem as follows:

> If random point mutations along the DNA string is taken seriously as the primary motivation of evolutionary change, then the chance of emergence of man is like the probability of typing at random a meaningful library of one thousand volumes using the following procedure: begin with a meaningful phrase; retype it with a few mistakes; make it longer by adding letters, and rearrange the subsequences in the string of letters; then examine the result to see if the new phrase is meaningful. Repeat the process until the library is complete.

Not only is the model of random mutations along the DNA chain untenable statistically as a means of increasing the information content of the molecular coding, it is without experimental verification. Professor H. G. Cannon[37] speaks to this clear lack of experimental supports in the following:

> A fact that has been obvious for many years is that Mendelian mutations deal only with changes in existing characters. . . . No experiment has produced progeny that show entirely new functioning organs. And yet it is the appearance of new characters in organisms which mark the boundaries of major steps in the evolutionary scale.

In addressing this question in college classrooms speaking with Probe Ministries, one of the authors has noted repeatedly the response that changes produced by mutations are too small to produce such a drastic alteration in the organism. Yet laboratory experiments in which countless thousands of mutations have been produced through the use of radiation on fruit flies have not given the fruit fly any new characteristic. Studies of this type always begin and end with the same organism. The distinguished French zoologist Dr. Grasse[38] has commented on the role of mutations in evolution as follows:

> Some contemporary biologists, as soon as they observe a mutation talk about evolution. They are implicitly supporting the following syllogism: mutations are the only evolutionary variations, all living beings undergo mutations, therefore all living beings evolve. This logical scheme is however unacceptable: first, because its major premise is neither obvious nor general;

> second, because its conclusion does not agree with the facts. No matter how numerous they may be, mutations do not produce any kind of evolution.

He goes on to use the illustration of bacteria that have the highest frequency of mutations, yet stabilized a billion years ago. He says once one has noticed micro-variations on the one hand and specific stability on the other, it seems very difficult to conclude that the former comes into play in the evolutionary process.

In summarizing this section on biotic evolution, the evidence for macroevolution seems very tenuous at best: "punctuated equilibrium" that causes such rapid change that no fossil record is left; caused by random mutations, a mechanism that produces such small changes that it is impossible to ever experimentally demonstrate that it produces new characteristics, rather than changes in existing characteristics. These two hypotheses for macroevolution essentially put it beyond the reach of scientific verification or refutation, making it essentially a metaphysical statement of faith that change occurs in some naturalistic way that can at present be neither explained nor observed. It is clear that special creation of the major types of plant and animal life is consistent with the scientific evidence currently available on the origin and development of plant and animal life.

C. Summary

Did God use miracle, process, or a combination of the two in creating plant and animal life as we see it today? Both the biblical and the scientific evidence seem to demand that "bara" and "asah" include some supernatural activity on God's part. The evidence, however, does not seem to preclude process being used as a supplement to the miraculous. The common usages particularly of "asah" seems to imply natural process and the ample evidence for microevolution (not discussed in this paper) would seem to support this hypothesis. Thus, we conclude that the "bara" and "asah" of Genesis should be properly interpreted to mean that God used a combination of miracle plus process to create life as we see it today. Theistic evolution is clearly not demanded at present by the scientific evidence (nor even well supported for that matter) and would appear to be quite dubious, based on the evidence from Scripture.

How much danger is there in attributing to miraculous activity on God's part that which science cannot explain today? The specific observations demanding either supernatural activity by God or a new mechanism all have to do with increasing information content and ordering, both in the origin of life and the development from simple to complex life forms. While it is possible that God used some natural but subtle mechanism to organize living systems, it seems reasonable *at present* to assume no such mechanism exists and attribute as we have the organizing of the major types of living systems to a supernatural activity on God's part.

III. GOD'S TIME FRAME IN CREATION

The question to be considered in this section is God's time frame in creation. Table 1 summarizes the possible positions with respect to time as they relate to mechanism(s) used by God in creating. We will consider first the biblical data followed by an evaluation of the pertinent scientific data.

A. Biblical Data

The Hebrew word "yom" and its plural form "yamim" are used over 1900[39] times in the Old Testament. In only sixty-five of these cases is it translated as a time period other than a day in the King James Version.[40] Outside of the Genesis 1 case in question, the two-hundred plus occurrences of "yom" preceded by ordinals all refer to a normal twenty-four hour day.[41] Furthermore, the seven-hundred plus appearances of "yamim" always refer to a regular day. Thus, it is argued by Morris that the Exodus 20:11 reference to the six "yamim" of creation must also refer to six regular days.[42]

These arguments have a common fallacy, however. There is no other place in the Old Testament where the intent is to describe events that involve multiple and/or sequential, indefinite periods of time. If the intent of Genesis 1 is to describe creation as occurring in six, indefinite time periods, it is a unique Old Testament event being recorded. Other descriptions where "yom" refers to an indefinite time period are all for a single time period. Thus, the absence of the use of "yamim" for other than regular days and the use of ordinals only before regular days elsewhere in the Old Testament cannot be given an unequivocal exegetical significance in view of the uniqueness of the events being described in Genesis 1 (i.e, sequential, indefinite time periods).

The terms "morning and evening" used in the Genesis 1 account in connection with the various "yoms" are sometimes argued to be compelling evidence for a literal day.[43, 44] Yet, it has been demonstrated that the "yom" of Genesis 1 cannot be unequivocally interpreted twenty-four hour day; it is unreasonable then to *demand* that "morning and evening" be given a literal significance. If "yom" can mean creative epoch, then "mutatis mutandis" (evening and morning) could reasonably be interpreted to have the metaphorical significance of beginning and ending. It should be emphasized that a figurative or metaphorical interpretation of the "yom" of Genesis 1 does not necessarily lead to a denial of the historicity of the Genesis 1 account (as some claim), but only rejection of the interpretation of the creative "week" as being of 168 hours duration. Furthermore, God's supernatural creative activity in these longer creative "days" is still affirmed, based on our previous discussion of the "bara/asah" of Genesis 1.

Exodus 20:11 is often suggested to be convincing evidence for a six-day creative week, but arguments by analogy can only be suggestive, and never conclusive. There is simply no reason why our seven-day week demands a creative week of seven twenty-four hour days. In fact Davis A. Young[45] has recently argued that God's creative week is still in progress, based on the absence of the "morning and evening" phraseology with reference to day seven (Gen. 2:2-3) and the references in Hebrew 4 to entering into God's rest, which suggests the seventh "yom" continues to the present.

Finally, it has been argued over the years that a twenty-four hour day translation for the "yom" of Genesis 1 creates more problems than it solves because the sense of the passage, and especially the sixth "yom" seems to suggest a much longer period of time. R. J. Snow[46] has recently discussed this problem, concluding that the activities of the sixth day as well as the response of Adam when he meets Eve clearly suggest a much longer time frame than a day. Snow notes with reference to the narrative of Genesis 1 and 2, we have the major types of land animals created, Adam created, the garden planted and made to grow by God, Adam being placed in the garden, Adam naming the animals and then feeling lonely, Adam being put to sleep and Eve being created, and finally the initial meeting at which Adam exclaims, "happa'am," or "now at length" (cf. similar usages in Genesis 29:34-35, 30:20, 46:30 and Judg. 15:3).

We conclude that the proper interpretation of "yom" in Genesis 1 is uncertain from an exegetical point of view. The interpretation of "yom" in this passage to be an indefinite period of time cannot be precluded; i.e., it is a legitimate interpretation. In fact Kaiser,[47] Snow, and others have argued it is the more compelling interpretation. The accusation that such an interpretation for "yom" is simply a capitulation to modern science is seen to be groundless when one recognizes that Josephus (first century),[48] Irenaeus (second century),[49] Origin (third century),[50] Augustine (fourth century),[51] Aquinas (fourteenth century),[52] and many others[53] held such an interpretation long before modern geology and astronomy adopted their current view of the antiquity of the universe including earth.

We will next look at the scientific data for the age of the earth to gain insight into the proper interpretation of "yom" in Genesis 1, deferring temporarily the question of harmonizing the details of Genesis 1, especially chronology, with current geological models.

B. Scientific Date

In this section we will summarize briefly some of the common scientific arguments for a young earth and for an old earth, presenting the assumptions required for each estimate. Then we will critique the assumptions in an attempt to draw some conclusions. All of the arguments have a similarity to the common problem of estimating how long you have been driving on a trip since breakfast. If you know the approximate distance traveled and the rate of travel, then the time may be easily estimated. All methods of dating assume something about the rate at which a given process occurs as well as the observed change over the time frame to be estimated. The variability between the estimates of 10,000 years versus several billion years for the age of the earth indicates that not all of the assumptions made by recent and ancient earth advocates can be simultaneously true.

1. Scientific Arguments for a Recent Creation

a. Decay of the Earth's Magnetic Field. Measurements of the earth's magnetic field over the past 130 years indicate that the strength of the field is decreasing. Assuming the decay follows an exponential decay pattern and that an upper limit to the magnetic field exists, the earth is estimated to be 6000 to 7000 years old.[54]

b. Missing Mass in the Universe. Clusters of galaxies can be observed throughout the universe. Random motion should have long ago dispersed these clusters: that is, only 2 to 14 percent of the mass necessary to hold these clusters close together has been observed. If they should have dispersed (due to insufficient gravitational attraction) and yet have not, it must be because of insufficient time for dispersion to have occurred; i.e., the universe is quite young.[55]

c. Poynting-Robertson Effect. The solar drag force exerted upon micrometeoroids in the solar system causes the particles to spiral into the sun. This solar drag results from absorption and reradiation of photons (from the sun) by the dust particles, resulting in a net loss of energy and an unstable orbit that spirals in toward the sun. Original estimates suggest dust particles of a typical size would be swept into the sun in about 10,000 years. However, many dust particles do currently exist in our solar system; thus, these particles must have originated very recently.[56]

d. Quantity of Dust on the Moon. Strong ultra-violet light and X-rays can destroy the surface layers of exposed rock and reduce them to dust at the rate of a few ten-thousands of an inch per year.[57] Hans Pettersson of the Swedish Oceanographic Institute calculated meteoritic dust settles to the earth at the rate of about $0.33''/10^6$ years.[58] From these two sources, one would expect to find at least several hundred feet of dust on the surface of the moon. Yet, only ⅛″ to 3″ of moon dust is actually found. Given the rapid rates of accumulation and the small total amount observed, the moon must be of recent origin, and therefore, the earth must be quite recent as well.

e. Cooling Rate of the Earth. Lord Kevin in 1911 estimated the earth to be only twenty-four million years old based on rate of cooling coupled with estimated initial temperature distribution and the present temperature distribution.[59]

The above five examples are only a few of the evidences cited by young earth advocates. Henry Morris has listed seventy-six different methods to calculate the age of the earth based on uniformitarian assumptions. The ages range from one-hundred years to five-hundred million years.[60] He concludes that such a wide variation in predictions must discredit uniformitarianism, further concluding that the earth is a very recent creation of God, as revealed in the Scriptures.

2. Scientific Arguments for an Old Earth

The proponents of an old earth (4.5 to 4.7 billion years old) also cite various evidences to support their claim. Some of the most prominent "clocks" will be reviewed next.

a. Radiometric Age Dating. Mathematical analysis of data from uranium/lead systems as found in meteorites gives their age as 4.5 billion years. This age has been independently confirmed by potassium/argon and rubidium/strontium dating of stony meteorites. This is the time since meteorites were differentiated, and it can be plausibly equated with the time of planet formation in the solar system. Earth rocks are dated to be on the order of 3.5 billion years old, which would be the time that the earth had cooled sufficiently to allow crystallization to occur. These results are considered to be in good agreement with the results from meteorites.[61]

b. Sea Floor Spreading. Molten matter is emanating from the mid-oceanic ridges, moving outward to the east and west toward the continents. As the molten matter cools, the direction of the magnetic field at that time is preserved in the rock. Magnetic surveys reveal a series of reversals in the magnetic field. The pattern is the same on each side of the oceanic ridges. Thus, the rocks are like recording tape making a record of the earth's magnetic field as a function of time. It is estimated that the sea floor spreading has moved the continents to their current locations in the last 200 million years.[62]

c. Coral Growth Rates. Some modern coral reefs are found to be over 4600 feet thick; e.g., the fastest rate of upward growth has been measured to be about 8mm/year.[63] Therefore, it would have taken at least 175,000 years to produce the Eniwetok atoll reef. An interesting sidelight here is that band structure in coral that is quite old (345-405 millions years) shows 400 daily bands between the annual bands, indicating a faster earth's rotation about its axis in the past than that which we observe at present.[64] The spacing of the rings also indicates that the ancient rate of growth was very similar to the rates observed today. Calculations by astronomers have shown that the rate of rotation of the earth is decreasing but that the period of the earth's revolution about the sun is essentially constant. Therefore, the age of the coral can be determined from the rate of decrease in the number of days per year. This allows the radiometric and fossil dating of the corals to be independently confirmed. The growth bands that have been observed on certain ancient bivalve mollusk shells are in essential agreement with the findings in corals.[65]

d. Sea Floor Sediments. Deep core drilling in the oceans have revealed deposits of calcium carbonate thousands of feet thick. These deposits accumulate from shells of living organisms. The current rate of deposition of these sediments rarely exceeds 20mm/1000 years.[66] Over thirty million years would be required to form only 2000 feet of such deposits. Very large areas of 2000′ thick calcium carbonate-anhydrite couplets are found in New Mexico. Such formations result from the evaporation of salt water which brings the mineral and/or salt content to a level of concentration that causes precipitation to occur. In the 2000 feet deposits are found over 200,000 alternating layers, indicating major changes in the sea water chemistry took place at least that many times.[67] Furthermore, each precipitation event had to occur in quiet water to allow the mineral to settle to the bottom and form a thin, uniform layer.

e. Age of Universe Estimates from Astronomy and Astrophysics. The age of the universe may be estimated in at least three ways from astronomy and astrophysics.[68] First, the "big bang" theory suggests that the universe was born in a fiery explosion in the past. By noting the current rates of expansion of various galaxies and noting the distance traveled from the common focal point of the universe, the time since this "traumatic" birth may be estimated to be ten to twenty billion years. A second approach is to determine the size of the universe that we can observe at present and then use this information in conjunction with the speed of light to suggest a minimum age of the universe; i.e., the time it took the light to travel from distant stars to earth. An age of ten billion years is suggested. A third estimate is obtained through the modeling of the birth, maturing and finally the death of stars. This approach gives an estimated age for our sun of five to ten billion years. Note these ages are in good agreement with the earlier radiometric dates of 4.5 billion years for the age of the earth, moon, and meteorites.

In summary, the universe and the earth are seen to be quite old (15 and 4.5 billion years) with many additional indications of great antiquity contained in the formation of various kinds of sediment and coral. The contrast between the young and old earth advocates' positions is obvious. In the following section, the validity of the various assumptions used to establish these positions will be more carefully examined to see if the physical basis for these conflicting claims can be better understood.

3. Critique of Assumptions Made by Young Earth Proponents

The assumption that the earth's magnetic field has decayed from some initial value is very suspect in view of the large number of areas where the sediment is found to have periodic reversals, indicating that the earth's magnetic field follows a sinusodial function, rather than decay from some initial value.[69] These magnetic reversals are well documented and cannot at present be explained by any physical or chemical processes except a sinusodially varying magnetic field for the earth. This would invalidate the time estimate based on an assumed decay from some maximum value. It should be added that recent studies have indicated that magnetic reversals on the sea floor are not as simple as originally thought.[70] For example, the polarity changes vertically as well as horizontally and there is a lack of lateral lithologic and stratigraphic continuity in the crust.

The missing mass argument for a young earth is not as simple as it appears in view of the many discussions in *Physics Today* over the past several years. It is obvious that there is much that we do not presently understand about dissimilar matter, antimatter, and creation of matter from black holes.[71] In estimating the age of the solar system based upon closeness of galaxies, calculations are made by young earth advocates to arrive at the mass in these galaxies. The statement is then made "there is a vast discrepancy found when the mass derived from consideration of the motion of galaxies in clusters is compared with the mass that we can observe. . . ." The term "vast discrepancy" is an exaggeration since secular scientists recognize their current measurements of mass of various galaxies as being only order of magnitude estimates at best. Thus, predictions of the age of the universe based on an area of physics that is so poorly understood and in which good empirical data is almost impossible to obtain is very speculative at best.

Slusher calculations for the Poynting-Robertson effect assume isotropic reradiation. Since in fact the Mic[72] scattering which occurs with particles of the size discussed by Slusher is higher anisotropic, it is not surprising that Slusher arrives at a meaningless conclusion.

The amount of dust on the moon has been estimated based on the recent visits there to vary from several centimeters to several meters.[73] It may be assumed that that rate of dust accumulation is dependent primarily on meteoric sources rather than ultraviolet light and X-rays, since these would effectively be screened once a small layer of dust accumulated. Furthermore, the rate of moon dust accumulation should be less than on the earth due to a smaller gravitational attraction. Approximately 1/8 the rate of accumulation of meteoric dust on earth estimated by Pettersson and often cited by young earth proponents would be reasonable. Actual photographs of moon soil specimens 6″ deep are found in many textbooks. Depending on which rate one chooses, or which maximum depth of moon dust one assumes (3″ to 3 meters), the age of the moon is estimated to be between 10 million and 2.5 billion years using this method. This calculation assumes dust accumulation after the first several inches is only meteoric in nature. It is clear that the method is crude at best, but it is also seen to give results that may be more easily reconciled with an old earth than with an earth that is 10,000 years old.

Finally, the cooling rate of the earth calculations of Lord Kelvin were made before we had any accurate knowledge of the material composition of the earth's crust or core. The temperature profile through the earth was also unknown to Lord Kelvin and is still uncertain at present (though it has been estimated with some confidence in recent years). Since the thermal conductivity depends *dramatically* both on the material as well as on the temperature, it was clearly not possible for Lord Kelvin to accurately estimate the earth's age using heat conduction type calculations. If one accounts for heating due to radioactivity and recognizes that much of the earth's matter is materials with a very low thermal conductivity (such as silicates), then a very long time is required for the earth to cool to its present temperature. Again, the use of incorrect models or empirical data is seen to lead to erroneous predictions of a recent earth.

4. Critique of Assumptions Made by Old Earth Advocates

Radiometric dating assumes that the rate of decay remains essentially constant and that the original parent/daughter ratio of elements may somehow be estimated. In a 1975 article entitled "Some Recent Developments Having to do With Time" Slusher attempts to document the uncertainty in the constant decay rate assumption by citing the work of physicist G. T. Emery. However, Emery's experimental results show a maximum change of no more than 4%.[74] He has since noted that there is no evidence for greater than a 1% variation in the decay rates used to date the age of the earth. These magnitudes of variation in the decay rate could hardly explain an earth whose actual age is 10,000 years giving an apparent age of 4.5 billion years.

A stronger issue is generally made of the uncertainty in the initial composition of the elements at the time of crystallization of a given mineral. Where this is uncertain because of chemical leaching or because of atomic diffusion in the case of argon in a mineral that has been reheated since crystallization, an accurate date cannot be obtained. The system must be closed and uncontaminated for reliable dating. An often cited example is that of lava formations in the Pacific Ocean near Hawaii which are known to be several hundred years old, yet have been dated by potassium/argon dating to be millions of years old.[75] When a volcanic eruption occurs in deep water, argon from earlier decay is liberated and will tend to move to the surface of the molten rock. Because the cooling rate is rapid for lava eruptions in water, much of this argon may not reach the surface, but rather is trapped or frozen in near the surface. If one radioactively dates this material, the excess or argon trapped in this region will give an erroneous indication of antiquity. Other examples may be cited. Nevertheless, there are many thousands of examples of dating where the initial composition can be accurately established. For example, in strontium/rubidium dating using certain minerals, the chemical solubility in the crystal lattice is very well defined so that we can know with confidence the initial composition within well defined limits.[76] In the case of uranium/lead, several isotopes may be used to date independently the same mineral. A consistent result from these two independent clocks gives confidence that the initial compositions have been accurately estimated.[77] An earlier work by Zeuner[78] and more recent works on geochronol dating summarize the painstaking results of geologists all over the world. Zeuner is quick to acknowledge the uncertainty that may accompany such measurements for reasons just cited and other similar ones. The intersection of the data, (over all consistency in predictions using many different methods) however, is fatal to the arguments of recent earth advocates. One cannot simply dismiss this evidence by pointing to occasional mistakes that occur for physically understandable reasons. Segraves and Kofahl[79] cite great uncertainty in radiometric dating of moon rocks as evidence of the lack of reliability in this method; yet the range they give is 2.3 to 4.9 billion years. As a second example, they cite the dating of lunar soil by various methods to give dates of 4.67 billion years (Pb^{207}/Pb^{206}), 5.41 billion years (Pb^{206}/U^{238}), 4.89 billion years (Pb^{207}/U^{235}), 8.2 billion years (Pb^{206}/Th^{232}), and 2.3 billion years (K/Ar-used on rocks in same region as lunar soil). This represents to us a remarkable support for the idea that radiometric dating is indeed quite accurate. It would be quite fortuitous for all of these initial parent-daughter compositions to give these same, consistent indications of antiquity for a moon that is only ten thousand years old. In summary, where a system is closed from external contamination or leaching and where the initial parent-daughter ratios of composition may be established through geochemistry, radiometric dating is found to give remarkable consistent predictions of an ancient earth. One cannot discredit this overwhelming body of evidence by pointing to occasional anomalous dates obtained where these two assumptions are not properly satisfied.

The criticism of the dating through slow processes of sedimentation is that much of this could have been deposited during the flood in a very short time. While some sedimentation undoubtedly was rapidly deposited during the flood, the examples cited in this paper clearly could not have been formed in this way (e.g., evaporative deposits, etc.). Dan Wonderly has documented many more examples in his recent book.[80] While these various nonradiometric methods of dating may be inaccurate for giving absolute ages, they occur at rates that give incontrovertable evidence that the earth is much older than ten thousand years. Furthermore, one cannot postulate here an uncertainty in assumptions as is done with radiometric dating since no assumptions are involved. Unless God chose to create the universe with this clear impression of great antiquity, the earth must actually be quite old.

The indications of age from astronomy based on the size of the universe and the present expansion are not critiqued in a physical way to our knowledge except to suggest that God created light "in transit" from the stars and placed the galaxies in their current positions to give an apparent age.[81] It is further argued that "apparent age" is unavoidable in fiat creation; for example, Adam was in all probability created full grown. Yet the historic arguments of this type have never been very compelling.[82] Why would God choose to create many things in the universe that give an apparent age that is very consistent in predicting antiquity if the earth is indeed quite young?

We believe in summary that the data from science for an old earth to be overwhelming. To argue based on a few anomalies (which have adequate explanations without appealing to a recent creation) that the earth is quite young while ignoring the tremendous body of evidence that the universe and the earth are quite ancient is simply untenable. A new theory in science is adopted only when it is able to explain more data than the existing theory. Clearly mature creationism is no threat to conventional geology and astronomy in the area of dating.

IV. DISCUSSION

We have presented arguments for God creating ("bara/asah") through a combination of miracle plus process over a very long period of time. The longer time frame may be reconciled with the Genesis 1 account in one of several ways. First, the "yom" of Genesis 1 may be interpreted to be an epoch rather than day. A second possibility is that the "days" of Genesis 1 are literal but not sequential days; i.e., they are days separated by long periods of geological history. A third possibility is that they are revelatory days; i.e., God revealed creation in six days. The strengths and weaknesses of each of these "models" are summarized in Appendix I[83] along with other models we have already rejected including mature creationism and theistic evolution. We prefer the day/age model in which "yom" is interpreted to be some indefinitely long period of time. The major remaining problem with which we must concern ourselves is the question of harmonizing the details of Genesis 1 with geological history if the day/age model is to be adopted.

It should be noted that there is very good general agreement between the Genesis 1 account and geological history. Both describe the creation of the atmosphere and dry land, followed by the appearance of plant life. This in turn is followed by the appearance of increasing complex forms of animal life culminating in man's appearance. The areas of particular concern would be the indications of certain kinds of plants (seed bearing) in day three prior to the appearance of any animal life, the creation of plant life over a long period of time prior to the creation of the sun, and the creation of birds prior to the creation of any other land animals. Ramm[84] argues that the treatment of Genesis 1 may be topical and/or logical rather than chronological. Thus, the creation of all of the plant life is mentioned in the third revelatory day without necessarily requiring that it chronologically appeared in total before any animal life was created. E.T. Kalem[85] and Newman and Eckelmann[86] have all noted that the "yamim" (plural for "yom") of Genesis 1 could also be overlapping rather than mutually exclusive. Young notes that light was created on the first day and would have been available to illumine the plants. He suggests that maybe the earth and the moon were placed in their current proximity to the sun in the fourth "yom." Newman and Eckelmann suggest a very interesting explanation assuming that Genesis 1 is written from the point of view of an observer on earth. They suggest that the appearance of plants in "yom" three and the resultant change in the atmosphere that occurred subsequently might have made the sun and the stars directly observable for the first time in "yom" four. Their interpretation of "yom" one and two based on astronomy and astrophysics is also quite interesting though speculative. It is our opinion that there are a number of possible ways of harmonizing Genesis 1 "data" with geological "data." It is not imperative to our purpose to suggest which one is correct but only that it can be done with assumptions that are much more palatable than those made in arguing a young earth interpretation from Genesis 1, geology and astronomy.

Finally, we wish to comment on the criticism of the progressive creationism model we have adopted based on the assumption of death prior to the fall of man that is implicit in such a model. A careful exegesis of the appropriate passages in Genesis 2 and 3 clearly indicates the death penalty to be prescribed for man as a result of sin. Furthermore, the primary death prescribed as punishment must have been spiritual since the consequence of sin was to be a penalty that was to be immediate ("in the day you eat of the fruit, you shall surely die"). To interpret "yom" of Genesis 2:17 as an indefinite period of time might weaken the present argument with reference to death but would simultaneously strengthen the arguments for a "yom" of other than twenty-four hours in Genesis 1. The spiritual consequences of sin were indeed realized immediately when man sinned with physical death being prescribed by God subsequently (Gen. 3:19). Plant life had to die in pristine Eden for man and animals to eat. Furthermore, to assume that all animals were vegetarians before the fall is quite speculative in view of the large claws and sharp teeth some animals have always had. Large fish would have been unable to support themselves in the ocean and local microscopic "wars" fought between bacteria and antibodies in our system would be considered illegitimate (i.e., premature) in prefall Eden. It seems quite unreasonable and unnecessary then to assume no physical death occurred in the plant or animal kingdom prior to the fall.

V. SUMMARY

We believe that the "bara/asah" of Genesis 1 implies God working through miracle *and* process to effect creation. We believe that the "yom" of Genesis 1 may be interpreted either "day" or "epoch." In either case Genesis may still be interpreted to allow for the large total time indicated by geology and astronomy. This model, usually called progressive creationism, suggests that God created the major types of plant and animal life at various times in geological history in a miraculous way and then worked through process (God acting in His customary way) to develop the tremendous variety of plant and animal life we see today. To accept the compelling evidence for geological age should not be equated with accepting the general theory of evolution (macroevolution). While a large amount of time is a necessary requirement for evolution, it is clearly not a sufficient condition by itself. Some ordering mechanism more efficient than chance must be invoked, even given a time scale of billions of years. Time is not a sufficient hero for this story. Progressive creationism is much nearer to mature creationism than to theistic evolution, disputing only the time frame, but readily acknowledges God's supernatural activity in this area. It is quite obscure to the authors why mature creationists insist on lumping together theistic evolution and progressive creationism as being essentially the same position.

We believe that the current mature creationist position will ultimately be unproductive by focusing the argument on the wrong consideration, namely, time rather than on the more important question of mechanism for ordering. Recent articles in *Time* (See footnote 85) and *The Science Teacher*[87] well illustrate this point. If the earth could be shown to be recent, this would be fatal to the evolutionary argument. However, to press this argument without adequate scientific support only discredits by association the legitimate arguments against the accidental origin of life and macroevolution that can be made. It is interesting to note that mature creationists are careful to debate other issues than time frame and as a result meet with a fair measure of success. It is unfortunate that they are not willing to be equally prudent in other contexts where they are much more dogmatic in insisting the mature creationist model is the only acceptable one for Genesis 1.

In conclusion we believe that progressive creationism achieves a very acceptable harmony of the scriptural and scientific data without in any way compromising the inerrant view of Scripture or resorting to a metaphorical or figurative interpretation where the context does not seem to suggest this interpretation.

TABLE I

Model	Mechanism	Time Frame
Mature Creationism	Miracle only	6 days
Progressive Creationism	Miracle plus process	Long, indefinite period of time
Theistic Evolution	Process only	Long, indefinite period of time

APPENDIX I
"Yom of Genesis 1: Several Views"

Norman L. Geisler

I. SEVERAL VIEWS CONSIDERED

A. **Gap Theories**

1. *Local Creation:* Geological Ages (G.A.) come before Gen. 1:1, which is beginning of a local creation.

a) *Geo. facts:* Gives full sway to antiquity and activity of G.A.

b) *Merits:* Seems to fit Gen. 2. Tries to take both science and Bible seriously.

c) *Weakness:* It cheapens Gen. 1, weakens Theism, and makes God a Local Repairman.

2. *Gap Theory:* G.A. comes between Gen. 1:1, 2. 1:1 is original creation then ruination.

a) *Geo.facts:* Recognizes vast time of G.A.; fits them between Gen. 1:1, 2.

b) *Merits:* Recognizes need for G.A. and makes room for them in Bible.

c) *Weakness:* Poor exegesis for Gen. 1:2 (makes "was" into "became") Chaos. In Geo., Chaos is at beginning (pre-Cambrian) not end of series (Pliestocene).

3. *Alternate Day:* G.A. comes between the twenty-four hour days of special creation alternatively.

a) *Geo. facts:* Accepts both time and sequence of Geo. history.

b) *Merits:* Retains twenty-four hour days, maintains Geo. time and fits progressive history of the rock record.

c) *Weakness:* "Days" of Gen. 1 seem to be successive, and it doesn't seem to fit Exod. 20:11.

B. **Exact Parallel Views** (G.A. are equated with the days of Genesis).

1. *Solar Days:* World and all life was created in six twenty-four hour days (144 hours).

a) *Geo. facts:* Fossils are satanic deceptions, freaks of nature, or relics of Noah's Flood (most).

b) *Merits:* It takes Gen. account factually and historically, and attempts to explain the fossil record.

c) *Weakness:* It denies bases for modern geology and interprets Gen. 1-2 over literally.

2. *Age-Day:* Days of Gen. are eras that correspond to the geological record.

a) *Geo. facts:* Fully accepts long time span and the sequence of Geo. history.

b) *Merits:* It explains the *sequence* as well as the *time* in Geo. and Genesis.

c) *Weakness:* Must stretch Gen. to make it fit Geo. sequence. Makes "days" metaphorical not literal. Weak exegesis of word "day."

3. *Relative Time:* Days were twenty-four hours in another time context, but of years in our time context.

a) *Geo. facts:* It accepts the findings of modern Geo. in terms of our time context.

b) *Merits:* Holds to twenty-four hour days in Gen. and explains them by "relativity" to our time.

c) *Weakness:* This makes Geo. eras of equal time. Also Gen. seems to be speaking in our time context.

C. **Broad Parallel** (G.A. are broadly represented by "days" of Gen. though not in detail).

1. *Vision or Pictorial:* "Days" are twenty-four hours of *revelation*, not of creation.

a) *Geo. facts:* It accepts findings of Geo., though not uncritically.

b) *Merits:* Explains Geo. time and yet maintains literal interpretation of Gen. 1.

c) *Weakness:* Gen. 1 isn't in language of vision (e.g., "I beheld").

2. *Narrational Day:* "Days" are twenty-four hours of direct revelation and recording of creation story.

a) *Geo. facts:* It accepts them the same as the Vision Theory does.

b) *Merits:* It evades the weakness of non-vision language and still explains G.A.

c) *Weakness:* Exod. 20:7 says, "In six days God *made* (not told) the heavens and . . ."

3. *Literary Framework:* "Day" series is used as a literary framework (as a chapter) for the great creation topics.

a) *Geo. Facts:* It is willing to accept them as modern science does.

b) *Merits:* Accepts modern science and yet takes Bible literally.

c) *Weakness:* no real proof "days" were ever used as "chapters."

D. **Non-Gap and Non-Parallel Therories**

1. *Concurrent or Overlapping:* God isn't bound by time. Days could be any interval and could even be overlapping. They are placed in series for our minds (or are in poetic form).

a) *Geo. facts:* Acceptance of the time and sequence of Geo.

b) *Merits:* It explains both Geo. history and antiquity by Genesis "days."

c) *Weakness:* Time *is* relevant to man, and Gen. 1 is speaking to man in *Man's* terms. Evidence of overlap is lacking.

2. *Catastrophy (Flood) Geology:* G.A. come long after the six days as a result of Noahic Flood.

a) *Geo. facts:* Reinterpreted to fit biblical 4000 plus years B.C.

b) *Merits:* Takes Bible seriously. Thinks critically about Geo. theories.

c) *Weakness:* Depends on complete revision of geological science and time. Does not adequately explain much Geo. evidence.

3. *Religious only View:* Language of Gen. is purely religious, not scientific.

a) *Geo. facts:* Gives Geo. full freedom to prove what it will.

b) *Merits:* Resolves all conflict between Bible and science.

c) *Weakness:* Neglects factual and historical aspects of Genesis on which many crucial doctrines are built.

II. SOME CONCLUSIONS

A. Only one view is categorically opposed to evangelical theology, "Religious only" view.

B. No single view should be used as a test of evangelicalness.

C. Crucial problem is age of the earth.

D. Exegetical arguments for "twenty-four hour days" seem stronger (cf. Exod. 20:11), but are not absolute (e.g., "seventh day" is not twenty-four hours).

E. Granting long time periods (millions or billions of years) does not help evolution (*Man's origin* . . . p. 69).

F. Whichever view is accepted should be careful to preserve:
   1. The historicity of Gen. 1-2, and
   2. The historical-grammatical interpretation of Scripture.

NOTES

[1]R. Hooykas, *Religion and Rise of Modern Science* (Grand Rapids: Eerdmans, 1972), p. 19.

[2]Ibid., p. 38.

[3]Henry M. Morris, *Biblical Cosmology and Modern Science* (Grand Rapids: Baker Book House, 1970).

[4]Bernard Ramm, *The Christian View of Science and Scripture* (Grand Rapids: Eerdmans, 1954).

[5]Davis A. Young, *Creation and the Flood* (Grand Rapids: Baker, 1977).

[6]The impartation of a soul to man at some appropriate time would be considered the main exception to God's use of process for a theistic evolutionist who considers Adam as a real, historical person rather than a symbol.

[7]J. Lever, *Where Are We Headed?* (Grand Rapids: Eerdmans, 1970).

[8]R. H. Bube, *The Encounter Between Christianity and Science* (Grand Rapids: Eerdmans, 1968).

[9]P. Teilhard de Chardin, *The Phenomenon of Man* (New York: Harper & Row, 1959).

[10]Robert Young, *Young's Analytical Concordance*, p. 210.

[11]Ibid., pp. 629-31.

[12]Davis A. Young, *Creation*, p. 91.

[13]Robert Young, *Concordance*, pp. 629-31.

[14]Robert Jastrow, *Readers Digest*, (July, 1980), pp. 49-52.

[15]R. H. Bube, *Encounter*, p. 97.

[16]J. Lever, *Where Headed?*, p. 29.

[17]Cyril Ponnamperuma, *The Origins of Life* (London: Thames & Hudson, Ltd., 1972).

[18]I. Prigogine, G. Nicolis and A. Baboloyantz, "Thermodynamics of Evolution," *Physics Today*, (Nov., 1972), pp. 23-31.

[19]Walter J. Moore, *Physical Chemistry*, 3rd Ed. (Englewood Cliffs, NJ: Prentice-Hall, 1962).

[20]Victor F. Weisskopf, "Frontiers and Limits of Science," *American Scientist*, Vol. 65, pp. 405-11.

[21]Harold Morowitz, *Energy Flow in Biology* (New York: Academic Press, 1968).

[22]G. Nicolis and I. Prigogine, *Self-Organization in Non-Equilibrium Systems* (New York: Wiley, 1977).

[23]W. L. Bradley, "Thermodynamics and Origin of Life," Accepted for publication in *Journal of American Scientific Affiliation*.

[24]S. L. Miller and L. E. Orgel, *Origin of Life on Earth* (Englewood Cliffs, NJ: Prentice-Hall, 1974), p. 148.

[25]The metabolic motor common to all living plants and animals would not be present in simple "chemical soup" used in prebiotic synthesis experiments.

[26]S. L. Miller and L. E. Orgel, *Origin of Life*, p. 145.

[27]Francis Crick. *International Journal of Solar Systems Studies*, Vol. 19 (1973), pp. 341-46.

[28]Michael Polyani, *Chemical and Engineering News*, (August 21, 1967), p. 54.

[29]David B. Kitts, *Evolution* (Sept, 1974), p. 458.

[30]S. J. Gould, *Natural History* (May, 1977), p. 14.

[31]Pierre-Paul Grasse, *Evolution of Living Organisms* (New York: Academic Press, 1977), p. 31.

[32]E. Core, *General Biology* (New York: Wiley, 1961), p. 299.

[33]J. Kerby Anderson and Harold G. Coffin, *Fossils in Focus* (Grand Rapids: Zondervan, 1977).

[34]Francis Hitching, *Life Magazine*, April, 1982, pp. 48-52.

[35]Roger Lewin, "Evolution Theory Under Fire," *Science* (Nov. 21, 1980) Vol. 210, pp. 883-87.

[36]M. Eden, quoted by Robert Butler in, "Heresy in the Halls of Biology: Mathematicians Question Darwinism," *Scientific Research* (Nov., 1967), pp. 59-65.

[37]H. G. Cannon, *The Evolution of Living Things* (Manchester, England: Manchester University Press, 1958).

[38]Pierre-Paul Grasse, *Evolution*, p. 88.

[39]Robert Young, *Concordance*, pp. 227-34.

[40]Robert E. Kofahl and Kelly L. Segraves, *The Creation Explanation* (Wheaton: Harold Shaw Publishers), p. 232.

[41] Ibid.

[42]Henry M. Morris, *Cosmology and Science*, p. 59.

[43]Ibid., p. 58.

[44]Robert E. Kofahl and Kelly L. Segraves, *Creation*, p. 233.

[45]Davis A. Young, *Creation*, p. 84.

[46]R. J. Snow, "How Long is the Sixth Day?," Appendix III in *Genesis One and the Origin of the Earth* by Robert C. Newman and Herman J. Eckelmann, Jr. (Downer Grove, Illinois: Inter-Varsity Press, 1977), p. 125.

[47]Walter Kaiser, panel discussion (Wheaton College, May 2, 1978).

[48]Joseph Free, *Archaeology and Bible History* (Wheaton, Illinois: Victor Books, 1950), p. 20.

[49]Ibid., p. 20.

[50]Ibid., p. 20.

[51]Ibid., p. 20.

[52]Bernard Ramm, *Christian View*, p. 147.

[53]Ibid.

[54]T. G. Barnes, *Creation Research Society Quarterly* Vol. 9, No. 4, (March, 1973), p. 222.

[55]Harold S. Slusher, *Age of the Cosmos*, Institute of Creation Research Technical Monograph No. 9 (San Diego: Creation Life Publishers, 1980).

[56]Harold Slusher, *Science and Scripture* (Sept.-Oct., 1971), p. 26.

[57]Raymond Arthur Lyttleton, *The Modern Universe* (Harper Publishers, 1956), p. 72.

[58]Hans Pettersson, *Scientific American*, Vol. 202 (Feb., 1960), p. 132.

[59]Frank Press and Raymond Siever, *Earth* (San Francisco: W. H. Freeman & Company, 1974), p. 66.

[60]Henry M. Morris, *Institute of Creation Research Impact Series*, No. 17, Institute for Creation Research (San Diego, CA, 1975), pp. 1-4.

[61]Frank Press and Raymond Siever, *Earth*, p. 68.

[62]W. C. Pitman III and M. Talwani, "Sea Floor Spreading in the North Atlantic," *Geo. Soc. Amer, Bull.*, Vol. 83 (1972), pp. 619-45.

[63]A. G. Mayor, "Growth Rate of Samoan Corals, in papers from the Department of Marine Biology of the Carnegie Institute of Washington, Vol. 19 (Washington, D.C.: Carnegie Institute Pub. No. 340), pp. 51-72.

[64]W. B. N. Berry and R. M. Barker, *Nature*, Vol. 217 (1968), pp. 938-39.

[65]S. K. Runeorn, "Corals as Paleontological Clocks," *Scientific American*, Vol. 215, pp. 26-33.

[66]Dan Wonderly, *God's Time-Records in Ancient Sediments* (Crystal Press, 1977), pp. 157, 162. (Taken from Harry E. Cook, "North American Stratigraphic Principles as applied to Deep-Sea Sediments," *American Association of Petroleum Geologists Bulletin*, Vol. 59 (1975), p. 824.

[67]R. Y. Anderson, W. E. Dean, Jr., D. W. Kirkland, and H. I. Snider, "Permian Castile Varied Evaporite Sequence," (West Texas and New Mexico) *Geo. Soc. Amer. Bull.*, Vol. 83, pp. 59-86.

[68]Robert C. Newman and Herman J. Eckelmann, Jr., *Genesis One*, pp. 15-30.

[69]A. Cox, G. B. Dalrymple and R. R. Doell, "Reversals of the Earth's Magnetic Field," *Scientific American*, Vol. 216, No. 2 (1967), pp. 44-54. J. R. Dunn, M. Fuller, H. Ito, and V. A. Schmidt, "Paleonmagnetic Study of a Reversal of the Earth's Magnetic Field," *Science*, Vol. 172 (1971), pp. 840-45. D. W. Strangway, *History of the Earth's Magnetic Field* (McGraw-Hill Book Co., 1970), p. 168.

[70]J. M. Hall and P. T. Robinson, *Science*, Vol. 204 (1979), pp. 573-86.

[71]Many different articles and comments in this area have appeared in *Physics Today* during the past several years.

[72]Mic, G., *Ann. Physik*, vol. 25, 377 (1908).

[73]Frank Press and Raymond Siever, *Earth*, p. 803.

[74]Stephen G. Bush, "Creation/Evolution: The Case Against 'Equal Time,' " *The Science Teacher* (April, 1981), p. 29.

[75]A. Funkhouser and J. Naughton, *Journal of Geophysical Research*, Vol. 73, No. 14 (July 15, 1978), p. 4601.

[76]Davis A. Young, *Creation*, p. 189.

[77]Don L. Eicher, *Geological Time* (Foundations of Earth Science Series, ed. A. Lee McAlester (Englewood Cliffs, NJ: Prentice-Hall, Inc., 1968), pp. 137-38.

[78]F. E. Zeuner, *Dating the Past: An Introduction to Geochronology*, 3rd Edition (New York: Longmans & Green Co., 1952).

[79]Robert E. Kofahl and Kelly L. Segraves, *Creation*, p. 201.

[80]Dan Wonderly, *God's Time Record in Ancient Sediments* (Flint, MI: Crystal Press, 1977).

[81]Henry Morris, *The Remarkable Birth of Planet Earth* (San Diego: Creation Life Publishers, 1970), 62.

[82]E. T. Brewster, *Creation: A History of Non-Evolutionary Theories* (Indianapolis: The Bobbs-Merrill Co., 1927), p. 112.

[83]Appendix I was graciously provided by Professor Norm Geisler of Dallas Theological Seminary.

[84]Bernard Ramm, *Christian View*, p. 149.

[85]T. E. Kalem, "Putting Darwin Back in the Dock," *Time* (March 16, 1981), pp. 80-82.

[86]Robert C. Newman and Herman S. Eckelmann, *Genesis One and the Origin of the Earth* (Downer Grove: InterVarsity, 1977), 67-79.

[87]Stephen G. Brush, "Creation/Evolution: The Case Against 'Equal Time' " *The Science Teacher*, (April, 1981), pp. 24-31.

A Response to The Trustworthiness of Scripture in Areas Relating to Natural Science

Gleason L. Archer
Professor of Old Testament
and Semitics
Trinity Evangelical Divinity
School

A Response to The Trustworthiness of Scripture in Areas Relating to Natural Science

Gleason L. Archer

This clear and well-written discussion deals largely with the case against the Young Earth Theory espoused by advocates of the twenty-four hour interpretation of the creative days in Genesis 1. This is probably the most debated area of interpretation among inerrantists today and represents an issue of decisive importance to the science of biblical hermeneutics. The question of the trustworthiness of Scripture is definitely at stake in the reconciliation of Genesis 1 and 2. If these two passages are construed in such a way as to establish a basic contradiction between the two, the inerrancy of Scripture is fatally undermined. This then is an issue that must be honestly faced and dealt with according to sound hermeneutical procedure, such as is normally employed in treating all other matters of doctrine in which Scripture must be compared with Scripture.

But before we launch into an extended discussion of Young Earth geology and its hermeneutical assumptions, we should first observe that there are many other areas in which reconciliation is needed between scientific theory and biblical references to matters of science.

The legitimacy and appropriateness of phenomenal language should be dealt with very carefully, especially in view of the fact that modern twentieth century science textbooks employ different terms in referring to meteorological processes, to flora and fauna and the operation of physics and mathematical science. Criticisms leveled at biblical references to these matters are usually framed in complete disregard of contextual factors and characteristics of literary genres. Matters of common sense and prevalent contemporary practice are largely ignored to an amazing degree of naiveté and oversimplification.

By the term "phenomenal language" we refer to things as they appear to human observers outside of the laboratory or the astronomical observatory. Modern exponents of scientism often speak disparagingly of such phrases as "the four corners of the earth" (as if implying a rectangular earth-surface) and "from the rising of the sun to the going down thereof" (as implying a terracentric theory for the solar system). But honesty demands that we face the fact that our scientifically enlightened twentieth-century usage still adheres to the terms "sunrise" and "sunset" just as habitually as the ancients ever did. It would be utterly absurd for some future generation of scientific savants to fault our calendars and almanacs for giving the exact times for "sunrise" and assume therefrom that we are a terracentric, backwardly primitive culture in this twentieth century. The same is true of the term "eclipse," whether of the sun or of the moon, since there is actually no part of either of them that is removed or missing in their spherical structure (the Greek *ekleipsis* means "a forsaking; a disappearance" rather than "an overshadowing by an intervening spherical body").

A similar principle of recognition of phenomenal language is involved in the events of the fourth creative day (Gen. 1:14-19). Taken by itself, the final clause of verse 16 appears to say that God made (*wayya' aś 'ᵉlōhīm*) the sun, the moon and the stars in the fourth creative day. It is safe to say that scientific creationists who hold to a twenty-four hour day are heliocentric in their concept of the solar system, i.e., they understand that earth and the other planets revolve about the sun. Now if the sun was not actually created until three days or more after the earth, it gives rise to at least two serious problems: (1) a complete lack of orientation as to the orbit of earth until the sun was installed as the central focus for its annual revolution; (2) the difficulty of explaining the process of photosynthesis essential for the terrestrial vegetation created on the previous day, during which the most advanced seed-bearing plants and trees were brought to full development. The suggestion advanced by some writers that there was some kind of cosmic light that was created on day one in response to God's command, "Let there be light!" has little to commend it, and that for two reasons: (a) there is no reference to *'ōr* ("light") anywhere else in Scripture that is not connected with the sun or stars, or with moons or planets which reflect sunlight, or to fire resulting from combustion; (b) there is no scientific evidence whatever for photosynthesis resulting from cosmic light alone.

The harmonization of the creation of light on the first day and the role of the sun and the other heavenly bodies on the fourth day is quite obvious, in view of the specified purpose that God articulated in Genesis 1:14-15: that the heavenly bodies might serve as clear illuminators of the earth's surface and might indicate time-divisions with ascertainable accuracy: "Let them be for signs and for seasons and for days and for years." It is fair to deduce from the innovative element in verse 14 that previously the light from the sun had been filtered through a cloud cover thin enough to permit proper plant growth but too thick to afford accuracy in calculating the exact time of sunrise, the vernal or autumnal equinox, or the true length of the solar year itself. At last the cloud cover was parted and clear blue sky became visible to observers on earth. The Scripture makes use of a phenomenal approach in this passage.

On a smaller scale the same principle applies to such matters as the inclusion of the *shāphān* (identified with the *Hyrax syriacus*) as a ruminant in Leviticus 11:5. There it is stated that this "coney" or "rock badger" (NASB) "chews the cud, even though it does not divide the hoof." A similar comment is made about the "rabbit" (*'arnebet*) in Leviticus 11:6. Although it is true that neither animal does not regurgitate cuds from its stomach to chew them over again—as true ruminants do—they give the appearance of chewing their cud in the same way as genuine ruminants do. It is said that even Linnaeus at first classified them with ruminants because of this resemblance. They actually do practice "reflection," or the re-mastication of their droppings, while resting in the shade (ZPEB 3:33), and so their inclusion with ruminants is quite justifiable from the phenomenal standpoint. A similar observation pertains to the description of the whale who swallowed Jonah as *dāg gādōl* ("a large fish"), Jonah 1:17. The term *dāg* may well have included any aquatic animal of a bodily structure resembling that of a fish, even such mammals as whales and dolphins. If this was the semantic scope of the Hebrew term used, as established by literary usage, it is inadmissible to categorize such phenomenal terms as scientifically erroneous.

The examples above cited lead us to the guiding principle that applies to valid interpretation of any literary production, whether secular or sacred: the concern of the interpreter is to discover as accurately as possible what the original author meant by the words that he used, rather than imposing on his text meanings attached to terms used for translation purposes in some foreign language. Even earlier English works, such as those of Chaucer or Shakespeare, may be improperly construed by twentieth-century speakers of English who have not taken the trouble to discover what men of the fourteenth or seventeenth century meant or connoted by the words used differently then from what they signify today. A careful study of parallel usage elsewhere in Scripture is absolutely vital for valid interpretation of any biblical text. It should also be perfectly evident that it is wrong to take figuratively what the original author meant literally, or to take literally what the author intended in a figurative way. (In the latter class would be our Lord's dictum: "It is easier for a camel to go through the eye of a needle than for a rich man to enter into the Kingdom of God"—Matt. 19:24.) It is, therefore, ill-advised for any evangelical Bible teacher to urge the necessity of "taking the Bible literally." Anyone who takes literally what God means figuratively is right on the brink of heresy!

After this preliminary discussion of basic principles involved in valid interpretation of Holy Scripture, we revert to the particular issues raised by the Bradley-Olsen paper. Their purpose is to survey the objective scientific data bearing upon the antiquity of the planet earth, or of the universe in general, since the time of their first creation. Their analysis of the arguments advanced by the exponents of the Old Earth and Young Earth approach is very helpful and convincing, so far as this reviewer has any competence to make a judgment. It seems that their handling of the evidence provided by geological science has been fairly done, even though Recent Creationists might feel that there is throughout the discussion the influence of an underlying commitment to the Old Age Theory. Yet it should be observed that all investigations of a scholarly nature involve scholars who have already been attracted to one side or the other of the matter under discussion and that observation certainly pertains to the proponents of Young Earth geology. They, too, operate upon the basis of an underlying presupposition that has a strongly determinative effect upon their handling of the evidence.

The presupposition referred to in this case is that Genesis 1 actually does teach or reveal that the planet earth was fully created in six twenty-four hour days. If this is a valid interpretation of Genesis 1, then logical integrity demands that Christian scholars in the field of science should make every effort to show that there is no body of objective scientific data, whether in geology or in astronomy, which is not compatible with a maximum interval of 10,000 years since creation began. (Stricter constructionists of the genealogical material of Genesis 5 and 11 might find even the suggestion of 10,000 years impossible to accept, since their interpretation of those texts as a tight line of descent without any links omitted leads them to a starting date of no more than 6000 B.C. or even more recent than that.) Be that as it may, the perception of Genesis 1 as clearly teaching a succession of six twenty-four-hour days would certainly bind the conscience of the true believer, whether a scientist or a layman, to a very tenacious defense against the long-age theories of secular science. Their interpretation of Scripture really obligates them to do so. Nevertheless, it needs to be demonstrated that there are at least two main fallacies which discredit this viewpoint so seriously as to make it well-nigh untenable.

The more serious difficulty with the twenty-four hour theory is that it gives rise to an insoluble contradiction with Genesis 2. Since this contradiction is easy to prove, it results in a fatal undermining of the inerrancy of Scripture to which all consistent evangelicals are committed. The surrender of inerrancy is too high a price to pay for the preservation of the twenty-four hour day theory, and therefore it should be very firmly insisted that Genesis 1 be construed in a sense compatible with the data of Genesis 2.

The crucial passage in Genesis 1:27 tells us very clearly that Eve was created as well as Adam during the sixth creative day. "And God created man (*'ādām*) in His own image, in the image of God He created him; male *and female* He created them." Since man is not mentioned in the list of sixth-day creations until all of the other terrestrial animals had been produced (vv. 24-25), it is fair to assume that no more than an hour or two would have been left toward the close of the sixth day for the introduction of Eve upon the scene.

Chapter 2 of Genesis supplies more detailed information concerning the succession of events transpiring between the creation of Adam and the creation of Eve. These events are as follows:

1. Genesis 2:7 records the creation of Adam from the "dust" (or the chemical constituents) of the ground, and the special infusion or inbreathing of His "breath" (*n^e shamah*, or more exactly, *nishmat hayyīm*, "the breath of life") into the nostrils of this climactic creation, fashioned in the "image" (*selem*) of God. Since God forbids the worship of any graven image (in the Second Commandment) and emphasized to Israel that no graven image (*pesel*) or resemblance of any three-dimensional kind (*t^e munah*) was to be made or revered, we can only conclude that the *selem* in which Adam and Eve were fashioned bore only a spiritual resemblance or analogy to their Creator, "in knowledge, righteousness and holiness" (as the Westminster Shorter Catechism defines it).

2. Genesis 2:15 next records that God placed Adam in a specially prepared environment, the Garden of Eden, and assigned him the responsibility of cultivating and caring for this large and beautiful

park area, with its abundance of streams and lush vegetation. He was put in charge of this entire area as an administrator, under a covenant of obedience to God (especially in regard to the "tree of the knowledge of good and evil"). It is clearly implied that his general supervision of Eden went on for a fairly extended period of time.

3. Genesis 2:18 relates how the Lord perceived Adam's sense of personal unfulfillment as he carried on this arduous task, for he lacked companionship. "It is not good for the man to be alone," God observed, "I will make him a helper suitable for him" (*'ēzer kᵉnegdō*—literally "a helper corresponding to him"). This qualification could only be fulfilled by Adam's future wife, as Genesis 2:20 makes clear. Nevertheless, the Lord saw fit to bring Adam first into closer fellowship with the animals and birds of the Edenic environment, if not of the earth as a whole. This involved nothing less than carrying out a major project in taxonomy: the careful study and assignment for an appropriate specie's name for every single animal and bird known to the Middle East. Many hundreds of species must have been involved. Adam had no fund of earlier nomenclature to fall back upon; he had to decide upon all of these names by himself. Apparently they were to be official and permanent names, accepted by God Himself, since "whatever the man called a living creature, that was its name" (Gen. 2:19).

If this assignment was thoughtfully and carefully carried out, involving as it did a certain amount of personal attention and the study of each specimen from every angle, taking stock of factors of shape and color and texture and the sound of voice, it must have required a considerable period of time. The Swedish taxonomist Linnaeus back in the eighteenth century is said to have taken a good thirty years in carrying out his survey of the flora and fauna known to European scholarship. To be sure, his techniques of examination of internal structure and his concern for genera as well as species must have demanded more time than the pre-scientific approach of our first parent operating entirely upon his own. But in the absence of computer technology it is safe to conclude that Adam must have required several months at least to carry out this project in an adequate fashion—especially in view of the factor of personal fellowship with each specimen to be assigned a distinctive name. There is a clear implication that a cordial personal relationship was to be cultivated between Adam and all of his menagerie, for the announced purpose of this natural history project was to mitigate or temporarily (at least) to banish Adam's feelings of loneliness amid the green paradise of

Eden. Yet the latter part of verse 20 states "but for Adam there was not found a helper (i.e., a life's partner) suitable for him."

This introduces us to the third stage of Adam's career prior to the creation of Eve. The Lord induced him to fall into a deep sleep, during which the first bone operation performed under anesthesia was carried out. There is no suggestion that this deep sleep was very suddenly induced or very quickly brought to its determination by the removal of the rib within a few seconds. And yet this kind of speed would have been absolutely essential if Adam and God had been working on a very limited time frame while the sun was fast approaching the horizon at the end of a sixth twenty-four hour day. Nor is there any hint that Adam himself had to go through a frenetic performance of spitting out specie's names faster than the mind could think—as the twenty-four hour day theory demands. What we have here is not a comically speeded up movie scene, but a beautiful, dignified, leisurely account of a career completed by Adam as a bachelor prior to the appearance of Eve. Indeed it is safe to say that any unbiased reader, not previously committed to an adverse presupposition, would gather from the wording of Genesis 2 that there was a long and careful preparation of Adam by God in order for him to appreciate and adore that woman whom God fashioned from his rib. The impression of an extended period of time for the large taxonomic project would also be unavoidable.

If this be the case, we must face a very basic issue involved in the science of hermeneutics. All biblical scholars admit that *yōm* ("day") may be used in a figurative or symbolic manner, as well as in a literal sense. This is very evident in Genesis 2:4: "This is the account of the heavens and the earth when they were created, in the *day* that the LORD God made earth and heaven." Since we have just been told in chapter 1 that six days were involved in the creative process, it is perfectly evident that *yōm* in Genesis 2:4 could not refer to a twenty-four hour day. In the frequent phrase, *yōm Yahweh,* "Day of Yahweh" (Isa. 2:12; 13:6, 9; Amos 5:18, 20; Jer. 46:10; Ezek. 13:5; 30:3 and many more) it is impossible to take this period of God's vengeance upon His foes as restricted to a mere twenty-four hours. The same is true of *yōm gāsīr,* "(in the) day of harvest." Nowhere on earth is an entire ingathering of crops accomplished in a single day.

Since the term *yōm* may refer to an interval of time when the transaction referred to achieves completion (whether it be a twelve-hour period, as in Genesis 1:5, or in a twenty-four hour period, or in a more extended space of time), it is necessary to establish in the light of the context and of comparable usage elsewhere in the Scripture, in which sense *yōm* is used. In any serious study of Bible doctrine it is absolutely essential to bring together all biblical passages bearing upon the subject in hand. Failure to do so violates the principle of comparing Scripture with Scripture (1 Cor. 2:13). It results in the kind of false teaching that emanates from the Russelite, who argues that since Jesus did get tired and sleepy upon occasion, whereas God never slumbers nor sleeps, Jesus could not have been God. The fallacy lies in the failure to compare *all* that the Scripture says about the Lord Jesus Christ in His divine nature and in His human nature. It is through comparing Scripture with Scripture that we come to an understanding of the Holy Trinity and of the hypostatic union of Christ.

In the case of Genesis 1 and 2, therefore, a proper methodology requires us to line them both up beside each other and see how they fall into focus with each other. Unless we are to side with skeptics who maintain that Genesis 1 and 2 must come from two different authors at two different periods of time, we are compelled to see that the long interval of time between the creation of Adam and the creation of Eve utterly precludes a twenty-four hour interpretation—for the sixth creative day at least. And if the sixth day was much longer than a single rotation of the earth, then there is no reason to believe that the first five were twenty-four-hour intervals either. The days of Genesis 1 must have involved a longer process of time than a single calendar day. The *yōm* is rather to be understood as a symbol of the beginning and completion of a distinct stage in the unfolding work of creation. The wording "And the evening and the morning took place, as day one" or "as a second day" (the Hebrew text has no definite article for any of the first six days) emphasizes the process aspect of the creative stage from its earliest beginnings to its final completion. There may be some analogy also with the occasions when God commanded Ezekiel to lie on his left side, symbolizing the 390 years of Israel's apostasy, and on his right side for 40 days, "a day for each year." Or again to the celebration of the Feast of Booths (*Sukkōt*) for a period of eight days, in commemoration of the forty years of wilderness wandering under Moses during the Exodus. The argument that *yōm* never means anything else in the Hebrew Bible but a literal twenty-four hours is completely untenable in the light of scriptural usage elsewhere. Furthermore, it tends to set up a genuine and essential contradiction between two passages in Scripture (in view of the unavoidable inference of a long time interval between the creation of Adam and that of Eve). And if a true contradiction can be shown to exist (on the basis of an insistence upon a twenty-four hour day interpretation) between these two chapters, then the doctrine of Scriptural Inerrancy must be abandoned.

It is, therefore, on such basic grounds as these that we must insist that Genesis 1 was not intended by either the Divine Author or by the human author (Moses) to teach that the whole work of creation took only six calendar days to complete—even though we may freely concede that God *could* have done it that way had He chosen to do so. In other words, Moses never intended the creative days to be understood as a mere twenty-four hours in length, and the information he included in chapter 2 logically precludes us from doing so. It is only by a neglect of proper hermeneutical method that this impression ever became prevalent among God's people, during the post-biblical era. Entirely apart from any findings of modern science or challenges of contemporary scientism, the twenty-four-hour theory was never correct and should never have been believed—except by those who are bent on proving the presence of genuine contradictions in Scripture.

A comment should be made in this connection relative to the Sabbath ordinance in the Decalogue, which stipulates (in Ex. 20:10-11) that the seventh day of each seven-day week is to be honored as holy, because Yahweh God made the heavens and earth and sea in six days and rested on the seventh. By no means does this demonstrate that twenty-four-hour intervals were involved in the first six "days," any more than the eight-day celebration of the Feast of Tabernacles proves that the wilderness wanderings under Moses occupied only eight days. The reminder of God's marvelous power, wisdom, and grace, culminating in the completion stage of God's "resting" after His six earlier stages in the creative process, could only have been celebrated by sanctifying one whole day in seven for this purpose. It was the number and sequence of the successive phases of creation that was symbolized by the institution of a seven-day week, rather than a reproducing of the precise time-interval involved in each stage. In view of the fact that no terminus is indicated in Genesis 2:2-3 so far as the Seventh Day is concerned, and Hebrews 4:4-10 states that God's Sabbath continues on without delimitation, it is hardly justifiable to claim for the first six days preceding any more circumscribed duration than is true of the seventh.

If, then, the Bible does not teach a six-calendar-day creation, and if the purpose of Genesis 1 is to show forth that the God of the

Bible is the only God there is, and that He by Himself created the sun, the moon, the stars, the winds and the seas, the rocks and the mountains, and everything that lives and grows upon the surface of the earth—then what we really have in this opening chapter of Holy Scripture is a manifesto directed at all the perversions and superstitions of ancient polytheism as well as of modern scientism. For modern scientism also has its absurd superstitions, such as the belief in the eternity of matter, or the possibility of orderly development according to an intricate and integrated plan—without any transcendent planner or creator. In fact, we must point out that any scientific theorist who believes that uncontrolled fortuity as the explanation of life and the universe has already canceled himself of all rational validity or meaningful dialogue. The reason for this lies in his proposition that all matter results from a chance collocation of atoms. If that be the case, then the molecules of the brain with which the materialistic-humanist does his thinking is also a mere product of a chance collocation of atoms. As such, therefore, his analysis of issues and his construction of events may have no connection with ontological reality and the only thing he can be sure of is his own opinion. By his own premises, then, he has condemned himself to solipsistic subjectivism and has absolutely nothing of assured validity to share with anyone else. This observation carries with it an inevitable corollary: science itself is rendered impossible upon any atheistic hypothesis. For science is predicated upon the assumption of assured regularity and control. But if the atheistic premise is correct, all is dependent upon sheer fortuity, and there is no true connection between cause and effect. If chance is the real basis of physical law, then any result may follow from any cause, and the orderly observation and systematization of data becomes totally impossible. Only if there is an intelligent guiding force or controlling intelligence outside of material reality is it possible to conduct scientific investigation at all. Otherwise there is no guaranteed regularity to observe. So much for the challenge of atheistic evolutionism!

Passing now from the problem of contradiction between Genesis 1 and 2, we turn our attention to the second major difficulty with the Young Age Theory. The Creation Scientist scholars show an interest and concern with the data of scientific investigation which is certainly as sincere as any of the agnostic or atheistic exponents of philosophic evolutionism. Their resourcefulness in coping with problems and their innovativeness in constructing new avenues of investigation is impressive indeed. Their exploitation of such embarrassing discoveries as the hominid footprints crossing paths with the brontosaurus in the Paluxy River bed in Texas has served to alert the public as to the questionable nature of the chronological schemes and biological sequence patterns of the paleobiologists who presently control the university scene. But on the other hand, salutary as their iconoclasm may be, there seems to be throughout their handling of evidences an underlying preoccupation with the 10,000 year deadline that controls their entire line of investigation. Many of them appear to be superbly equipped and highly informed for the task of unraveling the geological past. They will undoubtedly force upon the scientific establishment many a needful correction in the formation of a valid paleontology. Many of the new discoveries appearing in Bible-Science Newsletter are delightfully damaging to the evolutionist Old Guard. But their objectivity is often compromised by their commitment to a misunderstanding of the Genesis chronology, and the result is that their impact upon the current debate is not as formidable as it ought to be.

The basic principle set forth by the Bradley-Olsen paper that God has revealed Himself both in Holy Scripture and in His created world can hardly be quarreled with by any Bible student who has ever read Romans 1:19-21 and Psalm 19. The added comment: "We believe these revelations are equally valid and essentially complementary" is a bit overdrawn, however, since the direct "Thus saith the Lord" in Holy Scripture surely surpasses in clarity the moral nature and the holy will of God for our lives. Our Lord's "eternal power and godhead" are certainly revealed by nature, and likewise His glory as sovereign Creator. But we do not come into redemptive contact with Him apart from Special Revelation. Moreover it is through God's written Word that we gain insight into the origin and significance of the created world about us. Nevertheless, the Bible itself teaches us to recognize both general revelation (through the evidence of nature) and special revelation (through God's written Word) in conjunction with each other and indeed, also in harmony with each other. This involves an openness to what the rocks and strata and fossils have to tell us concerning the marvelous works of God, both His works of creation and His works of preservation and development. This means that in our study of geological strata we are not compelled to regard what seems to be the result of alluvial deposits and magmatic intrusions and long continued erosion as a pattern already present at a recent date of creation. Nor must we assume that strata apparently laid down by gentle water action as well as the boulders and coarse gravel of more violent water run-off as all alike the result of a single year during Noah's flood. The realization that the six stages of Genesis 1 do not represent calendar days leaves the Christian geologist free to draw tentative conclusions from his data, even as the non-Christian scientist tries to do. And yet between them there is a great gulf fixed, so far as basic presuppositions are concerned.

The basic difference has to do with the underlying principle of development, which is often referred to as Evolution. As the term has been used (entirely apart from its non-committal Latin etymology), Evolution has acquired the connotation of spontaneous, self-directed change resulting in the production of new varieties or species. Some draw a distinction between micro-evolution and macro-evolution, and suggest that micro-evolution is consistent with biblical teaching. But if this implies that organisms that God has created have been invested with ability to alter their form on their own initiative, apart from the control and guidance of God, then it seems to me that even micro-evolution is to be rejected as well, for the Bible assures us of an ever-present all-encompassing involvement of God in all of His creatures. Christ "sustains all things by His Word of power" (Heb. 1:3), "all things consist, or hold together, in Him" (Col. 1:17), "all things have been subjected beneath His feet" (Eph. 1:22), God's eye is on every sparrow that falls, and the hairs of our head are all numbered (Matt. 10:29-30). These passages and many like them seem to preclude the idea that any smallest activity or genetic alteration can be carried on without God's superintending care. This would seem to me to eliminate even the concept of micro-evolution—as the term is normally understood. Nor is there the slightest leeway in Scripture for what is called Theistic Evolution, unless the term "evolution" is divested of its usual meaning. As in honest merchandising, we would be well advised to avoid confusing or misleading labels; it is best to abjure evolution in any form as compatible with scriptural teaching. Connected as it is with Charles Darwin's definition of the term as indicating a process of auto-genesis quite independent of divine observation and control.

On the other hand, we challenge the right of exponents of the Young Earth Theory to label as evolutionist those who interpret the geologic evidence as indicating a long period of time between primal creation and the appearance of man upon the earth scene. There is no inherent connection between evolution (with its implications of auto-genesis and fortuitous alteration) and the length of time indicated by rock formations, extinct fossils, and radioactive minerals. All of these geochronological indicators are just as directly under God's control and ordained by His sovereign will as if they came into being no earlier than 10,000 years ago.

Likewise we should understand clearly that there is no necessary connection between a belief in the gradual deposition of strata and the uniformitarian assumptions of secular paleobiologists. Rightly defined, the uniformitarians assume that throughout all ages preceding the rates of sedimentation proceeded substantially at the same rate as they do today; that continental drift must always have been at the same speed as now; that radioactive decomposition must have remained unaffected by varying conditions in their immediate surroundings. Like the dogmatic scoffers of Peter's day, they insist, "All things continue as they were from the beginning of creation," ignoring the catastrophic changes indicated by geology itself and the supreme catastrophe of all (as Peter goes on to point out—2 Pet. 3:3-6) the worldwide, universal flood of Noah's time, which covered even the highest mountain summits over the entire earth (Gen. 7:19). The startling changes in land surfaces, nearly all of which show prehistorical marine deposits, the discovery of former vegetation in the Sahara Desert and in the continent of Antarctica, the indications of varying direction and force of the earth's magnetism (as so clearly described in the Bradley paper) are sufficient to make uniformitarianism logically untenable. The immense pressures that produced the Alps, the Andes, and the Rocky Mountain systems cannot be even remotely paralleled by phenomena observable today—with the violent eastward thrust of one mountain range over another, and the Alps so violently overturned that their geological history is almost unreadable. Uniformitarianism amounts to a creed that must be clung to in the teeth of the evidence.

Let me conclude this Response by pointing to the apologetic implications of recognizing the Age-Day implications of Genesis 1. Who can calculate the large numbers of college students who have been turned away from the Bible altogether by the false impression that it bound the conscience of the believer to the 24-hour Day Theory? Once we understand that this is not really what Genesis teaches at all (in view of the information contained in chapter 2), we can demonstrate that there is no conflict between the explanation of nature revealed in Scripture and the geologic evidence of an ancient earth. And once this roadblock is removed, and the many amazing insights into scientific realities and factors that have only recently been discovered by modern man, the congruity between Scripture and the true science can only serve as a powerful encouragement to any open-minded seeker after life's meaning to find his answer in Jesus Christ, the God of the Hebrew-Christian Scriptures. These are days of expanding opportunities for demolishing the whole system of atheistic evolutionism, now that scholars of the stature of Robert Jastrow feel compelled to admit that outside of theism there is really no satisfactory explanation for the control of a system of order governing the entire universe. The foundations of materialistic humanism are now being eroded and the deluded millions who have put their faith in scientism have been alerted to the inadequacy of their false messiah. This opens the way for an agressive, logically compelling advance upon the forces of spiritual opposition to Christ and His gospel, and this is the time for us to exploit the opportunity for all it is worth.

A Response to The Trustworthiness of Scripture in Areas Relating to Natural Science

Henry M. Morris
President of the Institute for
Creation Research

A Response to The Trustworthiness of Scripture in Areas Relating to Natural Sciences

Henry M. Morris

Dr. Bradley has rightly emphasized the historicity and scientific accuracy of Genesis 1-2, a position which must be held without compromise by all who take biblical inerrancy seriously. His treatment of prebiotic evolution and macro-evolution is excellent, showing that these notions are refuted by the laws of probability, by the second law of thermodynamics, and by the ubiquitous gaps in the fossil record. He also recognizes that evolution is unscriptural. "Theistic evolution" seems to most creationists to be at best a contradiction in terms, on a par semantically with "Christian atheism." Evolution seems to us to be the most wasteful, inefficient, and cruel process that could ever be conceived by which to produce man, and yet some Christians are willing to charge God with such insensitivity and incompetence. In any case, we are firmly persuaded that both the Bible and all true facts of science support special creation. Dr. Bradley is to be commended for his unequivocal stand on this great truth.

I. THE BIBLICAL CASE FOR LITERAL-DAY CREATION

It is disappointing, however, that he is not willing to take a similar stand on the equally clear biblical teaching of *recent* creation. Here, despite his good intentions, he allows modern uniformitarian philosophy to determine his interpretation of Scripture, instead of taking the higher ground of interpreting the physical data in light of Scripture. Since, as he says, "Genesis may still be interpreted" to allow for the great ages demanded by uniformitarians and evolutionists, Dr. Bradley and other "progressive creationists" simply resort to whatever hermeneutical techniques they find necessary to accommodate these geological ages. This is not the normal and proper way to exegete the Word of God.

Since (as Bradley himself recognizes) *yom* almost always means a literal day, since the use of the ordinal with *yom* always in other

Scriptures limits the meaning to literal days, since the phrase "evening and morning" always in other passages has the literal meaning, and since *yamim* ("days," as in Exodus 20:11) elsewhere is always literal, the burden of proof surely lies heavily on anyone who would choose nevertheless to interpret the days of Genesis 1 in terms of geological ages. There is certainly nothing *in context* to justify it. If one were deliberately to set out to describe creation in six literal days, there is no language that would do this better than the words actually used in Genesis 1.

This compelling body of evidence, nevertheless, is all rejected with the remarkable argument that, since Genesis 1 is a special case, the normal meanings of words in other parts of Scripture do not apply here! The fact is, however, that the only reason for calling Genesis 1 a special case is because of the assumed necessity to accommodate the evolutionary geochronology.

It is common, of course, to deny that evolutionary thought has led to the long-age interpretation of creation. Ancient expositors such as Origen and others expounded Genesis in such nonliteral fashion long before Darwin's time. This argument defeats itself, however, for Origen and his followers were merely attempting (with the same purpose as Bradley) to conform biblical revelation to the then current evolutionary long-age cosmology of ancient Greek pantheism. Modern expositors tend to ignore the important fact that ancient religions and philosophies all assumed long ages and some form of evolution.[1] The concept of special, recent creation is essentially unique to Genesis. That is why the divine author of Genesis had to be so clear and emphatic in specifying real creation in six literal days—otherwise its early readers would have tried to interpret it allegorically in terms of one of the evolutionary cosmologies with which they were already familiar.

II. THE COMPLETED WORK OF CREATION

The contention that *bara* ("create") and *asah* ("make") point to two different types of divine activity during the creation week is valid to a limited degree, but certainly not to the degree that interprets the first process as a completed supernatural process and the second as a continuing naturalistic process. In Genesis 1, *bara* is used when a basic entity (e.g., space, mass, time, life) is created by God *ex nihilo*, *asah* when created entities are organized by God into specific complex systems. That *both* are essentially supernatural activities of God is affirmed by the summary verse of the chapter—"God blessed the seventh day, and sanctified it: because that in it He had rested from all His work which God created and made" (Genesis 2:3). That is, both the *bara* work of God and the *asah* work of God were "finished" by the end of the sixth day. Thus, present-day "natural" processes are *not* the processes which God used in creation week. These present processes can be considered as His "providential" work, that of conserving His completed creation (Colossians 1:16-17; Hebrews 1:2-3; 2 Peter 3:5-7; Nehemiah 9:6; Ecclesiastes 3:14, etc.), but not as part of His work of "creating" and "making" all things (Exodus 20:11) in the beginning.

This does not mean, of course, that God is unable either to "create" or "make" things today if He chooses to do so, but only that, when He does, it involves once again His miraculous intervention, not the everyday natural processes that reflect His continual providential care of His creation. Such verses as Isaiah 54:16, cited by Bradley, do not refer to natural development, but to God's special creation of all men. There thus seems no justification at all for Dr. Bradley's opinion that either *bara* or *asah* in Genesis 1 could refer to natural processes like those in operation today. Zechariah 10:1, which he also cites to support this contention, actually is promising a special answer to prayer, not the ordinary functioning of clouds and rain, thus itself illustrating the principle that when *asah* is associated with a work of God, that work is a special work, not what we would call an ordinary mechanistic process.

Furthermore, it is not at all clear what progressive creationists have in mind when they reject evolution and yet accept "processes" as a major part of God's creative activity. What processes do they mean, if not evolutionary processes? "Micro-evolution" is merely another name for "variation," and is quite irrelevant to the discussion, since such processes do not require millions of years, and are fully accepted and emphasized as integral to the creation model by all scientific creationists. Is he postulating a "god of the gaps" concept, calling for special creation at every gap in the fossil record, or is he actually allowing for macro-evolutionary processes operating through the long geological ages. If the former, then he is postulating many more acts of special creation than even the "mature creationist" accepts; if the latter, then such an exposition is practically indistinguishable from that of the theistic evolutionist.

III. THE THEOLOGICAL FALLACIES

As a matter of fact, theistic evolution seems actually to be a sounder concept theologically than progressive creation. That is, the theistic evolutionist at least credits God with enough power and foresight to plan and implement the entire process right at the beginning. The progressive creationist, on the other hand, visualizes a God who must repeatedly intervene in the process, one who must step in frequently to redirect it when it deviates and to re-energize it when it stagnates. Both theistic evolution and progressive creation, of course, are built on the framework of the geological ages, which are based specifically on the fossil record. And whatever one may think of the evolutionary implications of this system, it is crystal clear that the great fossil graveyards of the world speak primarily of suffering and death, on a worldwide, age-long scale. This spectacle has to be viewed by the evolutionist and progressive creationist not as the result of sin and judgment, but as integral to the creative process itself. Thus, both theistic evolution and progressive creation imply that the Creator Himself is to blame for such a system—an awesome spectacle of waste and inefficiency, suffering and death which, if true, makes atheistic evolution more understandable and reasonable than either of these compromising philosophies.

IV. OTHER PROBLEMS WITH THE DAY/AGE THEORY

There are other serious weaknesses in the day/age type of exegesis. The very first usage of *yom* clearly defines its meaning, in context. "God called the light Day, and the darkness He called Night. And the evening, and the morning were the first Day" (Genesis 1:5). God defines His terms! The *yom* is the "light" period in the cyclical succession of light and darkness, which began with the first *yom* and has continued ever since.

The so-called revelatory-day theory, along with every other form of the day-age theory, is completely demolished by God's unequivocal statement in Exodus 20:8-11. "Remember the sabbath day, to keep it holy. Six days shalt thou labor, and do all thy work: . . . For in six days the Lord made heaven and earth, the sea, and all that in them is, and rested the seventh day. . . ."

How could language possibly be any more clear and explicit than this? Man is to work six days (*yamim*) because God worked six days. The same word is used, the same construction—everything is completely parallel. If man's "days" are not the same as God's "days," then language becomes meaningless. At the very best, God was then using some kind of inept pun. Remember also that this section is part of the Ten Commandments, "tables of stone, written with the finger of God" (Exodus 31:18). All of the Bible is divinely inspired, but this passage was divinely inscripturated! If any part of the Bible must be taken seriously, this is it. And this passage says, as plainly and emphatically as any words that could ever be devised for such a meaning, that God made the entire universe in six days. Surely this should settle the question for anyone who *really* believes in biblical inerrancy.

Even if, for the sake of argument, we allow the creation week to correspond in duration to the geologic ages, it still would not help scientifically, since the order of events in the one is quite different from that in the other. One can easily discern at least twenty-three discrepancies[2] between the two sets of events. To try to harmonize these discrepancies by talking of "topical" rather than chronological arrangements, or overlapping rather than sequential "days" is merely a roundabout way of rejecting the accuracy and historicity of the record. Most liberal intellectuals, of course, do this directly, without bothering to devise any such equivocal exposition.

V. BIBLICAL QUESTIONS ABOUT THE LITERAL-DAY EXPOSITION

The two biblical arguments most commonly advanced against the literal-day meaning of *yom* in Genesis 1 are: (1) the seventh "day" is still continuing, thus indicating that the other "days" are also longer than twenty-four hours each; (2) the events described in Genesis 2 in connection with the formation of Adam and Eve could not have been accomplished within a twenty-four-hour period. Such arguments are, in our judgment, both tenuous and gratuitous, certainly not of the same weight as the many clear-cut Biblical arguments in favor of literal days.

The Bible does not say that "God *is resting* on the seventh day," but rather that "on the seventh day He *rested,* and was refreshed" (Exodus 31:17). The seventh day, like the other six, was a literal day. God finished His resting, as well as His creating. The Lord Jesus Christ said it plainly: "My Father worketh hitherto, and I work" (John 5:17). As soon as God had completed His work of creating and making all things, He began His work of upholding all things (Hebrews 1:3) and then, after man's sin, He also began His work of reconciling all things (Colossians 1:20).

The assertion that the events of Genesis 2 would take more than a day is merely an unfounded opinion, based on uniformitarian assumptions. On the basis of other assumptions, which are much more realistic in view of the unique character of the creation period, it can be shown that all these events could easily have taken place in one day.[3] God made the land animals, and then Adam, early in the morning, placed him in the garden and then had him quickly meet and name the major kinds of field animals and birds (Genesis 2:19), those with which he might normally have the greatest amount of contact and which might seem potential helpers for him in keeping the garden. Not included were the creeping things, the fish of the sea, or the beasts of the earth. None of the observed animals were suitable for this purpose, however, and towards the end of the day Adam would realize keenly the need of someone like himself. Therefore, before the end of the day, the Lord made the woman and brought her to the man. Finally, everything was complete and God placed everything under their dominion, pronouncing it all "very good" (Genesis 1:26-28, 31). The account is beautiful in its simplicity and honesty. On the other hand, for God to tell Adam and Eve that they were to have dominion over everything that He had made, when multitudes of animals, and even species, had already become extinct, was misleading at best. To tell them that everything was also "very good," when the rocks beneath their feet were filled with the fossilized remains of dead animals (and even "pre-Adamite" hominids) and the world over which they were supposed to exercise some kind of vague dominion was already "groaning and travailing in pain" (Romans 8:22), with all creatures involved in a fierce struggle for existence, would seem to be an unthinkable, even sadistic, deception, completely out of character for a loving and omniscient Creator.

VI. THE PROBLEM OF DEATH

The problem of death in the animal kingdom before the entrance of sin into the world is too lightly dismissed by progressive creationists, in view of such Scriptures as Romans 5:12; 1 Corinthians 15:21; Romans 8:20-22 and others, all of which surely seem to indicate that man's sin brought God's curse on man's entire dominion. Plants, of course, do not possess life (Hebrew *nephesh*) in the biblical sense, and so do not "die," but animals are so closely associated with mankind that their shed blood was accepted on the altar in atonement for human sin (Leviticus 17:11). There was no real *death* in the world until sin entered into the world. Even if such Scriptures are interpreted (incorrectly) as applying only to human death, the progressive creationist still has the vexing problem of identifying the particular point in history when sin and death entered the human family. He wants to accept the geological ages and their fossil record, but these systems specifically incorporate the supposed data of human evolution, extending over the past several million years. Where does Adam fit into the hominoid and hominid line? Was he an Australopithecine or a Neanderthal or what? According to the standard scheme as currently taught, the genus *Homo* goes back over a million years, and even the species *Homo sapiens* probably 100,000 years. How can this system possibly be accommodated in the Genesis record of human history, especially the chronologies of Genesis 5 and 11, which indicate a period of only a few thousand years, at most, between Adam and Abraham?

However, such biblical arguments have been shrugged off by progressive creationists for many years. Despite their apparently sincere commitment to biblical inerrancy and authority, their greater authority seems to be uniformitarianism and the system of geologic ages based on it. Dr. Bradley admits that he is committed to the "double-revelation" theory, which assumes that God's revelation in nature is of equal authority with His revelation in Scripture. While we certainly believe that the real *facts* of science will always agree with Scripture, the latter must never be interpreted on the authority of some current scientific model, especially when the modern scientific establishment is so thoroughly committed to evolutionary humanism. John Whitcomb has written a compelling critique of this double-revelation theory,[4] and it should be required reading for anyone considering it.

VII. THE IMPORTANCE OF THE GREAT FLOOD

One would suppose that the scientific evidence for the geological ages must be overwhelmingly strong, to constrain men who believe in biblical inerrancy to sacrifice the plain teachings of Genesis to this uniformitarian view of earth history. But this is not the case at all! The great weight of genuine scientific data fits the recent cataclysmic model of earth history far better than the uniformitarian model.

It is significant that Dr. Bradley has completely ignored the significance of the Genesis Flood in his exposition, even though the title of his paper involves the trustworthiness of Scripture in *all* areas of natural science. The question of the historicity and character of the Deluge is every bit as critical as that of the Creation; neither can be effectively treated alone.

The Bible teaches clearly that the Noahic Deluge was global and cataclysmic, not local or tranquil. Progressive creationists, on the other hand, must be committed either to a local flood (e.g., Bernard Ramm[5]) or to a tranquil flood (e.g., Davis Young[6]) for the simple reason that a worldwide hydraulic cataclysm would completely rearrange the sedimentary crust of the earth, thus destroying all the supposed evidences for the geological ages. That the Bible teaches a universal cataclysmic flood is so obvious from a mere reading of the passages involved that one feels almost redundant in even arguing the point. The book, *The Genesis Flood,*[7] has often been considered the catalyst that triggered the modern revival of creationism, and it has been subjected to more numerous and more bitter attacks by evolutionists and "neo-evangelicals" than just about any book of our generation. Yet it is significant that all of these attacks have been leveled against its *scientific* interpretations.[8] No one has ever even *attempted* to refute its foundational argument that the Bible teaches a universal cataclysmic flood! The fact that the Flood covered all the mountains of the Middle East (including Mount Ararat, now 17,000 feet high) for a whole year; the necessity for building a gigantic ark capable easily of accommodating two of every known species of land animal, living or extinct in half its volume, and the Noahic covenant, promising never to send such a flood again are three obvious proofs that the Flood was universal. The writer has listed one hundred biblical and scientific arguments for a worldwide flood.[9]

The concept of a tranquil flood is, of course, even more absurd than a local flood. A worldwide tranquil flood is a contradiction in terms, about like a worldwide tranquil explosion! The entire geological column is composed of water-deposited sediments, presumably formed in at least local floods (if "the present is the key to the past," as uniformitarians insist). That anyone could believe in a worldwide flood which would leave no significant geological traces is itself a commentary on the remarkable mindset of Christians who feel they must, at all costs, accept the geological-age system.

VIII. NATURAL CATASTROPHISM IN GEOLOGY

It is significant that there has been a strong resurgence of catastrophism in geological thought in recent years. A number of eminent geologists (e.g., Derek Ager,[10] recent president of the British Geological Association) have gone so far as to recognize that the entire geological column is a record of catastrophes. These neo-catastrophists are not creationists, nor do they believe the Bible, but they do acknowledge that traditional uniformitarianism is incapable of explaining the geological strata. In fact, the concept of intermittent regional catastrophes in evolutionary geology is being increasingly associated with the concept of punctuated equilibrium in evolutionary biology and paleontology.[11]

Thus, the geologic record, as far as its actual data are concerned, is a record of stable kinds of organisms, with complete gaps between kinds, and rapid sedimentary burials, with presumed gaps between catastrophes. Evolutionists may be able to imagine rapid evolution in the punctuations and uniformitarians may imagine long ages between the catastrophes, but they are arguing not from evidence, but from its absence!

Furthermore, in view of the complete absence of worldwide unconformities in the fossiliferous portions of the geological column,[12] there is good reason for believing that all these supposed intermittent local catastrophes are merely components of one single complex global hydraulic cataclysm. An "unconformity" represents an interruption in the depositional process and, therefore, a time gap in the formation of the sedimentary strata in the *local* geologic column in which it occurs. Since there is no worldwide unconformity between any two "ages" in the standard geologic column, there is no worldwide time gap. Thus the depositional process during the formation of at least most of the geological strata must have been continuous. Since each individual formation represents at least a local catastrophe, the entire column represents a complex of continuous, interconnected local catastrophes. This, to all intents and purposes, is synonymous with a global hydraulic cataclysm.

Certain types of formations that seem superficially to require long period of time for their production (e.g., evaporites, coral reefs, sea-floor sediments) have been mentioned by Bradley (relying on the discussion of these geological structures by biologist Dan Wonderly), but closer analysis of all of them will substantiate the fact that even these were formed quite rapidly.[13] Present process rates do *not* give the key to past process rates.

Once Christian believers realize that the whole geological-age system is based squarely on the philosophy of uniformitarianism, and that the actual data of the geologic column can be explained at least as well in terms of recent catastrophism, it seems inexcusable for them to continue to "wrest the Scriptures" (2 Peter 3:16) in order to accommodate these imaginary ages in Genesis. The apostle Peter long ago placed this vital issue in its prophetic context (2 Peter 3:3-6), noting that the basis for the widespread latter-day commitment to evolutionary uniformitarianism would be willful rejection of the overwhelming evidence for special creation of all things and their later cataclysmic destruction in the great Flood.

IX. ASSUMPTIONS IN GEOCHRONOLOGY

A close scrutiny of the few physical processes that *seem* to point to an old earth (e.g., uranium decay) in terms of the uniformitarian assumptions on which they are based will show that these assumptions are not only unproved but are also untestable and unreasonable. All the *real* history we have (that is, written human records) goes back only a few thousand years. Anything beyond that must necessarily be completely speculative, based on uniformist assumptions as applied to the changes occurring in some physical system.

There are only a very few such processes (uranium/lead, potassium/argon, rubidium/strontium) which, with such uniformitarian assumptions, will yield anything like the currently accepted five-billion-year age for the earth. On the other hand, there are scores of such processes[14] which, even with the same assumptions (that is, the assumptions of a closed system, constant rate of change, and zero starting point) will yield a young age for the earth. However, no one ever hears about these (except in creationist literature) for the simple reason that they do not allow enough time to make evolution possible. Dr. Bradley has discussed a few of these but (presumably for lack of space) his discussion is superficial at best.

Space admittedly *is* a problem, and the present writer can only urge Christians to give careful reading to recent creationist treatments[15] of geochronology and astrochronology before committing themselves to uniformitarian hermeneutics. There are thousands of qualified scientists,[16] coming from every field of science (including a fair number of geologists, astronomers and others whose sciences impinge directly on cosmic and earth history), who have repudiated evolutionary uniformitarianism and are now committed to special recent creation. The "progressive creation" interpretation is by no means a widely held position among Bible-believing scientists, and the writer would urge everyone who really believes in an inerrant Bible not to travel any such path of dangerous compromise. Progressive creationism is not a new theory, by any means, and it has already, for well over a hundred years, served as the camel's nose by which theistic evolution and eventually full-blown religious liberalism have come in and taken over hundreds of once-sound Christian churches and other institutions.

In fact, the current widespread defections in evangelicalism away from belief in biblical inerrancy—in other words, the very situation that led to the need for ICBI—are primarily the result of the widespread opinion that biblical foundations in Genesis have been undermined by modern science. Specialists in seminaries may argue about fine points of textual criticism, but the reason why most laymen, as well as scientists and other scholars in fields outside of philosophy and theology, reject the Bible is because they have been taught evolution and the great age of the earth, and they know that this presumed "fact of science" contradicts the Bible's very first chapter. This critical problem needs to be given high priority by ICBI, and the alleged evolutionary framework of history must be repudiated and replaced by the true biblical framework. A doctor does not cure a malignancy by diagnosing it as benign, nor by pointing out that other good people have had the same problem. Neither will men be brought back to faith in an inerrant Bible by directing them to the same old time-worn compromising hermeneutical system that led them away from it in the first place. God is able to say what he means and it is up to us merely to believe and obey what he says. "For what if some did not believe? Shall their unbelief make the faith of God without effect? God forbid; yea, let God be true, but every man a liar" (Rom. 3:3–4).

NOTES

[1]For analysis and documentation of evolutionary thinking in ancient times, see Henry M. Morris, *The Troubled Waters of Evolution* (San Diego: Creation-Life Publishers, 1974), pp. 51-75.

[2]See, for example, the writer's list in *Biblical Cosmology and Modern Science* (Grand Rapids: Baker Book House, 1970), pp. 58-62.

[3]This point is discussed at some length in the writer's commentary, *The Genesis Record* (Grand Rapids: Baker Book House, 1976), pp. 83-104.

[4]John C. Whitcomb and Donald B. DeYoung, *The Moon: Its Creation, Form and Significance* (Winona Lake: BMH Books, 1978), pp. 53-83 and 163-70.

[5]Bernard Ramm, *The Christian View of Science and Scripture* (Grand Rapids: Eerdmans Publishing Company, 1954), pp. 238-47.

[6]Davis A. Young, *Creation and the Flood* (Grand Rapids: Baker Book House, 1977), pp. 170-74.

[7]John C. Whitcomb and Henry M. Morris, *The Genesis Flood* (Philadelphia: Presbyterian and Reformed Publishing Company, 1961), 518 pp.

[8]Charles Clough, *A Calm Appraisal of "The Genesis Flood"* (Th.M. Thesis, Dallas Theological Seminary, 1968), 170 pp.

[9]Morris, *The Genesis Record*, pp. 683-86.

[10]Derek Ager, *The Nature of the Stratigraphic Record* (New York: Wiley, 1973), 100 pp.

[11]Stephen J. Gould, "Evolution's Erratic Pace," *Natural History,* Vol. 86, (May 1977), pp. 12-16.

[12]For discussion and documentation of this key point, see *Scientific Creationism* (ed. by H. Morris, Creation-Life Publishers, 1974), pp. 111-23. Also see H. Morris, *King of Creation* (San Diego: Creation-Life Publishers, 1980), pp. 147-69.

[13]Morris, *Scientific Creationism,* pp. 101-11.

[14]See H. Morris, *The Scientific Case for Creation* (San Diego: Creation-Life Publishers, 1977), pp. 55-59, for a tabulation of 70 worldwide processes which indicate a young earth.

[15]The Institute for Creation Research (Box 2666, El Cajon, CA 92021) will send a descriptive list including several such books, on request.

[16]For example, one such organization, the Creation Research Society, has a membership of over 700 scientists, each of whom has a postgraduate degree in some field of natural science and is committed to belief in recent creation, flood geology, and full biblical authority and inerrancy. The quarterly journal of this society should be required reading for anyone who writes or teaches on these subjects. For information, write Society headquarters, 2717 Cranbrook Road, Ann Arbor, MI 48104.

Adequacy of Language and Accommodation

Vern S. Poythress
Associate Professor of New Testament
Westminster Theological Seminary

6. Adequacy of Language and Accommodation

Vern S. Poythress

Objections to biblical authority are sometimes based on an appeal to the nature of human language. In the Bible, human authors write fully human language out of their fully human linguistic and cultural contexts. These authors speak to fully human audiences. Can such communication be adequate, fully true, and wholly without error in what it affirms?

I. OBJECTIONS BASED ON LANGUAGE

Three main sorts of objections rise up.

1. Human language is inadequate to speak about *God*.
2. Human language can never be wholly true, or infallibly true.
3. Human language from a "primitive" culture cannot be wholly true.

We may soften the sharpness and ethnocentrism of the third objection by reformulating it. The objector is claiming, perhaps, that it is inexpedient, unnecessary, and perhaps even impossible for human language coming out of a culture like that of the ancient Near East to speak wholly without error into all other cultural contexts. This is especially inexpedient if the language chooses to cover the range of topics actually covered in the Bible. Therefore, God has "accommodated himself" to mistaken notions of the ancient Near East in the course of adequately communicating the central truths of redemption.

What do we say about these objections? Objection 1, concerning "God-talk," typically springs up from philosophical and theological sources. Objections 2 and 3 are typically rooted more in linguistic and anthropological reflection. I intend to put forward first a brief biblically-based reply to the core concerns common to the three objections (§§ II-III). I then intend to leave aside objection 1. It has been skillfully answered already in an article by John Frame.[1] I will spend the bulk of my time exploring the complexities of language which contribute to the plausibility of 2 and 3 (Cf. §§ IV-XIII).

II. A BIBLICAL VIEW OF LANGUAGE

First of all, I believe that the teaching of the Bible itself provides some foundations for addressing the core concerns behind the three objections. What does the Bible's teaching imply about language? God is the all-sufficient creator of man. He created man with linguistic capacities in order that language should be one means of communication not only among men but also between God and man. As creator, God is a competent speaker of Hebrew, Greek, English, or whatever other language he chooses to use. Since he is sovereign, language offers no resistance to his purposes and cannot frustrate his desire to communicate. He is able to address men where they are, using idioms and style with which they are familiar, precisely because of his complete control over the medium that he uses.

It is true that human languages display various limitations. It is impossible to communicate some things by means of language alone. For instance, in English we cannot get very far in describing the smell of burning leaves or the taste of raw oysters to someone who has never had the experience. But it is God who has built in such limitations. He has no desire to achieve by human language what cannot be achieved by human language. What he has determined to achieve through the language of the Bible we find out through actually reading the Bible.

We may rephrase these truths in terms of biblical teaching on God's transcendence and immanence.[2] From a biblical point of view, God's transcendence does not mean that human language is alien to him or an inadequate means in which to express himself. Rather, it means that he has full control over the resources of language that he himself ordained.

Conversely, God's immanence does not mean that he is captured by human language so as not to be totally truthful or effective. In particular, it does not mean that he is forced to "accommodate" himself to error. Rather, it means that he succeeds in actually communicating to men so that they come to know him. God actually makes known his purposes and his demands, in all their concrete particularity. He is intimately in touch with man, as man resides in a cultural milieu. Therefore, "intimacy," "presence in particular cultures," or "culture-relatedness" is a more accurate description of the mode of God's communication than is "accommodation" or "cultureboundness."

In sum, God's transcendence and immanence are not in competition or tension with one another. God's control (transcendence) implies his power to meet man in the midst of culture (immanence). On the deepest level, we must say that there is no problem here. There may be deep and even insoluble problems for *us*. *We* may not be able to explain how God can adequately speak about himself, can be wholly true, and can be on intimate terms with all cultures. But such things are *not* a problem for *God*.

It is well for us to reflect on the simplicity and obviousness of God's abilities. Most objections to inerrancy based on supposed limitations or inadequacies of language are not ultimately motivated by a wisdom that sees more deeply into the problems of human language. Rather they are motivated by the folly that turns its back on a true knowledge of who God is and what he does. In that folly, man is also in danger of losing what insight he has into humanity and human language. Yet it is easy for the conservative believer to be trapped in presumption too. If there are no mysteries for God, there are mysteries for us. *We* cannot in a casual and unreflective way assume that we know how the language of the Bible does what it does. For example, it is possible to bring to the Bible a wooden concept of communication, and wrongly to insist on artificial standards of precision.

III. DIFFICULTIES CONFRONTING PEOPLE WHO OBJECT

Now let us look briefly at the roots of objections to the adequacy of language. Can such objections themselves have adequate foundations? Attempts to bring objections against the adequacy of human language run aground on three interconnected problems. The first is the problem of value. On what basis are we to make judgments about adequacy and inadequacy, truth and error, superiority and inferiority of cultures? What could we mean by saying that human language is inadequate to talk about God, or inadequate to convey only truth? In what way is it "inadequate?" And what do we expect talk about God and 'truth" to be like? Our expectations and definitions of "adequacy" and "truth" are themselves shot through with values, with preferences, desires, standards, and perhaps disappointments at goals that we set but are not reached. Where do these values come from? If God is Lord, we ought to conform our values to *his* standards. Hence there is something intrinsically rebellious about negatively evaluating biblical language.

Suppose that we are disappointed to find that the Bible uses round numbers and other "approximate" language. We expect a greater concern for a kind of mathematical and scientific precision. But that ought to lead us to ask whether we ourselves, together with our culture, have not set too high a value on a certain kind of precision. We might, of course, decide that we are here confronted with a "neutral" sort of cultural difference between the ancient Near East and the modern West. But we might also decide that there is here an implicit criticism of certain tendencies in the West. What we are not allowed to do is to make a transition later into a tacit affirmation of the *superiority* of the modern Western point of view.

The second problem about objections to language is the epistemological problem. How does the objector obtain the necessary knowledge about God, truth, and cultures in order to make a judgment about the adequacy of language for expressing theology and truth, and for achieving cross-cultural communication? How does he do this when he himself is largely limited by the capabilities of his own language and culture?

The third problem is more "metaphysical." What right does man have, being a creature, to draw limits to the language of the Bible when that language is *divine* as well as human? Who are you to make a reply to God (Rom. 9:20)?

IV. CAN LANGUAGE BE WHOLLY TRUE?

Consider now a more particular objection. Someone may say that human language can never be wholly true. Language is not infinitely precise. Hence it is always somewhat misleading. John Frame's article[3] gives a simple reply to this:

> (a) Some sentences are, in one sense, perfectly precise and comprehensive. Take "Washington is the capitol of the United States": could that fact be stated more precisely? more comprehensively? (b) Of course, even the aforementioned sentence is not comprehensive in the sense of "saying everything there is to say" about Washington and the U.S. But no human being ever *tries* to say all that, at least if he has any sense at all! Nor does the Bible claim to say "everything" about God. The claim to infallibility does not entail a claim to comprehensiveness in this sense. And where no claim to comprehensiveness is made, lack of comprehensiveness does not refute infallibility. (c) Nor is imprecision necessarily a fault. "Pittsburgh is about 300 miles from Philadelphia" is imprecise in a sense, but it is a perfectly good sentence and is in no usual sense untrue. An "infallible"

> book might contain many imprecise-but-true statements of this sort. Granted, then, that there is a sense in which language never conveys the "whole truth," we need not renounce on that account any element of the orthodox view of biblical authority.

In fact, the lack of infinite precision is a problem only if one wrongly adopts values putting too great a premium on infinite precision. Human language can be wholly true, provided that we are willing to adopt a sensible view of truth.

Something positive can still be gleaned from the above objection. Human language is indeed sometimes imprecise, often fluid and interconnected. There are complexities to expression and understanding. Let us, then, turn to a more positive reflection on language in which we will examine some of the complexities. We will no longer address objectors directly, but attempt to explore the problem areas for our own benefit.

V. BIBLICAL DISCOURSE AS A SELECTION FROM A LIMITED SYSTEM

Many people's naive intuitions about language run to the effect that language is an audible or visible mirror of thought or meaning. Meaning can unproblematically be "read off" of discourses by an audience, and can be unproblematically put into language by a competent speaker. Discourses are, as it were, created *ex nihilo* expressly to convey a speaker's meaning. But this cannot explain how anyone can understand anyone else's *new* meaning. As the later Wittgenstein[4] never tires of pointing out, there must be *public* criteria for interpreting new utterances, else there is no meaning. There is no purely "private" language. To express meaning successfully a speaker must have previously mastered through long experience a publicly available language system, a multidimensional complex of rules and regularities about how to create meaning. Someone who has imperfectly mastered a foreign language may be able to communicate many things, but not all that he would like to say.

Thus we must not think of each utterance as obtaining private meaning merely by the decision or decree of the speaker that it has such-and-such a meaning. It has meaning not as a creation *ex nihilo* but as a unit in a huge system. Its meaning arises from *relationships*. There are relationships of the words of the utterances to previous occurrences of the same words in the language. There are relationships of contrast between these words and others that could be used instead. There are relationships between words and the constructions in which they are or could be embedded: words in phrases, phrases in clauses, clauses in sentences, sentences in paragraphs, and so on, up to whole discourses embedded in still large social and cultural contexts.

I now propose to examine in greater detail the limitations on expression and communication at the level of words, of sentences, and of whole discourses.

VI. LIMITATIONS ON COMMUNICATION DUE TO WORDS

Every language has a finite vocabulary stock. New words can be created, of course. But because of the necessity for publicly accessible meaning, the capacity of language to absorb newly created words is quite limited. If new words are to be intelligible to others, they must be introduced in one of several circumscribed ways. They can be introduced using an explicit definition (rare outside of science). Or they can be introduced using a regular device for word-formation already at work in the language (e.g., "super-excessive"). Or they can be introduced with no explanation. In the later case, the repeated occurrence of the word in various contexts gradually allows the reader to zero in on the meaning, much as we zero in on the personality of a character in a novel by seeing him act in various situations. This third method, inferring meaning from context, is in fact the primary way in which we learn the meanings of most words in our mother tongue.

Not only do languages have finite vocabulary stocks. Any one word in the language has a meaning with some vagueness and non-precision. The meaning of a word is not infinitely precise. The words "vagueness" and "nonprecision," I have found, tend more or less automatically to have bad connotations with some people. I would rather that were not so, but I have not found better words. I would not want to quarrel over the label, as long as we understand the phenomena that I have in mind. Words are of limited precision in at least three respects.[5] First, they are capable of being applied not just to one absolutely particular case but to many cases. They have, if you will, a range of meaning, a denotational range. Second, the *boundaries* of this range of meaning are not themselves infinitely precise. We cannot always designate *exactly* where we come to the point where a word no longer is being used appropriately. Third, words with a range of possible meanings do not retain all these meanings when embedded in a sentence context. The context narrows down their function. Hence, meaning is "codetermined" by context, rather than being wholly a fixed function of the word in isolation.

Let us now look more closely at these three types of imprecision. First, a given word is capable of being applied to a whole range of situations and contexts. Words have a range of meaning or a denotational range. The word "dog" can denote not just a single animal but a whole class of such. The word "jump" applies to leaps both high and low, with the starting and ending points either the same or different, the start and end either at the same or different height, and so on.

Moreover, the meaning of a given word is largely determined by its contrasts with *other* words in the vocabulary stock. This can be well illustrated by considering the differences between the ways that different languages cover the color spectrum. The English vocabulary stock divides up the entire color spectrum into eleven primary parts: white, black, grey, red, orange, yellow, green, blue, purple, brown, and pink. In Bambara and Baoule of West Africa, by contrast, there exists only a threefold basic division.[6] It corresponds roughly to red, black, and green. But each of the three terms covers a broader region of the spectrum than do the terms in English. Because the meaning of each term is determined by contrast with only *two* other terms, it cannot be as precise as an English color term. Russian, on the other hand, achieves greater precision than English because it has two terms—*sinij,* "dark blue" and *goluboj,* "azure, sky-blue"—contrasting with one another, where English has only the one primary term—"blue."[7] (Of course, the situation is complicated by the fact that both English and Russian contain more technical terms to denote more precise shades: azure, aquamarine, beryl, cobalt, marine, turquoise, damson, indigo, periwinkle, cerulean, sapphire, etc. The observations still hold true, however, with respect to a kind of "basic vocabulary" of color, a vocabulary familiar to an average person who is beyond the range of technical influence.)

Second, the boundaries of the range of meaning of a word are themselves not fixed with infinite precision.[8] At what point is a word no longer used appropriately? Where *exactly* is the "boundary" to its meaning? There are, of course, cases where the word clearly does apply and other cases where it clearly does not. But there are in addition doubtful or disputed cases. For instance, how tall and how "treelike" does a shrub have to be to count as a "tree?" Can we answer precisely without drawing an arbitrary boundary on the spot?

Third, dictionary words with a whole range of possible meanings do not take on or retain all these possible meanings when embedded in a sentence context. For example, the English word "green" in a given discourse almost always means "unripe, immature" *or* "of the color green," but *not* both senses simultaneously (though a play on both senses is possible in the exceptional case). Similarly, the Greek word *parakaleō* in a given discourse almost always means "exhort" *or* "comfort," but *not* both senses simultaneously. Thus the dictionary entry for "green" or for *parakaleō* has a "vagueness" which it is the task of the context to eliminate.

The same points about vagueness can be made by considering words from the standpoint of the audience, instead of the standpoint of the language system in the abstract.

First, words have been learned by an audience because they are *used* repeatedly. A word with point-meaning (rather than a range of meaning) would not be learned and would die out of the language because it was too precise to be used frequently.

Second, words are learned by tacit inference from seeing them used in a *finite* number of contexts. The observations of their use in a limited number of contexts can never suffice to establish boundaries of their meaning with infinite precision. Would we be right in applying the word "dog" to something that looked like a dog but uttered a sound like a cat's meow? It is impossible to say definitively. We as speakers of English learned the word "dog" without ever seeing people use it or refuse to use it under "odd" circumstances.

Moreover, because different people have learned words from different sets of occurrences in different contexts, there is little possibility of infinitely precise coincidence to two people's impressions concerning the meaning of the same word. If we are looking for a certain kind of abstract mathematical precision, we will have to say that no two people see exactly the same meaning in a given word.

Such, then, are some of the ways that words are limited in precision. Their meanings have certain "vaguenesses." But this is not a threat to ordinary communication. Rather it is a virtually indispensable aid to communication! Many times artificial precision would tangle us up rather than freeing us. Words with very precise boundaries would be difficult to learn, because we would have to master the exact boundary. And they would be difficult to use, because we would have to check consciously that we were respecting that exact boundary. If, overnight, we could somehow introduce extra precision into the core language stock of a language, that precision would quickly be eliminated by the language users under the pressures and demands of day-to-day communication.

These limitations on the precision of words have definite implications for our conception of truth and the use of logic. Both Aristotelian logic and modern symbolic logic operate in terms of an ideal in which every word or word-like symbol should have two properties. (a) In each single instance of the occurrence of the word, the word is to apply to or refer to a range of objects, circumstances, actions, relations, or the like, circumscribed and distinguished from all others *with infinite precision.* (b) All of the occurrences of a given word are to be instances of exactly the same self-identical meaning.

Property (a) requires that there is no uncertainty about the "boundaries" of the meaning of the word. There must be no uncertainties that might, for instance, lead to quarrels over whether the word ought to be applied in such-and-such a new instance. This property is intended to eliminate so-called "semantic" questions, like the question whether tomatoes are a "fruit," a "vegetable," or both or neither. (Such questions have roots lying in the fluidity of use of words like "fruit" and "vegetable" in English.) Property (a) is seen, then, as necessary in order to achieve formal rigor. Property (b) is seen as necessary in order to avoid the "fallacy of equivocation," in which an invalid result is deduced by using a word in two different senses. For instance, consider the following:

All tigers are cats.
All cats are less than three feet long.
All tigers are less than three feet long.

The above syllogism is invalid because there is an equivocation between two meanings of "cat." In the first sentence it has the broader meaning in which the denotation covers the whole cat *family.* In the second instance it has a narrower meaning; the denotation includes only the domestic cat.

The above is an obvious case of equivocation. But language never absolutely attains the ideals expressed in (a) and (b), though it may try to approach them in mathematical formalism. Hence, if our standards for "equivocation" are based on these ideals, no syllogism will be immune from the charge of equivocation. If our standards of truth are based on these ideals, no sentence of ordinary language will be judged "wholly true," because the sentences are built out of "messy" words.

What do we say to this? We can answer merely that there is

something amiss with these standards. We need not deny that the ideal of infinite precision is of creative stimulus in mathematics, mathematical logic, and computer science. But its usefulness is limited. Applied uncontrollably, it tends to destroy itself (because the ideals are themselves formulated in ordinary language). And it tends to destroy the meaning of the words "truth" and "true" by refusing to use them in the way countenanced in ordinary language.

VII. THE INFLUENCE OF LEXICAL STOCKS ON THE POWERS OF LANGUAGE: THE SAPIR-WHORF HYPOTHESIS

One special aspect of the limitations related to words is the supposed limitation or constraint that language places on one's worldview. According to one common formulation of the Sapir-Whorf hypothesis, the vocabulary stock of a language together with its grammar influences and constrains the worldview of the speakers of the language. This hypothesis, though it has at least a grain of truth, must be qualified in many ways. It ought not to be used naively to "read off" a "Hebraic" or "biblical" worldview directly from linguistic facts (sometimes themselves inaccurately reported) about the vocabulary stock and grammar of Hebrew and Greek. Since James Barr[9] has already given an incisive critique of such procedures, I shall confine myself at this point to some summary remarks.

First of all, with regard to the positive adequacies available in *any* natural language, the following points are generally accepted in contemporary comparative linguistics (Cf., e.g., Nida[10]).

1. No natural language is ill-formed or "primitive." All are quite able to express complex, deep, or subtle ideas. Virtually anything that can be said in one language can be said in another, provided one takes enough time. Admittedly, poetry is notoriously difficult to translate. Phonological and rhythmic effects can seldom be reproduced effectively in another language, and some kinds of wordplay and allusion depend heavily on the metaphorical potential of a particular vocabulary stock of a particular language. But even in such cases some kind of "core" semantic meaning can usually be translated, and a footnote (as in the RSV of Amos 8:2 or Jer. 1:11-12) can shed further light.

2. The use of a certain lexical stock or of certain grammatical forms does *not* commit the speaker willy-nilly to theories about time, man, or the universe. The diversity of theories available in a single natural language, English, is positive proof of this. Hence, in partic-

ular, the use of terms *lēb* ("heart"), *k^elāyôt* ("kidneys"), *mē^cîm* ("intestines"), *rû^ah* ("wind," "spirit"), *nepeš* ("life," "soul"), *bāsār* ("flesh"), etc., in a psychological sense in Hebrew does not commit the speaker to a psychological *theory,* any more than the use of "mind," "heart," "emotions," "will," "conscience," "memory," do in English. This is certainly true with respect to words belonging to popular speech. It is even true, though with some qualification, of semitechnical terms. Jesus can, if he wishes, employ semitechnical religious vocabulary common to the Judaism of his day (altar, sacrifice, temple, priest, law, etc.) without agreeing with Pharisaism, Zealotism, or the apocalyptic currents of his day.

On the other hand, certain constraints bound up with the lexical stock should be noted.

3. The vocabulary stock will tend to be most developed, most rich, in those areas of thought and life in which the language users have consistently been interested. Eskimo languages may have seven or eight words for snow in its various forms; Near Eastern nomads may have an equal number for a camel in various conditions and stages of life. Hence it may take much longer to communicate the same amount of information in a language where the vocabulary is not equally rich.

4. Though virtually anything can be said in a language, not everything can be said with equal facility. The choices about what to emphasize, what to make precise, are constantly influenced by language resources. Seven terms available for snow are a standing invitation to be more precise about snow when one wishes. There is little or no cost in time, energy, or possibility of misunderstanding. But if there is only one word for snow, one will in many cases choose to be less precise: it is not worth the effort to be more precise. Indeed, being more precise could easily detract from the main point because hearers will be forced to puzzle through to an unaccustomed precision.

The above point I have made using a simple example involving vocabulary stock for snow. But the point is also true, sometimes in quite subtle ways, with respect to the whole language system. Consider the rich syntactic structure of Greek, both within clauses and between clauses. Contrast that with the relatively fewer options available in Hebrew. Translations can undoubtedly be made both ways. But the native speaker of Greek is constantly invited to specify logical, causal, and other such relations more precisely than would normally be the case in Hebrew.

VIII. DIVINE SPEECH AND VERBAL INSPIRATION: CAN *WORDS* BE INSPIRED?

What do these constraints on language imply in the case of divine speech in human language? Well, I think the first thing to be said is that God is quite happy with these constraints and freely works within them. After all, he is the one who ordained them in the first place. I firmly believe that God is Lord over all cultures and languages. Whatever structures and constraints languages and cultures have, either now or in the ancient Near East, they have because he specified them. As before, the transcendent sovereignty of God is the guarantee of his immanence through complete familiarity with the constraints.

Second, the constraints are in fact the instrument of communication rather than an opponent to communication. Without constraints, without regularities, there would be no human language and no linguistic communication. The regularities and constraints are the guarantee of publicly accessible meaning, meaning which is real but not infinitely precise. Let me use as an illustration the situation with motor vehicles. A vehicle can have four wheels, two wheels, three, five, or more. Any one of these is a "constraint." Any one limits the facility with which one can make certain types of motion under certain conditions of safety and loading. The choice between vehicles is like a choice between languages. Having made that most basic choice, one's further choices of locomotion "within the system" are limited. But without wheels, there will be no motion at all. The constraint is what enables the vehicle even to be a vehicle. Likewise, constraints are what make language language.

A third area of concern is with regard to the doctrine of verbal inspiration. Can we say that the Bible is *verbally* inspired if its *words* belong to a language system already in existence and if they have the meanings that they have as structurally constrained elements of this public linguistic system? I think that this question has depths to it that cannot be explored at this time. I hope that it will suffice to mark out the general area within which it is fruitful to develop further answers.

First of all, on the more positive side, I think that the major intent in the doctrine of verbal inspiration is to warn against the dilution of inspiration. It warns that it is not enough to affirm that only the "general thought" or direction of a passage belongs to God. According to theories of "general inspiration," the exact choice of words is merely left up to the human author who has received from God the "general thought." The clue here is the phrase "the exact choice of words." Theories of "general inspiration" show that they are tacitly aware of the fact that human authors work with an existing lexical stock and existing grammatical regularities. What distinguishes a particular author's message, within this broad linguistic context, is *not* his lexical stock but the choices that he makes from it. The human author makes choices to put such-and-such words in such-and-such an order one after the other, speaking within such-and-such an historical context. The choices *within* the constraints are what generate his particular meanings. Those meanings contrast with other meanings that might arise from a different series of choices. The doctrine of verbal inspiration, then, says that in the case of the Bible the choices of word-sequences are all choices that God made. Of course, it is true in addition that the human author made the choices. At the same time God takes responsibility for those choices of the human author. We will have to get used to the idea that a divine choice does not compete with a choice by human instruments. Do Christ's choices compete with God's plan? Do even the sinful actions of men in Acts 2:23 compete with God's predestinating purpose?

I can put the matter in another way. Hebrew and Greek are not "holy" languages, nor is their vocabulary stock "holy." It is not essentially easier in Hebrew than in English to tell the truth or to lie, to deceive or to enlighten, to be holy or to sin. What *is* holy, yes *divine,* is the particular message sent forth in a particular historical context by putting together, in the order specified in the Bible, words from Hebrew vocabulary—or Aramaic or Greek as the case may be. Each significant choice of one word of construction rather than another conveys a *divine* decision to say just this, not that.

So much, at least, is needed in the way of positive affirmation of the doctrine of verbal inspiration. But the doctrine has also been abused. It has been made to serve as the foundation for various types of questionable and even patently false inferences. For instance, verbal inspiration has sometimes been thought to imply an obligation on the part of Bible translators to reproduce as far as possible in their translations the syntactic structures and perhaps even the structures of vocabulary stock underlying and associated with the source-language texts. For instance, there is sometimes insistence on always translating a Greek genitive with English "of," and always or nearly always translating all occurrences of a given Greek word with the same English word. Whatever be the merits of such translation techniques, they have virtually nothing to do with the question of verbal inspiration as I have construed it. The doctrine of verbal inspiration makes pronouncements about the expression of meaning by means of choices *within* a given language system. It says nothing about the most effective means of taking a message given already in one language system and bringing it to expression in another system.

Also, I suspect that the doctrine of verbal inspiration has too often been one of the excuses behind etymologizing and elaborate word-studies incorporated into sermons by evangelicals. Many times etymologies and word-studies essentially provide facts about the lexical stock of the language. They are not themselves what is inspired. Only very rarely, it seems to me, does such material belong in a sermon at all. The sermon must convey the message, not the system which is its vehicle.

The improper use of etymologies and word-studies is but one instance of a problem of much greater magnitude among professional Bible interpreters. There is a very widespread tendency among professionals to read more into particular words than is there, while doing much less with whole discourses than they ought. The habit of "reading too much" into words could be brought under a good deal more control if people consistently paid attention to the fact that a speaker's choice in words *is* limited by the vocabulary stock. He can metaphorically extend the meanings of words here and there if he wishes. But even a metaphor must be solidly rooted in public meaning. And the individual speaker's ability to change the language *system* or the public meanings associated with the lexical stock is essentially nil. The distinctiveness of what a speaker says lies in his choices, which are manifested in nonrepeated sentences and discourses (Cf. Barr[11]).

IX. LIMITATIONS ON COMMUNICATION AT THE LEVEL OF SENTENCES: GRAMMATICAL LIMITATIONS

Reflections on the choice of words in particular combinations have already led us to the borders of reflection on larger units of discourse: the phrase, the clause, the sentence, and the paragraph. The sentence is a convenient intermediate-sized unit to focus on. But in the following reflections (§§ IX-XI) we will also extend our attention downward to the phrase and upward to the paragraph.

Let us first focus on the syntactical resources of grammar. Much of what has been said about words applies, if anything, with even more forcefulness to the syntactic apparatus which functions in the formation of grammatical sentences. In Greek, the case system, the tense-aspect system, the system of particles and conjunctions, and similar systems have a limited number of elements. The meaning of each element is determined largely by contrasts with the other elements in the same system. The accusative case, for example, is a kind of "garbage can" case used to express (a) that there is a syntactic connection and (b) that none of the other cases is appropriate (Cf. Louw[12]). The accusative takes "whatever is left over" from the other cases. Because there are only a few elements in the grammatical systems like the case system, each element has a wide range of meaning. The meaning of a choice of a given case or tense is therefore quite "vague."

Once again the tendency of professional Bible interpreters is to be much too precise in their deductions from grammatical phenomena. The aorist tense has suffered the most in the process. When interpreters come upon an aorist tense many are likely to talk about "action of a moment," "a definite occasion," "once-for-all action," or "a sharp break." In fact, the significance of the aorist is much more colorless (Cf. Stagg[13]). The aorist is used *rather than* the present or the perfect. It is used merely because there is no special desire on the part of the user to highlight the fact that the action is in progress or repeated (present), or to speak concerning the completed result of the action (perfect). For example, according to Leon Morris the aorist *metanoēson* of Revelation 3:19 is "aorist of once-for-all action."[14] This is over-interpretation of the aorist. Stagg[15] rightly replies by asking rhetorically whether we must therefore conclude that *poiēson* of Revelation 2:5 is also "once-for-all." In fact, both aorists should be thought of as aorist rather than present. In choosing the aorist the author merely indicates that he has no special desire to view the action as continuous or repeated. The aorist is "indefinite;" it "refrains from describing."[16]

The present tense can likewise be over-interpreted. It is common for people to solve the theological problem of 1 John 3:9 by translating the present tense *poiei* with an emphasis on progressive and continuous action: "the one born of God does not *continually* sin." But this is an overreading of significance of the present tense in the Greek text.[17] Consider: what alternative choices for tense were available to the author? The only other tenses used to express general truths are the future indicative and the aorist indicative. Both are unacceptable in the context of 1 John 3:9, because they would be understood as indicating future or past time. The present indicative is the *only* alternative available to the author for expressing what is true at the present time for the person who has been born of God. The author has no choice open to him, in terms of the tense-aspect system, between a progressive and nonprogressive alternative. If, then, he wishes to express the idea "continually," he must do it with a separate word such as *adialeiptōs*, *aei*, *pantote*, or *dia pantos;* in the context these would be coupled immediately with the negative *ou* to give the sense required.

The overall effect of this considerable fluidity in the grammatical apparatus is to create vast potential for ambiguity in sentences. For instance, take a sentence almost at random from the English Bible: "The weapons we fight with are not the weapons of the world." Grammatically speaking, "fight with" could be taken to mean "fight against." The "of" in theory could be taken as epexegetical rather than as an indication of possession. The word "world" could be taken in more than one sense. But all these ambiguities are "theoretical." The context effectively excludes them in practice. In fact, a good writer will automatically write in such a way that almost all ambiguities of a serious nature are eliminated by the interaction of (a) the reader's general feel for what makes sense referentially (people do not fight against weapons but fight using them), (b) the reader's previous knowledge of the writer and his views (e.g., familiarity with a special sense of "world"), and (c) the immediate literary context.

X. VALIDITY IN INTERPRETATION

One can, of course, still ask, "How can the reader be *sure* that his interpretation is right, in the presence of even theoretical ambiguity?" And then further, "What good is an infallible, inerrant message if the reader is not an infallible, inerrant interpreter of the message?" Still further one may ask whether the message even exists in an intelligible sense apart from the existence of some interpreter. If it does not, the fallibility of interpreters makes the message itself fallible. The argument for the last of these conclusions might go as follows. All meaning must be ultimately *personal* meaning. Persons (or entities behaving like persons in crucial ways) are necessary to construct meaning from marks on a page. Otherwise there is no way to exclude mechanically possible but wildly false alternative interpretations. Nor is there a way to go from the picture of language as an abstract system of counters (words) combining according to certain rules (grammar) to a picture in which language actually talks *about* something (a world already partially known to the interpreter).

What do we reply to this? Indeed, we do not have a certainty at *every* point of interpretation. Neither do we have an abstract, philosophical certainty based on a direct vision of the divine mind. We are finite creatures who are called upon to *trust* God. But inerrancy can still be affirmed within this viewpoint. There is an infallible interpreter—the Holy Spirit. Moreover, his infallible interpretation of an infallible message is not useless to us who *are* fallible. According to John 16 and related passages,[18] the Holy Spirit himself is the guarantee, not necessarily always of *present* understanding, but of *future* completion. *We* are guaranteed access to the Holy Spirit's definitive interpretation.

If, on the other hand, the Bible makes mistakes, *our* goal must be redefined. The eschatological goal of Christian living is not to persevere forever in error; hence the goal cannot be any longer to believe and conform to what the Bible says in detail. If the goal is changed in this way, the means of coming to the goal will also be changed. Along the way to the goal, we must at some stage be prepared to employ a kind of *Sachkritik*, content-criticism. Thus affirmations of inerrancy are not sterile "theories" merely because of the absence of contemporary infallible human voices. They have practical bite. Otherwise, why would they be so resisted?!

XI. PRESUPPOSITIONS, IMPLICATIONS, AND EXCEPTIONS TO SENTENCES

An additional complexity of language arising at the sentence level concerns presuppositions and implications of sentences. Roughly speaking a sentence *presupposes* all such facts as must be the case in order for the sentence itself to make good sense. A sentence *implies* all such facts as follow from the truth of the sentence.[19] Consider the sentence "the present king of France is bald." This sentence *implies* such facts as might be deduced about a bald man. It presupposes that there is a present king of France. Anything thus presupposing a falsehood will strike us as not so much false as unhappy or nonsensical.

Now take a biblical example. "As in Adam all die, so in Christ all will be made alive" (1 Cor. 15:22). This *presupposes* that Adam existed and that he died. It *implies* that there is a resurrection of the dead, that this resurrection is based on the resurrection of Christ, that it is similar to what happened with Adam's death, and so on.

What is a speaker responsible for? Can he be called to account for presuppositions and implications, as well as for what he states explicitly? In a general way I think that we want to say that a human speaker can be held responsible for the truth of both the presuppositions and the implications of what he says. He fails us (though it may be due to an honest mistake) if either the presuppositions or the implications fail to hold up. What shall we say concerning *divine* speech to men? Shall we say that *God* fails us if either the presuppositions or the implications of what he says fail to hold up? I think so.

But an objection can be offered. Perhaps divine speech is different from the speech of an ordinary human being precisely at *this* point. Perhaps *God does not* intend that we should use the presuppositions and implications. But no, the objection will not work. Ability to operate, at least in an elementary way, using presuppositions and implications is a very basic aspect in communicative competence. Only a little effort in self-conscious reflection will show that tacit use of presupposition and implication virtually pervades everyday language. If divine "speech" to men does *not* include *this*, we had better not call it "speech" at all, or at least admit that we are using "speech" in a tenuous metaphorical way. (Incidentally New Testament use of the Old Testament includes use of implications [Rom. 4:16-17] and presuppositions [Rom. 4:4-5].)

Perhaps here is one reason why retreats from inerrancy tend historically to end up a generation later in repudiations of the divine authorship of the Bible. A person abandons inerrancy at first because he finds some of the presuppositions or implications of biblical sentences contradictory, unpalatable, or out of accord with the modern worldview. Later on, he or his spiritual heirs wake up to realize that denial of divine responsibility for presuppositions and implications is tantamount to denial of any straightforward meaning to saying that "the Bible is the Word of God."

But there *is* a problem here. What counts as a presupposition or an implication of a biblical text? No exact mechanical definition is going to be able to capture the enormously, incalculably rich interaction of sentence and context influencing the alert reader's impressions of what he can count on and what he cannot. There is no infinitely sharp boundary between what is implied and what is not. Instead, there is a vague boundary. On the one extreme there are implications about which we are sure. On the other extreme, there are wild speculations not based on the text. In between, there is a kind of gradual slope of decreasing certainty and decreasing confidence.

An illustration of some of the problems is found in 1 Corinthians 15:22. Consider first the presupposition that Adam existed. Does this text or Romans 5:12-21 really require us to believe in an historical Adam? Could it be that Paul is doing no more here than what we might do illustratively? A person might say, "As the good Samaritan stopped to help the half-dead man, so Christ in his compassion lived and even died to help us." A person might say that much without either presupposing or implying that the good Samaritan and Christ both had historical existence on the same plane. So cannot Adam likewise be used illustratively? The other side of the dispute might reply as follows: "The cases are not parallel. Paul's audience assumed that Adam was historical, whereas the modern audience assumes that the Samaritan was not. If indeed Adam was not historical, 1 Corinthians 15:22 is reprehensible. It has built on the false assumptions of the audience rather than undermining them." But the reply in return is, "The main point of 1 Corinthians 15:22 is to say something about the resurrection of Christ. It is legitimate not to get sidetracked over the tangential question of the historicity of Adam. The text can therefore be seen as not arguing the case for Adam one way or another. Suppose that you spoke to an audience that believed that the good Samaritan was an historical figure. Might you not choose to ignore the disputed point?"

This last counter-reply confronts us with a difficulty at the level of discourse and culture, not merely the level of sentence. Suppose a given person speaks to a group of human beings who hold a whole complex of erroneous beliefs bound up with their social surroundings and their culture. Suppose further that the first person knows these beliefs to be erroneous. What counts as a legitimate strategy? To what extent can he legitimately draw on cultural elements bound up with these beliefs? Can he use illustrations or presuppose cultural background in a way that might lead people to suppose that he agreed with their beliefs? I think so. But only up to a certain point. Less direct uses, such as an illustration, would be more safely available than more direct uses. Moreover, a person's freedom will depend on how serious the effects are of the erroneous beliefs, how close the beliefs are to truth or half-truth,[20] and how much the straightening out or improving of the beliefs will be an aid to his cause rather than an irrelevancy. Because there would be so many factors involved, and because the person's own goals would be imperfectly known, it might be very hard to say in some cases whether or not he concurred in a cultural belief that he apparently presupposed.

Obviously I think that the same considerations hold in the case of divine speech. But there is one proviso: Old Testament history tells us that God tailored the Israelite culture and social situation specifically as the womb of special revelation. The later discourses spoken by God do not enter into a vacuum; they are not forced to undo the earlier discourses, in the way that Paul is forced to challenge Greek polytheism.

With regard to 1 Corinthians 15:22, I think that the argument for Adam's historicity will hold up, but only when it is further reinforced. I would like to see 1 Corinthians 15:22 brought into connection with 15:45-49, and the joint power of the two appreciated. I would also say that, to me at least, the most weighty point in the argument is not the historicity of *Christ:* that is granted. It is the historicity of the *all* in 15:22. If Adam does not stand in the same historical category as the "all," the illustration collapses into mush. How can real historical persons really die with Adam when Adam is not really there to die? It is as if we heard someone claiming that the Samaritan of Jesus' parable was an historical personage, and that the Samaritan had the experience described, but the man he helped was fictional!

1 Corinthians 15:22 can also serve as an illustration of the problems with implications and exceptions. Sentences in the Bible are not to be treated as well-sculpted statues, propositions independent of context, grist for a syllogistic mill. Rather they are more like paint-strokes on a canvas. The meaning of each must be interpreted in the light of the whole. One cannot blindly draw implications without attention to the qualifications of the context. And these qualifications, in the very nature of the case, have "fuzzy boundaries." We can almost never say *exactly* how limited or how unlimited, how qualified or unqualified a speaker intended many sentences to be taken. Some things are implied by his sentences, some are not. Some things are exceptions, some are not. But in between these definite cases there are areas of uncertainty.

Thus, for 1 Corinthians 15:22, Enoch and Elijah are at least partial exceptions to the first "all." New Testament scholars quarrel about whether the second "all" is to be taken as covering men generally or only those who are savingly united to Christ.[21] Then again, how far and in exactly what respects is the role of Adam parallel to that of Christ? We can draw implications from the parallel up to a point, but just exactly where do we leave off? Scripture will not tell us *exactly.*

Those of us who believe in inerrancy ought to ask whether stumbling blocks are sometimes created by us rather than by Scripture. Zealous inerrantists, in my opinion, too often overdraw the implications and presuppositions of sentences. We are afraid of a domino process that will leave us nothing. And so we prove prosaic, literalistic, unimaginative, arthritic, overdogmatic in claims about the implications. We fear to allow for vaguenesses, exceptions, and manners of speaking. For example, it is sometimes supposed that New Testament quotations prefaced by "Moses says" or "Isaiah says" presuppose Mosaic and Isaianic authorship respectively. This seems to me to show as little genuine thought as do the confident denials of such authorship. The use of "Moses" or "Isaiah" here is what one might still do with "Shakespeare says" or "Socrates says." Such expressions function to designate literary origin in a publicly familiar corpus, but do not *in themselves* commit one to a theory about actual authorship. Even a phrase like "Isaiah is bold and says" (Rom. 10:20) seems to me possible as a personification not *necessarily* presupposing authorship by the historical figure Isaiah the son of Amoz. (I realize that some will disagree with me here.) Only when we come to passages with the explicitness of John 12:41, 5:45-47, or Isaiah 1:1 does it seem to me that we have definite affirmations of the traditional views of authorship. These examples concerning authorship are but an illustration of a much more widespread problem concerning overreading.

XII. LIMITATIONS ON COMMUNICATION AT THE LEVEL OF DISCOURSE: HISTORICAL NARRATION

Finally, I should like to say two things about limitations on communication at the level of discourse. The first concerns historical narrative. Many of us are already familiar with the idea that historical narrative includes many possible subgenres. Historical writings differ somewhat in their interests, their rigor, their selection of facts, their claims to pedantic precision. The prologue to the Gospel of John tells us, for example, that we can expect to find in this gospel more overt interpretation and reflection on theology than we can expect in the Gospel of Luke.

But I should like to put into the background such questions about subgenres. I want to reflect for a moment on the question of the capabilities of narration in general. I will use as a foil for my own views a common naive view about truth in historical description. This common view goes as follows. True language is true because it correctly pictures the world; it pictures the facts. Truth is correspondence with the facts, ultimately in fact one-to-one correspondence. Therefore, an historical description is true to the degree that it produces mental pictures in one-to-one correspondence with the facts.

Floating behind such reasoning is what may be called a mental-picture theory of language. According to this view, language is true to the degree that it produces correct mental pictures. This theory is simply inadequate and misleading. Language does not function like a picture of the world.[22] Neither does it always function to produce "correct" mental pictures. Much of Wittgenstein's later writings may be understood as an endeavor to exorcise this bewitching theory. I shall confine myself to drawing some lessons about historical narration. Suppose I report, "Jesus touched a leper and healed him." Now let us form a "mental picture" of this. Imagine, that is, a videotape of the scene. When you have formed your picture answer the following questions. Which hand did Jesus touch the leper with? Did he touch with his finger only, did he lay his hand on him, or did he put his arm around him? Did the healing follow the touching or was it simultaneous? Did Jesus say anything to the leper or not? Were there others present at the time or not? Were the disciples of Jesus called on to participate actively in the healing or not?

A videotape, or a sufficiently robust "mental picture," automatically answers most if not all of these questions. My verbal report does not. It is far more "sparse." My language does *not* produce "mental pictures" in one-to-one correspondence with the facts. Ordinarily, at least, it is not *in the nature of language* to do this. The truth-claims of language are not of this sort. Historical narration is enormously selective in its reports. It is therefore also open-ended. It is capable of giving rise to hundreds of different mental pictures, each contradicting the rest. I have already said that in the case of *words* there is always a certain fuzziness about the boundaries of meaning. With regard to historical *narratives* I should like to say that there is always or nearly always fuzziness compounded, fuzziness cubed!

What can we rightly expect of true historical narrative? Positively, we can expect that not only each sentence but each choice of a word in the sentence makes a positive contribution to genuine understanding and knowledge of what happened. The truth of what *is* said contrasts with the error of what *might* have been said with different words and sentences. On the other hand, negatively, the nature of language and of history forbid us from expecting too much. We need to put some constraints on our expectations, as follows.

1. All historical narration is guided by human *interests*. There is no escaping one or another kind of "Tendenz" in the selection of material. The interests control in large measure the areas in which the reader does and does not have the right to expect a certain definiteness and precision.

2. Straightforward arguments from silence are almost worthless. For example, it does not follow that there was only one Gadarene demoniac because only one is mentioned in Mark and Luke. The amount of omitted information in *any* historical narrative is enormous. It is therefore rash to guess at what could *not* have been honestly omitted.

3. Deductions having to do with "filling out the scene" or completing one's "mental picture" are precarious. Only with the aid of a very good sense for a narrator's interests and intentions can one proceed at all confidently.

4. In general, for biblical narratives, reflections on the theological purposes of a whole book are perhaps a better guide to assessing the significance of a detail than is an attempt to fill out the mental picture on the basis of the detail. Such reflections, if sane, will frequently lead to the conclusions that the detail has subtle, almost unmeasurable effects. We cannot put our finger on the significance.

I think that inerrantists, as well as those who find "contradictions" between parallel accounts, have something to learn here. Both sides are disposed to "overread" historical narratives when they infer detail. As an example, take the gospel accounts of Peter's denial. Some have claimed that the different accounts contradict one another. On the other side, inerrantists have sometimes felt constrained to argue that Peter denied Christ six times in all.[23] But if they had had more sensitivity to the constraints of historical narration, they would have found it possible, perhaps, to see only three occasions of denial (cf. the explanations of Augustine, Bengel, Calvin, and Westcott).[24] There is still no contradiction, no "error," in the accounts! Noncorresponding mental pictures on the part of the readers do not constitute error.

XIII. LIMITATIONS ON COMMUNICATION AT THE LEVEL OF DISCOURSE: THE PARTICIPATION OF THE INTERPRETER IN THE PRODUCTION OF MEANING

My second concern with regard to discourse is an even more general topic: the topic of the interpreter's involvement.[25] What I have in mind is that discourses of any real complexity invite readers to ponder, to digest, to absorb, to be changed. Discourses are not "understood" without that response. On the logical plane, they invite inferences. But of course "inferences" in a *narrow* logical sense are not all they invite. Discourses of the Bible, in particular, implicate the reader in a personal encounter with the living God. The encounter includes the confrontation with the lordship of God and the consequent obligation to believe many propositions.[26] But it includes other things besides. Moreover, the divine obligations themselves are colored by the human recipient. The *way* in which they come to him is suited to *him*, in his uniqueness and individuality as well as in his generic humanness.

What I aim to say, then, is that discourses do not always strike *exactly* the same note or series of notes in all readers, nor is it desirable for them to do so. There is diversity in the body of Christ as well as unity. Of course, in some disagreements over interpretation, one person is right and another is wrong. But there may *also* be divergences in interpretation which are enriching differences of perspective. No one's knowledge of God is "merely" reducible to or included in another's. There may be divergences due to humanness and not to sin. I, for one, think that this is so and that it does *not* imply relativism. The diversity of insight and perspectives in the body of Christ does not swallow up or threaten the distinction between truth and error, sin and righteousness. Sin does not create diversity but twists it and makes it painful and contentious.

Whether or not others agree with me here, they may perhaps at least be willing to admit that exact identity of perspective and identity of meaning is seldom seen. Discourses are more than the mathematical sum of their sentences. They have extra richness. Setting the boundaries to that richness is a complicated affair, sometimes demanding the involvement of an interpreter's whole personality and experience.

In the face of such complexities, there are two routes to avoid. First, we cannot be relativists. We cannot be subjectivists who say, "Anything goes." *Some* interpretations of the Bible are proof of the interpreter's blindness. They call down condemnatory *judgments* on the interpreter, presaging the final judgment (2 Cor. 2:16, Titus 3:11, 2 Cor. 5:10).

Second, we cannot escape into objectivism. There is a kind of scholarship which is escapist. It pretends to itself that the most important questions for scholarship are the most "objectively controllable." Hence it would flood the journals with articles minutely discussing words and sentences, but refuse to wrestle robustly with discourse and surrounding cultures. It may discuss discourse, to be sure. But when it does it is still all too controlled by the idea of simply summing together what it has found from the words. The best students of literature would not think of treating discourse this way. They know that the profoundest interpretations *must* irreducibly involve the interpreter's perspective.

NOTES

[1]John M. Frame, "God and Biblical Language: Transcendence and Immanence," *God's Inerrant Word,* ed. John Warwick Montgomery (Minneapolis: Bethany Fellowship, 1974), pp. 159-77; see also James I. Packer, "The Adequacy of Human Language," *Inerrancy,* ed. Norman L. Geisler (Grand Rapids: Zondervan, 1980), pp. 197-226.

[2]Frame, "God and Biblical Language."

[3]Ibid., p. 160.

[4]Ludwig Wittgenstein, *Philosophische Untersuchungen.* 3e Aufl. With translation by G. E. M. Anscombe (New York: Macmillan, 1968).

[5]Stephen Ullmann, *Semantics: An Introduction to the Science of Meaning* (Oxford: Blackwell, 1964), pp. 116-28.

[6]Donald N. Larson and William A. Smalley, *Becoming Bilingual: A Guide to Language Learning,* Pre-Publication Edition (New Canaan, Conn.: Practical Anthropology, 1972), p. 124.

[7]Ullmann, *Semantics,* p. 246.

[8]Ibid., pp. 125-27.

[9]James Barr, *The Semantics of Biblical Language* (London: Oxford University, 1961).

[10]Eugene A. Nida and Charles R. Nida, *The Theory and Practice of Translation* (Leiden: Brill, 1969).

[11]Barr, *Semantics of Biblical Language,* pp. 234, 249, 263, 269.

[12]Johannes P. Louw, "Linguistic Theory and the Greek Case System," *Acta Classica* (1966), Vol. 9, p. 80.

[13]Frank Stagg, "The Abused Aorist," *Journal of Biblical Literature* (1972), Vol. 91, pp. 222-31.

[14]Leon Morris, *The Revelation of St. John* (London: Tyndale, 1969).

[15]Stagg, "The Abused Aorist," p. 227.

[16]Ibid., pp. 228-29.

[17]I am indebted to Moises Silva for pointing out this example.

[18]I hold that much of John 16 applies in a special, preeminent sense to the apostles in their eyewitness capacity (John 15:27). It applies secondarily and derivatively to the whole church. But this is not the place to discuss the complexities in interpreting John 16!

[19]Some people might prefer to talk about presuppositions and implications of

propositions rather than of *sentences*. The difficulty with *sentences* is that their meaning varies with context. Almost any piece of speech, for example, can be made ironical by insertion into an appropriate larger context. Even apart from irony, exact nuances depend on context a good deal more than most of us are aware of. At any rate, the sentences that I will henceforth consider are fixed in a context by their occurrences in the Bible. Hence there is no difficulty.

[20]For example, Scripture can pick up the statements of Caiaphas (John 11:50) or Aratus (Acts 17:28) without approving the sense in which the originators understood them. Can this be so in the area of presuppositions associated with a culture?

[21]Following Ridderbos (*Paul: An Outline of His Theology* [Grand Rapids: Eerdmans, 1975], pp. 555-58) I think that the second alternative is correct. But it should be noted that the second alternative is not supported by any very explicit qualification in the immediate literary context. It is supported only by our general knowledge concerning Paul's use of *zōopoieō* and the "in Christ" terminology, and by the general tone of the passage, whose concern is primarily with the fate of believers (Cf. 15:18-19, 15:54-58), not with humanity indiscriminately. Biblical writers are often very free about *not* explicitly qualifying what the academic theologian thinks needs qualification.

[22]In fact, rather than saying that language gives a "picture" of the world, we might better say that a picture is a "language-like" interpretation of the world. Phenomena of human vision and of visual arts, difficult to explain on the basis of any mechanical model of vision, become intelligible if we use language, translation, and verbal interpretation as a model for understanding visual processes. See M. Turbayne, *The Myth of Metaphor* rev. ed. (Columbia, S.C.: University of South Carolina, 1970).

[23]Harold Lindsell, *The Battle for the Bible* (Grand Rapids: Zondervan, 1976), pp. 174-76; John Brown McClellan, *The New Testament of Our Lord and Saviour Jesus Christ . . .* (London: Macmillan, 1876), Vol. 1, p. 501.

[24]Augustine, "Harmony of the Gospels," *Nicene and Post-Nicene Fathers*, ed. Philip Schaff (New York: Christian Literature Company, 1888), Vol. 6, pp. 187-89; John Albert Bengel, *Gnomon of the New Testament* (Philadelphia: Perkinpine & Higgins, 1860), Vol. 1, p. 710; John Calvin, *Commentary on a Harmony of the Evangelists, Matthew, Mark, and Luke* (Grand Rapids: Eerdmans, 1965), Vol. 3, Reprinted, pp. 262-63; Brooke Foss Westcott, *An Introduction to the Study of the Gospels*, 5th ed. (London: Macmillan, 1875), p. 298. In my opinion, the Evangelists are *not* obliged to give us notice of small-scale changes in posture and location, to give verbatim reports of the speeches, or to record group dialogues in full. They *would* have to do all these in order to protect the exact correspondence of reader's mental pictures with the facts.

[25]I think that the interpreter is involved in the production of meaning at the level of the word and the sentence, as well as at the level of discourse. But his involvement is most obvious at the level of discourse.

[26]John M. Frame, "Scripture Speaks for Itself," *God's Inerrant Word*, ed. John Warwick Montgomery (Minneapolis: Bethany Fellowship, 1974), pp. 178-200.

A Response to Adequacy of Language and Accommodation

Paul D. Feinberg
Professor and Chairman,
Division of Biblical and Systematic Theology
Trinity Evangelical Divinity School

A Response to Adequacy of Language and Accommodation

Paul D. Feinberg

I would like to divide my response to Professor Poythress' paper into two parts. First, I would like to make two very brief comments by way of clarification on matters in the paper. Second, I would like to amplify on some issues mentioned but not discussed in detail in the presentation.

I. COMMENTS BY WAY OF CLARIFICATION

There are two matters discussed in the paper which seem to me to need clarification. The first point is raised on pages 359 and 360. There Poythress is discussing the limits of a property. He shows us that in some cases we must know the boundaries of a concept or we may be guilty of the logical fallacy of equivocation. To demonstrate the problem he gives us an example of a syllogism that he thinks is invalid because of the lack of certainty about the term "cat." While it may be possible to reject that syllogism because of equivocation, I would suggest that there is an alternative understanding of it which I think most logicians would take that avoids the problem of equivocation. The problem with the syllogism given is *not* that there is equivocation, but rather that the second or minor premise is false. It is simply not true that "all cats are less than three feet long."

The second comment is related to the objection, "can language be wholly true?" which is discussed on pages 354 and 355. The locution "wholly true" is usually used in one of two ways. One way is incompatible with a biblical view of inspiration and inerrancy, while the other is not. Sometimes "wholly true" is used to mean that what has been said or communicated is a mixture of truth *and* falsity. Obviously, if all linguistic communication is a mixture of truth and falsity, then it would be true that an inerrant Bible would be impossible. However, such a contention would be in need of support or justification. It may be that the objection to propositional revelation (Brunner and Barth) discussed below is such a claim.

On, the other hand, "wholly true" may simply mean that we do not possess all the truth on the subject of God and his ways or works. Such a statement means that our knowledge is partial. Having said that, it in no way requires that the partial knowledge that we do possess is in any way false, because what knowledge we do have may be *all* or *completely* true. Furthermore, as Poythress argues, the language of the Bible need not be as precise as possible or even as precise as we might like. All that is required for an inerrant Bible is that all of the statements of Scripture be *true*.

II. COMMENTS BY WAY OF AMPLIFICATION

There are some issues which Poythress mentions but does not pursue that seem to me to be of great importance. I would like to discuss them in some detail. Poythress begins his paper by stating that objections based on language are of three general types: human language is inadequate to talk of *God;* human language is never wholly true; and human language from a "primitive" culture can never be totally true. The majority of the paper deals with the concerns that lead to objections two and three. I would like to focus our attentions on the matters that have led philosophers and theologians to advance the first objection. Then, finally, I would like to examine the question of accommodation and its relation to biblical interpretation and inerrancy.

A. The Adequacy of Human Language to Speak about *God*

There is no more important or fundamental challenge to the question of inerrancy, and propositional revelation for that matter, than the claim human language used to talk about God is in some sense inadequate. This claim has come from two quite different sources in the twentieth century. One root is philosophical, the other theological.

The philosophical root is found in logical positivism. This movement began in the early 1920s and was over by the late 1930s. However, its mark has been left unmistakably on Anglo-American philosophy. One of the concerns of the positivist's was to separate what they called pseudophilosophical questions from genuine questions. The tool which they devised to make this separation was called the verification principle. While the verification principle went through many formulations during its short but illustrious history, its central idea was this. For any statement to be meaningful *about the world* (putative), there had to be something in experience that would count for or against the truth or falsity of that statement. Or, put another way, a proposition could not tell us anything about the *world* if it was compatible with every state of affairs.

Statements that were not verifiable (that is, without experiential consequences) were placed in one of two classes. Either they were analytic or meaningless. Analytic propositions were statements that were true by definition or convention. The pedicate term was hidden in the subject term. "1 plus 1 equals two" and "bachelors are unmarried males" are two examples of such sentences. What is significant about analytic sentences is that while they are extremely important (the statements of math and logic make up this class), they tell us nothing about the world. The other class of statements is called meaningless. "Meaningless" is a misleading term. It is not synonymous with unimportant. Rather it is used to designate those sentences which *appear* to say something about the world, but are compatible with *every* state of the world. Nothing in experience counts for or against these propositions. All the statements of what had traditionally been called speculative metaphysics fell within this class. Statements like "the all is good" would be a member of the class of meaningless statements, because nothing in experience would count for or against that claim.

It was only a matter of time before theological discourse would be examined in light of this principle. In the Socrates Club (a discussion group sponsored by C. S. Lewis) at Oxford University, Antony G. N. Flew throws down the gauntlet to the theist over religious language. The interchange is recorded in "Theology and Falsification."[1]

Flew begins with a parable. Two explorers come upon a clearing in the jungle. In this clearing there are both flowers and weeds. One explorer thinks that this plot is tended by a gardener, the other does not. The two decide to find out who is right, and pitch their tents to watch for the gardener. Alas, they never see him. The explorer who believes in the existence of a gardener will not, however, give up his belief. He claims that the gardener is an invisible gardener. In hopes of finding if this is true, the two men put up barbed-wire fences. They electrify them, and patrol the area with bloodhounds. Still there are no cries of anguish as though someone has been shocked. Moreover, there is no movement of the wires. The believer still refuses to give up his belief in his gardener. He argues that the gardener is invisible, intangible, insensible to electric shocks, and has no scent and makes no sound. The gardener comes secretly to look after the garden which he loves. Finally, the sceptic demands to know in what way this eternally elusive gardener is different from an imaginary gardener or no gardener at all.

Flew thinks that this parable is an accurate picture of the disagreement between the theist and the atheist. The clearing is human experience. The existence of both flowers and weeds is indicative of the ambiguity of human experience with regard to the question of God's existence. The believer begins with what Flew calls a brash hypothesis. The garden is cared for by a gardener who loves it. However, as the believer's claim fails to be substantiated in experience, the bold claim dies what Flew calls the death of a thousand qualifications, killed by inches. The believer begins by making assertions that appear to be vast cosmological statements, but are reduced step by step to a expression of "picture preference."

Flew's point is this. Talk about God is not falsifiable; it is consistent with all and any states of affairs in the world. Therefore, religious language is meaningless. It tells us nothing about the world. At best it expresses the way in which the theist likes to *think* about the world.

Responses to the charge that religious language is meaningless can be placed into roughly three groups. First, there were those defenders of religious language who accepted the verification principle as the criterion of meaningfulness, but argued that the theist's case had not been dealt with fairly. Basil Mitchell and John Hick are examples of this approach. Mitchell was asked to respond to Flew at the Socrates Club.[2] His response went something like this. He argues that the theist does allow for the ambiguity of experience, and evil in particular, to count against God's existence, just not *decisively*. This refusal to allow final falsification is due to the fact that the Christian is committed by his or her faith to *trust* God.

Mitchell illustrates his point with a parable. The parable is set in a time of war in an occupied country. A member of the resistance meets a stranger one night. They engage in conversation for the whole night. The stranger tells the member of the resistance that he is on his side, in fact he is the commander of the resistance. He urges this member of the resistance to have absolute trust in him no matter what happens. This meeting so impresses the underling that he places his trust in his commander.

The stranger and the member of the resistance never meet in

similar circumstances again. During the conduct of the war, the actions of the stranger vary from help for the resistance to aid for the occupying power. Whatever the actions of the stranger are, the member of the resistance continues to trust because of the impression made on him at the initial meeting. When faced with the ambiguity of experience, he may either give up his faith or continue to believe, maintaining that God has reasons for withholding his help. He continues to believe, because he will not put God to the test.

A number of philosophers have seen John Hick's "Eschatological Verification"[3] as a further development of some ideas present in Mitchell's response. Hick's position is that theological discourse is verifiable, just not now. Hick argues that the term "God" and utterances like "God exists" are a *part* of a complex system of truth, and can only be grasped and verified in the context of the whole. This system of truth includes a certain understanding of the universe, man's place in it, the relationship between man's purposes and God's purposes within it, and the eventual fulfillment of God's purposes. It is in this context that the Christian expects a distinctive *future*, which is not anticipated by those who do not believe in the NT God.

On the way to the Celestial City human experience is ambiguous in support of God's existence. There are those things that seem to support it, as well as hardships and danger. However, around the last corner, it will finally be clear that the theist is right and the atheist is wrong. In the Celestial City there will be the experience of the fulfillment of God's purposes for us as recorded in the Bible, as well as communion with God and Christ. Thus, Hick holds that Christianity teaches an unambiguous state of affairs in the future. Their experience will verify Christianity. Hence, religious language is meaningful in the present.

Second, there were those who defended the meaningfulness of religious discourse by staking out some new ground for it. R. B. Braithwaite's "An Empiricist's View of the Nature of Religious Belief" is a good example of this approach.[4] He thinks that theological language is verifiable in terms of *use*. The primary function of religious assertions is to commit the utterer to a *way of life* or *policy of action*. This intention to act in a specified way is not only a test of sincerity but also of meaning. For Christianity religious assertions commit the utterer to an agapeistic way of life. This way of life is best described in 1 Corinthians 13.

Braithwaite's claim is this. Theological language avoids Flew's condemnation because it is verifiable in terms of its use. That use is to guide the conduct of the utterer into an agapeistic way of life.

Third, one may approach the problem of verifiability by denying that the verification principle is a criterion of meaningfulness. E. L. Mascall in *Words and Images* has done just that.[5] He looks with great suspicion on the verification principle because it has gone through so many reformulations, each successive version being weaker than the former. Why should this be? The answer is that the verification principle supposedly excluded too much. But, if this is so, how can we know that without some independent criterion of significance? Mascall says that it sounds as though the positivist has already decided what statements he wants to be meaningful, and is trying to tailor the verification principle to fit. The truly heroic course to take would have been to have formulated a manly and robust principle, and then allowed the chips to fall where they might.

Mascall then asks what kind of a statement the verification principle itself is. Meaningful statements are either analytic or empirically verifiable. Is the verification principle analytic? Mascall does not think so. That would require that "meaningful" and "empirically verifiable" are synonymous, since analytic statements have the characteristic that the predicate terms are hidden in the subject terms. Simple reflection will show us that that is not so. Neither does it appear to be an empirical generalization. No positivist has ever claimed to have examined a large body of meaningful propositions, and concluded that they all possessed the characteristic of being empirically verifiable. Nor can it be claimed that the verification principle is a rule of language, since that would make it a synthetic a priori statement. Synthetic a priori assertions happen to be just the kind of propositions that positivists deny exist.

Mascall also objects to the identification of "meaningful" with "empirically verifiable." "Meaningful" is not usually defined in terms of "empirically verifiable" but *intelligible*. If this is the case, then theological statements are not meaningless, since they are not unintelligible.

Finally, Mascall criticizes the positivist limitation of experience to *public* experience gained by the *five* senses. There is a good deal of experience that is not sense experience. A prime example of such experience is mystical experience, which is dismissed without consideration.

There is much more to say than space will allow. However, from these brief comments it should be clear that the philosophical challenge mounted against the meaningfulness and adequacy of religious language was not successful. If one accepts the verification principle as a criterion of meaning, then biblical Christianity is verifiable. There is the Incarnation, where God came into time and space in human flesh. Religious language does guide the believer's conduct. And at some future time there will be unambiguous evidence for the truth of Christianity.

On the other hand, one is surely not required to accept the verification principle as a criterion of meaningfulness. If verification is not the sign of empirical significance, then religious language is meaningful because it is intelligible.

The theological root of the claim that human language is inadequate to speak about God is to be found in neoorthodoxy. Emil Brunner and Karl Barth both hold this view, although for different reasons. I would like to examine each man's position in turn.

Brunner's objection grows out of the fact that the Bible is a *human* book. Inerrantists are guilty of a theological error akin to docetism (the human body of Christ was not real). A Bible that was free from error would no longer be human.[6] The Scriptures are the product of human research and selection. Its form is fallible; it comes in a human vessel. On the other hand, the content of revelation is infallible. Therefore, the Bible cannot be verbally inspired.[7]

Barth's rejection of the adequacy of human language is related to his belief in the radical transcendence of God. The pictures in which we view God, the thoughts in which we think of him and the *words* with which we define and speak of him are in themselves unfit for their object. It therefore follows that these pictures, thoughts and words are inappropriate to express and affirm our knowledge of God. Human language is finite; God is infinite.[8]

By way of summary, then, Brunner denies the adequacy of language, because it is human. Barth, on the other hand, thinks of human language as unfit to bear God's revelation because of God's radical transcendence and the finitude of human languages.

Are these objections justified? I think not. Brunner's objection is the easiest to answer. He does not take the biblical doctrine of a historical fall seriously. Sin, evil and error were not a part of the original creation. Man was created perfect. Therefore, a necessary or defining characteristic of humanity is *not* error or sin. Before the first pair sinned, they were human. At some future time there will be a group of men and women who cannot sin, and will still be human. The universality of sin and error is due to the Fall, not creation. Finite humanity does not necessitate error.

But there is more. The Bible is not simply a human book. While it is wrong to neglect the human character of the Bible, it is equally wrong to forget its divine character. The divine inspiration of the Scriptures protects the human authors from error. Let us never forget that the Bible is a *divine-human* book.[9]

Let me now turn to Barth. As has already been mentioned, Barth's objection to the adequacy of human language is related to his view on the radical transcendence of God. Even Brunner is critical of Barth's views at this point. He criticizes Barth's failure to distinguish between essence and being. In God there is a transcendence of essence. This means that God alone is God. His "Godhood" is absolutely and unchangeably different from all other forms of being. However, God is related to his creation by the *analogia entis* (the analogy of being). Barth vehemently rejects this, calling it an invention of the anti-Christ.[10] Barth's rejection of this doctrine is related to its connection with neo-Platonist ontology and the natural theology which is based thereon.

Yet Barth's position overlooks two important factors. The claim that God possesses a transcendence of being in some absolute sense logically leads to deism and the denial of the immanence of God. As Brunner points out, the biblical doctrine of God avoids both the extremes of a deistic doctrine of transcendence and a pantheistic doctrine of immanence.[11] Furthermore, there is an alternative to a doctrine of the analogy of being based upon neo-Platonic thought. There is the genuinely biblical doctrine of man as created in the *image* and *likeness* of God. The creator has stamped his imprint upon man. There is a point of contact.[12]

Before leaving this subject, it may be good to make explicit an assumption that is implicit in Barth's position and those like it. The assumption is that there is an antithesis between divinity and humanity, the infinite and the finite. The reasons for thinking this are numerous as one examines the history of Christian thought. Some have thought that they are contradictory. To bring them together would violate the law of noncontradiction. Others like the gnostics have felt that matter and finitude were inherently evil, and thus unworthy for contact with God. Neither of these views is substantiated by Scripture. That deity and humanity are not contradictory can be seen in the incarnation and the hypostatic union of natures in Christ. That matter is not inherently evil is clear from the pronouncement of God at the end of creation that the natural order was "very good." This is not, at the same time, to deny the vast differences between deity and humanity, the infinite and the finite.

It is not surprising that, given their views on religious language, both Brunner and Barth reject the Bible as propositional revelation. Revelation is personal, it is concretely in Jesus Christ. This is not to say that the words of Scripture are unimportant. They serve as a witness to revelation. The Bible has instrumental value in leading one to the experience of revelation.[13]

B. Accommodation

The concept of accommodation is both an important and often neglected principle of hermeneutics. More recently, it has begun to take a more important place in discussions on biblical authority and inerrancy.[14] Again, there is far more to be said on the topic than time and space will allow. Hopefully, what is said will encourage others to pursue this topic further.

The term "accommodation" has been used in three distinguishable ways. (1) It is used to explain how God, being infinite, could communicate his revelation to finite human capacity. Christ and his apostles also accommodated their teaching, so that those who heard would understand (cf. Jn 16:12; 1 Cor. 3:1-3). (2) The writers of Scripture and even Christ taught errors that were commonly believed in their time. They were culturally bound, or they deliberately taught error so as not to upset their hearers. (3) Accommodation is also used to refer the adaption of church order, liturgy, and so forth to the cultural situation. Today this would probably be called contextualization.[15]

It should be clear that sense (3) above would carry us to areas outside the scope of this paper. However, I would like to discuss senses (1) and (2) in the light of hermeneutics and inerrancy. Without question accommodation was a hermeneutical principle from the time of the fathers to the present.[16] In the first sense above accommodation was thought to express the way in which God condescends to communicate his truth to human capacity, a capacity that has been damaged by the fall. It was taken to be an appropriate tool to explain the *method* and *manner* of divine revelation, as well as an important hermeneutical principle for interpreting the language of the Bible. God used human language, human concepts, and objects of human experience to give his truth.

The importance of this principle can be seen in at least two areas. First, it leads to the revelation of God in anthropomorphic terms. How is pure spirit to be described? Christian divines have argued that in accommodating his truth to our capacity, God is spoken of in terms of physical properties and human emotions. Second, it explains why the realm of nature is spoken of in the language of appearance or observation rather than exact science. The Bible speaks of the sun setting and rising, not the more technical language of the natural sciences.[17]

The idea of accommodation is expressed in a number of different ways in the history of Christian thought. Origen uses an image that is later to be found in the writings of Augustine and Calvin. The picture is that of a parent or teacher trying to communicate with a child.[18] Calvin always uses the term as a verb, never as a noun. His use of the term is rooted in his profound sense of the differences between God and man. Man cannot overcome these differences, only God can. This he does through accommodation or condescension. Accommodation became one of the two most important and used hermeneutical principles in Calvin's thought. He points out that God has accommodated himself to man's capacity in a number of areas: revelation, Christ, the church and sacraments. In revelation Calvin says that God has chosen to speak baby-talk, to lisp, prattle, stammer and stutter so that we may know of him.[19]

Did God ever deliberately teach error in the communication of truth, or were the writers of Scripture unable to transcend the ignorance of their day in the inscripturating of God's revelation (sense 2 above)? Irenaeus clearly did not think so. He says that our Lord did not speak lies. He used neither fraud, deception, or hyprocrisy. Such an approach would not have healed their sickness.[20] Some of the later statements of Origen indicate that he came to think that God did accommodate himself to man in the sense that he deceived men *for their own good.*[21] God also used ambiguous words to cover the truth with a veil, if that truth might hurt us when openly stated.[22] Lindsley suggests that Origen's later views grow out of his allegorical hermeneutical method. If the allegorical sense of Scripture is always the fullest and most hidden, then it does not seem so troublesome that God should hide his truth from the unspiritual.[23]

Accommodation in the second sense given above never was widely held until the rise of liberal theology in the 18th century. This term then became the chief mode by which God communicated through the Bible. It resolved the problem of the temporal and cultural boundaries of the Scripture. The chief concern becomes how one goes about distinguishing the "essential content" from the "time related form."[24]

It should be clear from our discussion that accommodation to error (sense 2) is incompatible with inerrancy, but condescension to ignorance (sense 1) is not only proper but an important tool in the proper exegesis of the Bible.[25] As a matter of fact, such contemporary writers as Roland Frye, G. Ernest Wright, Floyd Filson and Paul Minear, while not associating the principle with biblical authority, have claimed that it constitutes a viable alternative to Bultmann's program of demythologizing.[26]

NOTES

[1]Antony G. N. Flew, "Theology and Falsification," in *The Philosophy of Religion,* Basil Mitchell, ed. (Oxford, Oxford University Press, 1971), pp. 13-15.

[2]Basil Mitchell, "Theology and Falsification," in *The Philosophy of Religion,* Basil Mitchell, ed. (Oxford, Oxford University Press, 1971), pp. 18-20.

[3]John Hick, "Theology and Verification," *Theology Today,* 17 (1960), 12-31.

[4]R. B. Braithwaite, "An Empiricist's View of the Nature of Religious Belief," in *God, Man and Religion,* Keith Yandell, ed. (New York: McGraw-Hill, 1973), pp. 215-29.

[5]E. L. Mascall, *Words and Images* (London: Longmans, Green, 1956).

[6]Emil Brunner, *Truth as Encounter,* trans. by A. W. Loos and D. Cairns (Philadelphia: The Westminster Press, 1964), pp. 176-77.

[7]Emil Brunner, *The Christian Doctrine of God,* trans. by Olive Wyon (Philadelphia: The Westminster Press, 1950), pp. 110-11.

[8]Karl Barth, *Church Dogmatics,* Vol. II: *The Doctrine of God,* ed. G. W. Bromiley and T. F. Torrance; trans. T. H. L. Parker, W. B. Johnston, H. Knight and J. L. M. Haire (New York: Scribners, 1957), Pt. 1, p. 188. See also John M. Frame, "God and Biblical Language: Transcendence and Immanence," in *God's Inerrant Word,* John W. Montgomery, ed. (Minneapolis: Bethany Fellowship, Inc., 1973). pp. 159-77.

[9]For further discussion of this point see Paul D. Feinberg, "The Meaning of Inerrancy," in *Inerrancy,* Norman L. Geisler, ed. (Grand Rapids: Zondervan Publishing House, 1979).

[10]Karl Barth, *Church Dogmatics,* Pt. 1, p. viii.

[11]Brunner, *Doctrine of God,* pp. 175-76.

[12]Ibid.

[13]See Karl Barth, *Church Dogmatics,* Vol. I: *The Doctrine of the Word of God,* trans. G. T. Thomson (New York: Scribner, 1936), Pt. 1, pp. 125, 155-56. Emil Brunner, *Revelation and Reason: The Christian Doctrine of Faith and Knowledge,* trans. Olive Wyon (Philadelphia: The Westminster Press, 1946), pp. 118ff.

[14]Jack B. Rogers and Donald K. McKim, *The Authority and Interpretation of the Bible: An Historical Approach* (San Francisco: Harper & Row, Publishers, 1979), pp. 11-12; 98-100.

[15]Arthur Lindsley, "The Principle of Accommodation," unpublished Ph.D. paper, pp. 1, 2. This is a very excellent treatment of the question. I am deeply indebted to Lindsley for his introduction into the problem.

[16]Jack Rogers, *The Authority of the Bible*, pp. 11-12.

[17]Arthur Lindsley, "Accommodation," p. 3.

[18]R. P. C. Hanson, *Allegory and Event* (London, SCM Press, 1959), p. 226 from Fragment on Dt. 1:21.

[19]For example, John Calvin, *The Deity of Christ and Other Sermons*, (Grand Rapids: Wm. B. Eerdmans Publishing Co., 1950), p. 18.

[20]Irenaeus, in *The Anti-Nicene Fathers*, Vol. 1 (Buffalo: The Christian Literature Publishing Co., 1885), pp. 417-18.

[21]R. P. C. Hanson, *Allegory*, p. 229.

[22]Ibid.

[23]Arthur Lindsley, "Accommodation," p. 10.

[24]Ibid., p. 2.

[25]Ibid., p. 5.

[26]See Roland M. Frye, *Perspective on Man: Literature and the Christian Tradition* (Philadelphia: The Westminster Press, 1961); G. Ernest Wright, *The Old Testament and Theology* (New York: Harper and Row Publishers, 1969); Floyd Filson, *Jesus Christ the Risen Lord* (New York: Abingdon Press, 1956); and Paul S. Minear, *The Kingdom and the Power: An Exposition of the New Testament Gospel* (Philadelphia: The Westminster Press, 1950).

A Response to Adequacy of Language and Accommodation

Kurt E. Marquart
Associate Professor of
Systematic Theology
Concordia Theological
Seminary
Fort Wayne, Indiana

A Response to Adequacy of Language and Accommodation

Kurt E. Marquart

The valuable paper by Professor Poythress suggests several observations, which however are best stated in light of more general perspectives to be sketched under the heads of philosophy and theology respectively.

I. PHILOSOPHICAL REMARKS

In the first place it seems to me that the usual empiricist scruples about "God-talk" have a very narrow, and in our context basically irrelevant, range of applications. Their proper targets are those vague and windy "theologies" which resemble bloated hot-air balloons and positively invite common-sense puncturings. Let Langdon Gilkey describe a representative specimen:

> For us, then, the Bible is a book of the acts Hebrews believed God might have done and the words he might have said had he done and said them—but of course we recognise he did not. The difference between this view of the Bible as a parable illustrative of Hebrew religious faith and the view of the Bible as a direct narrative of God's actual deeds and words is so vast that it scarcely needs comment. . . .
>
> we have induced . . . the theological generalisation that God is he who acts and speaks. This general truth about God we then assert while denying all the particular cases on the basis of which the generalisation was first made. Consequently, biblical theology is left with a set of theological abstractions, more abstract than the dogmas of scholasticism, for these are concepts with no known concreteness.[1]

One can hardly blame the empiricist Kai Nielssen for complaining of "a new or at least a radically altered language-game with Christian terms and an atheistic substance."[2]

There is no reason to believe, however, that the objections to ethereal ghosts of deceased theologies apply also to a robust, flesh-and-blood realism, which takes Holy Scripture at face value. Thus Malcolm Diamond, in his introduction to a book on the subject co-edited by him, explicitly argues that "fundamentalists are not vulnerable to the challenge of verification" because they can point to purported observations, even rather "startling" ones, such as "the parting of the raging waters of the Red Sea and . . . their standing in 'walls.' "[3] Diamond says: "Contemporary empiricists concede the factual meaningfulness of fundamentalist theology," and cites Rudolf Carnap himself in support. At the place indicated the latter does indeed concede "clear meaning" to what he calls the "mythological" use of the word "God," by which Carnap means (a) "physical beings which are enthroned on Mount Olympus, in Heaven or in Hades. . . ." or (b) "spiritual beings which, indeed, do not have manlike bodies, yet manifest themselves nevertheless somehow in the things or processes of the visible world and are therefore empirically verifiable."[4] Despite the condescending comparison with Mount Olympus, it is at least clear that on this view the religion of the Incarnation, of God-made-flesh, cannot in principle be charged with empirical vacuity. In the biblical context, at any rate, the proposition "God loves us" is not an optimistic platitude compatible with any and every actual state of affairs, but a highly specific assertion which logically presupposes truth-claims about concrete matters of fact like the life, death, and resurrection of Jesus. One might even quip with Alvin Plantinga "that if after death I were to meet Father Abraham, St. Paul, and St. John (I think I could recognize them), who united in declaring that they had been duped, perhaps I should have sufficient reason for concluding that God does not love us after all."[5]

Anchorage in the factual matrix of historical revelation, however, is not the only possible source of empirical relevance for religious assertions. This function is served, if anything, even better by the *scientific* connections of a robust *natural theology,* or what we today might call "philosophical" or even "scientific" theology. The whole point of natural theology in this sense is that it argues from the nature of the observable universe to certain conclusions about God (Rom. 1:20). And of course, unlike revealed theology, which deals with the certainties of faith, natural theology, together with empirical science generally, operates within the realm of probability and common sense.

Mortimer Adler, who wishes to "engage in thinking about God

that is not only philosophical but also pagan," concludes, by arguing from the contingency of the universe, "that God exists, either beyond a reasonable doubt or by a preponderance of reasons in favour of that conclusion over reasons against it."[6] In an even more recent book he crisply characterizes the analogy with scientific reasoning:

> The only justification for affirming the existence of something unperceived and, perhaps, imperceptible is that whatever it is that needs to be explained cannot be explained in any other way. This is the sound rule laid down by William of Ockham in the fourteenth century and it has been followed ever since by careful, cautious scientists and philosophers.
>
> The reasoning of nuclear physicists concerning the existence of certain elementary particles that are intrinsically imperceptible takes this form. So, too, does a valid argument for the existence of God.[7]

But of course, as everyone "knows" nowadays, natural theology came to an abrupt end as a result of Charles Darwin's work. As Sir Julian Huxley, grandson of "Darwin's bulldog," put it at the Darwin Centenary in Chicago: "Darwinism removed the whole idea of God as the creator of organisms from the sphere of rational discussion. . . . Darwin pointed out that no supernatural designer was needed. . . ."[8] Presumably, however, Darwin was engaged in rational discussion when he was removing God from the sphere of rational discussion! If one says with Neal Gillespie, for instance, that Darwin "effectively demolished William Paley's classical design argument for the existence of God,"[9] one can hardly maintain at the same time that Paley's design argument for God was cognitively meaningless or empirically vacuous. What was Darwin refuting then? One cannot "refute" meaningless statements—the "*refutatum*" must be at least as meaningful as the "*refutans*." For as Wesley Salmon put it, "the negation of any verifiable statement is verifiable."[10] If Paley's argumentation was meaningless, therefore, then so was Darwin's refutation of it. Or, if Darwin's refutation was meaningful, then Paley's argument was equally so.

The irony is that there is some doubt nowadays about the empirical meaningfulness (or vacuousness, respectively) of the Darwinian, or more accurately, neo-Darwinian, conjecture itself.[11] Fortunately, however, at least if with Sir Karl Popper we take "gradualness" to be, "from a logical point of view, the central prediction," if not the only one, of Darwinism,[12] then that prediction appears now to be not only falsifiable but actually false.[13]

On a more fundamental, radical level, Darwinism is today coming unstuck in the face of information-theoretic considerations. The distinguished astronomer Sir Fred Hoyle, who until recently had taken an atheistic view of origins, argued at the 1981 Kellogg Symposium that the higher life forms contained information "represented by the number $10^{40,000}$," and that the likelihood of such organisms arising by random, evolutionary processes was comparable to the chance that "a tornado sweeping through a junk-yard might assemble a Boeing 747 from the materials therein." Sir Fred added that he was at a loss to understand "biologists' widespread compulsion to deny what seems to me to be obvious."[14]

Hoyle's and Wickramasinghe's brilliant diagnosis of the bankruptcy of Darwinism retains its value, it seems to me, despite the implausibility of their exotic cure (a regress, à la Gnosticism, of ever higher intelligences, "even to the extreme idealised limit of *God*").[15] A single Creative Intelligence, as assumed by Mortimer Adler for instance, seems the more sober and efficient conclusion, given Ockham's razor. But the very outlandishness of the distinguished authors' flights of fancy is a measure of the desperateness which has befallen the Darwinian position. Perhaps, by way of poetic justice, we are in for a rash of imaginative absurdities (Rom. 1:21!), which it would be not inappropriate to dub "Paley's Revenge."

The point of all this is simply to illustrate, in support of Prof. Poythress' argumentation, the groundlessness in principle of defeatism in respect of "God-talk." Both a robust natural theology and a revealed theology based on Holy Scripture are, because of their factual moorings, beyond the reach of the standard empiricist objections to "religious language." I would venture to say even that the latter is a largely fraudulent category[16] designed to accommodate and legitimize a shapeless sort of religious rhetoric that is all froth and no beer. This normless chatter in "religious language" reminds one, in Thomas C. Oden's apt phrase, of "a physician forgetting the difference between disease and health, axe and scalpel, or a lawyer forgetting the difference between criminality and *corpus juris*."[17]

Finally, it must not be overlooked that even natural science itself has failed to meet the rigorous criteria set by Logical Empiricism. The nature and status of scientific knowledge are today the subjects of lively discussion, and no clear-cut consensus has as yet emerged.[18]

It is in light of all this that I want to comment briefly on Prof. Poythress' important distinction between "truth" (correctness) and "precision" (exactness), which of course I wholeheartedly endorse.

If anything, I would go even further. Truth and precision refer to entirely different dimensions of sentences. Take two existentially quantified statements, both about the number 7:

(1) There is an x such that x is a positive integer and x equals twice 7.

(2) There is an x such that x is a positive integer and x is greater than 7.

Now, (1) and (2) are equally true, but (1) is much more restricted in scope than (2). (1) is, if you will, "punctiliar," in that it requires x to be precisely 14, whilst (2) covers an entire range of numbers, which in fact turns out to be infinite. But the truth of (2) remains completely, rigidly unchanged, whether we let x equal 8, or 14, or 144,000, or any other integer greater than 7. Truth-functionally it matters not at all whether the scope of an assertion is macroscopic or microscopic, punctiliar, linear, or multidimensional. The more constrained or "pinpointed" is the value of x, the more precise is the statement—but this in itself does not affect its truth.

Nor is this relative independence of truth and precision simply a weakness of "ordinary language," avoidable, say, in science. Sir Karl Popper argues, convincingly in my view, that precision is a relative, not an absolute standard. As a function of specificity of interest or inquiry precision is context-dependent, and cannot anticipate all possible future demands for further specification.[19]

Philosophically, then, it is simply a category mistake to cite imprecision as an argument against inerrancy.

Although the topic of "truth" as such is treated elsewhere, in a separate essay, one or two comments about it may be in order here, since Prof. Poythress' essay adverts to this question occasionally. For instance, it is not clear to me whether on pp. 371-73 the essayist wishes to criticize only the fallacy that true historical descriptions produce accurate "mental pictures," or also the major premise that "truth is correspondence with the facts." I shall assume the former, since otherwise we should be faced with a *non sequitur,* as though the definition of truth as correspondence entailed the further view that in history what must conform to fact are the information-rich but intensional "mental pictures" rather than the informationally sparse but extensional sentences or statements.

The very notion of "inerrancy," which is not peculiar to theology, cannot be defined except in relation to truth. And the only notion of truth that seems at all relevant is that common-sense one which is presupposed in all ordinary discourse, including that of science, and is technically called the "correspondence" view and tagged with the name of Alfred Tarski (" 'Snow is white' is true if and only if snow is white").[20]

Finally, a word about "meaning." On p. 366 Prof. Poythress cites the objection that messages are meaningless without interpreters, but that all relevant interpreters are fallible. Hence what is the relevance of an infallible message, even if there were or could be one? (By the way, the perfect illustration of Poythress' "mechanically possible but wildly false alternative interpretations" is the computer "translation" of "the spirit is willing but the flesh is weak" as "the drinks are acceptable but the meat is spoilt").

The problem of the validity of biblical interpretation is of course primarily a theological one. The assumption that "all meaning must be ultimately *personal* meaning" is, however, a philosophical one, and may therefore be criticized philosophically. The trouble with this maxim about "personal meaning" is that it tends to disintegrate all discourse into a multiplicity of atomistic "personal meanings," that are, subjective, psychological, mental states or acts. A handy antidote against this subjectivism might be Popper's notion of an objective realm of ideas, a "third world," distinct from and in a sense autonomous in relation to the realms of mind or self-consciousness ("second world") and of matter-energy ("first world") respectively.[21] This "third world" contains ideas, theories, logical relations, problems, etc., which are objective in the sense that they are implicit and objectively discoverable within given frames of reference, even if no one in point of actual psychological fact should ever notice them, e.g., mathematical complexities, numbers larger than any number anyone has ever thought of, and the like.

This strain of Platonic/Kantian rationalism in Popper has served as a much-needed corrective to the shallow, one-sided empiricism which triumphed briefly in Logical Positivism. Popper's influence here can hardly be overestimated. Indeed he modestly accepts responsibility for having "killed" Logical Positivism.[22] The implications for the humanities (including "divinity") are liberating: the strangle-hold of the "verifiability criterion of meaning" was broken. Popper's own notion of "falsifiability" is meant to function not as a criterion of meaning—after all, we must know what a statement means *before* we can decide whether it is verifiable or falsifiable—but as demarcation criterion distinguishing science from non-science.

And even this demarcation criterion is not rigidly doctrinaire in Popper's thought.

Such developments may ultimately release philosophy from her bondage as "the charwoman of science" (Copleston), and may even rekindle her interest in her former noble role of handmaid to theology. In natural theology of course she might frolic to her heart's content. But in the area of sacred, or revealed theology, her duties are limited to purely ancillary, instrumental, linguistic ones. Whenever she aspires to anything more, anything that smacks of substantive domination, she must be told, as Luther bluntly suggests: "Let the woman be silent in church" (1 Cor. 14:34); and, "Listen to Him" (Matt. 17:5).[23]

Theology herself of course has no need to masquerade meretriciously as "science": she possesses, after all, infinitely more than the crumbs of empirical conjecture! Her treasure is the life-giving evangel of the Logos made Flesh, Whom to serve is true liberty.

II. THEOLOGICAL REMARKS

Theologically, it appears to me, Prof. Poythress' key sentence occurs on p. 363: "What *is* holy, yes *divine,* is the particular message sent forth in a particular historical context by putting together, in the order specified in the Bible, words from Hebrew vocabulary—or Aramaic or Greek as the case may be."

This way of putting the matter at once suggests the Christological parallel. And it is more than a parallel. If the Incarnation, climaxing in the Cross and Resurrection, is indeed the ultimate revelation of God (Heb. 1:1-2), then we may well expect it to be mirrored in various ways in all God's gracious dealings with men. In other words, it is no accident that the Bible is of a piece with Christ, that the "inverbation" or "inscripturation" of God's Word resembles in certain respects the Incarnation of the Word Who is God. As He is God and Man in one indivisible Person, so His Word is one divine-human unity. And as He took upon Himself the form of a Servant (Phil. 2:7), so His blessed Word wears the humble garb of common (*koiné!*) human language and "primitive" culture. But what holds of Him—"blessed is he whoever shall not be scandalized on My account" (Matt. 11:6)—holds also of His Word: "Whoever therefore shall be ashamed of Me and of My words in this adulterous and sinful generation, of him also shall the Son of Man be ashamed when He comes in the glory of His Father with the holy angels" (Mark 8:38).

If the "problem" is that humble human language serves as the bearer of infallible divine revelation in Scripture, then the solution lies in keeping inviolate the "Chalcedonian relationship" of distinction-without-separation obtaining, analogically, between the divine and human aspects of Scripture. Poythress' point, that the concrete, particular biblical message spelled out in the very *human* Hebrew, Aramaic, or Greek languages, IS *divine,* illustrates the Christological analogy perfectly: the starkly human blood of the God-Man has divine sin-cleansing power (I John 1:7), His very flesh is life-giving (John 6:51), and His audible, earthly words "are spirit and are life" (John 6:63).

Any retreat, in the name of human language as such or of its lowly "servant form" in particular, from the absolute divine authority of the concrete biblical text (John 10:35!) is therefore in principle a retreat from the Incarnation itself. Humanity *as such* implies error no more than it implies sin. The concrete once-and-for-all-ness of the apostolic-prophetic foundation of the church (Eph. 2:20) is part and parcel of the uniqueness of its Chief Cornerstone—Whose fleshly, historical particularity, combined with His absolute and universal claims, proved so offensive in Capernaum (John 6:66).

From this perspective we may indeed speak of God's gracious accommodation or condescension to our weakness and ignorance. But this can only mean that we honour and treasure all the more the earthly "masks" under which the Divine Majesty chooses to deal with us. There can be no question here of "errors": "Yea, let God be true, but every man a liar" (Rom. 3:4). To presume to "correct" Scripture is to misread the nature and purpose of the lowly form of the divine teaching among men: He means precisely to appeal to humble faith and to bless it—and not the intellectual arrogance which despises ordinary and simple things (Matt. 11:25).

But none of this entails the sort of "arthritic" rigidity of interpretation which Prof. Poythress rightly rejects. I fully accept his strictures against various forms of "over-interpretation."

As the reference to Ephesians 2:20 has already foreshadowed, Christ is more than a Paradigm for the Bible: He is its real scope and content. Even the "letter which kills," that is, the preaching of Law, judgement, and condemnation in the Scriptures must subserve their overriding purpose, which is to make us "wise to salvation through faith which is in Christ Jesus" (2 Tim. 3:15. Cf. John 5:39; 20:31). Here lies the deepest reason why the human and the divine, flesh and spirit, factual-historical and theological, earthly and heavenly, form a sacred, indissoluble unity that God has joined together and that man therefore may not put asunder. This applies in the first instance to the Mystery of the Incarnate Savior—"next to the article of the Holy Trinity the greatest Mystery in heaven and on earth"[24]—but also, *mutatis mutandis*, to the mystery of the God-breathed biblical text.

Troeltsch was quite right, therefore, from his own profane perspective, to denounce biblical history as dogma in disguise, and not genuine history at all:

> What stands in the centre here is miracle, the God-Man, who is history and timeless Being at once, the miracle of redemption, which is a cosmic event in historical garb; and all this is in principle withdrawn from all true history, from all research and criticism and from all genuine temporality . . . And as these events are not really history, so their theory is not philosophy, but faith, a doctrine based on authority and revelation . . .[25]

But what for Troeltsch is less than history, is for Luther more than history. Unlike all "dead histories" and "histories of the dead," says Luther, the Gospel histories are not (mere) histories, but are "sacraments," that is, "sacred signs through which God works in believers" the very things the histories of the Gospel are all about.[26]

In conclusion, a word or two about the problem of certainty, which so bedevils our age. One might have thought that given a clear and uncompromising confession of Holy Scripture as God's own infallible Word in human language, no toehold is left for sceptical objections. It may still be argued, however, as Poythress rightly points out: "Even supposing that the Bible is infallible divine revelation, we can never be certain whether we have understood or interpreted it correctly." What can be said about this in our context?

In the first place, it would be mistaken to try to settle this matter on the basis of our own judgements about *appearances* (John 7:24!), *e.g.*, "there are so many different interpretations and confessions; therefore no one can be sure that his is the right one; therefore Scripture doctrine cannot be known with certainty." The argument is as invalid as a similar one about a university mathematics test: "Only 1 percent of the class got a perfect score. The other 99 percent got at least one thing wrong. And even their mistakes differed wildly from one another. Therefore the textbook has no objectively ascertainable meaning, or even worse, mathematics itself is a highly ambiguous, subjective enterprise." The principle must be maintained that our doctrine about Scripture, like all other Christian truth, rests on the particular biblical texts that teach it—not on our impressions about various textual phenomena. (Example: What would one teach about the sinlessness of Jesus if one were allowed to base one's doctrine not on the relevant biblical claims themselves, but on our impressions and judgements about various incidents. *e.g.*, an apparent loss of nerve in Gethsemane, or a sudden fit of rage in the Temple, among the moneychangers?)

Secondly, nothing very relevant to our purpose is likely to emerge from technical discussions about language as such. A judge has judicial competence and jurisdiction only as a judge, not simply as a human being, even though all judges are necessarily also human beings. And just as the judicial authority of courts cannot be derived from general arguments about the human nature of judges, so the Bible's competence to impart infallible teaching cannot be based on general considerations of human language, in which the Bible happens (necessarily) to be written. Not the qualities of language as language are decisive here, but the qualities and functions of this particular language in this particular divine message.

Nor, thirdly, does it help to introduce, at this point of the argument, an appeal to the Holy Spirit in any sense suggesting that it is His function to complete and clarify somehow the arguments, descriptions, and teachings left incomplete and unclear in the text itself. Yes, He is the real Author of Scripture, "Who spoke by the prophets" (Nicene Creed). And yes, only He, the Lord and Giver of Life, can create the miracle of faith, so that we truly believe and confess that Jesus is Lord (1 Cor. 12:3)—but He does this through the external Gospel, the "dynamic of God for salvation" (Rom. 1:16). Therefore, no, there can be no appeal to the Spirit *from* the biblical text, as though He needed to supply missing arguments, but only an appeal to Him *in* the text that He Himself has given.

We are left, then, finally, with the inspired text itself. It can and must alone (*sola scriptura*) adjudicate the basic issues of hermeneutics. And the very first thing we notice in the sacred text is that our problem of how we can ever be sure of its meaning simply does not exist there. Scripture takes for granted that if we "continue" in Christ's Word, then we "shall know the truth" (John 8:31-32). Christian faith need not scale heights and depths to catch an elusive saving truth: "But what saith it? The word is nigh thee, even in thy mouth, and in thy heart: that is, the word of faith, which we preach" (Rom. 10:8). The Savior commands His church and her ministry to *proclaim* His truth, not to *discover* it (Matt. 28:19ff.), to *confess*, not simply to *discuss* Him before men (Matt. 10:32). And His Apostle expects his hearers to distinguish clearly between what is apostolic and what is apostatic, and to act accordingly (Rom. 16:17; Gal. 1:6-9, etc.). If this apostolic gospel seems "hid" to some, it is because "the god of this world hath blinded the minds of them which believe not, lest the light of the glorious gospel of Christ . . . should shine unto them" (2 Cor. 4:4).

Our extra-biblical problem, moreover, arises not from superior standards of intellectual honesty and humility, but from something else altogether. C. E. M. Joad was quite right, I believe, when he described the typically modern "preoccupation with the self and its experiences, promoted by and promoting the subjectivist analysis of moral, aesthetic, metaphysical and theological judgements" as *"stigmata of decadence."*[27] Decadence of course is beyond the reach of mere arguments. It requires stronger medication: regeneration, resurrection, perhaps even exorcism!

Even though Scripture is "clearer than the sun" (Luther), we can still go astray of course by misunderstanding the nature of this clarity and looking for it in the wrong place. As Prof. Poythress reminds us, "we do not have a certainty at *every* point of interpretation" (p. 367). Precisely. We should be bitterly disillusioned were we to seek that clarity and certainty in various ingenious schemes that have been spun round the numbers 666 and 144,000 in the Apocalypse, for example. It is not that the Bible is without obscurities, but that the evangelical substance, the articles of faith, are clearly stated in clear texts—that is the real point, too, of God's gracious condescension to us in a humble, down-to-earth-in-working-clothes Scripture, which is for that very reason clear and understandable. We can therefore meet the diffident scepticism of Erasmus with this happy counter-challenge:

> For what still sublimer thing can remain hidden in the Scripture, now that the seals have been broken, the stone rolled from the door of the sepulchre (Matt. 27:66; 28:2), and the supreme mystery brought to light, namely, that Christ the Son of God has been made man, that God is three and one, that Christ has suffered for us and is to reign eternally? Are not these things known and sung even in the highways and byways? Take Christ out of the Scriptures, and what will you find left in them?[28]

Of this we can be sure—and it is enough.[29]

NOTES

[1]Langdon B. Gilkey, "Cosmology, Ontology, and the Travail of Biblical Language," *Concordia Theological Monthly,* XXIII, 3 (March 1962):146-53.

[2]Kai Nielsen, *Contemporary Critiques of Religion* (New York: Herder and Herder, 1971), p. 110.

[3]Malcolm L. Diamond and Thomas V. Litzenburg, Jr., eds., *The Logic of God/Theology and Verification* (Indianapolis: Bobbs-Merrill, 1975), p. 44.

[4]Rudolf Carnap, "The Elimination of Metaphysics," in A. J. Ayer, ed., *Logical Positivism* (Glencoe, Illinois: The Free Press, 1959), p. 66.

[5]Alvin Plantinga, "Verificationism," in Diamond and Litzenburg, *Logic of God*, p. 450.

[6]Mortimer Adler, *How To Think About God* (New York: Macmillan, 1980), pp. 9 and 150.

[7]Mortimer Adler, *The Angels and Us* (New York: Macmillan, 1982), p. 56.

[8]Sol Tax and Charles Callender, ed., *Evolution After Darwin* (Chicago: University of Chicago Press, 1960), vol. III, pp. 45-46.

[9]Neal C. Gillespie, *Charles Darwin and the Problem of Creation* (Chicago: University of Chicago Press, 1979), p. 83.

[10]Wesley C. Salmon, "Verifiability and Logic," in Diamond and Litzenburg, *Logic of God*, p. 467.

[11]Paul S. Moorhead and Martin M. Kaplan, eds., *Mathematical Challenges To the Neo-Darwinian Interpretation of Evolution* (Philadelphia: Wistar Institute Press, 1967), pp. 5-19, 64-71.

[12]Paul A. Schilpp, ed., *The Philosophy of Karl Popper* (The Library of Living Philosophers, 1974), vol. I, p. 139.

[13]The new concept, forced by palaeontological realities, is "punctuated equilibria," that is, evolution by "sudden bursts." *New York Times*, 10 November 1980.

[14]*Nature*, vol. 294 (12 November 1981), p. 105.

[15]Fred Hoyle and Chandra Wickramasinghe, *Evolution from Space* (London: J. M. Dent, 1981), p. 144.

[16]According to one interpreter, "religious language" is true in the manner of "puns and witticisms," which are "irrelevant to truth and falsity in the usual propositional sense." So Sten H. Stenson, *Sense and Nonsense in Religion* (New York: Abingdon Press, 1969), p. 146.

[17]Thomas C. Oden, *Agenda for Theology* (San Francisco: Harper and Row, 1979), p. 48.

[18]See Mary Hesse, *Revolutions and Reconstructions in the Philosophy of Science* (Bloomington: University of Indiana Press, 1980); I. Lakatos and A. Musgrave, eds., *Criticism and the Growth of Knowledge* (Cambridge: Cambridge University Press, 1970); Frederick Suppe, *The Structure of Scientific Theories* (Chicago: University of Illinois Press, 1977); Bas C. van Fraassen, *The Scientific Image* (Oxford: Clarendon Press, 1980).

[19]Schilpp, *Philosophy of Karl Popper*, pp. 12, 17, 21, 71.

[20]Karl Popper, *Conjectures and Refutations* (New York: Harper Torchbooks, 1965), pp. 223 ff.

[21]Karl Popper, *Objective Knowledge* (Oxford: Clarendon Press, 1979), pp. 106-90. Note also the fascinating symposium on the irreducibility of mind to brain: Sir Karl Popper and Sir John Eccles, *The Self and Its Brain* (Springer International, 1977). Cf. Michael Scriven's argument that parapsychology is better founded empirically than psychoanalysis: Robert G. Colodny, ed., *Frontiers of Science and Philosophy* (London: Allen and Unwin, 1964), pp. 79-129.

[22]Schilpp, *Philosophy of Karl Popper*, p. 69.

[23]Martin Luther, "Disputation on John 1:14: The Word was made Flesh," in H. Lehmann, ed., *Luther's Works* (Philadelphia: Fortress Press, 1971), vol. 38, p. 240.

[24]Formula of Concord, Solid Declaration, VIII, 33, in T. Tappert, ed., *The Book of Concord* (St. Louis: Concordia Publishing House, 1959), p. 597.

[25]Ernst Troeltsch, *Der Historismus and seine Probleme*, 3rd vol. in *Gesammelte Schriften von Ernst Troeltsch* (Tuebingen: J. C. B. Mohr [Paul Siebeck], 1961), p. 14. My translation.

[26]*Martin Luther, Werke. Kritische Gesamtausgabe* (Weimar, 1883 ff.), vol. 49, p. 221 and vol. 9, p. 440.

[27]C. E. M. Joad, *Decadence: A Philosophical Inquiry* (London: Faber and Faber, n.d.), p. 117.

[28]Martin Luther, "The Bondage of the Will," *Luther's Works*, vol. 33, pp. 25-26.

[29]"For it is enough for the true unity of the Christian church that the Gospel be preached, unanimously and according to its pure understanding, and that the sacraments be administered in accordance with the divine Word" (Augsburg Confession, 1530, German text. My translation. A slightly inaccurate translation is given in Tappert, *Book of Concord*, p. 32).

Author's Intention and Biblical Interpretation

Elliott E. Johnson
Associate Professor of Bible Exposition
Dallas Theological Seminary

7. Author's Intention and Biblical Interpretation

Elliott Johnson

The International Council on Biblical Inerrancy has boldly affirmed that: "Being wholly and verbally God-given, Scripture is without error or fault in all its teaching, no less in what it states about God's acts in creation, about the events of world history, and about its own literary origins under God, than in its witness to God's saving grace in individual lives."[1]

One question remains unaddressed: what truth does the Bible teach? In a sense, evangelicals have lived with an interpretational truce. While we agree on doctrinal "essentials" we have also agreed to not talk very seriously about issues of disagreement. Yet Paul charted God's strategy for Christian growth when he wrote:

> "so that we all reach unity in the faith
> and in the knowledge of the Son of God
> and become mature
> attaining to the whole measure of the fulness of Christ."
>
> Ephesians 4:12, 13

In order to reach unity we need some way to talk about our different interpretations and to evaluate these differences. Too often the discussion moves quickly to the defense of a position or a reputation. This is not in the spirit of "speaking the truth in love." There is a need for an accepted central authority, a firm set of principles to rely upon to arbitrate disagreements about what a text truly means. This is the task of hermeneutics. It is the purpose of this paper to propose two items upon which we must agree in order to reasonably seek to pursue "unity in the faith and in the knowledge of the Son of God." The first item is the goal of interpretation. Where is the task of interpretation headed? The second item involves normative principles to guide the interpreter toward the goal. How do we reach the goal?

In seeking a "strategy of resolution," one dare not surrender the ideal of Scripture teaching the truth. Resolution does not imply compromise in truth to a level of mutual agreement. Rather resolution implies a mutual willingness to modify one's own interpretation in view of authoritative principles in interpretation.

I. THE GOAL OF INTERPRETATION

The first issue to be considered is the question of goal. Which of the possible meanings does the interpreter seek to know? Discussion of interpretation does not frequently consider the problem of a goal. Perhaps the question of goal is considered self-evident—the goal is the meaning of the text. But as is readily recognized, meaning is not given directly except to language speakers. Language signs are given directly in the text. These signs must be construed to perceive the meaning. And these signs functioning within conventional norms of public usage are often capable of sponsoring more than one meaning. Often these meanings are in direct conflict with each other. An instance is Job 19:26 where two translations are possible and capable of defense. One rendering "without my flesh I shall see God" yields a meaning that is diametrically opposed to "in my flesh I shall see God." The question is which one is correct.

Within the tradition of the Protestant Reformation there is a strong heritage which affirms that a biblical passage has one meaning. This single sense of a passage had determinate boundaries so that it was not capable of generating multiple or conflicting senses. The single meaning could sponsor implications but these were implications of that single meaning. Thus if the subject of a passage were interpreted to be *Christ*, it could not at the same time be *Beelzebub or Elijah or one of the prophets*. The sense of the passage was singular and determinate. Bernard Ramm designated this single sense as the literal interpretation.[2] Walter Kaiser feels this issue is the point of crisis in hermeneutics. "The issue must be put bluntly: Is the meaning of a text to be defined solely in terms of the *verbal* meaning of that text as those words were used by the Scriptural author? Or should the meaning of a text be partly understood in terms of what it now means to me, the reader and interpreter? There hangs one of the great dilemmas of our age. And there also hangs the fortunes of the authority of Scripture."[3] The goal of interpretation, then, must be to know this single sense. But which of the possible textual meanings is this single sense?

The first affirmation of this paper is that this single meaning is the author's intended meaning. This wording appears within the Reformation tradition. John Calvin reflects this goal. In discussing

James 2, "It is not possible to understand what is being said or to make any discerning judgment on the terms, unless one keeps an eye on the intention of the author."[4] Francis Turretin says, "literal describes not only that which is based on the strict, not figurative, meaning of the words, by which it is distinguishable from figurative meaning, as was done by the Fathers, but it also describes the meaning intended by the Holy Spirit and expressed either strictly or in figurative language."[5]

As an heir of the Reformation, Bernard Ramm seeks to present a system that most generally characterizes conservative Protestantism. "This is the primary and basic need of hermeneutics: to ascertain what God has said in Sacred Scripture."[6] I. Howard Marshall, as editor representing a number of evangelical scholars, defined the goal of interpretation: "our aim is to discover what the text meant in the mind of its original author for his intended audience. Exegesis seeks for an interpretation of a passage which will account satisfactorily for all the features of that passage, both on its own and in its context."[7] Thus there is a consistent testimony within the conservative Reformation tradition that the understanding of the author's intended meaning is the goal of interpretation.

In addition to the tradition of Biblical interpretation this question has been debated and defined more carefully within the tradition of general hermeneutics. E. D. Hirsch argues forcefully for this goal in interpretation.

> Almost any word sequence can, under the conventions of language, legitimately represent more than one complex of meaning. A word sequence means nothing in particular until somebody either means something by it or understands something from it. There is no magic land of meanings outside human consciousness. . . . To banish the original author as the determiner of meaning was to reject the only compelling normative principle that could lend validity to an interpretation.[8]

Hirsch's point demands a specific context of words from an author to make the various senses clear, still his argument is forceful. Yet the basis of his argument is limited. P. D. Juhl challenges Hirsch's pragmatic foundation.

> Whereas Hirsch is more or less explicitly offering a recommendation as to what critics ought to do in interpreting a text—namely, try to ascertain the author's intention—my view is that they are necessarily doing so already, in virtue of what it is for a literary work to have a certain meaning.

Juhl then summarizes his own thesis:

> I shall attempt to uphold the view that there is a logical connection between statements about the meaning of a literary work and statements about the author's intention such that a statement about the meaning of a work is a statement about the author's intention.[9]

Thus, the goal of the author's intention is not simply a pragmatic goal but a necessary goal. It is necessary because of the very nature of verbal communication. Verbal communication is the expression of a message by an author to an audience. Therefore, to banish the author is to redefine communication. Alonso Schokel, writing within the Roman Catholic tradition, recognized this:

> The whole theory of the four senses was not applied by the Middle Ages to the authors of Scripture, but to the books, to the works themselves: the allegorical sense, and the tropological and anagogic senses, were there in the text, visible to the Christian who read with faith. They never asked whether or not the author of this or that book of the Old Testament perceived these senses with the same precision that they did.[10]

He recognized that the interpreters saw meanings that the author did not and thus in effect authored the meanings themselves. The unique case of biblical authorship of course will demand further consideration, but first a definition of intention or intended meaning is needed.

The term chosen to designate the author's role in communication is INTENTION. This term has the advantage of both ancient usage and widely accepted modern usage among evangelicals. This does not mean that the term is not without liabilities. Its broad field of meaning and its abstract reference results in the term being indefinite in the minds of most students. Thus the first task must be to define the way the term will be used in this treatment of the goal. The question of definition is complicated by authors using the term in a wide range of usage. These will be treated in broad categories:

1. Intention is not to be identified with the psychological experience of the author. F. E. D. Schleiermacher stands in a prominent position in the history of general hermeneutics. His early writings designate two tasks of hermeneutics, grammatical and psychological. "An act of speaking cannot even be understood as a moment in a person's development unless it is also understood in relation to the language. . . . Nor can an act of speaking be understood as a modification of the person."[11] This early statement and broad conception

would find few who would object. His later refinements and emphases, especially as represented by Wilhelm Dilthey, focused an improper emphasis on the psychology of the author. "Before the art of hermeneutics can be practiced, the interpreter must put himself both objectively and subjectively in the position of the author. . . . On the subjective side this requires knowing the inner and the outer aspects of the author's life. . . . By a knowledge of the individuality of an author, grammatical interpretation can be brought to a level that it could not reach on its own. The goal is to reproduce the subjective bases for the combination of particular elements of a text in order to learn how to grasp the train of thought."[12] But such individual mental acts are private and really inaccessible to the interpreter.

In a related approach, similar psychological and private conceptions of intention are inadequate conceptions of intention. Wimsatt and Beardsley's conception of intention is the "design or plan in the author's mind."[13] P. D. Juhl argues that there are numerous conscious activities that are intentional but are not planned nor do they involve a detailed knowledge of the alternative actions. In order to talk to a friend, I intend to visit him. Such an intention seldom involves planning nor complex thought given to leg movements and raising of my feet. A second objection to this conception of intention is that it is a separate event which precedes or accompanies the performance of a speech act. "When we decide to speak to someone or to write something we usually do not plan in advance precisely what we will say; rather, our specific intentions are formed in the process of formulating the sentences we use."[14]

2. Intention is not to be identified with the relation between mental acts and mental objects. E. D. Hirsch adopts the analysis of intention found in Edmund Husserl's description of intentionality. Husserl's discussion rests on the theory of Franz Brentano. Brentano claimed that all acts of consciousness are directed toward an object. We think something, know something, or remember some object. Thus, these mental acts are directed toward mental objects. He called their directedness the intentional relation. To think, to fear, or doubt is to think, fear or doubt something. Husserl, as does Hirsch, used intentional as a basis for an attack against psychologism. Many different mental acts may be directed toward the same object. I can see it, analyze it and remember it two days later. Someone else can also analyze it. Although the mental actions are different and individual, still the mental object remains unchanged. Thus the conception, the mental object is not dependent on the individual mental activities.

Thus it is objective since it is independent of the mental acts. Hirsch summarizes:

> The general term for all intentional objects is meaning. Verbal meaning is simply a special kind of intentional object, and like any other one, it remains self-identical over against the many different acts which 'intend' it. But the noteworthy feature of verbal meaning is its supra-personal character. It is not an intentional object for simply one person, but for many—potentially for all persons. Verbal meaning is, by definition, that aspect of the speaker's 'intention' which, under linguistic conventions, may be shared by others.[15]

For Hirsch, intention involves the author's full awareness as he wrote. A portion of this awareness is expressed in the text. But if the author's intention is the goal of interpretation, and if it is broader than the shared meanings in the text, then his own goal of valid interpretation is undermined. The concept of intention must be related to the author's textual meanings.

3. Intention is not to be identified with the hoped for consequences of his writing. It is not even to be identified with the natural consequences of his writing. Since intention is not understood as a separate event, there is no difference between action conceived and action achieved. Rather intention is expressed in the public activity of writing.

4. Intention is to be identified with the "sense of the whole" by which the author arranges and relates each particular meaning of his composition. One may ask, why is the intention not the sense of each individual word? While the sense of each word must be considered, the "sense of the whole" is more than the sum of the parts. Rather, the intention of the author selects and arranges each individual part, and relates them into a coherent whole. This is the conception of intention presented by G. E. M. Anscombe in her work, *Intention.*[16] She writes, "What distinguishes actions which are intentional from those which are not? The answer that I shall suggest is that they are the actions to which a certain sense of the question 'why?' is given application; the sense is of course that in which the answer, if positive, gives a reason for acting."[17] Thus intention is that which gives the reason for acting. In this case, the acting is writing each particular word in the text. Thus intention is the "sense of the whole" which can naturally explain each particular meaning in the text considered as a whole. In this way, it gives the reason for that word, for each unit of meaning. It provides a reasonable explanation to relate the

particular to what preceded and to anticipate what follows. From the author's point of view this sense of the whole is his *intention*. From an interpreter's point of view, this "sense of the whole" is a synthetic construct of the whole composition. Thus the goal in interpretation is to know the author's "sense of the whole" which can give a reasonable explanation for all the particulars in the text.

There are, however, some unique features in biblical authorship. The intention must be discovered in the shared Divine/human expression of the text. J. I. Packer summarizes the two facets of the mystery well. "Evangelicals stress that Scripture is a *mystery* in a sense parallel to that in which the incarnation is a *mystery*—that is, that the identifying of the human and the divine words in the one case, like the taking of manhood into God in the other, was a unique creative divine act of which we cannot fully grasp either the nature or the mode or the dynamic implications. Scripture is as genuinely and fully human as it is divine. It is more than Jewish-Christian religious literature but not less. There is a true analogy between the written Word and the incarnate Word. In both cases, the divine coincides with the form of the human, and the absolute appears in the form of the relative."[18] Packer approaches the problem in a wise way. Rather than seeking to delineate the mystery by a distinction between divine and human, he discusses authorship in terms of true humanity and true deity. True human expression involves a share in the meaning that would enable the author to write in his language and in his style. While it is impossible to fully specify how the meaning was shared, that is not at issue in interpretation. What is at issue is the intention expressed in the text. Error is not a necessary and defining trait of human intention; it is a common trait of fallen man. Historical and cultural perspective is not a necessary and defining trait of human intention, it is a common trait of historical man. But such a limited perspective can be enriched by divine providential instruction. This does not necessarily imply dictation for even the believer is responsible to have his "mind renewed" through divine instruction (Rom. 12:1, 2). True divine authorship affirms that the content arose from God (2 Pet. 1:20, 21). The origin of Scripture is divine. God then providentially shared the meaning with the human author. The human authors "spoke from God as they were carried along by the Holy Spirit." The product is a verbally inspired text which is shared as God's word and the human writer's word (2 Tim. 3:16).

Within these parameters of authorship, the task of interpretation must take place. If the goal of interpretation is to determine author's intention, the immediate question arises, which author? Since intention involves the reasonable expression of the text, and since both authors share in the expression of the text, then the "sense of the whole" is a shared meaning. This "sense of the whole" is the one meaning of the whole text. Yet it seems clear in numerous passages that the human author did not share fully in the divine author's meanings. Peter most clearly described it: "Concerning this salvation, the prophet, who spoke of the grace that was to come to you, searched intently and with the greatest care, trying to find out the time and the circumstances to which the Spirit of Christ in them was pointing when he predicted" . . . (1 Pet. 1:10-11). This issue of authorial ignorance of time and circumstances will need to be considered in depth shortly but at this point the broad framework of the answer will be developed.

To state the nature of the shared meaning an additional distinction needs to be made. Gottlob Frege introduced a distinction, within the modes of verbal meaning, between sense and reference. Similar distinctions have been recognized under the terms connotation/denotation and intension/extension of a proposition. Frege's terminology will be accepted although it will be defined in somewhat different fashion. *Sense* focuses on the verbal meaning of the language expressed in the text irrespective of reference. Church identifies it as the content of meaning that is common to the sentence and its translation into another language. This content of meaning is a proposition reflecting an author's judgment which may be capable of being the common property of many sentences. The *defining sense* of the passage is to be identified as the author's/writer's intention. This meaning is shared by God and the human writer of the text.

Reference is first of all a question of meaning and then the question of truth-value can be judged. As a mode of verbal meaning, it includes the implications associated with reference to a particular reality in the real world or to a particular audience. The task of unfolding these implications is interpretive. A critical task may follow. It involves a judgment of truth-value of the proposition in reference to the world of reality. The proposition is true when its reference corresponds to reality. The proposition is false when there is no such reality or it is a faulty reference to reality. The nature of the divine reference, in His omniscience, will be fuller than the human reference in the shared meaning. The human author truly refers to the reality but not fully.

The distinction between sense and reference is not the same as the distinction between meaning and significance. Reference concerns implications of meaning that are apparent when the sense is related to the historical instance. In Zechariah 12:10, even if the sense *pierced through* is established, the reference is still not clear. It could refer to goring or a sword blow. Only when the sense is compared to Roman crucifixion is the reference clear. Yet the death by crucifixion is an implication of the prophet's meaning (John 19:37). Significance is distinguished from such meaning. "*Significance* names a relationship between that meaning and a person or a conception, or a situation or indeed anything imaginable."[19]

In order to illustrate the distinction, the important instance of Psalm 16 will be examined briefly. This illustration gives us the advantage of a divine interpretation by Peter in Acts 2:25-32 and by Paul in Acts 13:35-37. The problem may be defined in terms of David's reference. Both Peter and Paul affirm that David refers to Christ as the *hasîd*, the Holy One. Yet Delitzsch affirms without equivocation, "by *hasîd* David means himself."[20] Walter Kaiser defines the problem: "exegetes must squarely face the hermeneutical and theological problem arising from the distinctively Messianic use made of it. Were the various fulfillments that the apostles attributed to this text explicitly present in the psalmist's purposes and consciousness when he wrote the psalm?"[21] The answer proposed in this paper is that God and David shared a defining sense in the expression of the Psalm. God then was conscious of all the implications of reference to David and Christ while David may have been limited in his conscious reference.

While it is necessary to agree on the goal of interpretation—the Author's/author's intention—it is also necessary to agree in principle about reaching that goal. This is not an attempt to program a certain process of thought by which one reaches that goal. Rather it is an attempt to define at the level of general principle what tasks need to be accomplished to reach the goal. These principles will then mediate between various interpretive attempts to reach the goal.

II. THE PRINCIPLE OF RECOGNITION

There are two basic principles which guide the task. The first is *the principle of recognition: the interpreter recognizes the author's chosen type of meaning*. The term recognition is a term introduced by Emilio Betti. Writing soon after Gadamer's masterpiece work, *Truth and Method,* he sought to defend objective interpretation. "The interpretive object is an objectification of man's spirit (*Geist*) expressed in sensible form. Interpretation, then, is necessarily a recognition and reconstruction of the meaning that its author . . . was able to embody."[22] Such a recognition is first of all a rethinking of the meanings of the author as one reads the text. Every attempt should be made to share in the original language of the author as well as sharing in the historical occasion of communication. In this way the interpreter steps out of his world and into the author's world to recognize as many clues as the author shares.

Thus recognition involves "an inversion of the creative process."[23] The individual words viewed alone are capable of sharing multiple senses. The task of recognition is to discern which of the possible meanings is the author's intended sense. From the author's point of view, this verbal expression is a temporal process. It is also a conscious process. At one moment the author is conscious of the particular meanings he is expressing. But what guides the sequence of expression into a unified whole message? No author is able to entertain in conscious thought at any one moment all the meanings he intends to express. E. D. Hirsch draws upon Augustine for his analysis of the author's knowledge and for an explanation of his conscious but temporal process. Hirsch writes:

> How does a speaker manage to put one word after another unless his choices and usages are governed by a controlling conception? There must be some kind of overarching notion which controls the temporal sequence of speech, and this controlling notion of the speaker, like that of the interpreter, must embrace a system of expectations. For the words that are to be said are not yet present before the speaker's mind, and the words he has already said have gone by.[24]

He then selects a portion from Augustine's Confessions in which Augustine compares human consciousness with divine consciousness in foreknowledge. Augustine thereby descriptively illustrates the marvel of personal consciousness and speech:

> I am about to repeat a psalm that I *know*. Before I begin, my expectation alone reaches over the whole: but so soon as I shall have once begun, how much so ever of it I shall take off into the past, over so much my memory also reaches: thus the life of this action of mine is extended in both ways: into my memory, so far as concerns that part which I have repeated already, and into my expectation too, in respect of what I am about to repeat now; but all this while is my marking faculty present at hand through which that which was future is conveyed over that

> it may become past: which the more it progresses forward, so much more the expectations being shortened is the memory enlarged; till the whole expectation be at length vanished quite away, when namely, that whole action being ended, shall absolutely pass into the memory. What is now done is this whole psalm, the same is done also in every part of it, yea and in every syllable of it; the same order holds in a longer action too, whereof perchance this psalm is but a part.[25]

Since Augustine was concerned about foreknowledge he illustrated the concept of intention in a specialized system of expectations. However a speaker can say, "I *know* what I'm going to say" without having memorized each word. The common element in both cases of *knowledge* is a conception of the whole to be said. The parts then flow from this *knowledge* of the whole. This conception of the whole is the author's intention. Yet there is a more complete conception of intention. Intention is the "sense of the whole." That "sense" may be more comprehensively understood as a "type of the whole sense." For each piece of literature may be classified in relation to other pieces of literature. By this means, the "sense of the whole" can be understood not only with its own content but also in comparison to and in contrast with other types. In particular, all literary types have a purpose to express and a proposition. In distinction, each willed type has a distinct proposition.

The text, then, is the expression of this type of meaning. Hirsch focused attention on this chosen or willed type of meaning. He established it as the object of recognition as it is also the object of the author's intention. As one reads the text, his initial and overriding interpretive question is, What type of meaning is this?

This conception of an author's chosen *type of meaning* meets the basic requirements already set for interpretation and communication. It is a determinate object of interpretation, the one meaning of the text. It is also a sharable object since it can always be represented by more than one instance. This makes communication possible.

Recognition thus begins with the reading of the text. As one reads he asks the simple question: What type of meaning has the author chosen to express? It is an attempt to classify the meaning with one of the shared types of meaning within the reader's knowledge. Considered in general "a type, as its etymology suggests (from the Greek *typos*, an impression, a cast, a model) has recurrent, general, distinctive features which are not properties of the individual as such. Those essential features which stamp an aggregate with a certain cachet or physiognomy constitute the type."[26] The identification of these essential and defining features of the sense of the passage is the essential task of recognition. Hirsch has called these defining features the necessary traits of the type of meaning. They are traits necessary to define the type of meaning.[27]

Frege would identify this type of meaning expressed in the text with the sense of the text. It would be construed in the form of a proposition. The defining traits would be the subject and predicate of the proposition. A third defining trait is the purpose that is expressed in this type of meaning.

The role of such a chosen type of meaning becomes clear when the interpreter faces an ambiguous statement; "I am hot." If the author chose to talk about *temperature*, then "hot" means degrees. If, however, he chose to talk about *temperament,* then "hot" means anger In this way choice of a type of meaning is central to the author's task and to the interpreter's task of recognition of the sense of the text.

Some may find the choice of terminology, "type," as unfortunate and confusing. "Typology" is well established in biblical hermeneutics and seemingly unrelated to "type." But, in fact, biblical typology reflects the universal application of the general principle of "type of meaning." Typology is the recognition of a unique type of biblical narrative meaning. It is unique because the historical pattern implies predictive defining traits. It reflects the application of the general principle in a difficult context.

To further clarify the principle as applied to the text, the type of meaning in Psalm 16 will be examined. Walter Kaiser summarizes the defining sense as "From such a fellowship and enjoyment of God comes . . . remarkable consequences."[28] Derik Kidner says "the theme of having one's affections centered on God gives this psalm its unity and ardour . . . it sings of the chosen loyalty in verses 1-6, and the blessings that come to meet it in 7-11."[29] Both of these conceptions of the sense of the passage are helpful. Any addition would simply be in the precision of wording. My understanding of the type of meaning is: *Rejoicing in God, His portion brings His Holy One hope for resurrection.* Since the final portion the author's intention will be the focus of discussion in the next section, the definition of the sense "hope for resurrection" will be defended. The type of meaning "hope" is expressed in these textual particulars; "counsels me" . . . "instructs me" (16:7), . . . "he is at my right hand, I will not be shaken" (16:8), "my body will rest secure" (16:9), . . . "you will not abandon" . . . "nor will you let" (16:10), . . . "you will fill me" (16:11).

The type of meaning "for resurrection" is expressed both in these textual particulars; "my body . . . rests secure" (16:9) . . . "not abandon me to the grave" (16:10) . . . "you will fill me with joy in your presence" . . . (16:11), and in "made known to me the path of life . . . in your presence" . . . "at your right hand" (16:11). Thus the particulars in the text reflect a type of meaning which the author chose to express; "hope for resurrection."

III. THE PRINCIPLE OF EXEGESIS

There is a second principle around which agreement must be won. It is *the principle of exegesis: the interpreter exegetes the implications of the author's chosen type of meaning*. Many interpreters recognize exegesis as the heart of the task of interpretation. If exegesis is the heart of the task, distinguishing *implications* that are a part of the author's meaning is the issue in the problem of interpretation. E. D. Hirsch writes:

> The crucial issue is the problem of implication. Of course, this problem is not in itself more important than a good many others in hermeneutic theory, but when our central concern is validity we always have to ask whether a particular meaning is or is not implied by an utterance. The correct determination of implications is a crucial element in the task of discriminating a valid from an invalid interpretation. . . . At the center of them all is the question, Is this meaning implied or is it not?[30]

Biblical exegesis is the explanation of the meaning of a passage or a book of the Bible. The Greek word ἐξήγησις from which the English word exegesis is derived means literally "a leading out." This captures the purpose of exegesis, therefore, as to "bring out," "set forth," and explain an author's meaning.

However, as commonly practiced, the student may lead out lexical or grammatical meanings found in a lexicon or grammar. A question then arises. Are these lexical meanings the author's meaning? Which one of these grammatical meanings is the author's chosen (willed) meaning? Does the author choose all the options listed or which ones does he choose? By what principle does the interpreter choose which of these linguistic and literary meanings to lead out as the author's meaning? It is these questions which lead to what will be called type-logic.

The first principle (recognition) is inductive and thus the product is preliminary and tentative. The next principle (exegesis) is logical and reasoned. Exegesis is the leading out of the logical implications of the identified type of meaning. The form of the logic is simple:

1. IF the author's meaning is of this type and the text provides these language structures and the lexical or grammatical meaning possibilities are shared
2. THEN the author's willed (chosen) meaning for this textual particular is ______.

Each step of the process may be briefly described:

The premise of the syllogism is the recognition of the author's willed-type meaning. As the premise, it lends its perspective to judging between linguistic possibilities and actual meanings fitting the author's type of meaning. While the choice may not always be precise it will be determinate, consistently fitting the author's meaning.

In addition, the premise contains a unit of textual structure and a statement of the linguistic possibilities shared in the public medium of language. For the modern student these are not immediately available. Thus an analysis of ancient lexical, grammatical, literary meaning options is necessary to determine the meanings the author shared with his culture. The more thorough one's knowledge of these options, the more precise is one's knowledge of the author's implications.

The conclusion determines the actual implications chosen by the author for each particular in the text. The importance of recognizing this logic is found in the necessary power of determination resting in the type statement. Hirsch explains:

> From the standpoint of verbal meaning, then all implications without distinction are governed by the trait-type model. We know that a given partial meaning is implied by an utterance, because we know that such a meaning belongs in that type of utterance. With due qualifications and in different terms, this is the point J. S. Mills made about the function of the syllogism. We come to the conclusion that Socrates is mortal, that 'Socrates' implies mortality because Socrates is an instance of a type (man) which past experience has shown to have the trait mortality.[31]

In this fashion the interpreter unfolds the author's meanings expressed in each textual particular. The textual particular is the expression by the author of the chosen type of meaning. From the interpreters point of view, the particular words or phrases are the explicit implications of the type of the whole sense. This sense of "implication" is broader than normal usage. Normally implication is limited to unsaid meanings. But, since both explicit and implicit implications are unfolded from the type of sense as a whole, the term "implication" will be used to refer to both aspects of meaning.

There are two perspectives for leading out implications in the exegesis of an author's text. There is first, the exegesis of the full sense of the passage. The full sense of the passage unfolds the single defining sense of the whole passage. This is the single and determinate meaning of the passage and each particular in the passage. Each explicit particular has one meaning in the expression of the single willed type of meaning of the passage. Implied or unsaid implications are exegeted by type-logic from the type of the whole sense and what is not expressed explicitly. This single willed type of meaning which defines the sense of the whole is shared by the divine and human author.

The second perspective for the leading out of implications is implications of reference exegeted in the historical context. In Psalm 16, the implications of reference surround David and the references in the song to David's hope. Kidner comments on these implications of reference. "Admittedly some commentators see here no more than recovery from an illness (cf. Isa. 38:9-22); but the contrast in Psalm 49 and 73 between the end of the wicked and that of the righteous supports a bolder view. And at its full value, as both Peter and Paul insisted (Acts 2:29ff; 13:34-37), this language is too strong even for David's hope of his own resurrection."[32] Kaiser interprets the implications with a somewhat different sense. "David expects to arrive safely with his immaterial and material being in the presence of God."[33] In each case the implications of reference are determined by the interpreter's perception of the type of meaning in reference to David.

Exegesis of biblical prophecy and typology, however, introduces another dimension of implications of reference. The message that referred to David also refers to Christ. It must be affirmed strongly that the enlarged context of progressive revelation does not change the defining sense of the original passage. Its textual defining sense remains determinate and unchanged. Additional implications of reference often become evident in the unfolding of revelation. Thus Kidner adds, "this language is too strong even for David's hope of his own resurrection. Only he whom God raised up saw no corruption."[34] Does this reference to Christ change Kidner's understanding of one sense? Kaiser states clearly that it should not. "Therefore he rested secure in the confident hope that even death itself would not prevent him from enjoying the face-to-face fellowship with his Lord even beyond death, since that ultimate *hasîd* would triumph over death. For David, this was *one word* . . ."[35] But it is not clear how this was one word or one sense. In reference to David, the sense is resurrection (expects to arrive safely with his immaterial and material being) and eternal life (enjoying the face-to-face fellowship). In reference to Christ, the sense is simply resurrection (ultimate triumph over death). Kidner seems to suggest a change in sense. "Peter quoted this closing paragraph of the psalm, from the LXX, as a prophecy of the Messiah, for whom alone such words would be perfectly and literally true."[36] In reference to Christ, the literal sense is true while in reference to David, perhaps a figurative sense is true. Kaiser affirms that it is only one sense. But his exposition of this one sense is not clear. In reference to Christ, he writes of only resurrection. In Peter's day, Peter argues that David had not yet arisen but he surely enjoyed eternal life. Thus it is not clear, in the case of Psalm 16, how one sense is retained in reference to both David and Christ.

As has already been suggested, the defining sense of the passage is: Rejoicing in God, His portion brings His Holy One hope for resurrection. That sense does not change in progress in revelation. In reference to David, it refers to resurrection. In reference to Christ, it refers to resurrection. While the sense of the psalm is one, the implications in reference to David and in reference to Christ are distinct. When David affirms that "I have set the LORD *always* before me" (16:8), it was true but to a limited degree. In 1 Samuel 21:10-15 and 27:1-12 David took refuge with the Philistines with Achish of Gath. In 2 Samuel 11, David took Bathsheba. To the limited extent or degree that any sinful man can have allegiance to God, David could and did. But Messiah did without limit. Kidner recognizes this distinction,[37] but limited reference does not equal figurative reference. Similarly when "your Holy One" (16:10) identifies the author David, and Christ, it refers to David in a limited degree. Whether the term is active "one in whom God manifests his grace and favor" or passive "one to whom God is loyal, gracious or merciful" it is unlimited in reference to Christ and limited in reference to David.[38] This distinction in fullness of implications of reference is crucial in the development of the psalm.

It was the limits of David for God's purposes (Ps. 16:5, 6 and Acts 13:36) that necessitated God's instruction and counsel (Ps. 16:7). This instruction and counsel enabled David to know and to speak as a prophet (Acts 2:30). As a prophet, he anticipated his own death in spite of God's portion and lot (Ps. 16:8-10; Acts 2:30; II Sam. 7). But God would make known to him the way to life and reigning at His right hand (Ps. 16:11). In addition, his hope included the knowledge of the fully Holy One or Favored One. This knowledge came by prophetic instruction (Ps. 16:7). David's personal hope was limited in comparison to this One who would fully inherit God's favor. In a limited reference, David would not be abandoned to the grave. To a limited extent, he would not see decay. David would not remain in the grave eternally. David would not see decay eternally. In addition as a prophet, he also saw the One who would experience the full extent in resurrection. And in His experience of resurrection David would experience resurrection to life and reign. Thus both are affirmed as true. David's hope is a hope in Christ, the Heir.

While David, the prophet, knew the truth clearly it is doubtful that he knew the full implications in reference to Christ or even to himself. While he knew the fact conveyed in His words, the type of meaning "hope of resurrection" undoubtedly involved implications of which he was unaware. In this way, David was unaware of all that he was saying. This issue of human authorial ignorance is very crucial in Biblical exegesis.

There are two kinds of authorial ignorance that are possible. The first is ignorance with regard to the subject matter. As David spoke of death—both his own and the Holy One—there was much about that subject matter beyond which he spoke. He did not know the historical means, the historical occasion, the full reason or time of death. Similarly, there were many details about the subject of resurrection that even believers with a completed canon know but David undoubtedly did not know. The interpreter must not confuse his own greater knowledge of a subject with the interpretation of an author's meaning. This is not exegesis but rather eisegesis. While there is a valid application of the Canonical Process Approach to the Psalms developed by Bruce K. Waltke,[39] the confusion between subject matter and the author's type of meaning must be kept clearly in mind. Waltke says that "the Antiochian principle of allowing but one historical meaning that may carry with it typical significance are inadequate hermeneutical principles for the interpretation of the psalms. . . . By the Canonical Process Approach I mean the recognition that the text's intention becomes deeper and clearer as the parameters of the canon were expanded."[40] When Waltke abandons the one historical sense he is in danger of failing to define the type of textual sense.

Then when additional aspects of the subject are mentioned in the progress of revelation, it is possible that extrinsic implications may be read into the Old Testament textual meaning. The scope of Author's/author's intention must not be separated from the affirmations of the text.

A second type of authorial ignorance concerns not the subject matter but the author's meaning itself. Hirsch addresses the obvious question:

> How can an author mean something he did not mean? The answer to that question is simple. It is not possible to mean what one does not mean though it is very possible to mean what one is not conscious of meaning. That is the entire issue in the argument based on authorial ignorance. That a man may not be conscious of all that he means is no more remarkable than that he may not be conscious of all he does. There is a difference between meaning and consciousness of meaning, and since meaning is an affair of consciousness, one can say more precisely that there is a difference between consciousness and self-consciousness. Indeed, when an author's meaning is complicated, he cannot possibly at a given moment be paying attention to all its complexities.[41]

In biblical authorship, the existence of the human author's possible ignorance is very relevant. As already postulated the human and divine author share the defining sense of the passage. This defining sense sponsored the writing of the text by the human author. God, however, in authoring the revelation not only originates the defining sense and all the textual particulars through the human author but at the same time is aware of all the implications of all possible reference. It is possible that the human author does not share this knowledge as Peter seems to assert in 1 Peter 1:10-12.

Such a possibility is not recognized by Walter Kaiser. After he quotes 2 Peter 1:10-12, he asserts: "Does this text teach that the writers of Scripture 'wrote better than they knew'? Indeed it does not. On the contrary, it decisively affirms that the prophets spoke knowingly on five rather precise topics (1) the Messiah, (2) His sufferings, (3) His glory, (4) the sequence of events . . . and (5) that the salvation announced in those pre-Christian days was not limited to the prophet's audiences, but it also included the readers of Peter's day."[42] He then adds that the prophets "searched intently" without any success about the *time* when these things would take place. He concludes that "this passage does not teach that these men were curious and often ignorant of the exact meaning of what they wrote and predicted. Theirs was not a search for the *meaning* of what they wrote; it was an inquiry into the *temporal* aspects of the *subject*, which went beyond what they wrote."[43]

The issue is simply this. Does this type of meaning, "spoke of the grace that was to come to you," imply time. To answer the question, it is necessary to examine specific passages. It is true that numerous *promises* do not specify or imply time. Even promises of imminent action do not imply a specific time. Jesus affirmed that only the Father knew the time of the second Advent (Acts 1:5-7). However, the *prediction* of Daniel 9:24-27 does specify the time of the "Coming Prince." Thus, Daniel wrote beyond what he knew. The prophets themselves expected to find a notation of time in the prophecies. This is an example of an implication of reference in what they said which they did not know. So it seems quite clear that the human writers know accurately and precisely the defining sense of what they wrote. Had they lived at the time of Jesus Christ they could identify Jesus as the Coming Prince based on the true sense of what they wrote. This is, in fact, what the gospel writers did in reference to the triumphal entry. But they were limited in the fullness of their knowledge of the type of meaning which they spoke. God who spoke in the prophets did not share such a limit in knowledge. What we are therefore proposing is that the *author's intention* expresses a *single, defining textual sense of the whole*. The single sense is capable of implying a fullness of reference. This is not *sensus plenior* but *sensus singular* as expressed in the affirmations of the text. But it also recognizes the characteristic of *references plenior*. In Psalm 16, it agrees with Vaccari; "The words of verse 10 apply to both David and Christ in their proper sense, yet in a fuller sense to Christ who rose from the dead, while David's body knew corruption but will not be subject to *eternal* corruption."[44]

S. Lewis Johnson affirms a similar conclusion: "We should not be surprised that the authorial will of God goes beyond the human authorial will."[45] J. I. Packer affirms a similar conclusion with a qualification: "God's meaning and message through each passage, when set in its total biblical context, exceeds what the human writer had in mind . . . the *sensus plenior* which texts acquire in their wider biblical context remains an extrapolation on the grammatico-historical plane."[46] While both Johnson and Packer recognize the need for the control of the historical-grammatical, they also concede that divine implications of meaning transcend the historical setting. The solution proposed to this dilemma is a defining *singular sense* and *references plenior*. The single sense is defined in the affirmations of the text of Scripture. It is shared by human and divine. The full references are only divine and only fully recognized by the interpreter in the progress of revelation.

NOTES

[1]*The Chicago Statement on Biblical Inerrancy: A Short Statement*, p. 3.

[2]Bernard Ramm, *Protestant Biblical Interpretation* (Boston: W. A. Wilde Co., 1956), pp. 89-96.

[3]Walter C. Kaiser, *Toward an Exegetical Theology* (Grand Rapids: Baker Book House, 1981), p. 24.

[4]John Calvin, *Calvin's Commentaries*, trans. A. W. Morrison, eds. David W. Torrance and Thomas F. Torrance (Grand Rapids: Wm. B. Eerdmans Publishing Co., 1972), 3:285.

[5]Francis Turretin, *The Doctrine of Scripture*, ed. and trans. John W. Beardslee III (Grand Rapids: Baker Book House, 1981), p. 200.

[6]Ramm, p. 2.

[7]I. Howard Marshall, "Introduction," in *New Testament Interpretation* (Grand Rapids: Wm. B. Eerdmans, 1977), p. 15.

[8]E. D. Hirsch, *Validity of Interpretation* (New Haven, Conn.: Yale University Press, 1967), pp. 4-5.

[9]P. D. Juhl, *Interpretation* (Princeton, N.J.: Princeton University Press, 1980), p. 12.

[10]Luis Alonso Schokel, S. J., *The Inspired Word* (New York: Herder and Herder, 1965), p. 256.

[11]F. D. E. Schleiermacher, *Hermeneutics*, ed. Heinz Kimmerle (Missoula, MT: Scholars Press, 1977), p. 99.

[12]Ibid., pp. 113, 153.

[13]W. K, Wimsatt and M. C. Beardsley, "The International Fallacy," *On Literary Intention*, ed. D. Newton-De Molina (Edinburgh: Edinburgh University Press, 1976), pp. 1-13.

[14]P. D. Juhl, *Interpretation* (Princeton, N.J.: Princeton University Press, 1980). p. 134.

[15]Hirsch, p. 218.

[16]G. E. M. Anscombe, *Intention* (Ithaca, N.Y.: Cornell University Press, 1963).

[17]Ibid., p. 9.

[18]J. I. Packer, "Biblical Authority, Hermeneutics, Inerrancy," in *Jerusalem and Athens*, ed., pp. 144-45.

[19]Hirsch, p. 8.

[20]Franz Delitzsch, *The Psalms*, 3 vols. (Grand Rapids: Wm. B. Eerdmans Publishing Co., n.d.), 1:228.

[21]Walter Kaiser, "The Promise to David in Psalm 16 and Its Application in

Acts 2:25-33 and 13:32-37, *"Journal of the Evangelical Theological Society*, 23 (September 1980):219.

[22]Richard E. Palmer, *Hermeneutics* (Evanston, IL: Northwestern University Press, 1969), p. 57.

[23]Ibid.

[24]Hirsch, p. 78.

[25]Confessions XI:28.

[26]Edward A. Tiryakian, "Typologies," *International Encyclopedia of Social Sciences*, vol. 16.

[27]Hirsch, pp. 44-51.

[28]Kaiser, p. 223.

[29]Derek Kidner, *Psalms 1-72* (London: Inter-Varsity Press, 1973), p. 83.

[30]Hirsch, p. 89.

[31]Ibid., pp. 48-49.

[32]Kidner, 1:86.

[33]Kaiser, pp. 226-27.

[34]Kidner, 1:86.

[35]Kaiser, p. 229 (emphasis mine).

[36]Kidner, p. 86.

[37]Ibid.

[38]Kaiser, pp. 224-26.

[39]Bruce K. Waltke, "A Canonical Process Approach to the Psalms," in *Traditions and Testament*, eds. John S. Feinberg and Paul D. Feinberg (Chicago: Moody Press, 1981), pp. 3-18.

[40]Ibid., p. 7.

[41]Hirsch, p. 22.

[42]Walter C. Kaiser, Jr., "The Single Intent of Scripture," in *Evangelical Roots*, ed. Kenneth Kantzer (Nashville: Thomas Nelson, 1978), p. 125.

[43]Ibid., p. 126.

[44]Leopold Sabourin, S. J., *The Psalms* (New York: Alba House, 1970), p. 270.

[45]S. Lewis Johnson, Jr., *The Old Testament in the New* (Grand Rapids: Zondervan Publishing House, 1980), p. 50.

[46]Packer, pp. 147-48.

A Response to Author's Intention and Biblical Interpretation

Earl D. Radmacher
President and Professor of
Systematic Theology
Western Conservative
Baptist Seminary

A Response to Author's Intention and Biblical Interpretation

Earl D. Radmacher

Dr. Elliott Johnson has carefully and lucidly delineated the basic necessities in dealing with authorial intention, namely, the necessity of a goal, which is "the meaning of the text," and the necessity of a set of principles for arriving at the goal which are "recognition" and "exegesis."

In the case of the goal, he strongly and rightly emphasizes, I believe, the singular and sharable nature of the meaning in the text. He wisely warns against two ever-present dangers which are, first, to separate the words of the text from the author resulting in multiple meanings and thus no "meaning" and, second, to so identify the words of the text with the psyche of the author with the resultant impossibility of knowing the meaning. In either case, hermeneutical nihilism would be the result. Thus, the author's intention is not simply a *pragmatic* goal but a *necessary* goal. Because this necessity is so often overlooked in the academic dialogue, however, it bears reinforcing at this point. I am reminded of an encounter I had on a university campus after speaking in a class on comparative religions. A student approached me asking for further opportunity to "rap" with me. Obligingly, I set up a time and place for that same afternoon. Upon meeting, we got right into the discussion and had not proceeded very far until I appealed to Scripture for support of a position. At that point my challenger protested, "There are many different interpretations of that statement of Paul." Somewhat irritated, I responded, "Wait just a moment! Earlier today you asked for more time to "rap" with me. Now I have come to "wrap" but I don't see any presents to wrap or any wrapping paper. Now I don't know how we are going to wrap without presents or wrapping paper." He looked at me as though I had lost my mind and responded, "but, that isn't what I meant!" "Oh, I'm sorry," I said, "But after all, there are many interpretations to what you said. Now, let's wrap!" Despairing he said, "We can't even communicate." "Precisely!" I responded. "We can't continue an intelligent conversation unless I am willing to understand what you mean by what you say. Now, how about allowing Paul the same privilege?"

Such a dialogue demonstrates a universal expectation among men that an author-writer or speaker-is the obvious one to give original meaning to his own statements. All of us operate by this principle daily; however, we live in a day in which developers of hermeneutical procedures declare openly the impropriety or even impossibility of the authorial determination of meaning.

What seems so very strange, therefore, in this whole contemporary debate of semantic autonomy is the fact that a theory is being condoned by an author for the writings of others that would never be applied to his own. I thoroughly agree with Walter Kaiser:

> It never ceases to amaze me how those interpreters who wish to fight the theory that meaning is single-fold and always a return to the author's own meaning demand that all who read their own papers and books do so with the understanding that their meaning is single-fold and must be understood literally. But though we have granted this privilege to them, they then wish to resume interpreting all other texts as they advocate—with this polyvalent theory of meaning![1]

E. D. Hirsch presses the logic of this further:

> Whenever I am told by a Heideggerian that I have misunderstood Heidegger, my still unrebutted response is that I will readily (if uneasily) concede that point, since the concession in itself implies a more important point, namely, that Heidegger's text *can* be interpreted correctly, and has been so interpreted by an accuser. Since the accusation assumes the determinativeness and stability of Heidegger's meaning *and* the possibility of its being correctly interpreted, I admit the practical error for the sake of the theoretical truth. I was once told by a theorist, who denied the possibility of correct interpretation, that I had not interpreted his writings correctly."[2]

Pressing the logic still further, Hirsch continues:

> The question I always want to ask critics who dismiss authorial intention as their norm is one that could be transposed into the categorical imperative or simply into the golden rule. I want to ask them this: "When you write a piece of criticism, do you want me to disregard *your* intention and original meaning?" Why do you say to me, "That is not what I meant at all; that

> is not it at all." Why do you ask me to honor the ethics of language for your writings when you do not honor them for the writings of others? . . . Few critics fail to show moral indignation when their meaning is distorted in reviews and other interpretations of their interpretations. But their sensitivity is often one-way. And in this they show an inconsistency amounting to a double standard—one for their authors, another for themselves. They are like the tenant farmer whose belief in redistributing everybody's property extended to land, money, horses, chickens, and cows, but, when asked about pigs, said: "Ah hell, you know I got a couple of pigs."[3]

Simple logic seems to demand that the author must be the sole determiner of meaning.

A second area that would seem to be worthy of reinforcement in Dr. Johnson's paper is the relationship of the matter of authority to the singular meaning of the author. Within the International Council on Biblical Inerrancy there is the belief that, as the issue of inerrancy goes, so goes the final authority of Scripture. To the extent that correction is allowed in the autographa, to that same extent another authority is substituted for the authority of the Scripture. There is a parallel to this in the matter of meaning versus meanings in the interpretation of the Scripture. With the evaporation of the meaning of the author goes the authority of that author. Thus, it is of little profit to hold to the inerrancy of the original writings while at the same time banishing the author as the sole determiner of meanings. One writer claims,

> There is, because of the continuing activity of the Spirit, no final and authoritative interpretation, nor even, perhaps a final and authoritative principle of interpretation. It may even be, in the last analysis, that there is no need ultimately for Biblical theologians, at least in those places where Christians are aware of their role under the Spirit as interpreters of the Scripture.[4]

Such a view would certainly doom us to hermeneutical nihilism and subjectivism would reign supreme. Thus, there is a logical and necessary relationship between authorial intention and authority. Hirsch states it cogently.

> Whenever meaning is attached to a sequence of words it is impossible to escape an author. Thus, when critics deliberately banished the original author, they themselves usurped his place, and this led unerringly to some present-day theoretical confu-

> sion. Where before there had been but one author, there now arose a multiplicity of them, each carrying as much authority as the rest.[5]

In addition to the aforementioned areas of suggested reinforcement, there are two areas of question I would raise. The first of these relates to the issue commonly referred to as "dual-authorship." This theological formula that seeks to express the biblical evidence of both God and man as active in the origin of Scripture may have a built-in bifurcation that was never intended. While attempting to give due recognition to both the divine and human authors in Scripture, is it possible that we have *separated* them in an unnecessary and, perhaps, unscriptural way when we suggest that the divine author had understanding of the meaning of the text of which the human author of the text was ignorant. Often the analogy of the Theanthropic Person is used when we discuss the Theanthropic Book. In describing the former as to the relation of the humans and the divine, we are careful to caution against confounding the natures or dividing the Person. Is it possible that the charge of authorial ignorance has been guilty of "dividing the Person," so to speak, of the author of Scripture? Are we demanding the divine attribute of omniscience of the author when what is actually required is divine communication with understanding through the human author. Furthermore, is it not possible that the claim of authorial ignorance makes the Bible something less than a truly human document. Just as we do not want to describe the person of Christ as less than truly human, so we do not want to describe the Scriptures as less than truly human.

On the more positive side, 1 Corinthians 2:10-13 may give some clarification to this. It does not treat the human author as an ignorant and passive conveyor of truth beyond him. Rather, Paul says of himself and the other receivers of revelation:

> Now we have received, not the spirit of the world, but the Spirit who is from God, that we might know the things freely given to us by God . . .

It is interesting to note that Paul uses οιδα rather than γινωσκω at this point. Abbott-Smith helpfully comments: "SYN.:γ., *to know* by observation and experience is thus prop. disting. from οιδα, to know by reflection (a mental process, based on intuition or information);"[6]

The next verse goes on to emphasize, twice using the word διδασκω, that the Spirit taught them the things of God. The writers were not simply recipients of divine dictation that they did not understand. Rather, they were taught—divinely instructed—by the One who alone knows the deep things of God. This passage is worthy of a great deal more study with respect to its contribution to the qualifications of the human author. Let us not too quickly lay ahold of the idea of authorial ignorance in view of divine omniscience. For, indeed, there may well have been intelligent, divine communication with understanding through the human author. I appreciate the statement of Bruce Vawter in his article "The Fuller Sense: Some Considerations" wherein he states that the Scripture is:

> A fusion of the divine Spirit with human expression: something theandric. The Word of God has been spoken through the enlightened judgement of a human writer. Therefore the literal sense could now be recognized in its proper dignity and significance. What this human writer had intended to say was itself the very Word of God, the genuine meaning of Scripture.[7]

The second area of question I had in response to Dr. Johnson's paper was with reference to his identification of authorial intention with the "sense of the whole" in which he claims that "the human author did not share fully in the divine author's meanings." Inasmuch as the other responder to his paper, Dr. Walter Kaiser, has already challenged this at length, I would simply say that I see this as the Achilles' heel for an otherwise fine defense of the single meaning of the author.

NOTES

[1]Walter C. Kaiser, *Toward an Exegetical Theology* (Grand Rapids: Baker Book House, 1981), p. 113.

[2]E. D. Hirsch, *The Aims of Interpretation* (Chicago: The University of Chicago Press, 1976), p. 6.

[3]Ibid., p. 91.

[4]Peter Richardson, "Spirit and Letter: A Foundation For Hermeneutics" *Evangelical Quarterly*, 45 (Oct.-Dec. 1973): 318.

[5]E. D. Hirsch, *Validity of Interpretation* (New Haven, Conn.: Yale University Press, 1967), p. 5.

[6]G. Abbott-Smith, *A Manual Greek Lexicon of the New Testament* (Edinburgh: T. & T. Clark, 1954), pp. 92-93.

[7]Bruce Vawter, "The Fuller Sense: Some Considerations."

A Response to Author's Intention and Biblical Interpretation

Walter C. Kaiser, Jr.
Academic Dean and Vice President of Education and Professor of Old Testament and Semitic Languages
Trinity Evangelical Divinity School

A Response to Author's Intention and Biblical Interpretation

Walter C. Kaiser, Jr.

A literary work like the Bible can have one and only one correct interpretation and that meaning must be determined by the human author's truth-intention; otherwise, all alleged meanings would be accorded the same degree of seriousness, plausibility, and correctness with no one meaning being more valid or true than the others. As E. D. Hirsch warned, "To banish the original author as the determiner of meaning [is] to reject the only compelling normative principle that could lend validity to an interpretation."[1] This is so fundamental to the process of interpretation that one must temporarily assume this hermeneutical principle is true in order to successfully deny its legitimacy. It is humorous to see how many defenders of some form of multiple sense hermeneutic will demand that they be understood according to the single truth-intention of their use of their own words while arguing that Scriptural words have a plethora of meanings. What accounts for this quest for opening the door to secondary and fuller senses among evangelical interpreters?

It is no doubt to be explained by a confusion of the goal of interpretation with the implication(s) of an interpretation. While most will admit that Scripture has but one literal sense (the actual, explicit, or historical sense), they are also aware of the fact that there is a "consequent" or "implicit sense" which is somehow to be connected with that literal meaning. And there lies the problem in Elliott Johnson's paper.[2] He is clear on the point that the author's truth-intention is that which governs the single, defining sense of a text, but he also affirms that the authorial will of God goes beyond the human author, i.e., the instrumental agent of Scripture. While the divine and human will are joined in the single grammatical, historical meaning of a text, only the divine will stands behind the fuller references these texts acquire—presumably from the wider biblical context and the interpreter's use of reason.

This division of the tasks of the interpreter raises a very serious matter: does Scripture have a consequent sense as well as a literal sense, which both carry divine authority? Or to put the question in another way: are the significances, applications, implications, and contemporary uses of the grammatical-historical meaning of the biblical text as authoritative and "scriptural" as the single defined meaning of the text? Again, let it be clearly stated that the supreme rule of interpretation is to discover and to define exactly what the human writer had intended to express by the words he used as a result of receiving the revelation of God. But, we are now concerned with that elusive surplusage—that "consequent sense" or naming of contemporary relationships that exist between that single authorial meaning of the biblical words in their B.C. or first century A.D. dress and the needs of our day. How valid, how scriptural, how normative is that implied meaning?

The question must be raised: *Could* God see or intend a sense in a particular text *separate* and *different* from that conceived and intended by his human instrument? Notice the italicized words: *separate* and *different.* Therein lies the story. The situation would then be as Rudolph Bierberg has assessed it:

> . . . if they are really different from the literal sense, if they are not the subjective comprehensive and consequent extension of the inspired words, then they are not effects of inspiration, and hence, are not true senses of the Sacred Scriptures considered as inspired. They are at best implications or accommodations *per extensionem.*[3]

The key then is to be found in whether the divine implication attributed to a biblical text is both contained in, implied, and intended (whether actually or virtually) by the human author. If the extension is *different* from that which by any normal rules of grammatical interpretation may be attributed a concept or idea found in the word(s) used by the author, then the *sensus plenior* is a *different* sense rather than a fuller sense.

What we are dealing with, then, is a general or universal term which Bierberg defines with Coffey[4] as "one that applies '*in the same sense* to each of an *indefinite* number of individual things.' "[5] Legitimate implications, then, will adhere to the exegeted general or universal term in the same sense, rather than a separate or different meaning. In fact, that is why we should avoid referring to a "double sense" for any Scripture since that term usually means two different senses which have little or no relationship one to another.

Scripture itself supplies us with a number of illustrations of this very process. The best is Paul's use of Deuteronomy 25:4 in 1 Corinthians 9:8-10.[6] The apostle argued that the law itself contained the same principle he was propounding even though it did not offer the same application, viz. the right of the laborer for the gospel to expect a worthy financial remuneration. When Moses wrote, "You shall not muzzle the mouth of the ox that tramples the corn," Paul announced triumphantly that "these things were written for our sakes" and therefore pastors and workers in the cause of the gospel were owed a similar reimbursement for their efforts. God was not only concerned for oxen in the Deuteronomic legislation; he was even more vitally concerned about the attitudes, sensitivities and graciousness of the owners and users of oxen.

Accordingly, a passage has always one and the same meaning even though it may have manifold applications. This may be illustrated in our Lord's use of Hosea's remonstrance with Israel, "I [the Lord] desired mercy and not sacrifice" (Hosea 6:6). Jesus used this passage to justify his eating with publicans and sinners (Matt. 9:10-13) and to justify his disciple's action in plucking and eating grain on the Sabbath (Matt. 12:1-7). The applications certainly differed from each other and from that of the prophet, but this was neither a "double sense," different meaning or *sensus plenior* (as usually defined). The principle remained the same throughout; it was only brought to bear on different subjects. All three texts set forth what was necessary for acceptance on high while erring mortals focused on the physical externals at hand.[7]

Both of these examples, in Paul and Jesus, focus on a universal principle and apply it to a contemporary situation. But what of logical deductions which take an explicit proposition of the Scriptures as the point of departure and conclude with some new formula? Is this process legitimate and may we link these new formulas with "God says"? Certainly we may do so when the new formula is a simple clarification of a term in a scriptural statement. For example, C. F. Devine[8] forms from the biblical statement, "Christ died for all men," a new statement, "Christ died for Peter." Since this is simply a clarification of the term "all men," it cannot be regarded as a new truth or a different teaching from the original Biblical statement. The individual, Peter, is contained in the universal term. Needless to say, the deduction is legitimate and fully authoritative.

But what if the implication is not found in the revealed statement of Scripture as such (otherwise, it could be shown to be part of the grammatical, literal, meaning of the human author) and is not simply a clarification of his use of terms (whether explicitly or virtually contained in them)? Suppose it is known solely as a premise of reason, by metaphysical analysis or explanation of the middle term. For example, take two terms that are joined in Scripture by a simple copula: A is B (God is unchanging, Mal. 3:6). What if we reason that immutability is similar to eternality and set up this syllogism after DeVine:[9]

major premise:	God is absolutely immutable (assertion of Scripture)
minor premise:	What is absolutely immutable is eternal (known from reason)
Ergo:	God is eternal

It is clear that Malachi 3:6 has not claimed anything about the eternality of God; only his unchangeableness. Here is an implication that is theologically motivated, but not exegetically demonstrable. It is totally different from the original revelation of God, yet it bears some connection with it. Some will say that it is a further clarification of the subject, God. Others will say that it is virtually implicit, as DeVine does: "It is a distinction not of thing and thing, but of two diverse concepts of one and the same thing."[10]

But should not the clarification normally be of the predicate if we wish to remain with a revelational norm? And if we wish to clarify the subject as well, must we not rely on the presence of an explicit "antecedent analogy of Scripture" or "an informing theology" if we expect such to be part of the content of meaning found in these concepts, words or actions?[11]

What if these alleged divine implications were found in the whole of Scripture and attributed to one particular text even though they exceeded what a human author could conceive and intend by his own text? Recently, Bruce Waltke has described this as "the canonical process approach."[12] Thus, the full meaning of an earlier and smaller text could not be obtained without interpreting it in light of the entire Bible. This is similar to some of the concepts in the Jesuit scholar, Norbert Lohfink.[13] Now in addition to the meaning obtained by ordinary exegesis, there was a fuller, canonical, reinterpretation of that passage taught by the whole Bible.

But what is it that the whole or unity of Scripture teaches that cannot be found in the individual parts by the grammar and syntax? And if we must answer that a *different sense* is taught that went beyond the consciousness of the original instrumental agent who wrote that text, then we must argue that such is not an objective *sensus plenior.* In fact, we must deny that such a different sense is scriptural (i.e., *graphē,* "written") at all. Indeed, had it been written, we could have obtained it from the grammar and syntax at hand. Does not this conclusion deprive the *sensus plenior* (which is a *different,* not the same sense) of one of its most essential elements—its scriptural status?[14] Therefore, we easily dismiss it as having no force, authority, or as constituting no normative status over believers.

Should someone plead, "but that is a biblical sense which can be shown from another passage to be fully scriptural," we will reply, "Then let us go to that passage for that teaching rather than transporting it to odd locations in earlier parts of the canon. The unity of Scripture (an important truth of Scripture) must not be traded for the uniformity of all Scriptures on any topic any of them touches.

We are still left with this issue: what is the authority status of those clarifications, implications applications, illustrations of legitimately derived principles, universals, propositions, or laws of Scripture as determined by the single, truth-intention of author? We shall answer: (1) the process of deducing such implications is a valid and necessary part of the exegetical process. How can we assume that the interpreter's job is finished until the reader or listener has understood how that text impinges on his or her life, times, and acting? The two horizons of the writer and reader must be fused in the manner described here. We will balk only when the fusion starts linking up *different* or *separate* things. (2) The degree of authority that we attach to these "secondary senses" (a term which I would prefer to avoid since it confuses the word "sense" with the author's truth-intention[15]) or significances depends on how closely it reproduces the original statement, universal or idea. Surely, we must not demand that our applications be accorded the same status as Scripture; but some will be so transparent that they are only a rewording of the original proposition in Scripture. Thus, the answer will be mixed here: some applications are already made in Scripture, e.g., the second half of many of the Pauline letters. Others will be our own suggestions which we will ask for the helpful criticism of the priesthood of believers as they are enlightened by the ministry of the Holy Spirit in connection with a particular text. These we must refrain from calling "biblical" or authoritative in the same sense that the apostle's applications were normative.

Conclusion: God did not exceed the intention of the human

author either through a retrojection of the whole of the canon on an earlier text or by means of a hidden freight of meaning which awaited our discovery of it many centuries later. Both in prophecy and type, New Testament citation of the Old Testament and the practical use of historical, wisdom and legal portions of the Bible, there must be an objective basis in the individual text itself with the extension of that meaning into our contemporary culture consisting of the same, not a separate or different thing than what was mentioned in the text. Only on these grounds will the hard fought battle for inerrancy have been well worthwhile. To introduce through some subjective principle a teaching of the whole canon as an additional meaning of a particular text or through some alleged divine implication what is not found in the text is to give away with the left hand all that was won with the right hand in the contest for an inerrant Bible. We urge Christ's church not to do so.

NOTES

[1]E. D. Hirsch, *Validity in Interpretation* (New Haven, Conn.: Yale University Press, 1967), pp. 4-5.

[2]Elliott Johnson, "Author's Intention and Biblical Interpretation," *Hermeneutics, Inerrancy, and the Bible*, ed. Radmacher and Preus (Grand Rapids: Zondervan, 1984).

[3]Rudolph Bierberg, "Does Sacred Scripture Have A Sensus Plenior?" *Catholic Biblical Quarterly* 10 (1848): 187.

[4]Peter Coffey, *The Science of Logic* (New York: Peter Smith, 1938) I: 45.

[5]R. Bierberg, "Sensus Plenior," p. 188.

[6]See our extensive discussion of this passage, W. C. Kaiser, Jr., "The Current Crises in Exegesis and the Apostolic Use of Deuteronomy 25:4 in I Corinthians 9:8-10," *Journal of the Evangelical Theological Society* 21 (1978): 3-18.

[7]This is the argument of Frederic Gardiner, *The Old and New Testaments in Their Mutual Relations* (New York: James Pott and Co., 1885), pp. 268-69.

[8]C. F. DeVine, "The Consequent Sense," *Catholic Biblical Quarterly* 2(1940): 151.

[9]DeVine, "The Consequent Sense," pp. 151-52.

[10]DeVine, p. 152.

[11]See our discussion of these terms in W. C. Kaiser, Jr., *Toward an Exegetical Theology: Biblical Exegesis for Preaching and Teaching* (Grand Rapids: Baker, 1981), pp. 134-40.

[12]Bruce K, Waltke, "A Canonical Process Approach to the Psalms," in *Tradition and Testament: Essays in Honor of Charles Lee Feinberg*, eds. John and Paul Feinberg (Chicago: Moody Press, 1981), pp. 3-18.

[13]Norbert Lohfink, *The Christian Meaning of the Old Testament*, trans, R. A. Wilson (Milwaukee: Bruce, 1968), pp. 32-49.

[14]For the development of this argument, see Bruce Vawter, *Biblical Inspiration*, Theological Resources (Philadelphia: Westminster, 1972), p. 115.

[15]I believe the suggestion of G. B. Caird is very helpful when he distinguishes five different meanings of meaning using supralinear sigla. They include: meaning^{R} (=referent; identifies person[s] or thing[s] named), meaning^{S} (=sense; qualities of a person[s] or thing[s]), meaning^{V} (=value; "this *means* more to me than anything else"), meaning^{E} (=entailment; "this *means* war"), and meaning^{I} (=intention, that which a speaker or writer intends by his use of language). See G. B. Caird, *The Language and Imagery of the Bible* (Philadelphia: Westminster Press, 1980), pp. 37-40.

The Role of the Holy Spirit in the Hermeneutic Process: The Relationship of the Spirit's Illumination to Biblical Interpretation

Fred H. Klooster
Professor of Systematic Theology
Calvin Theological Seminary

8. The Role of the Holy Spirit in the Hermeneutic Process: The Relationship of the Spirit's Illumination to Biblical Interpretation

Fred H. Klooster

One who attempts to write a paper on this subject should earnestly desire the illumination he attempts to describe. Illumination by the Holy Spirit cannot be claimed, however, in justification of one's interpretation; nor can the Spirit's illumination be demonstrated. Hopefully, it can be recognized. Illumination does not provide new revelation; hence none will be claimed.

Illumination is a work of the Holy Spirit in the reader, hearer, interpreter of Scripture. That is to say, illumination concerns the correlation of Word and Spirit and the correlation of the Spirit's activity and human activity. While illumination is the Spirit's gift (*Gabe*), the gift comes when the interpreter engages in his task (*Aufgabe*). Whether the mysterious illumination of the Spirit has actually occurred can only be recognized by testing a person's interpretation by the text of Scripture itself; the success of that test also requires the illumination of the Holy Spirit. To that test the writer of this paper willingly submits.

The illumination of the Holy Spirit is regularly mentioned in theological literature; yet detailed discussion of this subject is rare.[1] Since Calvin, considerable attention has been given to the internal testimony of the Holy Spirit (*testimonium Spiritus sancti internum*) whereby the believer acknowledges the inherent authority of Scripture; the *testimonium* has also been given a place in many confessions, especially those of the Reformed churches.

What is the relation of this internal testimony to illumination? Are they distinguishable facets of the Holy Spirit's work? Is illumination a distinct activity of the Holy Spirit or is it simply a distinguishable aspect of a larger activity? Is illumination an integral part of the Spirit's work in regeneration, conversion, faith, and sanctification? or is it an additional activity of the Spirit, perhaps present only occasionally in believers, or only in some believers? Does the Spirit's illumination function distinctly in the scientific exegesis and interpretation of Scripture? Do biblical commentators possess a special gift of the Spirit for interpretation and does illumination occur uniquely in such interpreters? These and many other questions surface as one investigates this subject.

The Holy Spirit's illumination is indispensable for discerning the true meaning of the Spirit-breathed Scripture. Yet the task of analyzing the precise nature of the Spirit's illumination is extremely difficult. The difficulty is analagous to that of attempting to describe the exact nature of the process of inspiration. Perhaps one can only clarify the subject somewhat by distinguishing facets of the Spirit's illumination within the various stages of biblical interpretation.

The temptation exists to use the term "illumination" in either too broad or too narrow a sense. To use "illumination" as an umbrella term for regeneration, conversion, faith, the internal testimony, and sanctification would not promote theological precision nor facilitate clearer understanding. On the other hand, illumination cannot be separated from the activities of the Spirit just mentioned. The Spirit's illumination is not one additional activity; rather it is an aspect of each. One should attempt to be as precise as possible, that is, as precise as the scriptural givens warrant, in describing the nature of illumination. At the same time one should avoid the danger of isolating illumination from the broader context of the Spirit's ministry in renewing the children of God. That is why I prefer to designate the subject as "the role of the Holy Spirit in the hermeneutic process."

In the discussion that follows I am first of all concerned with the interpretation of Scripture that every believer must pursue. Interpretation of Scripture is the responsibility of the entire believing community; that task is not restricted to a priesthood of specialists. The priesthood of all believers was at the heart of the Reformation, and rightly so! After I have developed the subject from the perspective of the ordinary believer (1-13 below), I turn very briefly to consider "scientific exegesis" pursued by specialists and professionals. I maintain that they are but one species in the same genus. The scope of the paper has not permitted me to consider the aspects of the meaning of Scripture uncovered by non-Christian interpreters who do not reach heart-understanding. Yet there are implications on that subject along the way.

Two observations may help to prevent misunderstanding of what follows. I am not presenting a complete soteriology; only what is necessary for describing the role of the Holy Spirit in the hermeneutic process is included. Secondly, I am not describing the chronology of the Spirit's activity in this process. Understanding arises within believers' hearts in varied ways. I insist only on the chronological priority of the Spirit-inspired Scripture to our interpretation, and on the logical priority of the Spirit's regeneration to the other soteriological activities in the believer. I refer to the latter as a "logical priority" because the internal testimony and illumination may occur simultaneously with the radical rebirth.

I. THE SPIRIT-INSPIRED AUTHORITATIVE SCRIPTURE[2]

The interpretative process ought to start out from the confession that the Old and New Testament Scriptures are the inspired, authoritative Word of God. That is what the Holy Scriptures really are, even if that is not confessed. Scripture was produced in history by a special activity of the Holy Spirit through the instrumentality of human authors (2 Tim. 3:16; 2 Pet. 1:21).

The "driving activity" (*pheromenoi*, 2 Pet. 1:21) of the Holy Spirit was not "mechanical" or "dictational"; it can perhaps best be described as an "organic" inspiration since the Spirit "utilized the distinctive personalities and literary styles of the writers whom he had chosen and prepared."[3] The Spirit's inspiration (*theopneustos*) led these biblical writers to inscripturate the redemptive-history by which God worked salvation and faithfully to interpret that original special revelation.

Because the Scriptures were Spirit-produced, they claim and actually possess inherent divine authority. Scripture is God-breathed; therefore, what Scripture says, God says. For a more extensive statement of this biblical perspective, I refer to the major confessions of the Reformation and to the 1978 "Chicago Statement on Biblical Inerrancy."

II. THE PNEUMATICALLY CHRISTOLOGICAL THEOCENTRIC MESSAGE OF SCRIPTURE

The confession of the inherent authority of Scripture is basic to all sound biblical interpretation (cf. #11 below). This confession alone does not guarantee faithful biblical interpretation, however. Many Jews of Jesus' day claimed to acknowledge the authority of Moses and the Old Testament, but they did not really believe the Old

Testament since they rejected Jesus as the Christ of Scripture. Jesus denounced that unbelief (John 5:45-47)! A genuine confession of the authority of Scripture includes the confession of Jesus as Lord and Christ. That confession, however, is not simply a "flesh and blood" possibility (Matt. 16:17); it is not a possibility for the "natural man," that is, "the man without the Spirit" (1 Cor. 2:14).

That is not to say that the biblical message is only a "Christocentric" one. I refuse to choose between the alternatives of "Christocentric" or "theocentric." Scripture is really Christologically theocentric. One can state that even more accurately, for it is a pneumatically Christological theocentricity! Those complex words express what Paul stated so simply: "For through Him [Christ Jesus] we both have access to the Father by one Spirit" (Eph. 2:18; cf. 2:12-13).

The basic message of Scripture is the gospel, the good news of the triune God's redemptive activity for rebel sinners. Through that message God reveals Himself, His good creation in the beginning, Adam's fall into sin with its consequent guilt and corruption of the entire human race, and the covenant-kingdom work of God-triune in redemptive history.

This redemptive message from the triune God is conveyed by means of a book comprising many smaller books written by several human authors under the inspiration of the Holy Spirit. Scripture consists of words and sentences in contexts; it is linguistically qualified and historically rooted.

God's gracious purpose with this book is to bring about the living "encounter" with Him in an I-thou relationship for building His church and manifesting His kingdom. For the believer this I-thou relationship is not really an "encounter," with the negative implications of that term, but fellowship and communion with the living triune-God!

The words and sentences of Scripture present a message, a personal message from the living God to His fallen creatures, calling them to repent, to believe, and to love Him with their whole hearts. Hence Scripture must be seen as God's personal and gracious love letter aimed at reconciling His alienated creatures (John 3:16: 2 Tim. 3:15). Indeed, the Lover also expresses His anger and judgment upon the unfaithful, but He does that with an urgent call to be reconciled to Him, the living God, Creator, and Redeemer (2 Cor. 5:18-21).

Therefore the authority of Scripture is not truly confessed, nor is the biblical message really understood, unless one responds from the depths of the heart in love to the living God-triune. Jesus revealed that, "Now this is eternal life, that they may know You, the only true God, and Jesus Christ, Whom You have sent" (John 17:3). To "know" (*ginōskō*) in that statement carries the Old Testament sense of "to love" without excluding the intellectual; it is heart-knowledge, heart-understanding. Heart-knowledge of the Father through Jesus Christ is possible only through the Holy Spirit (Matt. 16:17; 1 Cor. 12:3).

The *order of revelation* is Father, Son, Holy Spirit; the Father reveals Himself through the incarnate Son and inscripturates that revelation through the Holy Spirit. The *order of knowing* in the believer is Spirit, Son, Father; the Holy Spirit enables one to confess Jesus as Lord and Christ, and the Son reveals the Father Who sent Him (Matt. 11:28-30; 1 Cor. 2:10-16). These richly personal dimensions of the biblical revelation are the ingredients of heart-understanding; Father, Son, and Holy Spirit restore the I-thou fellowship relationship with believers.

This perspective is crucial for the interpretative process. Unless one comes to heart-knowledge of the Father through the Son in the fellowship of the Holy Spirit, one has not really understood Scripture—God's love letter to humankind. The Ephesian Gentiles were previously "separate from Christ . . . and without God" (Eph. 2:12). The Jews who rejected Christ did not really believe Moses or the prophets (John 5:39, 46). A nonbeliever may read the love letter, but without knowing the Persons Who sent the letter, one reads words and sentences but does not truly understand the message. Heart-knowledge is possible only in true faith; for that the Spirit's regeneration and enlightenment are indispensable!

III. THE CORRELATIONS OF SPIRIT AND CHRIST, SPIRIT AND WORD

The relation between the ascended Christ and the Pentecost Spirit is intimate and crucial as Jesus taught in John 14-16 and the epistles emphasize repeatedly (1 Cor. 2; 12:3; Eph. 2:18). The Holy Spirit is the effective administrator of the ascended Christ. All the blessings Jesus won for us through His incarnation, obedient life, suffering, death, resurrection, and ascension are administered through the Holy Spirit as His Agent. What Christ earned for us is given to us by the Holy Spirit. No one knows the Father but the Son and those whom the Son chooses to reveal Him, and no one knows the Son but the Spirit and those to whom the Spirit chooses to reveal Him (Matt. 11:28-30; 1 Cor. 2:10-11)!

That correlation of the Spirit and Christ enables the believer to confess that the "glory of Christ," our ascended Lord, benefits us because "through His Holy Spirit He pours out His gifts from heaven upon us His members."[4] With that assurance the true believer confesses that the Holy Spirit "has been given to me personally, so that, by true faith, He makes me share in Christ and all His blessings, comforts me, and remains with me forever."[5]

This correlation of Christ and Spirit calls also for the acknowledgment of the correlation of Spirit and Word; Christ rules "by His Word and Spirit."[6] The Spirit-inspired Scriptures reveal Jesus Christ, and the Spirit employs His Word to unite believers to Christ in true faith. The Spirit is not tied to the Word so that wherever the Word is, there the Spirit of Christ is also; the Spirit remains sovereign over His Word. When the Spirit sovereignly brings sinners to Christ, however, He employs His own theopneustic Word.

In bringing the believer to faith in Christ, the Spirit witnesses "by and with the Word in our hearts."[7] That is also the case in the Spirit's bringing about the conviction that Scripture is the authoritative Word of God. The internal testimony of the Holy Spirit does not bring new revelation; Calvin rightly states that "the Word is the instrument (*organum*) by which the Lord dispenses the illumination of His Spirit to believers."[8] "The same Spirit . . . Who has spoken through the mouths of the prophets must penetrate into our hearts to persuade us that they faithfully proclaimed what had been divinely commanded."[9] Therefore, "those whom the Holy Spirit has inwardly taught truly rest upon Scripture. . . . And the certainty it deserves with us, it attains by the testimony of the Spirit."[10] I turn now to those distinguishable aspects of the Spirit's work whereby "Spirit and Word" unite us to Christ.

IV. ILLUMINATION AND REGENERATION

Adam's rebellious fall into sin corrupted his entire heart—intellect, will, and emotion. Hence the human subject to whom Scripture is addressed is a rebel, a fallen creature, blinded by sin, perverse in heart, "without hope and without God in the world" (Eph. 2:12; cf. 4:17-19). The "man without the Spirit," that is "the natural man," "does not accept the things that come from the Spirit of God, for they are foolishness to him, and he cannot understand them, because they are spiritually discerned" (1 Cor. 2:14).[11] Unless one is born again, one cannot see the kingdom or know the King (John 3:3).

Rebirth, regeneration by the Holy Spirit is the only remedy. The fallen sinner needs a renewed heart—eyes to see, ears to hear, a mind illumined to understand, a will freed from its bondage, feelings redirected. Calvin expressed this admirably in the Geneva Catechism:

> Our mind is too weak to comprehend the spiritual wisdom of God which is revealed to us by faith, and our hearts are too prone either to defiance or to a perverse confidence in ourselves or creaturely things. But the Holy Spirit enlightens us to make us capable of understanding what would otherwise be incomprehensible to us, and fortifies us in certitude, sealing and imprinting the promises of salvation in our hearts.[12]

The Holy Spirit's regeneration brings about a radical redirection that manifests itself in repentance and faith. The illumination of the Spirit is involved in that regeneration because the radical beginning of the interpretative process has now begun; the basic message of the gospel has been understood. Through the words of Scripture—read, preached, or witnessed—a regenerated sinner has come to know Jesus Christ, person to person. Heart-understanding has taken place. The regenerated believer is in a new and intimate fellowship with the living God.

Sometimes this change takes place immediately, as it did for the thief on the cross and for Saul on the Damascus road. In the normal covenant-nurtured experience, however, conversion may be less dramatic, though no less real. When the Holy Spirit's regeneration occurs, however, illumination, internal testimony, and enlightenment are all present to some degree. During the lifelong process of sanctification, the need for the Spirit's illumination continues (cf. #6), but rebirth, renewal of the heart in regeneration is the most radical form of illumination one experiences.

V. ILLUMINATION AND THE *TESTIMONIUM SPIRITUS SANCTI INTERNUM*

"The internal testimony of the Holy Spirit" is the term that has come to designate the Spirit's action by which a believer acknowledges the inherent authority of the Scripture as a whole. Just when this conviction emerges in the consciousness of a believer is impossible to say. There is undoubtedly a great deal of variety in the experience of believers on this score. Nevertheless, the confession that Scripture is God's address to us and normative for all faith and conduct is the result of the Spirit's *testimonium*.

Paul thanked God because the Thessalonians accepted the message that he preached to them, "not as the word of men, but as it actually is, the Word of God, which is at work in you who believe"

(1 Thess. 2:13). The same response is expected of us in relation to Paul's inspired writings, indeed, to the whole Scripture as the inspired, authoritative Word of God. The illumination of the Spirit enables the believer to reach that conviction and make that confession. Since Calvin's time, this aspect of the Spirit's illumination has been called the *testimonium Spiritus sancti internum*.[13]

The internal testimony is not a special revelation; the Spirit witnesses in our hearts by and with the Word." Three interrelated factors lead to the regenerated believer's conviction of Scripture's inherent authority. First, Scripture is inherently authoritative and specific passages refer to this inspiration and authority. Second, the person with this conviction has become acquainted with these scriptural claims and has reflected upon them. Third, the Spirit's illumination brings about understanding, conviction, and confession of Scripture's claimed authority. It is an organic process by which the Spirit's *testimonium* leads to the believer's confession. That confession may be only implicit at early stages of one's faith; when it becomes explicit, however, these three interrelated factors will be present, as the Reformed confessions clearly indicate. The Chicago Statement expresses it succinctly: "The Holy Spirit, Scripture's divine author, both authenticates it to us by His inward witness and opens our minds to understand its meaning."[14]

A few of Calvin's statements provide a good summary of the illumination of the Holy Spirit generally referred to as the "internal testimony:"

> For as God alone is a fit witness of Himself in His Word, so also the Word will not find acceptance in men's hearts before it is sealed by the inward testimony of the Spirit. The same Spirit, therefore, Who has spoken through the mouths of the prophets must penetrate into our hearts to persuade us that they faithfully proclaimed what had been divinely commanded.[15]

In this internal testimony or illumination, the Holy Spirit uses the Scripture: "The Word is the instrument (*organum*) by which the Lord dispenses the illumination of His Spirit to believers."[16]

As a result "those whom the Holy Spirit has inwardly taught truly rest upon Scripture . . . and the certainty it deserves with us, it attains by the testimony of the Spirit."[17] This certainty rests in the whole heart:

> Such, then, is a conviction (*persuasio*) that requires no reasons; such, a knowledge (*notitia*) with which the best reason agrees—in which the mind (*men's*) truly reposes more securely and

> constantly than in any reasons; such finally, a feeling (*sensus*) that can be born only of heavenly revelation.[18]

This heart conviction resulting from the Spirit's witness "by and with the "Word" is basic to all faithful interpretation of Scripture. There are however, other aspects of the Spirit's illumination needed in the process of sanctification.

VI. THE SPIRIT'S ILLUMINATION AND SANCTIFICATION

The regenerated believer has become the temple of the Holy Spirit (1 Cor. 6:19). The indwelling Spirit guides the believer in the ongoing process of santification. The sanctified life urgently needs the guidance of Word and Spirit. The Spirit's illumination is essential for the interpretation of Scripture that takes place in the process of sanctification. Perhaps most Bible study and interpretation occur within this context, and illumination is certainly crucial here, though, as we have seen above, it may not be restricted to this large phase of the believer's life.

How is one to use Scripture and profit from it in the sanctified life? Calvin answers that question this way:

> By receiving it with the full consent of our conscience, as truth come down from heaven, submitting ourselves to it in right obedience, loving it with true affection by having it imprinted in our hearts, we may follow it entirely and conform ourselves to it.[19]

Think of Peter at Caesarea Philippi, the Emmaus disciples on Easter night, and the Jerusalem disciples the same night. They were believers then, though highly confused. The illumination that came to each of them when Jesus opened their minds to understand the Scriptures took place within the process of sanctification (cf. Matt. 16:13ff.; Lk. 24:27, 45). Something like that happened centuries later when Luther rediscovered the scriptural way of justification by faith. The synthesis of "faith and works" prevented him from finding genuine peace with God in his personal struggle. Eventually the Spirit's illumination enabled him to grasp the liberating power of the Scriptural teaching that "the righteous will live by faith" (Rom. 1:17). The Spirit's illumination came "by and with the Word" in the context of interpreting Scripture within the process of sanctification. And the result, eventually, was the Reformation!

The illumination of the Holy Spirit operates in the lives of all believers as they progress in sanctification and discipleship, though often less dramatically. Paul repeatedly prayed that the believers might grow in understanding and knowledge through the illumination of the Holy Spirit (1 Cor. 2; 2 Cor. 4:4-15; Eph. 1:17-19; Phil. 1:9-11; Col. 1:9-13; cf. also 1 John 2:20-27). Believers, who through the Spirit have "the mind of Christ" (1 Cor. 2:16), are expected to bring every thought captive to the obedience of Christ "in whom are hidden all the treasures of wisdom and knowledge" (Col. 2:3; 2 Cor. 10:5). That requires the illumination of the Spirit in the correlation of Word and Spirit.[20]

VII. "ORGANIC ILLUMINATION" AND INTERPRETATION[21]

It seems particularly appropriate to designate the Spirit's illumination in connection with the sanctified believer's interpretation of Scripture as an "organic illumination." I use the term "organic" analogous to its application to inspiration. Just as the biblical writer used his own talents and investigation, so the biblical interpreter must read and study and struggle to understand the biblical text. The more self-consciously active the interpreter is in that process, the more likely is the Spirit's illumination. That is why I think the term "organic illumination" is especially useful in this connection.

To understand Scripture every believer must read and interpret intelligently. The Holy Spirit does not produce revelational insight that "automatically" provides the meaning of any passage. The interpreter's feeling does not provide an easy clue to the text's meaning. Not only the scientific exegete must struggle to grasp the intent of the text; every believer is required to do that. One must discern the author's purpose in writing a particular book of the Bible (cf. John 20:30-31). The immediate context of a passage is crucial for its correct understanding. The historical circumstances of the text and its literary style are important for faithful interpretation. All the issues that emerge in the grammatical-historical interpretation of Scripture (cf. #16 below) by exegetical specialists ought to emerge in biblical study by every believer. Of course, most ordinary believers will not even recognize these terms and will not be able to consult the original language of the text. Yet faithful interpretation calls for thorough work involving these issues on a nonscientific level. Word and Spirit are correlative; so too are Word-interpretation and Spirit-illumination!

In the *organic inspiration* of Scripture the Holy Spirit worked in the biblical writers to faithfully record and interpret the original revelation that God gave in redemptive history. In *organic illumina-*

tion the Holy Spirit works in the believing interpreter of the inspired Scripture to enable faithful understanding of the meaning of the passage under study.

The basic message of Scripture—creation, fall, redemption through Jesus Christ in the fellowship of the Holy Spirit—is clear so that one who runs may read. The insistence of the Reformation on the perspicuity of Scripture did not mean, however, that all parts were equally clear. The apostle Peter acknowledged that some parts of Paul's letters were "hard to understand" (2 Pet. 3:15-16). I must confess that some parts of Peter's letters are even more difficult to understand than Paul's (cf. 1 Pet. 3:18-20; 4:6). Peter's warning is also applicable to us: "ignorant and unstable people distort" Paul's difficult passages "as they do the other Scriptures, to their own destruction" (2 Pet. 3:16). Faithful biblical interpretation is a demanding task for every Christian, and the illumination of the Holy Spirit is indispensable for faithful human interpretation.

Sometimes the meaning of a biblical passage is readily grasped. At other times one may work long and hard on a difficult passage. The meaning of the text eludes the interpreter even after a strenuous effort to understand. Then a surprising thing occasionally happens. After one has left the laborious process of interpretation, perhaps taken the dog for a walk, the meaning of the passage suddenly seems to jump to mind. I suppose most interpreters have enjoyed that experience at times. The experience seems to involve intuition, perhaps even a special revelation. I believe that such an experience may be the result of the Spirit's illumination, but I do not think it may be considered a special revelation. The interpreter's struggle to understand always precedes that unique experience; it does not occur in connection with a text on which one has expended no effort. The human mind is a unique gift of God who formed us in his own image. Our minds often continue to function even while we rest and relax. Hence I am convinced that the experience of such sudden insight does not come apart from one's earlier study of the passage. That is also why I refer to the "organic illumination" of the Holy Spirit in connection with the demanding process of interpreting Scripture.

VIII. ILLUMINATION AND HEART-UNDERSTANDING

Throughout this paper I have referred to heart-understanding. Regeneration brings heart-knowledge. The internal testimony of the Holy Spirit is a heart-rooted conviction that Scripture is the authoritative Word of God. Similarly, the continuing process of biblical interpretation in the process of sanctification should aim also at heart-understanding. Interpretation of Scripture involves much more than head-knowledge or the gaining of information, historical or other. That is why illumination is a continuing need.

What does such heart-knowledge of Scripture involve? It involves heart-knowledge of the living God (John 17:3), a true knowledge of man and woman as God's creatures, fallen into sin, redeemed only through Jesus Christ, and redirected in the sanctified life of kingdom service. It includes also the redemptive knowledge of the world as God's creation in which that kingdom must increasingly reappear.

The goal of heart-knowledge requires a Christian epistemology for describing the hermeneutic process involved. *Who* understands; *how* such a person understands; and *what* is understood is basic to hermeneutics and Scriptural interpretation.[22] The biblical answer to these three questions requires that understanding be viewed basically as a matter of the heart, the religious concentration point of a person's entire being. That is implied in the confession that sin is a matter of the heart, that a new heart or rebirth is required (John 3:3), that the natural man "cannot understand" the "things that come from the Spirit of God" (1 Cor. 2:14), and that believers "have the mind of Christ" (1 Cor. 2:16).

Understanding is not only a matter of the mind or thought or reason, as Enlightenment hermeneutics implied—although the human mind is certainly involved in interpretation. Heart-understanding does not allow for the separation between faith and knowledge, as if knowledge were reached by reason common to all people while faith is restricted to trust in what reason has achieved. This separation between knowledge and faith has been promoted by the use of Scottish realism in the Old-Princeton apologetic and appears in a new context in Pannenberg's theology.

Furthermore, understanding the biblical message is not chiefly a matter of feeling as Schleiermacher's psychological hermeneutics maintained—although feeling or emotion is part of heart-understanding. Feeling, at the expense of the intellect, often appears dominant also in pietistic interpretation of Scripture. Nor is understanding mainly a matter of the will as existential hermeneutics insist (Heidegger, Bultmann, Ebeling, Fuchs)—although the will is also part of heart-understanding.

Understanding rooted in the heart does include the intellect, will, and emotion; it concerns the whole person. Understanding Scripture with its theocentric redemptive message (#2 above) is more than an intellectual grasp of words, thoughts, facts, and events. It obviously involves much more than the grammatical-syntactical analysis of sentences and paragraphs, although that too is essential for understanding Scripture's meaning. Understanding Scripture requires more than an intellectual grasp of the historical setting of the text or the literary structure of the passage. Of course, all that is necessary to discern the intended meaning of the text and its author's purpose. If Scripture is the reconciling love letter from the living God, then understanding God's message is more than a matter of the head; it concerns the heart, person to person! Heart-understanding demands the heart response in the totality of one's person to the living, triune God.

Heart-understanding is what Calvin referred to as "wisdom" (*sapientia*) in the opening line of the *Institutes*; "wisdom" includes the knowledge of God and the knowledge of self in their mutual interrelations, never the one without the other. Through the words and sentences of Scripture God reveals Himself to sinful persons for the purpose of restoring covenantal fellowship and redirecting them in the whole of life to know (*yada*) the Father through Jesus Christ in the fellowship of the Holy Spirit (John 17:3; Eph. 2:18). This is the scope of the heart-understanding that should always be the goal of authentic Scripture interpretation. Regeneration is indispensable for such knowledge rooted in the renewed heart; the ongoing illumination of the indwelling Spirit is likewise necessary for interpretation that contributes to progress in the sanctified life that promotes the kingdom of God.

IX. PREUNDERSTANDING AND THE HERMENEUTIC CIRCLE

If heart-understanding is to grow through the Christian's ongoing study of Scripture, that interpretation should proceed from the preunderstanding of genuine biblical faith. This confronts us with one instance of the hermeneutic circle.

Faith, of course, comes from hearing Scripture (Rom. 10:14-17; yet Scripture is truly heard only in faith; yet such heart-understanding is itself required for properly grasping the message of Scripture. This is the most basic sense in which the hermeneutic circle confronts us. This is not a vicious circle, however, for the same Spirit who inspired the Word also employs it in the process of bringing sinners to faith.

The Spirit's illumination occurs within that process. With Calvin we have become accustomed to speak of Scripture as the "spectacles"[23] through which the sinner understands God's revelation in creation. In terms of the hermeneutic circle, it can be helpful also to think of Scripture as the "spectacles" through which Scripture itself is to be read and understood!

As a matter of fact, no one approaches Scripture without some preunderstanding; presuppositionless exegesis is impossible. Even Bultmann acknowledged that! However, not every presupposition nor every preunderstanding is valid. Faithful interpretation of Scripture requires that one approach it with a preunderstanding that conforms to Scripture. Unbiblical presuppositions will short-circuit the interpretative process.

Regenerated believers are not immune from the danger of pursuing their study of Scripture with at least a partially unbiblical preunderstanding. Especially in academic work, foreign syntheses sneak in, often unwittingly.

A sound biblical hermeneutic demands that one approach Scripture with a preunderstanding that is wholly consonant with it. The unbeliever's preunderstanding must be fundamentally *redirected* by the regenerating power of the Holy Spirit. A believer's preunderstanding may require *reformation* (re-forming) within the regenerated heart through the Spirit's illumination. I am thinking of what happened to Luther when he finally grasped the true meaning of Romans and broke with the Roman Catholic synthesis, the both/and, and returned to the Scriptural *sola*.

Furthermore, the *re-formed* believer's preunderstanding, in the above sense of "reformed," must be continually *conformed* to the Word of God. The illumination of the Spirit in the sanctification process is necessary for that to occur. I am thinking of the subtle types of synthesis that frequently overpower Christians in advanced education and university study. Every synthesis of Christianity with Aristotle, Plato, Common Sense philosophy, idealism, existentialism, process thought, or any other type of non-Christian thought, must be eradicated so that the Christian preunderstanding will fully conform to the Word of God. The Spirit's organic illumination "by and with the Word" is indispensable in conforming one's preunderstanding to Scripture. Only from such preunderstanding can faithful biblical understanding result in real sanctification.

The preunderstanding of twentieth century secular man, as the preunderstanding of secular man in any century, must be fully eradicated; one's preunderstanding must be wholly conformed to the Word of God. A "fusion of horizons" in Gadamer's sense is unacceptable since it means that the understanding of the Bible results from a synthesis between Scripture's horizon and the interpreter's horizon. The biblical message is not truly grasped as a synthesis in a dialogical relation between modern man and the Bible. Every interpreter, including the true Christian, must be alert, however, to the constant danger of a "fusion of horizons" that results even if one unwittingly reads Scripture through the spectacles of the *Zeitgeist*. Scripture must be interpreted through the spectacles of Scripture; the preunderstanding with which the interpreter approaches Scripture must wholly conform to Scripture. This hermeneutic circle must be consciously embraced.

X. ILLUMINATION, PREUNDERSTANDING, AND THE TEXT

The preunderstanding that wholly conforms to the Scripture does not automatically render the genuine meaning of a particular text or passage of Scripture. Of course, it is a tremendous aid, indispensable, as has been noted earlier. The lover understands the letter while an outsider is baffled by it. Scripture is a rich mine whose treasures are never exhausted, and many passages call for great effort in order to understand them.

The Reformation doctrine of the perspicuity of Scripture may not be appealed to as an excuse to avoid the diligence required for faithful biblical interpretation. What it does exclude is a special priesthood or hierarchy; it places the responsibility for understanding Scripture upon every believer—the priesthood of all believers.

The need for organic illumination within the interpretative process is therefore of great significance. The faithful interpretation of Scripture continues to be a task with awesome responsibility. Individual believers can, of course, receive great assistance from the believing community (Acts 15). The Holy Spirit works in individual persons, but His work is not individualistic. As the administrative agent of the ascended Christ, the Holy Spirit gathers the church as the body of Christ. The Spirit's illumination may be expected therefore within the believing community and in the community of believing scholars as well. Christian scholars and professional exegetes can serve the believing community in very significant ways (cf. #14-16 below). Yet the responsibility of every believer before the Word of God remains. The process of sanctification calls for continued personal study of Scripture so that all of faith and life may truly be formed by the authoritative Scripture.

XI. ILLUMINATION AND AUTHENTIC BIBLICAL INTERPRETATION

How does an authentic preunderstanding function with the Spirit's organic illumination in biblical interpretation? Only a few examples can be given, but they are important ones.

Faithful interpretation of Scripture should proceed from the conviction that the Bible is God's revelation to us. The result of rejecting that biblical claim is clearly evident in liberal and other theologies. Presuppositions proved decisive! Furthermore, Scripture claims to be God-breathed, inspired by the Holy Spirit. When interpretation proceeds from the assumption that Scripture is simply a human product, misinterpretation and misunderstanding inevitably follow. The Spirit worked organically in the human authors of Scripture; if biblical interpretation proceeds from the assumption that human authors were not involved in the production of Scripture, misunderstanding and misinterpretation are sure to follow also. That is why grammatical-historical interpretation is required to get at Scripture's intended meaning.

To separate divine authorship from the human instrumentality or vice versa, is to misinterpret and misunderstand Scripture. Scripture did not drop ready-made from heaven; it is a Spirit-produced, humanly written, linguistically qualified historically-conditioned Book. The organic illumination of the Holy Spirit cannot be expected to function if these factors in the Spirit's inspiration of Scripture are ignored or denied.

Interpretation aimed at promoting heart-understanding must also proceed in accord with Scripture's claim to be a reliable, trustworthy (non-deceiving, non-falsifying, non-fallible, inerrant) revelation of the living, triune God. Christ and His apostles showed that attitude toward the Old Testament. Scripture claims that trustworthiness for itself in its entirety as well as in its parts, even to the words in their respective contexts. Today's interpreter should approach Scripture with the expectation of its trustworthiness. On this score one will not be disappointed or deceived, even when unable to resolve all difficulties of interpretation. Within that context one may expect the Spirit's illumination to guide the human interpreter in his interpretative struggle.

These are a few illustrations of how crucial authentic preunderstanding is in faithful scriptural interpretation. Several others could be mentioned such as the unity of Scripture, progressive revelation, the redemptive focus, and others. Space limitation does not permit elaboration, however. Hopefully the illustrations are adequately suggestive of the issue.

XII. ILLUMINATION AND THE WHOLE AND THE PARTS

There is another sense in which a hermeneutic circle confronts the interpreter (cf. #9 above). All parts of Scripture are needed to understand the whole, yet the parts are only understood in the light of the whole. The relation of the whole and the parts is undoubtedly true of most writings. In Scripture this relation is unique because the parts came from many human authors in a progressive revelation spanning centuries. Inspired by one Spirit, however, the parts contribute to a single message.

Sections of Scripture are correctly interpreted and understood only in the light of the whole, and the whole of Scripture is understood from the proper understanding of each of the parts. The one cannot be done without the other. Yet one cannot understand the whole without taking the time needed for studying all its parts. Growth in biblical understanding is a long process, part of the ongoing sanctification process—lifelong and never completed. God's Word is a rich mine whose depths are never fully plumbed.

This relation of the whole and the parts has been referred to as the *analogia Scripturae*, the analogy of Scripture. One must take into account what other passages say on the subject of a particular text. Another way of saying that is that Scripture must interpret Scripture; Scripture is the "spectacles" through which to read Scripture. The New Testament requires the Old for proper understanding; the Old Testament needs the New for its faithful interpretation. The illumination of the Holy Spirit can only be expected within that organic context of the interpreter's use of the whole and its parts, the parts and the whole.

This implies that the *sola Scriptura* emphasis of the reformers requires the correlation of *tota Scriptura*; if the whole of Scripture is not taken into account, the danger arises of a canon within the canon. Until one has made substantial progress in understanding Scripture, there is great danger of working with a narrow canon. Even after much biblical study that danger continues.

Any hermeneutical principle that isolates a canon within the canon is illegitimate and Spirit-mocking. The entire Scripture is God-breathed and "useful for teaching, rebuking, correcting and training in righteousness, so that the man of God may be thoroughly equipped for every good work" (2 Tim. 3:16-17). Whether that restricted canon is Luther's initial "*was Cristum treibet*" or "existential self-understanding" or "saving" content in distinction from "non-saving" content, or something else, the inevitable results is to barricade proper understanding. All Scripture witnesses to Christ, and all Scripture is God's authoritative revelation. The Spirit's organic illumination functions in correlation with the whole Scripture and all its parts.

XIII. HEART-UNDERSTANDING AND LIFE *(APPLICATIO)*

The aim of Spirit-illumined interpretation of Scripture should be heart-understanding. The goal of heart-understanding is the worship of God, and the service of God and fellowman with one's whole heart in all of life in the whole world. In short, heart-understanding is kingdom oriented!

We have already noted that intellectual understanding is not the sole end of the interpretative process. More than intellectual curiosity and gratification is involved, although the wisdom of God is truly satisfying and exhilaration accompanies new insight. Heart-understanding leads to confession and a life which advances Christ's church and promotes God's kingdom. Rebirth enables a believer to see the kingdom (John 3:3) and therefore to "seek first His kingdom and His righteousness" in obedience to Christ's command (Matt. 6:33).

The kingdom life of obedience directed by the faithfully interpreted Scripture may not exclude any facet of one's life. Academic life, the pursuit of science, ought also to be pursued from heart-understanding of the Spirit-illumined Scripture. The ongoing process of sanctification should not be taken in a narrow individualistic and pietistic sense; genuine sanctification should increasingly contribute to kingdom service in obedience to the Messianic King. Here too, God's gift calls forth man's task!

XIV. SPIRIT GIFTED INTERPRETERS

Some people have special responsibility in biblical interpretation because of special gifts of the Spirit. I am thinking primarily of the gifts mentioned in Ephesians 4—apostles, prophets, evangelists, pastors, and teachers. Those gifted and appointed to these offices are specially qualified by the Spirit of the ascended Christ; the interpretation of Scripture is a significant responsibility of such persons. For that purpose special training is generally required, including knowledge of Scripture's original languages and skill in interpreting Scripture.

In view of the professional character of such workers and the specialized skills they are expected to possess, I prefer to speak here of "scientific exegesis" of Scripture. As noted earlier, the same factors are involved as in all biblical interpretation. This is simply a specialized species within a common genus. Hence the preceding thirteen points are applicable also here. The main difference is that disciplined interpretation becomes a professional activity pursued in more analytical ways. Heart-understanding should also be the goal of the exegete. The illumination of the Holy Spirit functions in an organic way also in such scientific interpreters. The Spirit's illumination is no more guaranteed the professional exegete than the ordinary believer. Word and Spirit are correlative, but the Spirit remains sovereign over His inspired Word.

Scientific exegetes and professional biblical commentators ought to function in a servant-role within the believing community. They are not a professional priesthood with the only keys to correct biblical interpretation. For "pastors and teachers" the interpretative function will largely serve preaching and pastoral duties. The goal, according to Paul, must be "to prepare God's people for works of service, so that the body of Christ may be built up until we all reach unity in the faith and in the knowledge of the Son of God and become mature, attaining the full measure of perfection found in Christ" (Eph. 4:12-13).

When thus employed, such Spirit-gifted interpreters can be of tremendous service to the entire believing community. Yet every believer retains a personal responsibility before God for rightly interpreting the infallible Word; therefore the Berean attitude is always proper (Acts 17:11). Whether the scientific exegete has truly been illumined by the Spirit in his interpretation of Scripture can be judged only by the Spirit-illumined examination of the text of Scripture itself!

XV. INTERPRETATION AND SCIENTIFIC EXEGESIS

Scientific activity always presupposes the everyday experience of pre-theoretical thought. Scientific activity is never presuppositionless. Science is a specific kind of activity, but it is not of a higher order. Theological science does not attain a higher or truer knowledge than the ordinary believer does. Hence scientific exegesis, as a distinct theological activity, is not lord of correct interpretation. Yet, when it is obediently pursued, it can be of great service to the body of believers and to the world at large.

Scientific exegesis is not restricted to trained theologians. Although exegesis is always a rigorous activity, non-theologians can also pursue it when they engage in disciplined Bible study, using lexicons, dictionaries, commentaries and similar aids.

There is no presuppositionless exegesis; here too not all presuppositions are valid. One readily discovers this when several different kinds of commentaries are consulted. Faithful exegesis requires the preunderstanding that Scripture itself demands. Scripture is its own interpreter; that is also true for the professional exegete. The whole is to be understood in the light of its parts, and the parts must be seen in the light of the whole. The findings of other sciences may become the occasion for reviewing a standard interpretation of Scripture, but science may never control or dictate the interpretation of Scripture. Scripture must be its own interpreter and the Spirit-illumined understanding is needed for the faithful discernment of its meaning, the meaning which contributes to heart-understanding.

XVI. GRAMMATICAL-LITERARY-HISTORICAL-THEOLOGICAL-CANONICAL EXEGESIS

The illumination of the Holy Spirit is also urgently needed in the scientific exegesis of Scripture. The Spirit's illumination can be expected to function organically "by and with the Word" in the context of the following exegetical procedures.

Scripture is verbal and lingual; it is God's Word written. Hence exegesis must interpret and understand the words in their sentences, and the sentences in their contexts. The sentences are parts of a literary composition, and Scripture contains various literary types. Hence grammatical-literary exegesis is required in interpreting Scripture.

The words of Scripture report, interpret, reveal, and proclaim what God has done in history for man's creation and redemption, for the establishment of His covenants, for the building of Christ's church, and the establishment of God's kingdom. Scripture reveals the good *news*; it is concerned with historical events. The biblical texts are also set in an historical context and correct interpretation requires understanding Scripture in its original historical context. Hence historical exegesis is needed.

Scripture presents a message, a message from God and about God-triune. Exegesis must seek to understand this theocentric message. All the lingual expressions of revelation are partial and occasional. The exegete must attempt to understand the total message to which the various parts contribute. The message of the entire canon must be understood from an interpretation of the meaning of each of the individual books. Hence exegesis must be theological-canonical exegesis.

Each and all of these exegetical procedures must be combined so that interpretation may result in heart-understanding of the total message of all Scripture. Because Scripture is Spirit-inspired, the authoritative Word of God which the natural man cannot understand, all of the Spirit's activities previously enumerated—regeneration, internal testimony, organic illumination, sanctification—all are equally needed when one engages in the scientific exegesis of Scripture. The preunderstanding that conforms to Scripture is needed if the illumination of the Spirit is to be expected in discovering the riches of the Word of God.

CONCLUSION

The attempt to describe the relationship of illumination to the interpretative process, the initial assignment for this paper, forced me to consider the role of the Holy Spirit in the hermeneutic process. The biblical materials indicate that the Spirit's illumination is multifaceted: illumination occurs in a radical way in the miracle of regeneration; it contributes to the believer's acknowledgment of the inherent authority of Scripture; it is essential to faithful biblical interpretation within the life of sanctification. The indwelling Spirit guides the believer in organic ways in the sanctified life and in the continual biblical interpretation strategically significant for the kingdom life. Heart-understanding is both the result of and the goal of authentic biblical interpretation; the whole person is involved—intellect, will, and emotion. I pointed briefly to scientific exegesis as a specialized form of biblical interpretation.

A precise definition of illumination does not seem possible. Illumination, as the other works of the Spirit, are not empirically discernable as such, only the fruits of the Spirit's works are observable. The illumination of the Spirit may be requested in prayer and confessed as reality, but it cannot be empirically demonstrated or rationally proven. Yet the presence of the Spirit's illumination must be tested, Berean fashion, by the text of the inspired Scripture itself. And the test itself requires the illumination of the same Spirit. That is the standard by which this paper wants to be tested.

Calvin's words on the *testimonium* provide a fitting conclusion for this paper on illumination: "I speak of nothing other than what each believer experiences within himself—though my words fall far beneath a just explanation of the matter."[24]

NOTES

[1]Discussion of "the internal testimony" is generally more common and more extensive than of "illumination." A longer discussion of illumination by an older writer is that of J. Owen, *Works* (Edinburgh: T. & T. Clark, 1862), Vol. 4, pp. 118-234. R. L. Saucy is a recent writer who devotes more attention to illumination than most writers. See *The Bible: Breathed from God* (Wheaton: Victor Books, 1978), pp. 103-12.

[2]The sixteen points that follow are not parallel. All the subsequent points are actually subordinate to the first. Those following the third point are subordinate to it; those following number six again are subordinate to it. The discussion of "scientific exegesis" in the last three points, presuppose all the preceding ones. *All biblical quotations are from the NIV.*

[3]The 1978 ICBI "Chicago Statement on Biblical Inerrancy," #8.

[4]The Heidelberg Catechsim, Question 51. The translation is the official translation of the Christian Reformed Church adopted in 1975.

[5]Ibid., Question 53.

[6]Ibid., Question 31; cf. 49 and 50.

[7]The felicitous expression from the Westminster Confession I, 5, used repeatedly below as well.

[8]J. Calvin, *Institutes of the Christian Religion*, ed. J. T. McNeill, trs. F. L. Battles (Philadelphia: Westminster Press, 1960) [Library of Christian Classics, Vols. 20 and 21], 1.9.3.

[9]Ibid., 1.7.4.

[10]Ibid., 1.7.5.

[11]I am not persuaded by the exegesis of this passage which separates faith as trust from knowledge. See, e.g., D. Fuller in *Scripture, Tradition, and Interpretation*, eds. W. W. Gasque and W. S. LaSor, (Grand Rapids, Eerdmans, 1978), pp. 190-93.

[12]4154 edition in T. F. Torrance, *The School of Faith* (London: J. Clarke, 1959), p. 23. Cf. also Westminster Larger Catechism, Question 67.

[13]*Institutes*, 1.7 Cf. also 1.8; 1.9; as well as 2.1-4 and 6; 3:1-3.

[14]Short Statement, #3.

[15]1.7.4.

[16]1.9.3.

[17]1.7.5.

[18]1.7.5.

[19]Geneva Catechism in T. F. Torrance, op. cit., Question 302.

[20]See the Chicago Statement, "Preface," and "Short Statement," #2 and #3.

[21]This and the following points are to be understood as further elaboration of the Spirit's illumination in the process of sanctification (cf. #6).

[22]Parts of the following sections are adapted from an earlier paper, "Toward a Reformed Hermeneutic," *Theological Bulletin* of the Reformed Ecumenical Synod, Vol. 2, No. 1 (May, 1974).

[23]1.6.1.

[24]1.7.5.

A Response to The Role of the Holy Spirit in the Hermeneutic Process

Wilber T. Dayton
Professor of Biblical Literature and Historical Theology and Vice President in Planning
Wesleyan Biblical Seminary

A Response to The Role of the Holy Spirit in the Hermeneutic Process

Wilber T. Dayton

It is a pleasure, indeed, to express essential agreement with and enthusiasm for Dr. Klooster's paper. Such a response reflects the conviction that there is a fundamental unity among Bible-centered Evangelicals that goes deeper than theological labels and loyalties. Some philosophical and theological frameworks in which beliefs are cast might cause some to despair of unity, to say nothing of agreement, in as sensitive an area as the Spirit's illumination in the matter of biblical interpretation, either in the case of the professional scholar or of the layman. But obedience to the Word of God and to the Spirit of God, through whom it was given, makes it possible to give priority to the truth as revealed. Faithfulness to the Word is the prior demand. Any accommodation, if required, will have to be in the human framework and systems. The faithful Christian will not try to change the revealed Word.

It has been the experience of many to discover that vital Christians agree much more than they disagree. And the areas in which they agree are vastly more important than those in which they disagree. This, in large measure accounts for the lifelong love and respect that existed between John Wesley and George Whitefield, in spite of radically different positions on certain issues. They believed in each other's life and ministry. The same situation exists in the ICBI, in Evangelical seminaries, and in the various bodies of Bible Christians today.

No doubt, it was with this in mind that the assignments were made for respondents to Dr. Klooster's paper. Though a Wesleyan would sometimes speak a different language and come to the subject with different frames of reference, it is enriching, instead of debilitating, to meet at the Word of God and to find life as the Spirit of God illuminates the heart and applies the printed page to our needs.

The enthusiasm for this unity is no call for disloyalty to any tradition, with the divergent understandings of many things. It is simply to rejoice that we can all be "taught of God" by his Word as we are illuminated through the Spirit, whether through traditional interpretations or in spite of them. For the sake of clarity, it is well to recognize a few of these differences for their general relevance as well as at later points in the response. But our main thrust will be on the common heritage rather than on the differences.

It is well known that many in the Calvinian tradition give a great deal of attention to scholarly and technical formulations that lend to systematic presentation. John Wesley and the early Wesleyans disliked debate and, when possible without being unfaithful to the truth as they saw it, avoided formal statements that they feared might dull the message to a needy world. Wesley said:

> I design plain truth for plain people: Therefore, of set purpose, I abstain from all nice and philosophic speculations; from all perplexed and intricate reasonings; and, as far as possible, from even the show of learning, unless in sometimes citing the original Scriptures. I labor to avoid all words which are not in common life; and, in particular, those kinds of technical terms that so frequently occur in Bodies of Divinity; those modes of speaking which men of reading are intimately acquainted with, but which to common people are an unknown tongue.[1]

Oxford scholar and linguist that he was, he conceived of his task as an evangelist in the language of his hearers. With all due respect and enthusiasm for the scholarly and exact statements of Dr. Klooster's paper, it should be pointed out that Wesley and the Wesleyans say many of the same things in words that are simpler to some people. Seeming differences are often in semantics.

There are, of course, doctrines of substance that cast a shadow of difference worthy of note. Were it not for the basic unity already affirmed, there could be confusion over different theological understandings of the work of the Spirit in relation to regeneration. To Dr. Klooster, regeneration seems to be the beginning of true knowledge illuminated by the Holy Spirit. Wesley and most Wesleyans also emphasize the work of the Holy Spirit in "prevenient grace" that leads to repentance, faith, and regeneration. Likewise, Dr. Klooster treats sanctification almost exclusively as a process. Wesley had much to say of a crisis aspect. Again, there is a different tradition behind Calvin's Latin word *testimonium* and Wesley's "assurance." While time and purpose will not always permit one to expound the effect of these differences, attention will focus on the way the Wesleyan tradition witnesses to the same confidence in the Word of God as the heart and mind are illuminated by the Holy Spirit.

In using simple language, Wesley exposed himself to those who would twist his words and change his message. On the other hand, he cut past the "nice speculations" and challenged his hearers with the simple gospel call—a message that could be driven home by the Holy Spirit. In a brief but familiar account, Wesley reveals his strong commitment to the Word of God, his hermeneutical method, his dependence upon the Holy Spirit's illumination, his confidence in both the clarity and profundity (perspicuity) of the Word, and the help that can be found from God and man in handling difficult passages. In many respects this account is so nearly parallel to Dr. Klooster's paper that it could almost be a layman's resume of much that was said in the paper, or the paper could be a scholarly interpretation of the principles put forward by Wesley. The statement of Wesley will be quoted for its general relevance here and can be kept in mind later in connection with Dr. Klooster's outline. Wesley says:

> To candid reasonable men, I am not afraid to lay open what have been the inmost thoughts of my heart. I have thought, I am a creature of a day, passing through life as an arrow through the air. I am a spirit come from God, and returning to God: just hovering over the great gulf; till, a few moments hence, I am no more seen; I drop into an unchangeable eternity! I want to know one thing—the way to heaven; how to land safe on that happy shore. God Himself was condescended to teach the way; for this very end He came from heaven. He hath written it down in a book. O give me that book! At any price, give me the book of God! I have it: here is knowledge enough for me. Let me be *homo unius libri*. Here then I am, far from the busy ways of men. I sit down alone: only God is here. In His presence I open, I read His book; for this end, to find the way to heaven. Is there a doubt concerning the meaning of what I read? Does anything appear dark or intricate? I lift up my heart to the Father of Lights: "Lord, is it not thy word, 'If any man lack wisdom, let him ask of God'? Thou hast said, 'If any be willing to do Thy will, he shall know.' I am willing to do, let me know, Thy will." I then search after and consider parallel passages of Scripture, "comparing spiritual things with spiritual." I meditate thereon with all the attention and earnestness of which my mind is capable. If any doubt still remains, I consult those who are

> experienced in the things of God; and then the writings whereby, being dead, they yet speak. And what I thus learn, that I teach.[2]

It is immediately clear that Wesley's goal is parallel to Dr. Klooster's in that he is primarily "concerned with the interpretation of Scripture which every believer must pursue" (Klooster, p. 452). He also refused to allow any special category of erudition or "scientific exegesis" as exempt from the humble quest of a heart-understanding of God's will and a full purpose to obey. This goes far to explain the almost complete way that Wesley and the early Wesleyans ignored the "assured results" of negative biblical criticism. They did not accept the credentials of the critics.

With these background observations, attention will be turned to a Wesleyan interaction with Dr. Klooster's Sixteen Points on the relationship of the Spirit's illumination to biblical interpretation.

I. Wesley's starting point and constant assurance was also "the Spirit-inspired authoritative Scripture." "That book" stands forever as the Word of God. Without it, we are lost. With it, we have "the way to heaven." Wesley seldom, if ever, gave meticulous description of the process of inspiration, but he yielded no ground on the result. It was the Word of God without defect[3] or error.[4] This presupposition is implicit throughout and comes into vigorous expression from time to time.

II. Dr. Klooster's presentation of the "pneumatically Christological theocentric message of Scripture" is a scholarly explanation of the understanding of the gospel that sparked the Evangelical Revival in England and most other moves back to God. Wesley agreed in theory long before his "Aldersgate experience." Then, with a burning heart, he was used by the Spirit of God to proclaim the authoritative Word to others. Christ was, of course, the central message, as the perfect revelation of God and of His salvation. The authority of the whole process was revelation. The Triune God, through the Holy Spirit, speaks in and through the written Word to reveal Himself in His saving love and grace. Any dilution of this message slips, sooner or later, into a sterile humanism. The Christology of Luther and the soteriology of Wesley are not alternatives over against an infallible Scripture, as many imply. Certainty in matters of faith and practice does not require a limited inspiration or limited infallibility. It tends, rather, to indicate a totally trustworthy and truthful Word of God as the foundation for confidence in the saving message. Herein is the credibility of the concept that the "Spirit of truth" (John 16:13) takes the Word that is truth (John 17:17) and proclaims the truth that is in Christ (Eph. 4:21) to bring us to the only true God (John 17:3). Anything less is sterile and futile.

III. The correlations of Spirit and Christ, and Spirit and Word are fundamental to biblical theology and certainly to dynamic Evangelicalism. What Christ did for us, the Spirit makes vital and effective in us. Neither, without the other, would accomplish the Divine purpose in our salvation. And, without an authentic and tangible record in the Word, it would be hard to conceive of a way to disseminate a firm knowledge of the truth that is in Christ. The only solution must be that the Spirit speaks mediately through the written Word and then works immediately upon the human heart and mind, illuminating the person with the light of the gospel message. Thus Christ is revealed to us by the Spirit both mediately through the Word, and immediately as an indwelling Sovereign Spirit.

IV. Illumination by the Spirit must, indeed, be related to regeneration. Apart from grace, man is both dead and blind. It is the entrance of God's words that give light (Ps. 119:130) at whatever point human experience is touched. It is interesting to observe the presence and operation of the Holy Spirit throughout the Scriptures in connection with creation, redemption, healing, regeneration, sanctification, and the Christian life. It is also striking that God "spoke" the worlds into being. Jesus generally performed His miracles with a "word". The "word of the Lord came" or "the Spirit spoke" throughout the Scriptures. A unique feature of Scripture revelation is that the God who acts is also the God who speaks and gives meaning to the act. So, regeneration is not just a new sense of well-being. The Spirit, who raises us from spiritual death to regenerated life (Eph. 2:1), also "enlightens the eyes of our understanding" (Eph. 1:18) so that we can have some comprehension of the significance of what God has done. Regeneration is more than feeling. It brings light and life to the depths of our being.

Dr. Klooster is probably wise not to obscure this fact by undue attention to "the chronology of the Spirit's activity in this process" (p. 453). He rightly insists on "the chronological priority of the Spirit-inspired Scripture to our interpretation, and on the logical priority of the Spirit's regeneration to the other soteriological activities in the believer" (p. 453). A Wesleyan view of the matter would only make a less sharp distinction between the work of the Spirit in prevenient grace prior to regeneration and regeneration itself, together with the soteriological activities that accompany and follow it. The importance of this distinction hinges on the place of human choice and responsibility in "meeting the conditions" of the sovereign acts of God. In any case, Dr. Klooster is right that "rebirth, renewal of the heart in regeneration, is the most radical form of illumination one experiences" (p. 457).

V. The "internal testimony of the Holy Spirit," as explained by Dr. Klooster (p. 457) and in the Chicago Statement is, no doubt, a central aspect in the Spirit's illumination. Implicitly or explicitly, it must lie behind the strong confessions and bold stands of the early church, the Reformers, Reformed theology, the Wesleyan Revival, and such other renewals as have come to the church. As it pertains to Wesley, at least, there is a chronological problem and possibly a theological one. Wesley seems to have had this kind of assurance about the Scriptures long before the personal "witness" to his own salvation. As a good Anglican, in 1729, Wesley "began not only to read, but to study, the Bible, as the one, the only standard of truth, and the only model of pure religion."[5] This was nine years before his assurance of salvation at a chapel on Aldersgate Street in London. It may not be necessary to inquire how deep and how clear this early assurance about the Scriptures was or whether the illumination was a part of prevenient grace as distinct from regeneration. But in the Wesleyan tradition, the validity and authority of the Scripture was taken for granted as a Divine certainty. It is more common for Wesleyans to use the term "witness of the Spirit" with reference to one's own assurance of salvation. Wesley described his experience as:

> I felt I did trust in Christ, Christ alone for salvation: And an assurance was given me, that He had taken away my sins, even mine and saved from the law of sin and death.[6]

Before this Wesley was sure that God had spoken through the Spirit and the Word. The Word was a message of salvation. But on May 24, 1738, God, through the Spirit and the Word spoke peace to his own troubled soul. In October, 1738, Wesley further distinguished between an assurance of present pardon, which he claimed, and an assurance of final perseverance, which he did not claim.[7] The assurance which "was given," it is safe to assume, was, in any case, an illumination of the Holy Spirit and in the form of an "internal testimony." Wesley had long searched, reasoned, and debated. Finally, to put it in Dr. Klooster's words, there was a "certainty resting in the whole heart," "a conviction that requires no reasons," "a knowledge with which the best reason agrees," "a repose of mind more secure and constant than in any reasons," and a feeling that can be born only of heavenly revelation" (p. 459). In any case, the Holy Spirit gave him "joy and peace in believing" (Rom. 15:13). The *testimonium* to the Word which Calvin received may not be identical to the "witness of the Spirit" to salvation which Wesley received, but they must both be a part of the Spirit's illumination to a needy soul.

VI. The Spirit's illumination is certainly essential to sanctification whether one, as Calvin, emphasizes the lifelong process or, as Wesley, gives special attention to a crisis in which issues of purity and power come into focus through a special work of the Holy Spirit (Acts 1:8; 15:9). Those who hold to the latter concept tend to call the process one of growth in grace to avoid confusing it with crisis experience. But, whatever the nomenclature and chronology, the point is well taken. One is sanctified through the truth (John 17:17). God's Word, the instrument (or organ), must communicate through the illumination of the Divine Spirit to the human spirit for us to receive the intended benefits. Only thus can we have "the mind of Christ."

VII. The term "organic illumination" puts in balance concepts that are too often confused. Certainly sloth and inactivity on the part of man will no more receive the Spirit's illumination than human laziness would have produced the inspired Scriptures. Faith without works (human response and effort) is dead (Jas. 2:26). It is no faith at all. The biblical interpreter cannot wait for lightning bolts to hit him. He must study, read, and struggle to be in a position to receive the Spirit's illumination. It is not enough to open one's mouth and expect God to fill it at 11:00 o'clock on Sunday morning.

The opposite error, of course, must be avoided. Many are quoting Barth to say that inspiration is not complete until the writings are preserved, read, and preached to me. The distinction between "organic inspiration" and "organic illumination" should help prevent this confusion. A definite and completed act (or series of acts) produced the Scriptures that "stand written." A multitude of Divine providences (along with human heroism) preserved the documents. Now the Spirit illumines and quickens my mind and heart to receive the message in a vital heart-knowledge. Three distinct steps are evident. God took the initiative in each. And man is actively involved in each. When the Spirit illuminates my heart, it is no new special revelation. It is only the application to me of the revelation made long ago.

VIII. Heart-understanding is the very crux of the matter. Historical and geographical studies tell much about gospel events. But nothing short of the Spirit's illumination in regeneration, witness of the Spirit, and sanctification can bring the certainty of heart-knowledge that is fundamental to a sound hermeneutic. The fall of man involved more than a lack of erudition. Sin requires a remedy that is basically a heart-knowledge, received by faith when the Spirit illumines the heart to receive the Word that convicts and changes us.

"Understanding rooted in the heart" does indeed include the whole person. An instructed mind is not enough for sound hermeneutics. The will and emotions are also involved. Spiritual things are spiritually discerned (I Cor. 2:14). One must not only have knowledge; he must be "wise unto salvation" (II Tim. 3:15).

IX. The "hermeneutic circle" is a vital concept. If one has no valid anchor from which to interpret a new thought, chaos results. One must indeed have a preunderstanding of Scripture by faith. Wesleyans, in common parlance, might call it simply "an experience." The Scripture "spectacles" remind one of Wesley's "comparing Scripture with Scripture." The point is well taken that "a sound biblical hermeneutic demands that one approach Scripture with a preunderstanding that is wholly consonant with it" (p. 464). To the extent that one fails at this point, he wastes his time in hermeneutics and may well corrupt many disciples. History is full of examples.

X. Perspicuity, or clarity, of the Scriptures does not, indeed, answer all questions. One must dig deep for some gems. Though there is a place for a community of believing scholars, no individual of the believing community is exempt from personal illuminated study of the Word for his own needs and for others.

XI. Dr. Klooster makes a necessary point when he shows the devastation caused by misleading presuppositions. Authentic biblical interpretation cannot be made on a document that is mutilated by rejection of the biblical claims as to source. trustworthiness, and the like. The Spirit will not illumine the heart in the study of a document that is not believed.

XII. The "analogy of Scripture" is a strong point. To "harmonize" Scriptures is not an abuse of hermeneutics. Only as one believes the truth of each part and of the whole can he possibly grasp the message that the one true God has given through His Spirit. And to disallow the authenticity of any part is to break the authority of the whole.

XIII. Heart-understanding necessarily implies application to life. Otherwise, the knowledge is at most intellectual. The faith which becomes heart-acceptance is aimed toward obedience and action. Disobedient interpreters are no more reliable than Balaam, the son of Beor.

XIV. Dr. Klooster's treatment of Spirit-gifted interpreters is helpful. The gifts and appointments come from God but not to the exclusion of abundant human labor. Gifted ones are not a special class above the rules that apply to others. They are not infallible. They are called to be servants and, if they fill their part well, they can render tremendous service. Or they can do great harm.

XV. "Scientific exegesis," too, has no monopoly on truth. By wrong presuppositions it can fail where faithful amateurs succeed, if the latter use the resources available. "Scripture is its own interpreter" and, as Dr. Klooster says, "the Spirit-illumined understanding is needed for the faithful discernment of its meaning."

XVI. No "scientific exegesis" is sufficient without the illumination of the Spirit. But the Spirit's illumination "can be expected to function organically by and with the Word" when correct use is made of legitimate exegetical procedures. There is indeed a legitimate concern for the grammatical, literary, historical, theological and canonical considerations. When these are properly used in submission to the Spirit-illumination under the conditions described in Dr. Klooster's Sixteen Points, one does indeed discover the riches of the Word of God.

CONCLUSION

I can only agree with Dr. Klooster's conclusion. The multi-faceted Spirit's illumination occurs radically in regeneration, contributes to the believer's acknowledgment of the inherent authority of Scripture, is essential to faith biblical interpretation in the life of sanctification, and guides the believer in the continual biblical interpretation. Though not empirically demonstrated or rationally proved, it is seen in the fruits of the Spirit's work. "Yet the presence of the Spirit's illumination must be tested, Berean fashion, by the text of the inspired Scripture itself." This again is "Beyond the Battle for the Bible." The answer to the present debate is not retreat from faith but a grounding in the presuppositions of faith and the courage to draw life from the Spirit-inspired Word interpreted under the illumination of the same Spirit.

NOTES

[1]*Works*, 5:2, (14 Vol., Zondervan Reprint).
[2]Ibid., 5:2-4.
[3]*Explanatory Notes Upon the New Testament*, p. 10.
[4]*Journal*, 6:117.
[5]*Works*, 11:367.
[6]Ibid., 1:103.
[7]Ibid., 1:160.

A Response to The Role of the Holy Spirit in the Hermeneutic Process

Arthur W. Lindsley
Director of Educational Ministries
Ligonier Valley Study Center

A Response to The Role of the Holy Spirit in the Hermeneutic Process

Art Lindsley

Dr. Klooster has done an admirable job of relating the illumination of the Holy Spirit to a wide variety of subjects. It would not be possible to respond to all sixteen points. I have chosen to add a few comments on heart-understanding and application (points VIII and XIII.) I also wish to underline the importance of the illumination of the Holy Spirit for this conference.

As Dr. Klooster mentions, a detailed discussion of the illumination of the Holy Spirit is rare in theological literature. It is even more rare in modern hermeneutics than it is in earlier writings.[1] Modern hermeneutics has become a sophisticated field. In the midst of all the discussion of methodology it is easy to lose sight of the Holy Spirit's role in interpretation. The Holy Spirit's work has not been given the prominence it deserves.

Perhaps we can learn from earlier ages in this regard. C. S. Lewis says that each age has its blind spots. It is important to continually allow the "breezes of the centuries" to blow through our minds. Thus we can get a clearer perspective on our own time. Included in the following discussion are quotes from a number of writers from earlier ages. We might ask ourselves if their emphasis should be ours.

I. IMPORTANCE OF THE SPIRIT'S ILLUMINATION

Over and over again in church history, theologians have stressed that there is no full understanding of Scripture without the Spirit's light. The teacher may teach and the student not learn. We may preach and the message not get through to our hearers. Augustine recognized this:

> . . . behold, brethren, this great mystery the sound of our words strike the ear; but the teacher is within.[2]

If we are to know the truth of Christ, the Spirit must be the one to convey it to us. Theophylact says:

> Since it is when made intelligible and opened by the Holy Spirit, that the Scriptures show us Christ, probably the porter is the Holy Spirit.[3]

The Holy Spirit is the "porter" not only of the truths of the person and work of Christ, but of all the truths of Scripture. John Owen maintains that the "primary efficient cause"[4] of our understanding of the Scripture is the Holy Ghost of God alone. When Owen gives rules for the right understanding of Scripture, the first is prayer and meditation.

This is not to say that Owen or other earlier writers neglected the use of means such as the study of languages, commentaries, and rules of interpretation.[5] However, they did so highly value the spiritual understanding of Scripture that they gave it great emphasis. Jonathan Edwards speaks of this spiritual understanding as the highest gift God can give:

> Spiritual wisdom and grace is the highest and most excellent gift that God ever bestows on any creature: in this the highest excellency of a rational creature consists.[6]

II. SENSE OF BEAUTY AND EXCELLENCE

We could listen to this emphatic language and ask, "What does the illumination of the Spirit add to our understanding? If there is only one literal sense to Scripture, couldn't this be discovered by any objective study of the text? Couldn't a non-Christian arrive at a proper understanding of a text?" The answer is "yes" and "no." Throughout church history there has been a distinction between having a true opinion about a text and having the full sense of that which it signifies. It is possible to grasp an idea with the mind but not to have a deep sense of its truth, goodness, or beauty. The Holy Spirit helps us to sense the beauty and excellency of Scripture. Calvin says:

> . . . illuminated by Him, the mind receives as it were new keenness for the contemplation of heavenly mysteries . . . Thus the human intellect irradiated by the light of the Holy Spirit begins to have a taste for those things which pertain to the Kingdom of God.[7]

Prior to this illumination the splendor of God's truth had been blunted. The mind was "too stupid and senseless"[8] to have any relish for them. As a result of this illumination the mind has a new keenness and a new taste for truth revealed in Scripture.

The Holy Spirit does not add any new words, propositions, or doctrines to the Scripture. Illumination drives home in the heart what the mind grasps. Edwards maintains:

> This spiritual light is not the suggesting of new truth, or propositions not contained in the word of God. . . . It reveals no new doctrine, it suggests no new propositions to the mind, it teaches no new thing of God, or Christ or another world, not taught in the Bible, but only gives a due apprehension of those things that are taught in the word of God.[9]

This new sense is a feeling of the "divine and superlative excellency of the things of religion."[10] For instance, God's holiness is not only understood to be good, but it is felt to be excellent. The Spirit drives home in the heart and conscience what the mind understands.

Although non-believers can have an understanding of individual texts, it is difficult for them to see how they relate to each other. Edwards maintains that the Holy Spirit helps the believer to understand more clearly the mutual relations of truths. The Holy Spirit's illumination gives us a more lively sense of ideas by engaging:

> . . . the attention of the mind with more fixedness and intenseness to that kind of object, which causes it to have a clearer view of them and enables it more clearly to see their mutual relations, and occasions it to take more notice of them.[11]

In a similar fashion Owen says that without the Spirit's light people are drawn to emphasize the wrong things. Apart from the Spirit people are:

> inclined to all things that are vain, curious, superstitious, carnal, suited unto the interests of pride, lust and all manner of corrupt affections.[12]

He implies that with the Spirit's guidance we are drawn to those things which are profitable.

Both Owen and Edwards emphasize that the Spirit's illumination gives us a sense of the beauty of things that the mind understands. Neither believe that new truth or revelation is given. Yet both believe that the Spirit helps the believer to focus on important truths and to see the proper relationships between them.

III. CONVICTION AND ASSURANCE OF TRUTH

This deep sense of the beauty of God's Word leads to assurance and confidence of its truth. Only the Spirit can give a full assurance of the doctrines we believe. Paul's desire for the Laodiceans and Colossians was that they might come to a "full assurance of understanding" of the truth. (Colossians 2:2). It is of great importance for us to have this assurance. A lack of this confidence inhibits worship, obedience, service to others, and ability to undergo adversity. If this assurance is established the whole of the Christian life falls into place.

There are many difficult truths for us to grasp. We are in the tension between the "already" and "not yet." We are promised many things that we have not fully obtained. Calvin says:

> The Spirit of God shows us hidden things, the knowledge of which cannot reach our senses. Eternal life is promised to us, but it is promised to the dead; we are told of the resurrection of the blessed, but meantime we are involved in corruption; we are declared to be just, and sin dwells within us; we hear that we are blessed, but meantime we are overwhelmed by untold miseries; we are promised an abundance of all good things, but we are often hungry and thirsty; God proclaims that He will come to us immediately, but seems to be deaf to our cries. What would happen to us if we did not rely on our hope, and if our minds did not emerge above the world out of the midst of darkness through the shining Word of God and by His Spirit.[13]

We see here that the Spirit helps us to realize the truth of things that are yet to come and gives us assurance of His presence in perplexing situations.

Above all the Spirit gives us confidence and boldness in the present. Luther in his *Bondage of the Will* argues against Erasmus on the place of assertions in the Christian life. Erasmus is wary of assertions. On the contrary Luther maintains, "Take away assertions and you take away Christianity."[14] The mark of the Christian should be assurance and confidence in believing God's truth. The Christian is one who asserts because the Holy Spirit has given a firm, assured, grasp of the truth. Thus Luther says to Erasmus:

> Leave us free to make assertions and to find in assertions our satisfaction and delight; and you may applaud your skeptics and academics. . . . The Holy Spirit is no skeptic, and the things he has written on our hearts are not doubts or opinions but assertions—surer and more certain than life itself.[15]

The assurance and conviction caused by the Spirit's illumination is to be characteristic of the Christian life. Without this assurance we may feel overwhelmed by problems we encounter. With this assurance our problems seem to be smaller. A firm grasp of God's truth always gives us a clearer perspective on suffering.

IV. APPLICATION TO LIFE

The Spirit is the one who applies God's truth to our lives. The illumination of the Spirit leads us not only to feel the beauty of God's truth but also to the desire to obey it. Theology that leads to true worship inevitably leads to service. If we sense the excellence of God's Word we will desire to apply it. Edwards says:

> . . . this light and this only has its fruit in an universal holiness of life. No merely notional or speculative understanding of the doctrine of religion will ever bring to this. But this light, as it reaches the bottom of the heart changes the nature, so it will effectually dispose to an universal obedience.[16]

Where application of God's truth to the heart and life are highly valued the illumination of the Holy Spirit will also be highly valued. Where application to life is given a small place the illumination of the Spirit will be given a small place. We must keep clearly before us that the goal of inspiration and interpretation is application to life. Hermeneutics safeguards our lives from the effects of error. Correct interpretation leads to an obedient and fulfilled life. Theory always has consequences in practice.

If we value application of God's truth to our heart and life; if we desire a "full assurance of understanding" we will, as Jerome says, "Let reading follow prayer and prayer reading."[17]

During this conference there will be many necessary discussions and debates on hermeneutical methodology and its relation to inerrancy. We need the Spirit's assistance to see the issues clearly. We need His illumination to feel the importance of the issues we face. We need the Spirit's light to keep before us the goal of hermeneutics—correct application to life. Let's not fail to grasp the importance of the subject before us and ask for His light during our time together.

NOTES

[1]I have not found anything in modern writing on hermeneutics that even comes close to the thoroughness of John Owen's work on illumination. It is found in *The Works of John Owen* edited by William H. Goold, Vol. IV; William Whitaker in his *A Disputation on the Holy Scripture*, The University Press, Cambridge, 1588 (reprint 1849) p. 447-73, devotes significant space to this subject. Compare this

with the amount of space devoted to the subject in conservative texts such as Milton Terry *Biblical Hermeneutics*; Bernard Ramm *Protestant Biblical Interpretation;* Louis Berkhof *Principles of Biblical Interpretation*.

[2]Augustine cited in Whitaker op. cit. p. 453.

[3]Theophylact cited in Whitaker op. cit. p. 465.

[4]Owen op. cit. p. 124.

[5]See Owen op. cit. p. 126, "That whereas the means of right interpretation of the Scripture and understanding of the mind of God therein, are of two sorts—first, such as are prescribed unto us in a way of duty as *prayer, meditation* on the word itself, and the like; and, secondly *disciplinary,* in the accommodation of arts and sciences, with all kind of learning, unto that work—the first sort of them doth entirely depend on a supposition of the spiritual aids mentioned, without which they are of no use; and the latter is not only consistent therewith, but singularly subservient thereunto." Note the last part of the quote.

[6]Jonathan Edwards, *The Works of Jonathan Edwards* revised by Hickman, Banner of Truth Trust, Carlisle, PA, (reprint 1979), sermon "Divine and Supernatural Light," Vol. II, p. 16.

[7]John Calvin cited in E. A. Dowey *The Knowledge of God in Calvin's Theology,* Columbia University Press, New York, 1952, p. 183; Dowey has an extensive discussion of Calvin on illumination, p. 173-91; see also H. J. Forstman *Word and Spirit: Calvin's Doctrine of Biblical Authority,* Stanford University Press, Stanford, 1962, p. 74-85 for another helpful discussion.

[8]Ibid., p. 183.

[9]Edwards, op. cit. p. 13.

[10]Ibid., p. 14.

[11]Ibid., p. 14.

[12]Owen, op. cit., p. 176.

[13]John Calvin, *Commentary on Hebrews and I and II Peter,* edited by Torrance, William B. Eerdmans Publishing Co., Grand Rapids, Michigan, p. 157-58.

[14]Martin Luther, *The Bondage of the Will* translated by J. I. Packer and O. R. Johnston, Fleming H. Revell Co., Westwood, New Jersey, 1957, p. 67.

[15]Ibid., p. 70.

[16]Edwards, op. cit. p. 17.

[17]cited in Whitaker op. cit. p. 468.

Philosophical Presuppositions Affecting Biblical Hermeneutics

Winfried Corduan
Associate Professor of Religion and Philosophy
Taylor University

9. Philosophical Presuppositions Affecting Biblical Hermeneutics

Winfried Corduan

In one sense, the task of uncovering the philosophical presuppositions of hermeneutics is in a league with exploring a philosophy of life, the philosophical notion of God, or the analysis of everything. Hermeneutics necessarily touches on so many areas that it almost involves a total philosophy of the human intellect. For such an endeavor, the reader must wait for a further paper. At present, let us limit ourselves to a somewhat more modest, albeit slightly arbitrarily chosen, task.

Hermeneutics has been defined as the science of understanding.[1] For theology this means understanding divine revelation as given in Scripture.[2] We can see the act of interpretation as the verbal expression given to the understanding received. Thus, at least for a start, we can describe our task as the philosophical explication of understanding the propositions of revelation. We are beginning with the fact that such understanding is had by persons studying the Bible; it is a given. Utilizing a transcendental argument we want to answer the question, what makes such understanding possible?

I

Let us begin with a very general case, the understanding of any proposition, *p*. What is involved in this act[3] of understanding? First of all, we must distinguish between belief and understanding. Let *p* stand for any proposition whatever, and *S* for any human being. Then

(1) *S* believes that *p*.

implies that *S* has a certain mental attitude toward *p* which Roderick Chisholm has defined as

(2) *S* accepts the proposition that *p*.[4]

Essentially, believing a proposition means giving assent to it (viz. to accept it as true) on unspecified grounds or possibly on no rational grounds whatever.

Understanding seems to also involve a mental attitude, and it seems to be similar. On first glance, it might appear reasonable to expect

(3) *S* understands *p*.

to be implied by (1). Can one believe some proposition without understanding it? Surely not, one would want to say. But the reality is far more complicated. The relationship between (1) and (3) is not convertible in either direction. So, for instance, we can make out a case for believing a proposition without understanding it, in two ways.

First, we can cite an argument based on the partial descriptions of a proposition.[5] Smith is a Christian believer committed to biblical inerrancy. Thus we can say categorically

(4) Smith believes John 11:35.

which can be a partial description for

(5) Smith believes that Jesus wept.

But we may not infer from (4) to (5) as Smith may never even have read the verse in question and may be totally ignorant of its content. Presumably, however, if informed of the content of the verse he would readily assent to it. Then let *q* stand for the implied content of John 11:35, and it follows that even though it may be true that

(6) Smith believes that *q*.

it is not true that

(7) Smith understands *q*.

for Smith believes *q* only on principle under its partial description and is ignorant of its actual content.

An even simpler example may convey the same point. Smith, our biblical inerrantist, may accept as true a proposition on categorical grounds, even after he has heard its content spelled out without understanding it. On the basis of 1 Cor. 15:29 he may believe *r* which stands for

(8) Some were baptized for the dead.

but based on common experience it is likely that

(9) Smith understands *r*.

is not at all probable.

Of course we must quickly add that there is a serious problem here. For even though it is possible to say of Smith that he does not understand *q* and *r* while he believes them, intuitively we know that he must have some minimal understanding of what it is that he believes. No matter how obscure the proposition or how partial its description, Smith must have some rudimentary notion of what it is that he is assenting to. But with the same intuition we know that, whatever it is, his understanding is not what we might use to characterize as complete, accurate, or correct. Thus, even though understanding does not in itself involve a judgment of truth, the concept carries with it the accompanying notion of degrees of understanding. Where there is understanding, there can also be misunderstanding. So a proposition may be believed and yet not understood, or, perhaps more accurately, believed and not understood properly. How there can be a standard of rectitude at all is something which needs to occupy us in the subsequent pages of this essay.

The asymmetry between belief and understanding makes itself felt in the other direction as well. It is certainly possible to understand a proposition without believing it. We can easily stipulate a noninerrantist, Jones, who does not accept a proposition, such as *q*, even though she has no trouble understanding it. For some reason she may simply not wish to assent to its truth, even though she has no difficulty discerning its meaning.

Thus there is a basic difference between believing and understanding. Believing involves the judgment of truth, whereas understanding does not. Then what is understanding? As we already hinted above, understanding is the discernment of the meaning of a proposition. Thus we might define (3) in terms of

(10) *S* discerns the meaning of *p*.

Unfortunately such a definition is of only very limited use. The concept of meaning is not much clearer than that of understanding. There is a rich history of philosophical debate on criteria for the meaning of a proposition. This debate became especially important in the twentieth century with the coming of analytic philosophy. Thus, to overgeneralize on some representatives, for G. E. Moore the meaning of *p* would be its reference, for Bertrand Russell it would be its description, and for Schlick it would be the empirical observation statements that can be deduced from *p*.[6]

In recent years it has been increasingly the practice to resort to some form of conventional theory of meaning. The two great bearers of this tradition are Ludwig Wittgenstein and W. V. O. Quine. The philosophies they espouse are radically different from each other, but they have this in common, that for each of them meaning is in some way system-dependent. *p* cannot be understood apart from taking an entire context into account.

For Quine, the context is provided by a system of beliefs as a whole. He states,

> The statement, rather than the term, came with Bentham to be recognized as the unit accountable to an empiricist critique. But what I am now urging is that even in taking the statement as unit we have drawn our grid too finely. The unit of empirical significance is the whole of science.[7]

Thus when we want to understand *p* we must inquire into its position within the entire complex of beliefs which it occupies in the system of the person who uttered it. Such a system is uniquely maintained on pragmatic grounds by each person, based on his scientific heritage and empirical experience.[8] The point we need to glean here is that a proposition cannot be understood apart from its context within such a system.

For Wittgenstein, the hermeneutic context of a proposition is the language game.[9] He does not permit the same kind of individualism as Quine does, but relates all propositions to the linguistic community in which they are uttered. Within a certain language game, propositions have meanings which cannot be discerned apart from the language game; and to learn the meaning of *p* is to play the game in which *p* is used.

Both Quine and Wittgenstein present valuable insights and pose serious problems for us as we attempt to delineate philosophical presuppositions of hermeneutics. Despite their differences, there are two points of importance which arise out of both of them. We shall label these as "implicit understanding" and "opacity."

By "implicit understanding" we mean that once one is privy to a particular interpretative scheme, whether language game or belief grid, one is automatically given access to understanding any proposition within it. As Wittgenstein says, there is no further "act of understanding" which we must perform;[10] the understanding is part of the successful playing of the language game. If one does not understand a proposition, one cannot bring up independent hermeneutical criteria, but one must learn to play the language game. On the other hand, once one can play the game, the question of understanding becomes either redundant or irrelevant. Similarly, for Quine the understanding of a proposition is entirely linked to its role in the entire system. There is no question of learning meaning apart from the system, but within the system the meaning is transparent.

Linked to the notion of implicit understanding is its converse, the opacity of propositions from one context to the next. For Wittgenstein, there are no standards to adjudicate meaning across different language games. No overarching language game governs understanding the meaning of a proposition in one language game from the vantage point of another. Such a thing cannot be done reasonably. Quine makes the particular point that statements are transformationally opaque. A certain proposition, e.g., a causal relationship, may be meaningful within one system, but its meaning cannot transfer to another system, for there it could have an entirely different role, and consequently a meaning unique to that system.

Let us apply all of this to an example. The proposition,

(11) God so loved the world that He sent His Son.

is, on the one hand, immediately intelligible to anyone who is a member of the particular universe of discourse in which it functions. However, not to be within that context would appear to eliminate one from the possibility of understanding it. Thus, on these grounds, the hermeneutical task is purely and simply to assume a place in that particular context. But of course that is exactly the difficulty which seems to be insurmountable.

Even assuming that an interpreter can in fact place herself into a context in which the propositon has some meaning, there seems to be no way of telling whether the meaning gained may be diametrically opposed to the correct meaning, for instance the meaning intended by the original speaker or writer. Philip Payne[11] has rightly pointed out that meaning is not exhausted by the author's intent; at the same time intent could give us one criterion for telling us whether we have the right meaning or not. The only problem is that if meaning is opaque, the author's intent will be so *a forteriori*. Thus even if we could adopt a context as our own to gain understanding, we could not be sure that we are not falling into misunderstanding. But the question of whether the antecedent condition is even possible looms large. Three different considerations arise:

a) So far we have been talking about propositions in various contexts. But many philosophers[12] want to recognize a distinction between propositions and sentences. Even if the understanding of a proposition may be implicit due to its contextual transparency, what the interpreter is faced with is first of all a sentence, and not a proposition. A sentence expresses a proposition; it is the linguistic mechanism by which a proposition is conveyed. Thus the sentences, "it is raining," "*es regnet,*" and "*il pleut,*" all express the same proposition. So, before the interpreter can ever even begin to uncover the meaning of a proposition, she must first of all decide which proposition the sentence is trying to express. Many philosophers dismiss this distinction, but it certainly is an important one when trying to understand a sentence originally given in a language different from that of the interpreter's ordinary context, as is the case with modern biblical hermeneutics.

b) The central difficulty revolves around the possibility of ever even being able to adopt a different contextual system for the sake of gaining understanding. Can I learn to play a new language game? One is reminded here of Wittgenstein's remark that we could not understand a lion even if he could talk[13] because we do not have access to his experienced world. Then how can I take on a new world view?

This difficulty is one of the most ticklish problems in all of philosophy. It begins with the problem of other minds, touches on the question of private experience, and works itself into the issue of the basis for language. None of these are issues on which one can speak definitively in a few pages, yet they cannot be avoided. We must begin here when we resume the next section.

c) A further problem is presented by the fact that when we come to a biblical hermeneutic we are dealing with historical writing and are attempting to gain understanding of a contextual system on the overage more than two thousand years removed from ours. How can one bridge that kind of gulf?

Given our transcendental mandate to uncover the conditions under which understanding is possible, we are committed to finding a resolution to these problems. Point a) can be left up to language scholars by and large. Points b) and c) need the greatest amount of philosophical attention. Both of them are predicated on the idea of a chasm: the problem of linguistic opacity. The way to remedy the situation is to show that the chasm is not, in fact, unbridgeable. But where is the bridge to be found? It will not do to arbitrarily change the facts of linguistic usage and understanding.

However, I shall present a possible remedy which goes beyond language. What a hermeneutical grounding needs is itself to be grounded in an ontology. We shall seek to uncover an ontology of understanding which allows us to overcome the conventionalism of Wittgenstein and Quine.

II

So far our discussion has focused primarily on the *de dicto* aspect of language, viz. it was language about language. But language has another mode, namely *de re*, which is its referring role. We need not at this point enter into the whole question of the nature of language, particularly the issue of a correspondence theory vs. a functional theory. In the end, it is probably the case that the truth consists of a combination of these two. The fact is that language does at least imply a certain amount of correspondence in that its symbols refer to certain intentional realities.

We began the last section with the *de dicto* proposition,

(1) *S* believes that *p*.

Let us now look at what a proposition such as *p* entails. In any proposition a property is ascribed to a thing. By "thing" we mean here any, even the most general possible subject referent, and a property refers to anything which may be said about it, including a verb phrase. Then we can expand *p* in (1) and come up with

(12) *S* believes that *x* has the property *P*. or:
(12') *S* believes that *Px*.

Any instantiations of the variables suffice here. E.g.:

(13) *S* believes that the moon is made of green cheese.
(14) *S* believes that birds fly.
(15) *S* believes that his parrot has no wings.

It does not matter for our purposes whether the belief in question is true or not. It is still accepted as true by *S* (Cf. prop. (2)).

Let us look more closely at (13). The proposition in question is

(16) The moon is made of green cheese.

We can logically dissect this proposition into the symbolism:

(17) There is an *x* such that *x* is the moon and *x* has the property of being made of green cheese. or:
(17') (%A*x*) (*Mx* & *Gx*)

The case we are pursuing here focuses on the existential quantifier in (17'). A *de re* proposition of this nature is premised on a judgment of existence. There is an entity predicated to which it is intended to refer. We must be careful to distinguish between a particular proposition and a universal one. A universal proposition, such as the one entailed by (14),

(14') S believes that $(x)\ Bx > Fx$.

carries no existential, only a hypothetical, presupposition. But in a particular proposition, to attribute a property to a thing implies that it exists. If something is red, then something red exists; if something flies, then something flying exists, etc.

But what about (15) where the proposition of belief is the negative,

(18) My parrot has no wings?

Here, even though a property is being denied of a thing, the existential reference is still in place. For (18) breaks down into

(18') There is an x such that x is my parrot and x does not have wings. or:

(18'') $(\%\mathrm{A}x)\ (Px\ \&\ -Wx)$

Thus language inherently refers to being in its *de re* mode. We already made the point that truth or falsity does not alter this fact. But of course in a false proposition, even though it intends to refer to being, it does not. And we must theoretically be open to the possibility that all of our contingent propositions are false and therefore do not refer to any being at all (necessary propositions do not refer). Then there is obviously no existential reference and no ontological grounding to language, not even in *de re*.

In considering this problem, we are fortunate in two respects. First, we can circumvent another classic issue in philosophy, the question of reference to nonexistent entities, such as Bertrand Russell's puzzle with regard to the proposition, "the present king of France is bald." The reason we can circumvent that issue is our second item of good fortune, namely that we do have certain knowledge of at least some existent beings. We may not know whether any of the previous propositions refer to any being, but we do know this with regard to the proposition,

(19) I exist.

I cannot utter this proposition without referring to my being.

We must understand this notion clearly and avoid several misconceptions. First of all, (19) is not necessarily true. Its truth is always contingent. As opposed to God, whose existence is necessary, I can envision many different worlds in which I do not exist. But even though (19) may only be contingently true, that does not mean that its truth may not be inescapable. Second, I am not about to reintroduce Descartes' *cogito*. Such an argument and its kin have been debated widely, and they may even have some merit; but we need not use that method here.

Following Norman Geisler,[14] I want to let the case for my existence rest purely on its undeniability. It is not a violation of logic, but an existential absurdity for anyone to deny his own existence. But if I must truly assert my existence in uttering (19), then I am indubitably referring to it. Then we have taken the essential step in this argument, namely we have shown that there is an ontological connection between at least some language we use and its referents. And having shown that fact to be the case at least once, there is no philosophical warrant to deny the possibility of ontological grounding of some other *de re* utterances.

We may make reference here to Jacques Maritain's idea of the intuition of being.[15] Maritain argues that implicit in any act of knowledge is the self-evident knowledge of being. Regardless of whether one comes from a realist or an idealist position, the supposition that something exists is fundamental; the ascription of a particular mode of existence is secondary. And there seems to be no existence as intuitively certain as my own.

What I have attempted to show in this section so far is two-fold: That language makes ontological reference and that a primary locus for such reference is my own existence. Now, in order to apply this to the hermeneutical problem, we need to show that the same grounding applies to an intersubjective community of human persons. This leads us to the so-called problem of "other minds." Can I know that other minds, similar to mine, exist outside of myself?

All problems in the history of thought depend for their existence and solution on their presuppositions. An analysis of this particular problem shows that it rests on rather dubious premises. Its origin in its modern form lies in the philosophy of Descartes, who first of all methodologically reduced himself to a thinking thing.[16] Then, on the basis of those principles, he could hardly get himself out of a solipsistic box. But surely the Cartesian view of human persons is open to challenge. It may be possible to say that a person is essentially immaterial, viz. has the property of immateriality essentially,[17] but that is far different from saying that he is exclusively immaterial. (19) is hardly equivalent to

(20) My mind exists.

(20) is merely entailed by (19). When I refer to my existence, I am speaking of something far more comprehensive than my mental properties; I am also including my physical properties, for example.

I want to argue that entailed in my existence is a facet of communality with the rest of humanity, viz. that inter-subjectivity is given within my subjectivity. This is not a novel claim. It has been made by many different writers in the context of their various philosophies. An almost too simple defense for this claim could rest on the nature of language itself. We already pointed out that language, particularly on Wittgensteinian grounds, is a communal feature. Then there is no private language. But then if I utter any proposition, including (19), I am affirming my membership in a linguistic community, and hence in an intersubjective nexus. This argument would need to be seriously bolstered against the charge of *petitio principii*.

An argument to the same effect is provided by Alfred Schütz in his defense of the so-called "we-relation" in a phenomenological analysis of the human person. This point needs his particular defense since phenomenology, the philosophy initiated by Edmund Husserl, appears to be faced with a paradox: On the one hand it uses the methodology of epochē in which the only final point of reference is the transcendental ego, but on the other hand it affirms the essential reality of the life-world which certainly includes *alter egos*.[18] The solution to the paradox lies in the fact that in the reduced state, the transcendental ego directs its intentionality toward the stream of its life-world, and it thereby hits upon similar centers of consciousness, i.e., other egos to whom it is inextricably bound. Obviously the transcendental ego is not identical with *alter egos*, but that does not make the *alter egos* superfluous noematic appendages. Schütz states, "The world which is experienced after the completion of the reduction to my pure life of consciousness is an intersubjective world, and that means that it is accessible to everyone."[19] Thus phenomenology describes the essentiality of an inter-subjective dimension to the self.

Jacques Maritain, the existential Thomist, gives us a third perspective on this issue. He relies on the distinction between an individual and a person.[20] Now any material being can be an individual, for it is matter that provides individuality. But in the realm of nature only the human being is a person. Personhood is defined by spirituality. Maritain contends

> . . . that it is essential for personality to tend toward communion. We must insist on this point which is often forgotten: the person, by virtue of his dignity, as well as of his needs, requires to be a member of a society.[21]

Let us see where this argument has brought us. We began with the problem that understanding seems to be hampered by the supposed isolation of an interpreter from different linguistic circles. But we have now provided two major remedial states of affairs: We have shown that language is grounded in ontology, and that there is an ontological link between the individual and other subjects. Thus we have begun to bridge the gap between the interpreter and the community of origin of any proposition she wants to understand. They are all part of the same human intersubjective nexus which is grounded in being.

No one understood this point better than Friedrich Schleiermacher, who has unfortunately acquired the reputation as the apostle of subjectivity in modern theology. To be sure, Schleiermacher emphasized the subjective experience of the individual as the source for revelation, but for him all tests for truth were ultimately bound to a community.[22] Thus in his lectures on hermeneutics, even though he stressed the psychological experience of the individual, he put equal stress on the necessity of the communal relationship as a *sine qua non* for any understanding.[23] And the communal dialogue is ultimately grounded, not in its own collective subjectivity, but in being.[24] It must be considered a detriment to our understanding of Schleiermacher as well as to the study of hermeneutics in general, that Wilhelm Dilthey appropriated the subjective pole at the expense of the intersubjective pole of Schleiermacher's hermeneutics.[25]

Now we have arrived halfway at our goal of defining the philosophical presuppositions to hermeneutics. But the mere existence of an intersubjective bond is in itself not adequate to allow for an effective hermeneutic. We need to focus also on the subject matter which is the object of understanding. This leads us to problem c) at the end of the first section of this paper. How do we deal with the special problems presented by the historical nature of the material to be understood?

III

We now enter an area of inquiry highly controversial with regard to even the minimal question of the applicability of hermeneutics.[26] Worse than that, the particular spot of concern to us occupies a midway point between the two options at odds with each other. Let us again consider several representative propositions to prepare the case we need to make. We can start with

(21) Mary is apprehensive about the future.

We have here a descriptive proposition containing very little factual material apart from a report about Mary's psychological state. To understand the proposition we make use of the common bond of intersubjectivity we affirmed, and we somehow empathically identify with Mary's feeling of apprehension. We, as it were, vicariously experience her subjectivity. A showcase for the role of inter-subjectivity developed in the previous section!

But now look at this proposition:

(22) Water freezes at 0° C.

Again we have here a descriptive proposition, but of a very different order. The report this time is of a purely physical phenomenon. Now it is not at all a matter of consensus to what extent it is necessary to apply hermeneutics to such a scientific proposition.[27] To a large extent we can see that the answer to that question revolves around one's definition of hermeneutics. On the very broad basis by which we defined hermeneutics here, we can see that it does in fact apply. Specifically we can make quick reference to two reasons. First, insofar as we made the act of understanding any proposition the paradigm for hermeneutics, viz. along the line of proposition (3), there is not a priori reason why scientific propositions should somehow be exempted. They too are part of a language game (Wittgenstein) and carry out a pragmatic function in the entire system of science (Quine). Secondly, as a result of the work of Thomas Kuhn and others[28] it has been made increasingly clear how much scientific propositions depend on intersubjective communities for both their meaning and apparent truth value. Thus (22) is also subject to hermeneutics.

Still we must be cognizant of the essential difference between (21) and (22). Whereas (21) can be understood on the basis of not much more than the intersubjective nexus, (22) requires us to be additionally acquainted with certain concrete facts of nature. Intersubjectivity alone does not produce understanding here. An empirical element is also necessary.

Now let us examine a further proposition:

(23) Solomon succeeded to the throne of David.

(23) is a proposition fairly typical for a biblical assertion. It involves historical knowledge. Note that (23) in certain ways occupies a half-way house between (21) and (22). It is a proposition about human subjects and their experiences, but it also involves some very factual matters. Unfortunately, in distinction to (22), an empirical methodology is only indirectly applicable in understanding the factual content. Thus historical knowledge presents a very special problem in the task of hermeneutics.

I will not take the trouble at this point to work out a historiographical epistemology.[29] Suffice it to stipulate that on the basis of what Holmes calls "interpretative realism"[30] it is possible to have true historical knowledge. But what we are interested in now is the question of historical understanding as opposed to historical belief. Let us recall the distinction between belief and understanding, as exemplified by propositions (1) and (3).

Again the presence of the intersubjective nexus is essential, for both historical events and historical writing are the products of other persons who share with us in our human ontology. But now we also need to establish an ontological bridge between the historical event and ourselves. Historical understanding can only be had if we specify that events in history had the same status of being as events in our time. This stipulation has nothing to do with the kinds of events (viz. novelty is not prohibited by some kind of Ritschlian principle of analogy) or with their clarity of perception. It simply means that we must grant historical events the same kind of actuality as present actuality. Else there is no safeguard against historical opacity.

Such an ontology of historical events is so basic to human experience that it is almost impossible to defend. If an event occurred five minutes ago, it is no less actual than if it is occurring right now. All of human discourse is based on this fact. The ascription of a property to a thing in a proposition (as in (13) and (15)) necessitates the existence of the thing; and this existential base is not dissolved by the past tense of the property. So (23) transforms into

(23') (%Ax) (x as Solomon & x succeeded to the throne of David)

Of course existence in the past is not the same thing as existence in the present. At this point in time, Solomon does not exist, whereas Menachem Begin does, and that makes for a lot of difference. When we talk of ontological continuity we are then certainly not saying anything as absurd as that the things and events of the past exist now as well; we are saying that at their point in time, past things had just as much ontological actuality as present things do now.

None of these considerations, whether intersubjective or factual, are intended to facilitate exhaustive historical understanding. Sometimes we have very limited understanding of the meaning of a historical proposition, e.g., if (23) had read

(24) Solomon succeeded to the cubar of David.

Since we presumably do not know what a "cubar" is we do not understand the proposition, and consequently we do not need to provide a philosophical theory for its understanding either.

Now the meaning of historical propositions frequently goes beyond their literal signification. The proposition

(25) The Greeks defeated the Persians at Salamis.

has its particular basic meaning. But one can also say that its meaning goes far beyond that particular record of a victory to yield:

(26) Hellenic civilization assured its persistence at Salamis.

Historical events may carry significance far beyond their bare propositional description, and this significance may be seen as a secondary meaning of such a proposition. Thus let us understand (26) as expressing some secondary meaning of (25).

It is obvious that (26) is in no way logically entailed by (25). Rather (26) is a conclusion based on (25) plus any number of additional premises. It is clear then that this kind of meaning presupposes a system of historical propositions, only one of which is given by (25). A conclusion such as (26) is then derived from the system as a whole, or at least a large part of the system.

But then once again we appear to be stuck in a conventionalistic framework in which propositions such as (26) are purely system-dependent and inaccessible to external understanding. However this criticism fails because we have already provided for an ontological basis for the system, namely in the existence of the intersubjective nexus and in the supposition of an ontology of historical events. Certainly there are different systems of historical interpretation, but we do have bridges and bedrock data which allow us to remove the arbitrariness from many historical meaning judgments.

It may be helpful in clarifying this point to draw a contrast to Quine. What we have said about a system above sounds very much like Quine's system, and surely Quine also has an ontology. Yes he does, but Quine's ontology is very different from what we have been saying here. In Quine's celebrated slogan, "to be is to be the value of a (bound) variable."[31] In any of the formal propositions we have presented above, e.g., (17'), (14'), or (18''), *x* is a bound variable because it has been given either universal or particular quantification. If in addition *x* is also instantiated, viz. it performs a particular indispensible function within a system, then for that system it has been given a value and ontological status. Thus for Quine, ontology is also system-dependent and pragmatically determined. What I have been arguing for is that ontology transcends any particular system and provides a solid background against which any system can be judged or understood to a certain extent. This ontology can then also be applied to historical systems.

Still, in the light of the subject matter under consideration for a biblical hermeneutic, this point needs to be carried one step further. A variation of (23), or possibly a secondary meaning, may be:

(27) The Lord gave to Solomon the throne of David.

In that case, another dimension needs to be added to the system within which this meaning is derived; namely a theistic world view is presupposed. This is not to say that the entire set of Christian beliefs is presupposed, as in a presuppositional apologetic.[32] The truths of Christianity are derived by us from biblical data; one need not be familiar with all of doctrine in order to understand biblical propositions. At the same time, one can understand no biblical proposition involving mention of God or the divine realm without positing the existence of the God of theism. His existence is not a conclusion of arguments within Scripture.

Again it is possible to guard against making this an arbitrary assumption on the basis of ontology. It is possible to show that God exists. Once more we enter a field of controversy; let me merely indicate a possible way in which this can be attempted. Having begun with an assertion of my existence as an undeniable, yet contingent, truth, I need to look for a metaphysical cause for my existence. Contingent entities do not cause themselves; if they exist at all they must have been caused. Nor does a series of contingent entities, no matter how long, provide any better metaphysical justification of the existence of any of its members. I may thus show that my existence is ultimately grounded in the existence of a necessary being who is God.[33] Then God as existent being can become part of the ontological apparatus which I bring to my act of biblical understanding.

We have now isolated three ontological components which need to be presupposed to a biblical hermeneutic. The first one, an intersubjective nexus, is required for all acts of understanding. The second one, an ontology of events, is particularly required for historical understanding. Finally, biblical understanding in particular demands a theistic presupposition. At the end of the first section we posed the problem of understanding across different linguistic and conceptual boundaries. That problem will always be real. But we have tried to show that with these ontological elements, there is always a bridge between communities, and the opacity can always at least be reduced to translucence.

IV

Let me now show how these considerations apply to three particular areas of special concern to the hermeneutician: the perspicuity of Scripture, the history of interpretation, and the unity of Scripture.

Of these three notions, the first two represent equally valid poles of a hermeneutical continuum. By "perspicuity of Scripture" we mean that the Scriptures are understandable to any human being, not merely to those trained in technical skills of interpretation. Our philosophical suppositions show why this is indeed possible. For the assumptions we have made concerning intersubjectivity, an ontology of events, and a theistic world view are, stripped of their philosophical garments, actually part of the world of common sense. The facts that the Bible was written by and about people much like us, that the events in the Bible were real and were directed by God, these facts are certainly not outlandish. They are the most likely presuppositions a pious reader of Scripture would bring along. Consequently many of the truths of Scripture are immediately open to her. One need not be a Wittgensteinian or Quinean, perhaps not even a Thomist, to understand the Bible. Philosophical and theological discussions can only clarify our implicitly present principles at this point.

But not all of Scripture is equally intelligible to us (Cf. prop. (8)). The doctrine of the perspicuity of Scripture nowhere suggests that anyone can have exhaustive understanding of the Bible. There are differences based on expertise, background, and divine illumination. There will always be some opacity. In that case it is natural that people with different backgrounds will come up with different understandings. Although the gap between communities has been bridged, the difference between communities also still exists. Clearly this difference will make itself felt over the course of history, where we then have a history of interpretation in which undoubtedly each latest phase considers itself to be in possession of the best understanding. But note how the understanding of any particular community is governed by its own concepts and language games. The Middle Ages are characterized by, and sometimes criticized for, the method of allegorical interpretation. But in an age in which allegory dominated all of life, can we fault their theologians for also going the allegorical route?[34]

We can also see how the third doctrine, the unity of Scripture, follows from our three ontological supposits. Biblical writing, spanning roughly 1,500 years, itself represents different communities; but even apart from the theological dogma of inspiration, we can see how the intersubjective nexus, the ontology of events, and the existence of God provide all that is necessary to allow for as unified and cohesive a piece of writing as the Bible does represent (keeping in mind that there are internal distinctions, e.g., literary ones).

To summarize, Hermeneutics is the act of understanding, in contrast to the act of belief. Understanding is the discernment of meaning of propositions which may require transcending different linguistic communities. This is done on the basis of an ontological grounding to language which makes itself apparent in three different realities: an intersubjective nexus, an ontology of historical events, and the presence of an existent God.

NOTES

[1]E.g. in Charles Taylor, "Understanding in Human Science" *Review of Metaphysics* XXXIV (Sept. 1980), pp. 25-46.

[2]Cf. the article, "Hermeneutik" in *Kleines Theologisches Wörterbuch*, eds. Karl Rahner and Herbert Vorgrimmler (Freiburg: Herder, 1976), p. 191.

[3]I am for the sake of convenience using the phrase "act of understanding" throughout this paper. As I indicate below, Wittgenstein is certainly right in saying that understanding is actually not a separate "act" of the mind. Nonetheless, it is a helpful form of designation in separating various forms of mental attitudes from each other, and I shall continue to use the phrase, keeping in mind Wittgenstein's *caveat*.

[4]Roderick Chisholm, "On the Logic of Purpose" *Midwest Studies in Philosophy,* Vol. IV *Studies in Metaphysics,* 1979, p. 225.

[5]Ibid, pp. 225-27.

[6]For an excellent historical treatment of the development of contemporary language philosophy see Barry R. Gross, *Analytic Philosophy* (New York: Pegasus, 1970).

[7]Willard Van Orman Quine, "Two Dogmas of Empiricism" *From a Logical Point of View* (2nd ed.; New York: Harper & Row, 1961), p. 42.

[8]Ibid, p. 46: "Each man is given a scientific heritage plus a continuing barrage of sensory stimulation; and the considerations which guide him in warping his scientific heritage to fit his continuing sensory promptings are, where rational, pragmatic."

[9]Ludwig Wittgenstein, *Philosophical Investigations* trans. G. E. M. Anscombe (3rd ed.; New York: MacMillan, 1958), p. 5.

[10]Ibid, p. 60.

[11]Philip B. Payne, "The Fallacy of Equating Meaning with the Human Author's Intention" *Journal of the Evangelical Theological Society* vol. 20 (Sept. 1977): pp. 243-52.

[12]E.g. a recent advocate of this practice is Alvin Plantinga in *The Nature of Necessity* (New York: Oxford, 1973), vol. 1, no. 1.

[13]Wittgenstein, *Investigations,* p. 223.

[14]Norman L. Geisler, *Christian Apologetics* (Grand Rapids: Baker, 1976), pp. 143-44.

[15]Jacques Maritain, *Sept lecons sur l'etre et les premiers principes de la raison speculative* (Paris: Tequi, 1934), pp. 51-70.

[16]René Descartes, *Meditations on First Philosophy,* trans. Donald A. Cress (Indianapolis: Hackett, 1979), pp. 18-19.

[17]Cf. Plantinga, *Necessity,* pp. 65-70.

[18]Alfred Schütz, "Phenomenology and the Social Sciences" *Phenomenology,* ed. Joseph J. Kockelmans (Garden City: Doubleday, 1967), p. 453.

[19]Ibid, p. 456.

[20]Jacques Maritain, *Scholasticism and Politics,* trans. Mortimer J. Adler (Garden City: Doubleday, 1940), p. 63.

[21]Ibid, p. 71.

[22]Friedrich Schleiermacher, *Dialektik,* ed. Rudolf Odebrecht (Darmstadt: Wissenschaftliche Buchgesellschaft, 1976). Cf. also my paper, "Schleiermacher's Test for Truth: Dialogue in the Church" *Journal of the Evangelical Theological Society,* forthcoming.

[23]Friedrich Schleiermacher, *Hermeneutics: The Handwritten Manuscripts,* ed. Heinz Kimmerle, trans. James Duke and Jack Forstman (Missoula, Montana: Scholars Press, 1977).

[24]Schleiermacher, *Dialektik,* pp. 19-20.

[25]Cf. Schleiermacher, *Hermeneutics,* vol. 235, no. 1, where the editor makes reference to Dilthey's interpretations.

[26]See e.g. the discussion in the following articles, all of which are in *Review of Metaphysics* XXXIV (Sept. 1980): Hubert L. Dreyfus, "Holism and Hermeneutics," pp. 3-23; Charles Taylor, "Understanding in Human Science," pp. 25-38; Richard Rorty, "A Reply to Dreyfus and Taylor," pp. 39-46; as well as the ensuing dialogue, pp. 47-55.

[27]Ibid.

[28]Thomas S. Kuhn, *The Structure of Scientific Revolutions* (2nd ed.; Chicago: Chicago U., 1970). Also: Nicholas C. Mullins, *Science: Some Sociological Perspectives* (New York & Indianapolis: Bobbs-Merrill, 1973).

[29]See William H. Dray, *Philosophy of History* (Englewood Cliffs: Prentice-Hall, 1964); Arthur F. Holmes, *Faith Seeks Understanding* (Grand Rapids: Eerdmans, 1971), pp. 60-84; Geisler, *Apologetics*, pp. 285-304.

[30]Holmes, *Faith,* p. 78.

[31]W. V. O. Quine, "On What There Is," *From A Logical Point of View*, pp. 1-19. Of course Quine's theory is more subtle than this summary indicates. But the various qualifications, e.g., the one on page 15 which seems to be directed against much of the same kind of thing I am accusing him of, ultimately cannot rescue Quine from his ontological conventionalism.

[32]Nothing less than this seems to be required in Gordon Clark's theory of meaning. See his *Religion, Reason and Revelation* (Nutley, NY: Craig, 1961), pp. 142-46.

[33]For a much more thorough presentation of the cosmological argument, see Norman L. Geisler, *Philosophy of Religion* (Grand Rapids: Zondervan, 1974), pp. 190-226. Also see my work, *Handmaid to Theology: An Essay in Philosophical Prolegomena*, chapter VII, forthcoming.

[34]Richard Winston, *Charlemagne* (New York: Random House, 1954), p. 179 illustrates the all-pervading allegorical thinking with the following dialogue from Alcuin's *Disputation Between the Royal and Most Noble Youth Pepin with Albinus the Schoolmaster:*

PEPIN	ALBINUS
What is writing?	The guardian of history.
What is speech?	The revealer of the soul.
What produces speech?	The tongue.
What is the tongue?	The lash of the air.
What is air?	The guardian of life.
What is life?	The joy of the good, the sorrow of the wicked, the waiting for death.
What is man?	The bondsman of death, a passing wayfarer, a guest upon earth.
What is man like?	An apple (a play on words: *homo, pomo*).
What is sleep?	The image of death.
What is faith?	Certain belief in an unknown and wondrous thing.

Further:

What is the stomach?	The cook of food.
What is the moon?	The eye of night, the giver of dew, the foreteller of storms.

etc.

A Response to Philosophical Presuppositions Affecting Biblical Hermeneutics

R. C. Sproul
President of Ligonier Valley
Study Center

A Response to Philosophical Presuppositions Affecting Biblical Hermeneutics

R. C. Sproul

Winfried Corduan provides an excellent summation of the difficulties of hermeneutics posed by the peculiar problems inherent in the complexities of language analysis. Since biblical hermeneutics directly involves an interpretation of language, the issues raised in our day by Russell, Wittgenstein, Quine, et al., have an important application to the task of the biblical exegete and theologian.

Though the seminal principle of the application of presuppositions of language to the current crisis of hermeneutics are set forth in the paper, space, time, or disposition did not permit the author to paint the broader picture of how the linguistic issues affect the current debate of hermeneutics. Surely the issues explored have far-reaching implications and serve well as keys to understanding the current chaos in the field of hermeneutics. In addition, other philosophical questions which are prior, in terms of historical development, though not necessarily in terms of logical priority, have shaped the contemporary crisis. These are but touched on and hinted at in the essay and require, I think, some sort of broad-brush mention.

I. THE SUBJECT-OBJECT DILEMMA

Behind Corduan's technical treatment of the problems inherent in the whole problem of intersubjective understanding is the basic epistemological question of how one thinking subject can have any knowledge or understanding of the external world which includes within it other thinking and speaking subjects. Can I ever know that my contextual system has any real point of contact with objective reality? How much influence does my own subjective contextual system have on any understanding? Or, to put it another way, is the quest for an objective understanding of anything possible, or even desirable?

Classically, hermeneutics was dominated by a quest for objective understanding. A sharp distinction was evident between the categories of understanding and belief. That distinction still functions in the current debate, but often in a fuzzy way. The quest for objectivity had several foci:

1) An ever-expanding attempt for *lexicographic exactitude*;
2) A serious commitment to mastery of ancient language structures;
3) A serious investigation of the historical context in which the biblical content was written.

The first of such study was designed to give the exegete the tools necessary to bridge the historical chasm and achieve *understanding* of the biblical writings. Belief or assent to the biblical propositions was considered a different matter. The truth claims must first be understood before they can be evaluated with respect to assent.

Thus a kind of "tabula-rasa" approach to exegesis was prompted by the grammatico-historical method.

II. BULTMANN'S REJECTION OF TABULA RASA

With the advent of the "new hermeneutic" we see the rejection of the quest for objectivity and a wholesale capitulation to a strange form of subjectivism (yet with a concealed commitment to objectivity still intact.) Bultmann's principle of *Vorverständnis*[1] is central to the debate:

> The resulting or corresponding presupposition of exegesis is that you do have a relation to the subject matter (Sache)—in this case to the psychical life—about which you interrogate a given text. I call this relation the "life-relation." In this relation you have a certain understanding of the matter in question, and from this understanding grow the conceptions of exegesis. From reading the texts you will learn, and your understanding will be enriched and corrected. *Without such* a revelation and such previous understanding *(Vorverständnis) it is impossible to understand any text.*[2]

Here Bultmann makes a proper "prior understanding" an absolute prerequisite for "understanding" the text. It is at this point, with his use of "understanding" that confusion enters the picture. In a host of circumstances Bultmann demonstrates a classical tabula rasa type of exegesis by which he lucidly sets forth what the text says (indicating that he "understands" it) but then goes on to reject it as being prescientific, mythical, too Greek, etc.

When Bultmann speaks of "understanding" he seems to confuse understanding and belief. To gain the proper belief from the text you must bring the proper beliefs to the text, that is, for the New Testament to be meaningful to modern man, we must come to it with the proper questions asked from the vantage point of the proper contextual system. Bultmann finds that proper system in existential philosophy, particularly in the Heideggarian mode:

> Our question is simply which philosophy today offers the most adequate perspective and conceptions for understanding human existence. Here it seems to me that we should learn from existentialist philosophy, because in this philosophical school human existence is directly the object of attention.[3]

III. EXISTENTIAL PHILOSOPHY AND HISTORICAL SKEPTICISM

When Bultmann sets forth existential philosophy as the necessary *Vorverständnis* of hermeneutics the crisis of modern theology is made clear. The categories of existential thought do not merely influence the "new hermeneutic" but govern it. In Bultmann we find the accent on such features as punctiliar salvation, a theology of timelessness, (the *hic et nunc* motif), and the call to decision (*entscheidung*). All of these categories reflect an existential skepticism with respect to history as an "objective" sphere or arena of revelation. The net result is the biblical message as de-historicized, de-mythologized, and relativized, being recast in personalistic and subjectivistic categories. It is not by accident that Bultmann is often charged (most stridently by Oscar Cullmann[4] with being a neo-gnostic. The ancient gnostic disdain for empirical or rational knowledge is echoed in Bultmann's theology, a disdain traceable to the metaphysical skepticism of existential philosophy.

The roots of such skepticism may be found partially in Lessing's ditch where the contingent or "accidental" truths of history are deemed incapable of yielding eternal or transcendent truth. The ditch became a yawning chasm with Kant's critique of theoretical thought and his metaphysical agnosticism. Placing God in the noumenal realm made revelation fundamentally impossible by means of reason, sense perception, and/or history. Thus, since Kant, theologians and biblical scholars have tried to reconstruct faith on some premise other than the historical rational-empirical. With history eliminated as a viable source of revelation some other means of "revelation" was sought to rescue Christianity from the refuse-heap of the Kantian critique.

In broad terms what has happened in biblical studies and hermeneutics in the past two centuries may be viewed as a postscript to Kant. Existential philosophy as a whole may be seen as a conscious alternative to pre-Kantian historically based faith. The influence of Kant is especially evident in the phenomenology oriented brand of existentialism. (It is interesting to note that both Sartre and Heidegger were students of Husserl.)

Nineteenth century theology tended to follow Hegel's reconstruction of the shattered pieces of historical knowledge left by Kant's hammer. Here history was "rescued" by a dialectical idealism where God was reintroduced into the historical continuum via the inner process of the divine *aufgehoben*. The problem here was that God became not merely revealed in history but confused *with* history by the resulting immanentism.

The protest of Barth to 19th century immanentism reached its extreme point in Barth's concept of the "wholly other" (*totaliter aliter*) God. So jealous was Barth to combat immanentism with its necessary loss of divine transcendence that he denied any *analogia entis* between God and man. This had the effect of turning Kant's chasm into an unbridgeable gulf. Though Barth rhapsodized about revelation he cut himself off, philosophically, from any possibility of it. If God were indeed "wholly other" no communication of any kind could ever proceed from Him to man as His "contextual system" would be utterly dissimilar to man's. Barth's God would be very much like Wittgenstein's lion whom "we could not understand even if it could talk."

Barth's God led to the crisis of supra-temporal religion that culminated in the current God-talk crisis of whether our language has any degree of adequacy with respect to the knowledge of God.

Once history is eliminated as a possible ground basis for revelation then contact with God must either be ruled out altogether or rediscovered by some other means such as a mystical divine-human encounter. The horizontal plain of space and time which governs the Bible's own inner hermeneutic is supplemented by a supra-temporal encounter, a *vertical* saving act of God, a "*senkrecht von oben*." Here we step into the roller coaster without brakes where it really doesn't matter at all if there even was a historical Jesus. The very word "Jesus" becomes a contentless cipher, capable of being filled by the content of the believing subject. The character of Jesus, like a chameleon, changes his color to fit the *Vorverständnis* of the exegete—resembling anything from Ritschl's champion of values of Käsemann's symbol of "Freedom."

This hermeneutic is ultimately committed to relativisim and is patently anti-intellectual. The crucial distinction Corduan makes between understanding and belief is obscured. The Bible may now be "understood" in a new way to fit the belief that is brought to it. The Procrustean Bed is complete as the Bible's message is cut, sawn-off and denuded to fit contemporary categories of existential philosophy.

NOTES

[1]G. C. Berkouwer, *De Heilige Schrift I* (Uitgave J. H. Kok N. V. Kampen, 1966), See discussion p. 158f.

[2]Rudolf Bultmann, *Jesus Christ and Mythology* (New York: Charles Scribner's Sons, 1958), p. 50.

[3]Ibid., p. 55.

[4]Oscar Cullmann, *Salvation in History* (New York and Evanston: Harper & Row, Publishers, 1967), p. 24.

A Response to Philosophical Presuppositions Affecting Biblical Hermeneutics

John F. Johnson
Associate Professor of
Systematic Theology
Concordia Seminary
St. Louis, Missouri

A Response to Philosophical Presuppositions Affecting Biblical Hermeneutics

John F. Johnson

Professor Corduan's initial demurrer concerning the imposing task of uncovering the philosophical presuppositions of hermeneutics (namely, that "it is in a league with exploring a philosophy of life . . . or the analysis of everything") is well taken. Indeed, the same reservation can be extrapolated to the relationship between his paper and this rejoiner. It is simply impossible to comment on the many fine observations and helpful clarifications offered in his essay in a brief response. Rather, the purpose of my comments is but to underscore a most significant statement by Corduan and take it in a direction which seems to me to be the most challenging and fruitful for a consideration of the philosophical presuppositions of biblical hermeneutics.

At the conclusion of the first major section of his discussion, one in which some of the primary difficulties implicit in the hermeneutical enterprise are introduced, Professor Corduan announces that "what a hermeneutical grounding needs is itself to be grounded in an ontology." Subsequently, the author seeks to develop the notion that language makes ontological reference; that is to say, language inherently refers to being. In other words, Corduan suggests some relationship between hermeneutics and metaphysics.[1] This is an immensely important point and one that deserves more attention than it receives in contemporary thought. Indeed, the two words, "hermeneutics" and "metaphysics," indicate a fundamental problem of modern philosophy and theology regarding the opposition or relation between hermeneutics and metaphysics, which means between an historical and hermeneutical approach to understanding and any metaphysical, even a transcendentally founded, way of thinking. This relation is conceived today most frequently as mutually exclusive in the sense that metaphysics has been proved in modern philosophy to be impossible, even meaningless, and has to be viewed as an obsolete relic of the past. One can find this sentiment in almost the whole hermeneutical literature of both philosophy and theology in our time.[2]

I cannot enter here into all of the critical (mainly Kantian) objections against the meaning and possibility of metaphysics nor can I discuss what metaphysics properly is or at least should be. What I would contend, however, is that any hermeneutical understanding has previous conditions which lie ultimately in a properly metaphysical or ontological dimension. It therefore follows that there is no strict opposition but rather a dialectical relation of reciprocal condition and mediation between hermeneutics and metaphysics. This is basically the position of philosophical theologians of the "Transcendental Thomist" school, particularly Wilhem Coreth. I suggest that Coreth's analysis is pertinent to the issue raised by Corduan.[3]

First, there is the hermeneutical problem of understanding as it is widely posed and as Corduan outlines it at least in part. Since the real process of "understanding" became a subject of explicit philosophical reflection, an essentially circular structure has developed. While this structure is evidenced in Heidegger and Bultmann, Corduan considers Quine and Wittgenstein to be the most prominent spokesmen for hermeneutical difficulties.

The basic structure of the problem is this: any particular content, it might be a thing, an event, a word or a sentence, has to be understood within a totality of meaning that reveals the sense of this particular object. However, the background of this totality is never given immediately in itself. The problem of the world is that its concrete totality is never explicitly given, but only implicitly presupposed. We can never become conscious of all origins, influences, and conditions that enter into the determination of our total world it is said. Much less can we understand the world in which other men live and feel and think (these are the problems of "other minds" and private experience which Corduan rightly sees as part of the hermeneutical question). We cannot reconstruct perfectly their different world, the world from which, for instance, ancient texts and documents speak to us as something to be understood. How is it possible to bridge the difference that exists already in any personal understanding when we talk to each other and, much more, to overcome the distance in any historical understanding of language from the remote past?

Of course, two prominent explanations have been set forth. The first consists in Schleiermacher's principle of identification.[4] This means that I have to transpose myself into the other, to identify myself with the other in order to understand his action and language. The more I abstract from myself and identify myself with the other, the better I understand him in his own perspective, from his own situation, within his own world. But it is evident, it seems to me, that an identification like this is never perfectly attainable. Moreover, it would not explain "my" understanding of the other.

It is in the light of this problem that Gadamer offers a second explanation—what he calls a "fusion of horizons."[5] This term is intended to indicate that different horizons of understanding meet and penetrate each other, flowing and fusing together. This certainly hints at something that happens in the real process of understanding and yet, the same fundamental problem recurs. Just as a perfect identification can never be attained, so a complete fusion of horizons is never possible. However, in spite of these problems understanding does occur.

This leads to the second major step in the argument for the relationship between hermeneutics and metaphysics. As Coreth notes, in modern hermeneutics the world of understanding is portrayed as a closed, untranscendable horizon. In actuality, the world is quite different. It does indeed belong to the world of our experience and understanding that it be always and essentially limited, but at the same time it is never definitely fixed, never closed in itself, but always open to further dimensions of reality.[6] It is, on the one hand, essentially limited. We never comprehend everything (i.e., the total reality). On the other hand, we do comprehend limited sections of reality and understand each under particular aspects. But in so doing, through the limits of what we understand, we are pointed out beyond the limits into a larger totality of being and meaning. Coreth writes, "This limitation is a property of human experience. But this indicates already that it is also proper to this experience that we are conscious of this limitation and thus already transcend its limits. We know *about* other and wider dimensions of reality that we do not yet know, that have not yet entered into our own world of understanding. No matter what we know, we are conscious of our not-knowing."[7]

All of this has most important implications and consequences of both hermeneutical and metaphysical relevance. In contemporary hermeneutics the "pre-understanding" is frequently considered as a fixed and limited view so that we can understand any new content only from a restricted point of view within our previously determined world; we reduce the content that appears to us into the limits of our own previously fixed and restricted horizon. This is a basic error of Bultmann and his disciples. If this were the case, any real understanding would be eliminated. I would be ready to accept only elements that match to my way of thinking and fit into my previous world. They would not offer enrichment of my horizon but only a confirmation of myself. However, real understanding requires a permanent openness and readiness to accept new contents and relations of meaning, to acknowledge even the unexpected and uncalculated, to open oneself to new dimensions of being and sense. This process demonstrates at the same time—and this would seem to be most significant—that our world of experience and understanding is not and cannot be the ultimate horizon of human being and understanding. Constantly, we go beyond it, we pose new questions, we get new experiences and open ourselves for new contents of meaning; we transcend our previous world in the openness for a wider horizon of reality and meaning.[8] This, indeed, is the condition of any understanding, as well of personal as of historical understanding. For it presupposes in any case the community of a common horizon. Only on the basis of a total and comprehending horizon can different standpoints refer to each other, can different modes of expression meet each other in real understanding.

This common horizon is, immediately, the common historical world. All temporal, intellectual, and cultural diversities join, beyond centuries, in the broad community of human experience and knowledge in which we meet and understand each other. Not to overlook this aspect is most important, especially in a time when the historical evolution of all human conditions is frequently emphasized. Rather, we understand each other beyond all diversities; we are personally addressed by facts and text many hundreds of years old, which reveal human persons in the same basic experience of human existence. This phenomenon is the primary presupposition of any hermeneutic.[9]

But in this community of an historical world a properly metaphysical horizon is already opened in which we meet and understand each other. Man experiences himself at any time and in all conditions of history in the reality of being that comprehends and transcends himself and reveals an absolute element. The knowledge of any man, that is to say, is addressed by the absolute claim of truth which we must acknowledge. Therefore, when we try to exegete any word or written text of the past, we have to suppose that the author, unless he wanted to deliberately misrepresent, intends to say the truth in his perspective and with his words (i.e., he articulates being as it appears and reveals itself to him).

Man also lives in personal and social relations within human community. Coreth writes: "There he experiences that the other meets him on the same level and under the same value of personal being, that he cannot be taken as a mere thing, but demands personal respect and esteem. There is at any time a horizon of human values, of personal confidence and love. These fundamental experiences might take different forms and expressions in human history; they might become human problems in different ways. Still, they hold true always. Human thinking, feeling, doing, and expression is only to be understood in this human horizon that comprehends all of us."[10]

But this intimates already that essentially human activity and self-realization reveal, as the condition of their possibility, an absolute relation, an unconditioned horizon, which means a relation of openness to the absoluteness of being and meaning and value. It is the ultimate horizon in which all of us are united and in which all diversities of historical worlds are comprehended.

If everything we seek for, or know, or have to do with, we are accustomed to call a "being"—something that "is"—then this final horizon can be characterized in the language of metaphysics as the horizon of being. As that preeminent Christian philosopher of being, St. Thomas Aquinas, reminds us the world is only possible within being and under the condition of being. The world as a human world is not possible unless in the unlimited openness of being. And that means that the horizon of being is something transcendental; it is the ground of everything and every knowing and understanding.

Therefore, metaphysics is the ground that comprehends and transcends everything and reveals itself as the ultimate condition of human being and human understanding. Because we are open to being and understand being, we have a world as a human world. Only because we are, in your world, open to being and, being so, transcend the limits of our world, is hermeneutics possible at all.

This observation leads to the final point of this response. According to Transcendental Thomism, there is a reciprocal relation between hermeneutics and metaphysics. Any hermeneutics, in the philosophical sense of trying to understand understanding itself—which is as Corduan notes in the introduction of his essay the task of his paper—reveals a metaphysical problem and presupposes metaphysical conditions. However, it also is the case that metaphysics itself has to fulfil a properly hermeneutical function. "Metaphysics does not intend an isolated particular thing or any particular objective reality as such, but essentially the particular within the totality, which means within the context or the connection of everything with which we have to do, to which we refer in all our asking and knowing."[11] A being as such is not to be considered under a particular and restricted aspect but insofar as it is and therefore, as a being, is in community and connection with everything that is within the totality of being. This is the meaning of any metaphysical question: trying to understand the particular being within the totality of being, therefore integrating all particular points of view. But this is precisely a hermeneutical function of metaphysics in opposition to merely empirical science. This indicates a profound affinity between the modern hermeneutical problem and the traditional metaphysical problem. In both there is at work the dominant desire to understand the particular element within its general horizon. In hermeneutics this horizon is taken as the world of our experience, communication, and understanding, the world of history and language; in metaphysics it is seen as the ultimate and unconditioned totality of being that transcends even all of the differences in our human world. There is, then, an essential relation between hermeneutics and metaphysics. Hermeneutics transcends itself into metaphysics insofar as the openness to being is the transcendental ground of all understanding of the world, of history, and language. But metaphysics as the transcendental reflection on the ultimate condition of any understanding presupposes a hermeneutic of human existence in our conditioned situation with a limited world, still open to the totality of Being.[12]

As noted earlier, this response is rooted in the work of philosophical theologians such as Coreth, Lonergan, and others of the "Transcendental Thomist" school. They are set forth in response to Professor Corduan as an approach to the problem of philosophical presuppositions of biblical hermeneutics which is even more fundamental than the problem of propositions which his paper brings to the fore. Professor Corduan is quite correct in seeking to uncover an ontology of understanding which allows us to overcome the philosophical chasm upon which modern hermeneutics is predicated. However, the chasm is not just one of linguistic opacity (credible though his handling of the issue is). It is rather the problem of understanding the whole totality of our human world which is only mediated by language. This problem calls for a much more radical ontology and a much greater appreciation from Protestant evangelical philosophers and theologians for those in the Western philosophical tradition who have preserved that ontological orientation for us.

NOTES

[1]Corduan consistently uses the term "ontology" which in Thomistic philosophy can be distinguished from epistemology and theodicy as a concern of metaphysics. I simply prefer "metaphysics" in the context of this discussion for the study of being in general.

[2]It is a position which underlies Gordon Kaufman's perspective on systematic theology, for example. See his *Systematic Theology: A Historicist Perspective* (New York, 1968). But even more disturbingly, it is an opinion that seems to be frequently voiced by some evangelicals writing in the areas of anthropology and cross-cultural evangelism with an almost anti-metaphysical bias. Note, for instance, the work of Charles Kraft of Fuller Seminary.

[3]Coreth deals with this issue in his *Grundfragen der Hermeneutik* (Freiburg, 1969). For English readers his perspective can be gleaned from his essay, "From Hermeneutics to Metaphysics," *International Philosophical Quarterly* (1971), pp. 249-59. I synthesize his analysis in this response. Others belonging to this school of thought include Bernard Lonergan and, to an extent, David Tracy.

[4]For Schleiermacher, understanding involved the concrete reexperiencing of the mental processes of the text's author. This means I have to transpose myself into the other, to identify myself with the other in order to really understand him.

[5]Hans-Georg Gadamer, *Truth and Method* (London, 1975).

[6]See also Lonergan's treatment of insight as knowledge in *Insight* (revised ed., New York, 1978).

[7]Coreth, p. 254.

[8]Lonergan, *Insight,* pp. 634-41.

[9]Coreth, p. 254.

[10]*Ibid.*,

[11]*Ibid.*,

[12]*Ibid.* This approach to hermeneutics is especially challenged by phenomenology. For an example of the latter see Edward Farley's *Ecclesial Reflection* (Philadelphia, 1982).

The New Hermeneutic

Hendrik Krabbendam
Associate Professor in
Biblical Studies
Covenant College

10. The New Hermeneutic

Hendrik Krabbendam

I. A GENERAL ORIENTATION IN THE NEW HERMENEUTIC

A. Since the publication of the symposium *The New Hermeneutic*, edited by J. M. Robinson and J. B. Cobb, Jr., in 1964, the title of this work has become increasingly the standard designation of a theological approach of which E. Fuchs and G. Ebeling are the chief representatives.[1]

This approach is characterized by two essential features. The first one anchors it squarely within the larger modern hermeneutical movement which traces its origin to Schleiermacher and counts philosophers as Heidegger and Gadamer and theologians as Barth and Bultmann among its exponents. The second one identifies it as part of the later phase of this movement in which the thinking of Schleiermacher the early Heidegger and Bultmann has been transcended by Barth, the later Heidegger and Gadamer.

The first feature pertains to the subject matter of hermeneutics. Hermeneutics is no longer viewed as one of the many concerns of the theological enterprise which seeks to identify the principles, methods, rules and techniques that are prerequisite for the orderly interpretation of written documents. Instead it becomes coterminous with theology as the theory of understanding. The total theological enterprise, from exegetics through systematics to homiletics, is assigned the task of looking into the conditions that make understanding possible and of paving the way for its occurrence. In short, the fundamental concern of the hermeneutical discipline is no longer the theory of interpretation, designated as hermeneutics, but the theory or art of understanding often designated as hermeneutic (singular), to distinguish it from traditional hermeneutics.[2]

The second feature pertains to the method of hermeneutics. Hermeneutics is no longer regarded as a theory in which words or language, as they pose problems and require explanation, function as the object of understanding. Even the earlier phase of the modern hermeneutical movement, by taking this approach, failed to escape the domination of the subject-object scheme in which objectifying thought has the final say. Instead the primacy is given to word or language that as final hermeneutical principle both produces understanding and gives rise to hermeneutics as an aid to understanding. In short, hermeneutical theory, in which the interpreter determines, initiates and effects the access to understanding of the text, gives way to a new hermeneutic, in which the subject matter of the text is the originating origin of understanding and enlists hermeneutics to reach its goal.[3]

Both features can be combined in a maxim that fairly represents the later thought of the modern hermeneutical movement, "understanding through language,"[4]

Not even the evangelical world reacted to this maxim, that at the same time serves as the program of the modern hermeneutical movement, without a measure of appreciation.

In one instance, the early contribution made by Schleiermacher in the area of understanding has been hailed as a "noble service" for its much needed emphasis upon the "subjective side of interpretation."[5]

In a second instance, the question posed by Fuchs as to how language, specifically the language of ancient texts, will "strike home" with the modern hearer, is lauded as one of the more important questions to be asked.[6]

It must be conceded that it is difficult to see in the maxim, understanding through language, anything but a legitimate, if not central, concern for the student of Scripture. However, there appears to be more than meets the eye. A probe into the meaning and function of both understanding and language will bring this to light.

B. Fundamental for both understanding and language is that they are never at the disposal of man. They are beyond objectification and conceptualization. This is indicated by the constant emphasis upon understanding and language as events.

With regard to understanding, from the very inception of the modern hermeneutical movement it was sharply distinguished as non-objectifiable from "explanation" as objectifying. Explanation is characteristic of the scientific method that deals with objective facts. Understanding has a deeper concern. It endeavors to grasp reality, whether theologically or philosophically defined, as it transcends the objective facts. This accounts for the fact that hermeneutics as theory of understanding could never be satisfied with drawing up methods and rules to interpret an objectively present text. It had to go beyond it by inquiring, thus taking the place of classical epistemology, into the conditions that make a non-objectifiable understanding of a non-objectifiable reality possible and by seeking to initiate it.[7]

With regard to language, in the early phase of the modern hermeneutical movement, it was regarded as the objectification of a reality expressed in it and by it. Hence it was held that breaking through the objectifying language garment—in Bultmann's case negatively by means of a program of demythologizing and as its positive counterpart by means of an existential interpretation of the text[8]—would be both the condition for the possibility of understanding and serve to set it in motion. This, then, became the hermeneutical challenge. In the later phase, the resultant attempts were disqualified as failures. It was recognized that epistemologically these attempts were nothing but objectifying theories that did not bring understanding into view, let alone produce it. It was also recognized that the attempts of any interpreter, who as knowing subject deals with the text as passive object, even if it is with a view to understanding, can never transcend the level of objectification and therefore will constitute at best a hermeneutical theory.

This is an important moment in the modern hermeneutical movement, because at this point the hermeneutical flow is reversed. The subject matter of the text, designated as the language-event or word-event, is now posited as the originating, non-objectifiable, origin of understanding. The interpreter no longer interprets the text and is no longer asked to initiate understanding. Language determines the occurrence of language and through the text interprets the interpreter. In assigning the primacy to the language-event the modern hermeneutical movement truly turns the tables.[9]

It needs to be underscored that the language-event strikes as a flash of lightning.[10] It simultaneously reveals and conceals, arrives and withdraws. Hence it should not be equated with a series of oral sounds that can be recorded. Nor may it be visualized in terms of signs that can be printed. Language as event transcends mere speech, however profound it may appear, and sheer words, however informative they may seem. Mere speech is superficial and hides true reality from view. Sheer words are divisive and produce fragmentation. They threaten man with death by "language-poisoning."[11] Language as event, on the other hand, does precisely the opposite. It can be characterized as a "letting-be." As such it illuminates reality and unifies in community.[12] In "letting-be" it says "Yes" and therefore can be called a saving-event and a love-event.[13] However, this illumination and unification, which takes place in understanding, is equally non-objectifiable.

C. In order to effect understanding the language-event uses both the text and the sum total of theology, now transformed into a hermeneutical, or epistemological, tool. Both are needed as aids to understanding.

As to the text, it provides the room for the language-event. As such it is indispensable.[14] At the same time, the language-event may not be identified with the text. This is a *sine qua non* of the modern hermeneutical movement in its earlier as well as its later phase.

Bultmann and Ebeling, together representative of both phases, champion the propriety and necessity of the critical-historical method as well as a thorough application of its "acids" to the biblical text.

Its propriety is said to be rooted in the relative autonomy of the natural and social sciences. They must be allowed to examine the text critically in the realm of both facts and concepts and "to burn everything that will burn." To do otherwise would amount to an unacceptable sacrifice of the intellect.

Its necessity is said to be rooted in the Reformation doctrine of the justification by faith. It is the epistemological concomitant of the *sola fide* that no human words or human language will be allowed to function as the unshakable ground or final guarantee for salvation. To hold otherwise would be to substitute works for grace.

The application of its "acids" leads not only to a categorical rejection of biblical facts like the virgin birth and the bodily resurrection of Christ and biblical concepts like the substitutionary atonement and everlasting punishment, but also to a total relativizing of every word and all the language of Scripture.[15]

It is recognized, of course, that this makes the claim of the text as room for the language-event rather tenuous. An objectifiable entity is the room for an non-objectifiable event and functions as an aid to an non-objectifiable understanding!

To escape the force of this difficulty an important qualification is added. The room for the saving love-event of language is the text as it is preached. The sum total of theology, from exegetics through systematics to homiletics, discharges itself into "the textbook of preaching" as hermeneutical principle.[16] The new hermeneutic undoubtedly resorts to the act of preaching because of its seeming event character. But the fundamental problem merely shifts. Apart from the fact that the content of a new hermeneutic sermon will prove to be very meagre after the demolition of the text by the critical-historical method, the language of the sermon simply does not transcend the level of objectification. The difficulty, therefore, remains. An objectifying entity is said to be the room for a non-objectifiable event and is said to function as an aid to an non-objectifiable understanding.[17]

With regard to hermeneutics, it is used and needed by the language-event to arrive at the text-in-preaching and thus to effect understanding. In critical self-appraisal the modern hermeneutical movement has conceded that in its earlier phase the hermeneutical attempts remained under the domination of the subject-object scheme. This means very simply that thinkers like Schleiermacher, the early Heidegger and Bultmann failed to arrive at understanding. But how about the exponents of the later phase of the modern hermeneutical movement, like Barth, the later Heidegger, Fuchs, Ebeling and Gadamer? Did they succeed where their predecessors failed? Did the many volumes penned by them with the specific aim to solve the hermeneutical problem transcend the level of objectification?

In theory(!), the new hermeneutic suggests that progress has been made. The first claim is that hermeneutics operates between an earlier experience of the language-event and its consequent understanding and a later one. Otherwise its concern could not be explained. What else could be the driving force behind its program? The second claim is that hermeneutics as an aid to understanding must arise from the language-event. Otherwise its effectiveness could be challenged. What else could make the difference with the attempts of the earlier phase? The third claim is that hermeneutics as an aid to understanding must be of the same nature as understanding. Otherwise its propriety could be called into question. How else could it escape the liabilities of an objectifying theory?

At this point the famed "hermeneutical circle" is said to emerge. Hermeneutics appears to originate and terminate in the same understanding producing language-event and as such to assume its nature. If it did not originate there, it would not arrive. If it would not arrive, it did not originate there. If it were of a different nature, it would not originate there and would not arrive.[18]

D. The New Hermeneutic, in its own admission, stands or falls with the three claims and the resultant "hermeneutical circle." A further examination will have to determine whether they can be substantiated or not. But it is already evident that the maxim, "understanding through language," is far from harmless.

The language in view is not the language of the Bible. Much of that language ought to be discarded as obsolete from the point of view of science. All of that language must be rejected as essentially deficient from the point of view of the subject matter of the Bible.

Neither is it the language of the sermon. Even if it is purified by the science of hermeneutics, it is still essentially deficient as objectifying.

All that is known about the language in view, and this applies equally to understanding, is what it is not. Since it is beyond conceptualization, it is not known what it is.

Apparently it is known that it exists. But the only guarantee for that is the word of the New Hermeneutic. The question is, whether this word which is evidently final, is sufficient. Is the New Hermeneutic more than a hermeneutical theory? Has its language moved beyond the level of objectification? To settle this issue, it is advisable to begin with a more detailed look at the failure of the early phase of the modern hermeneutical movement in the thinking of Schleiermacher, the acknowledged father of this movement, and the early Heidegger. Following this the focus will shift to the later Heidegger, who precipitated the later phase, and to representatives of the theological wing of the modern hermeneutical movement, specifically the New Hermeneutic.

II. THE FUNDAMENTAL FAILURE OF THE NEW HERMENEUTIC

A. Schleiermacher, who is credited with defining hermeneutics as the art of understanding, holds that the process of understanding has two aspects. The first aspect is grammatical. It has as its task to understand a discourse in its full orbed lingual, cultural, historical and literary setting. As such it may be characterized as external, comparative and discursive. The second aspect is psychological. It seeks to understand the same discourse as "a fact in the thinker." As such it is to be characterized as direct, immediate, intuitive and divinatory.[19]

There are apparently two realms. The one is objectifiable. The other is not. Each one has a corresponding way of knowing. The one is objectifying. The other is not. Schleiermacher suggests a synthesis when he claims that the two aspects compose one unitary act of understanding. The definition of hermeneutics as the art of understanding substantially implies the same claim. As art the science of hermeneutics has transcended the level of objectification.[20]

However, the claim has no basis in fact and the term "art" veils the true state of affairs. This comes into view when Schleiermacher describes the relationship between the "grammatical" and "psychological" aspects in a later context as one of oscillation.[21] Apparently the science of hermeneutics has not transcended the level of objectification. The fusion of the objectifying and the non-objectifying has not materialized.

The failure to accomplish a synthesis becomes further evident in conjunction with the so-called "hermeneutical circle." It has correctly been observed that in Schleiermacher the process of understanding is simultaneously circular and explicative.[22]

It is circular inasmuch as the impression is given that understanding is not only the point of destination, but also the point of departure.

It is explicative inasmuch a methodological process, consisting of a systematic search for hermeneutical rules, is indispensable to effect understanding.[23]

The complaint is made that there is no "cohesion"[24] between the circular and the explicative aspect in the hermeneutical process. This point is well taken. Hermeneutics is either circular or explicative. It can not be both at the same time. The primacy either belongs to understanding in its immediacy which then comes into its own, appropriates itself, in and through hermeneutics. In that case the discipline is circular. Or the primacy belongs to the systematic process that seeks to initiate understanding. In that case the discipline is explicative. In Schleiermacher's hermeneutics the primacy belongs to the systematic process. Understanding as the point of departure appears to be (only) a general inkling which has to become a deliberate grasp through the indispensable tool of the hermeneutical discipline. The primacy of the explicable aspect caused H. Kimmerle, who is responsible for the widespread recognition of Schleiermacher as the father of the modern hermeneutical movement, to conclude that his hermeneutics must be characterized as an objectifying theory.[25]

B. In the early Heidegger a similar pattern emerges. According to Heidegger, "Philosophy is universal phenomenological ontology and takes its point of departure from the hermeneutic of Dasein, which as an analytic of *existence*, has made fast the guiding-line of all philosophical inquiry at the point where it *arises* and to which it returns."[26]

The first point of note in this definition is that philosophy aims at the disclosure of Being by means of the phenomenological method. The second point of note is that the horizon from which Being comes into view is disclosed by an analysis of existence that has its point of destination as its point of origin. Both the phenomenological method and the existential interpretation, however, appear to be deficient. They fail to meet the standards set by Heidegger himself, something he eventually admitted. They both appear to be objectifying.

With regard to phenomenology, its task is "to permit that which of its own accord manifests itself *(phenomenon)* to reveal itself *(logos)* as it is."[27] The circular structure is quite evident. The *phenomenon* has the primacy. It is said to manifest itself of its own accord. It is further said to use the *logos* in its self-revelation. However a complication arises. The *phenomenon* for the most part does not show itself. This necessitates the *logos* to wrest it from the objects of phenomenology. Further, because the concealment belongs to the essence of the *phenomenon,* it resists communication in the form of assertions and by means of conceptualization. This puts the *logos* in a precarious situation. Since it cannot escape assertions, the very phenomenological enterprise is in danger. Heidegger admits this and recommends that phenomenology must be self-critical. It ought always to be willing to renounce its own assertions in favor of preferable alternatives.[28] It should be noted, however, that the *logos* is the agent in the process of its self-criticism.

The picture that now emerges is somewhat ambiguous. The primacy has clearly shifted to the *logos* in its acts of violence against the objects of phenomenology and as agent in the process of self-criticism. At the same time, the *logos* is vulnerable. In its twofold activity it does not transcend the level of assertions and conceptualization. This is undoubtedly the reason why Heidegger acknowledges at this point already that his concept of phenomenology bears a preliminary character, even as he holds out the prospect that at the end of the phenomenological enterprise an unblemished phenomenology will be in evidence.[29]

With regard to the existential interpretation, philosophy is said to receive its impetus to disclose Being from a vague, preontological understanding of Being that is universally prevalent. Since this understanding is characteristic of human existence, philosophy takes its point of departure in an analysis of existence. Heidegger states that authentic existence will only be exhibited after the existential analysis has run its course. But then it will prove that the vague understanding of Being belongs to the essential constitution of authentic existence and that authentic existence lies at the root of the existential interpretation. In fact, he strongly insists that only authentic existence will justify the existential interpretation.[30]

The circle is again in evidence. At this point, however, in anticipation. At the conclusion of the analysis of existence the point of destination will appear to be the point of origin. Until that time the primacy must be assigned to the existential interpretation.

When finally, the existential interpretation has been thought through to the end, Heidegger gives the impression that it is no longer an arbitrary construction. In other words, he believes to have reached his goal, an existential analysis that has disclosed authentic existence, has arrived at the level of authentic existence and has now authentic, that is non-objectifying, force.[31]

Precisely at this juncture, however, the existential interpretation is said to need acts of violence to wrest authentic existence from its inauthenticity. This is puzzling, to say the least. Why are acts of violence introduced, when the existential interpretation seems to have reached its goal? In his effort to account for this violence Heidegger maintains on the one hand that the analysis of existence is governed by a general idea of existence, and on the other hand that it is rooted in an authentic understanding of existence. But this will not do. A general idea of existence is not sufficient to justify the existential interpretation. This was already conceded by Heidegger.[32] Further, while authentic understanding could give that justification, the claim that it is the transcendental condition of the existential interpretation with its acts of violence has clearly no basis in fact. It is admitted in the very same context that authentic understanding is effected through the hermeneutical analysis. The primacy remains with the methodological interpretation and the circle, that was introduced in anticipation, has in the final analysis not been established.[33]

Instead of a circle, in which authentic understanding and hermeneutic interpretation fuse together into one non-objectifying focal point, an elliptical structure is in evidence, in which objectifying hermeneutics and non-objectifying understanding are two irreducible focal points that are mutually exclusive.[34]

This explains why it could not be shown that authentic understanding was the transcendental origin of existential interpretation and that existential interpretation disclosed authentic understanding.

This also explains the violence inherent to the phenomenological method and the existential interpretation. It has correctly been observed that "in the final analysis the violence is very real. It is the violence of the fundamental antinomy . . . between the solitary position of authentic existence (non-objectifying!) and the general validity of the existential analytic (objectifying!)."[35]

This, finally, explains why the earlier phase of the modern hermeneutical movement was found wanting by its own exponents. Scientific hermeneutics, in whatever form, was unable to transcend the level of objectifying theory.

C. In retrospect, the later Heidegger concedes that he failed to accomplish his goal as a result of the objectifying characteristics of the existential interpretation. But it is the genius of the man that he explains this failure in a way that sets the stage for his later thinking and for the later phase of the modern hermeneutical movement in general.

In his later thinking Heidegger no longer construes the existential interpretation as responsible for the disclosure of Being. He rather posits Being as the origin of thought. In revealing itself Being is said to give rise to non-objectifying thought. However, Being does not only reveal itself, but also and simultaneously conceals itself. When this concealment, which by itself is presented as a virtue, was concealed, Being was forgotten. This forgottenness of Being gave rise to the era of objectifying thinking. This era, also called the era of metaphysics, begins to take shape in early Greek thinking and reaches its zenith in today's culture with its technocratic domination. It covers all of the history of Western thought and practice, virtually from its very dawn. This included philosophy, science as well as theology. Even the existential interpretation was not able to escape its blemishes altogether! The main characteristic of metaphysics is that it has lost sight of Being and dispersed itself in a futile preoccupation with beings in general, which makes it impossible to transcend the level of objectification.[36]

Heidegger's construction is not without a touch of brilliance. It accounts for the objectifying as well as the non-objectifying type of thought. Both are ultimately rooted in Being itself, the first one in its concealed concealment, the second in its revealed revealment.[37]

The question must be asked, however, whether this construction has a basis in fact. Heidegger's later thought consists of a series of determined efforts to show that the answer should be in the positive.

But is he successful?

In his first effort he concentrates upon Being as it reveals itself. For that he turns to the writings of the pre-Socratics. In his estimation these writings testify to the revealment of Being. However, since the concealment is equally ultimate as the revealment, the emergence of metaphysical blemishes was inevitable. This was already visible in the pre-Socratic fragments. For that reason the effort to disclose Being in its revealment took the form of a retrieve of Being in its revealment from the metaphysical error precipitated by Being in its concealment. In other words, retrieve must remove metaphysical error to bring the revealment of Being into view. According to Heidegger, it must do so forcibly. It must resort to acts of violence. However, these very acts of violence, as was the case in the existential interpretation, prove that retrieve does not transcend the level of objectification. As soon as Heidegger recognizes this, the concept of retrieve begins to fade from his vocabulary. The effort to retrieve Being in its revealment is clearly a failure.[38]

In his second effort he concentrates upon Being as it conceals itself in its revealment. The focus subtly shifts. The revealment no longer occupies center stage, but the concealment as the ground of the metaphysical era. Heidegger now proposes that thought, rather than forcing Being into the open by acts of violence, steps back; away from the entanglement of the metaphysical subject-object dichotomy and into the concealment of Being. Its disappearance into the concealment of Being will constitute its transcendence of the level of objectification.

Heidegger officially designates this thought as step-in-reverse or leap-backward. However, its arrival in the concealment of Being is far from a foregone conclusion. He states that the step-in-reverse constitutes a long road and that the leap-backward must leap over and over again. This thought is apparently not able to extricate itself from metaphysical error as easily as was suggested. This is, indeed, the case. Heidegger declares that the long road and the recurring leap are necessitated by the metaphysical deficiencies of the language garment of thought. He further declares that thought as step-in-reverse and leap-backward will not succeed until it backs out of metaphysics through language into a different way of, obviously non-objectifying, uttering. The first declaration is an admission that the second effort is equally as much of a failure as the first one. The step-in-reverse and leap-backward as step-in-reverse and as leap-backward never arrive in the concealment of Being. They are too objectifying. The second declaration sets the stage of Heidegger's third effort.[39]

In his third effort he concentrates upon Being as it in its revealment turns against its own concealment. When it does turn, it will overcome metaphysics. Since metaphysics is ultimately rooted in concealment, a turn against the latter will have implications for the former. That it will turn, is virtually a certainty in Heidegger's view. The pervasive domination of metaphysics is indicative of, and correlative with, the pervasive influence of the concealment. Since concealment and revealment are equally ultimate, it is only to be expected that revealment will assert itself with equal effectiveness.

In the turn Being will reveal itself as Language or Utterance that produces thought. Language is defined as summoning silence, to safeguard the equal ultimacy of concealment. Thought is defined as the silence of authentic utterance, to indicate its arrival in concealment.

Until the turn thought is characterized as waiting for Being or as on its way to language. Both, however, appear to be objectifying.

The notion of waiting is introduced to emphasize that the initiative rests with Being. But it should not go unnoticed that as long as thought waits, Being has not arrived. This is further acknowledged by Heidegger himself when he states that no one knows when that arrival will occur.

Thought is said to be on its way to language to indicate that it is being beckoned away from objectifying conceptualizations to authentic articulation. However, it should be recognized that as long as thought is beckoned it has not transcended objectification. This is further emphasized by Heidegger himself when he states that authentic utterances can not be captured in assertions and that not every attempt to transform language will necessarily fail. Apparently, the pathway of philosophical thought has failed, precisely because it is bound up with objectifying assertions.[40] Implicitly Heidegger acknowledges the failure of his third effort. Being has not revealed itself. Therefore, thought is still waiting. Language has not been reached. Therefore, thought is still on its way.

His failure, and the reason for it, is expressed most succinctly in one of his last lectures, when he concludes by saying that he has merely spoken in inauthentic utterances. The blueprint of the provisional phenomenology apparently is still in force. The *logos* is required to renounce every assertion concerning the *phenomenon* as soon as it is made.[41]

Pugliese, one of the most perceptive Heidegger interpreters, is of the opinion that he has succeeded in what he set out to do. He holds that Heidegger has conclusively shown that Being lies at the root of his philosophizing and that this philosophizing is therefore truly circular.[42]

However, if Heidegger is taken seriously in his reflections upon his own work, this conclusion is not warranted. All of his thought and all of his language in both phases of his philosophy appear to be objectifying and inauthentic. The structure of his thinking is not circular. The two irreducible focal points of the ellipse are as much in evidence in his later thinking as they were in his earlier thinking. The gap between Being and thought is no more closed than the gap between existential interpretation and authentic understanding. The objectifying focal point and the non-objectifying focal point are mutually exclusive. The failure of the later phase of Heidegger's thinking is undeniable.

The implications are far-reaching. We have only Heidegger's word for the justification of his philosophy, including the concepts of Being and language. However, this word is in Heidegger's own admission objectifying. Hence it does not transcend the level of a hermeneutical theory, which prevents it by definition from providing the much needed justification, including the justification for the concepts of Being and language as they function in his philosophy. In short, Heidegger's word is fundamental for his philosophy but because it is unable to escape the liability of metaphysical deficiency it simultaneously invalidates it.

D. It is hardly surprising that the theological wing of the modern hermeneutical movement, which virtually owes its existence to the later Heidegger, is facing the same fundamental failure and the same far-reaching implications.

One of the representatives of this theological wing, H. Ott, wishes to move beyond Barth and Bultmann in terms of the later Heidegger. He recognized that in the thinking of neither theologian the theological enterprise and the nonobjectifying were coextensive. This implied, in his estimation, that in the case of both thinkers their theology was neither authenticated nor binding. To remedy this he posits that theological reflection originates in authentic understanding and merges again with it. However, the claim of circularity does not have any basis in fact. First, Ott states that authentic understanding or faith spurs on theology to endless reflection. Theology apparently never arrives. Second, he declares that a genuine reflection upon the essence of language, in the footsteps of Heidegger, will provide the solution to the hermeneutical problem.[43] It has already been established, however, that Heidegger's later thought failed to do so.

One of the chief representatives of the New Hermeneutic, G. Ebeling, claims that hermeneutics as an aid to authentic understanding must arise from the language-event and that it must be of the same nature as understanding. He further states that this brings the famous hermeneutical circle into view. However, in the same context he concedes that from the point of view of authentic understanding hermeneutics as its aid and the language-event as its ground are irreconcilable.[44]

Apparently neither Ott nor Ebeling are able to establish that the modern hermeneutical movement is characterized by a circular structure in which authentic understanding and hermeneutical thought fuse together into one non-objectifying focal point. This determines the fundamental failure of this movement.

E. Fuchs, the second major representative of the New Hermeneutic, apparently endeavors to break through the impasse by identifying the language-event as a saving-event and a love-event in which the divine "Yes" illuminates reality and unifies in community. He intimates that theological thought with its theological concepts succeeds where philosophical thought with its philosophical terminology fails.[45] This, however, will not do. The question is not, whether a concept is theological or philosophical, but whether it is objectifying or not. In this regard the philosophical wing of the modern hermeneutical movement and the theological wing of this movement face the same problems. Both speak only in objectifying language. This implies that also the word of the New Hermeneutic is no more than a hermeneutical theory and is not sufficient to validate its theology.

In conclusion, therefore, the New Hermeneutic does not only disqualify part of the language of Scripture because it is scientifically obsolete and all of the language of Scripture because it is metaphysically deficient. It also should disqualify itself because it does not transcend the level of metaphysical objectification. This implies that terms as language-event, saving-event, love-event, divine "Yes," illumination and unification are intrinsically meaningless. They do not mean, indeed, can not mean what they say. Neither do they mean what they do not, indeed, can not say.

This leads us to the final appraisal of the New Hermeneutic in which an inquiry is made into the ultimate conditions that make its emergence and failure both possible and necessary.

III. A TRANSCENDENTAL APPRAISAL OF THE NEW HERMENEUTIC

A. It has correctly been observed that behind the hermeneutics of Schleiermacher lies the "philosophical scheme of the necessary indissoluble subject-object correlation and its hermeneutical transcendence."[46] However, this does not only apply to Schleiermacher, but to all of the modern hermeneutical movement. This movement is rooted in the nature-freedom dialectic propelled into prominence by the philosophy of Immanuel Kant.

The nature pole is characterized by the scientific, theoretical, subject-object relationship. Everything that is objectifiable properly belongs to the realm of nature. The freedom pole transcends the subject-object relationship. Nothing that is objectifiable may properly be assigned to the realm of freedom.

The nature-freedom dialectic became prominent when the scientific mind-set became such a dominant force that it threatened the realm of human freedom and religion. Kant embarked upon the gigantic task of securing the inviolability of human freedom and religion by determining both the foundation and boundaries of the scientific approach. He solved the problem, fundamentally, by positing the discontinuity of the realm of nature and the realm of freedom. Science is given absolute, be it limited, autonomy within the realm of nature, which is self-contained but not all encompassing. Religion is assigned to the realm of freedom which is beyond the reach of scientific thought, but at the same time may not interfere in the internal affairs of the realm of nature.

The discontinuity of the realm of nature and the realm of freedom, however, does not preclude their coexistence. On the contrary, the nature-freedom scheme is dialectic in character precisely because the two poles simultaneously exclude and presuppose each other.

First, the two poles are what they are only in dependence upon each other. Objectifying nature can only be understood as such against the backdrop of non-objectifying freedom and *vice versa*.

Second, the two poles are what they are only in contrast with each other. Objectifying nature can only be understood as such in opposition to non-objectifying freedom and *vice versa*.

It is this dialectic, with its two mutually presupposing and excluding poles, that determines both the task and the failure of Kantian thought in general and of the modern hermeneutical movement, in both its phases, in particular.

B. It determines the task. All of Kantian thinking, whether philosophical or theological, aims at the full recognition and acknowledgement of a bifurcated reality, comprising both nature and freedom, as universally valid and binding. This in turn is designed to secure a peaceful coexistence in which both the autonomy of the nature pole and the contribution of the freedom pole are safeguarded. In order to reach the intended goal an inquiry is made into both realms and then a concentration point, a point of synthesis, is sought in order to demonstrate that a peaceful coexistence is possible and necessary.

With regard to Kant, his *Critique of Pure Reason* sets out to determine the character and the boundaries of the realm of nature. His *Critique of Practical Reason* proceeds to set forth the nature and primacy of the realm of freedom. His *Critique of Judgment,* finally, seeks to establish a point of synthesis that bridges the gap between the realm of nature and the realm of freedom.[47]

The modern hermeneutical movement follows the same pattern. The realms of the objectifiable and the non-objectifiable, whether they are designated philosophically or theologically, are sharply contrasted and then the search is on for the focal point of the so-called hermeneutical circle, which is constituted by the fusion of the objectifiable and the non-objectifiable and thus will validate one's experiencing of reality as bifurcated.

However, the dialectic does not only determine the task, it also determines the failure of Kantian thought.

The *prima facie* evidence already points in that direction. The later thinkers in the Kantian tradition reject the solution of the earlier ones. There is disagreement among contemporaries. And the theologians claim to have it over their counterparts.

However, there is more. Ultimately Kantian thinkers must fail for principal reasons. None of them can escape a self-defeating and a self-destructive antinomy which is the unavoidable concomitant of the Kantian dialectic. What is this antinomy?

When the Kantian thinker seeks to secure an unshakable foundation for the freedom pole by means of arriving at a point of synthesis that will insure a peaceful coexistence of freedom and nature, his tools are thought and language. The only thought and language, however, that can succeed is universally valid thought and language. All other thought and language lack binding power. But universally valid thought and language are objectifying in nature. For that reason they must fail. Objectifying thought and language can never make meaningful predication about the realm of freedom, whether in philosophical or theological terminology. The only tools that can succeed must fail by their very nature. The dialectic will insure that the tools will be used again and again. The mutual presupposition of the poles will compel the Kantian thinker to seek for the point of synthesis. At the same time the dialectic makes it a foregone conclusion that the tools will fail. The mutual exclusion of the poles will prevent the Kantian thinker from arriving at the point of synthesis. The objectifiable and the non-objectifiable do not merge, can not merge and will not merge. The elliptical structure of Kantian thought, with its two irreducible focal points, can not and will not evolve into a hermeneutical circle with one focal point. The moment Kantian thought and language spring into existence, the rift with the non-objectifiable, which it seeks to secure, begins to emerge.

Because of all this Kantian thinkers are faced with the inevitable fact that all their thinking and all their utterances pertain to the unthinkable and unutterable that eludes all thinking and all utterances. To be sure, the language of the theologians is different from that of the philosophers. But this is completely incidental. All language, whether philosophical or theological, loses its naming power, its power of predication. This is the great crisis that no representative of the modern hermeneutical movement can escape.

What is more important, however, the very failure of the thinking and language of the thinkers in the Kantian tradition must lead to the conclusion that the reality, which is supposed to correspond to the two poles of the dialectic or to the point of synthesis, whether presented in terms of understanding (Schleiermacher), existence (the early Heidegger), Being (the later Heidegger) or Language (Fuchs, Ebeling), has not been demonstrated. Indeed, it should be argued that such reality does not exist. The fact that the dialectic with its two poles in the driving force behind Kantian thinking does not imply its existence. In the final analysis, one has only the word of the Kantian thinker for it. And that word is disqualified.

C. Against the backdrop of the Kantian dialectic the structure approach and failure of the New Hermeneutic comes into sharp focus.

First, it is clear why the New Hermeneutic is not interested in simply determining methods, rules and techniques or interpretation. This would restrict hermeneutics to the realm of nature. It would not only be too provincial, but also in a real sense irrelevant.

Second, it is clear why the New Hermeneutic concentrates upon the process of understanding. It aims at developing an epistemology in terms of the concept of understanding that will establish communication with the realm of the non-objectifiable and thus posit it as inviolable.

Third, it is clear why the New Hermeneutic applies the "acids of modernity" to the language of the Bible. Scientific thought has the final authority in the realm of nature. Therefore, it will remove whatever it regards as obsolete.

Fourth, it is clear why the New Hermeneutic regards all of the language of the Bible as metaphysically deficient. None of it transcends the level of objectification.

Fifth, it is clear why the New Hermeneutic designates hermeneutics as an art. The term suggests that the point of synthesis has been found, the bridge that spans the gap between the objectifying nature of thought and language and the non-objectifying character of understanding. As such it is suspect and should not be uncritically adopted.

Sixth, it is clear why the New Hermeneutic fails in reaching its objective. The very dialectic that made the New Hermeneutic possible and necessary also determined its failure. The later phase of the modern hermeneutical movement is no more successful than the earlier phase. One objectifying theory is replaced by another.

Seventh, it is clear why the realities that allegedly correspond to the terminology used by the New Hermeneutic can be denied existence. One has only the word of the New Hermeneutic for it. And this word has, admittedly, been found wanting.

D. The question arises why the Kantian tradition refuses to concede defeat and continues with such persistence in its search for the elusive synthesis. Over a century and a half of admitted failure has not convinced the modern hermeneutical movement that it is fighting not just a losing, but a lost battle. In fact, in view of this it is nothing short of astonishing that throughout this time period it has not only become increasingly influential, but also made significant inroads in the larger evangelical community. Not only Karl Barth with his orthodox sounding response to old-time liberalism, but also Rudolph Bultmann with his emphasis on authentic understanding in contrast to a wooden scholasticism have received a sympathetic hearing. The necessity of the battle for an inerrant Scripture, strongly opposed by both these theologians is only one of the many evidences.[48]

The reason why the modern hermeneutical movement has not faded is to be found, in the words of one scholar, in its underlying "conceptual scheme," which enjoys the "status of unquestioned and absolute assumption."[49] This scheme is the nature-freedom polarity. An inquiry into its controlling influence and a challenge to its dominant position are long overdue.

The nature-freedom dialectic, as I have argued elsewhere,[50] is rooted in an act of rebellion against the God of Scripture. When man in his apostasy dethroned God, he was forced to interpret the universe from his newly acquired, autonomous, vantage point. On the one hand, he concluded to a principle of discontinuity and disorder, since reality appeared to him as contingent, unconditioned and undetermined, an unpredictable flux and a random aggregate of unconnected particulars. On the other hand, he introduced a principle of continuity and order, since reality required necessity, determination and control, a predictable stability and a universal structure to connect the particulars. These two principles sustain a dialectic relationship to each other. Discontinuity or disorder and continuity or order, by definition, simultaneously presuppose and exclude one another.

Whenever men or methodologies, consciously or not, have their roots in an apostate stance, they are always and by necessity in the grip of the dialectic, however it is designated.

In ancient philosophy the dialectic emerges in the form-matter scheme. This scheme dominated ancient thought and determined the direction of philosophy from the Pre-socratics to Plotinus and beyond. The primacy was assigned to the form pole (the principle of continuity) to offset and control the disturbing characteristics of the matter pole (the principle of discontinuity).

In modern philosophy the dialectic is translated into the nature-freedom polarity. This polarity controls modern thought from the Renaissance to Heidegger and beyond. Here the tables are turned. The primacy is assigned to the freedom pole (the principle of discontinuity) to defend the humanity of man against the increasing threat of the stifling rationalism, peaking in modern technocracy, of the nature pole (the principle of continuity).

The dialectic appears to be a veritable trap. Men or methodologies, caught in apostasy, whether by design or in ignorance, are burdened with the task of putting up a defense against the threat of the one pole in terms of and for the sake of the other one. Note the difference with the warfare required in Scripture. The Bible does not ask for a battle against one of two dialectic principles, which supposedly make up reality, on behalf of the other, and to referee their relationship to insure a peaceful coexistence. It calls for a battle against sin as a transgression of God's law and for holiness as a reflection of God's nature. The battle is not metaphysical and, then, basically epistemological. It is ethical and, therefore primarily actual.

In the meantime, the task to which the dialectic summons will never cease and never go anywhere. Because the two poles presuppose one another, they will always be a mutual threat. Therefore the task must continue. Further, because they exclude one another, there will never be a peaceful coexistence. Therefore the task will continue. The dialectic produces a never ending dead end street. All this accounts for the persistence of the modern hermeneutical movement to pursue the search for the elusive synthesis in spite of its continuous failure. The dialectic is a hard taskmaster. It condemns its victims to a veritable Sysiphus labor. Note again the difference with Scripture. It holds out the prospect of the final defeat of sin and of a new earth in which righteousness dwells. The task will be successfully completed.

All this is not to say that the dialectic is simply a methodological dead end street. The case is much more serious. If the dialectic were to succeed in its search for the synthesis, its view of reality, including that of the world, life and God, would prove to be correct! In other words, the dialectic is on a direct collision course with Scripture. This will now be shown, specifically with regard to the dialectic in its theological language garb of the nature-freedom polarity.

First, the nature-freedom dialectic amounts to a declaration of independence from the God of Scripture. To begin with, the nature pole is removed from his jurisdiction and control. Scientific thought has the final, absolute and only say. A sacrifice of the intellect is not tolerated. God is by definition excluded from every and any area that is within the reach of the human mind. He may not interfere in word or in deed. He must remain silent and inactive. Further, the freedom pole is said to be God's territory. However, the characteristics of this pole determine not only the nature of God so that he cannot speak and will be silent, but also the function of God so that he actually serves the cause of man's independence. He is introduced to establish and safeguard man's non-objectifying nature against the threat of dehumanizing objectification. In short, God is told to produce the point of synthesis that will keep him out of his own creation, now reinterpreted in terms of the subject-object scheme, and will guarantee man's freedom, now reinterpreted in terms of the transcendence of the subject-object polarity.

Second, the nature-freedom dialectic leads to a program of suppression of the truth of God. To begin with, because the nature pole does not tolerate God's interference, his manifestation in created reality is denied, and because in the nature pole scientific thought is assigned the final authority, God's revelation in Scripture is subjected to a most destructive critical approach. Further, because the freedom pole is non-objectifying, the language of Scripture in its totality is not only regarded as inadequate, but as incapable of expressing the subject matter of the Bible.[51]

Let it be emphatically added that this declaration of independence and this program of suppression is not only found in the more radical wing represented by Bultmann and his school, including the New Hermeneutic, but also in the more orthodox sounding wing of Barth and his followers. Neither Bultmann nor Barth honor a God who acts and speaks in history and requires man's thought to be captive unto the obedience of Christ. Neither Bultmann nor Barth honor a creation in which God's glory manifests itself and a Scripture which is the written Word of God, in its concepts and facts in particular and in its language in general. The dialectic does not permit it.

All this warrants only one conclusion. The dialectic, whether couched in philosophical or theological terminology, and Scripture are mutually antithetical and exclusive. They are on a collision course on which both can not survive, and will not survive. Either Scripture is destroyed in the name of the dialectic, which is evident from the modern hermeneutical movement, or the trap of the dialectic is sprung in the name of the Scripture. If there is a fundamental commitment to God, but one's methodology is unconsciously determined by the dialectic, a recognition of this fact and a subsequent conscious renunciation of both the methodology and the dialectic will spring the trap. However, if the control by the dialectic and the consequent methodology are ultimately rooted in an apostate stance, their renunciation ultimately originates in a radical repentance and a heart's surrender to the God of Scripture.

It appears, therefore, in concluding this transcendental appraisal of the New Hermeneutic, that the penultimate condition of one's methodology is the dominant control of either the dialectic or Scripture and the ultimate condition either apostasy from or surrender to the living God. The dominant control of the dialectic leads to the demise of divine truth. The dominant control of Scripture leads to the promotion of divine truth. Apostasy from the living God leads to death. Surrender to the living God leads to life.

NOTES

[1]*The New Hermeneutic*, eds. J. M. Robinson and J. B. Cobb, Jr. (New York: Harper & Row, Publishers, 1964); cf. H. M. Kuitert, *De Realiteit van het geloof* (Kampen: J. H. Kok, 1966), p. 56; C. E. Braaten, *History and Hermeneutics* (Philadelphia: The Westminster Press, 1952), p. 131; J. D. Smart, *The Strange Silence of the Bible in the Church* (Philadelphia: The Westminster Press, 1970), pp. 37-38; C. Van Til, *The New Hermeneutic* (Nutley: Presbyterian and Reformed Publishing Co., 1974); and A. C. Thiselton, "The New Hermeneutic," *New Testament Interpretation*, ed. I. Howard Marshall (Grand Rapids: Eerdmans Publishing Co., 1977), pp. 308-333.

[2]*The New Hermeneutic*, eds. J. M. Robinson and J. B. Cobb, Jr., pp. 6, 67; G. Ebeling, *Word and Faith* (Philadelphia: Fortress Press, 1963), pp. 313, 317-318.

[3]*The New Hermeneutic*, pp. 23-24, 54-56, 58, 62; Ebeling, *Word and Faith*, p. 318; E. Fuchs, *Hermeneutik* (Bad Cannstatt: R.&Müllerschön, 1958), p. 79, 131; Thiselton, "New Hermeneutic," pp. 309, 312-313; and H. G. Gadamer, *Truth and Method* (New York: The Seabury Press, 1975), p. 477.

[4]Ebeling, *Word and Faith*, p. 318, "The primary phenomenon in the realm of understanding is not understanding OF language, but understanding THROUGH language."

[5]J. Julius Scott, Jr., "Some Problems in Hermeneutics for Contemporary Evangelicals," p. 7; a paper distributed and read at a regional meeting of the Evangelical Theological Society, held at Covenant College, Tennessee.

[6]Thiselton, "New Hermeneutic," pp. 308, 329.

[7]*The New Hermeneutic*, pp. 19ff.; Ebeling, *Word and Faith*, p. 313.

[8]R. Bultmann, "Neues Testament und Mythologie," *Kerygma und Mythos* ed. H. W. Bartsch, (Hamburg-Volksdorf: Herbert Reich, Evangelischer Verlag, 1951), Vol. I, pp. 15ff.; *Jesus Christ and Mythology* (New York: Charles Scribner's Sons, 1958), "Zum Problem der Entmytheologisierung," *Kerygma und Mythos*, Vol. II, pp. 179ff.; *Glauben und Verstehen* (Tübingen: J. C. B. Mohr, 1933-1965), Vol. II, pp. 211-35, Vol. III, pp. 81ff., Vol. IV, pp. 128ff.

[9]E. Fuchs, *Hermeneutik*, p. 111; *New Hermeneutic*, p. 54.

[10]H. G. Gadamer, *Truth and Method*, p. 478; *New Hermeneutic*, p. 68.

[11]G. Ebeling, *God and Word* (Philadelphia: The Fortress Press, 1967), p. 2.

[12]E. Fuchs, *Hermeneutik*, pp. 126-34, spec. 130-31; *Zur Frage nach dem historischen Jesus* (Tübingen: J. C. B. Mohr, 1965), p. 425; P. J. Achtemeier, *An Introduction to the New Hermeneutic* (Philadelphia: The Westminster Press, 1969), p. 91; G. Ebeling, *The Nature of Faith* (London, 1961), pp. 87, 183; *The New Hermeneutic*, pp. 54, 58.

[13]E. Fuchs, *Zur Frage*, p. 420; "The New Testament and the Hermeneutical Problem," *The New Hermeneutic*, pp. 143-44; *The New Hermeneutic*, pp. 45, 57, 60-61.

[14]E. Fuchs, *Zur Frage*, pp. 409-410, 420.

[15]R. Bultmann, *Glauben und Verstehen*, Vol. I, pp. 1ff., spec. 18-25; G. Ebeling, *Word and Faith*, pp. 51, 55-61, 307; E. Fuchs, *Zur Frage*, pp. 182-83, 216-17, 427; S. U. Zuidema, *Van Bultman naar Fuchs* (Franeker: T. Wever, n.d.), pp. 31, 59-60, 75, 77, 89-90.

[16]E. Fuchs, *Zum Hermeneutischen Problem in der Theologie* (Tübingen: J. C. B. Mohr, 1959), pp. 179-80; C. E. Braaten, *History and Hermeneutics*,

pp. 142-43; G. Ebeling, *Word and Faith*, pp. 328, 331, "Thus the text by means of the sermon becomes the hermeneutic aid in the understanding of present experience; the sermon is EXECUTION of the text."

[17]This appears to be acknowledged by Ebeling, *Word and Faith*, p. 60, when he declares that the nature of the hermeneutical problem "is acutely concentrated in the act of preaching."

[18]Ebeling, *Word and Faith*, pp. 320-22.

[19]F. D. E. Schleiermacher, *Hermeneutics*, ed. H. Kimmerle, trans. J. Duke and J. Forstman, (Missoula: Scholars Press, 1977), pp. 33-35, 99ff., 117ff., 153ff., 161ff.; R. E. Palmer, *Hermeneutics* (Evanston: Northwestern University Press, 1969), pp. 86, 88-90; H. W. Frei, *The Eclipse of the Biblical Narrative* (New Haven: Yale University Press, 1974), pp. 290ff., 300.

[20]Schleiermacher, *Hermeneutics*, pp. 35, 68-69, 98-100; Frei, *The Eclipse*, pp. 291-93, 299-300, 302-03.

[21]Schleiermacher, *Hermeneutics*, pp. 68ff. The term "oscillation" is suggested by H. W. Frei, *The Eclipse*, p. 292. See also pp. 303, 308-09.

[22]Frei, *The Eclipse*, pp. 300ff.

[23]Ibid., pp. 300ff., spec. p. 305.

[24]Ibid., pp. 319-20.

[25]Ibid., pp. 300, 305. Frei sees correctly that in terms of Schleiermacher's intention "explication becomes secondary, in part because understanding is in principle a self-completing operation or process of which explication is merely the external expression." However Kimmerle recognized that in reality this was not the case. H. Kimmerle, "Hermeneutical Theory or Ontological Hermeneutics," *History and Hermeneutic, Journal for Theology and the Church*, ed. R. W. Funk, (New York: Harper & Row, Publishers, 1967), Vol. IV, pp. 107ff.

[26]M. Heidegger, *Being and Time* (New York: Harper & Brothers, 1962), p. 62.

[27]Ibid., p. 59.

[28]Ibid., p. 61.

[29]Ibid., pp. 50, 60-63, 408.

[30]Ibid., pp. 25-29, 32-34, 333, 360.

[31]Ibid., pp. 350, 353, 357.

[32]Ibid., pp. 359-61.

[33]Ibid., pp. 362-63. See also pp. 32 and 195.

[34]The comparison with an ellipse has been suggested by J. P. A. Mekkes, *Scheppingsopenbaring en wijsbegeerte* (Kampen: J. H. Kok, 1961), p. 77; and J. van der Hoeven, *Kritische ondervraging van de fenomenologische rede* (Amsterdam: Buijten & Schipperheijn, 1963), p. 154.

[35]Van der Hoeven, *Kritische ondervraging*, p. 142.

[36]M. Heidegger, "On the Essence of Truth," *Existence and Being* (London: Vision Press Ltd., 1949), pp. 340-47; *Identität und Differenz* (Pfullingen: G. Neske, 1957), pp. 46-47, 51, 56, 59-71; *Was is Metaphysik* (Frankfurt a. Main: V. Klostermann, 1949, pp. 7, 8, 11, 19; *Über den Humanismus* (Frankfurt a. Main: V. Klostermann, 1947), p. 17.

[37]Heidegger, "On the Essence of Truth," pp. 346-47; *Holzwege* (Frankfurt a. Main: V. Klostermann, 1952), pp. 243, 310, 336; *Vorträge und Aufsätze* (Pfullingen: G. Neske, 1954), p. 264; and *Der Satz vom Grund* (Pfullingen: G. Neske, 1957), p. 98.

[38]M. Heidegger *Einführung in die Metaphysik* (Tübingen: M. Niemeyer Verlag, 1953), pp. 11, 29, 78, 87, 100, 102-9, 115, 120-26, 135-36; *Holzwege*, pp. 303, 310, 336, 341; *Vorträge und Aufsätze*, pp. 271-72.

[39]Heidegger, *Vorträge und Aufsätze*, pp. 176-81; *Nietzsche* (Pfullingen: G. Neske, 1961), Vol. II, pp. 355-58, 368, 379, 389-92, 397; *Der Satz vom Grund*, pp. 107, 129, 157, 159; *Identität und Differenz*, pp. 46-47, 71-72.

[40]M. Heidegger, *Discourse on Thinking* (New York: Harper & Row, Publishers, 1966), pp. 68, 74-75, 79-80, 86, 89; *Unterwegs zur Sprache*, pp. 15, 29-33, 134-35, 138, 141, 146, 148, 152-55, 169, 172, 195, 228, 236, 241-42, 250-54, 261-68.

[41]M. Heidegger, "Zeit und Sein," extensively quoted in O. Pugliese, *Vermittlung und Kehre* (München/Freiburg: Verlag Karl Alber, 1965), pp. 161ff., spec. p. 170, "Er (*i.e.* the lecture) hat nur in Aussagesätzen gesprochen."

[42]Pugliese, *Vermittlung*, pp. 12-14, 208, spec. 14, "Das 'Denken' *ist* bei Heidegger . . . -extrem formuliert-*selber* Geschichtlichkeit in transzendental-ontologischem Sinne."

[43]H. Ott, "Das Problem des nicht-objektivierenden Denkens und Redens in der Theologie," *Zeitschrift für Theologie und Kirche* LXI (1964), pp. 327ff.; "Language and Understanding," *New Theology No. 4*, eds. M. E. Marty and D. G. Peerman (New York: The McMillan Co., 1966), pp. 137-38, 141-45.

[44]G. Ebeling, *Word and Faith*, pp. 314-15, 322-23.

[45]E. Fuchs, *Philosophische Rundschau*, VIII (1961), p. 108; S. U. Zuidema, *Van Bultmann naar Fuchs*, pp. 6, 31, 58, 89-91; E. Fuchs, *Zum Hermeneutischen Problem*, p. 137.

[46]Frei, *The Eclipse*, p. 320.

[47]Fr. Copleston, *A History of Philosophy* (New York: Doubleday & Company, 1964), Vol. VI, 1, p. 239. "Kant tries, as far as our consciousness is concerned at least, to bridge the gulf between the mechanistic world of Nature as presented in physical science and the world of morality, freedom and faith."

[48]Karl Barth has left his mark upon the thinking of G. C. Berkouwer, Rudolph Bultmann upon that of H. M. Kuitert, both of which deny the inerrancy of Scripture. For Barth's influence upon Berkouwer, see F. W. Buytendach, *Aspekte van die vorm/inhoud-problematiek met betrekking tot die organiese skrifinspirasie in die nuwere theologie in Nederland* (Amsterdam: Ton Bolland, 1972), p. 333, where he quotes A. D. R. Polman in this matter. For Bultmann's influence upon Kuitert, see H. M. Kuitert, *De realiteit van het geloof, passim*.

[49]Frei, *The Eclipse*, p. 321.

[50]H. Krabbendam, "B. B. Warfield versus G. C. Berkouwer on Scripture," *Inerrancy*, ed. N. L. Geisler (Grand Rapids, Zondervan Publishing House, 1979), pp. 443ff.

[51]See for the issue of the adequacy of language, J. Frame, "God and Biblical Language," *God's Inerrant Word*, ed. J. W. Montgomery (Minneapolis: Bethany Fellowship, 1973), pp. 173ff., and J. I. Packer, "The Adequacy of Language," *Inerrancy*, pp. 197ff.

A Response to The New Hermeneutic

James I. Packer
Professor of Systematic and
Historical Theology
Regent College

A Response to The New Hermeneutic

James I. Packer

My response to Dr. Krabbendam's analysis of the proposals which the so-called new hermeneutic involves falls into three sections. First, I shall contextualize the analysis by locating the new hermeneutic within the wider hermeneutical discussion of which it really forms part. Second, I shall support the analysis with some comments on what is at stake here for Christianity. Third, I shall reflect a little on the principles of faithful hermeneutics, picking up some questions which the analysis raises.

I. THE WIDER HERMENEUTICAL DEBATE

How did the new hermeneutic of Fuchs and Ebeling ever come to birth? Thereby hangs a tale.

The word hermeneutics, in its Latin form *hermeneutica*, first appeared in the seventeenth century, when Protestant scholars began to use it in the titles of their books on biblical interpretation.[1] But their concept of interpretation was much older, going back to the start of Christianity and in formula terms to Aristotle's tract *Peri Hermeneias* (On Interpretation), written in the fourth century B.C.[2] Aristotle did not of course invent interpretation; as so often, he merely offered a precise description of what actually goes on. The activity of interpreting phenomena, and in particular documents, has been going on since history began. But Aristotle's formula is illuminating, and has been influential, and is worth setting out as a reference point.

Aristotle defined *hermeneia* as the process of stating what is true and false about objects of attention. Explains Richard E. Palmer:

> "Interpretation" in this sense is the primary object of the intellect in formulating a true judgment about a thing. A prayer, a command, a question or a deprecative sentence is not a statement, according to Aristotle, but is derived from a statement; it is a secondary form of sentence which appears in some situation which the intellect originally perceived in the form of a

> statement. (For Aristotle, typically, the intellect perceives meaning as statement.) . . . In general, Aristotle divides the basic operations of the intellect into (1) the understanding of simple objects, (2) the operations of composing and dividing, (3) the operation of reasoning from known to unknown things. Enunciation—Aristotle's name for *hermeneia*—deals only with the second: the constructive and divisive operation of making statements in which there is truth or falsity.[3]

In other words (putting it colloquially) interpretation means for Aristotle seeing what you are looking at and saying of it what is and is not there.

Applied to Bible study, Aristotle's approach yields at once the idea of interpretation as a process of perceiving, first, what the text is talking about, second, what it says about it, and third, what our reaction and response should be. This idea—which in any case is common sense, following from the fact that documents are written in order to communicate, and furthermore is plainly basic to the New Testament interpretation of the Old—was taken for granted by all throughout the patristic, mediaeval and Reformation eras. During these centuries it was bound up with a further unquestioned assumption—namely, belief in the divine inspiration and instrumentality of Scripture: belief, that is, that the biblical text is God's word to the world, and as such the channel of his particular instruction about salvation and righteousness to each individual, as is clearly expressed with reference to the Old Testament in, for instance, 2 Timothy, 3:15-17. The fact that the Reformers rejected the allegorical way of interpretation that had prevailed before meant, of course, that henceforth many passages were differently understood; however, the new insistence that what God says to us in and through texts is application of what their human authors were saying to their own envisaged readers, neither more nor less, did not change the basic notion of what biblical interpretation is. This historic notion, predicated on the further historic notions of the inspiration and instrumentality of Scripture, still determines conservative Protestant approaches to the task of understanding the Bible, approaches which rightly claim to stand in the succession of the Reformers: see, for proof of this, the hermeneutical handbooks of Terry, Stibbs, Mickelsen, Ramm, Sproul and Berkhof.[4]

But among rationalistic Protestants in the seventeenth and eighteenth centuries the sense of Scripture as the once-for-all, here-and-now utterance of God faded, and out of this came a double trauma for theology, comparable to the boxer's one-two (cross to the midriff, bringing down your opponent's guard, followed by a punch to his exposed jaw). Trauma number one was the critical philosophy of mind set forth by Kant the deist, which silenced God by making it methodologically unphilosophical to suppose that he sends men any messages by any means at all. Trauma number two was Schleiermacher's reconstruction of theology along culturally romantic lines as the descriptive verbalizing of corporate Christian experience (feeling, in the sense of emotionally-laden intuition)—in other words, as a phenomenological, as distinct from speculative, venture in what one has to call natural theology. Many saw Schleiermacher's reconception as vitalizing therapy for theology, and muzzy assertions of punch-drunk type were heard among professionals to the effect that the Schleiermacherian method stopped Kant from being a threat and made everything in theology feel pretty good. But in fact Schleiermacher's proposal was and remains a knock-out blow to every form of Christianity that seeks to live by words that proceed from the mouth of God, according to the example and instruction of the biblical Jesus (cf. Matt. 4:4).

Schleiermacher's redefining of theology was part of a larger programme whereby he aimed to blend theology into the German Romantic movement that was developing all round him, and so restore to culture the religious dimension which the rationalism of the Enlightenment had almost snuffed out. His pioneer reflections on hermeneutics belonged to the same programme. For him there was no distinction between biblical (sacred) hermeneutics and other literary (secular) hermeneutics: in both, the task was to understand the total experience and state of mind which the author's words expressed, and when this was accomplished the job was done. The technique for doing it was partly linguistic and logical, partly empathetic and divinatory. These ideas of Schleiermacher opened a new era of debate about the meaning and method of understanding.

A genealogical line runs from Schleiermacher to the new hermeneutic. It takes in Dilthey, who saw hermeneutics as essentially an imaginative reliving of the life reflected in the text under study, and who was the first to speak of the "hermeneutical circle" in which the interpreter's provisional sense of the whole and his specific conclusions about the parts challenge and correct each other at each stage of his enquiry. It takes in Heidegger, who in both his earlier and later periods was trying to show how the dynamic reality of Being impacts us, imparting a verbally expressible understanding of itself. It takes in Bultmann, phenomenological exegete, positivist historian, Kahlerian Christological dualist, Kantian philosophical dualist and existentialist preacher, for whom the New Testament was culture-bound mythological clothing for a new self-understanding through ineffable encounter with God, and Jesus, through whom the encounter was triggered, was not God, wrought no miracles and did not rise from the dead.[5] From this formidable family tree came the new hermeneutic of Bultmann's pupils Fuchs and Ebeling, who on the basis of their master's scepticism about New Testament facts want to give substance to the thought that the self-defining language-event that occurs through the study and preaching of Scripture begets understanding without appeal to "subject-object" thinking, and so without exposing it to the acids of relativism in which our positivist age immerses all "objective" assertions about supernatural facts or truths.

For the record, this is not the whole story of hermeneutics since Schleiermacher. From him, Dilthey and Heidegger has also stemmed a wider debate on hermeneutical principles and procedures involving practitioners of the humanities across the board—philosophers, linguists, teachers of literature, lawyers, historians of ideas and others. Disciplines involved include logic, linguistic philosophy, semantics, semiology, communication theory, history and literary criticism. Central to the discussion is the problem of achieving in our own era and cultural milieu a correct understanding of what was said or signified in another. The pot is stirred by a conflict of views as to what a correct understanding might be, and what criteria determine it. In literary study, for instance, the claim that the meaning of a text is the author's expressed meaning, and that there is a specifiable logic of validation by which that meaning may be known, does battle with the counter-claim that the meaning of a text is its meaning for this or that student of it, and that something new genuinely breaks forth from the text as students of it bring genuinely new questions and experiences to it.[6] Here the battle lines are parallel to those between exponents of the old and of the new hermeneutic in Protestant Christianity. But we cannot pursue discussion of the wider issue in this present response.

II. GOOD-BYE TO REVELATION AND RATIONALITY

Now I move to the substantive question on which Dr. Krabbendam concentrated throughout, namely the verdict which the new hermeneutic merits as a contribution to Christian thought.

What is "hermeneutic?"—or "hermeneutics": for the singular

and plural forms are used interchangeably. For me, as I think for most today, these terms denote the theory of the process whereby human beings come to understand God's current communication to them through Holy Scripture. To those who follow the old paths, this will mean on the one hand formulating right principles for exegeting and applying the biblical text and on the other hand showing how the Holy Spirit enlightens sin-darkened minds to grasp with clarity and certainty the reality of God's word and work set forth in Scripture as these bear on our lives. Theologically, the best overall presentation of principles of objective interpretation and subjective understanding properly combined seems still to be John Owen's treatise of 1678, *Causes, Ways, and Means, of understanding the Mind of God, as revealed in his Word, wih assurance therein, And a declaration of the perspicuity of the Scriptures, with the external means of the interpretation of them.*[7] Latter-day evangelical theology has tended in its textbooks and seminary courses to separate the study of interpretative principles from reflection on the conditions and means of spiritual understanding, with the result that the message-character of Scripture, its status as communication from God specifically applying to each hearer and reader, has not always been given proper prominence. By contrast (and to some extent in reaction) neo-orthodox and existentialist Protestantism in this century has made much of the instrumentality of Scripture as the medium of God's moment-by-moment speaking to us; it has however failed to see Scripture as God's given message in and of itself, and this has meant arbitrariness, more or less, due to lack of external control, in all its many attempts to state what God is telling us through Scripture here and now. Evangelicals (be it said) need urgently to recover Owen's perspective on what it means to be taught by God, so that we shall not any longer seem to be setting the given content of the Word, apart from any reference to the illuminating Spirit, over against the neo-orthodox and existentialist appeal to the illuminating Spirit, apart from any concept of the given content of the Word: for both extremes are lopsided and inadequate. Just at present, however, the point I would stress is that the older approach sets Scripture, the objective of interpretative study, in control of that study, in the sense that it will not accept any proposed account of God's gift or promise or command or will or work, past or present, which runs counter to one or more passages in Scripture itself. For it is here that the ways of the old and the new hermeneutic divide.

In the new hermeneutic of Fuchs and Ebeling there is no biblical control. Why not? Because these writers maintain a systematic distinction between what texts meant historically and what they come to mean existentially. Hermeneutics to them is the study of an intrinsically enigmatic process whereby two separate-seeming things occur together. On the one hand we enter empathetically into the personal thought-world, existence and convictions of the biblical writers in their culture long ago. Then, on the other hand, even as we do this, consciously "distancing" ourselves and our world from them and theirs, a language-event occurs that changes us; our "horizons" (presuppositions, view of ourselves in our world, prejudices, things taken for granted) get impacted by what we read, and the result is understanding that was not there before. This understanding, which Fuchs and Ebeling as good Bultmannian existentialists describe as a self-understanding achieved in and by decision, is understanding *through* the text; but how it relates to grammatico-historical understanding *of* the text is problematical. It is certainly not a precise application of universal principles which the text exhibits for every man's learning.

Professionally Fuchs, like Bultmann, is a New Testament scholar. What does he claim to have found through the New Testament? What New Testament language (not the words as such, but the linguistically-constituted dynamic of the language event) imparts is (says he) a call to selfless love. Faith is entirely a matter of answering this call by decision. "In the language event I give priority to love. . . . The essence of language"—he means biblical and churchly language, viewed as a dynamic of understanding—"is its movement toward love, derived from love. . . . In the world one must *believe* in love. And one can do that only when the word *to* love—as proclaimed word *of* love—puts us in decision as to what we think of our present."[8] So faith for Fuchs is not belief in Jesus who died and rose, nor in the propositions of the apostolic gospel which announces itself as God's own teaching about Jesus who died and rose. Fuchs thus sentences himself, as P. J. Achtemeier puts it, "to defend a view of faith based on some portions of the New Testament"—Achtemeier is referring to Fuchs's exegesis of some of Jesus' parables—"from a view of faith based on other portions."[9] This drastic narrowing of the New Testament outlook does not create confidence in the method which produced it.

Dr. Krabbendam criticized the new hermeneutic as being, first, incoherent (objectifying in its very attempt to get beyond subject-object objectification) and, second, apostate (having its roots in the

Kantian nature-freedom polarity, which is a denial of the sovereign, self-announcing God of the Bible). His criticisms were, I think, successful and indeed unanswerable. I want now to add two further criticisms, both of which I pose as questions.

First: Can the new hermeneutic state, even in principle, the relation between what it claims that individuals receive from the biblical text in the language-event and what that text meant historically, as grammatico-historical exegesis determines this? It seems not.

Fuchs leads with his chin at this point, claiming emphatically that in the word-event the interpreter is interpreted rather than the text.[10] Pinnock did not overstate when he wrote that for Fuchs "the text is in motion! . . . It stands in dynamic, existential relation with its interpreter, and may be interpreted"—meaning, may strike sparks off him— "in the opposite way from that which the writer intended."[11] For Fuchs' basic thought is that of Heidegger, who insisted that the word-event is on a different plane from subject-object thinking. Subject-object thinking, which in Heidegger means the "I-it" way of conceptualizing reality that grasping the text's message occurs within the limits and on the lines laid down by what the text "objectively" means. ("Objectively" here signifies historically, permanently and publicly, and "means" signifies "meant at, and has meant from, the time of writing.") Fuchs's belief that the new self-understanding emerges as the text is cut loose from the restraints of objective historical exegesis and so set free to interpret its interpreter, sets us off and running along a path of fundamentally uncontrolled linguistic mysticism, where almost anything, as it seems, could bring almost anything to speech. For the restraint of the text as object—i.e., as carrier of the precise meaning that its words express—has been withdrawn, and Fuchs's own account of Christian faith, being no more, in terms of his own theory, than his own personal self-understanding, cannot be determinative for the rest of us. It is evident that Fuchs does not see this, but it is also evident that his account of the language-event as transcending the subject-object way of thinking makes the above conclusion logically inevitable.

Second: Can the new hermeneutic provide any criterion of truth of value for assessing the new self-understanding(s) to which language-events give rise? Again, it seems not.

Remember where Fuchs has placed us. The criteria of correspondence with apostolic teaching in general and the historical sense of the text in particular no longer apply. What is now left? Is the mere fact of being more or less startling to us the criterion whereby new thoughts about ourselves and our lives, triggered by the text, are henceforth to be evaluated? Should the most startling be judged the most authentic? "In what way" asks J. C. Weber "can we know that language does not bring to expression illusion, falsehood, or even chaos? If the criterion of truth is only in the language-event itself, how can the language-event be safeguarded against delusion, mockery or utter triviality? Why cannot the language-event be a disguised event of nothingness? . . . Fuchs's ontology is in danger of dissolving into a psychological illusionism"[12]—by which, presumably, Weber means an inducing of the sense that something significant happens when nothing significant happens. There seems no counter to this criticism. Fuchs really has left us to sink in the swamps of subjectivist subjectivity, with no available criterion of truth and value for any language-events that happen. Those who know how mixed-up, obsessive, dishonest and perverse is the human heart may well shudder.

The new hermeneutic is the end of the Schleiermacherian road. Its denial of the reality of God-given truth, linked with its rejection of the subject-object frame for knowledge of God through Scripture, produces a state of affairs in which revelation and rationality have been lost together. Logically, the new hermeneutic is relativism; philosophically, it is irrationalism; psychologically, it is freedom to follow unfettered religious fancy; religiously, it is uncontrolled individualistic mysticism; theologically, it is illuminism; structurally, it is all these things not by accident but of necessity. It seems unlikely that it can live long.

III. AFTERTHOUGHTS

But when we have laid the new hermeneutic to rest, some questions still remain.

It is a good rule for the theologian, when criticizing others' positions, to evaluate their purposes separately from their positions and ask himself how, if those purposes seem right, he proposes to implement them in terms of his own convictions. We should do this in relation to the new hermeneutic before we turn our backs on its corpse.

What was its aim? There is no mystery here; Fuchs and Ebeling, standing on Bultmann's shoulders, made their goals perfectly clear. On the one hand, they sought to escape the historical relativism which they believed to be inescapably bound up with critical study of the Scriptures. It seemed to them that this relativism, as seen for instance in Troeltsch, was the direct result of subject-object thinking, and that the way to transcend it was to posit, against the background of the historical relativism which would otherwise be the last word, the self-generated language-event, the hermeneutical occurrence which interprets itself in and by its interpretation and the personal subject to whom it happens. Borrowing from Heidegger, they claimed that man's "linguisticality" is the clue to understanding his "existence," and that, as Fuchs puts it, "God, word, and faith in this context are not at all concepts and most of all not metaphors. Rather they are the expression of an event, they are "language event" and . . . are to be thought about as such."[13] Thus, on the other hand, they sought to show how texts that have been worked over and relativized historically as expressing one bygone viewpoint among many, can "speak" afresh, "striking home" to us by their transforming interpretations of us, in the event of preaching ("proclamation").

How, we ask, should the decisive absoluteness of Scripture, and its transforming power when preached, be explicated, if not in the terms proposed by the new hermeneutic? Can any of the bits and pieces which went into the making of the new hermeneutic serve evangelicals as means to this end? I raise for discussion the following questions.

(1) Should we not in our systematic theology set the inspiration of Scripture—that is, its giveness as the revealed Word (message) of God—in the context, perspective and frame of reference which are established by its instrumentality—that is, its God-announced function of being the means whereby God through his Spirit communicates with us, instructing us for faith and righteousness and salvation (cf. 2 Tim. 3:15-17)? Is our anti-Barthian habit of playing down instrumentality in order to play up inspiredness a good path to follow or not?

(2) Should we not in our theology of God communicating with us through Scripture take over, and redefine for our own purposes, the idea that understanding occurs through "language events" as our own "horizon" (outlook limited by presuppositions bound up with our cultural conditioning and our sinfulness together) is impacted by the different "horizon" possessed and projected by this or that biblical author? Is not the highlighting of the shock which this clash may and sometimes needs to impart an important move when explaining to ourselves and others what is supposed to be happening when the written Word of God is studied and preached? Is this not one mode of the Holy Spirit's teaching work?

(3) Should we not in our bibliology make much of the thought

that Scripture is intended to do more for us than give us information? The need to counter viewpoints, like that of Bultmann and the new hermeneutic, which deny that, in the words of Augustine's prayer, "what your Scripture says, you say," leads us often to talk as if the Bible were entirely a complex of revealed propositions, and to make little or nothing of its performative, imperative, evocative, imaginative dimensions of meaning and communication. Is this not a theological weakness? And does it not sometimes produce didactic preaching which lacks life-changing punch, and is to that extent unbiblical in character?

(4) Should we not in our spirituality make more than we do of the fact that my own "horizon" may become a hindrance to my knowing and hearing God, and being taught by him from his Word? Do we not need a more substantial understanding than is sometimes found in our predominantly defensive, apologetically-oriented evangelicalism of what it means to be interpreted, judged and corrected in relation to the day-to-day life that we actually live, by God's utterance in Scripture?

By prompting these questions the new hermeneutic, however nonsensical in itself, still renders us, I believe, a service.

NOTES

[1]E.g., J. C. Dannhauer, *Hermeneutica Sacra, sive methodus explicandarum Sacrarum Literarum* (1654).

[2]Aristotle, *On Interpretation*. Commentary by St. Thomas and Cajetan. Translated by Jean T. Oesterle (Milwaukee: Marquette University Press, 1962).

[3]Richard E. Palmer, *Hermeneutics: Interpretation Theory in Schleiermacher, Dilthy, Heidegger and Gadamer* (Evanston: Northwestern University Press, 1969), p. 21.

[4]Milton S. Terry, *Biblical Hermeneutics* (New York: Hunt and Eaton, 1883; reprinted, Grand Rapids: Zondervan, 1952); Alan M. Stibbs, *Understanding God's Word*, revised D. and G. Wenham (London: IVP, 1976); A. B. Mickelsen, *Interpreting the Bible* (Grand Rapids: Eerdmans, 1963); Bernard Ramm, *Protestant Biblical Interpretation* (Boston: Wilde, 1956); R. C. Sproul, *Knowing Scripture* (Downer's Grove: IVP, 1977); Louis Berkhof, *Principles of Biblical Interpretation* (Grand Rapids: Baker Book House, 1950).

[5]The measure of Bultmann's total position is well taken by Robert C. Roberts, *Rudolf Bultmann's Theology: A Critical Interpretation* (Grand Rapids: Eerdmans, 1976) and Anthony C. Thiselton, *The Two Horizons: New Testament Hermeneutics and Philosophical Description with Special Reference to Heidegger, Bultmann, Gadamer and Wittgenstein* (Exeter: Paternoster Press and Grand Rapids: Eerdmans, 1980), pp. 205-92.

[6]See E. D. Hirsch Jr., *Validity of Interpretation* (New Haven: Yale University Press, 1967), especially the critique of Gadamer, pp. 245-64. Palmer, a Gadamerian fellow-traveller, hits back at Hirsch, *Hermeneutics*, pp. 60-65, accusing him of narrowness and superficiality.

[7]J. Owen, *Works*, ed. W. Goold (London: Banner of Truth Trust, 1967), pp. 118-234.

[8]E. Fuchs, "Response to the American Discussion," in *The New Hermeneutic*, ed. James M. Robinson and John B. Cobb Jr. (New York: Harper and Row, 1964), pp. 241f.

[9]P. J. Achtemeier, *An Introduction to the New Hermeneutic* (Philadelphia: Westminster Press, 1969), p. 162.

[10]"Each science orients itself to its subject matter. In this case the subject matter is yourself, dear reader." *The New Hermeneutic*, p. 141.

[11]Clark Pinnock, *Biblical Revelation* (Chicago: Moody Press, 1971), p. 226.

[12]J. C. Weber, "Language-event and Christian Faith" in *Theology Today*, 21 (1965), p. 455.

[13]Fuchs, *The New Hermeneutic*, p. 242.

A Response to
The New Hermeneutic

Royce G. Gruenler
Professor of New Testament
Gordon-Conwell Theological
Seminary

A Response to The New Hermeneutic

Royce G. Gruenler

I. INTRODUCTION TO THE CENTRAL PROBLEM OF THE NEW HERMENEUTIC

A. Hendrik Krabbendam's paper has correctly described the intention of the New Hermeneutic to reverse the hermeneutical flow of interpretation by allowing language itself to address and interpret the interpreter. The primacy of the language-event in the New Hermeneutic reflects the priority of the more mystical and passive attitude of the later Heidegger who listened to and waited upon Being to "speak." Professor Krabbendam demonstrates astutely how this listening to the language-event is understood by the new hermeneuticians to transcend mere speech and objective knowledge, opening the door to a more radical historical criticism of the objective text of Scripture and "to burn everything that will burn."

B. As I have observed in my own hermeneutical study, *New Approaches to Jesus and the Gospels: An Exegetical and Phenomenological Study of Synoptic Christology*,[1] non-evangelical scholarship on the Gospels tends to contract Jesus as speaker out of the story, except as he discloses some non-objective understanding of personal existence to the hearer of the language-event. But since this is an entirely subjective experience, the objective texts of the Gospels are open to the most extreme kind of redactional criticism. Professor Krabbendam points out correctly how thoroughly Kantian this is and how Kant's discontinuity between the realm of nature (science) and the realm of freedom (religion) is perpetuated in the New Hermeneutic. Ironically, the New Testament critic, functioning as a scientist, has complete autonomy over the objective and historical biblical text, and complete autonomy in his subjective experience of the language-event. At the close of his paper, Professor Krabbendam goes to the heart of the matter when he describes from a biblical perspective how the nature-freedom dialectic of the New Hermeneutic is really traceable to a rebellious declaration of independence from the living God of Scripture. My paper continues this theme by employing Van Til's presuppositional hermeneutic to Gadamer and other representatives of the New Hermeneutic.

II. VAN TIL'S CRITIQUE OF THE NEW HERMENEUTIC

A. According to Van Til's hermeneutic, an authentic exegesis of the fact and facts of Jesus Christ in the Gospels does not mean the imposing of a set of dogmatic assumptions upon brute and unknowable "facts out there," in Kantian fashion. Rather, it means that God has already interpreted the facts of nature and history by creating and sustaining a world which is the proper vehicle for the incarnation of Christ and special revelation. Jesus Christ does not come into alien territory—occupied territory, yes, but not alien. Hence the physical laws of creation, wheat and wine, eating and fellowshiping, the language of persons and the movements of nations all become the materials Jesus uses to proclaim the inauguration of the kingdom of God and the time of salvation. Common grace and special grace find their union in him. This is the presupposition of proper exegesis.

The penetration of Van Til's analysis of presuppositions in contemporary hermeneutical thought is especially noteworthy in his study, *The New Hermeneutic*.[2] As in his earlier works, Van Til relentlessly moves the reader to the bare line of assumptions underlying the New Hermeneutic as it is represented principally by Ernst Fuchs and Gerhard Ebeling who are deeply in debt to Heidegger's epistemology, as he is in turn to Kant, the father of modern autonomy in the realm of ideas. It would be well for us to see how Van Til critiques the New Hermeneutic from a biblical point of view and reveals its essentially non-Christian presuppositions.

The goal of the New Hermeneutic is to attempt to present Christianity in such a way that it will bear more relevance to the modern setting. With a focus on human receptivity, Fuchs and Ebeling carry on the previous work of Barth, Brunner, and Bultmann, and farther back the impulse of post-Enlightenment theology via Kant. According to the school, one problem that remains unresolved is the place of the historical Jesus in the proclamation of the gospel. Why are the evangelists interested in him at all? In answering this question, modern phenomenalism and existentialism as Heidegger develops them are applied by Fuchs and Ebeling beyond the limitations of Bultmann's hermeneutic. If only (the New Hermeneutic says) we pay more attention to the Gospels and demythologize them more consistently than Bultmann did we will see that they reveal in their narratives the sovereign grace of God—not in supernatural terms but in their existential exhortation to listen to Jesus who makes God present for us. It is Jesus' words which present the hearer with the possibility of new and authentic existence. Jesus moves in the sphere of words and becomes God's "verb," God's "time-word,"[3] offering an exchange of life for death through God's love. The New Testament—and not only Paul and John, but the synoptic evangelists as well—becomes itself a textbook in hermeneutic by teaching the hermeneutic of faith in response to God's speech-event in Jesus.

B. Van Till now goes back to examine Fuchs' 1954 study on *Hermeneutik,* finding there the basis of his new quest of the historical Jesus in terms of language-event which speaks its Yes of love. Jesus is not seen as some objective factuality or messianic person but as "word of address," which can be translated into existential language that speaks today. Jesus is the material point of departure which makes it possible for us to recover a valid hermeneutic. We see directly at this point the influence of the later Heidegger on Fuchs, where the earlier Heidegger influenced Bultmann. Heidegger moved more in his later years to the poet's corner where he listened to the silent toll of being, seeking some sound or vision from that noumenal and ruminous wholly other in which the authentic self participates and becomes truly the free self. This is the true home of the self, the purely transcendent being which speaks to us of the possibility of future authentic Being in faith, love and hope. This purpose always remains hidden and can never be conceptualized in the empirical I-it terminology of science, metaphysics or objective theology, nor of course is it possible for the written Bible to contain it. One can only stand in the truth of being and participate supraconceptually in it, aware somehow that one is the loudspeaker of its silent toll.

For Fuchs this Being of the later Heidegger which addresses us is none other than the God of Christianity, and proper response to Jesus' address brings true self-understanding. But Jesus cannot be known as objective historical person with his own messianic self-consciousness; he can be known only in terms of his historic (geschichtlich) significance through the new hermeneutic as his language mediates the possibility of authentic existence "for me."[4] The same is true of Ebeling, who, though he sees Jesus as indispensable to Christian faith in terms similar to Fuchs, denies that the Jesus of the Gospels ever links the concept of faith with his own person or ever speaks of faith in himself. Rather, Jesus participates in the faith in which he speaks and points his language to the ground of faith and to participation in the essence of God.[5]

C. Van Til cogently points out that such knowledge of God reduces theology to anthropology, the implication being (as I would draw it out) that there is no interest in the New Hermeneutic in Jesus' language as revelatory of himself and as indicating his own correlativity with God. Instead, Jesus is important only as he speaks to us; he can be experienced only as he poses a question in an I-thou encounter. Jesus is located, accordingly, as is God, only in the conscience of the self when one is addressed in the language-event existentially in the present moment of decision. Jesus as historical person is not objectifiable; if he is objectified, then he is falsified and becomes an I-it manipulable being. Only in the historic, not historical, nature of reality does God address me through the language of Jesus. Subject (myself) and object (Jesus) are correlative; Jesus is known only as his language addresses *me*.[6]

D. The problem with this hermeneutic is that it simply substitutes the language of the self for God's own objective self-disclosure in the person of Jesus. The hidden presupposition of the New Hermeneutic is that the final authority as to what is authentic disclosure is the autonomous self. The interpreter is always in control, even when he claims to be addressed by God or by the language of Jesus. We can therefore appreciate the effect this sort of hermeneutic is going to have on one's exegetical method. There is no neutral exegesis, and the sooner the evangelical realizes that fact the wiser he will be in dialogue with non-evangelical exegetes. There will appear to be overlapping of exegetical methodology up to a point; but only when the biblical interpreter knows where his liberal colleagues are coming from will he be aware of hidden agendas which predetermine the eventual interpretation of the data, since it will always be the case in liberal exegesis that the Scripture as inspired and infallible objective revelation from God will be rejected in favor of the right of the autonomous interpreter to determine what, if any, and when, if ever, the Bible is the Word of God.

III. GADAMER AND THE NEW HERMENEUTIC

A. Another prominent representative of the New Hermeneutic needs to be considered in order to point up a present danger in present-day hermeneutical scholarship. Since he continues to be the leading theoretician of a post-Bultmannian hermeneutic and exercises considerable influence in both liberal and evangelical circles, Hans-Georg Gadamer invites careful attention. In *Truth and Method,*[7] Gadamer carries on the Bultmannian and New Hermeneutic legacy that the horizon of New Testament Christianity must be fused with our contemporary horizon, but in a radically critical sense. Hence both Kant and Dilthey, while basically correct in their assessment of the self, did not press the autonomy of the critical mind far enough. They did not see that the truly critical mind must reinterpret dogma itself in order to be free from it. Only in Heidegger, Gadamer argues, do we see the radical rejection of the notion of substance and its replacement by the absolute historicity of understanding.[8] A text that comes down to us from tradition puts a question to us as interpreters. The interpreter understands the text only as he understands the question and attains the hermeneutical horizon of questions (Fragehorizont) within which the direction of meaning of the text is determined. This penetration by the interpreter of what the text says opens up the horizon of questioning and necessarily invites a diversity of answers. Gadamer allows at this point that he is indebted to R. G. Collingwood's "logic of question and answering" as developed in *An Autobiography,*[9] and in the *Idea of History.* In the latter, Collingwood writes: "The fabric of human society is created by man out of nothing, and every detail of this fabric is a human factum, eminently knowable to the human mind as such."[10]

B. Van Til spends several pages exploring this brash but very widespread historicist hermeneutic which Gadamer shares along with many contemporary theologians and New Testament scholars. It is radically Kantian and Heideggerian and focuses epistemology not on isolated particulars or abstract universals but on the historical experience that can be defined only in terms of the life of the autonomous mind. The historical past exists nowhere else than in the world of ideas as the interpreter moves in his (or her) critical recreation of an imagined past. The historical past is therefore the present because it deals with the expression of thoughts that are relived in the mind of the historian. Van Til quotes the following statement by Collingwood which attempts a Copernican revolution in modern historiography and hermeneutic: "So far from relying on an authority other than himself, to whose statements his thoughts must conform, the historian is his own authority and his thought autonomous, self-authoring, possessed of a criterion to which his so-called authorities must conform and by reference to which they are criticized."[11] Perhaps the most widely quoted passage from Collingwood, one to which I warmly subscribed during my liberal years, is the following:

> Freed from its dependence on fixed points supplied from without, the historian's picture of the past is thus in every detail an imaginary picture, and its necessity is at every point the necessity of the a priori imagination. Whatever goes into it, goes into it not because his imagination passively accepts it, but because it actively demands it.[12]

This imaginative reconstruction of history by the historian does not give him license to create whatever he wants, for there is evidence to be taken into account, and this must be fitted into a coherent picture. But the "evidence" is never addressed as to whether it is true or false in and of itself, but as to its meaning for the historian as he or she reconstructs the historical event. Van Til observes how the hermeneutic of Collingwood and Gadamer controls the exegetical work of modern liberal scholarship on the question of the Jesus of the Gospels:

> This historic Jesus is constructed by the hermeneutical principles of the internally self-sufficient man. Jesus *must* be that which aids him in his attempt to find authentic self-existence. Reality must be of such a nature as to furnish Jesus with an infinite supply of grace with which man can develop his authentic self.[13]

True interpretation of the historical Jesus must be existential, that is, in terms of my needs and questions; hence the historical Jesus becomes the historic Jesus, or the contemporaneous Jesus *for me*. There is for Gadamer no objective revelation from outside history.[14] All historical data meets us only within present history and is therefore subject to continual reconstruction in the dialectic of question and answer. The Word that is Jesus is pure speech-event which is discerned by the listener-interpreter from the normative view-point of his own horizon. An historical fact is not past but present; and what is historical is contemporaneous as we fuse the horizon of the present with the horizon of the past (Horizontverschmelzung).[15]

C. Summing up his case, Van Til remarks that "Gadamer in German-language thinking and Collingwood in English-language thinking stand together in assuring the ultimate self-sufficiency of man as his own final source and criterion for meaningful linguistic expression.[16] In this connection one should read E. D. Hirsch's excursus on "Gadamer's Theory of Interpretation"[17] for a trenchant critique of the epistemological problems inherent in this interpreter-centered approach. His perceptive—and I believe correct—indictment of the Heidegger-Bultmann-Gadamer legacy confirms Van Til's analysis that this school represents a deep and destructive skepticism about the very possibility of ever rehabilitating a text's (or person's) original intentions. Gadamer directly attacks the premise that textual meaning is the same as the author's meaning. Accordingly, the historical Jesus as the objective incarnation of the preexistent Son who speaks and acts intentionally and authoritatively as the voice of God for our time is rejected by Gadamer and his school.

Here lies the central issue between an evangelical hermeneutic and a non-evangelical hermeneutic. With Van Til the evangelical exegete and theologian work from the presupposition that God is not only able to speak but has spoken authoritatively for all time in his inspired and infallible Scriptures, supremely in Jesus Christ the incarnate Son. By the ministry of the Holy Spirit the objective truth of Scripture and the continuing validity of the intention of Jesus that is embodied in his words and works confronts the interpreter with authoritative truth claims.

D. Van Til is sometimes faulted for overkill, of which his linking of Gadamer with the extreme idealism of Collingwood might seem to be an instance. For Gadamer wants to insist that the interpretation of a text is not totally at the mercy of the interpreter's horizon but has a horizon of its own, a tradition, that must be fused with that of the interpreter. He is aware of the danger of subjectivity. But then so is Collingwood, who reacts against any suggestion that his idealist historiography is identical to the craft of the novelist. After all, there are data that have to be interpreted. Van Til's rejoinder to both men is valid, however, for there is simply no way they can make good on the claim that there are objective data from past history whose horizons of meaning can be known by the interpreter, without the interpreter's hermeneutical horizon reconstructing those data. Gadamer may sense the problem, but he cannot resolve it. Indeed, the way in which he has set up the interpretation of historical texts through a dialectic of question and answer virtually determines the autonomy of the interpreter in deciphering the text, for both problems and answers are constantly changing and require a continuing reconstruction. The horizon of the critic must always remain normative. Hence,

Jesus' own understanding of his mission is unrecoverable; I can only try to find his understanding of authentic existence as it addresses my existential needs and questions.

Van Til's presuppositional approach to hermeneutics only points up the epistemological dilemma of the modern exegetical task. One might even say that Van Til as a representative of orthodox Christian faith, having demonstrated the irrationalism of an autonomous hermeneutic, shows the way to solve Gadamer's dilemma. The only way is to become an orthodox Christian and enter the authoritative horizon of the Scriptures by faith. Only by working from within the believing Christian community and by accepting the canonical authority of its biblical texts can the interpreter be addressed by the authentic Word of God. The authoritative self-disclosure of God in the Bible constitutes the special revelation which correctly interprets the historical data about Jesus of Nazareth and the church's proclamation of him. Without this presuppositional posture within the canonical revelation of God, there is no check on subjectivity and pluralism in the interpretation of Scripture.

E. Van Til's presuppositional approach to hermeneutics offers an important correction to E. D. Hirsch, who also criticizes Gadamer for his subjectivity and plumps instead for the right of the author of a text to posit a normative meaning or horizon for posterity. The meaning, says Hirsch, remains stable, while its significance for the individual interpreter may vary.[18] This is all well and good, and I agree with Hirsch (and expect Van Til would as well). But how can one be sure (1) what the real meaning of the text is (Hirsch suggests the analysis of genres as clues to the meaning), and (2) that the author has really intended that meaning? It is all very well to counter Gadamer's subjectivity with an appeal to authorial intent—if one can establish the genuineness of the text, and then fathom its meaning. If these two operations can be carried out successfully, then the text does indeed bear the signature of the author's intent, as I have elsewhere argued in analyzing Jesus' language by employing a phenomenology of persons. The problem with Hirsch's hermeneutic is that, impressive as it sounds, it does not assure us that we have analyzed the text properly so as to have arrived at the author's intended meaning. We may be only committing the intentional fallacy in thinking we have captured, or been captured by, the author's intended meaning, when actually we may have reinterpreted the text according to our own intended meaning and subtly, if unconsciously, missed the original meaning altogether. This happens regularly in literary and historical criticism.

F. The problem is a serious one and is, from a secular point of view, insoluble. It underscores the Kantian question of how I can know the thing in itself—in this case, the author's intended meaning—without passing it through the sieve of my own experience and understanding. In that case the original meaning has been melded with my meaning, so that only the fused phenomenon can be known, not the author's original meaning. Or at least I cannot be certain that I have recovered the author's intended meaning. There must always be a gnawing doubt that I have not got hold of the real thing. That, from Van Til's perspective, is the problem the finite interpreter faces in every realm. Without special revelation, God's revelation in nature cannot be properly interpreted. The Fall aggravates the problem, but even Adam in Eden prior to sinning required God's special interpretation of nature to help him understand God's disclosure in nature. This means that Hirsch's critique of Gadamer is on the right track, but fails because of the presence of ambiguity in all human interpretation, whether literary, historical, sociological, or scientific.

G. The only possible way out of this maze of criticism and subjectivism is to enter by faith into God's own interpretation of his own created data. This requires the autonomous critic to relinquish his claim to have the first and final word, and comes by his humbly confessing his creatureliness and sinfulness and experiencing a rebirth of his heart and mind by faith in Jesus Christ as Savior and Lord. The gift of God's Spirit then imparts a new wisdom which comes through the power of the cross—it is the mind of Christ (1 Cor. 1:18-2:16) through which all things are seen no longer from a human point of view (*kata sarka*, 2 Cor. 5:16-17). Such is the presupposition of every believing Christian; it is the hermeneutic by which the Christian stands within the believing community and accepts the canonical Scriptures of that long-standing body of believers as normative and infallible. This was true for nearly two thousand years until the rise of autonomous criticism in the modern age. It is also the testimony of the faithful evangelists and apostles to whom were imparted the oracles of God. The recipients of divine revelation put in writing their authorial intent—correlative with the divine intent—that Scripture is authoritative. Jesus uses the address of the authoritative "I say unto you" (e.g., Matt. 5:21-48), and is faithfully recorded in the Gospels as speaking the oracles of God; Luke claims reliable testimony (Luke 1:1-4; 24:25-27); as does Paul (1 Cor. 15:1-20; 2 Cor. 4:2; Gal. 1:12, 15-16; 2 Tim. 3:16); and Peter (1 Pet. 1:10-11; 2 Pet. 1:16, 20-21); and the author of Hebrews (1:1-2). The genre of the New Testament faith is clear: the believing community lives within the redemptive story of Jesus Christ and accordingly has high regard for the written testimony of Scripture to Christ.

H. With this presupposition of the all-sufficient Christ and the authority of Scripture, the believing Christian is supplied with the heuristic vision and commitment, to use Polanyi's terminology, to investigate the meaning of Jesus Christ and the story of Scripture. There is no possibility of finding neutral ground where the real meaning of the Scripture texts can be discerned with scientific tools apart from some commitment for or against the supernatural. A descriptive phenomenology of the language of Jesus is at best only a scratching of the surface grammar and does not get at the depth grammar of Jesus, which comes only through faith in him. Moreover, "neutral" exegesis is not purely descriptive, for the intention of the interpreter to approach the Gospels without presuppositions already discloses a tacit component of commitment to critical agnosticism in its desire to get at the *real* meaning of the text apart from the faith of the New Testament community.

IV. "MEANT" AND "MEANS" IN STENDAHL'S HERMENEUTIC

A. The meaning of the Gospels can not be so easily discovered from the outside. Presuppositionless exegesis is simply not possible, and it is naive to think that it is. This would be my criticism of Krister Stendahl's definition of the exegetical task which he shares, on the critical side, with the New Hermeneutic. Stendahl had argued in his famous and widely influential article on biblical theology that the historicocritical method underlies proper exegesis and aims to get at what the text *meant* by a purely descriptive methodology.[19] What the text means today is the task of hermeneutics. This is fundamentally wrong for two reasons. The first is that the historian's task involves hermeneutical assumptions in the very method it uses to get at what a text *meant*. To use Polanyi's term, there is a tacit component in the historicocritical approach, namely that it is possible to recover the Ding an sich or meaning of a past text, and that it is recoverable through the objective tools of critical research. Few evangelicals will deny that textual, historical, linguistic, literary, and sociological analysis will shed light on the setting and uses of language in the Gospels and their tradition. But when the most preliminary stage of critical research, text criticism, is acknowledged by one of its foremost exponents, Bruce Metzger, to be an art as well as a science and dependent on the judgment of the text critic as he weighs probabilities,[20] we are wise to acknowledge the role of the interpreter's grid in framing the questions and designing the tools to answer them in light of a given text.

Van Til, were he doing a critique of Stendahl, would probably point to the many interpretations Stendahl infers from the Scripture texts which reveal that he is not performing the purely descriptive task he has set for the New Testament scholar, but is in fact interpreting what he thinks the text actually *meant* by what he believes they really *mean*. For example, in discussing Christology in the article, he makes it clear that the writers of the New Testament are seen, in light of a critical historical approach, to have positions which "come miles apart from one another as contradictory," and that as far as Jesus' messianic consciousness is concerned—"yes-or-no," did he think of himself as Messiah?—the evidence descriptively would appear to be, no:

> Those who claim a straight messianic consciousness in Jesus overlook the evidence that the messiahship in Jesus' earthly ministry has a strong futuristic note.[21]

B. But of course Jesus looks forward to the fulfillment of his messianic work. If, however, Stendahl is really doing descriptive exegesis, he will see that Jesus does claim by his very words and acts that he is consciously acting as the Messiah. There must be something which is holding Stendahl back from the evidence, some hidden agenda which predetermines how he will describe what he thinks the text really meant, historically—not what the church thought it meant, but what is *really* meant, what the *real* Jesus, the Ding an sich, actually thought about himself. And when it comes to that, Käsemann is to be preferred, for he at least allows that he is speaking only his own personal opinion when he denies Jesus' messianic consciousness, in spite of evidence to the contrary. Stendahl's exegesis is more dangerous, however, for he actually thinks that he is scientifically and objectively describing the actual historical "meaning" of Jesus. From my point of view as a practicing historian and exegete, I see Stendahl's description of Jesus and New Testament Christology as a contemporary redaction in terms of what Jesus Christ means to him, given his hermeneutical horizon. This is the sort of thing to which Van Til makes us sensitive. Our presuppositions do play a determinative role in interpreting a textual tradition like the Gospels. The very questions we ask of the text and the tools we devise in going about that task betray our own attitudes toward the text and the kinds of answers we will get back. The hermeneutical circle is clearly operative here. Where the exegete goes in is where he comes out—unless in the process he accepts the evangelists' witness to Jesus as self-acclaimed Messiah and the texts as historically faithful. But then the interpreter goes in a different door.

C. Accordingly, any attempt to avoid Gadamer's Kantian dilemma is bound to fail, apart from an orthodox view of inspired Scripture. For Stendahl, the preacher may fuse the horizons of "means" and "meant"; but,

> it is once more clear that we cannot pursue the study of biblical theology adequately if the two tenses are not kept apart. For the descriptive biblical theologian this is a necessity implied in his own discipline; and whether he is a believer or an agnostic, he demands respect for the descriptive task as an enterprise valid in its own right and for its own sake. For the life of the church such a consistent descriptive approach is a great and promising asset which enables the church, its teaching and preaching ministry, to be exposed to the Bible in its original intention and intensity, as an ever new challenge to thought, faith, and response.[22]

Certainly, the serious exegete is going to do his homework in biblical languages and backgrounds, but the assumption that the descriptive biblical theologian not only can but must keep his discipline separate from Christian faith reflects in its very framing of the task a contemporary prejudice, and militates against such a biblical critic ever really getting at the original meaning of the texts—or as regards the Gospels, the authorial intent of the original speaker, Jesus, and the intent of the evangelists. Indeed, such a neutral and descriptive approach is impossible apart from just the opposite of Stendahl's hermeneutic; for a truly descriptive exegesis of the original meaning of a text is possible only (1) if the exegete enters into a personal relationship with Jesus Christ and enters the story from inside, and (2) accepts the authoritative witness of the evangelists who are also part of the hermeneutical community of faith. Only through the common faith engendered by the Holy Spirit can the exegete bridge the gap between then and now, and describe the reality of Jesus and the story about him at the level of their depth grammar.

This is precisely Van Til's point and the awesome challenge of his hermeneutic. Only in humble acceptance of God's own special interpretation of history in Jesus Christ can one properly use the tools of historical research; then the tools that arise from the common grace of God's general revelation help elucidate the texts of the special revelation in respect to their linguistic, historical, and sociological setting. The interaction of common and special revelation comes through a personal relationship with Jesus Christ and a humble obedience to the inspired text of Scripture. In this way, and only in this way, can the original authorial intent of Jesus and the evangelists be discovered. The dualistic approach of Stendahl's hermeneutic will only lead in the end, not to the depth grammar of the Gospels, but to the imaging of the interpreter's own face in the well of history.

D. This criticism of Stendahl's hermeneutic is all the more ironic in view of the fact that he sees the work of the Spirit in the formation of the canon, and indeed in the gift of prophetic and inspired teaching down to our own day.[23] But that openness of the canon also endangers its validity in interpretation, since subjectivity and relativity may now be more the rule than the exception. It is perhaps this problem of hermeneutical pluralism that forces Stendahl to limit the Spirit's inspiration to the realm of theological interpretation rather than to ensure the infallibility of the evangelists' witness. Whatever has prompted him to adopt his hermeneutic of "meant" and "means," he has laid out an unrealizable task for the exegete; for not only is it impossible to get at the deep meaning of Jesus Christ neutrally by critical tools of the human mind, but because of the notion of an open canon it is impossible to get at the normative interpretation of the New Testament canon itself, since it is not really normative if subject to continual revision. It would be fair to say that Stendahl's belief that we can get at the original meaning of a text is valid, but not in the way that he thinks. The search for the real meaning of facts in the created world of nature and history can only be achieved by the aid of God's own "canonical" interpretation of those facts. This requires the exegete to defer to the authoritative witness of Scripture. Otherwise, the autonomous critic will demand the right to give an authoritative statement on what the text actually meant; but it will really only be what the text means to him. For without the Holy Spirit as guarantor of past meaning there can be no sure knowledge of the past. There can be only a present subjective meaning of the "past" which is subject to change. And that, of course, is the state of contemporary liberal theology and hermeneutics, including the New Hermeneutic; it is constantly shifting ground. Kant was right if the critic rejects the authoritative canonical Scripture. He can never know the meaning of anything as it is in itself, not even contemporary persons or events, let alone persons and events of the past. But if canonical Scripture is accepted as authoritative, then Van Til is correct: God's self-disclosure in inspired Scripture and in Jesus Christ is his own interpretation of the deep grammar of nature, history, and of human existence. By the common grace of God's general revelation in creation there are many overlappings of knowledge on the level of surface grammar (Ps. 19:1-6; Matt. 5:45; Rom. 1:19-20) which allow evangelical and non-evangelical to agree on a considerable body of scientific, linguistic, social, and even religious data, for we share a common created world. But though we may agree on surface meanings, the deep and ultimate meanings are spiritually discerned (1 Cor. 2:6-16). Here it is crucial to get our presuppositions out in the open, for these have to do with the ultimate meaning of the phenomena. From this analysis we may conclude that the New Hermeneutic is not really new, but repeats a familiar theme.

NOTES

[1](Grand Rapids: Baker Book House, 1982). This paper is adapted from the last chapter, "Jesus as Self-Authenticating Authority: Presuppositions and Authorial Intent in Van Til's Hermeneutic."

[2]*The New Hermeneutic* (Nutley, New Jersey: Presbyterian and Reformed Publishing Co., 1974).

[3]See Ernst Fuchs, "The New Testament and the New Hermeneutical Problem," in *New Frontiers in Theology,* Volume 2, *The New Hermeneutic*, eds. James M. Robinson and John B. Cobb, Jr. (New York: Harper & Row, 1964), p. 136; Van Til, *The New Hermeneutic*, p. 6.

[4]See Van Til's discussion, *The New Hermeneutic*, pp. 8-12.

[5]Gerhard Ebeling, *Word and Faith,* trans. James W. Leitch (Philadelphia: Fortress Press, 1963), pp. 202-45. Van Til, op. cit., pp. 12-14.

[6]Ibid, p. 18.

[7]Trans. by Garrett Barden and John Cumming (New York: Seabury Press, 1975) from *Wahrheit und Methode* (Tübingen: J. C. B. Mohr [Paul Siebeck] 1965). See also Anthony C. Thiselton, *The Two Horizons: New Testament Hermeneutics*

and Philosophical Description with Special Reference to Heidegger, Bultmann, Gadamer, and Wittgenstein (Grand Rapids: Eerdmans, 1980), especially chapter 5.

[8]See Van Til, op. cit., pp. 82-88 for a critique of Gadamer's historicism. References in Van Til are to *Wahrheit und Methode*, especially pp. 206-57, 351f.

[9](London: Oxford University Press, 1939), pp. 30-31.

[10](London: Oxford University Press, 1946), p. 65.

[11]Collingwood, *The Idea of History,* p. 236; Van Til, op. cit., p. 85.

[12]Collingwood, op. cit., p. 245; Van Til, op. cit., p. 86.

[13]Van Til, op. cit., pp. 87-88. His italics.

[14]Gadamer, *Wahrheit und Methode*, p. 357.

[15]Gadamer, ibid., pp. 356-96.

[16]Van Til, op. cit., p. 87.

[17]In *Validity in Interpretation* (New Haven: Yale University Press, 1967), pp. 245-64.

[18]See E. D. Hirsch, "Gadamer's Theory of Interpretation," ibid.

[19]Krister Stendahl, "Biblical Theology, Contemporary," *The Interpreter's Dictionary of the Bible*, Vol. I (New York: Abingdon Press, 1962), pp. 419, 424.

[20]Bruce M. Metzger, *A Textual Commentary on the Greek New Testament* (New York: United Bible Societies, 1975), pp. xxiv, xxviii, xxxi.

[21]Op. Cit., p. 426.

[22]Ibid., p. 431.

[23]Ibid., p. 429.

Presuppositions of Non-Evangelical Hermeneutics

Millard J. Erickson
Professor of Theology
Bethel Theological
Seminary

11. Presuppositions of Non-Evangelical Hermeneutics

Millard J. Erickson

I. PRELIMINARY UNDERSTANDING WITH THE READER

Because of the very broad topic which has been assigned to me for treatment, it is essential that we note initially several definitional problems which we face. The first is involved in the use of the adjective, "non-evangelical."

To speak of "non-evangelical" is like speaking of "non-A." It suggests the contradictory of a particular position. There may be many contradictories, but only one contrary. Thus, Z is a case of non-A, but so also is B, C, D, E, etc. By the same token, there are many forms of non-evangelical thought. Some are diametrically opposed to evangelicalism. Yet other viewpoints differ from evangelicalism in only certain tenets, or on a given tenet, only to a rather limited degree. Thus, the idea of non-evangelical could cover a wide variety of views, each rather different from each of the others.

We are therefore faced with a choice in developing this paper. One option would be to attempt to describe every variety of non-evangelical hermeneutic. Such an endeavor, however, would either result in an almost interminable treatise, or would be hopelessly superficial treatment of these varied schemes. A second possibility would be to single out one specific hermeneutic, or at most a very few, and regard them as representative of non-evangelical hermeneutics. The very variety just spoken of, however, militates against the success of the effort. It might be possible to reject the presuppositions discussed, but not be evangelical; one might simply be non-evangelical in some other way. Yet a third approach would be to try to treat those assumptions which are common to all non-evangelical hermeneutics. Here, however, the problem is that such a "lowest common denominator" approach may yield conclusions of such a general nature as to be of little practical value in evaluating any given hermeneutic. For the most part, however, it will be a combination of the second and third options which will be followed.

A second preliminary issue to be discussed concerns the variety of presuppositions. A presupposition is a conception brought to the task of interpretation. It is a prior belief held as one of the givens within which the task of interpretation occurs. It is part of the very framework of the interpreter. Presuppositions, however, may be of several types. There are *theological* presuppositions. These are doctrinal beliefs, such as the nature of God, or of man, which affect the understanding of specific passages. There are also *philosophical* presuppositions. These are conceptions shared with other disciplines or pertaining to broader topics than the strictly theological or religious. Here are beliefs about truth, meaning, the nature and direction of history, etc. Finally there are *methodological* presuppositions. These pertain to the use of logic, inference, induction and deduction, and the like. It would obviously be impossible to isolate, identify, and analyze all of the presuppositions of even a single coherent non-evangelical hermeneutic. What will be done will be to sample presuppositions cutting across these several categories.

The scope of the paper then, should be conceived of with several limitations upon the original form as stated above. It will actually be something such as "Some Theological, Philosophical, and Methodological Presuppositions of Typical Non-Evangelical Hermeneutics."

II. THE NATURE OF PRESUPPOSITIONS

It is necessary now to take a closer look at the nature of presuppositions in order to come to a fuller appreciation of their influence upon interpretation. We have already noted briefly the general nature and the various classifications of presuppositions. We are not, by the use of terms such as "presupposition" or "preunderstanding," suggesting that these hermeneutical methodologies assume the conclusions, i.e., the meaning of given passages, in advance of the actual work of attempting to interpret it. To do so would be quite unfair, as the persons whose views we are examining reject this, both by their express declaration and by practice.[1] Rather we contend that because these elements presupposed are inseparable from the method utilized, they inevitably influence the outcome. Thus, to some extent at least, the conclusion may be implicit within the methodology.

A hermeneutical method is a device utilized to attain a conclusion, i.e., the understanding of the meaning of the text. There is a tendency to assume that the device is itself somehow neutral or sterile. If accurately applied, it will lead accurately to correct conclusions. Yet no matter how carefully and precisely used, a small deviation in the device itself will affect to a considerable extent, the end result. If I am hunting, for example, I will attempt to aim as accurately as possible at my target. Assuming that my target is not moving and that there is no significant wind to cause drift, and that the rifling of the barrel is such as to produce a straight flight of the bullet, then if I sight perfectly through the gunsight and hold the gun perfectly steady, I will hit my target perfectly. All of this, however, assumes that the sight is perfectly aligned with the barrel of the gun. If it is only one degree out of alignment to the left, however, then when I shoot at an object 100 feet away, I will miss the spot by nearly 2 feet to the right. If I continue repeatedly to sight and shoot accurately, I will continue to miss by that amount, assuming I make no compensation for the error.

A further compensation is navigation by dead reckoning, a method used by seamen and aviators. If I start from a given point and with an accurate knowledge of the direction and speed of the wind and of the distance between my starting point and destination and of my true airspeed, make wind corrections and adjustments for the variation between true north and magnetic north, I will at the end of the calculated elapsed time, be directly over my destination airport—if my compass is completely accurate. If, however, my magnetic compass deviates by as little as one degree, at the end of the flight of 200 miles I will be approximately 3½ miles off course, possibly enough to prevent my spotting the airport. The small error built in at the beginning has resulted in a large consequent error.

This is why presuppositions are so important in hermeneutics. We do right in attempting to apply our method of interpretation as thoroughly and carefully as possible. Built into that method, however, will be certain factors of which we may not be consciously aware. We do not work toward them, we work through them or with them.[2] A slight difference in those assumptions will make a large difference in the conclusions to which we come, even if we perfectly apply the method.

III. THE NATURE OF HERMENEUTICS

While there have been a variety of meanings attached to the term "hermeneutics," there has nonetheless been in evangelicalism a sort of common body of meaning attached to the term. It has meant the science of interpretation. As such, it has often designated a set of techniques for extricating the meaning from the (sometimes obscure) text. In practice, it even became reduced to a list of rules.[3]

In recent years, however, the term hermeneutics has taken on a much broader meaning. It has been especially concerned with the problem created by the historical gap between biblical times and the present situation of the interpreter. Traditionally, hermeneutics took note of the fact that the biblical author lived, thought, and wrote within a concrete historical setting. Interpretation involved, to a considerable extent, getting back into that context and understanding it, as a means to understanding the writing. Biblical backgrounds was an important subject for study. It might mean no more than being familiar with Edersheim's *Life and Times of Jesus the Messiah* when studying the gospels, but understanding idioms required knowing the background against which they were written. Now, however, the world of biblical scholarship became very much aware that the interpreter, just as the text itself, stands in a given historical context and tradition. Hermeneutics must therefore concern itself with understanding the interpreter's situation, and then finding ways to bridge the gap between these two. Thus, it was not sufficient to understand what the biblical text meant to persons living in biblical times. Hermeneutics must ask what the biblical text means to people living today. It has, to a large extent, become a question of how meaning can be transferred from one historical and cultural context to another, entirely different, one.[4]

This means that hermeneutics now requires additional skills and areas of knowledge beyond those formerly believed to be involved. In addition to a knowledge of biblical languages, familiarity with the cultural background, and an understanding of various types of literature, doing of hermeneutics in this new sense calls for an awareness of the history of the church and of the world in general, an understanding of contemporary culture, and of individual and social psychology, as well as of philosophy.

IV. AN EXAMINATION OF PARTICULAR PRESUPPOSITIONS

A. The Nature of Christianity

One of the most basic questions for any theological discipline concerns the definition of Christianity. While the title, "The Essence of Christianity" was perhaps overworked during the nineteenth century, the topic was and is significant, for the conception was undergoing change, which has had an influence even to our present time. And what one believes about the basic nature of Christianity affects the hermeneutical task, for it colors what one expects the message and purpose of the Scripture to be.

Until the nineteenth century, there had been a basic consensus that a major dimension of the Christian religion, if not indeed its primary character, was its intellectual content, or the doctrinal beliefs involved in it. Thus, the dispute between Roman Catholicism and Protestantism in the sixteenth and immediately succeeding centuries was primarily over doctrine. Luther's insistence upon justification by faith called into question the Catholic understanding of salvation, and his doctrine of the universal priesthood of believers similarly challenged the Roman Catholic Church's teaching regarding the nature of the church. Later Protestantism emphasized even more the importance of "rechte Lehre" or correct doctrine, and worked out in greater detail the refined definitions of belief. This (especially the seventeenth century) was the age of Protestant orthodoxy or scholasticism, as it was called.[5] The fact that the church throughout its history has formulated and in many cases required adherence to creeds and confessions, is evidence that doctrinal belief was considered to be of the essence of the Christian religion. The attempt of Luther and Zwingli to unite the German and Swiss segments respectively of the Reformation broke down over a doctrinal point, specifically the question of the real presence of the body and blood of Christ in the Lord's Supper. The existence of separate denominations was at this point often related in large part to doctrine.

With the nineteenth century, however, changes of conception began to appear. In 1799, Friedrich Schleiermacher published his *On Religion: Speeches to its Cultured Despisers*. In this he rejected the conventional idea that religion in general and Christianity in particular is a matter of belief or dogma. Nor is it a matter of a particular kind of action, which would reduce it to ethics of one sort or another. He said:

> In order to make quite clear to you what is the original and characteristic possession of religion, it resigns, at once, all claims on anything that belongs either to science or morality. Whether it has been borrowed or bestowed it is now returned.[6]

Rather than either doctrine or ethics, religion is concerned with feeling. At times, Schleiermacher seems to be saying that any and all feelings are religious.[7] At other places, he restricts it to one feeling above all others: the feeling of absolute dependence.[8] Thus, the real nature of Christianity is compatible with widely differing theologies or ethics, or combinations of forms of these.[9]

In so doing, Schleiermacher was accepting the argument advanced by Immanuel Kant in his *Critique of Pure Reason* in 1783 that religion cannot be based upon theoretical reason. Schleiermacher, however, declined to place religion where Kant did in his second critique, the *Critique of Practical Reason*, in 1788. Here Kant argued that religion is a postulate of the practical reason, necessary to the functioning of ethics. It might be possible to locate religion, as Schleiermacher understood it, within the sphere covered by Kant's third critique, the *Critique of Judgment*, which dealt with esthetic experience.

If one branch of liberalism took its lead from Schleiermacher, another more closely followed the thought of Albrecht Ritschl. Ritschl saw Christianity as less concerned with objective facts than with value judgments: judgments of the worth or goodness of things. The doctrinal confessions, such as regarding the person of Jesus Christ, stem from the experience of His effect in the life of the individual. Thus, the nature of God and Christ are known by us only in their worth for us.[10] Christianity for Ritschl became a utilitarian and moralistic activity. As such, he is closer to Kant than to Schleiermacher.

In later liberalism, particularly in the United States, these two streams became blended together. But in any event, there was deemphasis of the doctrinal or intellectual dimension (in the sense of involving acceptance of certain tenets). When fundamentalism insisted upon the retention of certain beliefs, while liberalism was more tolerant of doctrinal diversity, it was partly because liberals considered the older forms to be obsolete, and thus in need of replacement by more contemporary ways of understanding. But to a large extent it was simply because liberalism did not think doctrines to be all that important. True Christianity found its locus elsewhere.[11]

If this shift is accepted, then the aim of Christianity will not be seen as attempting to lead to any particular belief. And consequently, the Scripture will be interpreted in light of what type of experience or action it tends and intends to evoke, rather than what belief it might seem to be inculcating.

B. Changed Humanity

Another presupposition underlying much non-evangelical hermeneutics is the belief that "modern man" is radically changed from his counterpart of biblical times. If this were not so, hermeneutics would be relatively simple. It would merely be a matter of determining the meaning of the passage against the background of its cultural setting, of finding a cultural equivalent for our day and presenting it to humans where they are. In practice, however, say many non-evangelical biblical interpreters and theologians, it is just not this simple. Our contemporaries may not understand the biblical message, since it comes from such a strangely different world. Or they may understand it, just as they can understand what is being affirmed by various primitive religions, myths, and folklore. But though they understand it, they cannot accept it. It is not believable. It is comprehensible, but not credible. Paul Achtemeier considers it one of the primary reasons for the reemergence of hermeneutics as a discipline in our day:

> It is one of the great unsolved problems with which the era of "liberal" theology grappled, with its concern over how much of the historic faith was credible to the modern age. The problem was never really solved. . . . But unresolved problems have a way of refusing to lie dormant for long, and it ought to be cause of no surprise that it has again thrust itself to the center of our attention. It is, to put it simply, a problem that dare not be ignored. Until this problem is solved, until some clarity has been achieved concerning how the Bible may legitimately be appropriated in the modern era, theology will continue to thrash about, casting up all manner of solutions ranging from the bizarre to the naive, from resolute "fundamentalism" to the "theological" affirmation that God is dead.[12]

William Hordern, in his introductory volume to the *New Directions in Theology Today* series, noted the desire of many theologians of our day to engage in "dialogue" or "conversation" with the world. There are two basic varieties of these. The "translators" believe the problem lies primarily in the *intelligibility* of the Christian message. The task of the theologian (for our purposes here, the biblical interpreter) is to restate the biblical message in such a way that it can be understood by twentieth-century persons. In so doing, however, the essential content is to remain the same. The transformer, however, holds that it is *credibility*, not intelligibility, that is modern man's difficulty with biblical Christianity. Some portions, even when understood, are literally unbelievable for such a modern person. The message, therefore, must be changed.[13]

One example of this type of thinking is found in Rudolf Bultmann's treatise, *The New Testament and Mythology.* Here he notes that much of the content of the New Testament is mythical. The cosmos is regarded as a three-storied structure, with heaven (the locale of God and the angels) above, hell (with Satan and the demons) below, and earth (the sphere of man's activity) in between. In this human realm, supernatural forces intervene in the events of history, and in what people think and do. Evil spirits may take possession of one, or Satan plant evil thoughts in his mind. God, on the other hand, sends dreams and visions to man. Miracles take place. And the end of time will occur through the supernatural judge coming from heaven, raising the dead, judging them and consigning them to their final states. This is the biblical picture, but it is not tenable. Bultmann says:

> *Man's knowledge and mastery of the world* have advanced to such an extent through science and technology that it is no longer possible for anyone seriously to hold the New Testament view of the world—in fact, there is no one who does.[14]

It is neither necessary nor possible to believe this today. Anyone at all familiar with astronomy knows that there is no "up" or "down" in the universe. And the most elementary acquaintance with medicine informs a person that illness is not the result of demon possession. Instead, it results from bacteria, viruses, and other natural causes. Demon possession is therefore untenable.

Others find another aspect of this idea that man has radically changed since biblical times. It is with respect to his need for God. In the Bible, God was the solver of man's problems, the supplier of his needs. If there was a draught, biblical man prayed, and God sent rain. If his wife could not bear children he prayed and God gave a child ("opened her womb" is a biblical euphemism used to describe the case of Hannah). Modern man, however, has no need for God. Technology has enabled him to solve these problems. If rain is needed, he merely finds a cloud with some moisture content, flies over it, seeds it with silver iodide or a similar substance, and out comes the rain. The barren woman consults with a gynecologist, who prescribes a fertility pill—and a whole litter of children is born! Similarly, the mysteries of the world, which required God as the explanation, are now explainable on other grounds. The amazing complexity of the human organism, for example, which seemed to require an intelligent purposeful creator according to the argument of Paley and others, was now alternatively accounted for by evolution, through the process of natural selection. The modern has learned to solve his own problems, as well.[15] This, then, is "religionless Christianity," which does not hold to God out of some necessity for Him.

There is, finally, the foreignness of biblical concepts and experiences to our contemporaries. Some of these are foreign to the very experience of life. Take for example the biblical idea of guilt. For some present-day humans, strongly affected by Freudian psychology and holding to ethical relativity, there really is no such thing as objective guilt. There are only guilt feelings.[16] Or take the sense of mystery or awe described phenomenologically in some detail by Rudolf Otto in *The Idea of the Holy*.[17] This has withered for some modern persons, together with any idea of encountering God, as found in neo-orthodoxy. Augustine might have believed that all humans had a restlessness which could only be satisfied by God, but modern man finds him strange. He has no experience to which to relate these concepts.[18]

If, now, hermeneutics is understood not merely as the attempt to determine the meaning of the passage to the writer and his immediate audience, but as an attempt to interpret and state that biblical message for today's readers, it is apparent that considerable restatement must be done. Either one must affirm that what they were saying was, at least in part, untrue, and reject those parts, while retaining certain others. Or else one must say, as Bultmann does, that the real message being expressed was something of a rather different nature, and reinterpret it in the light of this new understanding.

C. Positivistic Historiography

Some but by no means all, non-evangelical hermeneutics, operate on the basis of a positivistic historiography. By this is meant a belief that history is a closed continuum, a tight causal web, in which events can all be understood as occurring in accordance with fixed "patterns," or "natural laws." Hence, a historical-critical method which approaches the interpretation of a miracle account from such a presupposition will necessarily give a different explanation of what has happened, then one which comes with a somewhat more "open" perspective.

While many interpreters of the Bible work from such a presupposition, some do so self-consciously. Thus Rudolf Bultmann states his presupposition as follows:

> The historical method includes the presupposition that history

> is a unity in the sense of a closed continuum of effects in which individual events are connected by the succession of cause and effect. . . .
>
> This closedness means that the continuum of historical happenings cannot be rent by the interference of supernatural, transcendent powers and that therefore there is no "miracle" in this sense of the world.[19]

This belief in a closed causal system then shows itself in the treatment of miracles. One example is the explanation of the miracles in the fourth gospel, as found in the *Interpreter's Bible*. The author of the commentary prefaces the discussion of the marriage at Cana by saying:

> With regard to the healing miracles, such an attitude is of course entirely out of date. Does not J. A. Hadfield, with his immense experience, tell us bluntly: "There was a time when people said that 'miracles do not happen,' the implication being that the narratives of miracles in the Gospels are untrue. Nowadays practically all the healing 'miracles' of the New Testament have been reproduced in shell-shock hospitals over and over again." Many things in the Gospels which were once scoffed out of court by confident and scornful voices are now accepted as self-evidently true; and in some sense the wonder of Christ's achievements is seemingly reduced to this, that in his own practice he antedated by a couple of thousand years the discoveries of modern science.[20]

From this, it can be seen that the miracles are thought of as fully within the laws of nature. So, what Jesus did in healing is really no different from what is being done by medical science in hospitals today. Those occurrences were thought of as miraculous because the processes by which they were accomplished were previously unknown. Thus, antibiotics when first introduced were referred to as "miracle drugs," for they overcame infections which had previously been very difficult to fight. Today, however, they are so commonplace as to be taken for granted. So the miracles which Jesus performed are not denied, as being impossible. Instead, they are accepted, but as necessarily being part of the causal web of nature. Or they are given a spiritualized meaning. The commentator says of the incident of turning water into wine:

> What water is to wine, what that embarrassing insufficiency was to the relief he wrought for his host, so is any other life

> compared to the fullness, the color, the adventure, the achievement that he gives.[21]

Ernst Troeltsch very rigorously applied a positivistic historical method to the study of Scripture. He argued that Christianity's early roots could not be preserved in a type of historical ghetto, regarded in terms of unique supernatural divine acts in history. Rather, these claimed historical occurrences must be seen as historical phenomena, subject to investigation by the same type of historical research as any other occurrence. If Jesus is an historical personage, then faith in Him depends upon the outcome of historical research, rendering likely the claims regarding Him.

For Troeltsch, however, commitment to the task of historical research involves commitment to a definite task: "to explain every movement, process, state and nexus of things by reference to the web of its causal relations." This web of causal connections is in reality part of a universal system of things.[22]

Troeltsch evaluates the historical probability of an event on the basis of a principle of analogy with a historian's present experience. This means that in considering the likelihood that a given miracle occurred, he will evaluate it in terms of whether he finds such currently occurring within his own experience. This places the perspective of the historian, even the Christian historian, in sharp contrast with the traditional approach of the Christian theologian. Van Harvey has observed:

> If the theologian believes that the events upon which Christendom rests are unique, the historian assumes (i.e. in Troeltsch's view) that those events, like all events, are analogous to those in the present and that it is only on this assumption that statements about them are to be assessed at all.[23]

This means that there is an inherent point of conflict between a supernaturalistic Christian theology and the application of historical method of Troeltsch's type to the documents of Christianity. Harvey put it thus:

> The problem was not, as so many theologians then believed, that the Biblical critics emerged from their libraries with results disturbing to believers, but that the method itself . . . was based upon assumptions quite irreconcilable with traditional belief. . . . If the theologian believes that the events of the Bible are the results of the supernatural intervention of God, the historian regards such an explanation as a hindrance to true historical understanding.[24]

More recently, Dennis Nineham has argued that there is inherent in the outlook of our historical age that belief "that all past events form a single causally interconnected web and that no event occurs without this worldly causation of some sort."[25] Divine intervention must, then, be understood not as an event, but only a way of seeing an otherwise ordinary event. In other words, miracles, like truth, beauty, and contact lenses, are in the eye of the beholder.

Not all non-evangelical hermeneutics make this positivistic assumption about the method of historiography. In particular, Wolfhart Pannenberg has rejected such a constricted view of history and of the historical method.[26] Nonetheless, it is a presupposition found in varying degrees of strength in a rather large number of non-evangelical systems of interpretation.

D. The Nature of Revelation

One of the crucial theological presuppositions is the idea of revelation. For a long period of time the Christian Church was rather uniformly committed to a view which identified revelation with the words of the Bible. God had, on this basis, communicated true, objective, information and this had been preserved in written form in the Bible. Thus the words of the Bible were the very words of God Himself. If one could accurately determine their meaning, he would know what God was saying.[27]

With the rise of "higher criticism," however, this identification collapsed. As the methods applied to the interpretation of literature and historical narrative in general were extended to the study of the Bible as well, it began to appear to be a very human book. Composite authorships were found, with conflicts among them. Historical references were believed to be quite inaccurate in many cases. Some of the miracle accounts were rejected as incredible. In short, much of what was asserted to have occurred just did not take place. Either God made a mistake, or these writings were the product of man, not God. There would have to be revision of the understanding of the nature of the Bible.[28]

Several types of restatement were made. One was to try to sift through the material, to separate revelation (the divine factor) from the chaff (the human element). L. Harold DeWolf, himself a rather moderate representative of the liberal tradition, put it this way:

> The writings in the Bible are the writings of men, conditioned and limited by their times and their individual peculiarities,

> though also rising frequently to great heights of expression under the illumination of God's self-disclosing presence. The reader who would hear the true word of God in the reading of the Bible must be prepared to discriminate between the word of God and the words of men.[29]

While some liberals went much further in their criticism of the revelatory nature of Scripture, this was a fairly representative way of characterizing liberalism's view: the Bible contains the Word of God.

Another strategy was also found for dealing with the problems posed by new learning in biblical studies and in secular knowledge. This was the redefinition of revelation. Rather than understanding revelation as informational or propositional, this view regarded it as a personal encounter. The words of the Bible are not God's Word *per se*. They are merely the words of men: Isaiah, Luke, Paul, and others.[30] When God presents Himself to a human person through the words of Scripture, they may in that moment be termed the Word of God. What has been given in revelation is not information about God, but rather, God Himself. William Hordern has expressed it thus:

> This is why the Bible is the indispensable medium of God's revelation; it alone records the events through which God was revealed. In the Bible we read the witness of the Biblical writers that through this Jesus of Nazareth God's revelation came to them. . . . But we may read the Bible from cover to cover and never hear the Word of God. On the other hand, at any moment God may use a word of the Bible to speak his Word to our hearts, and in that moment we can confess with Peter, "Thou art the Christ." . . . The Bible is the earthen vessel through which at any moment God may speak to man (2 Cor. 4:7).[31]

While this particular form of the doctrine was identified with what was known as neo-orthodoxy, it has in a general form been found in considerably wider circles. William Temple, for example said: "The revelation, if given at all, is given more in Himself than in His teaching."[32]

Now if this is a correct understanding of the nature of revelation, then the response that is to be made must be appropriate to what the revelation is. If revelation is the imparting of information from God, then faith should consist of mental assent, or believing these propositions to be true. If, however, revelation is a person-to-person meeting with the divine sovereign of all of reality, then faith should consist of a personal trust, a believing-in rather then a believing-that, or believing-about.

With this shift from the locus of revelation as communicating divinely-revealed truth to being the medium of a divine-human encounter comes a changed emphasis on the nature and purpose of hermeneutics, as well. It is not really objective meaning that is sought. It is, in the case of the liberalism described earlier, frequently an attempt to rediscover the religious experience described in the writing. Or, in the case of neo-orthodoxy, it is an investigation of the Scripture writers' attempt to describe the circumstances in which the encounter-revelation occurred in the past. This is coupled with the expectation and hope of a recurrence of the revelation. In neither of these forms, however, can the Bible be construed as being in its entirety the revealed Word of God, and there is no real point in attempting to set forth the exact meaning of its content.

E. The Dichotomy Between Fact and Interpretation

One of the virtual consenses which has characterized and even virtually dominated the twentieth century is the separation of interpretation from the fact to which it attaches. This has manifested itself in several ways.

One instance of this separation is evidenced in the idea of Old Testament *Heilsgeschichte*. This idea has especially been developed and disseminated by Gerhard von Rad, probably the most important Old Testament theologian of the twentieth century. In his *Old Testament Theology,* he contrasted two very different versions of the history of Israel. One is the picture drawn by Israel of her own history, in the sacred writings known to us as the Old Testament. This is a witness to a redemptive history, or *Heilsgeschichte*. Here God is seen as at work on behalf of His people, delivering them from bondage, giving them victory over their enemies, establishing them in the land which he had designated for them. The other is the picture of Israel's history drawn by modern historiographers, who work without a supernatural hypothesis. Von Rad is aware of the rather sharp discrepancy between these two types of history, but he feels that theology cannot dispense with either one. What it must do, however, is set forth Israel's self-remembered history, and not substitute for it the modern reconstructions.[33]

Another example of this separation is the distinction between *Historie* and *Geschichte*, especially with respect to Christology. This terminology goes back to Martin Kähler's famous, *Der sogenannte historische Jesus und der geschichtliche, biblische Christus* (the so-called historical Jesus and the *historic* biblical Christ).[34] The distinction was between the "historical Jesus" and the kerygmatic Christ, the subject of the Christian Church's preaching. In drawing this distinction, however, he was not minimizing the role of the historical, or the place of the earthly Jesus. It was rather the modern historiographical Jesus that he tended to depreciate. The geschichtliche Christ is the whole Christ of the Bible: Jesus of Nazareth, who was born, lived, died, rose again and now lives in the preaching of the church.[35]

Later employment of Kähler's categories has developed the distinction in quite a different way, however. Particularly in the writing of Rudolf Bultmann, the historische Jesus becomes all that which could be sensorily experienced and studied by the methods of historical research, while the *geschichtlich* Christ is that experienced and proclaimed by the church. There is considerable scepticism over really knowing *Historie*. That, however, is relatively inconsequential, for Christian faith is not based upon it, but rather upon *Geschichte*. The event is to a large extent indeterminable, and the interpretation placed upon it is separable from it.[36] So common has this distinction become, and so much emphasis placed upon it, that a noted theologian of our century developed his Christology, not through a consideration of the relationship between the two natures of Jesus Christ, but between the two histories.[37]

Perhaps the most thoroughgoing instance of this assumption is found in the method of redaction criticism. Much conservative New Testament study has proceeded on the assumption that the writers of the synoptic Gospels were in some sense historians, concerned to give us at least some basic contours of the historical development of the life of Jesus. Redaction criticism, however, sees them as actual theologians and authors. Each had a basic belief about Jesus, and was concerned to express this to his particular groups of readers. Thus, each one interpreted the events of Jesus' life in the light of this purpose, this theological understanding. Consequently, what we have as explanation of the events, and to some extent even the events themselves as presented were products of the writer.[38]

There is an evangelical form of redaction criticism, which regards the interpretation and application done by the evangelists as inspired by the Holy Spirit. Thus, even if these are not actually Jesus' words, they nonetheless carry the same authority that they would have if they were. In non-evangelical hands, however, these are treated as the opinion of the evangelist, and thus subject to the shortcomings and even errors that are inevitably attached to human efforts. The writer modifies the tradition and interprets the events in keeping with his own theology and his evangelistic purpose.[39]

The effect of this presupposition is to create a distinction as to authority between the events and the interpretations given by Scripture writers. In an earlier age, conservative biblical scholars had debated regarding where Jesus' words and John's commentary began, in John 3. In a sense, however, the question was of only academic not practical significance, for John's words were as inspired and hence as authoritative as were those of Jesus. On this newer scheme, however, they would carry only the weight which a human interpreter's words would possess.

F. Truth as Dialectical

A final presupposition of real significance for interpretation is the dialectical understanding of truth. We are here dealing with what is fundamentally a methodological presupposition, but which rests upon a conception of the nature of reality as well. Dialectic suggests that within ideas or reality there is tension, polarity, paradox, and the like.

We contrast two very different methods or approaches: the logistic and the dialectical. The logistic method proceeds in rather straight-line fashion from premises to conclusions. Definitions of terms, axioms, principles, are established and spelled out, and they remain fixed. One can reason by objective laws of logic: if A is true, then not-A must be false. If A implies B and B implies C, then A implies C. Algebra and geometry, while they have differing subject matters, are excellent examples of logistic thinking. In proceeding, one looks for and expects to find resolutions of contradictions. Harmonization is the aim.

Dialectical methodology, however, emphasizes contrasts and even contradictions. Here there is tension between conflicting ideas. Out of that contradiction, or even as a characteristic of it, is the truth. Hegel developed a theory of logic, history, and reality on this pattern. There is a thesis. Then an antithesis occurs. Out of the tension between these two a synthesis emerges, gathering up elements of both into a new reality. This synthesis serves as the new thesis, to which there is then in turn another antithesis, and so forth.[40]

In the thought of Søren Kierkegaard, however, the two poles of the tension do not become reconciled. They form instead, a *paradox*. The inability of the intellect to resolve the tension offends the intellect, resulting in an inward passion. And this inward passion constitutes the truth.[41]

The paradox may on the one hand be present because of the tension between the individual and the universal. This is seen in the case of Abraham. Abraham was commanded to sacrifice his son, Isaac. The universal, the ethical, said that one should not kill. Yet here God was commanding Abraham to sacrifice his son. There was proposed a teleological suspension of the ethical.[42] It may also result from the tension between the infinite and the finite. That the unlimited eternal God should become incarnate as an individual, limited human being at one particular place and time in history—that is the supreme paradox. It is the absurd. The intellect cannot assimilate it.[43]

This same dialectical relationship between two seemingly opposed factors is also found in some twentieth-century thought. Consider the question, "Is the Bible the Word of God?' This, for many theologians, does not admit of a simple yes or no answer. Hence, Emil Brunner, for example, in effect answered that question by saying: "The Bible is the World of God/the Bible is not the Word of God." In the moment in which God is encountering a human being through a passage of Scripture, one may appropriately regard that portion as being God's Word, but not as an intrinsic quality of the writing.[44]

Note that this conception of the paradoxical nature of reality is not predicated of all of reality. Rather, a distinction is drawn. In realms of natural science, mathematics, economics, and history, the reality dealt with is thought of as fitting logistic categories. When, however, we deal with human persons or with divine or supernatural reality, the very nature of the objects of study is such as to produce paradox. The thought is frequently expressed that when eternal matters are discussed using temporal, earthbound human ideas and language, there is a refraction of the truth resulting in inevitable paradox.[45]

Now what is the effect of such a presupposition as this upon the interpretation of the Bible? An interpreter working from such an assumption would not expect to find harmony among the Bible's teachings. There would consequently be little effort to reconcile apparently conflicting passages or concepts. Indeed, in some cases there may even be expectation of disharmony, so that interpretations are favored which highlight discord.

V. CONCLUDING OBSERVATIONS

In the foregoing, we have looked at a number of presuppositions which affect our interpretation of the Bible. In so doing, we have necessarily been selective. Among the other issues which might have been dealt with are the centrality of the concept of man and the emphasis upon and confidence in humanity, the transcendence and the immanence of God, and the subjectivity of truth. In particular, the idea of the subjective locus of truth was omitted, largely because another paper at this conference dealt especially with this concept, as highlighted by the new hermeneutic.

It has not been our aim in this paper to evaluate or criticize the presuppositions described. Rather, we have sought primarily to identify them, and to some extent, to note the effects of the particular presupposition upon one's interpretation of the Scripture.

What a study of this type should do for us is to make us aware of the importance of presuppositions, and thus make us diligent in ferreting out the assumptions which we bring to our work of biblical interpretation. Geoffrey Turner, in a perceptive article, notes that systematic theologians have inquired about and discussed the role of presuppositions for some time, but that this has not been true of exegetes.[46] This perhaps suggests the need for additional dialogue between exegetes and theologians. This is particularly important in evangelical circles, where systematic theologians presumably base their theology upon the results of exegesis of the Bible. It is quite possible that we may otherwise attempt to interpret the Bible using categories drawn from a method that at root is contradictory to our basic understanding of the nature and teaching of the Bible. And it suggests that at least logically prior to our doing of serious exegetical work, we must ask some serious pre-exegetical questions, such as the nature of history, of truth, of God Himself, and of man. As one student once said to me: "It sounds as if you are saying that before we can develop a systematic theology we must have a knowledge of Scripture, and before we can interpret the Scripture we must have a theology." With some qualifications and modifications of terminology, I would pronounce that statement true.

But do we not face an impossible problem here? How do we antecedently arrive at presuppositions that are consistent with biblical teaching, before we do our interpretation of the Bible's teaching? In part, the answer will be found in a circular endeavor. We may begin with a somewhat unsophisticated approach to the Bible, simply taking it at face value. This will yield for us some understanding of certain of its conceptions, such as the nature of truth, history, God, and the world. We will thereby gain some tentative boundaries, so that as we do the philosophical and analytical work of establishing our method, we can ask whether it really is consistent with biblical ideas. Then as we apply our method to the study of the Bible, we will begin to obtain a more precise understanding of its contents. As we do so, we may well adjust and refine the presuppositions feeding into our hermeneutical method. Thus, the circle becomes narrower, the understanding of Scripture deeper, and the consonance between the Bible and hermeneutical method closer.

NOTES

[1]Rudolf Bultmann, "Is Exegesis Without Presuppositions Possible?" *Existence and Faith,* selected, translated, and introduced by Schubert M. Ogden (London: Hodder and Stoughton, 1960), p. 289.

[2]Norman L. Geisler, "Philosophical Presuppositions of Biblical Errancy," *Inerrancy,* ed. Norman L. Geisler (Grand Rapids: Zondervan Pub. House, 1979), p. 307.

[3]Paul J. Achtemeier, *An Introduction to the New Hermeneutic* (Philadelphia: The Westminster Press, 1974), p. 14.

[4]Anthony C. Thiselton, *The Two Horizons* (Grand Rapids: Wm. B. Eerdmans Pub. Co., 1980), p. 11.

[5]A. C. McGiffert, *Protestant Thought Before Kant* (New York: Harper and Brothers, 1961), p. 142.

[6]Friedrich Schleiermacher, *On Religion, Speeches to its Cultured Despisers* (New York: Harper and Brothers, 1958), p. 35.

[7]Ibid., p. 46.

[8]Friedrich Schleiermacher, *The Christian Faith* (New York: Harper & Row Publishers, 1963), Vol. I, p. 12ff.

[9]Schleiermacher, *On Religion*, p. 53.

[10]Albrecht Ritschl, *The Christian Doctrine of Justification and Reconciliation* (Edinburgh: T & T Clark, 1902), Vol. III, pp. 203ff.

[11]William Hordern, *A Layman's Guide to Protestant Theology,* revised edition (New York: Macmillan Co., 1968), pp. 83-84.

[12]Achtemeier, *Introduction to New Hermeneutic*, p. 15.

[13]William Hordern, *New Directions in Theology Today* Vol. I, *Introduction* (Philadelphia: The Westminster Press, 1966), pp. 141-42.

[14]Rudolf Bultmann, "The New Testament and Mythology," *Kerygma and Myth, a Theological Debate*, ed. Hans Bartsch (New York: Harper & Row Publishers 1961), p. 4.

[15]Langdon Gilkey, *Naming the Whirlwind* (Indianapolis: The Bobbs-Merrill Co., 1969), p. 37. William Hamilton, "Dietrich Bonhoeffer," *Radical Theology and the Death of God* by Thomas J. J. Altizer and William Hamilton (Indianapolis: The Bobbs-Merrill Co., 1966), pp. 115-16.

[16]Donald Baillie, *God was in Christ* (New York: Charles Scribner's Sons, 1948), pp. 160-64.

[17]Rudolf Otto, *The Idea of the Holy* (New York: Oxford University Press, 1958).

[18]William Hamilton, *The New Essence of Christianity* (New York: Association Press, 1961), pp. 63-64.

[19]Rudolf Bultmann, "Is Exegesis Without Presuppositions Possible?" pp. 291-92.

[20]*The Interpreter's Bible*, ed. George Buttrick (New York: Abingdon-Cokesbury Press, 1952), Vol. VIII, p. 490.

[21]Ibid., p. 491.

[22]Ernst Troeltsch, "Historiography," *Contemporary Religious Thinkers*, ed. John Macquarrie (London: S.C.M. Press, 1968), p. 81.

[23]Van A. Harvey, *The Historian and the Believer. The Morality of Historical Knowledge and Christian Belief* (London: S.C.M. Press 1967), p. 5.

[24]Ibid.

[25]Dennis E. Nineham, *New Testament Interpretation in an Historical Age* (London: Athalone Press, 1976), p. 18.

[26]Wolfhart Pannenberg, "Hermeneutics and Universal History," *History and Hermeneutic* ed. Robert W. Funk (New York: Harper & Row Publishers, Inc., 1967), pp. 122-52.

[27]Benjamin B. Warfield, "The Church Doctrine of Inspiration," *The Inspiration and Authority of the Bible*, ed. Samuel Craig (London: Marshall, Morgan & Scott, 1971), pp. 105-28.

[28]John Herman Randall, Jr., *The Making of the Modern Mind*, rev. ed. (Boston: Houghton, Mifflin Co., 1940), p. 552.

[29]L. Harold DeWolf, *The Case for Theology in Liberal Perspective* (Philadlphia: The Westminster Press, 1959), p. 48.

[30]Emil Brunner, *Our Faith* (New York: Charles Scribner's Sons, n.d.), p. 10.

[31]William Hordern, *The Case for a New Reformation Theology* (Philadelphia: The Westminster Press, 1959), p. 65.

[32]William Temple, *Nature, Man and God* (London: Macmillan and Co., Ltd., 1953), p. 311.

[33]Gerhard Von Rad, *Old Testament Theology* (Edinburgh: Oliver & Boyd, Ltd., 1962), Vol.I, pp. 106-8.

[34]Martin Kähler, *The So-Called Historical Jesus and the Historic Biblical Christ*, ed. Carl E. Braaten (Philadelphia: Fortress Press, 1964).

[35]Carl E. Braaten, *New Directions in Theology Today*, Vol. II, *History and Hermeneutics* (Philadelphia: The Westminster Press, 1966), p. 61.

[36]Rudolf Bultmann, "Offenbarung and Heilsgeschehen," *Beiträge zur evangelischen Theolgie*, ed. E. Wolf (Munich: Evangelischer Verlag, Albert Lamp, 1941), Vol. 7, p. 66.

[37]Donald Baillie, *God was in Christ*, p. 20ff.

[38]Norman Perrin, *What is Redaction Criticism?* (Philadelphia: Fortress Press, 1969), pp. 25-39.

[39]Grant R. Osborne, "The Evangelical and Redaction Criticism: Critique and Methodology," *Journal of the Evangelical Theological Society*, Vol. 22, No. 4 (December 1979), pp. 307-9.

[40]Georg Hegel, *Reason in History, A General Introduction to the Philosophy of History* (New York: Liberal Arts Press, 1953).

[41]Søren Kierkegaard, *Concluding Unscientific Postscript* (Princeton: Princeton University Press, 1941), p. 180.

[42]Søren Kierkegaard, *Fear and Trembling* (Princeton University Press, 1945), pp. 79-101.

[43]Kierkegaard, *Concluding Unscientific Postscript*, p. 528.

[44]H. Emil Brunner, *Revelation and Reason* (Philadelphia: The Westminster Press, 1946), p. 145.

[45]Kierkegaard, *Concluding Unscientific Postscript*, p. 187.

[46]Geoffrey Turner, "Pre-Understanding and New Testament Interpretation," *Scottish Journal of Theology*, Vol. 28 (1975), pp. 227-42.

A Response to Presuppositions of Non-Evangelical Hermeneutics

Gordon R. Lewis
Professor of Theology and Philosophy
Denver Conservative Baptist Seminary

A Response to Presuppositions of Non-Evangelical Hermeneutics

Gordon R. Lewis

Millard Erickson helpfully raises the consciousness of Bible interpreters to the influence of their presuppositions in his objective survey of "some theological, philosophical and methodological assumptions of typical non-evangelical hermeneutics."[1] He admits that at least in part the effect of presuppositions means biblical interpretation is a circular endeavor.[2]

In my response, I seek to challenge the necessity of hermeneutical circles, so often regarded inevitable since existentialist philosopher Martin Heidegger and New Testament scholar Rudolph Bultmann stressed interpretive preunderstandings.[3] Instead of treating each of Erickson's presuppositions separately, I associate those that typically appear together among non-evangelical interpreters as a set, and list a second set typically held by evangelical interpreters.

I show the subtle influence of non-evangelical assumptions upon Erickson's formulation of the primary hermeneutical problem and propose a revision. Along the way I suggest some steps to take in order to avoid logically fallacious circularity in hermeneutics.

I. TWO INFLUENTIAL SETS OF PRESUPPOSITIONS

Conceptions held in advance of interpretation by some non-evangelical scholars in Erickson's research, assume that: (1) the essence of Christianity is a non-conceptual experience, (2) humanity today differs radically from humanity in biblical times, (3) history is now considered a closed causal nexus excluding verifiable miracles, (4) revelation happens in a noninformative encounter for which no objective meaning can even be sought, (5) the preaching of the early church inaccurately portrayed the first century life of Jesus and (6) God's thought is so totally different from human thought that religious "truth" involves irresolvable tensions or dialectical contradictions. The result of this set of presuppositions is biblical errancy.

Contrasting conceptions held in advance of interpretation by some evangelical scholars, as Erickson showed, affirm that: (1) the essence of Christianity is experience of God founded on conceptual truths, (2) humanity today, however different from humanity in biblical terms, shares much in common for both have been created and sustained in God's image, (3) the regularities of nature reflect God's ordinary ways of working through means and do not render impossible God's extraordinary, miraculous acts in history, (4) divine revelation not only happens in event and encounter, but also abides in conceptual assertions whose objective meanings can be sought, (5) preaching in the early church accurately portrayed the life of Jesus Christ in history and (6) the teaching of Scripture in varied types of literature by very different writers on subjects often complex and incomprehensible can nevertheless be formulated without logical contradiction. God created and recreates people in His image to think his thoughts after Him (Col. 3:10) and does not deny Himself. Given this set of assumptions, the inerrancy of biblical teaching remains a live option.

Although Erickson's paper attempts little evaluation of these alternative sets of presuppositions, their crucial importance stands out vividly. They affect a person's interpretation of Scripture regarding the very nature and essence of Christianity, humanity, history, revelation, Jesus Christ, theology and biblical inerrancy.

Realistically, can anyone claim total objectivity or complete freedom from the influence of any concepts held in advance of his biblical exegesis? In an essay highly influential in recent discussion of the hermeneutical circle, Rudolph Bultmann asked, "Is Exegesis Without Presuppositions Possible?" Yes, he insisted, a person can transcend his own biases, gifts and weaknesses, but No, he cannot interpret Scripture apart from some methodological approach such as the historical-critical method. It influences in considerable measure the types of questions asked and considered important. Also influential are the interpreter's picture of the first century world in contrast with his picture of the contemporary world.[4]

In spite of the influence of concepts, methods and world pictures, Bultmann argued that presuppositions only falsify the biblical picture if they are taken definitively and exclusively. On those very bases, however, he himself falsified biblical teaching. Bultmann definitively presupposed that nature is a closed system of causes excluding any supernatural concursive activity. And he definitively adopted Heidegger's existentialism as the exclusive framework for translating the meaning of the New Testament situation into a contemporary life-situation. Clearly this non-evangelical New Testament scholar did not escape the subtle influence of presuppositions.

To help evaluate not only nationalist and existentialist, but also Marxist, humanist, occult and Eastern religious presuppositions influencing Bible scholars today, dialogue with systematic theologians and apologists may become increasingly important. Carl Braaten wrote,

> In the history of Protestant theology, dogmatics has received the bad reputation of lording it over the Bible, prejudging what it has to say; historical and philosophical criticism in undermining dogmatics received the glorious reputation as liberators of the Bible. Now it seems that the roles might be reversed. Dogmatics will have to assert itself both constructively and critically, taking its place in the arena of debate on hermeneutics as a full partner with other disciplines to broaden the terms of the discussion and clear the way for understanding the message of the Bible in its fullness.[5]

The first step in breaking out of hermeneutical circles then asks interpreters, whatever their fields, to increase their awareness of presuppositions and critically to assess their potential for falsifying biblical instruction.

II. THE PRECISE HERMENEUTICAL PROBLEM

The subtle influence of preunderstandings appears even in stating the task of hermeneutics today. Properly Erickson traces the shift of interest from the ancient context of the biblical writers to the interpreter's contemporary situation. We must ask not only what the text meant in biblical times, but what it signifies for us now.

However, Erickson overstates the gap between the biblical and contemporary cultures when he claims that hermeneutics "has to a large extent become a question of how meaning can be transferred from one historical and cultural context to another, *entirely different one*."[6] This statement mistakenly assumes the second nonevangelical presupposition (above), that humanity today is radically different from humanity in biblical days. To say that human culture now is entirely different overlooks genuine similarities in all people of all times as a result of creation in the image of God. With all the differences in means of travel, media of communication, types of home heating devices, and technical apparatus for producing goods, people are still human.

People of all times have capacities for self-transcendence, moral discernment, and linguistic signs for communication, as I argued against a total relativism in Chicago.[7] The universality of language and the translatability of thought from one language to another confirms, as Eugene Nida found, that "(1) the processes of human reasoning are essentially the same, irrespective of cultural diversity; (2) all people have a common range of experience, and (3) all people possess the capacity for at least some adjustment to the symbolic 'grids' of others."[8]

Attempts to "transfer the meaning" of Scripture from its times to ours can succeed because of the similarities between the times underlying the differences. Across the centuries-gap people are human, persons possess inherent human rights, demand justice, need forgiveness, desire loving acceptance and seek faithfulness to what is and to one another in deed and word, as I argued elsewhere.[9] Teaching on such crucial matters may be shared in common by people of Bible times and ours.

Where real differences between Biblical cultures and contemporary cultures do affect a grasp of the Bible's teaching, we are not free to change its meaning but to spell out its intended meaning's relationship to a different situation. E. D. Hirsch stated an important distinction between meaning and significance that Walter Kaiser featured in his *Toward an Exegetical Theology*. The *meaning* of Scripture is conveyed by a text, its grammar and the author's intention as indicated by his use of words. The *significance* refers to a relationship between that meaning and another person, time, situation or idea.[10]

Since our situation is not entirely different, the task of hermeneutics is not to transfer meanings into totally different meanings. The task is to discover the author's intended, single meaning and then to consider its relationship to people in spaceships, automobiles, machine shops and modern kitchens. To alter the meaning of God's conceptual revelation given once-for-all in inspired Scripture is inconsistent with the ICBI's position on propositional revelation and inspiration. That inspired meaning is to be discovered by exegesis and applied to life here and now. Clear distinctions must be made, then, between what the Scripture taught as *given* and how that teaching as related to life in varied cultures today may be *taken*.

An influential strand of missiological thinking today considers the hermeneutical task to be one of finding in another culture a dynamic or functional equivalent by which to convey the same pragmatic result as the Scripture did originally in its culture, or in the missionary's culture.[11] Surely the missionary must relate the Bible's meaning to the people he seeks to reach, thus giving its significance for their situation. In the name of contextualization, however, missionaries consistent with the ICBI convictions, cannot fail to distinguish the given meaning of Scripture from their attempts to show its significance and application in other cultures. Is not the hermeneutical task, then, to seek first the conceptual or essential meaning and then the contemporary functional or existentialist significance? On the above set of non-evangelical existentialist presuppositions, existence may be prior to essence, and so the primacy of cognitive knowledge must be abandoned.[12] But on evangelical presuppositions of propositional revelation and verbal inspiration, essence is prior to existence, cognitive knowledge provides the guidelines for commitment. The interpreter's first task is that of exegeting the essence of revelation as given; the interpreter's second task is that of living authentically by revealed truths in his existential context. Both are indispensable, but the priority of revelational givens may easily be lost if the hermeneutical task is not carefully formulated.

As different as our cultures may be from biblical cultures, we may need the same message people needed in earlier centuries. Geoffrey Bromiley asks, If the Bible's "message is for all men of all cultures, how important is the cultural particularity of the message?"[13] Surely the relationship of the Bible or of Jesus Christ to their particular cultures is not so important that they fail to relate to other cultures. Inspired writers were culture related, but not "culture bound" as G. C. Berkouwer[14] and Charles H. Kraft[15] imagined. Inspired writers exercised their own powers of self-transcendence and received God's transcendent guidance in writing Scripture.

The second step, then, in breaking out of hermeneutical circles calls upon all sides to give priority to distinguishing the inspired meaning of Scripture from its contemporary significance in the context of our lives and cross-cultural ministries. Unless we address the same issue, our words about the Bible's teaching will pass each other like ships in the night. To formulate the overarching issue as one of changing the meaning of Scripture to make it suit our grasp of our totally different existentialist or functional societies is to render the affirmation of propositional revelation and verbal inspiration a charade.

III. THE LOGICAL STARTING POINT

It has been established that non-evangelicals are not more totally objective than evangelicals. Both begin interpretation with conceptual and methodological presuppositions. No exegete's mind is *tabula rasa* when opening the Bible.

It is also evident that non-evangelicals cannot justify their conflicting presuppositional claims on the basis of private experiences, or the personal witness of the Spirit. Mormon claims to additional revelations and special interpretations of Scripture based upon a "burning in the bosom" of the youthful Latter-day Saints at your door are unconvincing. Publicly verifiable contradictions and discrepancies discount private sincerity, however intense.

Neither can non-evangelicals imagine that the problem of conflicting presuppositions is settled by alleging that "all scholars agree." Clearly scholars at work within both conceptual frameworks argue fallaciously that anyone who does not agree with them is for that reason unscholarly.

Unless all sides critically assess their presuppositions, however, biblical interpretation becomes a matter of getting the book to teach what we had previously assumed it teaches. Exegesis, whatever our disciplines, becomes eisegesis. God then does not speak to us through the Scriptures, but like ventriloquists, we "hear" our own previous assumptions echoed there.

If our views of God, creation, human need, Jesus Christ, revelation and inspiration are sound, we need not fear that they will provide the best account of the given data. The Berean's testing of Paul's teachings, surely involved the apostle's most basic presuppositions, and received commendation as "noble." The Christians at Berea "examined the Scriptures every day to see if what Paul said was true" (Acts 17:11). Since an apostle's statements were not beyond reexamination, are those of biblical theologians, systematic theologians, liberation theologians, cultural anthropologists, psychologists and counselors?

The third step out of circular reasoning in hermeneutics calls upon every interpreter to consider his own and other's presuppositions and hypotheses to be tested, or claims to be verified or disverified. Presuppositions carry only provisional authority until adequately tested and confirmed. Erickson's paper suggests regarding them "tentative boundaries."[16] I agree and have sought to emphasize, a bit less briefly, that there is nothing in presuppositions too ultimate for examination and for which we ought not be able to give our reasons. Premature finality from non-evangelicals is no more commendable than from evangelicals. Let smugness disappear from both sides and let genuine investigation of the relevant data be wholeheartedly pursued.

IV. COMMON GROUND

Can people of radically diverse and deep commitments genuinely put their presuppositions to the test or "refine" them?[17] Can non-evangelicals reassess the validity of their assumptions? Can evangelicals? In spite of great differences there remain underlying, vitally important similarities that make thought and communication possible. Because all interpreters of Scripture on all sides are creatures of God, made in His image, and recipients of common grace, (if not special grace) to think God's thoughts after Him and share His work in the world, communication is possible. I did not say easy! Because of pride, previous investigations and sincere commitments dialog is far from easy. But by God's grace interpreters can reexamine interpretations, revise and accept those that are more adequate.

All biblical knowledge is interpretive. So we hear, "That's just your interpretation!" Another exclaims in return, "And that's just your interpretation!" True, but some interpretations are better informed than others. We are constantly called upon to decide between interpretations. We can, and we must, responsibly choose the better informed options closer to God's fully informed mind on the subject.

By creation and providence God has so constituted the human mind in His likeness that it can test, try, prove, and hold fast what is good and true. A way out of hermeneutical circles returns to our common humanity programmed by a wise Creator to think in general categories like His and His whole creation. As a result we share not only given, publicly observable data, but also the logical principle of noncontradiction a *sine qua non* of meaningful thought and communication, the supreme human value of love, holy love, faithful love, satisfying justice ethically and fulfilling human existence psychologically as well as spiritually.[18] With a common need for respect and love and a common responsibility before the data, coherently faced, can we not reassess our perspectives? Are not all, in spite of our fallenness, eventually accountable to God for our faithfulness in the use of these common abilities? Their recognition does not make man autonomous, but responsible.

In spite of presuppositional differences, then, we need to find and acknowledge our basic agreements where they do exist. Where differences remain, we need choose for one against another only when the assertions contradict each other or fail to fit facts. Statements in logically contradictory relationships cannot both be true. But many different assertions may express logically contrary relationships, in which both statements can be true. Choice is necessary when one asserts that no divine revelation is propositional and another asserts that some divine revelation is propositional. However, it would be unnecessary to choose for one against another if one said, "Some revelation is in mighty acts" and another said, "Some revelation is in propositional assertions."

The fourth step by which to break out of hermeneutical circles, then recognizes between schools of interpretation in our common humanity under God, our common requirements of relating to reality and to each other meaningfully. The reality of common ground means that no one need resort to violence or mind-control to achieve worthy educational objectives.

V. CRITERIA OF TRUE INTERPRETATIONS

Granting that as human beings non-evangelicals and evangelicals can discuss intelligently deep presuppositional differences about the Bible, how can we ever resolve the contradictory assumptions adopted? Out of the universal *imago dei* arise criteria of truth to which we all find ourselves accountable and to which we hold others accountable. Ultimately, our interpretations of Scripture are true if they correspond to God's interpretations. God knows what is and ought to be in the respective contexts of biblical meaning and contemporary significance. How then can we know when our interpretations correspond with the intended meaning of God and the authors God inspired?

God knows all the relevant data, does not deny Himself and leads us to eternal, spiritual life. So we can apply these criteria of truth in general to hermeneutics. A true interpretation is noncontradictory, fits all the relevant facts and leads to eternal, spiritual life unhypocritically. In disputed passages, the true interpretation is the proposed interpretation that without contradiction accounts for the converging lines of grammatical, historical, cultural evidence with the fewest difficulties. The criteria of truth in interpretation as elsewhere are: (1) logical noncontradiction, (2) empirical fit and (3) experiential viability.

Consider how such standard criteria of truth apply to typical nonevangelical presuppositions in the study of New Testament. Alan Richardson writes,

> The way in which one may attempt to state the theology of the NT . . . is by the framing of an hypothesis (whether consciously or unconsciously) and then testing it by continual

> checking with the NT documents and other relevant evidence from the period. This is in fact the way in which historical critical interpretation is done nowadays in every field of historical reconstruction. It necessarily involves a personal or subjective element, but this is now seen to be unavoidable, as the illusion of scientific or presuppositionless history recedes. It does not, however, involve an absolute subjectivism or historical relativism, for the pursuit of history as a humane science involves the conviction that one historical interpretation can be rationally shown to be better than another.[19]

Furthermore, the hypothesis-verification method of reasoning is not circular. It does not assume, but tentatively proposes the point to be established. Suppose, then, that Rudolph Bultmann's basic presuppositions concerning the New Testament be put to the test of coherence. In the words of Alan Richardson,

> R. Bultmann's hypothesis that the theology of the New Testament is a mythological conglomeration of Jewish apocalyptic and Hellenistic gnostic ideas which have somehow coagulated round the name of Jesus of Nazareth, about whom little certain historical knowledge can be attained, must be studied to see whether it gives a rational and coherent explanation of the New Testament evidence. In this respect it should be compared with the other hypotheses, such as that Jesus himself is the prime author of the striking reinterpretation of the Old Testament theology which is found in his own reported teachings and in the New Testament as a whole (the new covenant, the new Israel, the reinterpreted Messiahship, the reign of God, and so on).[20]

A verificational method cannot be abstracted from the larger philosophical and theological context of the age in which it is devised and used, but, as Carl Braaten argued, "The ultimate criterion of an appropriate hermeneutic is a material one; that is, does the hermeneutical method do justice to the matter to be interpreted? The historical method, as an essential component of hermeneutic, should be the servant, not the master, of the Biblical subject matter."[21]

A major criticism of non-evangelical sets of presuppositions and hermeneutical methods, then is their failure to fit the facts of the Bible's own subject matter. As Geoffrey Bromiley succinctly said, "Scripture understanding itself, not as an essay in human religion, but as divine self-revelation."[22] This view of Scripture is plainly taught by Scripture, neither arbitrarily imported into it nor fancifully extracted from it.

The new hermeneutic claims that if the meaning of Scripture is to be grasped, it must be accommodated to preunderstandings in people's experience. The preunderstanding of fatherhood may be enlarged and corrected, but without it understanding and appropriation are impossible. In condescending to communicate with humanity, God does use intelligible words and historical events, not ineffable intuitions. However, the new hermeneutic seems to infer that people cannot learn what is not yet within their experience. So it seeks completely to reconstruct Scripture that does not fit "modern" thought-forms and world pictures. So naturalistic presuppositions are imposed upon Scripture and God is reduced to the measure of mankind, rather than mankind brought under the measure of God. In the name of linguistic analysis the power of the Holy Spirit to disclose new areas of meaning to inspired prophets and apostles is denied. Hermeneutics must take account of the hearers of revelation, but not confuse the recipient with the Revealer! Non-evangelical hermeneutics must take account of the context of the Bible's readers, but not confuse the reader's presuppositions with biblical teaching, if in fact those preunderstandings do not fit the facts of the biblical record. A hermeneutical method that undermines the validity of the evangelical set of presuppositions, to that extent does not do justice to the givens in the book it seeks to understand.

Clearly interpreters must decide whether the scriptural givens, or their own presuppositions are the final court of appeal in determining meaning. If our preunderstandings are the ultimate authority, then exegesis reduces ultimately to ventriloquism. If the lordship of Christ comes to expression in the biblical data, then our presuppositions, conceptual and methodological, may need revision to provide the most coherent fit.

I conclude that an evangelical set of presuppositions like that briefly set forth above, constitutes the most consistent, factual and viable account of the biblical data with the fewest difficulties. A case for inerrancy is not itself inerrant. Not all who hold it need agree with every step of this hypothesis-verificational approach to it. But on this approach important to many evangelicals, the case for propositional revelation and inerrant inspiration and a literal-cultural-critical meaning is not logically fallacious, circular reasoning.

And the system that results is not closed, but open to further study, does not impose a contrived interrelatedness upon Scripture, but at the end of the interpretive endeavor seeks an authentic interrelatedness, makes no claim to exhaustiveness, but acknowledges the limited nature of a person's investigations and lack of full comprehension, and does not seek to educate by sheer indoctrination, but calls for the participation of scholars in defining the issue, proposing hypotheses, examining relevant evidence and arriving at his own conclusions on the grounds of their coherence.

The fifth step out of hermeneutical circles, then, asks each interpreter to confirm or disconfirm his presuppositions by their consistency, adequacy and viability in terms of the revelational givens in Scripture teaching. That set of presuppositions should be adopted which without contradiction accounts for the many diverse lines of relevant grammatical, historical, cultural, theological and experiential data with the fewest difficulties.

CONCLUSION

Although it has been impossible in this brief compass to include many lines of converging evidence in support, I conclude that the evangelical set of presuppositions above fits most coherently with given scriptural data.

The element of truth in the non-propositional view of revelation is that the Bible is not merely a handbook of statements along the lines of Wittgenstein's *Tractatus*. In the many types of literary genre in Scripture, however, cognitive assertions are implied, even though not in standard logical form (Subject, the verb to be, and predicate nominative). The element of truth in propositional views of revelation is even more important. Anthony Thiselton writing on "Wittgenstein and the Debate about Biblical Authority" concludes, "It is that the dynamic and concrete authority of the Bible rests, in turn, on the truth of certain states of affairs in God's relation to the world. As J. L. Austin succinctly put it, for performative language to function effectively, 'certain statements have *to be true*'."[23] We may become involved in biblical authority through careful exegesis with all the contextual processes that involves. But the basis of the Bible's authority is something broader than our present comprehension. It is God's inner integrity as faithful and true, and God's relationship to this world, similarly faithful and true, and our submission to His Lordship as revealed in God's inscripturated faithful and true words.

NOTES

[1]Millard Erickson, "Presuppositions of Non-Evangelical Hermeneutics" 594.
[2]*Ibid.*, p. 610.

[3]For a survey, see Anthony C. Thiselton, *The Two Horizons* (Grand Rapids: Eerdmans, 1980), pp. 104-10, 147, 165-66.

[4]Rudolph Bultmann, *Existence and Faith* (New York: Living Age, 1960), pp. 289-96.

[5]Carl Braaten, *History and Hermeneutics New Directions in Theology Today* Vol. 2 (Philadelphia: Westminster, 1966), p. 137.

[6]Millard Erickson, *op. cit.*, p. 596, italics mine.

[7]Gordon Lewis, "The Human Authorship of Inspired Scripture," *Inerrancy*, ed. Norman Geisler (Grand Rapids: Zondervan, 1980).

[8]Eugene Nida, *Message and Mission* (New York: Harper, 1960), p. 90.

[9]Gordon Lewis, "Three Sides to Every Story: Communicating the Absolutes of General and Special Revelation to Relativists," (Denver, CO 80210, C. B. Seminary, 1978).

[10]Walter C. Kaiser, Jr., *Toward an Exegetical Theology* (Grand Rapids: Baker, 1981), p. 32.

[11]Charles H. Kraft, *Christianity in Culture* (Maryknoll, NY: Orbis, 1979), p. 324.

[12]Calvin O. Schrag, *Existence and Freedom* (Evanston, Illinois: Northwestern University Press, 1961), p. 22.

[13]Geoffrey Bromiley, "The Interpretation of the Bible," *The Expositors Bible Commentary I*, ed. Frank Gabelein (Grand Rapids: Zondervan, 1979), p. 74.

[14]G. C. Berkouwer, *Holy Scripture* (Grand Rapids: Eerdmans, 1975), pp. 185-86.

[15]Charles H. Kraft, *op. cit.*, p. 300.

[16]Erickson, p. 610.

[17]*Ibid.*

[18]Gordon R. Lewis, *Testing Christianity's Truth Claims* (Chicago: Moody, 1976), pp. 288-89 and chapters 7-10.

[19]Alan Richardson, "New Testament Theology," *A Dictionary of Christian Theology*, ed. Alan Richardson (London: SCM, 1969), p. 229.

[20]*Ibid.*

[21]Carl Braaten, *op. cit.*, p. 137.

[22]Geoffrey Bromiley, *op. cit.*, p. 72.

[23]Anthony Thistleton, *op. cit.*, p. 437.

A Response to Presuppositions of Non-Evangelical Hermeneutics

Robert L. Saucy
Professor of Systematic Theology
Talbot Theological Seminary

A Response to Presuppositions of Non-Evangelical Hermeneutics

Robert L. Saucy

The paper to which we are responding has given us a good survey of some crucial presuppositions common to most non-evangelical hermeneutics. We would concur with Dr. Erickson's own acknowledgment that others could be added to this list. However, rather than simply attempt to add to the list, it seems to us that additional value can be gained by seeking some common factors which these presuppositions share and thereby attempting to get to the underlying root idea or ideas which differentiate the evangelical and non-evangelical in their approach to the interpretation of Scripture.

While the ultimate starting point of this distinction may be debated in that it is not always easy to determine the direction of flow between the ideas, we would suggest that theologically one's concept of man, if not the ultimate presumptive starting point, at least lies deep as a foundational element in a person's attitude toward the Scriptures. This in turn influences the concept of God and the world, which in turn has direct bearing on the understanding of the nature of the Bible and its interpretation. In the brief scope of this response we would like to sketch that flow noting at points its relation to some of the presuppositions mentioned in the paper.

I. MAN—HIS AUTONOMY

A. The Basic Presupposition

In order to be relevant to modern man, theology, according to many non-evangelicals must start from below and be structured by the questions posed by modern man rather than by some supposedly timeless message imposed from above.[1] As Karl Rahner has stated, theological formulas must ". . . make use of such presupposition as are self-evident to modern man."[2] Implicit in this approach is the acceptance of modern man's understanding of his experience in the world as a true interpretation of reality. Behind this acceptance lies the deeper presupposition of the autonomy of man.

Without attempting to trace the rise of this belief, its impact upon theology is readily apparent. From the Catholic side Hans Kung following Zahrnt accepts "the modern understanding of authority as vital to theology": "no truth is accepted without being submitted to the judgment of reason. . . ."[3] Tillich, likewise, in his autobiography refers to a "difficult and painful break-through to autonomy" which he testifies made him "immune against any system of thought or life which demands the surrender of this autonomy."[4] While perhaps not so patent in some other non-evangelicals, it is not difficult to see this assumption behind many of the canons of what is frequently referred to as historical-critical analysis. Indicative of the result of this presupposition is the comment of Gilkey in reference to the historical record of Scripture.

> The difficulty is that *our* theological affirmations about history and God's role in relation to it cannot be based exclusively or unequivocally on that biblical interpretation of history, i.e., on the history the Bible reports, for that is not a view of history which we ourselves can necessarily accept.[5]

In sum, the modern theologian frequently operates on the underlying premise of the modern historian set forth by Harvey when he says, "The historian *confers* authority upon a witness."[6] His right to do so is obviously derived from a higher authority namely, himself.

Implicit in this presupposition of human autonomy are at least two ingredients which should be noted in passing. The first is the real lack of a serious consideration of the noetic effect of sin. For it is not only the believer's mind which is allowed to establish the categories by which Scripture is to be interpreted, but that of the unbeliever as well. The second inherent assumption is the superiority of the modern man over his ancient counterpart. It is not at all apparent why the modern mind, which has for the most part turned away from God and his light, should be set forth as the criterion of truth.

Integral to the basic presupposition of human autonomy and one of its key elements is the evolutionary view of the universe. Not only does it tend to support modern man in his feeling of historical rational supremacy, but its implications are probably the strongest driving force behind the relativity of modern historical consciousness that is so influential in hermeneutics.

B. Some Hermeneutical Ramifications of Human Autonomy

It is beyond our task to indicate the full scope of the impact of this major presupposition of human autonomy upon the interpretation of Scripture. We would, however, like to briefly list four hermeneutical principles used by non-evangelicals which are rooted in this presupposition.

1. Truth is judged by human experience

Barr asserts forthrightly,

> . . . we have a right, and indeed a duty, to use the Bible critically. In using the word 'critically' I am not referring in the first place to biblical criticism, as usually so termed. . . . I mean more specifically that the sayings of scripture have to be weighed and measured by us. . . .[7]

Although in our judgment Thielicke does not entirely avoid this same problem he rightly notes what subtly takes place when man's analysis of human experience is accepted as the controlling factor of theological statement.

> . . . A tragic entanglement of thought occurs, since the arguments needed to throw light on the presuppositions of an understanding of revelation . . . unintentionally become means to determine in advance what revelation must be according to nature and form of communication. . . .[8]

2. Truth is relative

A second result of the acceptance of human autonomy is the overwhelming historic consciousness that prevails in so much of the modern approach to the Scriptures and truth. If human reason is the final authority it is only logical to understand truth in relativistic terms.

3. Truth is judged by human fulfillment

In the third instance, the elevation of man to autonomy carries with it the understanding of human existence primarily in terms of what benefits man. In modern terms this amounts to such concepts as authentic personhood, self-fulfillment, and personal freedom. It is only too obvious how such a man-centered starting point is presently affecting the interpretation of Scripture in the realms of ethics and politics.[9] But perhaps most of all it determines one's soteriology being concerned only with what happens *in* me rather than *for* me. In short it assigns truth the limited function of personal significance, "being the means whereby I master life."[10]

4. A preference for the new and creative

Finally, we would suggest a fourth influence that the presupposition of human autonomy has upon the hermeneutical procedure, that is, the propensity toward the preference for the new and creative rather than the traditional. We need care at this point not to deny the value of fresh insights into the understanding of the Word. The history of doctrine and the life of the church demonstrates that God does not intend his people simply to repeat the understanding of prior generations. He desires to lead us into new understandings and applications of His truth for our own age even as He has done in the past. Having said this, however, it is nevertheless true that one of the banes of modern theology is the high premium it places on creativity and novelty as opposed to tradition. In our mind Barr in his criticism of fundamentalism exemplifies this tendency. He writes,

> . . . the essence of scholarship does not lie in brains or learning: it lies in ideas, in fresh analysis, in new perspectives. On this side even the best conservative scholarship is shockingly defective. It is stodgy, apologetic and uncreative. Its dullness is monumental. What striking new line of approach, what creative new method, what fresh analysis has ever come from it, even in its most creditable modern forms?[11]

It is evident from the context of this statement that Barr attributes the creativity of scholarship which he applauds to the critical approach toward Scripture which we would suggest rests upon or is at least closely related to the modern presupposition of human autonomy.

II. GOD-HIS EXCLUSION FROM OBJECTIVE INVOLVEMENT IN HISTORY

A. The Basic Presupposition

Behind several of the presuppositions mentioned by Erickson, notably a positivistic historiography and the nature of revelation, lies a deeper fundamental presupposition about God and His relationship to creation. This is clearly expressed in this statement of Küng.

> . . . The present-day understanding of God presupposes the *scientific explanation of the world:* weather and victories in battle, illnesses and cures, fortune and misfortune of individuals, groups and nations are no longer explained by the direct intervention of God, but by natural causes. . . .[12]

On the basis of such an understanding of the relation of God to the world, Küng goes on to assert that "there is no action of God alongside world history, but only *in* the history of the world and of man's activity."[13]

In our opinion this understanding of God's relationship to the world is a direct and necessary result of the first presupposition of human autonomy. If man's understanding of his experience is made the criterion of reality and he is seen in his freedom as the creator of his history, there is no place for the direct intervention of God. To be sure the acceptance of human autonomy and creativity is seen in varying degrees among non-evangelical theologies. For some, such as process thought, it becomes central. In neo-orthodoxy, on the other hand, it is virtually denied in the heavy emphasis on the necessity of divine initiative. Yet even in neo-orthodoxy the acceptance of the so-called scientific world view with its empirical criterion of truth has the same effect of excluding God from direct objective entrance into the world. While God may be viewed as working differently, in all of those systems because this world is placed under human reason, God is limited to the immanent subjective realm.

B. Some Hermeneutical Ramification of the Exclusion of God from Objective Involvement in History

1. The denial of objective revelation

The modern concept of subjective non-propositional revelation is inherently related to the broader viewpoint of God's relationship to the world. In our opinion this modern viewpoint cannot be substantiated either biblically or empirically. Rather it stems directly from this underlying presupposition.

2. The disjuncture between human language and God's Word

Since human language is an objective aspect of human history, the exclusion of God in any objective form from that history of necessity entails the denial that any words can be both man's and God's. God's Word must always be behind the human Word speaking only in the subjective realm.

3. The priority of faith over objective truth

A common element in much of non-evangelical theology is the diminishing of the role of the objective revelation of God in Scripture in the entire process of bringing man into relationship with God. Some strains of existential faith, as Cobb points out, are almost totally void of a noetic element except for some knowledge of itself.[14]

This naturally allows faith to be somewhat indifferent toward the facts of Scripture. Although apparently not ignoring the objective basis of faith in fact, the following statement of Barr gives evidence of the application of this principle in one's attitude toward Scripture.

> The faith is not itself founded upon the Bible or upon biblical inspiration: it is founded upon persons of the past, especially of course Jesus Christ, and upon what they said and did. The Bible is the primary source for these persons and events; and yet it is not an exact transcript of what they were or what they said. . . . Faith is a personal relation to God through Jesus Christ, and the dealing with biblical texts is one part of the total functioning of faith in relation to God. The true believer is a believer in God and in Christ, not in the first place a believer in the Bible.[15]

How one comes to know God and believe in Him without first coming into contact with the objective truth of the Bible and believing it is not explained by Barr. His approach, however, is the logical result of disallowing God an objective involvement in history.

III. THE BIBLE-ITS PRODUCTION BY THE CHURCH

A. The Basic Presupposition

The presuppositions of human autonomy and the exclusion of God from objective involvement within history lead to the final concept which lies directly behind the non-evangelical hermeneutical approach to the Scriptures. We refer to the belief expressed forthrightly by some contemporary writers that the Bible is the product of the faith of the church. Barr states,

> The Bible is in its origin a product of the believing community. Modern biblical study has made this much more plain to us than it could ever have been in the past.[16]

In saying this he expressly denies the Protestant position which he correctly describes as giving ". . . scripture priority over the church in the *ordo revelationis*."[17]

Achtemeier, who has the same understanding, sets forth a corresponding concept of inspiration which in effect denies any unique work of the Spirit in the origin of the Scriptures. He explains that

> . . . if Scripture is to be understood as inspired, then that inspiration will have to be understood equally in terms of the community that produced those Scriptures. Inspiration, in short, occurs within the community of faith, and must be located at

> least as much within that community as it is with an individual author.[18]

How much the Spirit is excluded from the actual production of the Bible is seen when he asserts that "a unitary outlook on the reality of God would be possible only if the Bible were produced by a group of like-minded people writing to a like-minded people over a short period of time."[19] Another possibility, of course, is to see the Holy Spirit exert his influence throughout the production of Scripture and thus provide the unifying factor. But the presuppositions of human autonomy and the denial of the direct involvement of God in human history preclude such an operation of the Spirit.

B. Some Hermeneutical Ramifications of the Production of the Bible by the Church

It is obvious that when the principle is held that the Bible is the product of the church, even a church of devout faith, the impact on the hermeneutical procedure is extensive. The Bible as fundamentally a human writing must be interpreted in the light of what we know of contemporary man and what we believe concerning ancient man. Without attempting to elucidate all of the effects of this belief we would suggest the following as having major hermeneutical impact:

1. The interpretation of Scripture in the light of human fallibility

Viewing Scripture primarily as the product of man immediately influences the interpreter to explain any difficulties which he finds in terms of human fallibility. Thus problems of internal harmony are solved by different sources and problems relating to present human knowledge in all areas can be chalked up to the ignorance of the outmoded views. The obvious diversity among human thinkers as we know them leads also to an emphasis on the diversity of theologies within the Bible rather than laboring to find any overarching unity. Finally and perhaps most devastatingly of all, the relativity of all things in the modern historic consciousness of man leads to the conclusion that the statements of the Scriptures must likewise be viewed with that same relativity. Achtemeier gives evidence of this effect when he says:

> . . . The Bible is the result of the earnest search of God's will for his world in ever-changing situations, and the mark of the faithfulness of the respondents to the living traditions of God's acts in the past is seen precisely in the differing interpretations

> given to those acts in the differing situations faced by the various respondents.[20]

2. Explanation of the Scripture in terms of the historical conscious intent of the human author

A second hermeneutical impact of the human production of the Bible is the tendency to seek an explanation for the author's thoughts within his human context. As a result preference is given to all sorts of influences from the ancient world as the real sources for much biblical thought.

3. The final hermeneutical authority of the present believer

The ultimate result of viewing the Bible fundamentally as the product of man is the establishing of the contemporary believer as the hermeneutical authority. If the Scripture is nothing more than the fallible responses of believers to God's action in their midst and the responders have not, in fact, even agreed among themselves, but have continually reinterpreted God's acts in different situations as Achtemeier holds, then it surely makes good sense to see that process continuing even today. In addition, to define inspiration as belonging basically to the community of faith out of which the Scriptures arose is to provide oneself with a spiritual dynamic for such a present-day authority. For, according to this theory, the Spirit continues His inspiring work in believers today allowing them to interpret the Word in creative revelatory ways as needed in new historical contexts. Achtemeier reflects this whole scheme in the following statement:

> Here again, the process of appropriating Scripture closely reflects the process by which Scripture came into existence. The traditions incorporated into our Scriptures represent the way generations within the community of faith, in Israel and in the church, sought to appropriate the experience of those who had gone before. If then there are inconsistencies in that record and in those traditions, it is precisely the inconsistencies that are reflections of the life of the community of faith. A life in the twentieth century that exactly replicated a life in the eighth century before Christ or the first century after Christ would not be a life of faith, it would be a grotesque anachronism. The Bible reflects the life of the faithful community over a span of centuries, and in the process of faithfully hearing and interpreting traditions in the light of new historical situations, the

> life of that community changed, and differed, from its earlier stages. Failure to change does not mean faithfulness, it means death, and a community which seeks to respond to a living God can hardly do so with an unchanging response that characterizes death rather than life.[21]

This principle of the contemporary inspired believer as the final hermeneutical authority takes two forms. In its personal application it is used to affirm only what the Scripture says or means to me. Allegedly under the inspiration of the Spirit the individual decides what is normative for his life and thought. More generally among theologians it is the collective community through which the Spirit leads to give his people continual revelation of new truth. Barr explains,

> The Bible takes its origin from within the life of believing communities; it is interpreted within the continuing life of these communities: the standard of its religious interpretation is the structure of faith which these communities maintain. . . .[22]

In response to the whole concept of a present inspiration with its concomitant doctrine of continuing revelation we can do no better than concur with the words of Stephen Clark when he writes,

> . . . any "spirit" who leads someone to contradict the teaching of canonical scripture is exhibiting clear signs of not being the one Holy Spirit. One of the greatest values of possessing a canon of Scripture is that it provides a means of discerning spirits . . . For a Christian to neglect the highest teaching authority in favor of individual or collective revelation or inspiration is a major spiritual mistake.[23]

IV. CONCLUSION

In conclusion may we emphasize our agreement with Erickson's insistence on the necessity of a sort of hermeneutical circle involving theology and exegesis. Perhaps the circle could be enlarged to include even those factors which lie behind our theology. The issues of hermeneutics are multiple and complex. Yet, at least in most rational thinking, there are foundational premises which color our approach to all issues and more than likely bind our conclusions together.

We have sought in our response to trace what in our opinion is behind the non-evangelical view of the nature of the Scriptures which in turn dominates their hermeneutical outlook. At the risk of oversimplification and excessive reductionism, may we state that the final issue is whether we do hermeneutics from a center outside of ourselves or whether we do it ultimately from ourselves. We may disagree on certain biblical interpretations, but the ultimate question is whether we are seeking our theological understanding which affects our exegesis from within the Scripture itself or whether we are letting alien influences from outside determine our meaning.

NOTES

[1]Hans Küng, *On Being a Christian,* trans. Edward Quinn (Garden City, New York: Doubleday & Company, Inc., 1976), p. 83.

[2]Karl Rahner, "Die Forderung Nach Einer 'Rurzformel' des Christlichen Glaubens," in *Schriften zur Theologie,* Vol. III, pp. 154-55, cited by Burke, *Rahner and Revelation* (Unpublished doctor's dissertation, Yale University, 1974), p. 31.

[3]Küng, *On Being a Christian,* p. 81.

[4]Paul Tillich, "Autobiographical Reflections," in *The Theology of Paul Tillich* edited by C. W. Kegley and R. W. Bretall (New York: The Macmillan Company, 1956), p. 8.

[5]Langdon Gilkey, *Reaping the Whirlwind* (New York: The Seabury Press, 1976), p. 136.

[6]Van Austin Harvey, *The Historian and the Believer* (New York: The Macmillan Company, 1966), p. 42.

[7]James Barr, *The Scope and Authority of the Bible* (Philadelphia: The Westminster Press, 1980), p. 55.

[8]Helmut Thielicke, *The Evangelical Faith,* Vol. I, trans, and edited by Goeffrey W. Bromiley (Grand Rapids, Michigan: William B. Eerdmans, 1974), p. 54.

[9]Stephen Clark, *Man and Woman in Christ* (Ann Arbor, Michigan: Servant Books, 1980), pp. 507-40.

[10]Thielicke, *The Evangelical Faith,* p. 27.

[11]Barr, *The Scope and Authority of the Bible,* pp. 72-73.

[12]Hans Küng, *On Being a Christian,* p. 81.

[13]Ibid., p. 295.

[14]John B. Cobb, Jr., "Faith and Culture," in *The New Hermeneutic* edited by James M. Robinson and John B. Cobb, Jrd. (New York: Harper & Row, 1964), pp. 219-31.

[15]Barr, *The Scope and Authority of the Bible,* pp. 125-26.

[16]Ibid., p. 113.

[17]Ibid., p. 116.

[18]Paul J. Achtemeier, The Inspiration of Scripture (Philadelphia: The Westminster Press, 1980), p. 116.

[19]Ibid., p. 156.

[20]Ibid.

[21]Ibid., p. 146.

[22]Barr, *The Scope and Authority of the Bible,* p. 111.

[23]Clark, *Man and Woman in Christ,* pp. 360-61.

Unity of the Bible

John J. Davis
Professor of Old Testament
Grace Theological
Seminary

12. Unity of the Bible

John J. Davis

The beauty and charm of a well composed symphony is enjoyed by everyone whether or not they possess the technical skills to critically analyze it. Symphonic arrangements characteristically exhibit an overall unity, but within that unity there is considerable diversity of movement, tone, and purpose. Such compositions may include great crescendos in contrast to the tender notes of a single melody line. Movements in a minor key and the introduction of dissonant notes, when blended with skill, enhance the impact of the composition.

The Bible is a theological symphony whose composer is God the Holy Spirit and is no less intricate and diverse in its several parts. Over the centuries, however, some have isolated small segments of that symphony which appear to strike a discord with the whole, and then have called its unity into question.

Early attempts to deny the essential unity of Scripture go back to the second century when Marcion separated the two testaments completely and suggested that the Old Testament be removed from the Canon. Perhaps influenced by the Gnosticism of his day,[1] he concluded that the Judaism of the Old Testament Scriptures had no relationship to the redemption which was found in Christ. He viewed the God of the Old Testament as another inferior being, vindictive in nature and wholly opposed to the gracious God revealed in the New Testament.[2]

Since the second century there have been others who have questioned the value of the Old Testament for the Christian faith. Friedrick Delitzsch published a rather brutal rejection of the Old Testament in his two volume work entitled *Die Grosse Täuschung* ("The Great Deception").[3]

The Nazis of World War II Germany also discarded the Old Testament but kept the New, and in this sense approximated the position of Marcion.[4] It should be noted that the motives for the rejection were clearly anti-Semitic, while the rejection of the Old Testament by Marcion and more modern writers was probably done on purely theological grounds. Those who do not agree to the essential unity of the testaments do not normally reject the Old Testament outright, but place it on a level of value secondary to the New.

Among modern writers, Rudolf Bultmann stands out as one who has raised serious questions about the value of the Old Testament in comparison to the New. While he insisted that the New Testament gospel cannot be understood fully apart from the Old Testament,[5] he nonetheless viewed the Old Testament as having largely a pedagogical function and, therefore, did not stand on the same level as the New. He proposed that Israel's history is not a history of revelation and that Jerusalem is no more significant a city for Christians than Athens or Rome. Furthermore, he asserted that "for the Christian faith the Old Testament is no longer revelation, as it was and is for the Jews."[6] Because of these positions, some have associated Bultmann with Marcionism.[7]

Other writers, for different reasons, find the New Testament fully unacceptable as a completely authoritative revelation from God, and thereby deny the unity of the Testaments. Floyd V. Filson observes that "Albert Schweitzer in his works and his recent supporter, Martin Werner, in *Die Entstehung des christlichen Dogmas,* really reject the New Testament apocalyptic strain, which they discover dominating that Testament, and some of their followers find themselves more at home with the Old Testament prophets than with the allegedly apocalyptic Jesus or Paul."[8]

In contrast to those who deny the essential duty of the Scriptures is a vast army of writers from the Post Apostolic Period onward who have defended its unity and authority. Among the early fathers, Irenaeus[9] and Augustine of Hippo[10] stand out as champions in that defense.

I. APPROACHES TO UNITY

Of critical importance to this study are the assumptions that underlie any concept of unity between the testaments. While many might agree to general forms of unity or continuity between the testaments, there are divergent opinions as to what constitutes the basis for such unity. For some, an objective, verifiable unity of the Bible is unlikely in the light of more modern critical analysis.

A. Allegorical Interpretation

The ancient method of allegorical interpretation as a means to unify the Old and New Testaments has, according to McCasland, been forever set aside.

> As we come down into recent centuries, however, and the rise of the various forms of critical study, which have been gradually but inexorably applied to the Bible, as well as to practically everything else, one can hardly fail to observe that this ancient view which held the Bible together has now largely, if not entirely disintegrated. The plaster has dissolved and fallen out. For biblical students familiar with critical methods of study, there is a question whether the temple can be kept standing. The bonding of the stones is exceedingly tenuous. For some indeed the stones have already fallen into a disorderly heap, and those who pass by view the mound as a cairn, whose origin and meaning are forgotten, or as a tell, which one might dig up in search of a meaning.[11]

B. Existentialism

Disturbed by the nonverifiability of miracles, or the outmoded scientific concepts of ancient peoples, the assertion is then made that:

> We do not base our faith on an inerrant Bible, or on its esoteric meanings, its predictions, or even its miracles. It is clear to us that while these aspects of the Bible were in their time the expressions of genuine faith, they are not susceptible of historical verification, and they may have been a shaping of the account of external events to correspond with what was essentially an inner experience within the authors' own souls. Nevertheless, the Bible is becoming a living book again.[12]

But one might ask in what sense can the Bible be regarded as a "living book" in this scheme? Modern approaches to this problem have largely been resolved in existential thought. Driven into a scholastic despair by the apparent irresolvability of critical problems within Scripture, some, unwilling to cast Scripture aside, attempt to redeem it by a subjective faith which permits a bypass of the conflicts.

> This faith of biblical men was at times naively projected into strange distortions of historical facts. It is quite possible that a great many legendary elements have thus crept into the Bible. But this is of no consequence to us, neither the Bible nor anything else can ever be used to give objective, infallible validation of "the things not seen." Man's faith must always be in invisible things, of which there can be no rational proof because they are beyond the scope of reason. There is thus no rational certainty in faith.[13]

What then shall be said of the unity of Scriptures in the light of this approach? McCasland reflects the opinion of many who have resolved objective dilemmas by an existential experience:

> The essence of faith is that it is an immediate institution of things not seen. The heart of a religious man is cheered by the sense of a divine presence. But this certainty of the invisible never becomes objective knowledge, although it is itself the foundation of such knowledge and inevitably transcends it. In this experience lies the deepest and most abiding unity of the Scriptures.[14]

In such a conclusion, of course, McCasland is merely reflecting the widely accepted opinions of Barth[15] and Brunner.[16]

C. Confessional and Communal

In a somewhat different vein Roy L. Honeycutt, while acknowledging various categories of biblical unity,[17] sees serious levels of discontinuity between the testaments which are largely irresolvable.[18] Nonetheless, biblical unity can be established upon the unity of God, and the unity of history.[19] He then argues "It is perhaps obvious by now that any assertion of unity or authority for the biblical revelation is essentially confessional in nature. It is not a matter of demonstrable, tangible proof."[20] Unity is also established by communal tradition according to Honeycutt.

> We have the all but unbroken testimony of the Christian community across nearly two thousand years that the Old Testament bore legitimate witness to the mighty acts of the same God who was in Christ reconciling the world unto himself. To this is added the communal witness of Israel, a believing people who for over three thousand years have borne consistent testimony to the unity of God's action, sealing with their own blood in many cases the assertion of their faith.[21]

While such historic affirmations of unity are important, they rarely define that unity.

D. Revelational

There is a brighter prospect for discovering the unity of the Bible if the self-claims of Scripture are taken at face value. B. B. Warfield properly warns that the facts or the phenomena of Scripture should not be studied apart from the Bible's claims for its own origin and nature.[22] If the assertions of 2 Timothy 3:16 and 2 Peter 1:21 are true, then it is proper to assume the essential unity of the Bible on *a priori* grounds. The question then is, "Do the phenomena of Scripture attest to this unity and if so, in what form?" Gaebelein argues that:

> . . . it is our responsibility to examine in the light of Scripture's self-claims the phenomena of Scripture, such as the manifold facets of its historical, philological, and stylistic characteristics; and then, on the basis of this examination, to study the relation of these phenomena to the self-claim. But always the self-claim has prior consideration.[23]

Because God is true, His declarations are true and therefore the task of the scholar is not to test the veracity of God's declaration, but to determine the manner in which this truth is displayed (". . . let God be true, and every man a liar . . ." Rom. 3:4, NIV).

Syllogistically we may express the sequence of thought as follows: Major premise: All that God creates is in perfect unity with Himself and other elements of His creation; Minor premise: God created the Old and New Testaments; Conclusion: The Old and New Testaments are a perfect unity. A brief explanation of the syllogism is in order. First, we are assuming that the kind of God Scripture describes would not create anything in conflict with His essential attributes and being. The support for this assertion is, of course, Genesis 1. There all His creative acts were pronounced as "good." On the natural level there is evidence of symmetry, balance, and unity. One might therefore assume that His creative activity, with references to the inspiration of Scripture, would be equally harmonious.

The minor premise of our syllogism accepts the objective literality of 2 Timothy 3:16. If it can be shown that the revelation in Scripture is unique and without real parallel in the annals of literary activity, then an explanation of its origin must be sought beyond the realm of the purely natural. As will be noted below, there are compelling evidences for the fact that the Scriptures are distinctive in their scope, character, and nature, so much so, that only supernatural revelation properly accounts for their existence.

Many will immediately charge that this argument involves circular reasoning. Indeed, when one begins with the self-claims of Scripture there are some working assumptions which involve the conclusion. But after all, modern negative critical viewpoints also begin on assumptions which are characteristically antisupernaturalistic and nonrevelational and the reasoning is equally circular.

The validity of beginning with the self-claims of Scripture is found in the nature of God and His self-disclosure. J. Murray argues,

> It might seem analogous to the case of a judge who accepts the witness of the accused in his own defense, rather than evidence derived from all the relevant facts in the case. . . . It is fully admitted that normally it would be absurd and a miscarriage of justice for a judge to accept the testimony of the accused, rather than the verdict required by all the relevant evidence. But the two cases are not analogous. There is one sphere where self-testimony must be accepted as absolute and final. This is the sphere of our relation to God. God alone is adequate witness to Himself.[24]

The process of appealing to the authority of Scripture as a starting point would be suspect if Scripture originated other than from an infinitely perfect God. James Grier notes that,

> The immediate point to be noted is that the argument has dealt with the objective content of revelation and not with subjective religious experience. The appeal to Scripture to validate the authority of Scripture is an appeal to an objective content that is God-breathed.[25]

The search to find literary and conceptual parallels to the Old Testament is often pursued with this assumption, and quite often, significant differences are conveniently bypassed or overlooked. The Bible is then declared similar to other ancient Near Eastern literatures and its origin is traced to the normal literary processes of the ancient Near Eastern milieu. Evaluating this methodology, Carl F. H. Henry observes:

> A consequence of the critical approach was the tendency to evaluate materials from both biblical and non-biblical sources by philosophical assumptions alien to the Scriptural view. It imposed upon the Bible, for example, a theory of evolutionary dependence and theological continuity that runs counter to biblical inspiration.[26]

The current critical hermeneutic relies heavily on the authority of extrabiblical parallels. When the theological concepts of the Bible are interpreted solely in the light of these parallels, serious discontinuity is created within Scripture itself. This then becomes the basis for rejecting a supernatural revelation.

If Scripture is the product of the creative breath of God, should there not then be objective evidence of its unity? We believe the Bible does display rather interesting evidences for this unity.

II. KINDS OF UNITY

The unity of the Bible is displayed in a remarkable number of ways. The following are selected examples of these evidences of unity and they are by no means exhaustive:

A. Thematic Unity

The Bible is without parallel with respect to the consistency and the grandeur of its themes. What it states about God, man, and the world is consistently developed throughout Scripture. Concepts are enlarged and terms enriched. While there are observable quantitative differences due to progressive revelation, there are no qualitative distinctives. The affirmations about God in Genesis are just as accurate and profound as those found in Revelation.

The origin of the world and man by direct creation of God is a basic and persistent theme throughout the pages of Scripture. In addition to the historical and anthropological significance of this theme, there are the many calls to worship because of the majestic greatness of the Creator.[27] One cannot escape the prominence of this theme in the New Testament as well. Numerous passages associate Christ with the work of creation.[28] With this dominant theme in Scripture, and its rich theological implications, it is strange indeed that under modern scientific pressure some have surrendered the doctrine or relegated it to a place of unimportance. If biblical affirmations about the original creation of the world are not historically reliable, then where does our hope lie for the eschatological creation of the new heavens and the new earth?[29]

Not only is this theme persistent in the Bible but viewed against its ancient Near Eastern background, its cosmology is unique.[30]

Other themes involving sin, judgment, salvation, faith, Satan, Israel, and God are presented with perfect consistency throughout Scripture.[31]

B. Historical Unity

The first chapter of Matthew makes it abundantly clear that there is genealogical, and therefore historical, continuity between the testaments. The people of the days of Christ were the people of Israel,[32] and Christ's association with the line of David historically was not a matter of secondary importance.

Biblical perspectives on Israel are consistent throughout both the Old and New Testaments. The birth, growth, and ultimate captivity of this nation is viewed within the framework of God's special covenant with His people. Even the rise and fall of surrounding nations are measured in the light of God's purposes for this nation. History is not an uncontrolled fatalistic process, but completely under the power of a sovereign God who gives the kingdoms to whomsoever He will, a concept that took Nebuchadnezzar some time to fully appreciate (Dan. 4:28-37).

C. Prophecy and Fulfillment

One of the distinctive unifying features of the Bible is the process of prophetic promise and fulfillment. The importance of this feature to the unity of Scripture is discussed by Rowley:

> . . . the single hypothesis that the finger of God is to be found in expectation and in fulfillment is adequate, whereas if this is denied no single explanation of all can be found, but a variety of unrelated suggestions must be made in vain effort to count for each separate fragment of the whole, and none of the suggestions is really adequate for the work that is demanded of it.[33]

While the Christian church has traditionally seen predictive elements in prophecy,[34] Bultmann and others have largely rejected the idea of predictive prophecy and fulfillment as a vital link between the Old and New Testaments.[35] Under the influence of von Rad and others, many are inclined to discuss the subject under the heading "Promise and Fulfillment" rather than "Prophecy and Fulfillment."[36]

The characteristics of biblical prophecy highlight the distinctiveness of its process and provide yet another element in the Bible's unity. Ramm argues that since prophecy pervades the entire Bible, is very minute in its specifications, deals with the very remote in time and with people or kingdoms that do not as yet exist, whose fulfillment is clear, one is left with no alternative except to recognize the uniqueness and the supernatural character of such predictive prophecy.[37]

Space will not permit the discussion of other unifying features such as structural unity[38] and doctrinal unity.[39] We now focus our attention on the most significant unifying or integrating factor in Scripture, namely, the person of Christ.

D. Christological Unity

Without a doubt, the person and work of Jesus Christ is the most significant unifying factor between the testaments. This has been forthrightly expressed by numerous writers. ". . . It is no mere pious phrase nor theological subtlety to say that the unity of the Old Testament is really to be found in Jesus Christ."[40] Filson, while surveying an array of literature on the unity of the Bible, concludes "It is a Christocentric message or nothing. Unity will be found only on the basis of that Christ-centered message."[41]

Hints of this centrality come from the lips of the Lord Jesus Himself. To the two on the road to Emmaus He said,

> ". . . How foolish you are, and how slow of heart to believe all that the prophets have spoken. Did not the Christ have to suffer these things and then enter His glory?" And beginning with Moses and all the prophets, He explained to them what was said in all the Scriptures concerning Himself (Luke 24:25-27).

Later He stated that ". . . Everything must be fulfilled that is written about me in the Law of Moses, the Prophets, and the Psalms" (Luke 24:44). To the Jews He said, "You diligently study the Scriptures because you think that by them you possess eternal life. These are the Scriptures that testify about me yet you refuse to come to me and have life" (John 5:39–40). He also noted "If you believed Moses, you would believe me, for he wrote about me (John 5:46). Philip was also aware of the centrality of Christ in Scripture for when he was asked the meaning of Isaiah 53 he ". . . began with that very passage of Scripture and told him the good news about Jesus" (Acts 8:35).[42]

What is particularly significant about Old Testament Messianic prophecies is their specificity. They deal with matters of the place of His birth, the nature of his ministry and suffering, as well as His future kingdom.[43]

Caution needs to be exercised, however, in the pursuit of Old Testament Messianic ideas. Many interpreters have followed the early church fathers in an extreme form of allegorism by which virtually every agent, person, or place takes on specific Christological implications. On the surface this would seem to enhance the overall unity of Scripture, but ultimately the biblical text is removed from the hands of the layman and its interpretations restricted to a scholastic priesthood that operates under rather subjective notions. Doctrines established by purely allegorical methodology are highly vulnerable and can easily be destroyed by that same method of interpretation.

According to Gaebelein, once we recognize the Christological unity of Scripture,

> . . . We pass from a theoretical unity to an organic unity. For integration in a person means integration in life. And when that person is Jesus Christ, the unity, quite in keeping with the eternal horizons of the Bible, takes on infinite dimensions.[44]

When broadly viewed, Jesus Christ is the center or integrating factor in all these other objective forms of unity. Whether we speak of history, doctrine, structure, or themes, these all to one degree or another find their ultimate meaning in Christ. The explanation of the origin of all things as well as their end is to be found in Christ. The apostle Paul expresed it in the following words "For by him were all things created: things in heaven and on earth, visible and invisible, whether thrones or powers or rulers or authorities; all things were created by him and for him" (Col. 1:16).

III. THE NATURE OF UNITY

Our investigation now brings us to an evaluation of the precise nature of the Bible's unity. The traditional liberal argument is that the Bible represents a collection of traditions preserved either orally or in written form, over indefinite periods of time, and ultimately compiled and edited by certain scribes. It is argued that the diverse influence of these traditions over time, coupled with the theological subjectivity of the scribes, accounts for the disunity and contradiction many perceive in the biblical text. The difficulty with this reconstruction of the Canon's origin is that it glosses over the very obvious uniqueness of Scripture, which calls for revelational origin. No other people in the ancient Near East ever developed a monotheistic system of theology that approximates that of the Old Testament, much less, the unique ethical characteristics that attend this system.

Even more incredible from a purely human viewpoint is the Bible's unity and continuity when one notes that it was written over a sixteen hundred year span (including sixty generations) by more than forty different authors from virtually every walk of life. Three continents were included (Asia, Africa, and Europe) as well as three languages (Hebrew, Aramaic, and Greek).

Furthermore, the writings exhibit a great variety of literary types which include narrative history, law code, religious poetry, didactic and pedagogic portions, lyric poetry, biography, parable, and allegory.[45]

Even more remarkable is the monotheism which the Old Testament proclaims against a background of polytheism and idolatry. Such an elevated and majestic view of God within such a theologically hostile environment requires an explanation, and that is only adequately found in the process of special revelation supernaturally provided by God. With all the discussion of the evolutionary development of Israel's religion, no one has adequately demonstrated how this could have occurred within such a diverse and competitive environment.

In fact, the theological unity of the Bible is even more amazing when one realizes that hostility not only existed outside the nation, but at times within it. Note for example the syncretistic processes at work in Israel leading to periods of apostasy and open idolatry (Jude 2:13, 17; 8:33). Polytheistic idolatry found its way into the royal court during the monarchial period with some regularity (1 Kings 16:31-33; 2 Kings 3:2; 1 Kings 11:4-7), and at times this led to the brutal practice of child sacrifice (2 Kings 17:17). The prophets who carried the true message of God were often intimidated and persecuted (1 Kings 18:4).

In spite of these complexities and conflicts, the Bible remains a perfect theological unity. This is only adequately accounted for by the creative breath of God, who in the beginning made a perfect world (Gen. 1) and then produced a perfect Word (2 Tim. 3:16). Is it possible that those who have stumbled over the implications of Genesis 1, with its supernatural elements, are today finding difficulty with the implications of Paul's declaration which are also supernatural in character?

IV. CHALLENGES TO UNITY

Not all would agree that the unity of the Bible stands complete or that its doctrines are consistent. Serious contradictions and discontinuities are envisioned in the text which are viewed as destructive of any proposal of unity for the Bible.

A. Imprecations

The imprecatory Psalms have been viewed as being out of harmony with the spirit of the New Testament and, therefore, constitute disunity between the testaments. Honeycutt argues that

> . . . discontinuity of the testaments is reflected in the ethical disparity of the two. There are few, for example, who would defend the imprecatory Psalms (cf. Pss. 55:51; 69; 109; 139:22). There are fewer still who would place Christian approval upon the Psalmist's blessing those who would dash Babylonian children against the rock (Ps. 137:9). This does not sound like one who took little children upon His knees and blessed them.[46]

Others, too, have raised questions about the spiritual and moral value of these Psalms. One has classified the imprecatory Psalms as "cruel and vindictive . . . only a barbarous period could produce such songs."[47] Weiser thinks that Psalm 137 expresses "blind hatred and vulgar rage." It is a "frightfully cruel outcry." The poet "plunges into the abyss of human passion."[48] Oesterly refers to the imprecatory Psalms as "distasteful" and characterized by "vindictiveness and terrible sentiments."[49] Another calls the imprecatory Psalms "inferior . . . which belong to a primitive stage in the evolution of religious knowledge."[50] It is very clear that many question the ethical appropriateness of such statements in the light of New Testament truth.

On the surface this might seem like an insurmountable objection to the concept of biblical unity. This argument against the unity of the Bible, however, can only survive if the context of Scripture is ignored. It might be noted here that imprecations are not only characteristic of the Psalter, but many portions of the Old and New Testament as well.[51] The argument in favor of moral disunity, based on imprecatory Psalms, ignores the fact that David was a very patient man with his enemies.[52] Let it further be noted that these Psalms were not written by an unbelieving, bitter nationalist, but by one who deeply feared the Lord and possessed true piety.

These Psalms reflect the fact that the writer takes his concerns to the Lord for justice and does not execute these imprecations as a matter of personal or national pride. Furthermore, in many of the Psalms there is the expression of concern for the enemies of the Lord and a hope for their conversion (Ps. 2:10-12).

One also gets the impression that the writers were assuming God's view of evildoers and since immediate physical judgment was common in Old Testament times, the sentiments of these writers are understood. There is a sense in which it was appropriate for the Psalmist to pray for the destruction of the wicked because they were requesting God to do something which was in harmony with his nature for him to do. The utterances of the Psalmist reflect a deep zeal for God and his kingdom. It must be remembered that attacks on David were essentially attacks on the theocratic office established by the Lord and he was, in effect, the Lord's anointed. Finally, we might note that these were expressions of the abhorrence of sin. In fact, one might be surprised if such outbursts were absent from the Old Testament in the light of the evil that surrounded God's servants. C. S. Lewis makes the intriguing observation that "If the Jews cursed more bitterly than the pagans, this was, I think, at least in part because they took right and wrong more seriously."[53]

When the immediate context of selected passages, along with the theological framework of Scriptures is examined, the imprecatory Psalms and other such curses do not represent a discontinuity in biblical ethics, but an expected cry of the righteous when wicked men challenged the Lord's anointed and divinely revealed moral principles.

B. An Unmerciful God

Others reject unity on the basis that the Old Testament presents a view of God that is in direct conflict with the New Testament revelation. Honeycutt, for example, sees the wholesale extermination of enemy tribes (cf. Josh. 6:15ff) in serious conflict with the Lord's refusal to bring fire from heaven upon noncooperative Samaritans (Lk. 9:54ff).[54] Here again, however, the problem is more imagined than real. More often than not the difficulty with these passages is in the mind of the interpreter who attributes to God a form of love more characteristic of philosophical humanism than the divinely revealed attribute of absolute holiness. One needs to remember that the destruction of these cities was done on the basis of a divine command (Ex. 17:14; Dt. 7:2; 20:16; John. 8:2), and one should conclude *a priori* that anything God commands is just and morally right. Since these commands originated with God, the very moral character of God is at stake, not just of Joshua or his contemporaries. Furthermore, it is clear from other Scripture that while Israel was the instrument of judgment, ultimately God was dealing with sin on his own terms, which of course, is his prerogative. It should be remembered that the populations of Canaan were not "innocent peoples," but grossly evil people, upon which a righteous God must pour out his judgment.[55] It was God's prerogative, for example, to destroy the sinful cities of Sodom and Gomorrah (Gen. 19), while permitting other wicked cities in the land of Palestine to survive. God's only obligation to the sinner is judgment. That he extends mercy and exercises patience with others is the great mystery of his eternal love and grace.[56]

C. Statements of Jesus

Some have envisioned discontinuity in Scripture due to Jesus' statements regarding the Old Testament. B. H. Branscomb asserted that He ". . . flatly rejected a portion of it by appealing to another portion."[57] Another argues that ". . . the clearest testimony to such ethical disparity is the manner in which Jesus Himself corrected the Old Testament by His own ethical idealism (cf. Matt. 5-7)."[58]

The focal point of such concern has been the expression, "It was said . . . but I say . . ." used frequently in the Sermon on the Mount (Matt. 5:17-48). It has been assumed that Jesus was rejecting the ethics of the Old Testament in favor of a higher ethic. But what our Lord did was not to negate any of the Old Testament commands but to show their full scope and to strip off current misinterpretations of them."[59] With very clear statements Jesus established the fact that he did not come to destroy the law, but to fulfill it (Matt. 5:17-20). The Scribes and Pharisees had cluttered up true Old Testament teaching with tradition and speculation. Their emphasis was more on the letter of the Law than on its spirit.[60]

Other areas of concern with respect to the Bible's unity are discontinuity reflected in hermeneutical principles,[61] and the coming of Christ and the value of the Old Testament,[62] but space will not permit consideration of them here.

V. SUMMARY AND CONCLUSION

Our discussion of the unity of the Bible has taken a two-pronged approach. First, we have pointed to the self-claims of Scripture and what these imply. On the basis of the declarations of Scripture, it is appropriate for one to *expect* a unity in the Word of God. Our second area of concern dealt with selected phenomena of Scripture and whether or not these data reflect this unexpected unity.

We have seen that on the basis of theological, historical, and ethical considerations the Bible displays a remarkable unity, and this in spite of a hostile environment that historically existed within and outside the nation of Israel.

Needless to say, if there is no genuine and consistent unity in the Bible, the claims for inspiration and inerrancy would be suspect, indeed. But the self-witness of Scripture points to a perfect unity and the data of Scripture affirm it.

It is appropriate to observe here the important role of the Holy

Spirit in illuminating and clarifying this unity. As van Til notes "And Scripture in turn cannot be seen for what it is except it be by the testimony of the Holy Spirit enabling man to see the Bible, and therewith natural revelation, in their true light."[63] There are a number of notices both in the Old and New Testaments that point to a desire for, or need of, illumination in properly understanding the Word of God. The Psalmist makes the following request, "Open my eyes that I may see wonderful things in your law" (Ps. 119:18, NIV). The key to this passage is the Hebrew expression גַּל־עֵינַי. The intensive (pi'el) imperative meaning "uncover, disclose" comes from the root גָּלָה which has as its core the following ideas: "lay bare, make known, show, reveal."[64] The nature of this request appears to be for divine illumination of the Word of God. Similar requests are made in verses 33-34, and verse 130 of this Psalm.[65]

The apostle Paul seems to emphasize this truth in 1 Corinthians 2:14-15. His argument is that the natural man is incapable of properly discerning spiritual truth. The spiritual man, that is the regenerated man, possesses the Spirit of God and thus has this capability.[66] As Packer has observed:

> . . . the Holy Spirit has been sent to the church as its Teacher, to guide Christans into truth, to make them wise unto salvation, to testify to them of Christ and to glorify Him thereby. To the apostles, He came to remind them of Christ's teachings, to show them its meaning, to add further revelation to it and so to equip them to witness to all about their Lord.[67]

The affirmation of the essential unity of Scripture does not deny its literary diversity and variety, however. On the contrary, Scripture itself alerts us to the fact that this revelation came in such a way as to produce such variety and diversity. The writer of Hebrews explains "In the past God spoke to our forefathers through the prophets at many times and in various ways . . ." (Heb. 1:1).

Therefore, in this divinely inspired and inerrant theological symphony, we hear the great crescendos of majestic expression, the tender subtones of intimate relationships, the minor keys and dissonance of human suffering because of the presence of evil,[68] but all these are blended into a perfect harmony because its author was none other than God Himself.

NOTES

[1]See John Bright, *The Authority of the Old Testament* (Nashville: Abingdon Press, 1967), pp. 61-62.

[2]For more complete studies on Marcion see E. C. Blackman, *Marcion and His Influence* (London: S.P.C.K., 1948); A. von Harnack, *Marcion, Das Evangelium vom fremden Gott,* 2nd ed. (Leipzig: J. C. Hinrichs Verlag, 1924); and John Knox, *Marcion and the New Testament* (Chicago: University of Chicago Press, 1942).

[3]Friedrich Delitzsch, *Die grosse Täuschung* [The Great Deception] (Stuttgart: Deutsche Verlags-Anstalt, Vol. I, 1920; Vol. II, 1921).

[4]See Eugene Tanner, *The Nazi Christ* (Ann Arbor, MI: Edwards Brothers, Inc., 1942) and the views of Emanuel Hirsch in his *Das Alte Testament und die Predigt des Evangeliums* (Tübingen: J. C. B. Mohr, 1933).

[5]Rudolph Bultmann, "Die Bedeutung des Alten Testaments fur den Christlichen Glauben," *Glauben und Verstehen* (Tübingen: J. C. B. Mohr, 1933), p. 325.

[6]Ibid., 333-34.

[7]See Eric Voegelin, "History and Gnosis," *The Old Testament and Christian Faith,* ed. B. W. Anderson (London, 1964).

[8]Floyd V. Filson, "The Unity of the Old and the New Testaments," *Interpretation* 5:1 (1951), p. 135.

[9]See J. Barton Payne, "The Biblical Interpretations of Irenaeus," *Inspiration and Interpretation,* ed. John F. Walvoord (Grand Rapids: Wm. B. Eerdmans Publishing Co., 1975), pp. 11-66.

[10]See David W. Keer, "Augustine of Hippo," Ibid., pp. 67-86.

[11]S. Vernon McCasland, "The Unity of the Scriptures," *Journal of Biblical Literature,* 73 (1954), p. 3.

[12]Ibid., p. 8.

[13]Ibid., p. 9.

[14]Ibid., p. 10.

[15]See Karl Barth, *Church Dogmatics* (Edinburgh: 1956, English translation) I, 2, pp. 561-63.

[16]Emil Brunner, *Dogmatik* (Zurich, 1950), I, p. 115 and II, p. 307. See also Emil Brunner, *The Scandal of Christianity* (Richmond, VA: John Knox Press, 1965), pp. 25-28 and G. Ernest Wright, "The Unity of the Bible," *Scottish Journal of Theology,* 8:4 (1955), p. 343-44.

[17]Roy L. Honeycutt, Jr., "The Unity and Witness of Scripture," *Foundations,* 8:4 (1965), pp. 293-297.

[18]Ibid., pp. 297-304.

[19]Ibid., pp. 305-7.

[20]Ibid., pp. 307-8.

[21]Ibid., p. 307.

[22]Benjamin B. Warfield, *The Inspiration and Authority of the Bible* (Philadelphia: The Presbyterian and Reformed Publishing Co., 1948), pp. 203-8.

[23]Frank E. Gaebelein, "The Unity of the Bible," *Revelation and the Bible: Contemporary Evangelical Thought,* ed. C. F. Henry (London, 1959), p. 389.

[24]J. Murray, "The Attestation of Scripture, *The Infallible Word,* ed. N. Stonehouse (Philadelphia: Presbyterian and Reformed Publishing Co., 1946), pp. 9-10.

[25]James M. Grier, Jr., "The Apologetical Value of the Self-Witness of Scripture," *Grace Theological Journal* 1:1 (1980), p. 75. See also J. Frame, "Scripture Speaks for Itself," *God's Inerrant Word,* ed. J. W. Montgomery (Minneapolis: Bethany Publishers, 1974), p. 179ff.

[26]Carl F. Henry, *God, Revelation and Authority,* IV (Waco, TX: Word Books, 1979), p. 452.

[27]Compare Pss. 8, 19, 29, 65, 104.

[28]Jn. 1:3; Rom. 11:36; Eph. 3:9; Col. 1:16; Heb. 1:2; etc.

[29]Compare 2 Pet. 3:13 and Rev. 21:1.

[30]See William F. Albright, "The Old Testament and Archaeology," *Old Testament Commentary,* Alleman and Flack, eds. (Philadelphia: The Muhlenberg Press, 1948), p. 135; John J. Davis, *Paradise to Prison* (Grand Rapids: Baker Book House, 1975), pp. 67-72; and Alexander Heidel, *The Babylonian Genesis* (Chicago: The University of Chicago Press, 1951), p. 140.

[31]For further discussion of this subject see Rene Pache, *The Inspiration and Authority of Scripture* (Chicago: Moody Press, 1969), pp. 111-19; Newman Watts, *The Incomparable Book* (New York: American Tract Society, 1940), pp. 83-90; Bernard Ramm, *Protestant Christian Evidences* (Chicago: Moody Press, 1957), pp. 242-48; and Roy L. Honeycutt, "The Unity and Witness of Scripture," pp. 296-97.

[32]C. H. Dodd, *The Bible To-day* (Cambridge, 1946), p. 3. See also Carl F. Henry, *God, Revelation and Authority,* p. 468-69.

[33]H. H. Rowley, *The Unity of the Bible* (Philadelphia: Westminster Press, 1953), p. 13.

[34]See J. Barton Payne, *Encyclopedia of Biblical Prophecy* (New York: Harper & Row Publishers, 1973), pp. 8-10.

[35]See D. L. Baker, *Two Testaments, One Bible* (Downers Grove, IL: InterVarsity Press, 1976), pp. 166, 292-93.

[36]For a fuller discussion of these trends see D. L. Baker, *Two Testaments: One Bible,* pp. 293-95. Also see Walter Zimmerli, "Promise and Fulfillment," trans. by James Wharton, *Journal of Bible and Theology* 15:3; pp. 310-38.

[37]Bernard Ramm, *Protestant Christian Evidences,* pp. 84-87.

[38]Newman Watts, *The Incomparable Book,* pp. 86-88; Rene Pache, *The Inspiration and Authority of Scripture,* pp. 111-16.

[39]Rene Pache, Ibid., pp. 116-19; Roy L. Honeycutt, Jr., "The Unity and Witness of Scripture," p. 297 and Arthur T. Pierson, *Knowing the Scriptures.* (New York: Gospel Publishing House, 1910), pp. 53-58.

[40]Robert C. Dentan, "The Unity of the Old Testament," *Interpretation* 5:1 (1951), p. 173.

[41]Floyd V. Filson, "The Unity of the Old and the New Testament," p. 151. See also T. Glyn Thomas, "The Unity of the Bible and the Uniqueness of Christ," *The London Quarterly and Holborn Review* 35 (1966), pp. 219-27; J. Stanley Glen, "Jesus Christ and the Unity of the Bible," *Interpretation* 5:1 (1951), pp. 259-67.

[42]Other examples of this phenomenon are the times when Jesus applied specific Scriptures to Himself. Compare Mt. 21:42-46 with Ps. 118:22-23; Mk. 14:27 with Zech. 13:7. See Frank E. Gaebelein, "The Unity of the Bible," pp. 392-95.

[43]Examples of this are discussed in Josh McDowell, *Evidence that Demands a Verdict* (Campus Crusade for Christ, Inc., 1972), pp. 151-74.

[44]Frank E. Gaebelein, "The Unity of the Bible," p. 395.

[45]See F. F. Bruce, *The Books and the Parchments* (New York: Fleming H. Revell, 1963), p. 88 and Josh McDowell, *Evidence that Demands a Verdict,* pp. 18-20.

[46]Roy L. Honeycutt, Jr., "The Unity and Witness of Scripture," p. 293.

[47]Edyth Sage Armstrong, *Studies in the Psalms* (Chicago: Associated Authors, 1937), p. 50.

[48]Arthur Weiser, *The Psalms* (London: SCM Press, 1962), pp. 796-97.

[49]W. E. E. Oesterly, *The Psalms* (London: S.P.C.K., 1962), p. 331 (Cf. p. 457).

[50]Rudolf Kittel, *The Scientific Study of the Old Testament,* trans. by J. Caleb Hughes (New York: G. P. Putnam's Sons, 1910), p. 143.

[51]Compare Num. 10:35: Jud. 5:31; 2 Ki. 1:10, 12; 2:24; Neh. 4:4-5; 6:14; 13:29; Jer. 11:20; 15:15; 17:18; 18:21-23; 20:12; Mt. 23:32-36; 1 Cor. 16:22; Gal. 1:8, 9; 5:12; 2 Tim. 4:14 and Rev. 6:9-10.

[52] Sam. 24, 26 (Saul) and 2 Sam. 16:11; 19:16-23 (Absalom).

[53]C. S. Lewis, *Reflections on the Psalms* (New York: Harcourt, Brace and Co., 1958), p. 30. For additional discussion on the interpretation of these Psalms see T. Barns, "Psalms of Vengeance," *Expository Times* 19 (1907-08), pp. 185-87; H. H. Bernard, "The Vindictive Psalms," *The Expositor* 17 (Mason (1884), pp. 131-44; Talbot W. Chambers, *The Psalter* (New York: Mason D. F. Randolph and Co., 1876), pp. 167-79; F. G. Chalmondeley, "A Vindictive Psalm (109), *Expository Times* 30 (1918-19), pp. 183-84); William B. Greene, "The Ethics of the Old Testament," *Princeton Theological Review* 27:3 (July, 1929), pp. 214-16; Johannes G. Vos, "The Ethical Problem of the Imprecatory Psalms," *Westminster Journal* 4:2 (May, 1942), pp. 123-38; J. L. McKenzie, "The Imprecations of the Psalter," *American Ecclesiastical Review,* 3 (1944), pp. 81-96; Howard Osgood, "Dashing the Little Ones Against the Rock," *Princeton Theological Review,* 1 (1903), pp. 23-39; J. J. Owen, "The Imprecatory Psalms," *Bibliotheca Sacra* 13 (1856), pp. 551-63; Ragner C. Teigen, "Can Anything Good Come from a Curse," *The Lutheran Quarterly,* 26:1 (1974), pp. 44-51.

[54]Roy L. Honeycutt, Jr., "The Unity and Witness of Scripture," p. 303. Also see in this regard James Muilenburg, "The History of the Religion of Israel," *The Interpreter's Bible*. ed. George A. Buttrick (New York: Abingdon Press, 1952), p. 310 and H. H. Rowley, *The Rediscovery of the Old Testament* (Philadelphia: The Westminster Press, 1946), p. 32ff.

[55]Cf. Gen. 15:16-21 ("Sin of the Amorites")

[56]For further discussion of this problem see John J. Davis. *Conquest and Crisis* (Grand Rapids: Baker Book House, 1969), pp. 48-50).

[57]B. H. Branscomb, *Jesus and the Law of Moses* (London: Harper, 1930).

[58]Roy L. Honeycutt, Jr., "The Unity and Witness of Scripture," p. 301.

[59]John W. Wenham, "Christ's View of Scripture," *Summit Papers* (Oakland: International Council on Biblical Inerrancy, 1978), No. 1, p. 19. See also Roger Nicole, "New Testament Use of the Old Testament," *Revelation and the Bible,* pp. 138-41.

[60]For further study of this problem see Pierre Ch. Marcel, "Our Lord's Use of Scripture," *Revelation and the Bible,* pp. 121-34; Roger Nicole, "New Testament Use of the Old Testament," Ibid., pp. 137-51; John W. Wenham, "Christ's View of Scripture," *Summit Papers,* No. 1, pp. 1-27.

[61]Roy L. Honeycutt, Jr., "The Unity and Witness of Scripture," pp. 297-99.

[62]Ibid., p. 299-301.

[63]Cornelius van Til, *The Defense of the Faith* (Philadelphia: The Presbyterian and Reformed Publishing Co., 1955), p. 204.

[64]Francis Brown, S. R. Driver, and C. A. Briggs, *A Hebrew and English Lexicon of the Old Testament* (Oxford: Clarendon Press, 1962), p. 163. Important discussion of this verse relating to the doctrine of illumination can be found in Albert Barnes, *Notes on the Old Testament: Psalms*, and Herbert C. Leupold, *Exposition of the Psalms* (Columbus, OH: Wartburg Press, 1959), pp. 826-27.

[65]On v. 130 see F. Delitzsch, *Psalms*, in *Commentary on the Old Testament in Ten Volumes*, by C. F. Keil and F. Delitzsch, trans. by James Martin (Grand Rapids: William B. Eerdmans Publishing Company).

[66]See Paul Woolley, "The Relevancy of Scripture," in *The Infallible Word*, a symposium by the members of the faculty of Westminster Theological Seminary (Philadelphia: The Presbyterian Gardian Publishing Corporation, 1946), pp. 193-94.

[67]J. I. Packer, *"Fundamentalism" and the Word of God* (Grand Rapids: William B. Eerdmans Publishing Company, 1958), p. 111. Other passages dealing with the general idea are Eph. 1:17-18; and 1 John 2:20, 27; 5:20. Additional passages where interpreters have seen special enlightenment or illumination are Deut. 29:29; Psalm 36:9; 97:11; 112:4; 119:97-100; 104-105; Prov. 4:8; 25:2-3; Isa. 6:9-10; 29:10-12; 42:20; 54:13; Jer. 5:21; Matt. 11:25-27; 16:15-17; Luke 10:21-24; 14:35b; 18:34; 24:13-45; John 6:45; 10:3; Acts 16:14; Rom. 8:16; 12;2; 1 Cor. 12:3; 2 Cor. 1:21-22; 3:14-18; 4:3-4, 6; Eph. 3:9; 4:23; Phil. 3:15-16; Col. 1:9-10; 2:2; 1 Thess. 1:4-5; 2 Tim. 3:7; Heb. 6:4-6; 10:32; 2 Pet. 3:16.

[68]Even the evil deeds of men (a musical discord) are blended into God's perfect plan (Gen. 50:20) for *all things* are under His control (Rom. 8:28).

A Response to Unity of the Bible

James Montgomery Boice
Pastor, Tenth Presbyterian
Church
Philadelphia, Pennsylvania

A Response to Unity of the Bible

James Montgomery Boice

John J. Davis must be commended for a comprehensive treatment of a complex theme. The complexity may be measured from the fact that scholars have taken hundreds of pages to deal with just limited aspects of the unity problem as, for example, D. L. Baker's 550-page study of the relationship between the Old and New Testaments.[1] Davis has surveyed the chief approaches to biblical unity, the various kinds of unity, the nature of the Bible's unity and several difficulties with the idea of unity growing out of the Bible itself. His bibliography contains a wealth of diverse writings on the subject.

In response I wish to retrace some of the ground covered in Davis' study and make a few further suggestions, doing so in a Trinitarian context. My chief point is that evangelicals, in an expression of their valid concern for the Bible's christological unity, may neglect an equally valid emphasis upon its theological unity and a unity of effect arising out of the Holy Spirit's work through Scripture in individual lives.

I. THE BIBLE IS GOD'S BOOK

Davis and others are quite right in affirming that "if the assertions of 2 Timothy 3:16 and 2 Peter 1:21 are true, then it is proper to assume the essential unity of the Bible on *a priori* grounds."[2] The Bible is a unity because God is its author, and God is not a confused or self-contradictory being. If "all Scripture is God-breathed" and if the men who composed the various books of the Bible "spoke from God as they were carried along by the Holy Spirit" (NIV), then the Bible is marked by unity in its essential nature and worldview, even if these are not everywhere and at all times equally evident to us.

A. The Bible's Nature

The nature of the Bible flows from the nature of the sovereign, omniscient, holy God who inspired it. There is a unity in the *au-*

thority of Scripture, related to God's sovereignty. The Bible does not merely express viewpoints, as other books do. It makes declarations. It issues commands. This is as true of Genesis as of Revelation. It is always, "Thus says the Lord."

There is a unity of *insight* in the Bible, related to God's omniscience. Particularly, there is insight into the nature and psychology of man. As Emile Cailliet has written, the Bible is "the book that understands me."[3] This is true of the most diverse passages, and what is learned from one is not contradicted elsewhere. We are not convicted by Romans and let off the hook by 1 Corinthians.

There is a *moral framework* in the Bible growing out of the holiness of God. It is frequently said, especially by evangelicals, that there is nothing in all literature equal to the sublime ethical passages of the Old and New Testaments—the Ten Commandments or the Sermon on the Mount, for example. This is true, but it is not saying enough. Not only are these passages sublime. They are infused with a sense of God's holiness, which is their ultimate standard, and, the imprecatory Psalms notwithstanding, that holiness and standard are everywhere the same. There are differences of emphasis and application. These grow out of the writers' and readers' different historical needs and settings. But the standard is one: moral uprightness that corresponds to the character of God.

Points like these could be expanded for each of the divine attributes: mercy, love, wrath, and so on. This should be done as answer to the view that "the Bible is not a unified writing but a composite body of literature."[4]

B. The Bible's World-View

That the Bible is God's book affects not only its nature but its content as well. This is usually expressed by saying that there is a unity of doctrine in the Bible. It may equally be said that it has one world and life view. Carl F. H. Henry writes of this in *God, Revelation and Authority*:

> The unity of the Bible is not to be found in its literary genres nor in its human writers. It is found in the message and meaning of the book, namely, that the living sovereign God stands at the beginning of the universe—man and the worlds—as Creator and Governor, and at the end of history as final Judge; that he made mankind in his likeness for moral rectitude and spiritual fellowship and service; that human revolt precipitated disastrous consequences for humanity and the cosmos; that the manifested

> mercy of God, extended first to the Hebrews, proffers the only prospect of salvation; that the divine promise of deliverance, disclosed in the course of Hebrew redemptive history to the prophets, finds its fulfillment in Jesus of Nazareth; that the incarnation, crucifixion and resurrection of the Logos of God marks the beginnings of the new and final age; that the church is a new society of regenerate persons of all races and nations over whom Christ presently rules; that the history of mankind has a dual track, issuing in final and irreversible doom for the impenitent and in eternal blessing for the righteous; that Christ will return in awesome vindication of the holy will of God, to judge men and nations, and will in the resurrection of the dead conform the people of God to his moral image; that the benefits of redemption will embrace all creation both in a final subordination of evil and of the wicked, and in the eternal vindication of righteousness.[5]

Other biblical themes are consistent with and subordinate to this outlook.

II. THE BIBLE IS ABOUT JESUS CHRIST

When we pass from the first person of the Godhead to the second we come to that aspect of the Bible's unity so strongly emphasized by Frank Gaebelein, G. Campbell Morgan, Floyd Tilson and others,[6] particularly evangelicals. It can be viewed in many lights—as the unity of a person, as history, as the focus of the Bible's promises and fulfillment—but the chief point is that Jesus is what the Bible is about. He is the author of Scripture (together with the Father and Holy Spirit); the answer to the problem of human misery and sin, which the Bible so carefully analyzes; and the goal of all God's working, which the New Testament, as well as the Old, anticipates.

One important feature of this aspect of the Bible's unity is that the Old Testament, being written before the coming of Christ, is by itself an incomplete book. Extensive as it is, it is nevertheless only a preparation for the central act of God's salvation drama. Without Jesus Christ it lacks the play's chief actor and decisive events. Moreover, the Old Testament knows this incompleteness. Its prophecies of a Messiah are one sure indication. Equally striking are the wistful endings of so many Old Testament books: the death and embalming of Joseph (Gen. 50:26), the death of Moses (Deut. 34), the record that each Jew "did as he saw fit" (Judges 21:25), and so on. These do not reflect the proper end of men and women or of the people of

God as a whole. They call for a new chapter in God's working and look forward to it.

Similarly, the New Testament is incomplete without the Old. To prepare for Christ's appearance John the Baptist proclaims the coming of God's kingdom, an Old Testament concept. Matthew and Luke introduce Jesus as a descendant of Abraham and David, both Old Testament figures. John begins his gospel with a clear reference to Genesis 1:1 ("In the beginning . . ."). Indeed, Jesus explained the nature and necessity of his work by Old Testament prophecies and concepts (Luke 24:25-27).

Jesus is the one who ties these two individually incomplete works together and completes them in his own person and achievement. As Gaebelein says, the Bible's "unifying principle is nothing less than the Person of our Lord Jesus Christ, the incarnate Son of God and the Savior of the world of men whose lost condition in trespasses and sins is so faithfully disclosed within its pages."[7]

III. THE HOLY SPIRIT WORKS THROUGH THE BIBLE

Various writings on the unity of Scripture speak of the Bible as "a living book" or of its unity as "organic."[8] These are not ideal terms in our age. By themselves they might suggest that the Bible is somehow growing (perhaps needs to be added to) or changing. What these and other similar phrases are attempting to express—and rightly express—is that by the active working of God the Holy Spirit the Bible produces effects in its readers analogous to the impact of one living being on another. On the receiving end of this working are many human beings. On the giving end is the one holy God operating through his Holy Spirit to conform his people to the character of his unique and holy Son, Jesus Christ.

A. Repentance and Faith

A proper reading of the Bible always leads to repentance from sin, on the one hand, and faith in God as Savior from sin and its consequences on the other. Sometimes the Bible is misused the other way, that is, by seeking in it statements that seem to justify one's sinful conduct. But this is patently an error growing out of sin itself. To read the Bible properly is always to meet its author, and this is to be confronted with the reality of his holiness and our transgressions. It is always: "Woe to me! . . . For I am a man of unclean lips, and I live among a people of unclean lips" Isa. 6:5) or "Go away from me, Lord; for I am a sinful man" (Luke 5:8).

It is not only a matter of meeting the holy God, resulting in an awareness of and turning from sin, however. God is also the merciful, saving God. So to meet him in a repentant frame of mind is also to hear the gospel and be turned to faith in the Savior. This is a recurring effect found throughout Scripture as well as the effect of Scripture on those who read it today.

B. Sanctification and Service

Repentance and faith in God does not leave a person unchanged, nor is it all that the Holy Spirit works to accomplish as the Bible is read. A proper reading of the Bible also leads to growth in personal holiness and efforts to serve others in the spirit of Jesus Christ.

Personal experience of these items—repentance, faith, sanctification and service—obviously differs from individual to individual. There are different sins to be repented of, different aspects of the character of God to be known and responded to, different areas of life to be redeemed and developed, different works to be done. But this variety of application should not blind us to the overriding unity of effect achieved in responsive human beings by the Spirit of God working through the Word. Those in whom God thus works are one body, after all. And it is God's desire that this "body of Christ may be built up until we all reach unity in the faith and in the knowledge of the Son of God and become mature, attaining to the whole measure of the fullness of Christ" (Eph. 4:12–13).

NOTES

[1]D. L. Baker, *Two Testaments, One Bible: A Study of Some Modern Solutions to the Theological Problem of the Relationship Between the Old and New Testaments* (Leicester, England: InterVarsity Press, 1976).

[2]John J. Davis, "Unity of the Bible," pp. 644-45. Davis cites B. B. Warfield, Frank E. Gaebelein, John Murray, James M. Grier and Carl F. H. Henry as sharing this perspective.

[3]Emile Cailliet, *Journey Into Light* (Grand Rapids: Zondervan Publishing House, 1968).

[4]James Barr, *The Bible in the Modern World* (New York: Harper & Row, 1973), p. 157.

[5]Carl F. H. Henry, *God, Revelation and Authority,* Vol. IV, *God Who Speaks and Shows: Fifteen Theses, Part Three* (Waco, Tex.: Word Books, 1979), p. 468.

[6]Frank E. Gaebelein, "The Unity of the Bible" in *Revelation and the Bible: Contemporary Evangelical Thought*, ed. by Carl F. H. Henry (Grand Rapids: Baker

Book House, 1958), pp. 387-401; G. Campbell Morgan, *The Unfolding Message of the Bible: The Harmony and Unity of the Scriptures* (London: Pickering & Inglis, 1961); Floyd V. Tilson, "The Unity of the Old and the New Testaments," *Interpretation* 5:1 (1951). Davis gives other references.

[7]Gaebelein, "The Unity of the Bible," pp. 392, 393.

[8]Papias called Scripture "the living and abiding voice (quoted by Eusebius, *Church History,* III, 39, 4). Gaebelein argues that the Bible is "alive, not dead," *Exploring the Bible: A Study of Background and Principles* (New York: "Our Hope" Publication, 1929), p. 75, and calls its unity ("organic" ("The Unity of the Bible," p. 395).

A Response to
The Unity of the Bible

Robert D. Preus
President and Professor of
Systematic Theology
Concordia Theological
Seminary
Fort Wayne, Indiana

A Response to The Unity of the Bible

Robert D. Preus

Few theological concepts have been more confused, unclear, and undeveloped throughout the course of the church's history than the concept of the unity of Scripture. The term was not used in the early church, nor by the Reformers, nor even in the post-Reformation era. The terms most closely approximating the idea to be found during that vast span of church history were κανὼν Πίστεως and *regula fidei*, ἡ πίστις (a common term for creeds in the early church), and ἀναλογία πίστεως, or *analogia fidei*, terms with different meanings derived from Romans 12:7 and sometimes 2 Timothy 1:13. Whether the idea expressed by these terms constitutes simply a summation of Scripture or a hermeneutical norm as well is not always clear, but it usually includes both. And the actual meaning of these terms as to what they affirm about the nature of Scripture is not uniform and not even always clear. What do these phrases say in reference to the nature of biblical unity? Usually they simply assume an organic doctrinal unity within the entire Scriptures and offer a summation of that body of doctrine. The authority and truthfulness of the Bible and its doctrine are clearly presupposed, since such divine properties underlie the divine doctrinal content of Scripture. Also, the unity between the two testaments in simple terms of prophecy and fulfillment is explicitly affirmed, and emphatically so, by the church fathers, although not explicitly always by the aforementioned terms.[1]

During the Reformation and during the period of orthodoxy almost to the eighteenth century the idea of the unity of Scripture was expressed in many ways. And the aforementioned terms prevalent in the early and medieval church suggestive of the unity of Scripture were used freely in contexts much the same as in the early church. Thus, commentaries on the earlier creeds and new creeds and symbols were written as summaries of the biblical *corpus doctrinae* and adhered to, often with avidity by subscription to such documents. That the theology (doctrine) of Scripture was an organic (Luther) unity (the following terms connoting an organic unity of biblical theology were commonly used: *corpus doctrinae, articuli fidei, caput, pars, locus,* etc.) or a coherent system (Calvinism?) of doctrine was assumed and affirmed in the dogmatic and exegetical writers of the day. Furthermore, all the Reformers believed and asserted in their writings a unity of the Old and New Testaments in terms of prophecy and fulfillment; that is to say, verbal and cognitive predictive assertions of the Old Testament had a corresponding fulfillment in the words and deeds of Christ and other events recorded accurately in the New Testament. Coupled with this basic idea of unity was the conviction, held by all the Reformers (and even Socinians and Roman Catholics with certain modifications) in one form or another that all of Scripture, both Old and New Testaments, was Christocentric; that is, the main theme running through all of Scripture and cognitively set forth there is the person *and work* of Christ.

Thus, in the Reformation and post-Reformation era, as in the early church, there are many complementary ideas and convictions, all or any of which might give rise to a total integrated concept of the unity of Scripture. And yet the term "unity of Scripture" was not yet in vogue, nor was there any attempt to bring together the various convictions and ideas into a coordinated synthesis expressing the concept of biblical unity. Nor, I might add, was it always clear whether these firmly held views concerning (a) the divine origin and authority of all Scripture (the one God is the *autor primarius*), (b) the agreement between the testaments in terms of prophecy and fulfillment, (c) the Christocentricity of all of Scripture, and (d) the total doctrinal agreement of all Scripture were considered to be simply conclusions drawn from Scripture and thus part of the *corpus doctrinae,* or in addition hermeneutical principles drawn from Scripture and necessary for the correct and evangelical explication and application of Scripture. Of course, all the four principles mentioned above were held by the Reformers and to varying degrees became underlying working principles of hermeneutics as they plied their exegetical trade, as it were. Luther might have employed the principle of Christocentricity with more consistency and vigor, Calvin the principle of doctrinal unity, although I am not sure about this.[2] We must remember, of course, that in the early years of the Reformation no thorough studies on hermeneutics were written until the *Clavis Scripturae* of Matthias Flacius in 1567, although Andrew Hyperius as early as 1556 after Luther's death had taken up many hermeneutical concerns, spiritual, academic and theological, in his *De theologo, seu de ratione studii theologic libri IIII.* Even so, a full-blown and conscious treatment of the unity of Scripture incorporating the four basic principles annunciated above just did not appear, and it is only in recent times that the term "unity of Scripture" has been employed, and that one or more of the above principles has been included in the definition of the term.[3]

It is my contention that the concept of unity adumbrated clearly by Luther and the Reformers and structured on the four pillars of (a) divine authorship of Scripture, (b) agreement between prophecy in the Old Testament and fulfillment in the New, (c) Christocentricity, and (d) doctrinal agreement throughout Scripture is biblical; that is, each pillar of the construct is based squarely upon the exegesis of Scripture. Since the time of the Enlightenment and the advent of the historical-critical method initiated by Semler, this Reformation view of the unity of Scripture has not been considered viable as a doctrine or hermeneutical principle. However, the theologians of the Enlightenment, the higher critics, the Romantics, the mythophiles, the classical Liberals, and even the Deists all conjectured some principle of unity pertaining to Scripture. Ironically, what seemed to be a much greater *conscious* interest in the notion of the unity of Scripture becomes apparent in the eighteenth and nineteenth centuries and in our own day among just those theologians who abandoned every one of the four pillars of the Reformation doctrine, except in some cases a vague notion of biblical Christocentricity. Ironic too although understandable is the fact that throughout the course of church history those theologians who believed in (and took for granted) an intrinsic unity of Scripture never bothered to articulate the notion of the unity of Scripture as a unified principle of interpretation, whereas those theologians arriving later on the scene who could find no essential and objective unity in Scripture struggled with great effort and conviction to find some spiritual truth or religious principle which would give meaning to Scripture in spite of the fact that its historical references and factual claims could not be accepted and its theology was contradictory and often inane and irrelevant.

A tracing of the history of the concept of the unity of Scripture since the time of the Enlightenment yields some interesting conclusions. Having abandoned the four pillars underlying the Reformation concept, but persuaded that there was abiding spiritual truth or value in the Scriptures, the theological progeny of the Enlightenment, using the historical-critical method, and with all the developing historical scholarship and shifting philosophical insight of their day at their disposal, worked out a veritable welter of theories of biblical unity.

Usually the unity was found to apply to the *res* referred to by the Scriptures rather than the *verba,* or Scripture itself; and this seemed consistent enough, since Scripture itself was not God's Word or revelation, but only a human and primitive account of revelation (Semler), if that. And the unity of Scripture, its principle of coordination, was its meaningfulness which consisted usually in a coordinating motif or spiritual truth. To Semler this principle was the Bible's witness to the growing movement of man's spirit toward God according to universal moral and religious principles. To Zachariä the principle was a unity of concepts or religious ideas (but not explicit doctrine). To von Hofmann it was *Heilsgeschichte.* To Herder unity was the historical continuity of spirit and "content" between the two testaments. Even Strauss, the mythophile, found in Scripture a unifying theme, unrelated to its historical reference or fact claims; namely, the (philosophical) idea of reconciliation, or the uniting of the finite and infinite in man in his history.

Passing to our day and the theories of unity being propounded of late, we find that our modern theological pundits are not so original as their eighteenth- and nineteenth-century theological forebears. Roughly speaking modern liberal exegetes—and for convenience and with no pejorative implication I call everyone who admittedly or latently follows the lead of historical criticism, Romanticism, *Heilsgeschichte* (Beck, von Hofmann, Neo-orthodoxy), Idealism, or demythologization a liberal exegete—are equally disagreed among themselves as to just what constitutes the unity of Scripture. Let me offer some random, disparate examples. Herman Diem, a Lutheran Existentialist, sees the unity of Scripture to be a "proclamatory unity" (in contrast to a "doctrinal unity") in that in the witness of Scripture Jesus Christ is heard to be proclaiming Himself.[4] J. Stanley Glen, a Reformed theologian, after stating that there are "many [conflicting?] unities in the Bible," sets forth a thesis similar to Diem's, suggesting that the unity of Scripture is in its *kerygma* (proclamation) rather than in its *didache,* although he has his doubts whether there is any unity in the *kerygma* itself, except for the fact that it points to Jesus.[5] Ernst Käsemann,[6] a Lutheran and post-Bultmannian, who, like his mentor, rejects the facticity of the Resurrection and therefore of the atonement of Christ, finds the doctrine of justification the unifying center of Scripture, and "canon within the canon" which is able to test the spirits within the canon itself. Ed Schroeder, a Lutheran, who believes in the historicity and the resurrection of Christ and in the atonement, agrees with Käsemann.[7] Roy L. Honeycutt, Jr., a Baptist, offers us one of the more ingenuous and artless theories of unity. Finding theological aberrations and misunderstandings and poor rabbinic exegesis throughout the New Testament, and finding the New Testament notion of God incompatible with the Old and finding no unitary Christology in the New Testament at all, he opts for a unity within both testaments in that they witness to the "mighty acts of God."[8] Honeycutt's theory (which could apply to the Koran) is similar to that of the hard-headed critic, G. Ernest Wright, who, rejecting the doctrine of the Incarnation because it is "unbiblical," nevertheless yields to the mystique so common among liberal theologians, that there must be some unifying theme running through the Scriptures, and he offers in a magnificent *tour de force* the "rule of God" (but not in any ontological or historical sense) as constituting the unity of Scripture.[9] H. H. Rowley opts for a number of theological motifs such as monotheism, election, the cross, etc. to be the "unity in diversity" of Scripture.[10] Wolfhart Pannenberg, rejecting the orthodox Protestant doctrine of doctrinal unity and moving behind the *kerygma,* sees in the "Christ-event itself," that is, "the public ministry, death, and resurrection of Jesus Himself" the "standard by means of which to judge the Scriptures and their witness to Christ."[11] Foster R. McCurley sees the "Gospel" as the nucleus or unity of Scripture, but only in the formal sense (the Old Testament knows nothing of Christ).[12] S. Fernon McCasland, a committed and condescending higher critic, in a desperate *testimonium paupertatis* concludes that in the experience of faith (formal faith, *fides qua creditur*) "lies the deepest and most abiding unity of the Scriptures."[13]

A few comments on what has just been said. First, among those theologians since the Enlightenment who have rejected the traditional orthodox and classical notion of the unity of Scripture there seems to be no common understanding concerning a formal definition of such unity or what the term refers to. Does the unity of Scripture refer to the "wholeness" of Scripture, to a theme running through the Scripture (e.g., reconciliation, justification), to a historical continuity, to a person, or what?

Second, those who break with the orthodox Reformation doctrine of unity do not in any case derive their notion of the unity of Scripture from the explicative sense of Scripture, but rather by its applicative meaning. Like the Alexandrians (Clement and Origen) they are often unable to find abiding meaning in the literal explication of the biblical text. And yet they believe that there is some kind of unity (spiritual value, theme, insight, historical truth) underlying the

Scriptures (although not necessarily exegetically derived from the Scriptures) which is both important in itself and useful and even indispensible for interpreting the biblical text. But whereas for the Alexandrians and medieval allegorists the "rule of faith" pointed to an inherent doctrinal unity of Scripture as well as a consensus entering into the life of the church, and was employed to shed light and enhance the literal sense of Scripture, for liberal exegetes since the Enlightenment the principle of unity, or central meaning, of Scripture has taken on a more radical and critical function. Subjecting the Scriptures to critical historical scrutiny, these theologians not only saw the intended sense of Scripture to be irrelevant and of no spiritual value, but concluded it was patently false on historical or religious grounds. In this they went beyond the Alexandrians and medieval allegorists.

I will devote the remainder of this study to making a number of comments which hopefully will be relevant and even helpful to a discussion of the unity of Scripture.

1. Davis is correct when he agrees that the basis for the unity of Scripture must lie in the fact that it has one single, divine Author.[14] This was the basic argument of the Reformers and post-Reformation theologians who inferred from the divine authorship of Scripture the truthfulness and inner unity of its doctrinal content. It is a common contention among them that the Holy Spirit as the author of all of Scripture is the best interpreter of it and that since He inspired the Scripture in words the sense can never be separated from the *verba*.[15] In this view the doctrine of the unity of Scripture has the same *sedes* as the doctrine of the divine origin of Scripture; namely, 2 Timothy 3:16. Here Paul says that on the basis of its divine inspiration every single Scripture is profitable πρὸς διδασκαλίαν (singular), true doctrine (which Paul has spoken of previously) and is unequivocal and noncontradictory. Notice that Paul goes on to say that the Scriptures will render the theologian ἄρτιος . . . ἐξηρτισμένος.

2. The denial that the Old Testament predicts Christ and therefore preaches and promises Him destroys the unity of Scripture, at least in respect to the unity of the two testaments.[16] This view, so common today, finds Christ in the Old Testament, but only virtually, or implicitly. Thus Christ can be found not because the prophets spoke of Him directly in the sense that their immediate audience could believe in a Savior to come; but Christ can be found only by the utilization of a *sensus plenior,* or extended typology. And so the New Testament merely *fills in (Einfühlung*: Herder) the Old Testa-

ment prophetic word; it in no way cognitively refers to a correspondent fulfillment (*Erfühlung*) in the person and work of Christ. Meanwhile the Israelites were saved by God's "grace" apart from any faith in Christ, or perhaps by a different covenant, that of works. And so the unity of biblical soteriology is denied. The unity of Scripture is *eo ipso* undermined if there is no correspondence between prophecy and fulfillment, between type and antetype, between the meaning of a text and its referent. The New Testament writers are correct in their understanding and interpretation of the Old Testament, that is, they actually represent the *sensus literalis* and intention of the Old Testament, not a distorted interpretation, or *ex eventu* explanation or typology, or religious insight as they witness to the fulfillment of Old Testament prophecy. We must distinguish between predictive prophecy and typology at this point. In the case of predictive prophecy we have a rectilinear correspondence between an Old Testament descriptive and cognitive prediction and a thing, person, or event described in the New Testament. In typology there is also a straight correspondence, but between a thing or person or event in the Old Testament and a person, thing, or event in the New Testament. In the case of predictive prophecy the *words* of the Old Testament predict; in the case of typology the reference of the words predict. The correspondence, or unity, between type and antetype in the case of biblical typology is therefore only a unity of two references, type from the Old and antetype from the New Testament. Except in cases where the New Testament itself clearly marks out an Old Testament type the practice of typological exegesis can become open-ended and precariously arbitrary as a hermeneutical principle, since it is an application not of the unity of Scripture, but of the unity of the references of Scripture. It is thus no more based on explicative meaning of the biblical narrative than the application of unitary principles of Semler and his followers who believed that there was no unity of Scripture except that which was applicatorily derived. This is the reason that Hans Frei accuses Johannes Cocceius, a strict Calvinist, with his emphasis upon typology and the difference between the two testaments of unwittingly helping to cause the dissolution of the traditional unity of literal explicative sense and historical reference.[17]

3. The terms "Christocentricity" and "Christological unity" need clarification. Theologians as different from each other as Luther and Socinus, Karl Barth and Paul Tillich speak of Christ being the center of the Scriptures. For Socinus the metaphor meant merely that Christ is the subject matter of Scripture, just as Caesar is the subject matter

of Caesar's *Gallic Wars*. To Luther Christocentricity was always affirmed in a doctrinal and realistic soteriological context, in the context of justification through faith *propter Christum*, that is, on account of His redemptive work, and this is particularly the case when he urges Christology as a hermeneutical aid against legalism.[18] To Karl Barth the principle of Christocentricity is a doctrinal principle, but also a historical thematic continuity.[19] To Tillich all Christological terms are religious symbols without historical or ontological referents having anything to do with Christ. If biblical Christology is restricted to Christ's person (nineteenth century German positive theologians) without reference to His work of atonement, or if biblical Christology is presented as representing mere general spiritual truths, religious ideas, symbolic language, eternal truths, experience, myth, anthropology, then the very term Christocentricity of Scripture is a piece of deceptive theological blather. The Christological language of Scripture refers to reality, whether it refers to God's grace, forgiveness and salvation in Christ, whether it refers to Christ's eternal deity and attributes, His historic virgin birth, life, miracles, preachment, death, resurrection, ascension, and future return to judgment. And the effects of Christ's life and death and resurrection are real: God has been reconciled, the world has been redeemed, the sinner will be saved forever through faith in Christ—really and truly. All this must be included in the affirmation, "Christ is the unity of Scripture." Otherwise the phrase is deceptive, unbiblical, and without meaning.

The importance of maintaining the reality of biblical referents cannot be overemphasized, especially in our day of radical historicism. Of course, we must read the biblical text in its historical context, but that context must be determined by the biblical text, not *vice versa*. And the actuality of the historical references of the text must be maintained. Otherwise the religious truth of Scripture and of its Gospel center and Christology is severed from its roots in history and fact, and the meaning of the biblical text reduced to mere application (Strauss, Bultmann, Priebe[20]). Hans Frei in his very helpful and informative book, *The Eclipse of Biblical Narrative*,[21] mentions that the English Latitudinarians and the Neologists (Semler and others) in Germany also believed that "the *religious* (emphasis his: note that he does not say "theological") content of the Bible [was] dependent on the historical factuality of the occurrence narrated in it"—but only "in muffled and ambiguous tones." This is a charitable and gratuitous comment; for after the anti-supernaturalist or liberal critic has finished his surgery very little real history remains as a real basis of biblical religion or theology, say nothing of Christology. Thus, the historical or theologico-ontological matrix (e.g., divine revelation, theophanies, miracles, etc.) of cognitive and meaningful biblical theology—and every text of the Bible is cognitive and meaningful theology—reduced to almost zero, so that real referents in effect do not underlie biblical assertions at all.

What is to be done in such a situation, if any hermeneutical principle of Christological or biblical unity is to obtain? Some religious idea or motif, not explicatively, but only applicatively "derived" from Scripture, must be brought to bear as a unifying principle of hermeneutics, if Scripture or its content is to make any religious sense. But surely, no mere applicatively derived principle of hermeneutics is valid, any more than a principle utterly foisted upon Scripture from the outside, especially since every such applicatively derived principle of biblical unity conjured up since the Enlightenment has been in opposition to clear teachings explicatively derived from Scripture. And surely a valid principle of interpretation cannot be in conflict with the explicative meaning, or intention, of Scripture. In other words, because modern liberal theologians since the Enlightenment cannot accept the historical or in many cases the theologico-ontological (Incarnation, Trinity, etc.) referents of biblical assertions—and it seems always for this reason!—they impose upon Scripture an alien interpretive principle of unity which amounts to little more than an uncertain cipher which conflicts with Scripture and renders a theology or ideology which must be heretical, sub-Christian or even anti-Christian, but which ironically is the goal at which the exegete probably intended to arrive all the time. And all this expense of labor and life because the exegete has abandoned a first principle of hermeneutics, namely this, that when a biblical assertion in its intended sense has a referent, it is a real referent, whether the referent is a historical occurrence (Christ's resurrection), a state of being (the personal union), an act of God in history (personal justification through faith in Christ) or whatever.[22] There can be no Christological unity of Scripture or biblical and Christian Christology at all where the historicity and reality of biblical referents are not accepted with utmost seriousness as part of the intention of the biblical text. The same must be said if the biblical witness to Christ (the center of Scripture) is erroneous, truncated, or contradictory.[23]

4. If the phrase "Christ is the unity of Scripture" is not a satisfactory description of the unity of Scripture, neither is the theory that the Christ event is the unity of Scripture. To Pannenberg[24] the

"Christ event" within the nexus of historical events and having "its meaning in itself" and divorced from any Christological dogma gives unity to the Bible. In this view the unity of Scripture is not Christological, but the unity of history is Christological, and that unity of history is imposed upon Scripture, giving meaning to it.

5. The idea of the unity of Scripture which was adumbrated in the early church and by the Reformers always involved doctrinal unity. If there is not doctrinal unity throughout Scripture, the other three pillars on which the orthodox view rests collapse, and there is no unity at all. For instance, to say that Christ is the unity of Scripture but to maintain that there are conflicting or erroneous Christologies within or between the Testaments is only possible if one makes the principle of Christocentricity purely ontological. But that is nonsense, a μετάβασις εἰς 'άλλο γένος, like using the category of color to measure density. Scripture, like other writings, is cognitive discourse; it is our *principium cognoscendi,* the source of our knowledge of God. Thus, its unity must be cognitive, theological, in nature, or it has no unity appropriate to its nature. In fact, the other three aspects to the orthodox doctrine of the unity of Scripture involve doctrinal unity, and all pillars of the doctrine are implicatorily and inextricably related; if one pillar falls, they all fall. And when the unity, the doctrinal unity of Scripture, is abandoned, so is the entire structure of biblical bibliology: the entire structure! The history of hermeneutics since the Enlightenment has illustrated this point with clarity and even pathos.

6. There can be no cleavage between the doctrinal unity of Scripture and the unity of the gospel. Paul makes it very clear that there is only one gospel (Gal. 1:7-8). And this gospel is doctrine (what Melanchthon felicitously called the *doctrina evangelii*), it renders information, it is a cognitive *kerygma* to Paul, a message with a specific material content. This fact is made clear throughout his entire epistle to the Galatians. And Paul sees his teaching of the gospel as identical to the ἐπαγγελίαι of the Old Testament (Gal. 4:18; Rom. 1:2, 4:14). And his one gospel entails the total framework of the entire Old Testament doctrine. Thus, the singleness and unity of Paul's gospel is consistent with the doctrinal unity of all Scripture. It is interesting that the New Testament uses the term "doctrine" in the singular, except when speaking of doctrines of devils. And so it was in general among the Reformers and post-Reformation theologians; in this way they indicated their belief in the singleness and unity of biblical doctrine, just as of the biblical gospel.[25]

In what I have just said I am opposing all modern theologians who would find some kind of unity in the gospel which is not found in the Scriptures and then substitute the (unity of the) gospel or *kerygma* (which I suppose they have putatively drawn from Scripture) for the unity of Scripture.[26]

7. A word about the biblical basis for the unity of Scripture. Any concept of biblical unity which is to operate a presupposition or principle of hermeneutics lies, like the doctrine of the divine origin of Scripture, the divine authority, internal clarity and inerrancy of Scripture, prayer, and the guidance of the Holy Spirit, within the discipline of *hermeneutica sacra* which is peculiar to the interpretation of the Bible (in contrast to *hermeneutica profana* which employs canons of interpretation common to any and all writings) and must be drawn from Scripture itself. A solid principle of profane hermeneutics (and also surely of *hermeneutica sacra*) is that application of a given text or piece of literature cannot contradict, correct, mitigate, or take precedence over the explication of the text, lest the seriousness of the text and the explication of the *sensus literalis* which is the basic goal of both sacred and profane hermeneutics be undermined and all exegesis erode to the level of fanciful and arbitrary interpretation based upon some abstract principle of biblical unity without any connection to the biblical text and its intended meaning. In such a case there would be no need for the text itself.

8. In the history of the church through the time of the Reformation the unity of Scripture was employed by the application of the *analogia fidei* or *regula fidei* to the explication of biblical texts. What was this analogy of faith? On what biblical basis was it founded? How did it work? The answer to these questions is quite vague, if attainable at all, in the early church and even in the Reformation era. So I shall repair to some post-Reformation Lutherans for answers, again not always very complete, to our questions.

The notion of the analogy of faith, or Scripture, was discussed only in sections of dogmatics books dealing with the interpretation of Scripture or in treatises on hermeneutics. I do not recall it ever referred to as a principle in any exegetical work of the sixteenth or seventeenth century. A clear and typical definition of the analogy of faith is offered by John Adam Osiander, "The analogy of faith is the harmony of Bible passages, or the pattern of doctrine (*typus doctrinae*) structured according to clear and perspicuous statements of Scripture."[27] We notice that there are two aspects to this hermeneutical principle. First, it is a harmony of what is taught throughout

Scripture, a harmony between the two testaments and between Christ and the Old Testament,[28] a beautiful congruence, like a symphony.[29] Second, the analogy of faith is a pattern (ὑποτύπωσις, 2 Tim. 1:13) of doctrine, a summation of the doctrine of Scripture. Olearius does not shrink from calling the ecumenical creeds or the Augsburg Confession such a summation or analogy of fatih. Abraham Calov defines the analogy of faith as follows: "The analogy of faith is the inner conformity (*conformitas*) of the doctrine of faith, set forth clearly in the sacred Scripture, but especially in those passages where each doctrine has its own *sedes*."[30] John Conrad Dannhower calls it a "harmony of the truth."[31] Commenting on these words of Calov's Hollaz states, "Now if therefore the doctrine of faith is drawn and extracted from clear passages of Scripture, certainly every interpretation, consistent with the faith, ought to rest on the foundation of sacred Scripture." Hollaz believes that the interpreter of Scripture does his work according to the analogy of faith when his interpretation agrees with the fundamental articles of faith drawn, as they are, from Scripture. At just this point the principle of the unity of Scripture takes on a hermeneutical force. But only in a ministerial sense, in the sense that Scripture interprets Scripture. The very question Hollaz is addressing himself to in this discussion is, "Whether Scripture must be explained through Scripture." The analogy of faith helps the exegete in a twofold sense: First, as a harmonious pattern (Hollaz uses the words *complexio*-summary, *consensus*-agreement, and *concentum*-harmony) of sound words it enables him to arrange and coordinate the great *loci,* or themes, of Scripture with the doctrine of Christ as the center and to see them in their organic relationship (*proportio*) with each other. Second, as a summation of the articles of faith, it assists the exegete in applying the principle that Scripture interprets Scripture, that is, the clear passages dealing with a given article of faith will show light on less clear and obscure passages dealing with the same article. As far as I can discern this is *all* the freight that Hollaz or any of the orthodox Protestant theologians ever put on the analogy of faith as a hermeneutical principle. He avers that the principle is no different from a principle of analogy used in interpreting any human piece of literature which has inner connection and coherence. In the case of human writings we may well discover incoherence and incongruity. "But God is always the same, never inconsistent and totally without change and free from error." Thus, the unity of Scripture, hermeneutically operative by employing the principle of the analogy of faith, is a part of *hermeneutica sacra*, based upon the unity and trustworthiness and truthfulness of God. And so Hollaz concludes confidently, reverently and almost doxologically, "Therefore it can never happen that the true meaning of even one divine passage will not beautifully agree with the chief parts of the divinely revealed doctrine."

The unity of Scripture presupposes, in contrast to post-Enlightenment exegesis, especially the New Hermeneutic, that there is an inextricable union between the meaning (*sensus internus*) of Scripture and the words (*externa littera*): the meaning, or intention, of Scripture is always expressed by the words. It was not the Enlightenment with its sophisticated contempt of orthodoxy which first rejected this identification of meaning with the *sensus literalis* of the biblical text, but Roman Catholic theologians, especially the Jesuits, who insisted that unwritten tradition was the Word of God along with Scripture and could authenticate and elicit the meaning from the external word of Scripture. Robert Bellarmine[32] distinguished between the literal, or historical, sense of Scripture, the obvious meaning of the words (which was often unclear), and the spiritual, or mystical, meaning "which refers to something other than what the words immediately signify." The plain words of Scripture he likened to a sheath, and the meaning (*sensus*) of Scripture—bear in mind, not the *sensus literalis*—to the sword of the Spirit: the meaning can only be provided by tradition. Thus, the meaning of the text was wrenched from the intention of the words, from the text itself.[33] The unity of Scripture was destroyed as something intrinsic, as it came under the dogmatic domination of unwritten tradition.[34] But really the same thing takes place today when modern theologians, finding no meaning in the *sensus literalis* of Scripture in its original setting, or unable to believe the text, seek and find a *sensus plenior* or existential meaning or whatever different from the clear explicative meaning of the text under consideration!

How does the exegete use the analogy of faith as he carries out his work? John Gerhard offers five important steps to be applied in the proper use of the principle.[35] (1) The interpretation of a given text of Scripture ought to consist of the search for the intended *sensus literalis* which is appropriate to the given text. (2) The exegete must not depart from the plain, literal sense of the text, especially when it pertains to the articles of faith, unless Scripture itself elsewhere ostensively compels us to depart from that seeming literal sense. (3) Nothing should be affirmed as dogma or an article of faith which is not clearly based upon Scripture. (4) The rule of faith is consistent (*integra*) in all its parts: everything having to do with the rule of faith is from the Spirit of God and cannot contradict itself. This means that one article of faith cannot militate against another article of faith which is clearly taught in Scripture. For instance, passages teaching the unity of God cannot be used to mitigate the intention of passages which clearly teach the plurality of persons in the deity; rather the two biblical truths must be held in tension, even though they seem to conflict with each other. To Gerhard the unwillingness of human reason to allow the articles of faith to remain unimpaired according to the integrity of the rule of faith, but to insist on seeming contradictions between them is "the source of all heresy." (5) We must never depart from the rule of faith when interpreting passages which are not clear because of context, reference, or grammar.

The *regula fidei* actually aids the exegete in solving apparent contradictions and other difficulties in Scripture; never, however, by denying or mitigating the *sensus literalis* of a text, but by getting at the given text's intention and referents (time, situation, person, etc.), and thus, in the optimistic conviction that Scripture is in harmony with itself, solving some of the difficulties which arise between passages and *loci*, rather than just giving up on the undertaking. Never is the *regula fidei* imposed upon a text to deny its *sensus literalis*. Obviously the enterprise of harmonization will not always succeed. Above all the integrity of the text must be upheld.

If Gerhard's position is correct, the theologian can summarize in a *regula fidei* a message (in Scripture) or piece of cognitive discourse which transcends reason at various points and presents paradoxes; but one cannot summarize into any *analogia fidei* a piece of literature which is incoherent and self-contradictory.[36]

The analogy of Scripture as understood and applied by orthodoxy, based as it is on the divine origin and authority of Scripture, means that Scripture is analogous with itself (*Scriptura Scripturam interpretat*): it is not an analogy of Scripture with science (*scientia*), or philosophy (Thomas Aquinas), or mathematics (Descartes), or reason (Ritzschl), or an existentialist anthropology (Bultmann), or the "Gospel" (Schlink), or historical coherence, facts, and reality (Troeltsch, Historical-Critical Method). Biblical unity cannot be forced to correspond in analogy to some extra-biblical subject matter, norm, criterion, motif, or interpretation of reality.

9. The unity of Scripture, or *regula fidei*, as a principle of hermeneutics is *never*, as in Romanism, above the text of Scripture. The serious and devout search for the intended sense of the biblical

text must remain inviolate and unimpaired as the first principle of interpretation, in the sphere of sacred and profane hermeneutics. No concept of biblical unity, no doctrinal synthesis, *regula fidei*, or ecclesiastical symbol can fault, mitigate, or falsify the intention of the biblical text in any case whatsoever. Neither can the unity of Scripture be used as a cipher to transcend or cut through the serious, fundamental search of the exegete for the *sensus literalis*, so that the exegete need not abide by that *sensus literalis* in every case. Nor can the unity of Scripture or a *regula fidei* impose a forced meaning on any passage of Scripture. It can only be used to correct false or hasty exegesis, to amplify the meaning of passages and to complete the pattern (υποτύπωσις) of biblical *loci* and articles of faith. Essentially, the hermeneutical use of the principle of the unity of Scripture is summed up in the principle, *Scriptura Scripturam interpretat*, that is, the clear passages of Scripture clarify the less clear passages *which deal with the same article of faith or subject matter* of the biblical text by a principle of unity. If two passages or pericopes of Scripture seem to conflict with each other, the exegete, believing in the unity of Scripture and that Scripture does not contradict itself, will make every legitimate attempt to reconcile the seeming conflict. But any attempt at such harmonization which mitigates the *sensus literalis* of the biblical text or imposes a forced meaning on the text violates the integrity of the text and denies the divine authority of Scripture (*sola Scriptura*). This means that seeming contradictions between passages of Scripture which cannot be reconciled without doing violence to the biblical text must be allowed to stand; and the exegete, as Luther said, must simply tip his hat to the Holy Spirit and concede that the difficulty may never be solved in this life.

10. If the unity of Scripture, or analogy of faith, cannot force or mitigate the meaning of the intended sense of any Scripture passage, then the same principle is true *a fortiori* in the case of the articles of faith which are based upon clear *sedes doctrinae*. Some articles of faith, based upon solid *sedes*, seem *prima facie* to be at odds with other clearly derived articles of faith or clear biblical data.

For instance, Christ's vicarious atonement in which He endures the punitive wrath of God against the sins of the world seems to be in conflict with God's love toward all sinners (Ritzschl). So also the doctrine of hell seems to conflict with God's universal love. Particular election and predestination seem quite out of harmony with a doctrine of universal grace. Law ("This do and thou shalt live," Luke 10:28) and Gospel ("Believe on the Lord Jesus Christ, and thou shalt be saved," Acts 16:31) seem to teach different ways of salvation. In no case may the exegete, using a Cartesian mathematic model or a Lockian rational model of coherence, discount or attempt to mitigate the seeming paradox to be found between the articles of faith. In other words, in such cases the unity of Scripture which is an organic unity can only be held in (sometimes paradoxical) tension with such seeming conflict between articles of faith.

Even more vexing for the exegete is the fact that there seem to be inconsistencies or conflicts within certain articles, or mysteries, of faith. The personal union, or incarnation, is an article of faith clearly taught in the Scriptures (John 1:14; Luke 1:32,35; Gal. 4:4; 1 Tim. 3:16), but it is a union of disparates, something quite beyond human understanding. So too with the article of the Trinity, based as it is on a large number of passages and pericopes which directly or in passing refer to the unity of the Godhead or the plurality and deity of the persons of Father, Son, and Holy Spirit. Such articles, or mysteries, which transcend our comprehension and are revealed in Scripture to be believed by us can be clarified as we apply the analogy of faith in the sense of accumulating all the biblical data pertaining to the article of faith. *But* no principle of unity or analogy can be used to mitigate the plain meaning of texts and *sedes* or to force biblical data in order to make one aspect or element of the doctrine compatible with another. The disastrous results of employing such a principle can be seen in the welter of ancient and modern heresies concerning the doctrine of Christ and the Trinity.

Neither can the doctrinal unity of Scripture be used hermeneutically to discount what have lately been called the phenomena of Scripture. The fact clearly taught in Scripture that Jesus became tired, that He learned things, that He became very angry cannot be used to discount His deity. The fact that Scripture affirms things which seem to conflict with each other or with generally accepted scientific, historical, or geographical data and that we cannot harmonize these seeming discrepancies ought not be used to discount the divine origin and utter truthfulness of Scripture.

If passages are left according to their ostensive meaning and then seem to contradict each other, or if the articles of faith, based solidly upon clear *sedes doctrinae*, are left to conflict seemingly with each other, this in no way undermines the inerrancy of Scripture. Rather, it is an instance of upholding in faith the unity of Scripture and its utter inerrancy, even though one cannot demonstrate in every case Scripture's agreement with itself or the total (logical) coherence of all Scripture. To force reconciliation between Bible texts which seem to conflict or to force agreement between articles of faith which transcend reason by ever so subtle a violation of the *sensus literalis* of clear texts and pericopes from Scripture is rather an inappropriate, if not arrogant, admission that Scripture according to ostensive meanings of clear texts contradicts itself. To read something into another's words which is contrary to what that person says constitutes a criticism of that person's words or content. This is the case, even if we are graciously and reverently attempting to harmonize what that person says. When we cease to read something into another's words, even if these words seem absurd or contradictory to what he has said elsewhere, but simply accept the clear words and ostensive meaning of that person in every case, then we consciously or unconsciously concede that the person's thinking and expression is higher than our understanding or critical judgment. This simply is our posture toward the Scriptures, and toward Scripture alone, because Scripture differs from all other books in that it is the Word of God.[37]

NOTES

[1]See J. N. D. Kelly, *Early Christian Doctrines*, (London: Adam and Charles Black, 1958), pp. 64-69.

[2]Luther's Christological principle "Was Christum treibet" is based upon the conviction that Scripture agrees doctrinally with itself and James must agree with Paul if the book is to be considered apostolic, i.e., Scripture.

[3]In his fine discussion of the "Unity of the Bible" John J. Davis lists four "kinds," or aspects, of biblical unity which correspond to the four principles mentioned above: thematic unity (doctrinal unity), historical unity, prophecy and fulfillment, and Christocentricity. He assumes throughout his study the divine origin of Scripture. The best definition of the traditional doctrine of the unity of Scripture I have found is by Ralph Bohlmann, "Confessional Biblical Interpretation: Some Basic Principles" in *Studies in Lutheran Hermeneutics*, ed. John Reumann (Philadelphia: Fortress Press, 1979), p. 205: "Because the same God speaks the same message of Christ and his salvation throughout the Scriptures, the Scriptures present an organic unity of doctrine both within and between the Old and New Testaments. The unity of authorship, content, and purpose is reflected in the principle that Scripture interprets Scripture, whether applied to individual passages or articles of faith.

[4]Hermann Diem, *Dogmatics*, translated by Harold Knight (Edinburgh: Oliver and Boyd, 1959), p. 234, *passim*.

[5]"Jesus Christ and the Unity of the Bible" in *Interpretation*, 5:1 (1951), p. 260ff.

[6]"Is the Gospel Objective?" in *Essays on New Testament Themes*, tr. W. J. Montague (London: SCM Press, 1969), p. 58, *passim*.

[7]Edward Schroeder, "Law-Gospel Reductionism in the History of The Lutheran Church-Missouri Synod" in *Concordia Theological Monthly* (XLIII, 4, 1972, April), pp. 232-51. See also Paul Bretscher, *After the Purifying* (River Forest, Illinois: Lutheran Education Association, 1975).

[8]"The Unity and Witness of Scripture" in *Foundations*, 8, 4 (1965), p. 292ff., 298, *passim*.

[9]"The Unity of Scripture" in *Scottish Journal of Theology*, 8, 4 (1955), p. 341, 348, 350.

[10]*The Unity of the Bible* (London: The Carey Kingsgate Press Ltd., 1953).

[11]*Basic Questions in Theology*, translated by George H. Kehm (Philadelphia: Fortress Press, 1970), p. 197, *passim*.

[12]"Confessional Propria as Hermeneutic—Old Testament" in *Studies in Lutheran Hermeneutics*, p. 249-50.

[13]"The Unity of the Scriptures" in *Journal of Biblical Literature*, 73, (1954), p. 10.

[14]Ibid., p. 6.

[15]See John Gerhard, *Loci theologici* (Tübingen: John Georg Cotta, 1763), I, 43, 45. See also Horace Hummel, "The Influence of Confessional Themes on Biblical Exegesis" in *Studies in Lutheran Hermeneutics*, p. 220. Hummel understands the unity of Scripture to mean that it contains "one theology because it has only one author."

[16]See Foster R. McCurley, ibid., pp. 233-35. McCurley, like many others, particularly Lutherans, maintains that there is Gospel in the Old Testament, but not predictions of Christ. Thus there is only a purely formal gospel in the Old Testament.

[17]See Hans W. Frei, *The Eclipse of Biblical Narrative* (New Haven: Yale University Press, 1974), p. 46ff.

[18]WA 2, 73; 2, 334; 3, 63, 1; 3, 620; 4, 153, 27; 9, 560, 1; 14, 97, 2; 18, 606, 29; 40 III, 652, 15; 52, 509; 54, 29, 3; 54, 414, 13; 56, 59.

[19]*Christian Dogmatics* (Edinburgh: T. & T. Clark, 1958), IV, 2, 193, *passim*. cf. also IV, 3, 1, 53-55.

[20]Duane A. Priebe, "Theology and Hermeneutics" in *Studies in Lutheran Hermeneutics*, pp. 295-311. As an eager and enthusiastic devotee of the New Hermeneutic Priebe really is more radical than Strauss or Bultmann, for he sees no constant or abiding meaning even in the application of the biblical text. Priebe is an advocate of what E. D. Hirsch, Jr. in his excellent book, *Validity in Interpretation* (New Haven: Yale University Press, 1967), calls "semantic autonomy," the notion advanced by Heidegger and a host of modern literary critics that the text's meaning is not dependent upon the author's intention, a notion which to Hirsch leaves no principle for the judging of the validity of any interpretation.

[21]Frei, *The Eclipse of Biblical Narrative*, p. 118.

[22]For an excellent discussion of the necessary relationship between the historicity of the biblical narrative and Christology see Kurt Marquart, "The Incompatibility between Historical-Critical Theology and the Confessions" in *Studies in Lutheran Confessions*, pp. 323-30.

[23]Honeycutt, 298.

[24]pp. 196-98.

[25]See *Formula of Concord*, Solid Declarations, IX, 31.

[26]Warren Quanbeck believes in the truth and centrality of the Gospel and its

unity, but maintains the Scripture presents a number of contradictory theologies concerning God's work in Christ. "The Confessions and their Influence upon Biblical Interpretation" in *Studies in Lutheran Hermeneutics*, pp. 174-87. See also J. Stanley Glen [footnote above], who substitutes the unity of the *kerygma* for the unity of Scripture.

[27]See David Hollaz, *Examen theologicum acroamaticum* (Leipzig, 1750), Prol. III, q. 48, Obs. 4, prob. a3, p. 161.

[28]Hollaz, Prol. III, q. 30, prob. d, p. 112.

[29]John Olearius, *Theologica Exegetica* (Frankfurt and Leipzig, 1674).

[30]*Biblia novi testamenti illustrata* (Frankfurt, 1676), II, 207. We find the same understanding of what the analogy of faith is in the Reformed theologians of the era. See John Henry Heidegger, *Corpus Theologiae* (Zürich, 1700). For a brief, very useful summation of the Reformed position on the analogy of faith see Milton S. Terry, *Biblical Hermeneutics* (Grand Rapids: Zondervan Publishing House, n.d.), pp. 579-81.

[31]*Hermeneutica sacra* (Strassbourg, 1669), p. 366.

[32]*Disputationes de controversii christianae fidei* (Milan, 1721), *de Verbo Dei*, III, III, col. 141.

[33]Bellarmine, IV, IV, col. 178.

[34]Bellarmine said (*de Verbo Dei*, Lib III, c. 9), "Scripture cannot tell us what its true sense is." The result of such an opinion according to Gerhard (I, 50) is that the church must give us the *sensus* (meaning) which does not come from the words of Scripture. Gerhard claims that this is against the very nature of knowledge. For knowledge is a relationship (*adaequatio*, correspondence) "between the thing to be known and the knowing intellect." "Knowing something in the intellect (*intellectio*) is a receiving in the intellect a kind of abstract picture of the object to be known." The Roman view would impose a view whereby knowledge of something would not necessarily have any relation to the thing to be known, but would be provided by something else (church, pope, authority, etc.).

[35]Gerhard, I, 72ff. Gerhard speaks of the *regula fidei*, but he means by the term the same as the *analogia fidei*. He defines the rule of faith as follows: "We understand the rule of faith to be the clear passages (*loci*) in which the articles of faith are set forth in clear and distinct words."

[36]See John Andrew Quenstedt, *Theologia didactico-polemica, sive systema theologicum* (Leipzig, 1715), C. IV, S. II, q. 6, ekth. 3-5, I, 119-120.

[37]The finest treatment of the pitfalls of applying the analogy of faith, or unity of Scripture, illegitimately is by John P. Koehler entitled "The Analogy of Faith" and first appearing in *Theologische Quartalschrift* and later translated in *Faith-Life*, XXIV, 10 (Oct., 1951) to XXV, 5 (May, 1952). I do not think I will burden the reader by quoting him at length on the point just mentioned above.

> If it is obvious that the Holy Ghost has expressed a *definite* line of thought or a *definite* thought, is it permissible to change (*umgestalten*) this according to *other* lines of thought so that it is deprived of its characteristic content for the reason that we think it contradicts what the Holy Spirit has said elsewhere in Scripture?
>
> I believe every one will agree with me when I say that every *reasonable* conception of interpretation will *deny* that because we are dealing with *infallible* statements of God.
>
> The thought that the words of the Holy Spirit form a harmonious whole

cannot alter this judgment. By the way, this is a later objection which we do not meet with in the youthful, fresh days of theology. The harmony of Scriptures is not the starting-point of our understanding; we arrive at it when we cease learning piecemeal.

Nevertheless I admit at the outset: the Scriptures are a harmonious whole. But suppose that is not evident to me in a certain case? Then I effect (*vermitteln*) a harmony by means of the analogy of faith. But who vouches for this harmonizing if it is not contained in Scripture in the very same form?

All *reliability* of exegesis would collapse by this method. A *criticism* of the connections of thought of the Holy Ghost would be granted to the interpreter. He would be permitted to find on the basis of *his own judgment* a reconciliation with the other statements of Scripture. In spite of his holding fast to other statements of the Bible this method would bring at least so many *purely human elements* into the results of the exegesis that anything which God has revealed would be omitted or given a different turn.

This sort of exegesis cannot be accepted by sound reason, for our human faculty of conception self-evidently cannot cast light upon the background of apparent contradictions of the Holy Ghost unless this explanation is given by God Himself. Why, then, such attempts?

We shall, therefore, always find in the history of exegesis along these lines all sorts of *attempts* which do not wish to *exclude* one another mutually. Even the proponents of the analogy of faith often say this.

But why is it done? It only disturbs our *trust* in the reliability of the divine word. In such a case it is always the correct procedure simply to register our *inability* which is not capable of following the line of thought of our great God in all its ramifications and then to *be satisfied with what is clearly stated* (emphases his).

Cf. also my discussion of the same topic in "The Hermeneutics of the Formula of Concord" in *No Other Gospel*, ed. Arnold J. Koelpin (Milwaukee: Northwestern Publishing House, 1980), pp. 309-36.

Contextualization and Revelational Epistemology

David J. Hesselgrave
Professor of World Mission
Trinity Evangelical Divinity School

13. Contextualization and Revelational Epistemology

David J. Hesselgrave

Liberation theology, Waterbuffalo theology, Pain of God theology; The Living Bible, Good News for Modern Man, the Cotton Patch Gospel; *Gospel in Context,*[1] *Gospel in Culture,*[2] *Christianity in Culture*[3]—there can be little doubt that contemporary Christianity is characterized by a concerted attempt to get its message out of the cathedral and into the marketplace. And the word that has come to supply a linguistic umbrella for these intense and diverse efforts is the word "contextualization." Still in its infancy, that word has already been defined and redefined, used and abused, amplified and vilified, coronated and crucified. Not without reason, Bruce Fleming concludes that it has already outlived its usefulness and urges evangelicals to lay it to an untimely rest.[4] Now that evangelicals have adopted it into their linguistic family, however, it is more likely that it will get no rest whatsoever. And even if euthanasia could be applied to the *word,* the *endeavor* gives every promise of a long life.

Academicians tend to play games with words. Missiologists are no exception. Currently, missiologists are "having a ball" with the word "contextualization." In the first place, they sometimes make it appear that contextualization endeavors began with the coinage of the word in the early 1970s. Actually, the endeavor is as old as missionizing activity. Secondly, they sometimes define the word so as to *prescribe what should happen* in the contextualization process rather than to *describe what actually is happening*. Of course, it is incumbent upon us to establish criteria for legitimate and effective contextualization. But this can only be done by critical analysis and evaluation; it cannot be done simply by definition. Thirdly, the subject of contextualization is often treated as though it were solely a Christian concern. In reality, it is a concern of all communicators—and particularly cross-cultural communicators. Therefore, to disregard the insights of such theorists as Ludwig Wittgenstein,[5] I. A. Richards,[6] Kenneth Burke,[7] and Robert Oliver[8]—to name but a few—is a mistake. Likewise, to disregard non-Christian representatives who contextualize their respective faiths with a view to communicating them across cultures is self-defeating parochialism.

It would be most helpful to begin our discussion with a consideration of the secular theorists on related subjects, but time and space preclude all but a few references to their conclusions. Nonetheless, our present considerations are inclusive of a variety of contextualization materials—theoretical and practical, linguistic and nonlinguistic, legitimate and illegitimate. Accordingly, we will opt for an inclusive working definition: "Contextualization is the process whereby representatives of a religious faith adapt the forms and content of that faith in such a way as to communicate and (usually) commend it to the minds and hearts of a new generation within their own changing culture or to people with other cultural backgrounds."

In this very broad sense, and with special reference to the Christian message and mission in the world, contextualization is primarily undertaken in six areas with respect to any given culture or subculture: the translation of the Scriptures, the interpretation of the Scriptures, the communication of the gospel, the instruction of believers, the incarnation of truth in the individual and corporate lives of believers, and the systemazation of the Christian faith (theologizing).

In this monograph our special focus will be on the epistemic pre-understandings that undergird the contextualization of the religious writings that have the status of Scripture. In regard to this focus and my procedure I would like to make three points.

First, by limiting our discussion to a type of special revelation I do not imply that general revelation is unimportant. The Bible, our consciences, and our missionary experiences all attest to the presence and importance of general revelation. But the task of contextualization as we have come to know it fundamentally relates to special written revelation—in the case of Christianity, to biblical revelation. A perusal of the works of even those Christian contextualizers who take a low view of the Bible will reveal how dependent they are on the biblical text—using or misusing it, as the case may be, in the development of their theses and theologies. Kenneth Hamilton, for example, concludes that "liberation theologies and kindred theologies . . . that seek to concretize salvation . . . are offering another salvation from one spoken in the Bible because they proclaim another God than the God and Father of our Lord Jesus Christ.[9] We must not infer from this that liberation theologians do not point to the

Bible, however. In his *A Theology of Liberation*, Gustavo Gutierrez includes 412 references to the Old and New Testaments![10]

Granted this kind of dependence upon the Bible in the case of even the more liberal Christian theologians and a corresponding dependence upon their respective scriptures on the part of non-Christian theologians, there can be little quarrel with our focus on special written revelation.

Second, I am concerned with epistemic pre-understandings for a personal reason. My own involvement, research, and contributions are primarily locatable in the area of cross-cultural communication.[11] But time without number as I come across contextualization proposals I am driven back to the subject of revelational epistemology. Epistemic pre-understandings impact with terrifying force upon gospel communication, determining in large measure both the message itself and the modes of its presentation. Time and time again I am impelled to examine the epistemological and revelational soil which nourish the larger contextualization tree. I want to know whether the soil, roots, trunk and branches are compatible with each other, or whether some ecclesiastical botanist has been shifting ground, planting strange trees, or grafting in new branches. Again and again I pull up short and stand incredulous before the maturing contextualization tree and wonder how Christian soil can nourish such strange fruit.

Third, of the six areas of contextualization mentioned above, those having to do most intimately with the text of scriptures—namely, translation and interpretation—are most crucial and therefore constitute a special concern. In these areas, epistemological presuppositions on the one hand, and cultural considerations on the other, intersect with remarkable intimacy. For example, as relates to Bible interpretation, H. G. Gadamer has argued that both the text and the interpreter (and, by extension, the contextualizer) are conditioned by their respective historical milieus.[12] "Two horizons" must therefore be kept in view. Anthony Thiselton regards "the issue behind Gadamer's formulation" so important for hermeneutics that he uses his imagery as the title for a book on the subject.[13] Thiselton goes on to say that to insist upon the importance of the interpreter's pre-understanding

> does not give grounds for the cynical response that the modern interpreter understands the Bible only on the basis of his own presuppositions. For there is (an ongoing) process of dialogue with the text in which the text itself progressively corrects and reshapes the interpreter's own questions and assumptions.[14]

In refusing to be "unduly pessimistic" about the effect of presuppositions, Thiselton is reflecting Gadamer's view that "tradition is not only a bridge between the past and the present, but also a filter which passes on interpretations and insights which have stood the test of time."[15] However, Thiselton's optimism assumes that the interpreter's pre-understanding encourages an attitude of responsiveness to the text and tradition! In cases where that is in fact true we can share his optimism. Be that as it may, there can be no doubt that pre-understandings are of paramount importance. Consequently, in the consideration of any attempt to interpret or contextualize scripture-based religious faith, one is inevitably driven to a consideration of the contextualizer's epistemic pre-understanding—how he views the scripture text with which he is working.

In accordance with the above, we will proceed as follows in this monograph. First, we will look at four genres of written revelation categorized on the basis of the kinds of authority adherents of the various religions have traditionally ascribed to their respective scriptures. Second, we will examine some primary characteristics and representative examples of non-Christian contextualization in an attempt to show how the epistemic pre-understandings affect these contextualization efforts. Third, we will consider approaches to contextualization being advocated by certain Christian spokesmen in an endeavor to show that truly Christian contextualization requires an evangelical orthodox epistemic pre-understanding. Finally, we will relate our findings to the doctrine of biblical inerrancy and state our conclusions.

I. GENRES OF WRITTEN REVELATION

As all will know, the holy books of the world's religions are extremely numerous and diverse. Their authors and apologists ascribe varying degrees of authority and authenticity to them; their adherents and interpreters hold to them with variant degrees of loyalty; and their opponents attack them from varying epistemological vantage points.

If, in the final analysis, the Bible is the holy book of Christianity and contextualization is undertaken in order to commend its message to the minds and hearts of the world's peoples, it is imperative that we understand more than the Christian message and the larger cultural milieus into which it is to be sent. We must also give consideration—deep consideration—to the revelational roots of the source and receptor traditions. As Eric Sharpe says:

> For a full understanding of a religious tradition, it is necessary to view Holy Scripture in the light of the totality of that tradition. It is, of course, important to know what a written source meant to the writer, and what was the precise message which it was originally intended to convey, but it is equally important to study traditions of scriptural interpretation. So while on the one hand the student will ideally use all the tools of Western scholarship to establish original texts and to collate variant readings, he must on the other hand attempt to read with the eye of the faithful and to treat, say, the Bhagavad Gita, the Qur'an or the Gospel of John as representing divine revelation. And since virtually all scripture is understood in revelatory terms . . . there must be some prior understanding of Hindu, Jewish, Christian, Muslim and other doctrines of God and doctrines of revelation.[16]

Depending upon what Sharpe means by "reading with the eye of the faithful" and treating the Gita and Qur'an as "representing divine revelation" he seems to be saying more than we would want to say. But he is at least saying as much as we want to say. Namely, that if we are to understand a religious tradition (the receptor religious context) we must know its god (or gods) and its sacred scripture—not just the scripture text but how that scripture is viewed (the doctrine of revelation). Contextualization attempts and analyses that do not take this into account are not only ill-advised, they may well be illegitimate.

This is true for at least two reasons. First, as Sharpe implies, we cannot understand the people of a respondent culture until we understand any attempt at contextualization must of necessity be inadequate. Second, attention to the scriptures of the respondent culture provides a point of reference for the study of what we might call "comparative contextualization"—the inquiry into questions having to do with the demands that the scriptures of the various religious traditions make upon contextualizers, and the relationship between types of revelation and contextualization. Apart from this kind of inquiry any analysis of contextualization must be deficient in the nature of the case.

Sharpe is correct when he says that, generally speaking, scriptural revelation is present in all faiths. In speaking of Judaism, Christianity and Islam as "revealed" religions we use the term "revealed" in a narrow sense as referring to "the self-communication of the supernatural to chosen individuals or groups."[17] Here the divine reality is personal and there is a certain definiteness about the channels and products of divine revelation.[18] (Of course, there are significantly different understandings even within these faiths and to some of these differences we will turn later.) When we categorize religions according to this narrow definition of revelation, however, we imply that the other great religions are necessarily "non-revealed religions." To this implication they can be expected to object since they too claim to have a body of divine truth even though they may believe that the "divine" goes beyond personhood and that the "truth" is not so circumscribed as to channel or product. For present purposes, therefore, we include non-theistic religious systems and non-self-communicational types of relation within our purview.

A. "Myth" as a Genre of Special Revelation

We may think of myths as phantasmagoric narratives thought to convey basic information about god(s), the world and men which bind a people together in a common origin, loyalty and destiny. In modern as in ancient times, however, mythical language has been viewed differently by various peoples. Generally speaking, we may say that moderns divide into rationalists and existentialists as regards their views of mythical language. Rationalists—Spinoza, Hobbs, and Jung among the philosophers, and Tylor, Lang, Marrett and Frazer among comparative religionists—have tended to understand myths as erroneous interpretations of nature and natural phenomena. Intuitionalists (Heyne and Herder, and more recently Cassirer and Schelling) understand mythical language as growing out of inner states—generally as a function of the faculty of intuition. Herder also suggested that myths are created more by the genius of nations (*volksgeist*) than by the genius of individuals, and this sociological interpretation has been adopted by Voltaire, Comte and Durkheim.

Whether myth is understood as the aberrant product of intellect or the creative product of intuition, myths do command the loyalty of individuals and societies. Moreover, *to the people who hold to them*, they usually represent something more than the product of mere intelligence or intuition. They represent the truth as revealed by god(s) or, at least, by revered ancestors who occupy a status that is almost divine. They may be handed down orally from generation to generation and never reduced to writing. Or, they may be "inscripturated" at some point in time or over a period of time. In any case, for those who hold to them, they come with the force of divine revelation.

A classic case of such a myth—and one with which all will be acquainted—is that of the ancient Yamato people of Japan which became the basis of Shinto and ultimately of Imperial Japan. To avoid being cut off from their roots by the incursion of foreign ideas and faiths (particularly the Buddhist faith) the ancient Japanese committed the Yamato myth to writing in the Kojiki and Nihongi (primarily) by the middle of the eighth century. For over a millennium and in spite of the vicissitudes and vagaries of history, this aetiological myth has provided the foundation for Japanese nationalism.

The Kojiki and Nihongi purport to be historical and to trace the origins of Japan and its people right back to the gods. Every reputable scholar recognizes that these books present pseudo-history. And no conscientious person would make a serious attempt to defend either the existence or character of the numerous capricious and cavorting deities therein presented. Certainly these books do not constitute a basis of study or meditation on the part of the overwhelming majority of the Japanese people. Nevertheless, the Shinto myth which they contain has conferred a divine authority on a religio-sociopolitical system that has commanded the total allegiance of millions of Japanese in our own day.

B. "The Writings of the Enlightened" as a Genre of Special Revelation

In Hinduism we encounter a different understanding. A very inclusivistic religion, Hinduism has been able to encompass a wide variety of deities, sacred books, and religious expressions. If there are any basic epistemological commitments that run through this extensive divergency, however, they are: (1) the knowledge of Ultimate Reality comes in the experience of *moksha* (enlightenment); and (2) the highest written authority is that of the Vedic literature.

To briefly expand upon this, Hinduism admits to two types of knowledge—primary and secondary. Primary knowledge accrues to the enlightenment experience alone. All other knowledge—including both the theological and scientific varieties—is secondary knowledge. The Hindu scriptures are also divided into two types: *shruti* ("that which is heard" or "revelation"); and, *smriti* ("that which is remembered" or "tradition"). Strictly speakig, the Vedas alone come into the *shruti* category though brahmanical (priestly) and upanishadic (philosophical) appendages are usually included as a matter of course. *Smriti* literature is a voluminous and ever-expanding corpus.

Although the Vedas have always held a unique place in Hindu literature, there has been some disagreement as to how they are divinely authenticated. A minority believe that the Vedas were communicated directly by the great lord of the universe who, for this purpose, is considered to be personal. They recognize the need for this kind of authority, but, generally speaking, they do not offer an historical frame of reference for the Vedas nor do they put forward objective proofs for their position.

Philosophically inclined Hindus have recognized the weakness of the above position while nevertheless realizing that the authority of the Vedas requires some explanation. They think of eternal ideas of Reality as resounding in the highest spheres of the universe. Highly spiritual, disciplined *rishis* (sages) of old were translated into these higher spheres where they could "hear" (directly intuit) these truths. They then conveyed them to posterity in the words of the Vedas. *Shruti* depends on direct perception of the kind experienced by these unidentified *rishis* of long ago. With a greater or lesser degree of sophistication, this is the view held by the majority of Hindus.

In sum, for most Hindus primary knowledge is attainable only in the enlightenment experience. The experience itself being ineffable, any propositional report—no matter how genuine and authentic—comprises and conveys secondary knowledge only. The Vedas are accorded a special authority in this scheme of things because they report the experiences of the earliest *rishis* and therefore are the most normative. Nevertheless, even they can do no more than aid readers and hearers in the quest for experiential knowledge of the Reality behind the phenomenal world.

Buddhism furnishes us with more scriptures of this genre, but they also grow out of the Indian tradition. For another example, turn rather to a very different religious stream, that of China. Sinologists are not in agreement as to whether or not Laotzu existed and, if he did, when he lived. Like Homer, he may have been a composite of the insights of later men. But he, or they, had a vision of reality that has helped to shape the lives of multiplied millions of Chinese down through history.

Unlike Confucius who was a bibliographer and collected ancient wisdom, Laotzu caught a vision of the Tao in nature. Discouraged by the decadence of his native state of Cheu, he prophesied its decay. As a consequence he had to leave, but he was met at the border by an officer with the name of Yin-hi who asked him to write down his teaching. The result was the *Tao-Teh-King*, a short book of about 5000 characters. Max Stilson says that some of its statements are "easy to understand, some are hard to understand, and some are impossible to understand."[19] That assessment would not have disturbed Laotzu because he knew that the wisdom men need could be but dimly reflected in the propositions of a book—even his own book. It must be experienced directly. And it is ineffable. That is why he was reluctant to write down his teachings in the first place. And that is why when he did write them down he wrote, "The one who knows does not speak; the one who speaks does not know."[20]

C. "Divine Writing" as a Genre of Special Revelation

Orthodox Muslims recognize two types of inspiration—*ilham* or "lower level" inspiration and *wahy* or "higher level" inspiration.[21] It is widely believed that the *ilham* type of inspiration may be experienced by holy men as well as prophets. It is a gift of Allah which accords knowledge to men, but it is subjective and cannot be trusted fully.

Wahy, on the other hand, confers knowledge that is objective and fully trustworthy. It comes directly from Allah through true prophets. The inspired messages of prophets antedating Muhammad which came in this category were corrupted. Therefore, the Qur'an alone fully qualifies today as being the product of *wahy*-type inspiration and as possessing infallible authority. W. Montgomery Watt says that the absolutely essential features of Muhammad's *wahy* experience are three: "the words in his conscious mind; *the absence of his own thinking*; and the belief that the words were from God" (italics mine).[22]

It is important to recall that orthodox Muslims consider the Qur'an to be a partial reproduction of an eternal original called the "Well Preserved Tablet" or "Mother of the Book" which is in heaven. The reverence that Muslims entertain for the prophet Muhammad is not simply attributable to Muhammad's personality, character or gifts as such (though they would not impune any of these). The unprecedented importance of Muhammad rests in the faith that Allah delivered his message to the prophet by an angelic messenger (usually said to have been Gabriel) over a period of time and subsequent to his prophetic call.[23] Allah had already spoken through a number of prophets, but in revealing his word to Muhammad he gave his final word. Note that. It was Allah's word. Muhammad was a passive receptor and recorder. His mind, heart, feelings—none of these entered into the recording of the words of the Qur'an. It is the eternal, uncreated word of Allah which has existed through all time as an expression of his will. Furthermore, in view of the distortions which had overtaken his previous revelations Allah undertook to insure this final revelation against distortion for all time to come.

This understanding lies at the very heart of the Muslim attitude toward the Qur'anic scriptures. In the first place, the Qur'an is the undisputed and supreme authority in Muslim law and theology, faith and practice. Secondly, it is on the heart, mind and tongue of millions of Muslims who have memorized it, at least in part. Thirdly, the Qur'an has traditionally been held as being untranslatable—the very Arabic words being the words of heaven and therefore divine in their very sound and rhythm.

D. "Inspired Writings" as a Genre of Special Revelation

All will be aware of the fact that Christians characteristically speak of the Old and New Testament Scriptures as being the "inspired Word of God." This appellation grows out of the King James rendering of the Greek adjective *theopneustos* in 2 Timothy 3:16. As B. B. Warfield pointed out a number of years ago, the word really means "breathed out by God."[24] In context the reference is specifically to the written word of the Old Testament. But by extension it is applied to the New Testament as well.

As Warfield was careful to point out (with special reference to the New Testament authors), inspiration in this sense does not have reference to the psychological state—or even the spiritual state—of the human writers as such, but rather refers to the activity of God whereby He "breathed out" His Word through the biblical authors. It is obvious that in this process God did not discount the personality, background, experience, or research of the authors. Nevertheless, all of these human elements were divinely employed in such a way that the end product is more than the word of the author—it is also, and in an even more profound sense, the Word of God. This claim is everywhere made in Scripture and is made most incontrovertibly and arrestingly by our Lord Himself. What Scripture says, God says. When men hear the words of Scripture they hear the Word of God. Of course, a further work of the Holy Spirit is necessary for them to perceive and receive it as the Word of God. The Westminster Shorter Catechism refers to this as "effectual calling."[25] Nevertheless, the Bible does not *become* the Word of God when hearers are called; it became the Word of God when its authors were "in-spired" to write it.

We must insist that this is not the understanding of the Bible and our Lord Christ alone. It is the traditional understanding of the

Christian Church regarding the nature of the revelation which we have in the Holy Scriptures. Not a few writers have disputed this—most recently Jack Rogers and Donald McKim in their book *The Authority and Interpretation of the Bible: An Historical Approach.*[26] Rogers and McKim assert that the authority of the Scripture does not stem from its form or words but rather from Christ and his message to which the words point. They further insist that this is the historic position of the Church regarding Scripture from the time of the Church fathers such as Origen and Augustine up to and including the great reformers such as Luther and Calvin. As John Woodbridge has shown, however, Rogers and McKim have carefully managed the evidence in such a way as to reinforce their own position. Woodbridge demonstrates conclusively that the notion that biblical authority relates to the very words of Scripture is not the invention of post-Reformation European theologians and nineteenth-century Princetonians. It was the view of many of the fathers and reformers to whom Rogers and McKim make reference![27]

II. NON-CHRISTIAN CONTEXTUALIZATION

In the light of the foregoing to state that contextualization attempts can be expected to reflect the genre of written revelation with which it is concerned is to state the obvious. Rather than argue the point, therefore, we will illustrate it—first in the products of non-Christian contextualization and, later, in those of Christians.

A. The Contextualization of Myth

Within the genre of myth one is at a loss to find parameters which contextualization attempts could not legitimately cross. After all, though the myth may include some historical data, it characteristically will reach far beyond history into fantasy with little or no regard to the difference. While the myth may contain something of truth, it characteristically will mix truth and falsehood without providing criteria for distinguishing between them. In short, whatever claims may be made for a myth by the people who hold to it, the myth itself neither demands, nor lends itself to, the kind of critical analysis that leads unbiased minds to accept its genuineness and authenticity.

The only impingements that bear upon the contextualization of a myth, therefore, are brought to the myth by the pre-understanding, ethic, and imagination of the contextualizer himself. The myth provides the basic raw materials for contextualization—the symbols, the *leitmotiv*, the *dramatis personae*—and, of course, these are somewhat limited in quantity and kind. But the only other limitations are those imposed by the contextualizer—what he *can* do with the given materials and what he *will* do with them. He will be praised or blamed largely on bases extrinsic to the myth itself.

As an illustration of non-Christian contextualization within this genre, look again at the Japanese case. Just as many untutored Japanese have thought of their icons as deities while others have thought of them as symbols of the deities, so some have taken the myth of the Kojiki and Nihongi literally while others have taken it symbolically. But the important thing is that at critical stages in the history of Japan the myth has been made to fit the particular mentality of the people and the purposes of their leaders by well-constructed and effective presentments. We may confidently call this "Shinto contextualization."

One such notable attempt occurred at the time of the Meiji Restoration in the late nineteenth century when Japan turned its back upon feudalism, reinstated the emperor, established a parliamentary form of government and sent out government-sponsored propagandists to reinforce the new system. At the base of their message was the Yamato cosmogonic myth. Holtom explains,

> The center of the world is the Eight Great Islands of the Japanese archipelago. The lands that they loved and knew constituted the real universe to the early mythmakers. The islands were brought into being by the creative purposes of the gods and are the direct offspring of the union of Izanagi and Izanami, the sky-father and the earth-mother. Hirata Atsutane, the early nineteenth-century theologian of Shinto, merely gave expression to a typical conception when he declared that the Japanese islands were produced first by the greatest of the ancestral *kami* [gods] and that the inferiority of the rest of the world was indicated by the fact that it was produced later out of seafoam and mud.[28]

But the case with which most of us are best acquainted would undoubtedly be that monumentally successful effort on the part of the militaristic government of Japan in the 1930s and early 1940s to convince the Japanese of the validity of this same myth and its implications. Namely, that their divinely-ordained destiny was to share the beneficent rule of the *Tenno Heika* (Heavenly Emperor) with the rest of the world. There were two major aspects of that endeavor—persuasion and, when that failed, coercion. The fact that hundreds of thousands of Japanese willingly gave their lives, and millions of others stood ready to give their lives, attests to the fact that the persuasion attempt was enormously effective.

How did the militarists convince highly literate and intelligent Japanese of the validity of the phantasmagoric myth such as that which is unfolded in the Kojiki and Hihongi (as summarized above)? Not by marshalling evidence for the historicity of the text. Of course not. Such an undertaking—if it betrayed any kind of objectivity—was likely to be met with government opprobrium and opposition.[29] Not by undertaking a new translation designed to convey the meaning of the texts with more accuracy and contemporaneity. Of course not. The ambiguity and inaccessibility of the language of the texts constituted an advantage. No, let the texts be as products of their time and place. As D. C. Holtom makes abundantly clear, the ancient texts simply provided the symbols out of which a very "contemporary" faith could be constructed. Holtom says,

> We find, then, that, in order to understand modern Japan and her significant trends, we must deal first and foremost with a highly successful, rigorously centralized, religiously founded educational program whereby the national mentality is fixed in terms of forms that are governmentally expedient and necessary to military control. But these forms are not arbitrarily manufactured out of makeshift materials in the social and political life. They have come down out of an ancient past, they are erected on literary foundations that have the sanctity of holy scripture, and they survive as almost instinctive elements in the folkways. In all this we come to recognize that the center of that ethical certitude that stands so firmly in the midst of the storm of Far Eastern politics is lodged in the conviction of the possession as a race of unique divine attributes, of a peerless national structure, and of a sacred commission to save the world.[30]

Such was the case. It was a case of Shinto contextualization" par excellence!

B. The Contextualization of the "Writings of the Enlightened"

This genre has been contextualized quite differently. Since the report and teachings of enlightened persons are involved, textual criticism becomes more important than is the case with myth, but not as important as in the cases of the other two genres. After all, if a given text purports to contain the teachings of an inspired seer who "experienced truth," it is to be expected that the reader will want to know: (1) if whether or not it is the seer who spoke (or wrote), and (2) whether or not this is what the seer said (or wrote).

One does not proceed very far in his studies of scriptures of this type, however, before he discovers that, though adherents do address themselves to authorship and textual questions, these questions are not of the essence. Why? Because the overriding purpose of such writings is not so much to provide objective, authoritative knowledge as to assist the adept in attaining his own authoritative enlightened experiences. In a very real sense, the validity of the text, therefore, depends more upon its utility, effect and impact than upon its genuineness. Indeed, to place *too much* confidence in the teachings of the enlightened (or even on the enlightened teacher!) betrays one's ignorance of the true source of knowledge.

Contextualizers of writings of this sort, therefore, may and do exercise a considerable freedom both in translation and interpretation of the text. Form is not crucial. Both the purpose and the proof of the contextualized pudding are to be found in the eating of it. Indeed, the "revelatory corpus" is neither final nor closed. Experiencing enlightenment, the interpreter or contextualizer may translate and interpret existing texts in the light of his own experience or even offer his own teachings as "divine."

Consider two examples. One from the Indian (Hindu) tradition and one from the Chinese (Taoist) tradition.

Swami Prabhavananda and Frederick Manchester offer an introduction and translation of the Upanishads for Westerners in *The Upanishads: Breath of the Eternal*, copyrighted by the Vedanta Society of Southern California.[31] In the introduction, they point out the importance of the Vedas: "All orthodox Hindus recognize in them the origin of their faith and its highest written authority."[32] Then they explain that there are four Vedas, each of which is divided into two parts: Work and Knowledge.

> The first is mainly made up of hymns, instructions regarding rites and ceremonies, and rules of conduct. The second is concerned with knowledge of God, the highest aspect of religious truth, and is called—Upanishads.[33]

Next they proceed to explain how they selected 12 Upanishads out of an extant 108; the characteristics of the Upanishads; the necessity of a *guru* for the study of the Vedas; and the type of authority to be found in the Vedas:

> We have said that the orthodox Hindu regards the Vedas as his highest written authority. Any subsequent scripture, if he is to regard it as valid, must be in agreement with them: it may expand upon them, it may develop them, and still be recognized, but it must not contradict them. They are to him, as nearly as any human document can be, the expression of divine truth. At the same time it would be a mistake to suppose that his allegiance to their authority is slavish or blind. If he considers them the word of God, it is because he believes their truth to be verifiable, immediately, at any moment, in his own personal experience. If he found on due examination that it was not so verifiable, he would reject it. And in this position the scriptures, he will tell you, uphold him. The real study, say the Upanishads, is not study of themselves but study of that "by which we realize the changeless." In other words, the real study in religion is firsthand experience of God.
>
> Indeed the term Vedas, as used by the orthodox, not only names a large body of texts handed down by generation after generation, but in another sense stands for nothing less than the inexpressible truth of which all scriptures are of necessity a pale reflection. Regarded in this second aspect, the Vedas are infinite and eternal. They are that perfect knowledge which is God.[34]

Prabhavananda and Manchester approach this task of translation in a manner that is entirely consistent with this epistemic pre-understanding. They "allow themselves the freedom" as "seems desirable" to convey the "sense and spirit" of the original in English. Though the original Sanskrit is verse, they render it in prose, except in some special instances where they use "a form which is not verse perhaps, save by courtesy, but *which has seemed to us to produce a heightened effect not readily attained in prose*" (italics mine).[35] This, I maintain, is not only permissible, but commendable within this genre. The form is relatively *unimportant*. The "sense and spirit" are *very important*. Why? Because the impact, the effect, the result of reading and study in the experiences of the reader are *all-important*.

Representatives of this genre of revelational epistemology are so numerous and come clothed in so many religious habits that it would be well to consider another example—this time from someone of the Taoist persuasion. Over half a century ago Dwight Goddard attempted a translation and Henri Borel an interpretation of Laotzu's Tao-Teh-

King.[36] Goddard's introduction is highly interesting. He says that he loves Laotzu and wants his readers to love him. He says that Laotzu was "perhaps the first of scholars (6th century B.C.) to have a vision of spiritual reality. . . ."[37] He decries scholarship that questions Laotzu's existence and the genuineness of the text of the Tao-Teh-King (a considerable number of scholars!) with the words "Shame on scholarship when, sharing the visions of the illuminati they deride them!"[38]

Regarding the Tao-Teh-King itself, Goddard says that Chinese ideographs are "ill-adapted to express mystical and abstract ideas."[39] He insists that Sinologues, by their very scholarship, have done the book an injustice because they have stayed too close to the text. Then he writes, "I have tried to peer through the clumsy characters into his [Laotzu's] heart and prayed that love for him would make me wise to understand aright."[40] Accordingly he admonishes his readers,

> As you read these verses, forget the words and phrases, poor material and poor workmanship at best, look through them for the soul of Laotzu. It is there revealed, but so imperfectly that it is only an apparition of a soul. But if by it, vague as it is, you come to love Laotzu, you will catch beyond him fleeting glimpses of the splendid visions that so possessed his soul, visions of Infinite Goodness, Humility and Beauty radiating from the Heart of creation.[41]

If these examples are at all representative of contextualization of the "writings of the enlightened" genre of revelational epistemology as I believe them to be, we certainly should be able to appreciate their approach for it is entirely compatible with the genre. After all, even the autographs of the texts with which they are dealing could be no more than "inciters" of enlightening experiences. "Correctness" of translation (Goddard's word) at the expense of impact would be a bad tradeoff. The overriding concern must be to reproduce the experience of the *rishis,* the illuminati, the sages, and the seers in contemporary "seekers of the vision." Accordingly, good teachers (translators, interpreters, communicators) will aim for this.

C. The Contextualization of the "Divine Writing" Genre

Islamic contextualizers have a very different sort of problem. After all, what does one do—what *can* one do—with a book that is "made in heaven" and that admits of no human element? A book written, so to speak, in the "language of God"? Consistency here demands that the book be delivered, interpreted, preached, and taught—but not translated. And as we know, this has been the traditional position of Islam: the Koran translated into another language is not really the Koran. In a sense, all inquirers into the faith must themselves become "contextualizers." They must learn the Arabic language and culture! As Islam has come to rely less on power and more on persuasion to propagate the faith, of course, practicality has demanded translations. Nevertheless, translators sympathetic to Islam reflect a loyalty to the Arabic text that is unmistakably characteristic of the genre.

A. J. Arberry who has provided us with one of the most popular of these translations, writes nostalgically of his past when he heard the Koran recited in Egypt. He says that during the months of translations,

> I have been reliving those Ramadan nights of long ago, when I would sit on the veranda of my Gezira house and listen entranced to the old, white-bearded Skeykh who chanted the Koran for the pious delectation of my neighbour. He had the misfortune, my neighbour, to be a prominent politician, and so in the fullness of his destiny, but not the fullness of his years, he fell to an assassin's bullet; I like to think that the merit of those holy recitations may have eased the way for him into a world free of the tumult and turbulence that attended his earthly career. It was then that I, the infidel, learnt to understand and react to the thrilling rhythms of the Koran, only to be apprehended when listened to at such a time and in such a place. In humble thankfulness I dedicate this all too imperfect essay in imitation to the memory of those magical Egyptian nights.[42]

Arberry writes as though he possessed an inner compulsion to bring the Koran and its message to his English-speaking contemporaries. He concedes that the Koran is untranslatable. Granted "the rhetoric and rhythm of the Arabic," he says that "any version is bound to be a poor copy of the glittering splendour of the original."[43] He says that his chief reason for attempting a new "translation" is that no "serious attempt has previously been made to imitate, however imperfectly, those rhetorical and rhythmical patterns which are the glory and sublimity of the Koran."[44] Though an "infidel," Arberry seems to exude a disciple's passion and a missionary zeal when he explains what he means and what he has set out to accomplish.

> There is a repertory of familiar themes running through the whole Koran; each Sura elaborates or adumbrates one or more—often many—of these. Using the language of music, each Sura

> is a rhapsody composed of whole or fragmentary *leitmotivs*; the analogy if reinforced by the subtly varied rhythmical flow of the discourse. If this diagnosis of the literary structure of the Koran may be accepted as true—and it accords with what we know of the poetical instinct, indeed the whole aesthetic impulse, of the Arabs—it follows that those notorious incongruities and irrelevancies, even those 'wearisome repetitions', which have proved such stumbling-blocks in the way of our Western appreciation will vanish in the light of a clearer understanding of the nature of the Muslim scriptures. A new vista opens up; following this hitherto unsuspected and unexplored path, the eager interpreter hurries forward upon an exciting journey of discovery, and is impatient to report his findings to a largely indifferent and incredulous public.[45]

All of this accords well with what we know about the people, religion, and language of Arabia in Muhammad's day. In pre-Islamic Arabia, the *kahins* (pagan priests) regularly gave oracles in rhythmed prose that were similar in form and content to the Koran, especially the earlier suras. The form of Muhammad's pronouncements, therefore, were of special significance to his earliest hearers and have remained so down to the present day.[46]

Wilfred Cantwell Smith's assessment is that Arberry's work is "certainly the most beautiful English version, and among those by non-Muslim translators the one that comes closest to conveying the impression made on Muslims by the original."[47] It is highly significant that Arberry has accomplished this by giving close attention to the literary *form* of the Koran, and that he is content to call his work an "interpretation."

III. THE CONTEXTUALIZATION OF THE BIBLE

To a degree unmatched by the adherents of any other faith, as Christians we should rightly be concerned not only about the "two horizons," but also about the "double vision" which sees both the integrity and uniqueness of the text of our sacred Book, and also the importance of the task of contextualizing its message for the "unreached" people of post- and pre-Christian cultures. To the extent that one is both concerned and informed, however, this double vision results in a terrible tension. On the one hand, there is the Book, unique in its message and authority, authored by divinely-inspired authors far removed from us historically and culturally. We must be faithful to that sacred text with all that faithfulness requires. On the other hand, there are the people, desperate in their need of the Word of God, also separated from us religiously and culturally. We must be faithful to our commission to disciple these people, with all that faithfulness requires. Knowledge coupled with concern, therefore, results in what we might term the "tension of the double vision."

With this in mind, we should not impugn the motives of those who undertake either to protect the integrity of the text or to contextualize its message. God must be the judge of all such endeavors. At the same time, we must constantly inspect the pre-understandings and methods which are employed. To lean too far in one direction from a truly Christian (biblical) epistemic pre-understanding may lead to syncretism. To lean too far in the other direction may lead to sterility.

Let us see how this is so.

A. Demythologization and Christian Contextualization

Various meanings have been assigned to the word "myth" by proponents of demythologization. Paul Tillich says that "Myths are symbols of faith combined in stories about divine-human encounters."[48] Rudolf Bultmann defines myth in several ways which some critics say may not be entirely consistent with each other. In one meaning myth has to do with speaking about the other world in this-world terms. In another meaning it explains unusual phenomena in terms of the invasion of the supernatural. In still another sense, myth has as its purpose an objective description of the world.[49] My own assessment is that, unless these definitions are pressed too far, they are not only compatible with each other but are also compatible with the definition proposed earlier in this monograph. At least, they are all recognizable as members of the same family.

Both Bultmann and Tillich are attempting to update the message of the Bible in such a way as to make it possible for twentieth-century man to believe while maintaining his integrity. In this attempt Bultmann takes issue with a liberalism which simply reduces the number of items that must be believed in order to be a Christian. He feels that wholesale rejection of Scripture militates against the kind of hard decision which Christianity requires. Among other things, myth implies the pre-scientific world view of the Gospels. He writes, "To demythologize is to reject not scripture . . . but the world-view of scripture, which is the world-view of a past epoch." By separating out the myth, "it will eliminate a false stumbling block and bring into focus the real stumbling-block, the word of the cross."[50]

But if Bultmann parts company with the liberal interpretation of the faith, he also parts company with the literal interpretation of the text because it turns out that the "word of the cross" is not to be "objectified." The notion of a god becoming man and dying for his fellows is part and parcel of primitive mythology. It is part of the old pre-scientific world view. Bultmann says,

> To believe in the cross of Christ does not mean to concern ourselves with a mythical process wrought outside of us and our world, with an objective event turned by God to our advantage, but rather to make the cross of Christ our own, to undergo crucifixion with him.[51]

Not the death of Jesus on the cross, but the hearing of the gospel story to which it is central, "saves" a man. It does so by calling him to an awareness of his own enslavement to the powers of the world and to a new life of spontaneity and freedom from that tyranny. It is this "change of existence" that the New Testament calls "atonement."

For Paul Tillich, as we have said, myths are "stories of the gods" uniting the "symbols of faith." Myth is not confined to polytheistic religions. It is also characteristic of the monotheistic religions. That is why Bultmann and others can talk about demythologization. Tillich accepts the term if it is taken to mean recognition of "a symbol as a symbol and a myth as a myth." But he rejects it if it is taken to mean "the removal of symbols and myths altogether."[52] When a myth is understood as a myth and its symbolic character is revealed, the myth is "broken." Christianity is a religion of "broken myths." But note that these myths—whether biblical, doctrinal or liturgical—are not to be dispensed with because there can be no substitute for symbols and myths. They constitute the "language of faith."

During his later years especially, Tillich became interested in the history of religions and in interreligious dialogue. In a most friendly way, he was critical of the theology of his older colleague, Adolph Harnack, who "narrowed down his own constructive theology to a kind of high bourgeois, individualistic, moral theology."[53] He thanked Mircea Eliade who, from the perspective of the history of religion, introduced him to a "new intensity of meaning" in the doctrines and rituals of Christianity.[54] And he half-apologized for his own *Systematic Theology* which he said was written to answer the "questions coming from the scientific and philosphical criticism of

Christianity."[55] I remember Tillich saying in 1960 that if he had it to do over again he would rewrite his theology from the perspective of the history of religion—a method which he contrasted with the methods of supranatural theology and natural theology in his "The Significance of the History of Religions for the Systematic Theologian."[56] There he talks about gaining new understandings of religious symbols by studying them in the social matrices in which they developed in order to reintroduce them today.

If my readers will forgive the personal references, I have entertained an intense interest in Tillich's methodology and conclusions because I attended a series of lectures which he gave at the Kyoto and Doshisha universities in Kyoto, Japan during the spring of 1960. I have no doubt that the lectures were carefully prepared and delivered with the educated of Shinto, Buddhist and other religious persuasions in view. Moreover, they came very late in Tillich's career. We will make no mistake, therefore, in taking one of these lectures as an example of contextualization by demythologization or, as Tillich preferred to call it, "deliteralizing the myth." I choose the lecture "Religious Symbols"—the one for which I have the most copious notes. Even at that they are incomplete and for that also I apologize. But I am quite confident that they substantially convey what Professor Tillich said. Of course, their correctness can be checked indirectly because even though the lecture was not published, (as far as I know) my notes seem to be entirely consistent with what he has written elsewhere.

The primary points made in the lecture as I recorded it were as follows: Introduction:

> *Religion* is the state of being ultimately concerned about the ultimate.
>
> A *symbol* is a word or thing expressing something outside the thing being explained. *Signs* simply point but could be different if the circumstances were different. But in symbolism there is mutual participation. This I call "relation of participation," e.g., the sculpture and God which it represents are somehow in each other. Another difference is that the symbol opens up a dimension of reality that cannot be reached in any other way. It also opens up our inner self to the reality. Thirdly, signs are invented for expediency. Symbols are born in the inner need of man and exist as long as there is a community to which they

have meaning. The history of religions is a cemetery of dead symbols and a fertile field for new ones.

Art and religion are realms where symbols are all we have for communication. Religious symbols have a relational character. Any statement without an existential aspect is not religious. All religious statements are existential, i.e., they concern our existence in its totality. If not, they belong to science or another discipline. If in theology they do not have this character they are only a preparation for a truly religious approach.

Today we will deal with three main symbols of Christianity.

I. Creation from Nothing

This has nothing to do with an event 6000 or 5 million years ago. Rather it is as related to the past or future, a part of the raw material with which we express our finitude—from earth and to earth—in the present. To express this we say we were created in the past and have a consummation in the future.

A. We are creatures. We are not by ourselves, but are dependent on the Ground of our Being. Therefore our ultimate concern.

B. There is the creature idea of substantial identity. The infinite demands participation with the finite and vice versa. This symbol excludes the possibility of identifying either one separately.

C. We are not surrendered to the naturalistic. We are always in the lap of the eternal from which we come and to which we go.

D. The world is good in as far as it is rooted in the Divine. God saw it and it was good. Evil results from humans acting freely or independently. In other religions we have different ideas of evil and cannot have salvation by the transformation of the finite but only by the annihilation of it.

II. Christ

I do not say Jesus Christ. The meaning of Christ is Messiah, i.e., the one who brought the new age, new hope, etc. Therefore the New Being. It is used of Jesus (a man who lived 2000 years ago) to convey the idea that this new hope began in Jesus in principle. That idea is supported by other symbols—Savior, Logos, Son of God, Lord, etc. Sometimes this story is put together in such a way as to form a myth of the coming of the Son of God to save the world. This is a myth—i.e., the putting together of symbols in such a way as to make them sound like an event. This is dangerous when done by primitive man; when done on top of thinking as by the fundamentalist, it is catastrophic. [Laughter] When someone puts you in a trap by asking "Is Christ the Son of God?" I always recommend to my students that they reply by asking what this means. Then the inquirer is in a trap. He cannot answer. But as for the myth, we need that. Therefore I told Bultmann that he should not say "demythologizing" but "de-literalizing the myth."

So Jesus is a historical event. The question of the historical Jesus has plagued men for centuries. The quest never comes to an end and results in a confession of ignorance. And yet many have realized that something happened as recorded in the N.T. that changes all reality. As a matter of fact, the unity of the non-symbolic in history and the symbolic as in the idea of Christ is fundamental. We cannot find the historical Jesus in certainty. Certainty comes only in participation. And here is the triumph of Protestantism—it has survived even the uncertainty of the historical quest.

I would like to add that Buddhism is not intimately related to a historical question. The question of what Siddhartha really said is not therefore an existential question. Buddhism is a mystical religion which is fundamentally different and results in philosophical questions. It is mainly the concern of scholars. Only recently and as a result of textual critical studies in Christianity has it tended to take on some existential aspects.

III. The Kingdom of God

It is absurd to use this idea non-symbolically, i.e., as though it were a fulfillment of history in history. But it is also wrong if thought of as a place of some ecstatic happiness. Every scientist can undercut these ideas. They also contradict our world experience which is not somewhere between heaven and hell. No, this is a childish idea, the fulfillment of dreams. Positively the Kingdom of God has various meanings:

A. As a socio-political symbol, it emphasizes the idea of a community built on love and justice. A return to the eternal where individual has eternal destiny though no one knows in what sense.
B. As a history-directed symbol, it means that in and through history a decisive event happens. The New is born. History itself is revelatory.
C. As a dynamic symbol, it fights in history, but win or lose it brings an ambiguous solution. The demonic is broken but not removed. We are no longer bound by evil—or need not be. We have a latent but not an ultimate power.
D. As an eschatological symbol, it means that time runs toward something new. In the present we are being created and can experience eternal of the past and future.

Tillich has explained something of his purpose in terms of the *telos* or inner aim of the history of religions. Namely, to become a "Religion of the Concrete Spirit."[57] This entails struggle against all tyrannies that war against us both within the historic religions and outside of them. The Holy provides a sacramental basis for life which is free from religious dogmas, ecclesiastical impositions, and a secularism that seeks to dominate the Holy. It involves a "theonomy" where the "autonomous forces of knowledge, of aesthetics, of law and morals point to the ultimate meaning of life."[58] It occurs in fragmentary ways in the history of religion, but its ultimate fulfillment is beyond time in eternity.

It is significant that Tillich was born and educated in a Germany that fathered Hitler's fascism; that he emigrated to an America which was the bastion of Christian fundamentalism; and that during his later years he was attracted to a Japan that had been wholly committed to Shinto chauvinism. His system evidences a reaction against all three. Of the tyrannies of fascism and chauvinism, his Japanese audience was well aware. As for fundamentalism, the only overt response he received from the very proper and staid audience that attended the lecture reviewed above was mild laughter when he said,

> Sometimes this story [the Gospel] is put together in such a way as to form a myth of the coming of the Son of God to save the world. This is a myth—the putting together of symbols in such a way as to make them sound like an event. This is dangerous when done by primitive man; when done on the top of thinking as by a fundamentalist, it is catastrophic.

In some ways, Tillich's presentation was brilliant. His Japanese audience must have been impressed by the reassurance that a "fundamentalistic interpretation" of the Bible is analogous to the discredited chauvinistic interpretation of the Kojiki; by the homeomorphic hermeneutics of Christianity and Japanese religion; and the existential and mystical emphases. At the same time, my readers will not be surprised to learn that the daughter of a prominent professor at Kyoto University who had been in my Bible class reacted to Tillich's lectures by becoming disinterested and dropping out of the studies. As far as I was able to learn she did not associate with any other Christian group.

When the Bible is understood as myth, the method of contextualization—whether done by an avowed Shintoist or a professing Christian—remains essentially the same. I do not say that scholars such as Bultmann and Tillich neglect or discourage textual studies. Certainly not. But I do say that they engage in them with the bias that says that, *in the nature of the case*, the text cannot be accepted as literally true. More than that, they make of the symbols what they will. *This hermeneutic*—not any responsible orthodox one—represents "Christian chauvinism." Far from freedom, the persuaders become victims of a tyranny that is as ominous as, and more subtle than, that proposed even by a Shinto chauvinist. I am reminded of a conversation concerning Tillich carried on years ago by one of my philosophy professors and Sidney Hook in which Hook reportedly said, in effect, "I like Tillich, but I have this against him. I am an agnostic and want to remain one. But he won't let me choose. He makes me a believer by definition!"

B. "Dynamic-Equivalence" and Contextualization

There is another and much less radical method of contextualization that has gained considerable attention. It is modeled after the dynamic equivalent approach to translation which has been so ably advanced in recent years by Eugene Nida of the American Bible Society and others. It has been developed most fully by Charles Kraft in his book *Christianity in Culture*.[59] In chapter thirteen of that work Kraft compares his understanding of formal-equivalence with that of dynamic-equivalence (as explained by Nida and Taber) by noting some of the characteristics of the two approaches (see chart on following page).[60]

Kraft believes that one of the greatest obstacles to the acceptance of Christianity by peoples of other cultures is its foreigners. In various writings he refers to his missionary experiences among the people of

Formal-Equivalence	*Dynamic-Equivalence*
1. Simply transfers word forms	1. Each language has its own genius
2. Attempts to render each word form by same term in receptor language	2. One must respect this uniqueness
3. Adheres to 19th century concepts of the nature of language	3. Anything said in one language can be represented adequately (though never exactly) in another unless the form is an essential element of the message as in poetry
	4. To preserve the content of message the form must be changed
	5. The language of the Bible is subject to the same limitations as other natural languages
	6. Writers of the biblical text expected to be understood
	7. The translator must attempt to reproduce the meaning of the passage as understood by the writer

Nigeria—of their questions concerning the Bible, of the mutuality of the search for answers, and of the excitement that attended the discovery of new understandings. Kraft combines a missionary heart with a disciplined mind. He wants the "apostolic faith" to flourish around the world. He calls for dynamic-equivalence "transculturation of the message," dynamic-equivalence theologizing and dynamic-equivalence churches. He calls upon cross-cultural Christian workers and Christian nationals to "transform culture with God."

Kraft believes that we are now prepared to accomplish these goals to an extent not possible previously, thanks to the sciences of cultural anthropology and linguistics. Bicultural anthropologists and linguists are better able than historians and philologists to appreciate and understand cultural forms, functions and meanings and therefore to interpret the Scripture and contextualize its message. The importance of the insights of anthropologists and linguists can hardly be overestimated. Thanks to these insights, we are now in a position to sort out the cultural and the supracultural; we can now go beyond grammatico-historical interpretations of the Scriptures to ethnolinguistic interpretation. And we can now communicate biblical Christianity to receptor cultures, rather than a Christianity encrusted with "Westernness." Of course, a risk is involved, but Kraft believes that the "Christianity of the New Testament is *not conservative but dynamic, adaptive, unafraid to risk* the old understandings . . ."[61]

In an article in the *Journal of the Evangelical Theological Society* entitled "Interpreting in Cultural Context"[62] Kraft backgrounds and demonstrates his approach. He defines meaning as "that which the receiver of a message constructs within his head and responds to."[63] He explains that all communication including interpretation is approximate and that "accuracy of interpretation is, therefore, a matter of coming to understand what is said or written within an allowable range."[64] He explains that the interpretational reflexes of all people are conditioned by their culture and that the "plain meaning" approach to Bible interpretation is, therefore, inadequate. But, by harnessing the perspectives of anthropology and linguistics "we can develop dynamic-equivalent translations and highly interpretive 'transculturations' of God's Word" thereby communicating God's message "in today's languages and cultures so that the members of these cultures will be able to trust their interpretational reflexes when they study the Scriptures."[65] Finally, he proposes a model for interpretation which is designed to help us sort out levels of abstraction and accomplish these transculturations.

To take one example of how this works, Kraft recalls the Nigerian church leader who asked why missionaries taught Nigerians to obey the command not to steal but ignored the command that prohibits women from praying with their heads uncovered.[66] Kraft does not think that he was able to provide a very good answer at the time but he believes that he could do so now.

The key to this new understanding is that in communication we (and the Bible) mix various levels of abstraction. In the Nigerian case before us we have two of these levels. "Do not steal" is a general command which is understood within all cultures and within a fairly narrow culturally-conditioned range. The headcovering command, however, is different. It leads to a command that requires different cultural forms depending on the culture. In Greek culture for the female to pray with her head uncovered probably would have been interpreted as "this woman is immoral" or "this woman does not have the proper respect for men." Paul therefore commanded that women not pray with their heads uncovered. In Nigeria and the United States the interpretation would be different. Kraft proposes that we recognize three levels of abstraction. The varying degree of abstraction of the two commands would then become apparent:[67]

1. Basic Ideal Level	2. General Principle Level	3. Specific Cultural Form/ Symbol Level
More General		More Specific
A. Love your neighbor as you love yourself (Matt. 22:39)	1. Do not steal (Exod. 20:17)	a. Do not take your neighbor's donkey (Hebrew)
		b. Do not take your employer's money (U.S.A.)
B. Everything must be done in a proper and orderly way (1 Cor. 14:40)	1. Christian women should not appear out of line	a. They should cover their head when praying (1 Cor. 11:10) (Greek culture)
		b. They should not wear their clothes too tight (U.S.A.)

The basic ideals tend to be similar in all cultures, but the specific culture forms and symbols by which those ideals are made meaningful may be very different from culture to culture.

Kraft does not tell us what the appropriate specific (i.e., low level abstraction) commands would be in Nigeria, but his method is clear. And for an application of the method to Nigeria one need only consult another Nigerian case which Kraft has discussed in at least three different contexts.[68] The case involves the qualifications for church leadership listed in 1 Timothy 3 as they would vary at the "specific cultural form/symbol level" in three cultures: Greco-Roman, American and Higi.

Basic to Kraft's solution to the problem of what qualifications should be required of church leaders in "Higiland" is the notion ("general principle"?) that in any given culture a church leader should have a good reputation in his community. That is the "function" behind the "church form" indicated in the Pauline list. If we want churches in Higiland which are dynamically equivalent to (have the same impact as) the New Testament churches in their Greco-Roman culture, we must change the form of leadership in order to fulfill their function. This must take into account the fact that both our American and Higi cultural expectations are distinct from those of the Greco-Roman culture. In our culture, for example, we take a different attitude toward remarriage and youthfulness so we would want to amend the list so as to allow for remarried leaders (though perhaps not for a pastor who remarries after a divorce) and to include some young people. In Higi culture, generosity, membership in the "royal social class," and a healthy polygamous relationship (managing a household with only one wife requires little ability) are valued. These should be reflected in the list.

Kraft emphasizes that this is a starting-point for translation, interpretation and church polity. Though he does not make clear the significance of this for American churches, in the Higi churches polygamy, for example, may ultimately give way to monogamy. But at any given time "God chooses to work in terms of the forms of each culture in order to attain his purposes. We deduce, therefore, that the principle of dynamic-equivalence in leadership patterns is the ideal recommended by the Scriptures."[69]

Kraft provides for us the epistemic pre-understanding out of which he has fashioned his approach. First, that which provides a proper response to God is revelatory.[70]

Second, the difference between general and special revelation is not so much a difference of kind as it is a difference of effect, not so much a matter of the information which is provided as a matter of the way the information is used. General revelation is sufficient for salvation, but since it is general and predictable it is not likely to attract attention. Special revelation attracts attention because it is uncommon.

Third, the informational product of God's revelational activity in the past is called "revelation" by evangelical orthodoxy, but this is so only in a potential sense. God's purpose is that in combination with a Spirit-guided stimulus (synonymous with "illumination") this informational product recreates "revelational meanings for contemporary receptors."[71]

Fourth, the Bible is both "inspired by God" and presents an "accurate record of the Spirit-guided perceptions of committed men."[72] It is verbally inspired in that inspiration attaches to the words that are employed, but this is more a byproduct of the process because the inspiration is really in the meanings. The Bible is free from error "where intended meanings are concerned" but not in the whole extent.[73] Scripture is not like the sinless Christ but is more like an erring human being who nevertheless has the function of serving God. The important thing, therefore, is that Scripture be used to bring a proper response to God. Used improperly it is neither God's revelation nor God's Word.[74] Scripture can be likened to an ocean with supracultural truths floating in it; to a "tether" which keeps us from wandering too far from God; to a "yardstick" by which to measure our beliefs and efforts; and to an "inspired casebook" which provides us with a record of God breaking through barriers to communicate with men in the past.

Fifth, revelation has a continuing dimension, it is not merely "objective" and complete.[75] More Scripture is not to be expected, not because revelation is not happening, but because more Scripture is not needed. What is needed is that we imitate, for example, the process that Luke went through in producing his gospel.[76] Careful attention to purpose, audience and contextualization (as is evident, for example, in *Letters to Street Christians* and The Cotton Patch Version of portions of the New Testament) will result in the discovery of God's Word and proper response to God. This "discovery" can be termed "revelation" as it is in the case of Peter in Matthew 16.[77]

Kraft's writings fairly bristle with helpful insights. To neglect his dynamic-equivalence approach is to run the risk of perpetuating some cultural forms that have no significance to receptors in other cultures and still other cultural forms that have consequences deleterious to the cause of Christ. But to adopt his approach uncritically entails an even greater risk—that of eating his contextualization cheese and getting caught in an epistemic trap. If we do so, the fault will be ours because Kraft is honest with us. He has not camouflaged his revelational epistemology. He makes it crystal clear. But in so doing he gives evidence of being too easily persuaded to the view of his colleague Jack Rogers and others that a completely authoritative Scripture is a recent—and largely American—invention. In fact, he displays a certain willingness, if not eagerness, to accept uncritically some of the questionable conclusions of men like Rogers and Daniel von Allman that have been shown to be untenable by the careful research of evangelicals such as John Woodbridge and I. Howard Marshall.[78] And he gives no evidence whatsoever of a knowledge of the great religions of the world and of a realization of how close he is to the "writings of the enlightened" epistemology of Hinduism, Buddhism and Taoism. If those who would learn from him have the same blind spots the result could be disastrous. Just as Tillich was alarmed by the death of God theology which his own pre-understandings encouraged in some of his students, so Kraft's pre-understandings may result in any given case in the death of the apostolic Christianity which he proposes to champion.

The reasons for this warning will be more evident to those who have had missionary experience in Asia and who are familiar with Asian religions and culture. Revelation as potentiality, the crucial importance of the stimulus, functionalism, the dynamic model, continuous revelation, the importance of the "*guru*"—all of these concepts are already there sustaining religious faiths and practices inimical to biblical Christianity. Kraft, of course, will demur. But in his insistence that the meanings and not the words of the Bible are inspired he has parted company with *apostolic* Christianity. In agreeing with "one knowledgeable estimate" that "at least half of the early church controversies labeled 'heresies' by the 'Orthodox' ought rather to be seen as valid cultural adaptations"[79] he has parted company with historic orthodoxy. In the end, we are dependent upon the anthropologically and linguistically trained cross-culturalist himself to supply us with the meaning of Scripture, the use of Scripture in effecting "revelation" and "apostolicity," and even for the assurance that no more Scripture will be forthcoming since it "is not needed."

C. "Providential Preservation" Contextualization

It is not easy to find a reputable Christian scholar who believes in the mechanical dictation theory which orthodox evangelicals are often accused of espousing. If someone were to hold to the dictation theory while also believing that we have copies of the autographs that are correct in every detail, only then would we have an instance of "Muslim revelational epistemology" wearing the cloak of Christianity. There is a serious and reputable Christian scholarship that does maintain a position vis-a-vis the Received Text and Authorized Version of the Bible that is somewhat analogous to the Muslim view, however.[80] For comparative purposes it will prove instructive to review that position.

Edward F. Hills, who holds the Th.M. degree from Colombia Seminary and the Th.D. from Harvard University, is wary of textual criticism as usually practiced. He accepts Warfield's view of inspiration along with most other orthodox evangelicals, but he goes considerably beyond Warfield in his insistence that the providential preservation of Holy Scripture has secured for us a text that is correct in almost every detail.

Hills makes a sharp distinction between "orthodox Christian faith" and "naturalistic New Testament textual criticism." The former begins with an affirmation of the divine inspiration and the providential preservation of the Bible and draws its principles of criticism from the Scriptures and the creeds and writings of the Church. The latter ignores all of this and treats the Bible like any other book.[81] Hills accepts Warfield's understanding of inspiration and propounds providential preservation as an inferred doctrine, believing that an inspired text demands the preservation of an almost pure text. He elucidates six axioms of the providential preservation of the New Testament text:

1. "The purpose of the providential preservation of the New Testament is to preserve the infallibility of the inspired original text."[82] In the providence of God, the texts of many ancient books have come to light in modern times. Since God's purpose is to preserve not only the text of the New Testament but also its infallibility, God has not simply preserved the original text of the New Testament (as one text among many), but He has preserved it *in a public way* so that all the world knows what and where it is.

2. "Providential preservation concentrated itself on the Greek New Testament text."[83] There is a fundamental difference between the Greek text and translations of that text into other languages because in the case of the Greek text God's providence operates directly while in the case of translations it operates indirectly. By maintaining a pure Greek text, God encourages translations into other languages, furnishes the means for translation, and provides a standard against which translations can be measured.

3. "Providential preservation within the sphere of the Greek Church."[84] Since it was God's purpose to preserve a pure *Greek* text, divine providence operated in a special way in the Greek Church, not because it was a superior church, but simply because it was, of course, Greek-speaking.

4. "Providential preservation operated through the testimony of the Holy Spirit."[85] All Christians have experienced the Holy Spirit's inward testimony to the truth of the Bible, but in regard to the text this testimony came with special force to the Christians of the Greek Church. Other ancient Christians knew only the translations and therefore did not receive this testimony so clearly. The Syriac, Coptic and

Latin versions of the Bible, therefore, included many erroneous readings. The Holy Spirit operated continuously and progressively within the Greek Church so that during the first three centuries of the Christian era the canon was formed and after that the Greek Church was led to embrace the true text.

5. "The text of the majority of the manuscripts is the providentially preserved and approved text."[86] Special providence operating in the Greek Church resulted in the production of trustworthy copies; the reading and recopying of these trustworthy copies; and, the eclipsing of untrustworthy copies which were not read and recopied.

6. "The text of the majority of the manuscripts is the standard text."[87] Through providential preservation, then, the Greek text which is found in the vast majority of manuscripts is the standard text. This Byzantine Text—embraced by the entire Greek Church was the basic text of the Byzantine Period (312-1453)—became the basic text of the Textus Receptus, the Protestant Reformation, the King James and other early versions. God has in this way witnessed to its authority and authenticity.

Hills does not claim that the Byzantine Text is an absolute reproduction of the original text. He even finds it necessary to make certain disclaimers. For example, he says that the Byzantine Text "should be followed *almost* always in preference to the non-Byzantine texts"[88] (italics mine). He admits that some of the non-Byzantine readings introduced into the Textus Receptus are probably genuine.[89] And he admits that it contains a few obvious but minor errors.[90] But he insists that the Byzantine Text is a trustworthy reproduction of the original text and should be received as such.[91] And he insists that the few errors in the Textus Receptus can be corrected in marginal notes.[92]

Various scholars have responded to the contentions of men like Edward Hills and Wilbur Pickering concerning the biblical text.[93] To go into textual questions here would both take us far afield and beyond my expertise. But insofar as Hills' conclusions relate to the translation and contextualization of Scripture they are most germane to this discussion.

Hills displays a clear understanding of the nature and implications of inspiration and a commendable concern for the integrity of the biblical text. R. B. Kuiper is justified when, in his preface to the book, he places Hills in the train of James Orr who also warned of a type of textual criticism which "tends to widen out illimitably into regions where exact science cannot follow it, where often, the critic's imagination is his only law."[94] Hills is correct in pointing out that if the Scriptures are divinely inspired, then textual criticism of the Bible must be different from that of ordinary books.[95] He is also right in claiming that providential preservation is a necessary corollary of divine inspiration.[96]

It is Hills' particular understanding of providential preservation that occasions problems, not only textual and logical problems but also very practical ones. It turns out that the Textus Receptus—true to the Byzantine text and almost universally by Protestants for over 300 years—is the "true text of the Greek New Testament" that will always be preserved by divine providence and honored by consistent Christians.[97] Furthermore, all that has been said of the Byzantine Text and Textus Receptus constitutes a defence of the King James Version in Hills' view. For English-speaking Christians to exchange the King James for another version, therefore, may well involve a change of theology and even religion.[98] To *supplement* the King James is acceptable, but to *substitute* for it is "to fly in the face of God's providence."[99] "Its majestic rhythms easily lend themselves to memorization"—a use to which modern translations do not lend themselves."[100] It is superior to all other versions in that it is the "historic Bible of English-speaking Protestants." To reject it is to break the tie with millions of English-speaking fellow-believers who span 350 years of history and cover the earth.[101] Some expressions may be modernized and certain renderings bettered, but changes should be minimal and introduced only with great care

> in order that the matchless beauty of this great piece of classic English prose may in no wise be impaired. Thus slightly revised, the King James Version will doubtless continue for another three hundred and fifty years (if the Lord tarry so long) to preserve for faithful readers the true New Testament text undamaged by the ravages of naturalistic New Testament criticism.[102]

The practical problems here are serious ones. In the first place, Hills has provided a rationale for that host of Christians who, for a variety of lesser reasons, hold to the King James Version as they might hold to the autographs but without recognizing the difference. In the second place, this approach tends to discourage English translations that accomplish precisely that kind of communication which made the original message intelligible and attractive to the common man. In the third place, and most importantly from a missionary perspective, this approach promotes a kind of religio-cultural imperialism that has all too long prevailed in the Western Church. In effect it says to the people of the non-English-speaking world, "If you want to know Christ and Christian truth (really know) and if you want to fellowship with God's people (really fellowship), then you must study us, our language and our Bible." It is precisely this attitude—consciously or unconsciously held—that has militated, not against the sending of missionaries and the translation of the Scriptures into non-English languages, but against the people of the world looking upon Christianity as anything other than a Western religion. It is precisely this attitude that makes Christianity seem as culturally circumscribed to the people of the Third World as Islam has appeared to be to the West. It is precisely this attitude and approach in the past that has made the contextualization of the message of Christ so imperative for His people today!

D. "Relational Centers" Contextualization

Viewed against the backdrop of emphases such as those advocated by Tillich, Kraft and Hills, the less radical proposals of evangelical orthodoxy often attract little attention. These proposals however evidence a new awareness of the critical role of culture on the one hand, and a renewed commitment to biblical authority on the other. While that balance may not attract short-term attention, it does provide long-term stability for the missionary effort.

It is not a simple matter to choose one single representative of this balanced approach for illustrative purposes because, to my knowledge, no one has proposed a really comprehensive contextualization system of the depth and breadth of that put forward by Kraft, for example. Numerous authors have made significant contributions to the literature, but each has written within definite parameters dictated by time, expertise, interest or whatever. In spite of misgivings of this kind, we will briefly overview the contextualization proposals of Bruce Nicholls, executive secretary of the World Evangelical Fellowship Theological Commission, since he has focused on the issue central to this monograph within the scope of one representative work.[103] For want of a better identifying appellation we will term Nicholls' approach "relational center" contextualization.

Nicholls distinguishes between the efforts to understand biblical and dogmatic theology on the one hand, and the contextualization of theology on the other. Concerning the former he elucidates two opposing pre-understandings. One is the contemporary assumption exemplified by Bultmann which says that there is no pure gospel or neutral exegesis, and that by the "authority" of the Bible we mean that the Bible makes God's Word audible and leads to faith.[104] In this understanding, inspiration is understood in terms of the "inspiring character of encounters with God."[105] All interpretation is conditioned by the situation. In speaking of the Bible, attention is called to its "role," "influence," and "function."

The traditional (evangelical) pre-understanding, on the other hand, is that the authority of the Bible is external to our experience and rests on the fact of its inspiration. Words such as "infallible," "inerrant" and "autograph" are used to draw attention to the Bible's authority. Evangelicals recognize that historical and cultural factors influence their choice of these words, but they believe that "behind them stand supra-cultural verities which are inherent in the Word of God itself."[106]

Nicholls points out four hermeneutical principles for understanding biblical authority that accrue to the historic evangelical view:[107]

1. The lifestyle principle of faith-commitment. Confidence in, and submission and obedience to, God is essential to biblical understanding.

2. The objective-subjective principle of distancing from, and identification with, the text. Using the linguistic tools and the historical method known as the grammatico-historical method, the interpreter attempts to discover what the writer said. This is not to be confused with attempting to discover the author's intention—a more speculative process. He responds to the text by "fusion or identification" with its message. (A reference to Gadamers "fusion of horizons" referred to earlier.)[108] This same two-way process pertains to the contextualization of the Word. The contextualizer must distance himself from both his own culture and that of his respondents. Prophetically, he allows the text to judge the pre-understandings and both cultures. For example, instead of "semi-absolutizing culture" and changing the category of God as "father" in a matrilineal society, he will "allow the biblical revelation to judge the interpreter's image of 'father'."[109]

3. The body-life principle of the believing community. The hermeneutical task is the responsibility of the whole body of Christ. It must be done in the context of the Church in both its present and its past extensions.

4. The mission-in-the-world principle. The framework for the hermeneutical and contextualization tasks is the mission of God in the world. This framework preserves the biblical distinction between

the kingdom of God and the kingdom of Satan, and Church and the world. Only when these distinctions are maintained will the contextualization of the gospel conform to Scripture.

Moving from biblical theology to contextualized theology, Nicholls notes that the latter is always relative. No contextualized theology can claim the comprehensiveness of the Bible; even though it may be valid and true to the gospel. Contextualization, therefore, has its starting point in the circle of a faith commitment and the faith content which that commitment entails. The faith commitment is to God's self-revelation in Christ. The faith content has to do with the uniqueness of the acts of the Trinitarian God as revealed in the Scripture.

Cultures—always in process, always changing—provide, not the starting point, but the relational centers for contextualized theologies. There have been many of these in the history of the Church. They represent "varying responses to the work of the Spirit of God in particular historical contexts."[110] At the same time, "The truer they are to the givenness of biblical theology the more complementary and the less contradictory they become."[111] For example, the relational center of Luther's theology was the doctrine of justification by faith. It was a contextualized theology which related the biblical truth to the confused thinking of the Church at that time. As such it was and is a Western contextualized theology. But from his knowledge of Hinduism and Christianity in India, Nicholls insists that the recovery of this doctrine by the church in India is exceedingly important because in that context the Hindu notion of karma is strong and assurance of salvation on the part of Christians is greatly needed. He writes, ". . . I believe the recovery of justification by faith is one of the greatest needs of an Indian Christian theology. However, a commentary on Galatians by an Indian Christian theologian will be contextualized in a very different way from that of Luther's commentary."[112]

Similarly, the relational center of the covenant in Reformed theology is needed in Islamic culture and that of the power of the Holy Spirit in Pentecostal theology is needed in Latin cultures. Theologies with other relational centers need to be contextualized in the Third World: Hindu and Buddhist Asia needs a fresh contextualization of the doctrine of creation and resurrection; Latin America needs a contextualized theology of the kingdom of God; Africa and the Pacific area need a contextualized theology of the "joyous experience of the lordship of Christ;" those portions of the world living under tyranny need a contextualized theology of the liberating Christ. "But if these contextualized theologies are to quench the spiritual thirst of people of the world, they must be constantly subjected to the norms of biblical theology."[113]

It remains for Nicholls or someone who reflects his revelational epistemic pre-understanding to effect a much more complete system of contextualization, one that is truly worthy of the historic orthodox evangelical commitment that it reflects. But here we see, at least in preliminary form, an approach to contextualization that is distinct from the non-Christian and imbalanced Christian approaches heretofore considered. Here is an approach that grows out of that unique blending of prophetic and apostolic witness and teaching, and of Divine inspiration and superintendence, that make biblical revelation the inspired Word of God. Here is an approach that recognizes both the Divine supra-cultural origin of revelation and the human cultural condition in which it was inscripturated without allowing either to obscure or denigrate the other. Here is an approach that recognizes that form and function are both servants of the truth of God and refuses to allow either to emasculate the other.

IV. INERRANCY AND CONTEXTUALIZATION

It may seem that we have taken a circuitous route in this monograph to the subject of inerrancy. But what we have attempted to do is illustrate some of the crucial practical outcomes of the acceptance or rejection of this doctrine for contextualization discussions and endeavors. Let us see how this is so.

History has a way of dealing decisively with language—sometimes beneficently, sometimes maliciously, but always profoundly. That is why glotto-chronology and historical linguistics are so important. That is why we should examine the semantic routes traveled by certain critical words in receptor cultures—words that we employ in contextualizing the gospel for the people of those cultures, as Charles Corwin suggests and illustrates.[114] And that is why we examine the changing meanings of words and phrases which are of critical importance to both sending and receptor cultures.

I take it that there was a time, and not so long ago, when phrases like "divinely inspired," "Word of God" and "infallible Bible" were sufficient to express and guard the integrity and authority of Holy Scripture. That is no longer so. Divine inspiration and human inspiration have become almost indistinguishable in many contexts. "Infallible" is often used to equivocate—retaining the advantage of the old meaning while pertaining to a new understanding. So we are wise to adopt new phraseology such as "inerrancy" and "inerrant autographs." The *meaning* of inerrancy seems much more clear to us—at least for now. But of what *importance* is it, right now in this "new era" of contextualization? After all, "inerrancy" as a word has its own characteristics. It also "stands for" a concept and a doctrine. It even represents in some way the motivations and purposes of those of us who decide to employ it in this context. Infused with all of this signification, what negative and positive potential consequences does its employment entail—practical consequences, not only those dictated by logic?

On the negative side, we must recognize that the employment of "inerrancy" language itself represents a contextualization. The doctrine is not new. Assuredly not. But as a primary "identifier" of the doctrine, the word "inerrancy" is new. And it represents a contextualization with primary reference to the North American context. Therein lies a very real danger because, for different reasons, many if not most Christians in the First and Third Worlds do not view the problem of biblical authority in the same way that we do. Speaking very generally, First World Christians have been so profoundly affected by higher criticism, the struggle for survival and other concerns that they have not held the line against the fallibility of Scripture. Indeed, this may be one reason for the inglorious state of the church in much of the First World. Tradition simply cannot sustain the additional weight that is placed upon it when biblical authority is allowed to errode, even when that tradition is as prolonged and pervasive as it is in Europe.

Again, speaking generally, most Third World Christians have not really faced up to the challenge of textual criticism. They have learned of Christ and his gospel from the Bible. They have forsaken all gods and sacred authorities. They have believed the Bible and trusted the Christ. Their lives have been transformed. They have been given new hope. Now they share the message with their fellows. Indeed, this relatively untested faith in the veracity and authority of the Scriptures—untested not in life but in the halls of academia—may constitute one of the most vulnerable chinks in the armor of the churches in the Third World.

If the foregoing analysis is true to any significant degree whatsover, it would seem to follow that one of the greatest dangers facing orthodox evangelicalism today is the failure to contextualize inerrancy doctrine for Christians in the First and Third Worlds. For their own reasons, noble or ignoble, opponents of the complete authority of Scripture will insist that the struggle for inerrancy is simply a fight over words, a parochial concern of Christians in North America. They will insist that to bring the issue of inerrancy to the Third World is to export problems that are peculiar to the Western churches. They will reinforce their misrepresentation of our fidelity to Holy Scripture as being similar to the Muslim commitment to the "divine writing" of the Koran; as one that reveres the antiquated King James Version; as one that refashions the Bible into a "paper Pope"; as one that results in bibliolatry.

There is, in short, a tremendous potential for misunderstanding in propounding inerrancy. A concerted effort in contextualization on the part of orthodox evangelical missionaries in general, and scholars in particular, will be required in order to communicate what we mean by inerrancy, why we speak in these terms and what is at stake. Christians in the First World must understand that this doctrine represents the faith of the Fathers—*their* Fathers. Christians in the Third World must understand that this doctrine represents the faith of those who brought the gospel to them. And all must understand that this doctrine is true to the testimony of Christ and his apostles.

In undertaking this formidable task of contextualization, care must be taken that we maintain a balanced perspective and a genuinely Christian attitude and approach. It must be made clear that inerrantists are not obscurantists; that textual questions are being addressed in a forthright and scholarly manner. It must be remembered that however important it might be that we defend the Bible it is even more incumbent upon us to proclaim its message; that, in fact, the integrity of Holy Scripture is maintained in order that the purity of the gospel might be retained.

The positive consequences of inerrancy doctrine for the Christian world mission in this "new age" of contextualization are of incalculable importance. In the first place, it is the mixture of truth and error, and of history and phantasy, that makes the Scriptures of non-Christian faiths so vulnerable to misinterpretation and exploitation. Myths, like clay, lend themselves to the designs of the user. The "writings of the enlightened" represent little improvement because the human element in the enlightenment experience, and in the reporting and recording of it, is so dominant that the human interpreter is fully justified in making his own determination as to which portions will be accepted as true and elevating and which parts will be disregarded as irrelevant or even discarded as erroneous. There can be little doubt that, no matter how pure the motives and brilliant the proposals of the contextualizer might be, if the biblical text he contextualizes is errant even in part, that text will ultimately be treated as different only in degree and not in kind.

In the second place, biblical inerrancy demands an attention to the text that lower views do not—not just to the author's intentions but also to the author's words, not just to the nonverbal functions of the message but also to its verbal forms. We need the reminder of the general semanticists that meanings are in people. But we must take with a grain of salt their idea that meanings are not in words because language constitutes the primary means whereby meanings are conveyed from one person to another. The notions that anthropology is the arbiter of theology and that grammatico-historical interpretation has been superseded by ethnolinguistic interpretation must be challenged. Carried to an extreme this approach comes frighteningly close to that of the Buddhist master who by virtue of his kind of discipline is able to get "beneath the letter" of the scripture to its "true meaning." The truth is that by virtue of their understanding of how cultures function and their exposure to diverse cultures, anthropologists can bring important insights to bear upon peoples and cultures of even ancient times. But culture is not a skeleton key which will unlock meanings stored in the minds of first-century authors and readers; it is more like a number in a combination which unlocks part of that meaning. The trust is that we *have* the author's word; we *search* for the intent of the author and the effect on the receptor. Words and meanings go together. Form and function are like Siamese twins. In this sense, formal-correspondence and dynamic-equivalence are not enemies; they are friends. Pressed with too much vigor to conform to the verbal form of the source a translation becomes static and sterile. Pressed with too much vigor to produce a heightened effect in the respondent a translation becomes loose and even libertarian. Previously in this monograph we have spoken of the "two horizons" of the interpreter—his own cultural background and that of the authors of the text. We have spoken also of the "double vision" which keeps in view the uniqueness of the text and the need for contextualization. Now we must emphasize the need for "double translations" which balance form and impact. Our study has illustrated the fact that it is an inerrant text that safeguards biblical meaning. Though inerrancy does not necessarily protect us from the excesses of formal-equivalence, it does help to protect us from the excesses of dynamic-equivalence.

V. CONCLUSION

Christian contextualization does not occur in a vacuum. It occurs in a pluralistic world in which religious messages—*contextualized* religious messages—intercept each other in the ideological marketplaces of the world. But religious contextualizations are not undertaken *de novo*. They come with the imprimaturs and revelational-epistemological pre-understandings provided by the originators of the great traditional faiths. Contextualized religious messages, therefore, are not tendered simply on the basis of intrinsic qualities alone. If that were the case they might be justifiably accepted or rejected in accordance with the religious tastes of respondents. They are tendered also, and even more significantly, on the basis of an authority or authorities. In the final analysis, contextualized religious messages, including the Christian message, are no better than the authority of the source. To accept them or reject them is to accept or reject the authority or authorities behind them.

Our Lord Christ made it clear that He came, not to destroy the Law and the Prophets, but to fulfill them. He insisted that both His message and He himself came from God the Father. He promised that He would send the Holy Spirit to bring to the minds of His apostles all that He had delivered to them and to guide them into all truth. In every part the Old and New Testament Scriptures, therefore, bear the imprimatur of the Triune God. They display the characteristics of their known authors and the marks of their cultural settings. But they retain, in all, the authority of God Himself. Contextualization is fully Christian only when both the message of the Bible *and* the authority of the Bible have been faithfully contextualized so that *both* are distinguishable from non-Christian competitors.

Christian contextualizers, take care lest you lend the impression that your message is so divine as to be obtainable only to a culturally select few, or so human and culture-bound as to be epistemologically indistinguishable from all others. Christian contextualizers, take courage. People from the East and the West, the South and the North, will sit down together in Christ's kingdom.

NOTES

[1]Partnership in Mission, *Gospel in Context: A Dialogue on Contextualization* (Abington, PA: Partnership in Mission).

[2]John Stott and Robert T. Coote, eds., *Gospel & Culture* (Pasadena, CA:

William Carey Library, 1979; reprint ed., *Down to Earth,* Grand Rapids: Eerdmans Pub. Co., 1980).

[3]Charles H. Kraft, *Christianity in Culture: A Study in Dynamic Biblical Theologizing in Cross-Cultural Perspective* (Maryknoll: Orbis Books, 1979).

[4]Bruce C. E. Fleming, *Contextualization of Theology: An Evangelical Assessment* (Pasadena, CA: William Carey Library, 1980), pp. 77-78.

[5]Ludwig Wittgenstein, *Tractatus Logico-Philosophicus,* German and English (London: Routledge & Kegan Paul, 1961).

[6]I. A. Richards, *A Philosophy of Rhetoric* (New York: Oxford University Press, 1936).

[7]Kenneth Burke, *A Grammar of Motives and a Rhetoric of Motives* (Cleveland: World, Meridian Books, 1962).

[8]Robert T. Oliver, *Culture and Communication: The Problem of Penetrating National and Cultural Boundaries* (Springfield: Charles C. Thomas, 1962).

[9]Kenneth Hamilton, "Liberation Theology: An Overview" in *Evangelical and Liberation,* ed. Carl E. Armerding (Grand Rapids: Baker Book House, 1977), p. 9.

[10]Gustavo Gutierrez, *A Theology of Liberation* (Maryknoll: Orbis Books, 1973).

[11]David J. Hesselgrave, *Communicating Christ Cross-Culturally: An Introduction to Missionary Communication* (Grand Rapids: Zondervan Publishing House, 1978).

[12]Hans-Georg Gadamer, *Philosophical Hermeneutics* (Berkeley: University of California Press, 1976).

[13]Anthony Thiselton, *The Two Horizons: New Testament Hermeneutics and Philosophical Description* (Grand Rapids: William B. Eerdmans Publishing Co., 1980), pp. 16, 17.

[14]Ibid., p. 439.

[15]Ibid.

[16]Eric Sharpe, *Fifty Key Words: Comparative Religion* (Richmond: John Knox Press, 1971), pp. 64-65.

[17]Winston L. King, *Introduction to Religion* (New York: Harper and Brothers Publishers, 1954), p. 40.

[18]Ibid. p. 41.

[19]Max Stilson, *Leading Religions of the World* (Grand Rapids: Zondervan, 1964), p. 47.

[20]Laotzu, *Laotzu's Tao and Wu Wei,* trans. Dwight Goddard; *Wu Wei,* an interpretation by Henri Borel, trans. Mabel Edith Reynolds (New York: Brentano's Publishers, 1919), p. 39.

[21]H. A. R. Gibb and J. H. Kramers, *Shorter Encyclopedia of Islam* (Ithaca: Cornell University Press, 1965), pp. 163, 622-24.

[22]W. Montgomery Watt, *Islamic Revelation in the Modern World* (Edinburgh: University Press, 1969), pp. 69-70.

[23]Samuel Zwemer, *The Heirs of the Prophets* (Chicago: Moody Press, 1946), pp. 17-25.

[24]B. B. Warfield, *The Inspiration and Authority of the Bible* (London: Marshall, Morgan and Scott, 1951), pp. 245f.

[25]Westminster Shorter Catechism, Question 31.

[26]Jack Rogers and Donald McKim, *The Authority and Interpretation of the Bible: An Historical Approach* (San Francisco: Harper & Row, 1979).

[27]John Woodbridge, "Biblical Authority: Toward an Evaluation of the Rogers and McKim Proposal," *Trinity Journal,* Vol. 1 n.s., No. 2 (Fall 1980): 165-236.

[28]D. C. Holtom, *Modern Japan and Shinto Nationalism* (Chicago: The University of Chicago Press, 1943), p. 14.

[29]Ibid., pp. 24-25.

[30]Ibid., p. 25.

[31]Swami Prabhavananda and Frederick Manchester, *The Upanishads: Breath of the Eternal* (New York: The New American Liberary, 1957).

[32]Ibid., p. IX.

[33]Ibid.

[34]Ibid., pp. XI, XII.

[35]Ibid.

[36]Laotzu, *Laotzu's Tao and Wu Wei.*

[37]Ibid., p. 1.

[38]Ibid., p. 2.

[39]Ibid., p. 1.

[40]Ibid.

[41]Ibid., p. 6.

[42]Arthur J. Arberry, *The Koran Interpreted* (New York: The Macmillan Company, 1955), p. 28.

[43]Ibid., p. 24.

[44]Ibid., p. 25.

[45]Ibid., p. 28.

[46]Zwemer, *Heirs of the Prophets,* pp. 19-25.

[47]Arberry, *The Koran Interpreted,* front cover.

[48]Paul Tillich, *Dynamics of Faith* (New York: Harper & Row, Publishers, Harper Torchbooks, 1958), p. 49.

[49]Thiselton, *The Two Horizons: New Testament Hermeneutics and Philosophical Description,* pp. 252-58.

[50]Rudolf Bultmann, *Jesus Christ and Mythology* (London: S. C. M. Press, 1960), pp. 35-36; quoted in Thiselton, *The Two Horizons: New Testament Hermeneutics and Philosophical Description,* pp. 258-59.

[51]Rudolf Bultmann, "New Testament and Mythology" in *Kerygma and Myth* (2 Vols.), ed. by Hans-Werner Bartsch (London: S.P.C.K., 1962 and 1964), I., p. 36; quoted in Thiselton, *The Two Horizons: New Testament Hermeneutics and Philosophical Description,* p. 269.

[52]Tillich, *Dynamics in Faith,* p. 50.

[53]Paul Tillich, *The Future of Religions* (New York: Harper & Row, Publishers, 1966), p. 91.

[54]Ibid.

[55]Ibid.

[56]Ibid., pp. 92-94.

[57]Ibid., pp. 84-94.

[58]Ibid., p. 90.

[59]Kraft, *Christianity in Culture.*

[60]Ibid., pp. 265-75.

[61]Ibid., p. 38.

[62]Charles H. Kraft, "Interpreting in Cultural Context" in *Journal of the Evangelical Theological Society,* Vol. 21, No. 4 (December 1978), pp. 357-67.

[63]Ibid., p. 359.

[64]Ibid., p. 360.

[65]Ibid., p. 363.

[66]Ibid.,

[67]Ibid., p. 365.

[68]Kraft, *Christianity in Culture,* pp. 323-27; Stott & Coote, eds., *Gospel & Culture,* pp. 309-10; Charles H. Kraft, "Dynamic Equivalence Churches," *Missiology* Vol. 1, No. 1 (January 1973), pp. 39-57.

[69]Kraft, *Christianity in Culture,* p. 325.

[70]Ibid., p. 183.

[71]Ibid., p. 221.

[72]Ibid., p. 33.

[73]Ibid., p. 208.

[74]Ibid., p. 188.

[75]Ibid., p. 184.

[76]Ibid., p. 283.

[77]Ibid., p. 164.

[78]Woodbridge, "Biblical Authority," pp. 165-236; I. Howard Marshall, "Palestinian and Hellenistic Christianity: Some Critical Comments," *New Testament Studies* 19, pp. 271-87. We have referred to Woodbridge's argument earlier in this monograph (see footnote 27). Von Allmen subscribes to the four-stage approach to the Hellenization of Christianity and propounds the notion that in the later part of this process Paul "contextualized" a new Hellenized theology. (See "The Birth of Theology" *International Review of Mission* 44, pp. 37-55.) Kraft accepts uncritically Von Allmen's argument and uses it to reinforce his position. (See Kraft, *Christianity in Culture,* pp. 232, 287, 295-96.) But Marshall cites T. W. Manson's reference to "the building of Hellenistic castles in the air." He quotes O. Cullman who writes; "It is not possible to distinguish so sharply as is usually done between a theology of the Hellenistic Church and that of the original Church." And then he proceeds to show that "We cannot rigorously separate two cultures, but must admit that Jewish material reaches the church in a mixture of forms which cannot be easily disentangled" (see pp. 274-75).

[79]Kraft, *Christianity in Culture,* p. 287.

[80]Wilbur N. Pickering, *The Identity of the New Testament Text* (Nashville: T. Nelson, 1977); Edward F. Hills, *The King James Version Defended* (Des Moines: The Christian Research Press, 1956).

[81]Hills, *The King James Version Defended,* pp. 16-17, 21.

[82]Ibid., p. 30.

[83]Ibid., p. 31.

[84]Ibid., p. 32-33.

[85]Ibid., p. 32.

[86]Ibid., p. 34.

[87]Ibid., p. 35.

[88]Ibid.

[89]Ibid., p. 123.

[90]Ibid., p. 132.

[91]Ibid., p. 142.

[92]Ibid., p. 132.

[93]D. A. Carson, *The King James Version Debate: A Plea for Realism* (Grand Rapids: Baker Book House, 1979).

[94]Hills, *The King James Version Defended*, p. 4.

[95]Ibid., p. 8.

[96]Ibid.

[97]Ibid., 133.

[98]Ibid., p. 139.

[99]Ibid., p. 142.

[100]Ibid.

[101]Ibid.

[102]Ibid., pp. 142-43.

[103]Bruce Nicholls, *Contextualization: A Theology of Gospel and Culture* (Downers Grove, IL: InterVarsity Press, 1979).

[104]Ibid., p. 39.

[105]Ibid., p. 40.

[106]Ibid., p. 43.

[107]Ibid., pp. 48-52.

[108]Ibid., p. 50.

[109]Ibid.

[110]Ibid., p. 54.

[111]Ibid.

[112]Ibid.

[113]Ibid., p. 55.

[114]Charles Corwin, *Biblical Encounter with Japanese Culture* (Tokyo: Christian Literature Crusade, n.d.). Out of 222 "general thought categories" Corwin selects 33 word symbols for study. He then studies their semantic changes in the past and their modern range of meaning; he compares their Japanese meaning with the meaning of parallel word symbols in the Hebrew and Greek of the Bible and in English; finally, he notes the significance of this information for the encounter between Christ and Japanese culture.

A Response to Contextualization and Revelational Epistemology

Morris A. Inch
Chairman of the
Department of Biblical,
Religious and
Archaeological Studies
Wheaton College

A response to Contextualization and Revelational Epistemology

Morris A. Inch

Perhaps no author has presented as consistently a sane and thoughtful treatment of the contextualization issue as David Hesselgrave. I am especially pleased to be able to interact with his paper as an extension of his already significant contribution to the subject area.

I. CONCERNING TRUTH/ERROR MODELS

I use the concept of model as a representation of some aspect of reality, as we understand it from a given perspective. It is not the reality itself, but an effort to delineate for ourselves and others. It is also tentative by nature and subject to correction or revision.

Models are significant because they suggest how we objectify reality and subjectify our experience in reference to reality as a social construction. It is not an overstatement to suggest that the choice of models may be a matter of life or death. Man hangs onto life not by the seat of his pants but the weave of his thinking.

Hesselgrave provides us with a clue as to his model structure with reference to "double vision"—"which sees both the integrity and uniqueness of the text of our sacred Book, and also the importance of the tools of contextualizing its message for the 'unreached' people of post- and pre-Christian cultures" (p. 710). He adds that this double vision results in a terrible tension for those who are both concerned and informed. Therefore, we ought not to impugn the motives of those who mean to protect either the integrity of the text or the need to contextualize its message. We must allow God to judge all such endeavors, and strive to exercise our task responsibly. The alternatives may lead to syncretism on the one hand, or sterility on the other.

This is an interesting variation on the trichotomous model: a position to each side and one in the middle. C. S. Lewis gave the trichotomous model a classic expression when he suggested that Satan "always sends errors into the world in pairs—pairs of opposites. And he always encourages us to spend a lot of time thinking which is the worse. You see why, of course? He relies on your extra dislike of the one error to draw you gradually into the opposite one,"[1] so that we must keep our eyes fixed on the goal and press straight through between both errors.

Hesselgrave also allows for the three options: a singular concern for biblical integrity or the contextualization of its message, and the both together. His remaining comments advise how we can best manage with the tension of living with both ends in view.

The most obvious alternative to Hesselgrave's preference is the dichotomous model—two categories instead of three. Francis Schaeffer has established a reputation for dichotomous modeling. For instance, he comments that "Bultmann has some good exegesis in details . . . yet this is not the place for ambivalent judgment—that is, mere disagreement in details—we must realize that their system *as a system* is wrong."[2] He reminds us of the "antithesis" between Bultmann's radical departure and orthodox Christian faith. We must opt for one or the other.

It seems to me that there is considerable slippage between those who advocate one model or the other. The trichotomous alternative comes through as ambivalent to those who favor a dichotomous model, and the dichotomous model appears simplistic and perhaps censorious to the proponents of trichotomous thinking.

I suspect that there is a place for both, but even this suggestion is an example of the middle ground of the trichotomous approach. More pertinent to the task at hand is to recognize the perspective from which Hesselgrave develops his topic, the possibility of modifying whatever model we chose so as to improve our understanding.

It remains only to commend Hesselgrave's choice of model. For instance, Donald McGavran demonstrates the importance of taking a high view of Scripture, a high view of culture, and of making provision for legitimate differences of opinion.[3] The high views of Scripture *and* culture reflect the middle premise, and the additional provision for legitimate difference is a tension-reducing device that makes the course easier to negotiate.

There are many additional ramifications for Hesselgrave's approach, but rather than exploring them further, we will turn to some of the particulars in his provocative paper. We shall also have to be selective in terms of which of these to consider, and in what connection. And thereafter we shall attempt to pull some of the loose ends of our discussion together by way of conclusion.

II. GENRES OF WRITTEN REVELATION

Hesselgrave draws our attention to the need to inquire into "the demands that the scriptures of the various religious traditions make upon contextualizers and the relationship between types of revelation and contextualization" (p. 697). Apart from such an inquiry, any effort to analyze contextualization will be deficient.

He sets forth the following genre of written revelation: myth, the writings of the enlightened, divine writing, and inspired writings. He opts for the last of these as the orthodox Christian alternative, setting the others aside in the process. So far as the trichotomous model is concerned, the unacceptable alternatives lie to one side or the other—either as a simplistic appeal to revelational authority or cultural adaptation to the contrary. Presumably, divine writing constitutes an example of the former, while myth and the writings of the enlightened illustrate the latter. Only that of inspired writings provide the necessary tension between high views of Scripture and culture that allows Hesselgrave to proceed on course.

Hesselgrave is no doubt correct in pointing out that one's view of sacred writ affects how he contextualizes and the subsequent relationship between the two. This is certainly an important step, without which a discussion of the topic would be deficient, if not utterly misleading.

I will limit my comments to only one of the alternatives Hesselgrave sets aside, but what I say in this connection suggests at least an approach that could be taken to the others. We center our attention on the alternative of myth. The term myth activates a wide range of response, from the enthusiastically positive to the categorically negative. Few authors have labored as effectively as Helmut Thielicke in working through a concept of myth that reduces the negative factors and accentuates the positive factors.

Thielicke views myth as a temporal expression of the eternal. "Thus the story of Peter's denial seems to be only about a police action and its consequences, about everyday people, . . . but behind the everyday guise is a basic event. Peter exemplifies conflict and a situation of decision. An action on earth, irrespective of its concrete here-and-now reality, signifies not only itself but something else as well, which relates to eternal and not just to tempoal destiny."[4] More precisely, myth incorporates an awareness of a transcendent dimension to the situation and the insight that throws on man's character and responsibility. It focuses on the divine-human encounter.

Myth tempts us to commit idolatry by making absolute the partial, and so as to advantage self over others. That is, we employ myth against God and our fellowman, with the result that we also suffer—for violating the conditions of life in God's world. However, a properly restrained myth allows for the wonder and mystery of God and the integrity of man as the basis for constructing life. Thielicke uses the term *kerygmatic myth* to describe the adulterous presumption of myth, and *disarmed myth* as myth properly restrained.

Thielicke reasons that the victory of the gospel with regard to kerygmatic myth not only leaves the battlefield strewn with former gods, but disarms myth to be creatively employed. He confidently concludes that "The status of the gods have been broken to pieces and can be made into new mosaics."[5]

It is not my purpose to critique Thielicke in regard to his approach to myth, but illustrate how someone might opt for one of the alternatives, modify it so as to incorporate the preferred elements from the inspired writings' option, and promote it as a more adequate substitute. This implies that there may be some features of the inspired writings' alternative, as represented, which do not capture all of the richness of a biblical doctrine of revelation. More particularly, there seems to be an inherent tendency to reduce revelation to a consideration of inspiration. So while I would be counted with Hesselgrave in his choice of alternatives, I recognize that whatever position one assumes, he elects the problems that go with it.

III. CONTEXTUALIZATION

Rather than argue the point that the demands of sacred writ effect the approach to contextualization and their subsequent relationship, Hesselgrave chooses to illustrate it—first in regard to non-Christian contextualization, and then to that of Christians. The former is instructive and provides some helpful distance from a subject loaded with emotional content, but the latter is more directly to the issue. We shall turn our attention to the latter discussion.

Hesselgrave reminds us that we as Christians, "to a degree unmatched by the adherents of any other faith," should be rightly concerned about the integrity and uniqueness of the Biblical text and the importance of the task of contextualizing its message (p. 710). He then analyzes four approaches, ranging from Tillich, through Kraft and Hill, to Nicholls, and he designates these contextualization alternatives as demythologization, dynamic-equivalence, providential preservation, and relational centers.

Hesselgrave finds it easier to illustrate a singular appeal to cultural sensitivity than a singular appeal to biblical fidelity in current Evangelical writing on the contextualization issue. He explains that "It is not easy to find a reputable Christian scholar who believes in the mechanical dictation theory which orthodox evangelicals are often accused of espousing" (p. 723). However, he sets forth the providential preservation alternative as one that tends in that direction, while demythologization and dynamic-equivalence obviously lie in the opposite direction—toward a singular appeal for cultural relevance.

If one grants the truth/error model Hesselgrave employs and the case he builds for the effect of one's view of revelation for the practice of contextualization, his preference and line of criticism of other alternatives seems essentially correct. There is much in this section that one might profitably explore, but we shall have to limit ourselves with care. I shall comment only in regard to the Kraft proposal, that in a select connection, and as relates to the Nicholl's alternative—which has Hesselgrave's support.

Some are inclined to write off Kraft's critique of a formal-equivalence mentality as an attack on the inept character of traditional missionary activity, but I think Hesselgrave has effectively demonstrated that it is a more basic challenge to the theology of missions in general and Biblical understanding in particular.

Hesselgrave exhibits an ambivalence in reference to the dynamic-equivalence alternative. He admits that "Kraft's writings fairly bristle with helpful insights. To neglect his dynamic-equivalence approach is to run the risk of perpetuating some cultural forms that have no significance to receptors in other cultures and still other cultural forms that have consequences deleterious to the cause of Christ. But to adopt his approach uncritically entails an even greater risk—that of eating his contextualization cheese and getting caught in an epistemic trap" (p. 722). I could not agree more with his perception, although I would express my disagreement in a bit different fashion.

It seems to me that when we get to the heart of Kraft's approach, we discover that he surrenders the needed distance between biblical revelation and conventional wisdom—in this case, as reflected in a certain social theory setting. The result is that he comes up with a "Bible" within the Bible, a biblical "sound alike" that becomes a hermeneutical tool for rewriting biblical teaching according to a cultural concensus.

Nicholls resists this incursion on the biblical teaching with his principle of distancing from and identification with the text. "Using the linguistic tools and the historical method known as the grammatico-historical method, the interpreter attempts to discover what the writer said. . . . The contextualizer must (also) distance himself from both his own culture and that of his respondents. Prophetically, he allows the text to judge the pre-understandings and both cultures" (p. 728). This is a legitimate extension of what we have sometimes identified as the primacy of Scripture, but we will have more to say on this subject as we sum up.

Nicholls' remaining hermeneutical principles are also pertinent. We need to recognize the community of faith as the proper locus for reflecting on biblical truth. Otherwise we fall prey to the danger documented by Karl Barth: "Nineteenth-century theology ascribed normative character to the ideas of its environment. Consequently it was forced to make reductions and oversimplifications, to indulge in forgetfulness and carelessness, when it dealt with the exciting and all-important matters of Christian understanding."[6] We allow the world to dictate our theological agenda, priorities, and substance rather than the Word of God. We are held in cultural captivity.

But, it must be added for proper balance, the church exists in the world as God's sent ones. "The framework for the hermeneutical and contextualization tasks is the mission of God in the world. This framework preserves the biblical distinction between the kingdom of God and the kingdom of Satan, and church and the world. Only when these distinctions are maintained will the contextualization of the gospel conform to Scripture" (p. 729). Only then may we hope to preserve the uniqueness and integrity of Scripture and contextualize its message. The dynamic-equivalence alternative, as developed by Kraft, reduces the tension between a high view of Scripture and a high view of culture and subverts the endeavor as a result.

But we are indebted to Kraft, as Hesselgrave volunteers, for his insights into the contextualization issue, and I would go beyond Hesselgrave at this point to say that Kraft rightly senses the danger of slippage in the opposite direction, as should we, if we take seriously Hesselgrave's trichotomous model for understanding the problem before us and the tension created by the attempt to retain a balanced approach.

IV. INERRANCY

Hesselgrave takes a surprisingly long time to get to the topic of inerrancy (seeing the nature of our study commission), and disposes of it in relatively short order. He admits that "It may seem that we have taken a circuitous route in this monograph to the subject of inerrancy" (p. 730). This ought not to give us too much concern because his route has been beneficial, and what he has to say is on target.

Hesselgrave gathers that there was a time when phrases like "divinely inspired," "Word of God," and "infallible Bible" were sufficient to express and guard the integrity and unqualified authority of Scripture, but that this is no longer the case, "so we are wise to adopt new phraseology such as 'inerrancy' and 'inerrant autographs' " (p. 731). The doctrine is not new, but "as a primary 'identifier' of the doctrine, the word 'inerrancy' is new. And it represents a contextualization with primary reference to the North American context" (p. 731).

The repetition of the term *primary* in Hesselgrave's selection of words is striking: inerrancy as a *primary* identifier and *primary* reference to the North American context, which underscores the contextual nature of theology in general and the concept of inerrancy in particular. Inerrancy has assumed a primary role in identifying an orthodox conviction regarding Scripture. (Jack Rogers' and Donald McKim's thesis seems oblivious to the nature of theological refinement and ends up sanctioning their own preference by a historically uncritical appeal to the Church Fathers.[7]).

I doubt that few of us who affirm the doctrine of biblical inerrancy would object to an alternative that better represents and communicates our confidence in Scripture as the inspired and authoritative Word of God, but we want it demonstrated that the alternative will do the job better in the light of the tensions created by the Enlightenment and theological accommodation to it. Time honored phrases like "divinely inspired" and "biblical infallibility" have seemed to have lost their cutting edge. They no longer serve the purpose they once did.

"Words and meanings go together" (p. 733). We do not worship as Christians a paper pope but the One who revealed Himself in no uncertain terms through the Holy Scriptures. Hesselgrave's preference for the concept of inerrancy observes that words and meanings, form and function, formal-correspondence and dynamic-equivalence belong together in our thinking, and our commitment to an inerrant Bible dictates the way in which we will go about our contextualization of the message and how we view the resulting relationship between the two.

LOOSE-ENDS AND LOGGERHEADS

Hesselgrave's thrust seems to me essentially correct: revelational epistemology sets the scope for contextualization. He effectively illustrates this through Christian and non-Christian alternatives. I pointed out that the alternatives are not necessarily categorical except perhaps as they have been described. One may modify the alternatives in such a way as to make them more or less acceptable.

Hesselgrave's preference for a trichotomous model is of course open to debate. He finds it much easier to illustrate the wrong turn in one direction than the other, toward a singular appeal to culture instead of a singular appeal to Scripture. This may imply a weakness in the model, but it may also indicate a fault in the position or a deliberate positioning.

I prefer Hesselgrave's model, problems notwithstanding. I do not think there is a critical fault in his position, although I suspect one could readily develop in a compatible but less balanced theorist. In what particular regard? Likely in stressing the precision of Scripture to the exclusion of the larger issue with its primacy. As I suggested earlier, we may for all practical purposes reduce the issue of revelation to inspiration or inerrancy. The latter are proper topics but should be perceived within the broader concern.

This leads us to the possibility that there has been a deliberate positioning in Hesselgrave's perspective that accounts for the ease by which he illustrates the risk on one hand and the difficulty on the other hand. I believe this is the case, and that the positioning does in fact have to do with a conviction about the primacy of Scripture. The alternatives for primacy that are clearly in view are reason—what may be commonly understood by man of God's revelation through the created order, the working of divine providence in nature and history, and the distinctive nature of mankind, and Scripture—the advent of Christ, the preparatory account of the people of God leading up to it, and the subsequent account of the new people of God extending from it. Tradition, as the privileged insight and reflection of God's people on the meaning and intent of divine revelation, seems to play only a supporting role in the discussion. Hesselgrave plainly opts for the primacy of Scripture over reason as a theological resource. He does not exclude reason, for were he to do so, the idea of primacy would be meaningless. But opt he does, taking a stand with the primacy of Scripture, and defending it consistently throughout the paper.

The tension he describes as a result is not a tension between two equal attractions (Scripture and reason), but one so not as to disregard the other. I suspect the tension is greater as a result rather than less, and the temptation to surrender to a singular appeal for Biblical fidelity ought also to be greater.

However, it appears that in fact Hesselgrave discovers the drift in Evangelical circles in the opposite direction—toward a singular appeal to cultural relevance. This at first seems puzzling, but it may have a simple explanation. Much, and I would say most, of the Evangelical literature on contextualization up to this point has been generated from the basis of expertise in cross-cultural studies, but lacking in theological expertise. We need the former input, but we need the latter as well, and we need it badly.

Hesselgrave has rendered an important service in getting our discussion of contextualization on target—with reference to revelational epistemology. I should like to conclude my response with a reminder of the need for divine revelation. I quote the words of John Stott: "Now when man's mind begins to concern itself with God, it is baffled. It gropes in the dark. It flounders out of its depth. It is lost. . . . He is altogether beyond us. Therefore our minds, wonderfully effective instruments as they are in other realms, cannot immediately help us here. They cannot climb up into the infinite mind of God. There is no ladder."[8] The situation would have remained so had God not taken the initiative to remedy the matter. But he has taken the initiative to reveal himself. The question is no longer with God's initiative but our response.

Hesselgrave reminds us of the importance of our concern with inerrancy to let us hear the revealed Word of God above the clamor of men's voices. Otherwise, it may degenerate into partisan theological polemics, and go wide of its target.

NOTES

[1]C. S. Lewis, *Mere Christianity* (London: Collins, 1952), p. 156.

[2]Francis Schaeffer, *The God Who Is There* (Downers Grove: Inter-Varsity Press), p. 51.

[3]Donald McGavran, *The Clash Between Christianity and Cultures* (Washington: Canon Press), pp. 51-81.

[4]Helmut Thielicke, *The Evangelical Faith* (Grand Rapids: Eerdmans Publishing Co., 1974), p. 73.

[5]Ibid., P. 100.

[6]Karl Barth, *The Humanity of God* (Richmond: John Knox Press, 1960), p. 19.

[7]Jack Rogers and Donald McKim, *The Authority and Interpretation of the Bible: An Historical Approach* (San Francisco: Harper and Row, 1979).

[8]John Stott, *Basic Christianity* (Grand Rapids: Eerdmans Publishing Co., 1958), p. 10.

A Response to Contextualization and Revelational Epistemology

Wayne A. Grudem
Professor of New Testament
Trinity Evangelical Divinity School

A Response to Contextualization and Revelational Epistemology

Wayne A. Grudem

I found Dr. Hesselgrave's paradigms of the kinds of contextualization found in non-Christian religions extremely helpful. I share his objections to contextualization of the Bible as it is carried out by methodologies that he categorizes as "demythologization," "dynamic equivalence," and "providential preservation" (of a text which is not able to be translated). I agree with Dr. Hesselgrave that these methods are inappropriate to a Bible that speaks truthfully in every area it touches, and to a Bible whose very words are important because they are God's words as well as man's.

Furthermore, I agree with and wish to reinforce Dr. Hesselgrave's call to communicate the doctrine of inerrancy to Third World churches. He is right in saying that we must work diligently to communicate to these churches (1) a careful definition of inerrancy, (2) an explanation of the basis for belief in inerrancy, and (3) a clear explanation of the reasons why the doctrine of inerrancy is important. In short, I find that I have no substantive disagreement with Dr. Hesselgrave at any point.

Nevertheless it may be possible to add to Dr. Hesselgrave's discussion of contextualization some additional analysis from the perspective of biblical theology, especially New Testament theology. The theological consideration that is most relevant in this discussion of contextualization is the doctrine of the clarity (or perspicuity)[1] of Scripture. Therefore, I would like to analyze briefly the relationship between the Bible's teaching about its own clarity and the problems of proper contextualization of the message of Scripture in various cultures and societies.

I. THE APPROPRIATENESS OF TRANSLATION INTO INTELLIGIBLE CONTEMPORARY SPEECH

Dr. Hesselgrave said that the doctrine of inerrancy saves us from the dangers of dynamic equivalence, but that it does not necessarily protect us from the dangers of formal equivalence (page 733). From the standpoint of biblical theology, we can observe that Scripture itself shows that it would be wrong to think of it after the paradigm of "divine writings" that cannot be translated. The New Testament authors used a *translation* of the Hebrew Old Testament when they used and often quoted from the Septuagint. In doing this they affirmed the validity of the work of translating the Bible into the language of the people to whom one is communicating. In addition, Paul's insistence in 1 Corinthians 14 that the Corinthians speak intelligibly during public gatherings of the church for worship and instruction gives further confirmation to the idea that God is pleased when we attempt to communicate the teachings of the Bible in ways that can be understood readily by the people to whom we are speaking.[2]

This New Testament data suggests that we should resist the efforts of those who in any age would try to keep the Bible in a language people do not understand (whether it be Latin or Koine Greek or seventeenth-century English). Whatever we may later conclude about the doctrine of the clarity of Scripture, we must at the outset realize that this doctrine does *not* affirm that the Bible is clear without being translated into words commonly used and understood by the society to which we are attempting to communicate. We should encourage "contextualization" in at least this very limited sense of translating the Bible into the contemporary language of each receptor culture.

However, the great variety of Greek style in the New Testament should remind us also that it is not necessary that all Scripture be translated so that it is understandable to any intelligent ten year-old child. In the New Testament itself we find Luke, Peter, James, the author of Hebrews, and sometimes Paul using complex and often very polished Greek that would no doubt have challenged many of their readers. A translation that requires active and careful reading in order to be understood is not necessarily a bad translation.

II. SOME REMAINING UNRESOLVED QUESTIONS ABOUT CONTEXTUALIZATION

To say that the Bible should be translated into the language of each receptor culture does not solve all the problems of contextualization, of course, There are other types of problems which occur at a higher level of abstraction or synthesis than the level of the meaning of an individual word.

For example, there are problems in the communication of unfamiliar historical or cultural ideas which are found in Scripture.

How can we communicate to modern culture the meaning of phrases like "kick against the goads" (Acts 26:14) or "gird up the loins of your mind" (1 Pet. 1:13)? How can people in large urban societies understand "the Lord is my shepherd" (Ps. 23:1), or "your children will be like olive shoots" (Ps. 128:3), or "faith as a grain of mustard seed" (Mat. 17:20)? Even more challenging is the problem of making clear how it can be a compliment to tell a young woman that her teeth are like a flock of shorn ewes newly come up from washing and that her neck is like the tower of David (Song of Songs 4:1-5)!

Yet more complex are the problems relating to the communication of theological ideas. How can cultures with no knowledge of the history of Israel understand John the Baptist when he calls Jesus the "lamb of God" (John 1:29), or the author of Hebrews when he speaks of Jesus as our High Priest (Heb. 3:1)? Can the biblical concept of God as Father be rightly understood in a predominantly matriarchal society, or the idea of God as judge in a society with a long history of corrupt judges?

Perhaps most difficult of all are the questions relating to the communication or contextualization of moral commands or ethical standards found in Scripture. Is it always necessary for church elders to be "the husband of one wife" (Titus 1:6)? Must women pray with their heads covered (1 Cor. 11:5)? Should we "greet all the brethren with a holy kiss" (1 Thess. 5:26)? In addition to these individual questions there are larger questions about whether the Bible endorses liberation theology or some kind of Christian socialism or something like a free enterprise system.

We begin to realize that the task of communicating and applying the message of Scripture in the context of hundreds and hundreds of different cultures and societies is an exceptionally complex task. Indeed, when questions like these begin to proliferate, critics might charge those of us who believe in inerrancy with avoiding the real issues. What good does it do to talk about an inerrant Bible, they might ask, when we cannot decide exactly how it should be interpreted and applied?

Yet it is precisely at this point that the doctrine of the clarity of Scripture can be of help to us.

III. THE TEACHING OF SCRIPTURE CONCERNING ITS OWN CLARITY

The Bible repeatedly reminds us of its own clarity, its own ability to be understood rightly, not only by scholars or specialists, but by all believers. We see this first at several points in the Old

Testament. Moses tells the people of Israel, "And these words which I command you this day shall be upon your heart; and you shall teach them diligently to your children, and shall talk of them when you sit in your house, and when you walk by the way, and when you lie down, and when you rise" (Deut. 6:6-7). All the people of Israel were expected to be able to understand the words of Scripture, and not only to understand them so that they would be upon their own hearts (vs. 6), but also to be able to "teach them diligently" to their children. This teaching could not have consisted merely of rote memorization devoid of understanding, for the people of Israel were to *discuss* the words of Scripture during their daily activities of sitting in the house or walking or going to bed or getting up in the morning. God expected that all his people would both know and understand his Word. Thus, the "blessed man" was one who meditated on God's law "day and night" (Ps. 1:2). In this Psalm there is an expectation that all the righteous people in Israel would be meditating on (and presumably understanding) God's laws every day.

The character of Scripture was said to be such that even the "simple" could understand it rightly and be made wise by it. "The testimony of the Lord is sure, making wise the *simple*" (Ps. 19:7). And again we read, "The unfolding of thy words gives light; it imparts understanding to the *simple*" (Ps. 119:130). The "simple" here are not merely those who lack intellectual ability, but rather those who lack sound judgment, who are prone to making mistakes, who are easily led astray. God's Word is so understandable, so clear, that even these people are made wise by it. Similarly, the Proverbs of Solomon are able both to instruct the "simple" and the "youth", and to increase the understanding of the "wise man" as well (Prov. 1:4-5).[3]

We find a similar emphasis in the New Testament. Jesus himself in his teachings, his conversations, and his disputes, never responds to any questions with a hint of impugning the clarity of the Old Testament Scriptures. Even though he spoke to people who were removed from David by 1,000 years, from Moses by about 1,500 years, and from Abraham by about 2,000 years, he still assumes that they are able to read and rightly to understand the Old Testament Scriptures.

Not once do we hear Jesus saying anything like the following: "I see how your problem arose—the Scriptures are not very clear on that subject." Instead, whether he is speaking to scholars or to untrained common people, his responses always assume that the blame for misunderstanding any teaching of Scripture is not to be placed on the Scriptures themselves but on those who misunderstand or fail to accept what is written. He asks Nicodemus with incredulity and more than a touch of reproach, "Are you a teacher of Israel and yet you do not understand this?" (John 3:10). He rebukes the Sadducees with the blunt sentence, "You are wrong because you know neither the Scriptures nor the power of God" (Matt. 22:29).

Many further examples could be given, but perhaps the following list of Jesus' statements from the Gospel of Matthew will establish the point:

Matt. 9:13:	"Go and learn what this means, 'I desire mercy . . .' "
Matt. 12:3:	"Have you not read . . ."
Matt. 12:5:	"Have you not read . . ."
Matt. 12:7:	"If you had known what this means, 'I desire mercy, and not sacrifice,' you would not have condemned the guiltless."
Matt. 15:3:	"Why do you transgress the commandment of God for the sake of your tradition?"
Matt. 19:4:	"Have you not read . . ."
Matt. 21:13:	"It is written . . ."
Matt. 21:16:	"Have you never read . . ."
Matt. 21:42:	"Have you never read in the Scriptures . . ."
Matt. 22:31:	"Have you not read what was said to you by God . . ."

In all of these instances it is clear that the blame for misunderstanding, for wrong interpretation, or for wrong application of the Bible's teachings is *never* placed on Scripture itself, but *on the hearers* who have not studied or who have not believed what Scripture says. Jesus assumes in his conversations that the Old Testament Scriptures are *clear* and able to be understood by those who will read them.

By contrast, Jesus can speak of every true believer as one who hears the Word and "*understands* it" (Matt. 13:23). This is true even though those who are believers may not be wise according to the standards of the world, for it is not the wisdom of the world which enables one to understand the Scripture, but the work of God in giving people an ability to understand. So Jesus can say, "I thank thee, Father, Lord of heaven and earth, that thou hast hidden these things from the wise and understanding and revealed them to babes" (Matt. 11:25).

The New Testament authors, both in their actions and in their specific statements, also affirm the clarity of what they write. Most of Paul's epistles are written not to church leaders but to entire congregations. He writes "to the *church* of God which is at Corinth" (1 Cor. 1:2), "to the *churches* of Galatia" (Gal. 1:2), "to *all the saints* in Christ Jesus who are at Philippi, with the bishops and deacons" (Phil. 1:1), etc. He assumes that his hearers will understand what he writes, and encourages the sharing of his letters with other churches: "And when this letter has been read among you, have it read also in the church of the Laodiceans; and see that you read also the letter from Laodicea" (Col. 4:16). (Compare James 1:1; 1 Pet. 1:1; John 20:30-31; 1 John 5:13.)

It is important to realize that in many cases these New Testament epistles were written to churches that had large proportions of Gentile Christians, relatively new Christians who had no previous background in any kind of Christian society, and little or no prior understanding of the history and culture of Israel.

Even though the problems of "contextualization" may have seemed immense, the New Testament authors show no hesitancy in expecting even these Gentile Christians to be able to *understand* it rightly. Timothy was to "attend to the public reading of Scripture" (1 Tim. 4:13), and Peter's hearers were to "pay attention" to the prophetic word (2 Pet. 1:19) and to long for the pure spiritual milk of the Word like newborn babes (1 Pet. 2:2).

In writing to Christians at Rome, Paul does not hesitate to base a major theological argument on detailed events in the life of Abraham (Rom. 4). He can write a long exhortation to the Christians at Corinth based on detailed events in the Exodus and expect that they will understand his argument (1 Cor. 10:1-11).

Furthermore, the New Testament authors sometimes explicitly affirm the clarity of their own writing. Paul tells the Corinthians, "We write you nothing but what you can read and understand" (2 Cor. 1:13).[4] Paul writes in Eph. 3:4, "When you read this you can perceive my insight into the mystery of Christ." Even the fact that all Scripture is "profitable for teaching, for reproof, for correction, and for training in righteousness, that the man of God may be complete, equipped for every good work" (2 Tim. 3:16-17), seems to imply that Scripture will be *able to be understood* by any who would be taught or trained in righteousness by it, or by any who would be "equipped for every good work."

Like Jesus, Paul affirms that when people misunderstand the gospel message the fault is not with the message but with the hearers: "And even if our gospel is veiled, it is veiled only to those who are perishing. In their case the god of this world has blinded the minds of the unbelievers, to keep them from seeing the light of the gospel of the glory of Christ" (2 Cor. 4:3-4). James similarly implies that all believers are able to understand God's Word when he encourages them all not only to be "hearers" of the Word but also those who are "doers" (James 1:22-25).[5]

The New Testament writers also echo Jesus' teaching that the ability to understand Scripture rightly is more a moral and spiritual ability than it is an intellectual ability: see 1 Cor. 1:18-3:4; 2 Cor. 3:14-16; 2 Cor. 4:6; Heb. 5:14; James 1:5-6; 2 Pet. 3:5.

In summarizing this NT data on the clarity of Scripture, it would *not* be appropriate to say that the NT supports the idea that *all believers* will agree on *all the teachings* of Scripture. But once we have guarded against such a misunderstanding, we still need to be reminded that these passages which affirm the clarity of Scripture for ordinary believers do have much positive application to ourselves today. We need to be reminded, for instance, that whenever we misunderstand or disagree on something in Scripture, we should never place any part of the blame on the Bible itself. We should not begin to wish that the Bible had been written differently or written more clearly. We need to affirm that it has been written perfectly, exactly the way God wanted it to be written.

In this connection it might be appropriate to say that the Bible is "inerrant" not only in that it always tells the truth about all that it affirms, but also in that it does not need improvement in the area of clarity: it *is* understandable.

Furthermore, where there are areas of doctrinal or ethical disagreement (for example over baptism or predestination or church government) we should recognize there are two possible kinds of situations which would lead to these disagreements. On the one hand it may be that we are making mistakes in our *interpretation*, either because the *data* we used to decide a hermeneutical question was wrong or incomplete or because there is some *personal inadequacy* on our part, whether it be, for example, personal pride, or greed, or lack of faith, or selfishness.

On the other hand, where we have areas of disagreement it may be that we have made or that we are seeking to make affirmations where *Scripture itself is silent.* In such cases we should be more ready to say, "We don't know."

IV. APPLICATION OF THE DOCTRINE OF THE CLARITY OF SCRIPTURE TO THE PROBLEM OF CONTEXTUALIZATION

If we are right in thinking that God has caused the Bible to be written in such a way that it is understandable even for ordinary believers, then certain implications follow with regard to the problem of contextualization.

(a) This biblical teaching on the clarity of Scripture implies, I think, that the single most important thing we can do to solve the remaining problems of contextualization in hundreds of different societies and cultures is to translate the whole Bible into the language of each receptor culture. This sounds like an overwhelmingly difficult task, yet we must face the fact that the *whole* Bible with both the Old Testament and the New Testament read as a unity is its own best interpreter.

The historical narratives both in the Old Testament and in the Gospels and Acts give much necessary background for understanding not only figures of speech but also more complex historical and theological concepts in Scripture. Even someone who has never seen a shepherd can learn much about shepherds from the stories in the Bible itself. While someone who had no previous Bible knowledge or Christian experience would have a very difficult time understanding what was meant by "the lamb of God," or the work of the High Priest, the same person who could not understand those concepts from the New Testament alone could understand them if given an opportunity to read the Old Testament as well as the New Testament in his own native language.

Moreover the *whole* Bible is its own best interpreter because it is necessary to have the *entire picture* of the development of the history of redemption throughout Scripture if we expect to be able to take advantage of the clarity with which Scripture is written. (The New Testament authors are able to recognize that there will be some Christians without a New Testament, or with only a partial New Testament. But they did not envisage any believers without access to an Old Testament!)

Many questions of biblical interpretation turn on one's understanding of the development of the history of redemption over time.

And in the history of the development of God's work with his people, there are many divinely controlled examples of the application of theology and ethics to several different societies at several different times in history. Of particular significance to us is the fact that the Bible contains the narrative of the "contextualization" of the gospel to Gentiles in major cities of the Roman empire.

Do we really believe that the Bible is able to be rightly understood by ordinary believers who can read it in their own language? Then we should do everything we can to give them the Bible in their own language and then be confident that they will contextualize it rightly. Too many of our mistakes on the mission field have come about because we have been unwilling to do this: it wasn't from the Bible that many African Christians got the idea to build churches with steeples and to have pastors wear a coat and tie every Sunday morning, even in blistering heat.

(b) We as Western Christians must beware of becoming an elite of "contextualizing experts." Certainly it is good to improve and refine our hermeneutical skills, our tools for exegesis of Scripture, our knowledge of Hebrew and Greek and biblical theology and church history, etc. But we must *never* give the impression that because we have these tools and skills *we alone* are the final authorities in interpreting or applying Scripture. We must not give the impression that *we alone* can be confident that our interpretations of Scripture are correct or that *we* are the ones who can best carry out contextualization for other societies. The more "expert" we become, the more necessary it is for us to remind ourselves that God has made Scripture in such a way that ordinary believers are able to do a very good job of understanding it for themselves.[6]

Is there then any role for specialists, for scholars who have additional technical ability for training in interpreting Scripture? Certainly there is a role for this kind of person in at least four areas of activity: (1) *Teach*: God has given to the church some who are "teachers" (1 Cor. 12:28; compare Eph. 4:11), and those given this responsibility should be able to communicate, synthesize and apply the message of the Bible clearly and effectively. (2) *Explore*: biblical scholars have more opportunity to think about new areas of application and of understanding Scripture. (3) *Defend*: they have a positive role in defending biblical teaching against attacks by other scholars or specialists who have similar training and tools. (4) *Supplement*: those who have specialized scholarly skills in the study of Scripture can do much to relate the teachings of Scripture to the rich history of the church, and to help the task of interpretation be more precise by using a knowledge of the biblical languages and history and culture.

Now these abilities and their corresponding roles naturally will lead to a greater precision and accuracy in the interpretation of Scripture. I certainly do not wish to deny this or to see it as something that is harmful. Nonetheless the tendency in every generation will be toward the creation of a scholarly elite of biblical interpreters. In order to keep this generation of scholars from becoming a North American and European scholarly elite, it would be right to encourage deeper and more advanced study of the Bible at *every level* by people in receptor cultures. For church officers at the local level or for other lay persons who wish to do advanced Bible study it would be very helpful to have available a quite literal translation of the Bible, something like the New American Standard Bible but in their own language.[7] For this purpose also it would be very helpful if in other languages we could make available concordances such as the *Word Study Concordance* (recently revised edition of the *Englishman's Greek Concordance*; edited by Ralph D. Winter; Pasadena: William Carey Library, 1978). These concordances would enable people to do much more serious and precise word study on their own.

For pastors of churches, and for those who have ability to become writers and more highly trained Bible scholars within their own cultures, of course all that can be done to encourage them in the knowledge of Hebrew and Greek (and in access to and ability to use more advanced tools and skills in exegesis) will help in preventing churches in receptor cultures from becoming dependent on Western "contextualizing experts."

(c) Yet this biblical teaching on the clarity of Scripture would be misunderstood if anyone used it to argue that each culture and society should carry on the task of contextualizing the Bible's teaching in isolation from the rest of the church around the world and throughout history. The interpretation and application of Scripture is certainly enriched and strengthened when it is done in fellowship with the whole church. It is of course right to encourage continuing contact and interaction between each receptor culture and other Christians around the world, and to encourage continuing acquaintance with the rich history of the church. "Having gifts that differ according to the grace given us, let us use them" (Rom. 12:6). It is right that we use our various gifts in advancing our mutual goal of building and strengthening the church.

NOTES

[1]The older term for this doctrine in systematic theology was "perspicuity", but that word is no longer perspicuous. The term "clarity" is therefore preferable, and is the term I shall use.

[2]Small examples of translations of individual terms can be found in the New Testament books themselves. For example, in John 1:38-42, John translates for his Greek speaking readers the Hebrew terms "rabbi", and "Messiah", as well as the Aramaic term "Cephas."

[3]See also Ps. 119:99-100: the Psalmist who is instructed by God's Word has more understanding than all his teachers, and than the aged.

[4]The subsequent statement, "I hope you will understand fully" (2 Cor. 1:13), encourages the Corinthians to give Paul a sympathetic hearing but does not negate his basic affirmation of the clarity of his writings.

[5]Two verses in 2 Peter may be urged against the view that the New Testament authors affirmed the clarity of Scripture. First, 2 Pet. 1:20, someone may claim, teaches that "no prophecy of Scripture is a matter of one's own interpretion," and that this means that ordinary believers are not able to interpret Scripture rightly for themselves. It is unlikely that this implication should be drawn from 2 Pet. 1:20, for the verse is probably discussing the origin and not the interpretation of Scripture. Thus the NIV translates, "no prophecy of Scripture came about by the prophet's own interpretation"; compare M. Green, *The Second Epistle of Peter and the Epistle of Jude, T. N. T. C.* (Grand Rapids: Eerdmans, 1968), pp. 89-92. Second, even if the verse were held to speak of interpreting Scripture, it would still tell us no more than the fact that the interpretation of Scripture must be done within the fellowship of believers. It still would not imply that authoritative interpreters are needed to tell the true meaning of Scripture.

The other passage which might be urged against the idea that the NT affirms the clarity of Scripture is 2 Pet. 3:16, where Peter says of Paul's letters that "there are some things in them hard to understand, which the ignorant and unstable twist to their own destruction, as they do the other Scriptures." This verse reminds us of the evident fact that some parts of Scripture are much more difficult to understand than other parts, but it should also be kept in mind that this verse appears in the context of an appeal by Peter to the teachings of Paul's letter(s) which Peter's readers had read and understood (2 Pet. 3:15), and that there is some moral culpability assigned even here to those who misinterpret the difficult sections (verse 16).

[6]When I have a chance to teach adult Sunday School classes on the question of interpreting the Bible, I regularly tell them that the three most important rules for understanding Scripture rightly and the three most basic principles of biblical interpretation are the following: (1) Read it. (2) Read it. (3) Read it. I say this because I am convinced that not only Christians in other cultures but also (or especially) Christians in our own 20th century American culture are in danger of being convinced that they are unable to read and understand the Bible for them-

selves. As pastors and scholars we have a special responsibility to say to them clearly, "You *can* read the Bible and you *can* understand it rightly."

[7]I am not saying that all Bible translations should be quite "literal", for translations with different degrees of literalness are certainly good for different needs and situations. I am saying, however, that there is certainly a place for "more literal" translations which do less interpretation for the reader and thereby enable him to do more of the interpretation for himself, thus making him less dependent on the translator.

Patrick Fairbairn and Biblical Hermeneutics as Related to the Quotations of the Old Testament in the New

Roger R. Nicole
Professor of Theology and
Curator of the Library
Gordon-Conwell Theological
Seminary

14. Patrick Fairbairn and Biblical Hermeneutics as Related to the Quotations of the Old Testament in the New

Roger R. Nicole

Although a number of very worthwhile and sometimes monumental contributions on the subject of the quotations of the Old Testament in the New Testament have appeared in recent years, few if any can favorably compare with the treatment given to this matter in the last century by Patrick Fairbairn (1805-1874). It would appear that this man who can well be characterized as a master in the understanding of revealed truth did in a special way correlate his life ministry in relation to the subject of biblical hermeneutics. His earliest major work, and perhaps the one for which he is best known, was *The Typology of Scripture* in two volumes. This appeared first in 1845-1847 and has seen many successive editions and reprints. In this work a masterly presentation was made of the principles of typology with an application to the relation of the patriarchal age and of the age of the law to the fullest revelation of God's redemptive plan in the New Testament. The work is characterized by cautious restraint combined with a breadth of vision which readily perceives the lines of force of the biblical revelation which passed through all the ages of the redemptive purpose. Fairbairn developed his hermeneutical principles more fully in three major volumes dealing respectively with the Law,[1] Prophecy[2] and the New Testament.[3]

Fairbairn was not content to set forth hermeneutical principles, but he made a conscious effort to apply these in the production of commentaries. Thus, we have from his pen a commentary on Ezekiel (1851) and another on the Pastoral Epistles (1874) as well as a popular study of the prophet Jonah (1849). He furthermore used his thorough knowledge of the German language to publish translations of certain German commentaries, notably those on the Psalms and Revelation by Hengstenberg. He edited the very large *Imperial Bible*

Dictionary in two volumes (sometimes reprinted in six volumes) for which he contributed a multitude of articles. When one considers that he also published some papers on the history of doctrine and gave regularly lectures in pastoral theology (published after his death), it will be apparent that this man was a consummate scholar with an admirable breadth of vision.

Specifically, Fairbairn was exceptionally well-qualified to deal with the quotations of the Old Testament in the New. Beside many passages in his writings which relate to this general subject he dealt expressly with this topic in a rather extended form in two places.

We will mention first Appendix A found in his *Typology of Scripture*.[4] In this well-organized treatment he undertook to indicate first the framework of understanding of the Old Testament Scripture within which the quotations are advanced. He developed the view that this framework had its foundation in the direct teaching of our Lord. He further shows that the same framework was at the root of the quotations adduced by the Gospel writers in their presentation of the life of Christ and furthermore that it is the background of the quotations made also by Paul and by the author of the Epistle to the Hebrews.

In the *Hermeneutical manual . . . of the New Testament* Fairbairn returned to this topic and devoted a special part of the total work to "The Use Made of Old Testament Scripture in the Writings of the New Testament." There he considers at some length the manner of citation (pp. 357-415) and then the mode of application of the Scriptures (pp. 416-60).

It is this important work which we would undertake to summarize in this paper in order to focus the attention once again in our century upon the very valid considerations made more then one hundred years ago by this splendid exegete.

I. TYPOLOGY OF SCRIPTURE

In his introduction to the subject Fairbairn emphasizes the difference between formal quotations and references in the New Testament where the wording of Old Testament Scripture is used without implying that there is a relation of prophecy and fulfillment between the two situations. Obviously, in those cases there is no difficulty in understanding the use of the Old Testament Scripture, since the authors of the New Testament were from their youth suffused with scriptural ideas and formulations that would naturally come under their pen when they presented their own message. Similarly, it must be acknowledged that many of the quotations that are presented are featured in their natural sense as, for instance, when the commandments of the decalogue are quoted. The difficulty occurs principally in the passages of the Old Testament that are presented as prophetic and in which the authors of the New Testament appear to project a direct relation of prophecy and fulfillment. It is this area particularly that Fairbairn is concerned to explore. But before he launches into his major discussion, he adverts to the suggestion often made that in their methodology the New Testament writers have followed the rabbinical method of application of the Old Testament texts. This method would appear to us to be characterized by very considerable arbitrariness and therefore to distort the legitimate meaning of Scripture and to move by dint of allegory almost in any direction that an individual interpreter might desire.

Fairbairn emphasizes that Jesus distanced Himself from the rabbinical method of interpretation and rebuked the Jewish leaders for having made void the Word of God by their tradition (Mark 7:11-13). One purpose, therefore, of the ministry of Christ was to reassert the proper meaning of Old Testament Scripture, and it appears doubtful that the disciples would then revert to rabbinic methods in spite of the clear warnings of our Lord.

Fairbairn furthermore contrasts the sobriety of the New Testament handling of Old Testament Scripture with some of the very artificial interpretations that are found in some sectors of the early church, in the Apostolic Fathers, in Justin Martyr, and in Irenaeus. These, Fairbairn holds, have really no substantial base of correlation between the Old Testament incident and the New Testament truth. An example of this type of interpretation may be found in the Epistle of Barnabas in which the 318 trained men who accompanied Abraham in his pursuit of the four kings (Gen. 14:14) are considered to represent Jesus Christ on the ground that when this figure is written in Greek, the letters representing eighteen are the first two letters of the word "Jesus" and the letter T which means 300 portrays the shape of the cross. The Epistle of Barnabas compounds this artificially by saying "I never taught to anyone a more certain truth."[5] Allegorical interpretation of that type is damaging because it relies on elements of the Old Testament that are wrested out of their proper context and applied to a situation with which no correlation of meaning exists.

Fairbairn adverts here to three passages of the New Testament that are sometimes claimed to manifest a rabbinical type of interpretation, and he seeks to show that in each of those cases there is a substantial correspondence between the original Old Testament Scripture and the context in which the New Testament brings it to the fore. The first passage is the argument of Jesus for the Resurrection on the basis of the statement "I am the God of Abraham, the God of Isaac, and the God of Jacob." (Matt. 22:32, Mark 12:26 and Luke 20:37). Fairbairn emphasizes that the basis of the argument is not in the tense of the verb, but rather in the willingness of God to connect His own name with that of some people who were dead at the time. Since God is the God of the living, not of the dead, this implies that future life is foreseen for Abraham, Isaac and Jacob in this title of Jehovah.

In Galatians 4:21-31 many have felt that Paul's application of the history of Sara and Hagar to the doctrine of justification is fanciful (and indeed Paul himself uses the word "allegory" in this instance). Fairbairn emphasizes that the apostle here simply draws a parallel without asserting that there is a prophetic significance. He merely reads out the spiritual lessons that lay infolded in the history of Abraham's family as significant of things to come (p. 432).

In 1 Corinthians 10:1-4 another instance is found where Paul is accused of having a recourse to rabbinical methods. Here Fairbairn emphasizes that the great deliverance out of Egypt is only a type of that greater deliverance brought about by Christ for His people. This latter is symbolized by the sacraments of baptism and the Lord's Supper. Now baptism precisely represents the deliverance from the dominion of sin, the cleansing of the soul by the blood of Christ and the incorporation into the new life which God has opened for us. There is, therefore, a real parallel with the situation of the crossing of the Red Sea. The Lord's Table, on the other hand, among the various elements which it so richly symbolizes, bespeaks the truth that we are the guests of the living God, receiving that which is essential for our souls from Him from day to day. This truth also was made manifest in the experience of Israel since they were dependent upon a miraculous manifestation of God throughout their journey in the desert, both for food and for drink. There is therefore a true correspondence here, not an artificial and far-fetched application.

Fairbairn proceeds in his development by giving special attention to those prophecies actually presented by Jesus Christ Himself in the days of His flesh, and which He contemplated as fulfilled. Fairbairn views these as especially important since they indicate the fulfillment which Christ perceived to take place in His own life. He lays stress on the use made by Christ of Isaiah 61 at the very beginning of His public ministry. This indicates an affirmation that the wonderful and sometimes mysterious Person of the Servant of the Lord announced by Isaiah would be made manifest in His own life and ministry. Later on in other parts of the New Testament a number of the Servant passages from Isaiah were then also quoted in that way.

Our Lord sees a fulfillment of Old Testament prophecy in the ministry of John the Baptist as a preparation for His own ministry. Here the witness of Isaiah joins that of Malachi and the last prophecy of the Old Testament rejoins one of the first words of the New since it is a theme which Zechariah, the father of John the Baptist, includes in his song. The Old Testament in announcing the coming of Elijah obviously did not mean that he would return in person but that someone would be sent by God with the same spirit and power which characterized the ministry of the ancient prophet.

Another area in which Christ used Old Testament prophecy to confirm His own ministry relates to affirmations of the supreme dignity of the anointed of the Lord. One of the clearest texts in this respect is the use by Jesus of Psalm 110 in which King David, although the ancestor humanly speaking of the Messiah, still addresses Him as Lord. Jesus furthermore used the prophecy of Zechariah relating to the smiting of the Shepherd both as an announcement of His own suffering and as a way to emphasize His unique dignity as made explicit in Zechariah 13:7.

The New Testament indicates that our Lord discussed many more Scriptures of the Old Testament with His apostles (Luke 24:44) and we don't know precisely which ones He used in His teaching although the practice of the early church in the Book of Acts might very well indicate to us something of the teaching of Christ which they had imbibed and which was bound to come to the apostles' lips as they presented the gospel. We do find therefore that in the life of Christ there was an approach to the interpretation of the Old Testament that enabled the disciples to understand the major orientation of Old Testament Scripture and to apply with propriety to Jesus Christ things which had been stated sometimes in a rather cryptic manner in the Old Testament. These prophecies which our Lord applied to Himself "and the affairs of His kingdom, during the period of His earthly ministry, were such as admitted of being so applied in their most direct and obvious sense. In nothing else could they have found a proper and adequate fulfillment" (p. 440).

There were some statements, however, one public and the other made in private, in which our Lord presented prophecies "which could not be said to bear immediate and exclusive respect to New Testament times." In these in a special way we need to explore what are the hermeneutical principles which justify the use made by Jesus of the Old Testament Scripture. These same principles may extend to quotations made later by the apostles.

The first passage that Fairbairn mentions is the reference by Jesus to Psalm 118: "The stone which the builders rejected. . . ." In the context of the Psalm it appears that reference is made to a situation in which God's people join to praise Him for the time of blessing which follows a period of depression and contempt. Such a situation might occur after the captivity in Babylon, where God permitted a nation, so sorely oppressed as to be ruled out of existence, once again to come to life and to fulfill the divine purpose. Here the reference seems to be to the nation rather than to an individual. It is precisely to this point that the parallelism that our Lord perceives is of great instruction for it was characteristic of our Lord's approach to see a close connection between the providential purpose of God with Israel and the course of redemptive events in His own life. In a supreme sense the Lord Jesus is true Israel in whom the sum of the blessings promised to Abraham is realized and in whom also the redemptive intervention of God, manifest among His ancient people in type, is now fulfilled in its plenitude. One aspect of this connection between Israel and Jesus Christ which receives considerable elaboration can be seen in the parallelism between the situation of David as the epitome of the kingship of Israel (in spite of his personal failings) and Jesus Christ in Whom the supreme rule of God is particularly made manifest. When this general background is understood, it appears clearly that the application of Psalm 118:22 to Jesus Christ is profoundly appropriate, as are also a number of statements made by David and which are even truer of his greater counterpart than was the case for the King of Israel who first wrote them. Thus, Fairbairn sees a very significant principle of correspondence that binds the Old Testament and the New and which the Lord articulated in a most illuminating way. It is this insight into the correspondence of the Old Testament and of the New which must inform our hermeneutic, and it is in this framework that some of the interpretations which might at first surprise us will turn out to be perceived as appropriate and very insightful.

Fairbairn then turns to applications made by the evangelists of Old Testament prophecies, as distinguished from passages advanced by Christ Himself in His teaching ministry. He finds that under the leadership of Christ the Gospel writers also perceive a profound correspondence between the calling and destination of Israel and those of the Messiah as well as between the kingdom of David and the kingdom of righteousness which God will establish in His own purpose. The Gospel writers in emphasizing from the start the supernatural character of the ministry of Christ are preparing the way for an insight in the fulfillment of prophecy in Christ. It is in this fashion that Fairbairn accounts for the legitimacy of the quotations made in the early part of the Gospel of Matthew. It would be too long to summarize here those excellent passages in which one by one some difficult quotations are examined and shown to be remarkably appropriate.

Another section relates to the writings of the apostle Paul. The propriety of the application to justification by faith of the promises made to Abraham is first explored, then the difficult passage of Galatians 3:16 in which the singular "his seed" is construed by the apostle as an announcement of the Messiah. Then the passages in Romans that relate to the situation of the Jews, the conversion of the Gentiles and the return of blessings upon the Jews are the object of a careful scrutiny. In all of these passages, Fairbairn perceives the complete propriety of the application to Christ and the gospel of the statements made in the Old Testament.

In a final section Fairbairn discusses the hermeneutics of the Epistle to the Hebrews. Some of these passages are indeed difficult but once again Fairbairn makes plain that in using the Old Testament passages (very largely of the Psalms) as he does, the author of the Epistle to the Hebrews has proceeded on a basis analogous to that of Christ. He accounts for some of the difficulties that we have on the basis that we are not prepared to place ourselves on the same ground which the New Testament occupied in their apprehension of the relation between the Jewish and the Christian dispensation. It is because the inspired writers went so much farther in this respect than many of their readers and commentators are disposed to do now, that great difficulty is experienced in sympathizing with this part of their writings. They saw everything in the Old Testament pointing and tending toward the manifestation of God in Christ; so that not only a few leading prophecies and more prominent instructions, but even subordinate arrangements and apparently incidental notices in matters connected with the ancient economy, were regarded as having a significance in respect to Christ and the Gospel. No one can see eye-to-eye with them in this, if he has been wont practically to divorce

Christ from the Old Testament. In proportion as an intelligent discernment of the connection between the two economies is acquired, the course actually adopted by the New Testament writers will appear the more natural and justifiable (p. 470).

II. HERMENEUTICAL MANUAL

In the *Hermeneutical Manual . . . of the New Testament,* 1858, Fairbairn, as mentioned above, reverted to this topic and he organized the quotations first in terms of their textual relation to the Old Testament. He grouped them in four classes:

A. Those in which the Greek exactly corresponds with the Hebrew. He lists seventy-two of those.

B. Those in which the Greek subsequentially agrees with the Hebrew with only substantial differences not affecting the sense. There are thirty quotations in that class.

C. Those in which the Septuagint is followed though it diverges to some extent from the Hebrew. This class includes seventeen quotations, and finally,

D. Those which agree with neither Hebrew nor the Septuagint text. He has seventeen such quotations. Where substantial differences occur, Fairbairn has undertaken to explain them without opening the door to the charge that the New Testament writers were cavalier in their handling of the text.

In a second section Fairbairn discusses singly a number of quotations, some nineteen of them to be exact, in which the meaning of the Old Testament in its context does not seem to have been properly considered in the New Testament usage. Here again Fairbairn comes forth with extremely helpful comments in which he supports the practice of the New Testament writers in every case. It is high time that in the midst of controversies in which all kinds of accusations are levelled against the use of the Old Testament by New Testament authors the painstaking work of Patrick Fairbairn and his monumental scholarship be once again taken into consideration. I am sure that those who will read his volumes will find themselves amply rewarded.

It may be appropriate to conclude this survey of Fairbairn's contribution with a statement of a few principles that relate to the bearing of the Old Testament quotations in the New upon hermeneutical issues.

1. The New Testament authors almost without exception drew heavily from the Old Testament. Almost one-tenth of the New Testament actually consists of Old Testament quotations. More distant

references and allusions, furthermore, abound from Matthew to Revelation.

2. The New Testament authors viewed, and expected their readers to view, the Old Testament as a divinely authoritative document. This they made plain in a number of ways: the frequency of their quotations, the formulae of introduction which emphasized divine authorship, the personification of Scripture (as in Rom. 9:17 and Gal. 3:8), the readiness to build up an argument on just one word of Old Testament Scripture, the use of the present tense rather than the past tense as a means to feature the permanent relevancy of Scripture, are all indices of this high level of confidence. Not only evangelical scholars, who might be inclined to project on the New Testament authors their own view of Scripture, but many others who never claimed to have an outlook that coincides with that of Scripture have readily recognized that fact.

3. In quoting the Old Testament the New Testament writers have manifested a considerable liberty in adjusting the language to their needs. This, on the face of it, might at first be interpreted as a disregard for the sacredness of the inspired text. Rather, it should undoubtedly be seen as related to the kind of liberty which has often been enjoyed in literary productions of the past.[6] The type of punctilious (or notarial) accuracy which is nowadays required in works of scholarship was simply not a standard in biblical times. We are therefore not in a position to judge the performance of the biblical writers as if they had to abide by this standard or else explain why they do not do so. Because of this freedom and because of the lack of clear-cut signs as to what is intended as a quotation, it is often difficult to ascertain the precise limits of the quoted materials.

4. With respect to the meaning that they ascribed to Old Testament Scriptures it is not always easy to discern what principles of hermeneutics the New Testament authors used. It is apparent that they did recognize a fundamental unity in the redemptive purpose of God which led them to perceive deep-seated analogies between the Old Testament economy and the New Testament fulfillment of the redemptive purpose. Those who insist on perceiving the Old Testament as a closed system without opening toward the future will obviously find great difficulty in acknowledging the propriety of the use of Old Testament texts in the New Testament. Fairbairn, by contrast, with his far-reaching grasp of the lines of force which run across both testaments and with his willingness to be taught by the examples of the New Testament authors in their interpretation of the Old Tes-

tament, was in a position to give a full recognition to the hermeneutical insights that are apparent in the New Testament ways of handling the Old Testament Scripture. Even H. C. Toy said, "The deeper the reverence for the departed Lord and for the divine Word, the greater the disposition to find Him everywhere."[7] It is this devotion to Christ in Fairbairn that has illumined the propriety of New Testament usage. Is it too much to hope that in our day as well a similar devotion may lead us also to recognize Christ in the prefigurements provided in Old Testament history and symbolism?

5. In a number of cases the New Testament authors made a combination of various passages of the Old Testament, bringing together Scriptures which in the Old Testament had no contextual relationship. This is a procedure that can easily be abused and in which preposterous combinations may be suggested. In the New Testament, however, we find this practice used with great sobriety, and we are therefore encouraged to see the character of complementarity which is one of the features of inspired writ. It is when the Bible is seen as one large contextual unit that the ultimate in interpretation is also reached. This is, at least in part, what is meant by emphasizing the principle of the analogy of Scripture as a hermeneutical norm.

NOTES

[1]*The Revelation of the Law in Scripture*, Second Series of Cunningham Lecture, (Edinburgh: T. & T. Clark, 1969).

[2]*Prophecy Viewed in Respect to Its Distinctive Nature, Special Functions, and Proper Interpretation*, (Edinburgh: T. & T. Clark, 1856).

[3]*Hermeneutical Manual or Introduction to the Exegetical Study of the Scriptures of the New Testament,* (Edinburgh: T. & T. Clark, 1858), Vol. XII, p. 480.

[4]Sixth Edition, (Edinburgh: T. & T. Clark, 1882), pp. 427-70.

[5]Epistle of Barnabas, Chapter IX, *Ante-Nicene Fathers*, Vol. I, p. 143.

[6]One should consult with profit the able and extensive treatment of Franklin Johnson, *The Quotations of the New Testament from the Old, Considered in the Light of General Literature*, (Philadelphia: American Baptist Publication Society, 1896), Vol. XIX, p. 409.

[7]Crawford Howell Toy, *Quotations in the New Testament*, (New York: Scribner's 1884), Vol. XXV.

A Response to Patrick Fairbairn and Biblical Hermeneutics as Related to the Quotations of the Old Testament in the New

Ronald F. Youngblood
Professor of Old Testament
Bethel Theological
Seminary West

A Response to Patrick Fairbairn and Biblical Hermeneutics as Related to the Quotations of the Old Testament in the New

Ronald Youngblood

Inscribed on a wall plaque in the office of a friend is the following epigram: "I know you believe you understand what you think I said, but I am not sure you realize that what you heard is not what I meant." If adequate comprehension of *spoken* words is beset by obstacles too numerous to mention, is it not much more difficult for us to draw meaningful conclusions from a *written* Word from which we are separated by thousands of miles and thousands of years?

Under ordinary circumstances the answer to that question would be "yes." But in point of fact we do not approach the study of Scripture in a total vacuum. Our confidence in our ability to understand Holy Writ, though admittedly imperfectly by virtue of our fallen humanity, is not misplaced. For alongside the already impressive and continually multiplying number of excellent exegetical tools at our disposal—we have seen and used them, and they are marvelous in our eyes—we possess additional resources, which are spiritual in nature: an unshakable belief in the fact that "the Bible alone, and the Bible in its entirety, is the Word of God written and is therefore inerrant in the autographs";[1] the doctrine of the perspicuity of Scripture, which originates in the loving desire of our God to communicate his revelation in ways that are completely intelligible to his children, the objects of his love; the promise of our Savior that he would send a Counselor to guide us into all truth (John 16:13-15), and the resulting illumination of the Holy Spirit that all of us experience whenever we sincerely seek it;[2] and the recognition that, throughout the long history of the Church, devout men and women who have preceded us have used the exegetical tools available to them, have believed in an inerrant Bible, have reveled in the perspicuity of Scripture, have sought to be led by God's Holy Spirit as they have interpreted the text for themselves and for others, and have thus placed at our disposal a rich legacy of commentary and exposition.

Such a man was Patrick Fairbairn, the importance of whose work has been so well summarized by Roger Nicole. I remember with genuine delight and fond appreciation my first encounter with Fairbairn's *Typology of Scripture* in its Zondervan reprint edition more than twenty-five years ago. If it be true, as D. L. Baker argues, that the relationship between the Testaments is one of the most fundamental problems in current Biblical studies,[3] and if it be further true, as Baker summarizes Leonhard Goppelt's "simple and important" conclusion in his *Typos: Die typologische Deutung des Alten Testaments im Neuen*, that "typology is the dominant and characteristic method of interpretation for the New Testament use of the Old Testament,"[4] then Nicole has indeed chosen well and has provided for Lewis Johnson and myself a fertile topic for exploration and interaction.

But was Goppelt right? Is typology in fact "the dominant and characteristic method of interpretation for the New Testament use of the Old"? This summer I had the privilege of teaching a seven-week course at Bethel Theological Seminary West entitled "Christian Roots in the Old Testament." Near the end of the course I asked the students this question: "If you were forced to choose only one solution to the problem of the relationship between the Testaments, which would it be?" I then gave them four choices:[5] (1) Christology—witness and identity; (2) salvation history and actualization; (3) continuity and discontinuity; and (4) typology—example and analogy. The responses to my query, which will perhaps not be quite so surprising to you as they were to me, revealed that the class was just about evenly divided in their preference for one of the first three options, but no one—not one student out of the nineteen enrolled in the course—chose typology. Further discussion revealed that some students shied away from committing themselves to typological interpretation in any form because of past abuses (allegorical, symbolic, and so on) of the method and that others would have made it their second or third choice. But if my experiment with these students is at all typical, the fact remains that Goppelt's dictum applies primarily to the scholarly study of Scripture rather than to the hermeneutical practices of the Church at large.

Nevertheless, typology in the general sense that Fairbairn understood it has been enjoying a resurgence in our day, and distinguished theologians have led the way. For example, Gerhard von Rad's "programmatic essay on 'Typological Interpretation of the Old Testament' (1952) has been one of the most influential factors in the revival of typology in recent years."[6] Typology is associated by Nicole with numerous related terms, among them (cor)relation, context, representation, preparation, connection, application, analogy, parallel, example and complementarity. These are the "lines of force" (Nicole's phrase) that run across both Testaments and pass through all the ages of the divine purpose. Two other terms used by Nicole, prefigurement (=prefiguration) and correspondence (Nicole's favorite), are stressed as well by Baker, who isolates them as the two main categories of definitions for typology that modern scholarship has proposed.[7] The first is illustrated by C. T. Fritsch: "A type is an institution, historical event or person, ordained by God, which effectively prefigures some truth connected with Christianity."[8] G. W. H. Lampe exemplifies the second category by defining typology as "primarily a method of *historical* interpretation, based upon the continuity of God's purpose throughout the history of his covenant" and seeking "to demonstrate the correspondence between the various stages in the fulfillment of that purpose."[9] To Nicole's list Baker would add such terms as historicality, continuity, repetition, similarity, pattern, model, comparison, consistency and concreteness. Baker's own definition resembles that of Lampe:

> A *type* is a biblical event, person or institution which serves as an example or pattern for other events, persons or institutions; *typology* is the study of types and the historical and theological correspondences between them; the *basis* of typology is God's consistent activity in the history of his chosen people.[10]

Similar is the attempt of Roland E. Murphy:

> Typology connotes two factors: a set of correspondences between objects or actions in both Testaments, and an indication that their interrelations are God-willed. The correspondences will be subjected to imaginative flights unless they are controlled by the second factor, which for all practical purposes is to be sought in the insights of the New Testament.[11]

My colleague Lewis Johnson, in his excellent little volume on *The Old Testament in the New* as an argument for Biblical inspiration, generally concurs with the above as he gives his own definition among others that he cites: "Typology is the study of the spiritual correspondences between persons, events, and things within the historical framework of God's special revelation."[12]

Although a type—by definition—must precede its antitype chronologically, the significance of a type is neither found completely in nor exhausted by its antitype. On the contrary, it has a meaning of its own within its own historical context. This fact Patrick Fairbairn understood well:

> While . . . types speak a language that can be distinctly and intelligently understood only by us, who are privileged to read their meaning in the light of gospel realities, they yet had, *as institutions in the existing worship, or events in the current providence of God*, a present purpose to accomplish, apart from the prospective reference to future times, and, we might almost say, as much as if no such reference had belonged to them.[13]

Although by definition they are predictive,[14] types must be sharply distinguished from predictive prophecies, the very meaning and validity of which depends on their ultimate fulfillment. A type must always experience contemporary realization in some sense, whereas a predictive prophecy need not do so but may be entirely future in its orientation.

At the same time a type—by definition—is a mere prefiguring, a foreshadowing, of its future antitype. The greater reality to which it points is always grander and higher and more magnificent than itself. "The type is enlarged and developed in the New Testament fulfillment," says Johnson, due to "the progressive nature of divine revelation."[15] As might be expected, Fairbairn would agree wholeheartedly—while at the same time adding an important refinement: "The typical is not properly a different or higher sense, but a different or higher application of the same sense."[16]

The heightened sense discerned in the antitype is of course due to the nature of Scripture itself. Because it is "the Bible, Word of God in words of men,"[17] "the biblical interpreter is interested not only in what the inspired author meant but also in what God meant."[18] As Wenham puts it, "the Holy Spirit knew beforehand the course of history with its consummation in Christ, and so in guiding the writers he intended a deeper meaning than they understood."[19] Authorial intent (or "the author's willed meaning," to use Hirsch's phrase[20]), when applied to Scripture, ultimately must refer to the purposes of God himself, as Johnson affirms: "The total context of a passage is necessary for its correct understanding and, therefore, the intention of the secondary author must be subordinated to the intention of the primary author, God Himself."[21]

How are we to distinguish between predictive prophecy on the one hand and typological prefiguration on the other? Jesus interpreted Old Testament prophecies (and here I am using the term "prophecy" in its broadest sense) sometimes literally and sometimes typologically, and, says Wenham, "it is not always easy to discern the principles of interpretation which govern our Lord's understanding"[22] in such cases. Moreover, our inability to determine whether Jesus was using literal or typological hermeneutics in this or that specific case extends to his disciples' methodology as well. How did *they* view the Old Testament?

To illustrate the problem, I would like to do what Nicole in his paper modestly declines to do: examine and summarize Patrick Fairbairn's discussion of the Old Testament quotations found in the early part of the gospel of Matthew and affirm, with Fairbairn, their legitimacy and appropriateness—although I will disagree with Fairbairn on his methodology in connection with one of the five Old Testament quotations in Matthew 1-2. Let us look first of all at the four citations in Matthew's second chapter.

(1) Matt. 2:6: "But you, Bethlehem, in the land of Judah, are by no means least among the rulers of Judah; for out of you will come a ruler who will be the shepherd of my people Israel." Thus did the chief priests and teachers of the law quote Micah 5:2 (5:1 Hebrew), neither from the Hebrew nor from the Septuagint (which closely follows the Hebrew) but from memory (giving, nevertheless, its general sense). One can only agree with Fairbairn's comment: "The prediction is so plain, that there was no room for diversity of opinion about it."[23] I would simply make two observations, the first in the form of a question: Did the priests and teachers omit the last part of Micah 5:2 ("whose origins are from of old, from ancient times") because of its implications that the coming ruler was preexistent—a possibility that they were not quite prepared to acknowledge? My second observation is this: The miracle of the fulfillment of Micah 5:2 in Jesus is not so much the *place* of his birth (for *any* messianic ruler might be legitimately expected to be born in Bethlehem, "the town of David") as it was the *timing* of his birth: A Roman census was decreed at just the right moment to compel Joseph and the pregnant Mary to make the arduous journey from Nazareth to Bethlehem in order to fulfill Micah's prediction to the letter.

(2) Matthew 2:15: "Out of Egypt I called my son." The statement is cited precisely from the Hebrew text of Hosea 11:1, with which Aquila, Symmachus and Theodotion agree (the Septuagint differs somewhat). In a section entitled "Combination of Type with

Prophecy," Fairbairn comments thus on Hosea 11:1 as quoted in Matthew: "The scripture fulfilled was prophetical, simply because the circumstance it recorded was typical."[24] Note also his further statement: "What [Hosea 11:1] records to have been done in the type, must again be done in the antitype."[25] Again one can only agree with Fairbairn, as Wenham does (by implication) in such cases: "Jesus understood the Old Testament typologically, and it is to him that we owe the identification of himself (and of his disciples) with Israel."[26] Just as God called his son, Israel, out of Egypt in the days of Moses, so also God has now called his Son, the greater Israel, Jesus Christ, out of Egypt.

(3) Matthew 2:18: "A voice is heard in Ramah, weeping and great mourning, Rachel weeping for her children and refusing to be comforted, because they are no more." The citation, from Jeremiah 31:15, is closer to the Hebrew than to the Septuagint, although Matthew seems to have had recourse to both in this case. Fairbairn's discussion is again right on target, for he sees in Matthew 2:18 what Johnson would refer to as a "typical fulfillment."[27] There is correspondence between what happened in Jeremiah's day and what happened in Jesus' day, a correspondence at once subtle and profound. To accuse Matthew of seeing in his own time an instance of *predictive* fulfillment of Jeremiah 31:15 is to do him a gross injustice. In the words of Wenham:

> Matthew knows as well as we do that Moses was speaking of the people of Israel when he said, "Out of Egypt I called my son" (Mt. 2:15; Ho. 11:1); and that Jeremiah was speaking of the exile of his own days when he spoke of Rachel "weeping for her children" (Mt. 2:18; Je. 31:15).[28]

(4) Matthew 2:23: "He will be called a Nazarene." Although no verse in the Old Testament is clearly and unequivocally the source of this quotation, and although commentators do not agree among themselves on this matter, I would certainly concur with Fairbairn that the most probable solution is to look at the New Testament *Nazōraios* ("Nazarene," Hebrew *noṣrî*) as related typologically by Matthew to the messianic *nēṣer,* "Branch," in passages such as Isaiah 11:1. It may well be that Matthew 2:23 should read as follows: "So was fulfilled what was said through the prophets, (that) he would be called a 'Nazarene' "—that is, the quotation marks should be restricted to the final word in the verse. In any event a citation from Isaiah 11:1, which introduces an important section of the so-called

Book of Immanuel (Isa. 7:1-12:6), would form a fitting conclusion to Matthew's first five quotations from the Old Testament—a series of quotations that begins with another verse from the "Book of Immanuel." To that citation we now turn.

(5) Matthew 1:23: "The virgin will be with child and will give birth to a son, and they will call him Immanuel." The quotation of Isaiah 7:14 differs slightly from both the Hebrew and the Septuagint. The Syriac and Vulgate translations have a passive form in Isaiah, possibly reflecting the reading *wqr'* in 1QIsa[a] (probably to be vocalized as a *Pu'al* passive; see especially Isaiah 62:2, and note *kalesousin,* "they will call" [his name] = [his name] "will be called," in Matthew 1:23).

Traditionally Isaiah 7:14 (in the light of Matthew 1:23) has usually been understood as a prophetic prediction of the virgin birth of Christ, which therefore exhausts its meaning. Formidable arguments in favor of such an understanding have been set forth by scholars of the stature of Alfred Edersheim,[29] J. Barton Payne,[30] E. J. Young[31]—and Patrick Fairbairn himself. Since I have agreed completely with Fairbairn up to this point, it is with both reluctance and regret that I part company with him here and side with those—such as Gleason Archer,[32] Kenneth Barker[33] and Herbert Wolf[34]—who see typological prefiguration in Isaiah 7:14. The context of the Isaianic passage demands, in my judgment, a preliminary fulfillment in the days of King Ahaz—especially in the light of Isaiah 8:8, where Immanuel is addressed as one already born.

The scenario I propose runs as follows:[35] Isaiah 7:10-17 is similar in form and content to 8:1-4. This leads to the likelihood that Immanuel and Maher-Shalal-Hash-Baz are two names for the same child, the first given by his mother and the second by his father. Just as Shear-Jashub (7:3), the name of Isaiah's older son, has double-edged significance ("a remnant *will* return" and "*only* a remnant will return"), so also Immanuel ("God is with us") and Maher-Shalal-Hash-Baz ("quick to the plunder, swift to the spoil") represent salvation and judgment respectively, Alternate names are common throughout the Bible (see especially Naomi, "pleasant," and Mara, "bitter," in Ruth 1:20-21). The interplay between promise and threat in Isaiah 7-8 corresponds to the alternation between Immanuel and Maher-Shalal-Hash-Baz in the same section. Isaiah 7:15-16 and 8:4 refer to the same period of time (about two years, ending in 732 B.C. when the Assyrians destroyed Damascus and replaced Pekah king of Israel with the puppet-ruler Hoshea, spelling doom for Israel within a decade). The term "sign," referring to Immanuel in Isaiah 7:14, is echoed in 8:18 where the prophet Isaiah refers to himself and his children as "signs" and symbols in Israel. The context thus indicates that the eighth-century Immanuel is to be regarded as one of Isaiah's sons.

Apparently, then, Isaiah's first wife, the mother of Shear-Jashub, had died. In 7:14 Isaiah predicts that the girl who is to become his second wife—a virgin at the time of the prediction—will become pregnant and give birth to a son, whom she will name Immanuel. The wedding ceremony is referred to in 8:1-2. Isaiah takes his new bride to himself and soon she bears the promised son, whom Isaiah names Maher-Shalal-Hash-Baz. That Isaiah and his children were viewed typologically at least once in the New Testament is clear from Hebrews 2:13, which quotes Isaiah 8:18 and applies it to Christ as the father of his adopted children.

Thus the relationship of the "virgin" in Isaiah 7:14 and the Virgin Mary in Matthew 1:23 is that of type and antitype. Matthew's "God with us" reflects Deity incarnate and lifts the Immanuel of Isaiah 7:14; 8:8 to an infinitely higher plane. In the words of Wenham, "the Immanuel sign that the land would be freed of its dangers in the days of Ahaz prefigured the saving of Israel from its ultimate dangers by the advent of the true Immanuel."[36]

That I must disagree with Fairbairn on the nature of the Isaiah 7:14 prophecy is unfortunate, but his own insistence on paying careful attention to the context of an Old Testament passage when relating it to its New Testament fulfillment has led many evangelicals to occasionally find typological prefiguration where Fairbairn found prophetic prediction and vice versa. In any case I agree with him on four out of five of the Old Testament citations in Matthew 1-2, a respectable percentage indeed. And that a book on so arcane a subject as Biblical typology is still read and appreciated after 120 years is a tribute to the meticulous and devout scholarship of its author, Patrick Fairbairn.

"The whole relation of New Testament to Old is summed up in the one word 'fulfillment'," says John Wenham.[37] Whether that fulfillment be expressed in terms of prophetic prediction or typological prefiguration or a *tertium quid,* the *hina plērōthēs* of the New Testament remind us that "without the New Testament the Old Testament would be a magnificent failure" and "without the Old Testament the New Testament would be an inexplicable phenomenon."[38]

And Jesus Christ himself is the bridge between the two halves of the inerrant Word. F. F. Bruce summarizes as follows:

> In Jesus the promise is confirmed, the covenant is renewed, the prophecies are fulfilled, the law is vindicated, salvation is brought near, sacred history has reached its climax, the perfect sacrifice has been offered and accepted, the great priest over the household of God has taken his seat at God's right hand, the Prophet like Moses has been raised up, the Son of David reigns, the kingdom of God has been inaugurated, the Son of Man has received dominion from the Ancient of Days, the Servant of the Lord, having been smitten to death for his people's transgression and borne the sin of many, has accomplished the divine purpose, has seen light[39] after the travail of his soul and is now exalted and extolled and made very high.[40]

Or, to use the now classic statement of Gerhard von Rad, "Christ is given to us only through the double witness of the choir of those who await and those who remember."[41]

NOTES

[1]The doctrinal basis of the Evangelical Theological Society.

[2]John W. Wenham, *Christ & the Bible* (Downers Grove: InterVarsity Press, 1972), p. 18.

[3]D. L. Baker, *Two Testaments: One Bible* (Downers Grove: InterVarsity Press, 1977), p. 5. See the even stronger statement of Bernhard W. Anderson, ed., *The Old Testament and Christian Faith* (New York: Harper & Row, 1963), p. 1: "No problem more urgently needs to be brought to a focus than the one to which the following essays are addressed: the relation of the Old Testament to the New. . . . It is a question which confronts every Christian in the Church, whether he be a professional theologian, a pastor of a congregation, or a layman. It is no exaggeration to say that on this question hangs the meaning of the Christian faith."

[4]Baker, *Two Testaments,* p. 246, summarizing Goppelt, *Typos* (1939), pp. 239-49.

[5]The options are those listed by Baker, *Two Testaments,* pp. 367-72.

[6]Ibid., p. 292.

[7]Ibid., p. 242.

[8]C. T, Fritsch, "Biblical Typology," *Bibliotheca Sacra* 104 (1947): 214.

[9]G. W. H. Lampe, "Typological Exegesis," *Theology* 56 (1953): 202 (italics his).

[10]Baker, *Two Testaments,* p. 267 (italics his); see also p. 369.

[11]Roland E. Murphy, "The Relationship Between the Testaments," *Catholic Biblical Quarterly* 26 (1964): 357. The entire article is well worth reading.

[12]S. Lewis Johnson, Jr., *The Old Testament in the New* (Grand Rapids: Zondervan Publishing House, 1980), p. 55.

[13]Patrick Fairbairn, *The Typology of Scripture*, 2 vols. (9th edition; New York: N. Tibbals & Sons, n.d.), 1. 14 (italics his).

[14]See Johnson, *Old Testament in New*, p. 56.

[15]Ibid., p. 70.

[16]Fairbairn, *Typology*, 1. 3.

[17]The title of a volume by Jean Levie (London: G. Chapman, 1961).

[18]Johnson, *Old Testament in New*, p. 94.

[19]Wenham, *Christ & the Bible*, p. 103.

[20]E. D. Hirsch, Jr., *Validity in Interpretation* (New Haven: Yale University Press, 1967), p. 125.

[21]Johnson, *Old Testament in New*, p. 51.

[22] Wenham, *Christ & the Bible*, pp. 24-25. See also Richard T. France, *Jesus and the Old Testament* (London: Tyndale Press, 1971), chapters 3 and 4.

[23]Fairbairn, *Typology*, 1. 380.

[24]Ibid., p. 110. On p. 109 he states unequivocally that Hos. 11:1 refers to a past historical occurrence.

[25]Ibid., p. 381.

[26]Wenham, *Christ & the Bible*, p. 106.

[27]Johnson, *Old Testament in New*, p. 34.

[28]Wenham, *Christ & the Bible*, p. 99.

[29]Alfred Edersheim, *The Life and Times of Jesus the Messiah*, 2 vols. (2nd edition; New York: Randolph, n.d.), 1. 156, 215-16.

[30]J. Barton Payne, "Right Questions from Isaiah 7:14," *The Living and Active Word of God*, ed. Morris Inch and Ronald Youngblood (Winona Lake: Eisenbrauns, 1982).

[31]Edward J. Young, *Studies in Isaiah* (Grand Rapids: Wm. B. Eerdmans Publishing Company, 1954), pp. 143 ff.; *New Bible Dictionary*, ed. J. D. Douglas (Grand Rapids: Wm. B. Eerdmans Publishing Company, 1962), pp. 556-57.

[32]Gleason L. Archer, Jr., "Isaiah," *Wycliffe Bible Commentary* (Chicago: Moody Press, 1962), pp. 617-9; *Decision* (December 1976): 6, 12.

[33]Kenneth L. Barker, "A New Look at Isaiah 7:14 in Its Context (Isaiah 7:1-9:7)" (unpublished manuscript, 1980).

[34]Herbert M. Wolf, "A Solution to the Immanuel Prophecy in Isaiah 7:14-8:22," *Journal of Biblical Literature* 91 (1972): 449-56.

[35]The argument summarizes my fuller treatment in the article "Immanuel," *International Standard Bible Encyclopedia*, revised edition (forthcoming).

[36]Wenham, *Christ & the Bible*, p. 100.

[37]Ibid., p. 37. See also Rudolph Bultmann, "The Significance of the Old Testament for Christian Faith," in Anderson, ed., *Old Testament and Christian Faith*, pp. 27-29.

[38]A. F. Kirkpatrick, "How to Read the Old Testament" (1903), p. 9.

[39]See Isa. 53:11 NIV and first footnote.

[40]F. F. Bruce, *The New Testament Development of Old Testament Themes* (Grand Rapids: Wm. B. Eerdmans Publishing Company, 1968), p. 21.

[41]Gerhard von Rad, "Typological Interpretation of the Old Testament," *Essays on Old Testament Hermeneutics*, ed. Claus Westermann (Richmond: John Knox, 1963), p. 39.

A Response to Patrick Fairbairn and Biblical Hermeneutics as Related to the Quotations of the Old Testament in the New

S. Lewis Johnson
Professor of Biblical and Systematic Theology
Trinity Evangelical Divinity School

A Response to Patrick Fairbairn and Biblical Hermeneutics as Related to the Quotations of the Old Testament in the New

S. Lewis Johnson

Professor Nicole has been asked to address a very significant subject, since the study of the use of the Old Testament in the New Testament, of high import for many areas of systematic theology and exegesis, is absolutely vital to the consideration of hermeneutics as it relates to inerrancy. The importance of the matter may be clearly seen in the use that has been made of the subject by the critics of the doctrine of inerrancy. In fact, in the criticism of some scholars it has seemed to form the bellwether of the defense of their position. And, one must admit, the criticism has not always been answered very effectively by the inerrantists.

I am particularly glad to read and respond to Professor Nicole's comments, because it was an article of his, written about a quarter of a century ago, that was one of the incentives to further study of the area on my part.[1] I have since come to regard it as a most crucial clue to the understanding of the Bible, believing as I do that the meaning of the sacred text is to be found by the perusal of the sacred page. In other words, *Scriptura ex Scriptura explicanda est.*

In Charlotte, North Carolina, there is a section of the city called, or known, as Myers Park. It contains a maze of streets in which it is quite easy to lose one's sense of direction and get lost. Fortunately, however, there is a thoroughfare that runs through the section and, if one keeps its location in mind, then finding the way through the Park is immeasurably eased. The name of the thoroughfare is, appropriately enough, Providence Road. The use of Scripture in Scripture is a Providence Road that gives direction to the student of the Word, enabling him to hold to a straight course through it.[2]

There are, of course, different ways in which the use of the Old Testament in the New affects the question of biblical inspiration. It affects it *textually* through the differences that exist between the texts of the Old Testament and the New Testament citations of them. It affects it *theologically* through the differences that to some appear to exist between the doctrine taught in the Old Testament and that taught in the New. And it affects it *hermeneutically* through the differences that some see between the sense of the Old Testament passage cited and the meaning of it in the New Testament citation. It is with this last aspect of the study that we are concerned.

Professor Nicole has pointed us to the great significance of Patrick Fairbairn for this area of study, and against the background of his contribution I will make my response.

I. THE PRINCIPAL PROBLEM AND AREAS OF CONCERN

The principal problem in the study of the use of the Old Testament in the New as it relates to hermeneutics is the accuracy of the New Testament authors' exegesis of the Old Testament texts. Is their exegesis sound, conforming to hermeneutical principles taught preeminently in the Scriptures themselves? In this Fairbairn is a good guide, for he writes:

> And on the supposition of the authors of the New Testament being inspired teachers, the character of these citations is of the gravest importance—first, as providing, in the hermeneutical principles they involve, a test to some extent of the inspiration of the writers; and then as furnishing in those principles an infallible direction for the general interpretation of ancient Scripture. For there can be no doubt that the manner in which our Lord and His apostles understood and applied the Scriptures of the Old Testament, was as much intended to throw light generally on the principles of interpretation, as to administer instruction on the specific points, for the sake of which they were more immediately appealed to.[3]

Over and over he makes that point. The key of knowledge in this matter is "the sense of Holy Scripture as understood by inspired men themselves."[4]

In considering the principal problem of the use of the Old Testament as it concerns hermeneutics and inerrancy, three areas of concern should be isolated. We turn to them now.

A. Grammatico-Historico-Theological Exegesis

The meaning of the common term, grammatico-historical, is, of course, known to all the readers of this brief paper. I have added the term *theological* in order to indicate that in the Bible dual authorship, with all the questions pertaining to it, exists. Hirsch's highly regarded *Validity in Interpretation,* while referring to dual authorship's possibility, does not address itself to questions that arise from it.[5]

Two matters are the concern of the interpreter here. In the first place, the New Testament author's handling of the Old Testament *text* must be studied. Variations in texts, resulting from purely textual considerations, that is, unintentional variations arising from the use of different text forms, belong to the province of the textual study of the use of the Old Testament in the New Testament. These are not our concerns, in spite of their own importance.[6] Intentional variations, usually made by the New Testament author to capture and emphasize a particular point in the Old Testament text, are important. The Old Testament quotations often reveal by the New Testament author's modifications of them the desired emphasis he wishes.[7]

In the second place, the New Testament author's handling of the Old Testament *context* must be carefully studied. It is in this procedure that almost all of the serious problems of the use of the Old Testament in the New Testament find their solution. Many of the well-known *cruces interpretum* are relatively easy to handle, if only the interpreter gives himself to a careful analysis of the context of the Old Testament citation. Fairbairn's handling of the Old Testament citations in Matthew 1:23, 27:9-10, and Acts 1:20 illustrates the point.[8] The difficulty in 1 Corinthians 9:7-10 lies largely in the failure of the commentators to notice the context of Deuteronomy 24:5—25:4.

The objections of Ladd and Beegle to inerrancy, particularly those based on the New Testament author's supposed misunderstanding of the Old Testament text, are resolved through careful attention to context.[9]

I would not wish to be understood as saying that all talk of problems in this area of study is misguided. There are many nagging questions about the use of the Old Testament in the New Testament, but the way out of the problems lies in this direction, I believe.

It is here that evangelicals need to devote a great deal of work, since it is only by the painful, laborious, perspiring pondering of the problems, one by one and with the use of all our exegetical tools and procedures, that we shall be able to bring some conviction to our "friendly enemies" of the sensibility of a solution to the exegetical problem of the use of the Old Testament in the New Testament.

Robert H. Gundry's work on Matthew is an illustration of what I am suggesting.[10]

B. Biblical Typology

Typology, the study of spiritual correspondences between persons, events, and things within the historical framework of God's special revelation, is closely connected to the relationship between the use of the Old Testament in the New and the biblical doctrine of inspiration.[11] The failure to appreciate the amount of typological material in the Bible has upon occasion accounted for the inability to see the validity of the ways the Old Testament is used in the New. For example, Beegle contends that Matthew's use of Hosea 11:1 in Matthew 2:14-15 is invalid. Matthew says that the text from Hosea 11:1, "Out of Egypt have I called my son," a clear reference to the exodus of Israel from Egypt under Moses, is "fulfilled" by the return of the young Jesus from Egypt to Nazareth after the death of Herod. Beegle thinks he has found an error in the evangelist's hermeneutics, commenting, "The sense of the passage and the intention of the prophet point backward, not forward. There is not the slightest hint that the statement was intended as a prophecy."[12] Beegle has failed to appreciate Matthew's use of typology and his understanding of the term "fulfilled." Fairbairn's treatment here is sound, although brief.[13]

Of course, it is possible to overdo typology and offer interpretations, a la Barnabas and Arthur W. Pink, that are bizarre and weird. For example, the "two wings of the great eagle" of Revelation 12:13 are probably not the U. S. Air Force nor our F-16s. Further, Ezekiel's vision of the living creatures and wheels probably does not refer to UFOs operated by the cherubim, as a radio preacher suggested a few years ago. The many wives of Solomon are not a typical representation of the many virtues of his character, nor is Samson's meeting of the young lion a type of Christ's encounter with Saul on the Damascus road. When Jacob purchased Esau's birthright with red pottage, there is no reference to Christ's purchase of heaven for His people by His red blood. Jacob's being clothed with Esau's garment when the blessing was stolen does not picture Christ's being clothed with our nature when the purchase was consummated.[14]

We reject all of that, but we must not succumb to the biting ridicule of those who denigrate typology. We may then be guilty of ignoring what God has stressed. One of the happier results of twentieth-century scholarship has been the rediscovery of the importance of typology for the understanding of the Bible. I am hopeful that evangelicals, who so often follow rather than lead in biblical scholarship, will follow once again, for in this case modern scholarship is surely right.

Typology is grounded in good theology, being built squarely on the sovereignty of God, the immutability of God, and the wisdom of God (cf. Isa. 11:10-16; Jer. 23:1-8; Eph. 3:11). The fact that its recognition is the basis for the solution of a number of problems in the use of the Old Testament in the New is an indication of its importance for inerrancy. The use of Isaiah 8:17-18 in Hebrews 2:13 illustrates the point. Fairbairn's handling of it is an acceptable one.[15]

C. Allegorical Exegesis

As far as I can tell, there is no clear instance of allegorical exegesis of the Old Testament in the New. In spite of the derivation of the English word *allegory* from the word Paul uses in Galatians 4:24, *allēgoreō,* the usage of Paul is not that of allegory, as we usually understand the term. Webster defines the term as, "the expression by means of symbolic fictional figures and actions of truths or generalizations about human existence."[16] Now, if that is so, Paul's treatment is not allegorical, for he speaks of things historical. Therefore, both ancient (Theodore; Chrysostom; Theodoret) and modern exegetes agree that this is *typology,* not *allegory*. Ellis writes, "Even in this passage which Paul designates as ἅτινα ἐστιν ἀλληλορούμενα (Gal. 4:24), one finds an interpretation more in accord with Pauline typology than with Alexandrian allegory."[17] Lightfoot agrees, saying, "St. Paul uses ἀλληγορία here much in the same sense as he uses τύπος 1 Cor. x. 11 ταῦτα δὲ τυπικῶς συνέβαινεν, not denying the historical truth of the narrative, but superimposing a secondary meaning."[18] Contrary to Bunyan's *Pilgrim's Progress*, a true allegory, there is here correspondence and historicity, salient features of a type.

II. THE APPROACH OF PATRICK FAIRBAIRN TO THE PROBLEM

A. Its Strengths

When I think of Fairbairn's work, having just reread the portions of it that are the background of Professor Nicole's comments, I am reminded of an article by David Steinmetz, Professor of Church History and Doctrine at the Divinity School of Duke University. The article was entitled, "The Superiority of Pre-Critical Exegesis," and it appeared in *Theology Today* in 1980. While not overly important for what I want to say, Steinmetz' point was put in this way, "The medieval theory of levels of meaning in the biblical text, with all its undoubted defects, flourished because it is true, while the modern theory of a single meaning, with all its demonstrable virtues, is false. Until the historical-critical method becomes critical of its own theoretical foundations and develops a hermeneutical theory adequate to the nature of the text which it is interpreting, it will remain restricted—as it deserves to be—to the guild and the academy, where the question of truth can endlessly be deferred."[19]

Steinmetz' observation deserves fuller discussion, but there is one thing that is sometimes overlooked in our search for the latest research in biblical matters: The old is not seldom better than the new. Fairbairn is a case in point, perhaps. His discussions of the biblical contexts of the Old and New Testaments are the product of a mind filled with knowledge of Scripture in its breadth and depth and with devotion to the Lord Jesus Christ. The peculiar nature of his deepest interests, typology, prophecy, and hermeneutics, makes his work still a valuable source for study in the area of the use of the Old Testament in the New.

B. Its Limitations

Put very simply and briefly, the weaknesses of Fairbairn's work is largely the necessary weakness of biblical studies done without the benefits of the knowledge derived from technical development in the study of the biblical languages, and without the benefits of knowledge derived from the biblical research of the last century or so. He can hardly be held responsible for these things.

III. SUGGESTIONS FOR A FRESH APPROACH TO THE PROBLEM

A. A Serious Consideration of the Old Testament Use of the Old Testament

In the interests of the brevity imposed upon me in this response, let me make a few suggestions for consideration and discussion. The tendency of research to concentrate on the use of the Old Testament in the New has resulted in neglect of the study of the use of the Old Testament in the Old Testament. There, too, there is evidence of a fundamental hermeneutical theory, and it relates not only to the question of eschatology, but also to the question of inspiration, although I will admit that its most intriguing possibility relates to the former.

I am referring to the use of the Pentateuch by the authors of the Psalms, the use of the Pentateuch by Isaiah, the use of Jeremiah by Daniel, the use of Genesis by Amos, and the use of Isaiah by Zechariah. Old Testament scholars will immediately be able to enlarge the list of research possibilities. The attitudes of later authors to previous Scripture reflects a certain view of Scripture. This is the goal of the suggested research.

Further, there is evidence of possible development of earlier prophecies in later prophecies and, in fact, in this there may be solutions to some of the peculiar difficulties found in citations of different Old Testament texts at one New Testament location (cf. Matt. 27:9-10; Mark 1:2-3). Fairbairn himself has some comments on this that are worthy of further thought.[20]

B. An Evangelical Reconsideration of Typology in Exegesis

D. L. Baker in his Sheffield dissertation has again made the point that typology is not to be confused with fanciful interpretation. It is the scholarly study of correspondences in God's sovereign control of human history, a study related both to the unity of the divine purpose in history and to the unity of that record in the Holy Scriptures.[21]

The usefulness of a detailed understanding of the subject and its contribution to biblical exegesis can best be appreciated by those who have sought to find unity in the Bible without a recognition of its place in Scripture. It is particularly useful in the solution of problems arising from the use of the Old Testament in the New. The apostles had a well-developed conception of biblical typology and made extensive use of it in their use of Scripture.

C. An Intensified Consideration of the Interpretation of Prophecy

I would suggest that, following the lead of such older students as Fairbairn and Davidson, further attention be given to the solution of problems pertaining to the interpretation of prophecy. The subject of the dual authorship of Scripture and its ramifications is important, and I am glad to see that it is being addressed by this gathering. The problem of the authority of the New Testament apostle to "reinterpret" the Old Testament needs careful consideration. I have strong misgivings about this, in spite of its sponsorship as a biblical truth.[22]

The New Testament interpretation of New Testament prophecy, illustrated by Paul's and John's use of the Olivet Discourse calls for study as it might relate to the doctrine of inspiration.

And, finally, a well thought out and formulated structure for the interpretation of messianic prophecy, in both its broad and narrow sense and with delineation of its application to directly and indirectly predictive prophecies, is a desideratum. Fairbairn will be of use here, but we must go beyond the work of the great Scottish theologian.

NOTES

[1]Roger Nicole, "New Testament Use of the Old Testament," *Revelation and the Bible*, ed. by Carl F. H. Henry (Grand Rapids: Baker Book House, 1958), pp. 135-51.

[2]The illustration was suggested by the editor of *Theology Today* in comments commemorative of Carlyle Marney, the well-known Southern Baptist preacher, volume 35, p. 450, of the January, 1979, issue.

[3]Patrick Fairbairn, *The Typology of Scripture*, 6th ed. (Edinburgh: T. & T. Clark, 1876), pp. 427-28.

[4]*Ibid.*, p. 428.

[5]E. D. Hirsch, Jr., *Validity in Interpretation* (New Haven: Yale University Press, 1967), p. 126.

[6]An excellent illustration of this important aspect of the field is found in the work of Kenneth J. Thomas, "The Old Testament Citations in Hebrews," *New Testament Studies*, XI (1964-1965), pp. 303-25. The article is an updating in large measure of his Manchester dissertation.

[7]A simple illustration of variation for purposes of emphasis is found in Paul's handling of Genesis 15:6 in Romans 4:3. The modification of the LXX's καί by δέ serves to lay stress upon ἐπίστευσεν.

[8]Patrick Fairbairn, *Hermeneutical Manual* (Edinburgh: T. & T. Clark, 1858), pp. 357-58, 381, 416-26, 440-46, 449-50.

[9]Cf. George Ladd, "Historic Premillennialism," *The Meaning of the Millennium: Four Views* (Downers Grove: InterVarsity Press, 1977), pp. 20-21. His claim for "reinterpretation" of the Old Testament text by the New Testament author is summed up in the words, "The fact is that the New Testament frequently interprets Old Testament prophecies in a way *not suggested by the Old Testament context.*" On Matthew 2:15 and the use of Hosea 11:1 he says, "*The Old Testament is reinterpreted* in light of the Christ event." Dewey Beegle argues also that Matthew's use is "a distortion of the context" (*Scripture, Tradition, and Infallibility* [Grand Rapids: William B. Eerdmans Publishing Company, 1973], p. 237).

[10]Robert Horton Gundry, *The Use of the Old Testament in St. Matthew's Gospel* (Leiden: E. J. Brill, 1967).

[11]The literature on the subject is vast. A place to begin is with G. W. H. Lampe and K. J. Woollcombe, *Essays on Typology* (London: Allenson, 1957), and with R. T. France, *Jesus and the Old Testament* (London: Inter-Varsity, 1971), pp. 38-82.

[12]Beegle, *Scripture, Tradition, and Infallibility*, p. 237.

[13]Fairbairn, *Hermeneutical Manual*, pp. 426-29.

[14]Cf. R. W. Dale, *The Jewish Temple and the Christian Church* (London: Hodder and Stoughton, 1896), p. 61.

[15]Fairbairn, *Hermeneutical Manual,* pp. 459-60.

[16]*Webster's New Collegiate Dictionary,* p. 29.

[17]E. Earle Ellis, *Paul's Use of the Old Testament* (Grand Rapids: Eerdmans, 1957), p. 53.

[18]J. B. Lightfoot, *Saint Paul's Epistle to the Galatians* (London: Macmillan and Co., 1896), p. 180.

[19]David C. Steinmetz, "The Superiority of Pre-Critical Exegesis," *Theology Today,* 37 (April, 1980), pp. 27, 38.

[20]Fairbairn, *Hermeneutical Manual,* pp. 445-46.

[21]D. L. Baker, *Two Testaments, One Bible* (Downers Grove: InterVarsity Press, 1976), pp. 239-70.

[22]In addition to George Ladd's contention that the New Testament authors "reinterpreted" the Old Testament, we now have some comments of Clark Pinnock along the same line. He has written, "Let us by all means begin with the original sense and meaning of the text," adding in a new paragraph, "But when we do that, the first thing we discover is the dynamism of the text itself. Not only is its basic meaning forward looking, the text itself records a very dynamic process of revelation, in which the saving message once given gets continually and constantly updated, refocussed, and occasionally revised. Just consider the progression between the Old and New Testament, how the coming of the Messiah introduced crucial reinterpretations into the earlier revelational process." Cf. Clark Pinnock, "The Inspiration and Interpretation of the Bible," *TSF Bulletin,* 4 (October, 1980), p. 6. I do not see how this can be squared with the doctrine of inerrancy.

Homiletics and Hermeneutics

Haddon W. Robinson
President
Denver Conservative Baptist
Seminary

15. Homiletics and Hermeneutics

Haddon W. Robinson

Once upon a time an explorer discovered an ancient sundial. Realizing its value, he chipped away the dirt accumulated on its face and restored it to its original condition. He then placed the sundial in a museum where it would be shielded from the elements—including the sun. Although he valued the instrument, he did not use it. Evangelicals sometimes resemble that explorer with his sundial. What they prize in theology, they ignore in preaching.

Homiletics deals with the construction and communication of sermons. As a communicator, the preacher borrows from rhetoric, the social sciences, and communication theories. Yet because he handles religious content, he must also involve himself with hermeneutics. A homiletician, therefore, cannot merely ask, "How do I get the message across?" He must also ask, "How do I get the message?"

Men and women who believe the Bible to be the Word of God without error insist, "You find your message in the Scriptures." If we regard the Bible as God's tool of communication through which He addresses people in history, then it follows that preaching must be based on it. Expository preaching, therefore, emerges not merely as a type of sermon—one among many—but as the theological outgrowth of a high view of inspiration. Expository preaching then originates as a philosophy rather than a method. It reflects a preacher's honest effort to submit his thought to the Bible rather than to subject the Bible to his thought.

Not all preaching from evangelical pulpits, however, finds it source in the Bible. Declaring to a congregation that the Bible is God's Word—even in a sweaty voice—does not mean that it is expounded. Nor does all preaching or orthodoxy necessarily build on a biblical base. Ministers often repeat "the old, old story" without taking a fresh look at the Bible or without demonstrating to a thoughtful hearer that what they proclaim does indeed come from the Scriptures.

When preachers announce a text they sometimes practice slight of mind—now you see it, now you don't. The passage and the sermon may be nothing more than strangers passing in the pulpit. Yet, it is a rape of the pulpit to ignore or avoid in the sermon what the passage teaches. Topical preaching common in American pulpits flirts with heresy. Deuteronomy 18:20 warned that the prophet who spoke in the name of God what God had not spoken should be executed.

Admittedly, sound doctrine can be taught without referring to specific biblical passages, but grounding his sermons in Scripture protects a preacher from error. More positively, through expository preaching a minister speaks with authority beyond his own and those who sit before him have a better chance of hearing God address them directly. An expositor possesses confidence that his message is not "the word of men", but that "It really is the Word of God, which also performs its work in you who believe" (1 Thess. 2:13).

What this means in practical terms is that the concepts set forth in the sermon must have their source in the Scriptures. At its heart, this is a moral matter. In the ancient world the herald not only had to possess a powerful voice, but qualities of character as well. Hauch Friedrich observes:

> In many cases heralds are very garrulous and inclined to exaggerate. They are thus in danger of giving false news. It is demanded then that they deliver their message as it is given to them. The essential point about the report which they give is that it does not originate with them. Behind it stands a higher power. The herald does not express his own views. He is the spokesman for his master. . . . Heralds adopt the mind of those who commission them and act with the plenipotentiary authority of their masters. . . . Being only the mouth of his master, he must not falsify the message entrusted to him by additions of his own.[1]

Expository sermons are derived from and transmitted through a study of a passage (or passages) in context. Not only should an expositor find the substance of his sermon in the Bible, but he communicates it to his hearers on the basis by which he received it. As he studies, therefore, the preacher wrestles with exegesis and hermeneutics—the materials of grammar, history, literary forms, the thought and cultural settings of his text. In the pulpit he deals with enough of the language, background and context of his passage so that an attentive listener can follow the message from the Bible. The proper response to biblical preaching does not lie in pronouncing the pastor a skilled communicator but rather in determining whether God has spoken and whether or not He will be trusted and obeyed.

Since effective expository preaching deals largely with the explanation and application of Scripture, it reflects exegesis and hermeneutics on every hand. For one thing, the theme of the sermon should develop from the thought of the Bible. While this sounds like keen insight into the obvious, it is observed more often in the breach than in the keeping. Every Sunday ministers claiming high regard for the Scriptures preach on texts whose ideas they either do not understand or have not bothered to study.

As a case in point, scores of sermons on prayer have been based on the wording of Matthew 18:19 and 20. "Again I say to you, that if two of you agree on earth about anything that they may ask, it shall be done for them by My Father who is in heaven. For where two or three have gathered together in My name, there am I in the midst."[2] At first glance, Jesus endorses prayer offered in groups of two or three and promises that if Christians agree together about a prayer request somehow they bind the Father in heaven. Good sense, if nothing else, would drive us to scrutinize the context of those verses (If two or three Christian Dallas Cowboy fans agree to ask God for victory in an upcoming game and if a few Christians on the opposing team pray for a Cowboy defeat, which group is God bound to answer?).

Actually, Jesus' Words here have little to do with the subject of prayer but instead with how sinning Christians should be restored. In the immediate context, the "two or three" does not refer to a small group prayer meeting but to the witnesses summoned in verse 16. "But if he (the sinning brother) does not listen to you, take one or two more with you, so that by the mouth of two or three witnesses every fact may be confirmed." All that Jesus says, therefore, applies to Christians dealing with someone who has sinned. The old maxim reminds us that "a text without its context becomes a pretext." In battling for the inspiration of individual words of Scripture we sometimes forget that words are merely "semantic markers for a field of meaning." Particular statements must be understood within the broader thought of which they are a part or what we teach may not be God's Word at all.

In fact, an emphasis on verbal inspiration sometimes lures a preacher into eisegesis and error. For instance sermons on "How to know the will of God" advance the thesis that "Inward peace gives assurance of God's direction in our decisions." Colossians 3:15, "And let the peace of Christ rule in your hearts," is offered in support of that idea, Since every word of Scripture is God-breathed, the preacher provides a word study of *braxzeo* "to rule" or "to umpire." Christ's peace, the sermon goes, serves as a referee who "calls" each decision we make. When a Christian lives within God's will, he experiences peace which "surpasses all comprehension." Through this peace the referee, Christ, affirms our correct decisions. Should Christians make wrong choices, they will experience inner anxiety—a sign that they have stepped out of God's will.

Such an approach has the ring of exposition. It focuses on the Greek text and sounds extremely practical. Unfortunately it is not biblical. A reading of the context reveals that Paul is not talking about decision making, but instead about how Christians should relate to one another. T. K. Abbott comments that the phrase *peace of Christ* "is not to inward peace of the soul, but to peace with one another as the context shows." Using Colossians 3:15 to preach on God's guidance ignores completely the idea the apostle intended. When sermons proceed from such a cavalier handling of the Bible, they divorce sound hermeneutics from homiletics.

The common practice of using a single verse or fragment of a verse as a "text" can be blamed for leading many preachers away from the intended meaning of the biblical writer. For instance, many ministers calling people back to God, to the foundations of faith or to a lost morality, have posed the question found in Psalm 11:3, "If the foundations are destroyed what can the righteous do?" The question appears rhetorical. Without the foundations the righteous can do nothing at all. Yet, the question apparently comes from friends who speak as enemies of God. They ask in desperation, "If the foundations are destroyed what can the righteous do but give up." In the second half of the psalm, however, David replies that righteous men and women have splendid options open to them. Their faith does not depend upon foundations but instead upon the sovereign God who judges both the wicked and the righteous. While sermons taking off from the question in verse three may offer stirring pleas to secure the foundations both in the church and society, they are not biblical. In fact, such preaching proceeds from a methodology that itself undermines the foundation of biblical thought.

R. W. Dale in his lectures on preaching told of a minister in England preparing a sermon on a verse he imagined was in the Book of Proverbs. Before leaving for the church on Sunday morning he decided to look up the exact reference. Upon leafing through the

Proverbs he could not find his text. In desperation he turned to his concordance but could not locate it there either. So when the moment came to start his sermon he began, "You will all remember, my friends, the words of the wisest of kings"—and then launched into his message. On the basis of this incident Dale offered this advice, "When you take a text be sure it is in the Bible"[3] to which we should add, when a preacher finds a statement in the Bible, he must be sure that what he declares the Bible to say, is what the Bible actually says. To fail to do so is to sacrifice hermeneutics for homiletics.

A concern for hermeneutics in determining the basic idea of a sermon is a matter of integrity. Over one hundred years ago Nathaniel J. Burton spoke to all who propose to represent God when he asked in his *Yale Lectures on Preaching*,

> What is slander? Well, one form of it is reporting that a man has said something that he did not say. And why is not the Bible slandered when some inaccurate and unexegetical fumbler spends hours every week in public discoursings on what the Bible says?
>
> So then, our very veracity forces us to philology, to exegesis, to profound interpretation. If we intentionally misrepresent meanings, we are liars, plain as day. But if we misrepresent meanings through carelessness, or through laziness, it shows that we have in us the making of a liar. We are willing to make statement after statement that we have never taken the trouble to verify.[4]

Biblical preaching should not only be true to the Bible in its central ideas but in the development of those ideas as well. Many sermons that begin in the Bible stray from it in their structures. Homiletical methods sometimes tempt the minister to impose an arrangement of thought on a text foreign to that of the inspired writer. The shoe must not tell the foot how to grow. To be truly biblical, the major assertions supporting the sermon's basic concept must also be taken from the passage on which it is based. Of course, a preacher may sometimes rearrange his material along psychological lines, but whatever outline the sermon assumes—and this can vary with the audience, speaker, or occasion—its content should reflect the argument of the biblical author and ought at every place be controlled by the writer's thought.

As a case in point, in Philippians 3:13-14 Paul sums up the passage that begins at verse one. "But one thing I do: forgetting what lies behind and reaching forward to what lies ahead, I press on toward the goal for the prize of the upward call of God in Christ Jesus."

During the previous twelve verses Paul argues that "the overwhelming value of knowing Christ and having his righteousness makes every other value worthless and worth surrendering." One common development of the major idea in this passage takes off on what things should be given up for the sake of knowing Christ. Usually such values as power, possessions, position, passions, receive mention. In the passage itself, however, Paul refers to none of those indulgences. It is doubtful whether such things ever proved much of a problem to Saul the Pharisee. What the apostle abandoned for the sake of Christ were advantages that provided spiritual status—his knowledge and obedience to the law, a zeal for God's cause, his heritage, and his religious discipline. Paul turned his back on the self-effort and self-esteem of legalistic righteousness to gain a completely different kind of righteousness, one that comes through faith and identification with Jesus Christ.

The apostle's development of thought differs markedly from popular handlings of these paragraphs. As a consequence, the preacher not only loses the power of a great biblical theme settling for something closer to platitudes, but more basic, homiletics wanders off from exegesis and accurate hermeneutics. If God superintended the writing of Scripture and protected its details, then biblical preaching must reflect God's thought both in theme and development. Should a minister protest that such sermons suffer from a variety deficiency, he might discover that submitting his thought to the biblical author can produce vitality that no other homiletical method can offer. Donald Miller addresses himself to this when he writes:

> Someone has remarked that the Bible is not marvelous for the number of its ideas, but for the infinite variety of ways in which it presents a few very great ideas. To reflect the Bible's own variety in successive sermons would, in most cases, be a more effective savior from monotony than the efforts of the preacher's own individuality.[5]

A sermon constructed out of honest exegesis and sound hermeneutics will also be true to the Bible in its purpose. In theory, at least, every sermon has a purpose—the answer to the question, "Why am I preaching this sermon?" While the idea of the sermon is the truth to be presented, the purpose describes what the truth is intended to accomplish. A statement of purpose recognizes that truth exists not as an end in itself but as an instrument through which men and women establish a relationship with God and one another.

A biblical sermon finds its purpose not merely in a study of the audience but primarily through exegesis and hermeneutics. Behind every section of the sacred writings lies the reason why the author included the material. In some books, the purpose is clearly stated (i.e., 1 Timothy 3:14-15; John 20:31) while in others the purpose must be discovered through a study of the broad sweep of the content. Preachers who honor the Bible will align the purposes of their sermons with the aims of the biblical writer.

An accurate interpretation of a book like Job requires that a minister determine the purpose of the writer. While the speeches of Job's friends are in the Word of God, they are not necessarily God's Word. Job's comforters offer many explanations for suffering—most of them half or three-quarter truths—yet at the conclusion of the book God declared them wrong. A sermon showing why those ancient counselors worked from an inadequate theology would be in line with the purpose of Job, but to handle their ideas and their development as though they uttered God's truth would ignore completely the aim of the book.

A less obvious but just as harmful way of ignoring the purpose of a biblical author lies in the common practice of employing the historical narratives as case studies in morals, virtues, or spiritual struggles. In such sermons the camaraderie between David and Jonathan models an ideal friendship which all Christians should imitate; the conversation of Jesus with the woman at the wellside provides lessons on personal evangelism; the story of Ruth and Naomi turns into an example of how Christians should relate to their in-laws; Jacob's struggle at Peniel demonstrates how one must wrestle with God for blessing; Nehemiah becomes a case book for leadership. What is not asked in these sermons is whether the biblical writer intended for these histories to be used in this manner.

The use of the Bible as a collection of examples springs from homiletics and the preacher's search for relevance in his sermon. When confronted with historical narrative the preacher has to ask, "What does this event from the long ago and far away have to do with God's people in the here and now?" One solution is to use the incidents as examples—either of good or evil—of virtues to be cultivated or evils to be avoided. Dwight Stevenson states the case this way:

> As superb literature the Bible is a mirror. Most of the men and women whom we see there are reflections. We can see ourselves mirrored there. The hearer of the sermon or reader of the Bible

> does not need to be smuggled into the passage. He is already there in the passage. This is possible because of the dynamics of psychological identification, such as that experienced by a spectator at a play with an actor on the stage, or that of a reader of a novel with its hero.[6]

This illustrative approach is reflected throughout modern American homiletical literature. Lloyd Perry speaks for the tradition in his *Manual for Biblical Preaching* when he writes about biographical sermons.

> This is an excellent means of demonstrating the contemporary relevance of the Scriptures, for preaching on Bible characters gives the minister an opportunity to set forth in a clear fashion the modern counterpart to the experience of a biblical person. Furthermore, the use of this type of subject matter helps to make the Scriptures come alive with real persons who faced real situations, and with whose lives, difficulties, hopes and relationships God was immediately concerned and intimately involved. A wealth of biblical material exists for the purpose of biographical preaching, and this type of subject matter also includes the possibility of bringing messages on the lives of men and women whose names are not found in the Scriptures but who lived for God and contributed much for the cause of his kingdom.[7]

The practice of using the historical narratives as examples is occasionally defended by using 1 Corinthians 10. In this chapter Paul recounts several episodes in the history of Israel and uses them to warn his readers in verse 6, "Now these occurred as examples, to keep us from setting our hearts on evil things as they did." Then after spelling out what the Corinthians should have learned from the experiences of their forefathers, Paul observes in verse 11, "These things happened to them as examples and were written down as warnings for us on whom the fulfillment of the ages has come."

Before homileticians can offer this passage as the biblical base for exemplary sermons, they must struggle with its exegesis. First, the Greek word *tupos* translated "example" does not mean "illustration" in the common use of that word. *Tupos* comes closer to the words "evidence" or "pattern." A *tupos* refers to an event in Israel's history that demonstrated how God deals with His people when they sin. God's working in that event shows how God keeps His promises. What is more, the event became part of Scripture to serve as a warning to the community of faith in every age. God creates the "typical" relationship and that explains why it "was written down."

Not only does the past event prefigure similar present or future events because God keeps His promises, but the emphasis in the Corinthian letter is that these events actually happened. In talking about an example, Paul does not mean that his readers should "see themselves in the story" but instead urges them to learn from what actually took place in sacred history. As Heinrich Miller puts it, "Against some supposed metaphysical interpretation, salvation history is interpreted as the self-fulfilling activity of God in concrete human history.[8] A *tupos*, therefore, lies closer to a "proof" or "model" than to an illustration or example that throws light on a truth.

Clearly, then, Paul must not be taken to justify introducing scriptural incidents into sermons to be used pictorally, pedagogically, or illustratively with the unstated assumption that they carry divine authority. While the Bible may serve as a source of illustration to explain or apply a point or to convince an audience that a proposition is valid, if the historical event is separated from its purpose, then it does not carry the weight of Scripture and examples from church history, modern literature or the morning newspaper would serve as well. In fact, we could argue that modern non-biblical illustrations might be more effective since they would more likely illustrate the unknown by the known and would not imply that stories from the Bible carry the force of inspiration.

When a preacher ignores the purpose of a passage when using an incident as the text of his sermon, he has no defense against liberal theology. If he uses the historical narrative in order to speak about the temptations and problems of men and women in the pew, he would do as well to put aside the biblical text rather than to draw illegitimate parallels not intended by the biblical author. Sidney Greidanus in his stimulating book *Sola Scriptura* states the matter this way:

> The *Sola Scriptura*, so ardently confessed in theory, barely functions in the practice of exemplary preaching: one hardly needs the Bible for exemplary sermons. Ironically, the exemplary preacher, earnestly toiling to portray the man in the text in his personal struggles, therewith the better to draw a line to the man in the pew, could, methodologically, have saved himself the trouble and sketched merely the man in the pew, for motivated by the search for analogy (relevance), he loses precisely

> that distinctiveness which occasioned the appearance in the Bible of the man in the text.[9]

Obviously, a preacher must draw a parallel between the persons in the Scripture and the people in the pew. The objection lies in unwarranted parallels that ignore the purpose of the passage in its historical context and draw authoritative principles for living from one example.

How, then, can a preacher handle historical narrative passages so that they carry the authority of inspiration? First, he must understand that the writers of Scripture do not pretend to write with antiseptic detachment. They were not morally or spiritually neutral. The historians of the Bible were theologians and they wrote from a divine point of reference. The writers of the four gospels, for example, did not give us four chronologies of the life of Jesus. They were evangelists writing history from a theological perspective. Narratives in both the Old and New Testaments proclaim God's acts in history. Before a preacher can deal with a particular passage, therefore, he must look to the larger context of the book to ask why this writer recorded this story for his particular audience. Until he can sit where the biblical author sat as he addressed his readers, he cannot determine the relevance of the book or any of its passages for Christians today. The purpose of the sermon must flow out of the purpose of the historical narrative. We must read the text as the first readers read it before we can read it into the life-situations of people in the twentieth century.

This means that the preacher deals with the passages as parts of the canon. While source studies may provide guidance to the meaning of the text, he does not deal with the traditions or "sub-textual" sources. His primary concern is with the Scripture in its final, canonical form, for in the way the history is assembled the message is framed. As in any other kind of biblical literature, the narrative must be left in its own immediate and broad context. The preacher cannot clip the story from the page and move it around to suit his own purposes.[10]

The preacher finds the purpose of narration by studying the arrangement of materials and noticing editorial comments offered by the writer. For example, in recording David's affair with Bathsheba and his consequent murder of her husband, Uriah, the writer of Second Samuel tells us, "When Uriah's wife heard that her husband was dead, she mourned for him. After the time of the mourning was over,

David had her brought to his house and she became his wife and bore him a son." At that point in the narrative, it might appear that David had protected his reputation by shrewdly covering up his sins. The historian, however, becomes a theologian when he adds, "But the thing that David had done displeased the Lord" (2 Samuel 11:27). In the pages that follow, the historian-theologian recounts a series of tragedies in David's family—Amnon rapes his half-sister, Tamar, and then in revenge is murdered by Absalom. Absalom, David's favorite son, rebels against his father and rapes David's concubines in public. Later Absalom meets death at the hand of Joab, the same general who arranged the killing of Uriah. All of them emerge as wages of David's disobedience. While the historian does not moralize, his editorial comments and the orderings of the incidents demonstrate his purpose—to show that forgiveness does not necessarily wipe out consequences, and God brought open punishment on what was done in secret.

The narrative of Eglon's victory over Israel and his grisly assassination by Ehud (Joshua 3) has been used as evidence that God approves of killing tyrants. Others see in the account the moral that all men are Ehuds and have murder in them. Yet, the author of Judges comments, "The Lord strengthened Eglon," (Judges 3:2) and again "the Lord raised up for them a deliverer, Ehud" (Judges 3:15). Clearly, the purpose of the historian was not to provide a case study of a political assassination but to demonstrate that God works through the Eglons and the Ehuds of the world to accomplish His purpose for His people in history.[11] Although the ethical element remains, it develops from the author's view of God and demonstrates that even shocking political intrigues are controlled by God.

All of this is to say that in expository preaching the idea, the development, and the purpose of the sermon must precede from proper exegesis and hermeneutics and then be directed to the church today. The minister must exegete the passage and the people. He must recognize what the people to whom he ministers have in common, and what they do not share, with God's men and women in the first century and the centuries beyond. Relevant application as well as accurate exegesis raise hermeneutical questions that must be solved.

Exegesis and hermeneutics should also be reflected in the sermon's mood. While the emotion of a writer may be more difficult to pin down than ideas and their development, every passage has a mood. The mood involves the feelings of the writer and also the emotions his writings evoke in the reader. Some passages are alive with hope, some warn, some create a sense of joy, some flash with anger at injustice, others surge with triumph. A true expository sermon should create in the listener the mood it produced in the reader. Marvin R. Vincent stated the case for mood this way:

> The expositor must . . . aim to put himself for the time into the very *atmosphere* and *spirit* of the age out of which the word comes; not only to know, but to *feel* the motives of its acts and sayings. He must catch the quality of Jacob's shrewdness; he must glow with Deborah's warlike ardor; he must appreciate the political sagacity, no less the fatherly tenderness of Jephthah; he must thrill, like the singers of the Pilgrim Psalm, with inspiring and mournful memories of Jerusalem; he must be touched with the grateful affection which overflows in Paul's letter to the Philippians, and burn with the righteous indignation of his words to the Galatians and Corinthians.[12]

The personality of the preacher must submit to the atmosphere and spirit of a passage. As a case in point, a sermon on the opening verses of Peter's first letter should radiate with praise to God for a Christian's living hope. Yet, a minister bent on scolding his congregation can create a mood of guilt by charging that his hearers lack this hope. While other passages may have a spirit of rebuke, this one does not, and to fail to ring the changes on thanksgiving and victory is to live in the atmosphere of a defeated church of today rather than of the apostles.

As there are dominant and supporting ideas in a passage so, especially in larger passages, major and minor moods occur. Yet, as there are controlling ideas so there are dominant moods. That dominant mood, at least, should mark the spirit of the sermon. While recreating the atmosphere requires thought, feeling and skill, expository preachers need to be as true to the mood as to the message of the passage. The tasks of the poet, the playwright, the artist, the prophet and the preacher overlap at this point—to make people feel and see. Peter Marshall described the challenge to the preacher this way:

> What we have to do is to take a passage of Scripture and so carefully and accurately reconstruct the context of it that the scene comes to life. We see it first ourselves. Then we take our listeners to the spot in imagination. We make them see and hear what happened so vividly that the passage will live forever in their minds and hearts. It is like a newsreel from the Scriptures . . . a film from the world's big drama.[13]

Exegesis, hermeneutics and homiletics, therefore, link together as supporting disciplines. The biblical preacher builds bridges that span the gulf between the written Word of God and the minds of men and women. He must interpret the Scripture so accurately and plainly and apply it so truthfully that the truth crosses the bridge. In Paul's last letter to Timothy he urges Timothy to "cut straight" the Word of God. The Greek word *orthotomounta* was used of road making—the writers of the Septuagint used it in Proverbs 3:6 "He will make your paths straight." Exposition of the Scriptures should be so simple and direct, so easily followed that it resembles a straight road. To do that the minister as a good workman must be faithful to both the Bible and to his listeners, and in doing so will gain the approval of God.

NOTES

[1]Hauch Friedrich, *Theological Dictionary of the New Testament,* III (Grand Rapids, Eerdmans, 1965), pp. 687-88.

[2]Examples used to demonstrate the points come from specific sermons preached by men whose position on inspiration would qualify them to join I.C.B.I. My purpose is not to criticize such individuals or to point out their inconsistencies—all of us have nasty homiletical skeletons hanging in our basement—but to illustrate my point. Therefore, I have refrained from giving footnotes for this illustration.

[3]R. W. Dale, *Nine Lectures on Preaching* (New York: George H. Doran Company, 1878), p. 125.

[4]Nathaniel J. Burton, *Yale Lectures on Preaching and Other Writings* (New York: Charles Webster & Company, 1888), pp. 340-41.

[5]Donald Miller, *The Way to Biblical Preaching* (Nashville: Abingdon Press, 1957), p. 99.

[6]Dwight Stevenson, *In The Biblical Preacher's Workshop* (Nashville: Abingdon Press, 1967), p. 55.

[7]Lloyd Perry, *Manual for Biblical Preaching* (Grand Rapids: Baker Book House, 1965), p. 107.

[8]Heinrich Miller, *Dictionary of New Testament Theology,* Vol. III (Grand Rapids: Zondervan, 1971), p. 906.

[9]Sidney Greidanus, *Sola Scriptura* (Toronto: Wedge Publishing Foundation, 1970), p. 70.

[10]Greidanus, *Scriptura,* pp. 221-22.

[11]Ibid., pp. 225-26.

[12]Quoted in *The Way to Biblical Preaching,* p. 148.

[13]Peter Marshall, *John Doe, Disciple,* p. 124.

A Response to Homiletics and Hermeneutics

John F. MacArthur, Jr.
Pastor-Teacher, Grace
Community Church
Panorama City, California

A Response to Homiletics and Hermeneutics

John F. MacArthur, Jr.

I. INTRODUCTORY COMMENTS

A. General Critique

Erwin Lutzer has thoroughly critiqued "Homiletics and Hermeneutics" by Dr. Robinson (see following response) so I will not duplicate his efforts. However, a few general responses to the paper are in order.

Although the assigned title was "The Relationship of Inerrancy To Preaching," Dr. Robinson proposes to deal with the related issues of hermeneutics and homiletics. He only assumes the matters which link inerrancy to expository preaching and does not adequately define any of these terms. Nor does he show the relationship of the interpretive process to exegetical theology and to expositional preaching. Thus, he assumes rather than presents the subject assigned for this paper, i.e., the relationship between inerrancy,[1] exegesis and exposition.

It does not seem to be within the purview of my response to react to Dr. Robinson's philosophy of preaching (about which I have some questions) as presented in his paper. Therefore, I will rather move ahead to present some precise thinking on the originally assigned subject.

B. Preliminary Thinking

In approaching a proposition for our consideration, we must recognize that this is the most important subject in the entire series. It is the link between affirming truth and confirming people in truth through proclamation. It is in a real sense the confluence of all previous papers and the capstone to the careful handling of God's Word. To miss this is to miss God's purpose for revelation.

God gave His Word to be proclaimed for the redemption of the world. Thus, anything that fails to complete that intended purpose and design of God falls short of the divine plan. J. I. Packer has eloquently captured the pursuit of preaching:

> Preaching appears in the Bible as a relaying of what God has said about Himself and His doings, and about men in relation to Him, plus a pressing of His commands, promises, warnings, and assurances, with a view to winning the hearer or hearers . . . to a positive response.[2]

The only logical responses then to inerrant Scripture is to preach it expositionally. By expositionally, I mean preaching in such a way that the Bible is presented *entirely* and *exactly* as it was intended by God. Expository preaching is the proclamation of the truth of God as mediated through the preacher.[3]

Admittedly, not all expositors have an inerrant view. See William Barclay's treatment of Mark 5 or John 6 in *The Daily Study Bible Series*. It is also true that not all with an inerrant view practice expository preaching (Jerry Falwell, Jack Hyles, *et. al.*). These are, however, inconsistencies because an inerrantist perspective demands expository preaching, and a non-inerrantist perspective makes it unnecessary.

Putting it another way, what does it matter that we have an inerrant text if we do not deal with the basic phenomena of communication, e.g., words, sentences, grammar, morphology, syntax, etc? And if we don't, why bother preaching it?

In his much-needed, recent volume on exegetical theology, Walter Kaiser pointedly analyzes the current anemic state of the church due to inadequate flock feeding in the absence of expository preaching:

> It is no secret that Christ's Church is not at all in good health in many places of the world. She has been languishing because she has been fed, as the current line has it, "junk food"; all kinds of artificial preservatives and all sorts of unnatural substitutes have been served up to her. As a result, theological and Biblical malnutrition has afflicted the very generation that has taken such giant steps to make sure its physical health is not damaged by using foods or products that are carcinogenic or otherwise harmful to their physical bodies. Simultaneously a worldwide spiritual famine resulting from the absence of any genuine publication of the Word of God (Amos 8:11) continues to run wild and almost unabated in most quarters of the Church.[4]

The cure is expository preaching.

C. A Theological Imperative

The mandate then is clear. Expository preaching is the declarative genre in which inerrancy finds its logical expression and the church its life and power. My assertion is simply stated, "Inerrancy demands exposition as the only method of preaching which preserves the purity of God's Word and accomplishes the purpose for which God gave it."

R. B. Kuiper agrees in the matter when he writes, "The principle that Christian peaching is proclamation of the Word must obviously be determinative of the content of the sermon."[5]

II. INERRANCY, EXEGESIS AND EXPOSITION

A. Postulates and Propositions

I would like to begin the main discussion with these logically sequential postulates which introduce and undergird my propositions (as well as form a true basis for inerrancy).

1. God is (Gen. 1:1; Pss. 14, 53; Heb. 11:6).
2. God is true (Exod. 34:6; Num. 23:19; Deut. 32:4; Pss. 25:10, 31:6; Isa. 65:16; Jer. 10:8, 10:11; John 14:6, 17:3; Titus 1:2; Heb. 6:18; 1 John 5:20, 21).
3. God speaks in harmony with His nature (Num. 23:19; 1 Sam. 15:29; Rom. 3:4; 2 Tim. 2:13; Titus 1:2; Heb. 6:18).
4. God speaks only truth (Pss. 31:5, 119:43, 142, 151, 160: Prov. 30:5; Isa. 65:16; John 17:17; James 1:18).
5. God spoke His true Word as consistent with His true Nature to be communicated to people (a self-evident truth which is illustrated at 2 Tim. 3:16-17; Heb. 1:1).

Therefore, we must consider the following propositions.

1. God gave His true Word to be communicated *entirely* as He gave it, that is, the whole counsel of God is to be preached (Matt. 28:20; Acts 5:20, 20:27). Correspondingly, every portion of the Word of God needs to be considered in the light of its whole.
2. God gave His true Word to be communicated *exactly* as He gave it. It is to be dispensed precisely as it was delivered without the message being altered.
3. Only the exegetical process which yields expository proclamation will accomplish propositions 1 and 2.

B. Inerrancy's Link To Expository Preaching

Now, let me substantiate these propositions with answers to a series of questions. They will channel our thinking from the headwaters of God's revelation to its intended destination.

1. Why preach?

Very simply, God so commanded (2 Tim. 4:2), and the apostles so responded (Acts 6:4).

2. What should we preach?

The Word of God, i.e., *Scriptura sola* and *Scriptura tota* (1 Tim. 4:13; 2 Tim. 4:2).

3. Who preaches?

Holy men of God (Luke 1:70; Acts 3:21; Eph. 3:5; 2 Pet. 1:21; Rev. 18:20, 22:6). Only after God had purified Isaiah's lips was he ordained to preach (Isa. 6:6-13).

4. What is the preacher's responsibility?

First, the preacher needs to realize that God's Word is not his word. But rather:

a. He is a messenger, not an originator *(euagglizō)*.
b. He is a sower, not the source (Matt. 13:3, 19).
c. He is a herald, not the authority *(Kērussō)*.
d. He is a steward, not the owner (Col. 1:25).
e. He is the guide, not the author (Acts 8:31).
f. He is the server of spiritual food, not the chef (John 21:15, 17).

Second, the preacher needs to reckon that it is *ho logos tou theou* (the Word of God). When he is committed to this awesome truth and responsibility,

> His aim, rather, will be to stand under Scripture, not over it, and to allow it, so to speak, to talk through him, delivering what is not so much his message as its. In our preaching, that is what should always be happening. In his obituary of the great German conductor, Otto Klemperer, Neville Cardus spoke of the way in which Klemperer "set the music in motion," maintaining throughout a deliberately anonymous, self-effacing style in order that the musical notes might articulate themselves in their own integrity through him. So it must be in preaching; Scripture itself must do all the talking, and the preacher's task is simply to "set the Bible in motion."[6]

A careful study of the phrase *logos theou* finds 47 uses in the New Testament. It is equated with the Old Testament (Mark 7:13). It is what Jesus preached (Luke 5:1). It was the message that the apostles taught (Acts 4:31, 6:2). It was the word that the Samaritans recevied (Acts 8:14) as given by the apostles (Acts 8:25). It was the message that the Gentiles received as preached by Peter (Acts 11:1).

It was the word Paul preached on his first missionary journey (Acts 13:5, 7, 44, 48, 49, 15:35-36). It was the message preached on Paul's second missionary journey (Acts 16:32, 17:13, 18:11). It was the message Paul preached on his third missionary journey (Acts 19:10). It was the focus of Luke in the Book of Acts in that it grew (Acts 6:7, 12:24, 19:20). Paul was careful to tell the Corinthians that he spoke the Word as it was given from God, that it had not been adulterated and that it was a manifestation of truth (2 Cor. 2:17, 4:2). Paul acknowledged that it was the source of his preaching (Col. 1:25; 1 Thess. 2:13).

As it was with Christ and the apostles, so Scripture is also to be delivered by preachers today in such a way that they can say, "Thus saith the Lord." Their responsibility is to deliver it as it was originally given and intended.

5. How did the preacher's message begin?

The message began as a true word from God and was given as truth because God's purpose was to transmit truth. It was orderd by God as truth and was delivered by God's Spirit in cooperation with holy men who received it with exactly the pure quality that God intended (2 Pet. 1:20-21). It was received as *Scriptura inerrantis* by the prophets and apostles, i.e., without wandering from Scripture's original formulation in the mind of God.

Inerrancy then expresses the quality with which the writers of our canon received the text we call Scripture.

6. How is God's message to continue in its original true state?

If God's message began true and if it is to be delivered as received, what interpretive processes necessitated by changes of language, culture and time, will ensure its purity when currently preached? The answer is that only an exegetical approach is acceptable for accurate exposition.

Having established the essential need for exegesis, the most logical question is, "How is interpretation/exegesis linked with preaching?"

Packer answers best:

> The Bible being what it is, all true interpretation of it must take the form of preaching. With this goes an equally important converse: that, preaching being what it is, all true preaching must take the form of biblical interpretation.[7]

7. Now, practically pulling our thinking all together, "What is the final step that links inerrancy to preaching?"

First, the true text must be used. We are indebted to those select scholars who labor tediously in the field of textual criticism. Their studies recover the original text of Scripture from the large volume of extant manuscript copies which are flawed by textual variants. This is the starting point. Without the text as God gave it, the preacher would be helpless to deliver it as God intended.

Second, having begun with a true text, we need to interpret the text accurately. The science of hermeneutics is in view.

> As a theological discipline hermeneutics is the science of the correct interpretation of the Bible. It is a special application of the general science of linguistics and meaning. It seeks to formulate those particular rules which pertain to the special factors connected with the Bible . . . Hermeneutics is a science in that it can determine certain principles for discovering the meaning of a document, and in that these principles are not a mere list of rules but bear organic connection to each other. It is also an art as we previously indicated because principles or rules can never be applied mechanically but involve the skill (technē) of the interpreter.[8]

Third, our exegesis must flow from a proper hermeneutic. Of this relationship, Bernard Ramm observes that hermeneutics,

> . . . stands in the same relationship to exegesis that a rule-book stands to a game. The rule-book is written in terms of reflection, analysis, and expereince. The game is played by concrete actualization of the rules. The rules are not the game, and the game is meaningless without the rules. Hermeneutics proper is not exegesis, but exegesis is applied hermeneutics.[9]

Exegesis can now be defined as the skillful application of sound hermeneutical principles to the Biblical text in the original language with a view to understanding and declaring the author's intended meaning both to the immediate and subsequent audiences. In tandem, hermeneutics and exegesis focus on the Biblical text to determine what it said and what it meant originally.[10]

Thus, exegesis in its broadest sense will include the various disciplines of literary criticism, historical studies, grammatical exegesis, historical theology, biblical theology and systematic theology. Proper exegesis will tell the student what the text says, what the text means, and how the text applies personally.

Fourth, we are now ready for a true exposition. Based on the flow of thinking that we have just come through, I assert that expository preaching is really exegetical preaching and not so much the homiletical form of the message. Merrill Unger accurately notes:

> It is not the length of the portion treated, whether a single verse or a larger unit, but the manner of treatment. No matter what the length of the portion explained may be, if it is handled in such a way that its real and essential meaning as it existed in the light of the over-all context of Scripture is made plain and applied to the present-day needs of the hearers, it may properly be said to be expository preaching.[11]

As a result of this exegetical process that began with inerrancy, the expositor is equipped with a true message, with true intent and with true application. It gives him preaching perspective historically, theologically, contextually, literarily, synoptically and culturally. His message is God's intended message.

Now, because this all seems so patently obvious, we might ask, "How did the church ever lose sight of inerrancy's relationship to preaching?" Let me suggest that in the main it was through the "legacy of liberalism."

III. THE LEGACY OF LIBERALISM

A. A Recent Example

Robert Bratcher is the translator of the American Bible Society's *Good News For Modern Man,* a research assistant with ABS and also an ordained Southern Baptist pastor. As one of the invited speakers to the recent Christian Life Commission of the Southern Baptist Convention, he addressed the topic, "Biblical Authority for the Church Today." Bratcher was quoted as saying:

> Only willful ignorance or intellectual dishonesty can account for the claim that the Bible is inerrant and infallible. No truth-loving, God-respecting, Christ-honoring believer should be guilty of such heresy. To invest the Bible with the qualities of inerrancy and infallibility is to idolatrize (sic) it, to transform it into a false god.[12]

This thinking is typical of the legacy of liberalism that has robbed preachers of true preaching dynamics. I ask, "Why be careful with content which does not reflect the nature of God, or with content whose truthfulness is uncertain?"

B. False Notions

Bratcher and others who would subscribe to "limited" or "partial" inerrancy are guilty of error along several lines of reasoning.[13]

First, they have not really come to grips with that which Scripture teaches about itself. Benjamin Warfield focused on the heart of the issue with this inquiry:

> The really decisive question among Christian scholars . . . is thus seen to be, "What does an exact and scientific exegesis determine to be the Biblical doctrine of inspiration?"[14]

The answer is that nowhere do the Scriptures teach that there is a dichotomy of truth and error nor do the writers ever give the slightest hint that they were aware of this alleged phenomenon as they wrote. The human writers of Scripture unanimously concur that it is God's Word; therefore it must be true.

Second, limited or partial inerrancy assumes that there is a higher authority to estabish the reliability of Scripture than God's revelation in the Scriptures. They err by *a priori* giving the critic a place of authority over the Scriptures. This assumes the critic himself is inerrant.

Third, if limited inerrancy is true (first class condition), then its promoters err in assuming that any of the Scriptures are a trustworthy communicator of God's truth. An errant Scripture would definitely disqualify the Bible as a reliable source of truth.

Presuppositions are involved either way. Will men place their faith in the Scriptures or the critics? They cannot have their cake (trustworthy Scripture) and eat it too (limited inerrancy). Pinnock aptly notes:

> The attempt to narrow down the integrity of the Bible to matters of "faith" and its historical reliability is an unwarranted and foolish procedure.[15]

If the Bible is unable to produce a sound doctrine of Scripture, then it is thus incapable of producing, with any degree of believability or credibility, a doctrine about any other matter. If the human writers of Scripture have erred in their understanding of Holy Writ's purity, then they have disqualified themselves as writers for any other area of God's revealed truth. If they are so disqualified in all areas, then every preacher is thoroughly robbed of any confidence and conviction concerning the alleged true message he would be relaying for God.

C. The Bottom Line

G. Campbell Morgan, hailed as the twentieth-century's "prince of expositors," was a messenger widely used of God. However, there was a time in his life when he wrestled with the very issue we discuss. He concluded that if there were errors in the biblical message, it could not be honestly proclaimed in public.

Here is the account of young Campbell Morgan's struggle to know if the Bible was surely God's Word:

> For three years this young man, seriously contemplating a future of teaching and ultimately of preaching, felt the troubled waters of the stream of religious controversy carrying him beyond his depth. He read the new books which debated such questions as, 'Is God Knowable?' and found that the authors' concerted decision was, 'He is not knowable.' He became confused and perplexed. No longer was he sure of that which his father proclaimed in public, and had taught him in the home.
>
> Other books appeared, seeking to defend the Bible from the attacks which were being made upon it. The more he read the more unanswerable became the questions which filled his mind. One who had never suffered it cannot appreciate the anguish of spirit young Campbell Morgan endured during this crucial period of his life. Through all the after years it gave him the greatest sympathy with young people passing through similar experiences at college—experiences which he likened to 'passing through a trackless desert.' At last the crisis came when he admitted to himself his total lack of assurance that the Bible was the authoritative Word of God to man. He immediately cancelled all preaching engagements. Then, taking all his books, both those attacking and those defending the Bible, he put them all in a corner cupboard. Relating this afterwards, as he did many times in preaching, he told of turning the key in the lock of the door. "I can hear the click of that lock now," he used to say. He went out of the house, and down the street to a bookshop. He bought a new Bible and, returning to his room with it, he said to himself: 'I am no longer sure that this is what my father claims it to be—the Word of God. But of this I am sure. If it be the Word of God, and if I come to it with an unprejudiced and open mind, it will bring assurance to my soul of itself.' "That Bible found me," he said, "I began to read and study it then, in 1883. I have been a student ever since, and I still am (in 1938)."
>
> At the end of two years Campbell Morgan emerged from that eclipse of faith absolutely sure that the Bible was, in very deed and truth, none other than the Word of the living God. Quoting again from his account of the incident: ". . . This experience is what, at last, took me back into the work of preaching, and

> into the work of the ministry. I soon found foothold enough to begin to preach, and from that time I went on."
>
> With this crisis behind him and this new certainty thrilling his soul, there came a compelling conviction, This Book, being what it was, merited all that a man could give to its study, not merely for the sake of the personal joy of delving deeply into the heart and mind and will of God, but also in order that those truths discovered by such searching of the Scriptures should be made known to a world of men groping for light, and perishing in the darkness with no clear knowledge of that Will.[16]

May God be pleased to multiply the tribe of men called "preachers" who, being convinced of the Bible's inerrant nature, will diligently apply themselves to understand and to proclaim its message as one commissioned of God to deliver it in His stead.

IV. OUR CHALLENGE

One of the most godly preachers ever to live was Scotland's Robert Murray McCheyne. In the memoirs of McCheyne's life, Andrew Bonar writes:

> It was his wish to arrive nearer at the primitive mode of expounding Scripture in his sermons. Hence when one asked him, if he was ever afraid of running short of sermons some day, he replied—"No; I am just an interpreter of Scripture in my sermons; and when the Bible runs dry, then I shall." And in the same spirit he carefully avoided the too common mode of accommodating texts—fastening a doctrine on the words, not drawing it from the obvious connection of the passage. He endeavoured at all times to preach the mind of the Spirit in a passage; for he feared that to do otherwise would be to grieve the Spirit who had written it. Interpretation was thus a solemn matter to him. And yet, adhering scrupulously to this sure principle, he felt himself in no way restrained from using, for every day's necessities, all parts of the Old Testament as much as the New. His manner was first to ascertain the primary sense and application, and so proceed to handle it for present use.[17]

The expositor's task is to preach the mind of God as he finds it in the inerrant Word of God. He understands it through the disciplines of hermeneutics and exegesis. He declares it expositorily then as the message which God spoke and commissioned him to deliver.

John Stott has deftly sketched the relationship of the exegetical process to expository preaching:

> Expository preaching is a most exacting discipline. Perhaps that is why it is so rare. Only those will undertake it who are prepared to follow the example of the apostles and say, 'It is not right that we should give up preaching the Word of God to serve tables. . . . We will devote ourselves to prayer and to the ministry of the Word' (Acts 6:2, 4). The systematic preaching of the Word is impossible without the systematic study of it. It will not be enough to skim through a few verses in daily Bible reading, nor to study a passage only when we have to preach from it. No. We must daily soak ourselves in the Scriptures. We must not just study, as through a microscope, the linguistic minutiae of a few verses, but take our telescope and scan the wide expanses of God's Word, assimilating its grand theme of divine sovereignty in the redemption of mankind. 'It is blessed', wrote C. H. Spurgeon, 'to eat into the very soul of the Bible until, at last, you come to talk in Scriptural language, and your spirit is flavoured with the words of the Lord, so that you blood is Bibline and the very essence of the Bible flows from you.'[18]

Inerrancy demands an exegetical process and an expository proclamation. Only then can God's Word be delivered exactingly.

V. THE CONCLUSION

Only the exegetical process preserves God's Word entirely and exactly as He intended it to be proclaimed. Thus, it is the essential link between inerrancy and expository preaching. Expository preaching then is the result of the exegetical process. It is mandated to preserve the purity of God's originally given inerrant Word and to proclaim the whole counsel of God's redemptive truth.

NOTES

[1]Paul D. Feinberg, "Infallibility and Inerrancy," *Trinity Journal*, VI:2 (Fall, 1977), p. 120, rightly articulates critical inerrancy as . . . "the claim that when all facts are known, the scriptures in their original autographs and properly interpreted will be shown to be without error in all that they affirm to the degree of precision intended, whether that affirmation relates to doctrine, history, science, geography, geology, etc."

[2]James I. Packer, "Preaching As Biblical Interpretation," *Inerrancy And Common Sense*, ed. Roger R. Nicole & J. Ramsey Michaels (Grand Rapids: Baker Book House, 1980), p. 189.

[3]D. Martyn Lloyd-Jones, *Preaching And Preachers* (Grand Rapids: Zondervan Publishing House, 1971), p. 222.

[4]Walter C. Kaiser, Jr., *Toward An Exegetical Theology* (Grand Rapids: Baker Book House, 1981), pp. 7-8.

[5]R. B. Kuiper, "Scriptural Preaching," *The Infallible Word,* third revised edition, ed. Paul Woolley (Philadelphia: The Presbyterian And Reformed Publishing Company, 1967), p. 217.

[6]Packer, *Inerrancy And Common Sense,* p. 203.

[7]*Ibid.,* p. 187.

[8]Bernard Ramm, *Protestant Biblical Interpretation,* third revised edition (Grand Rapids: Baker Book House, 1970), p. 11.

[9]*Ibid.*

[10]This definition has been adapted from John D. Grassmick, *Principles And Practice of Greek Exegesis* (Dallas: Dallas Theological Seminary, 1974), p. 7.

[11]Merrill F. Unger, *Principles of Expository Preaching* (Grand Rapids: Zondervan Publishing House, 1955). p. 33.

[12]"Inerrancy: Clearing Away Confusion," *Christianity Today* (May 29, 1981), p. 12.

[13]These arguments have been adapted from Richard L. Mayhue, "Biblical Inerrancy In The Gospels" (Winona Lake: Grace Theological Seminary, 1977), pp. 12-15.

[14]Benjamin Breckinridge Warfield, *The Inspiration And Authority Of The Bible* (Philadelphia: The Presbyterian And Reformed Publishing Company, reprinted 1948), p. 175.

[15]Clark H. Pinnock, "Our Source of Authority: The Bible," *Bibliotheca Sacra* 124:494 (April-June, 1967), p. 154.

[16]Jill Morgan, *A Man Of The Word: Life Of G. Campbell Morgan* (Grand Rapids: Baker Book House, reprinted 1972), pp. 39-40.

[17]Andrew A. Bonar, *Memoir And Remains Of Robert Murray McCheyne* (Grand Rapids: Baker Book House, reprinted 1978), p. 94.

[18]John R. W. Stott, *The Preacher's Portrait* (Grand Rapids: Wm. B. Eerdmans Publishing Company, 1961), pp. 30-31.

A Response to Homiletics and Hermeneutics

Erwin W. Lutzer
Senior Pastor
Moody Church
Chicago, Illinois

A Response to Homiletics and Hermeneutics

Erwin W. Lutzer

Dr. Robinson is to be commended for his forceful plea for expository preaching and his concern that a preacher's message be truly biblical, i.e., that the ideas presented are based on solid exegesis, along with contextual and historical considerations. No doubt heresy is often preached from many evangelical pulpits because the preacher has based his message on a verse or fragment of a verse taken out of context. Equally serious is the practice of imposing upon a passage the preacher's own ideas and thoughts.

However, there are some issues which Dr. Robinson raises which necessitate discussion and/or clarification. I shall enumerate some of these, not so much to disagree with what is written but to highlight different points of view for interaction and evaluation.

First, though we would grant the danger inherent in topical preaching, we may question whether there is no place for topical preaching at all as Dr. Robinson seems to imply. He writes:

> Topical preaching common in American pulpits flirts with heresy. Deuteronomy 18:20 warned that the prophet who spoke in the name of God what God had not spoken should be executed.[1]

Of course topical preaching may flirt with heresy, but it need not. Dr. Blackwood whose books on preaching are well-known, has said that the best preachers were topical in their sermonic development.

For example, a preacher who prepares a message on biblical inerrancy may wish to explain Paul and Christ's view of Scripture. Several different passages may be used to expound this topic. If done carefully, with due regard to contextual and grammatical considerations, this would not be heresy, but good theology. Indeed, systematic theology is largely a topical study of the various themes of Scripture. Certainly topical preaching has been misused, but it can also be done effectively and with biblical integrity. The message on the topic can grow out of the intended meaning of Scripture.

Also, many effective preachers are textual preachers who use their message to develop the teaching of a verse or part of a verse (Spurgeon, for example). Here again the legitimacy of such a message depends on whether the preacher has given proper consideration to the context and meaning of the author. The fault is not with the methods; the fault lies with the preacher.

Second, Dr. Robinson questions the common practice of:

> . . . employing the historical narratives as case studies in morals, virtues, or spiritual struggles.[2]

For example, preachers often use the camaraderie between David and Jonathan as models of an ideal friendship, the conversation of Jesus with the woman at the well as a model for witnessing, and the story of Ruth and Naomi as an example of how Christians should relate to their in-laws. These accounts Dr. Robinson says, should not be so used because it was not the author's intention that we "see ourselves in the story." Dr. Robinson believes that such a use of Scripture violates the intended purpose of the author. He explains that I Corinthians 10:6, "Now these occurred as examples to keep us from setting our hearts on evil things as they did," does not say what some have thought it says. Paul, must not be interpreted to justify introducing scriptural incidents into sermons to be used pictorially, pedagogically, or illustratively with the unstated assumption that they carry divine authority.

In other words, since the author's intention was not to provide an example of friendship (David and Jonathan) or to give us a lesson in personal evangelism (Christ at the well) or to teach us how to relate to our in-laws (the story of Ruth) these narratives cannot be used for such purposes. In fact, Dr. Robinson says about the preacher:

> If he uses the historical narrative in order to speak about the temptations and problems of men and women in the pew, he would do as well to put aside the biblical text rather than to draw illegitimate parallels not intended by the biblical author.[3]

Here however several questions could be asked. (1) Since Peter wrote that "Christ also suffered for you, leaving you an example" (1 Peter 2:21) does not this give the preacher the right to use at least one aspect of Christ's life as an example? The authors of the synoptic Gospels have given us details that occurred during Christ's suffering in Gethsemane, subsequent trial and crucifixion. It seems apparent that their purpose was not to say to us, "Here's the way you ought to suffer." The details were given so that we could better comprehend what Christ did in our behalf. Yet Peter, says that Christ is our example of suffering. He seems to be asking us to use the narrative of Christ's suffering for a purpose other than the primary intention of the biblical writer.

This raises a question: Might not an author have one main purpose but also other subsidiary purposes in writing what he did? Is it unreasonable to suppose that John may have written about Christ's conversation at the well to give a discourse on eternal life but also to provide a model for how it should be presented?

Dr. Robinson claims if we use biblical characters as examples we might just as well go outside the Scriptures. But in the case of Christ's sufferings, his method of resisting Satan, and his approach to presenting the gospel, we have no one comparable to him; and the authors of the synoptic Gospels may have intended that he be our example in these encounters. Paul also presents Christ's incarnation as an example of humility for believers (Philippians 2).

Then (2) we must also bear in mind that Christ made logical deductions from a text of Scripture to prove a point which was clearly quite different from the intended purpose of the author. The Sadducees believed in the authority of the Pentateuch but denied the existence of the resurrection of the dead because they could not find this doctrine taught in the first five books of the Old Testament. Christ however, argued that the doctrine was taught in Exodus chapter 3 where God identified himself at the burning bush, "I am the God of Abraham, the God of Isaac and the God of Jacob." Our Lord's argument was this: God is the God of the living, which means that Abraham, Isaac, and Jacob were still alive though they had died long before God spoke these words to Moses. Becuse God used the present tense, "I am" He was still their God at the time he was speaking to Moses. That would not have been possible if when Abraham, Isaac, and Jacob died they ceased to exist.

On the basis of a present tense rather than a past tense Christ used the words that were given to Moses to support the doctrine of resurrection. Yet when God said to Moses, "I am the God of Abraham, Isaac, and Jacob," He was simply identifying himself, he was showing his continuity with the patriarchs of the past. Clearly, he did not say these words to Moses to convince him of the doctrine of resurrection.

Logical deductions therefore, may be drawn from the Scripture which are quite different than the author's intended purpose. Obviously, this is done when we attempt to defend a doctrine such as biblical inerrancy. Passages such as Matthew 5:18 were not given in the New Testament to defend verbal plenary inspiration. Christ was assuring his listeners that he did not come to abolish the Law or the prophets but to fulfill them. Thus he says that all the Law shall be accomplished . . . even to the very last letter. Yet, from this we may draw certain conclusions about our Lord's regard for the Old Testament, even though such conclusions were not the primary reason for Christ's statement.

Then (3) I think it is necessary to recognize that though a text has only one meaning, an author may write what he did for a variety of reasons; he may wish to communicate several ideas rather than the one that may be uppermost in his mind. For example, the miracles John selected were designed specificially to show that Jesus is the Christ, the Son of God (John 20:31). Does this mean that nothing else can be learned from them? Would it be incorrect to draw lessons about the benefits of obedience from the servants at Cana who drew the water at Christ's command? Is there nothing to be learned from the little boy who gave his lunch to Christ so that Christ could use it to feed the multitude? Indeed, if one is already convinced that Jesus Christ is the Son of God, should he ignore John's miracles since the intended purpose of John has already been accomplished?

The Book of Ruth may represent a similar instance. Once again the text has only one intended meaning, but if we ask why the book was written, we might find several intentions that the author wishes to accomplish. One certainly is to show how the geneology of David was preserved. But perhaps there are other lessons to be learned. Since some of the major characters are the object of prayers that are answered, the author may have intended that we see how God responds to the cry of the humble. Such secondary intentions are no doubt part of the central theme, but contain their own lessons as well.

This of course, is not to say there are hidden meanings in the text; I'm not suggesting that there are several levels of meaning that the author was unaware of—but the authors of Scripture, like authors today, may have had several reasons for writing what they did. There is only one intended meaning of the text, but several themes may be treated within the text; an author may have several reasons for writing what he did.

Finally (4) we must ask how limiting ourselves to the author's intent would affect our study of prophecy. We have all heard theories of "double fulfillment," or "a fuller sense of Scripture," in order to account for the fact that several prophetic passages in the Old Testament apparently had only local significance (Hosea 11:1 and Jeremiah 31:15, quoted in Matthew 2:15, 18 would serve as examples). In such cases, it would appear that we have a better understanding of what the prophets wrote than they did themselves. Undoubtedly Matthew used these quotations consistent with the prophet's intentions. But once again we have to recognize the possibility of multiple purposes though not multiple meanings. Jeremiah 31:5 has only one meaning, namely a description of the suffering of the Jews. But the prophet may have intended that it be applied both locally and prophetically.

To conclude, Dr. Robinson's plea for limiting preaching to the intended meaning of the author is necessary if we are to have an authoritative word from God. But we must distinguish between the intended meaning of the text (which is one) and the intended purposes for writing (which may be many).

NOTES

[1]Haddon W. Robinson, "Homiletics and Hermeneutics," p. 804.
[2]Ibid., p. 809.
[3]Ibid., p. 811.

The Role of Logic in Biblical Interpretation

Paul Helm
Senior Lecturer in
Philosophy
University of Liverpool

16. The Role of Logic in Biblical Interpretation

Paul Helm

> Must a book on every subject be inspired in order to be true? Have we lost all faith in inductive logic? Have we abandoned human testimony as a source of information? Is there no longer a place for the common sense of mankind?
>
> —Francis L. Patton

> The power of God is infinite without any limitations and above the grasp of our reason. It may seem to be our duty to want to limit this power and to want to say, God can do all possible things. But Scripture speaks in a different way and says, With God nothing is impossible.
>
> —John Gerhard

The task of interpreting an ancient document is often said to involve two stages: understanding the original, intended meaning of the author and (where appropriate) making that meaning relevant to today's readers. In what follows we shall be concerned only with the first stage.

What is involved in understanding a simple, declarative sentence such as, "The cat is on the mat"? Understanding such sentences consists in the mastery to a degree of some or all of the following capabilities: the ability to say or otherwise indicate under what circumstances the sentence is or would be true, or false; the ability to say what "The cat is on the mat" does not mean (it does not mean, for example, "The cow jumped over the moon"); and the ability to say what the sentence implies. These are capabilities which, like all capabilities, can be had to different degrees. I think that we would say that someone who had no such capabilities had not begun to understand what the sentence means. "Understanding" is not the name of a characteristic, purely mental state that could exist *apart from* such capabilities.

Now such capabilities are essentially *logical* in characters, as a moment's reflection reveals. To indicate under what circumstances a sentence would be true implies some knowledge of the circumstances that would make it false. To say what a sentence does not mean shows knowledge that, say "mat" does not mean the same as "moon," and also knowledge of certain syntactical matters: "The cat is on the mat" implies "At least one cat is on something."

The interpretation of a document involves understanding of this kind, but to such a degree that the meaning of the original is preserved in the sentences of the same or another natural language. So a logically necessary condition for success in the interpretation of a document whose statements are taken to be true or false is that the translation is *cognitively synonymous* with the original, that is, that both the original and the translation have the same truth and falsity conditions.[1]

In what follows it will be argued that, as already intimated, the role of logic in such an activity is logically inevitable, that understanding, of which the provision of an exact translation is one sort of limiting case, *could not* be achieved without logic. But it is important to keep in mind what is meant by "logic" here. It is *not* to be identified with *any* of the following: (1) with "reason" and "reasonable" when these mean "expectation," "fairness," "probable," "likely" and so on; (2) with the idea that "religion" has its own logic or that it is logically distinctive or logically odd.[2] Rather by "logic" is meant certain basic, purely formal principles of thought and of deductive reasoning. (Something will be said later about inductive reasoning.) To remove any doubt here are five such principles. The list is not meant to be exhaustive but the five given are essential to the activity of interpreting just because they are essential to any intellectual activity.

1. Everything is identical with itself and distinct from anything else.
2. If A is identical with B then whatever is true of A is true of B.
3. No proposition can be both true and false.
4. If a proposition p is true, and q follows logically from p then q is true.
5. If p and q contradict each other then they cannot both be true.

In saying that such principles are necessary conditions for thought it must be borne in mind that logic, in the sense in which we are using the term here, is a purely formal, topic-neutral discipline. It is concerned solely with what follows from what. It asks, taking for granted the truth of a proposition or propositions, what other proposition(s) can be inferred? To suppose that one proposition follows logically from another carries this consequence: that *if* the first proposition is true the entailed proposition must be true. Logic does *not* provide an initial stock of true propositions. These must be quarried elsewhere. So far as establishing true conclusions is concerned, logic is irreducibly hypothetical in character, concerned with what follows *given* some proposition or propositions. Logical validity preserves truth in virtue of the fact that the alternative to a logically valid deduction is a self-contradiction, that is, the alternative is an expression that represents no possibility at all.[3]

Such principles as 1-5 above are logically necessary for the interpretation of any document, hence they are logically necessary for interpreting the Bible. This position has not gone unchallenged. We shall look at five challenges before proceeding further.

1. All logic, including 1-5 above, is "merely human," a set of human constructions or conventions. Thus its value is suspect for the purposes of interpreting a divinely-inspired document since logic represents an alien, purely human intrusion into the divine. In reply, (a) there is some truth in the idea that human beings can choose to employ the principles of logic or not. But to suppose that 1-5 represent a convention is to suppose that there is an *alternative* set of principles. But what could they be? The choice is between intelligibility and babbling, and this is no choice at all.[4] (b) When such an objection comes from a theological quarter it is usually in the form of a point about divine power (the medieval theological debates, Descartes, some Protestants such as Gerhard) or divine objectivity (Karl Barth, T. F. Torrance) or about the sufficiency of the Scriptures (some evangelicals).[5] As it is an adequate answer to the medieval worry about divine power to say that not even God needs to be able to do what is logically impossible, to do something which is *not a possibility,* so it is a sufficient answer to the evangelical to say that it is no slur on the sufficiency of the Bible that it does not teach a "scriptural logic" that denies some or all of 1-5. We could not understand the Scriptures if they did. Texts such as Isaiah 55:8-9 and Luke 18:27 are to be understood as referring to the power of divine grace, not to a logic-transcending omnipotence.

To say that logic delimits the possible is not to say that only what we believe to be logically possible is logically possible. We may come to see that what we thought was an impossibility is not and *vice versa*.

2. Logic is "cold" but the Scriptures are "warm," God's personal address to men. The point about the Scriptures can be granted. Further, they are not in the form of a deductive system with axioms, derivations, theorems and the like. And the reason for this is obvious, that the Scriptures deal preeminently with redemptive history, with matters which are not, from a logical point of view, necessary but which are the product of free, divine choice. Nevertheless they are inspired by the Supreme Mind and are therefore not out of accord with 1-5. If a father says to his child "I love you" this is warm and personal. Nevertheless "I love you" means something different from "I hate you" and from "Mommy loves you" and "I love Mommy."

3. Logic is a post-Enlightenment imposition upon the biblical text or (a slightly different thesis) the expression of a Greek rather than a Hebrew mentality. This is in effect to argue that questions of meaning and truth are culturally relative. The way to respond to this position (to be found in its most blatant and uncompromising form in Professor Denis Nineham's *The Use and Abuse of the Bible*) is to see whether in fact the biblical writers observe 1-5, whether the language of the Scriptures is syntactically and semantically in accord with 1-5, whether the writers reason, guard against logical fallacies, reply to objections, and the like. And there seems little doubt that they do. The biblical writings often explicitly exemplify logical principles[6] and there are connected narratives (e.g., Luke/Acts) and sustained arguments (Romans, 1 Cor. 15). There is also reason to think that the more extreme forms of cultural relativism cannot be consistently sustained.[7]

In reply it might be said that it can be granted that the biblical writers observe rules of logic, but that to suppose that this closes the question is to confuse first- and second-order questions. *They* may observe such rules, but it does not follow that *we*, their interpreters, must. But what could be more relevant to what the biblical writers mean than what they say? The onus is very much on the shoulders of someone who holds this position to justify it.

4. A more formal objection to the use of logic in interpretation has been made on the grounds of intellectual economy.[8] But this is to confuse logical implication with causal explanation. Other things being equal, the most economical explanation of some phenomenon is to be preferred. But if the teaching of the Scriptures logically implies the doctrine of the Trinity it is irrelevant to object that to maintain the doctrine of the Trinity as scriptural unnecessarily complicates matters. For if the Scriptures entail the doctrine of the Trinity

then that is what (in part) the teaching of the Scripture *means*. If a consequence is logically necessary then why not draw it?

5. A final objection is that the use of logic involves treating Scripture as dogma, which it is not. It can be granted that Scripture is not dogma, but the use of logic in the interpretation of Scripture does not involve treating Scripture as dogma. It involves treating Scripture as having a meaning and therefore treating its declarative expressions as having truth-values. "The difference between Scripture and dogma is to be sought at the level of genre, or form, not at the level of principle."[9]

I

After this brief attempt to defend the role of logic in the interpretation of Scripture and to allay some fears, it is now time to look at the roles that logic plays. We shall look at four.

A. Deductive inference from single texts. From certain propositions in Scripture certain other propositions follow as a matter of logic. Thus from "The Lord shall descend from heaven with a shout" (1 Thess. 4:16) the following propositions follow:

(1) Paul believed that the Lord will come down from heaven at some time in the future from the time he wrote.
(2) Paul believed that the Lord's return will be accompanied by a noise.

These propositions do not follow:

(3) Paul believed that the Lord will shout when he descends from heaven.
(4) Paul believed that the Lord will visibly descend from heaven.

These do not *follow,* though doubtless Paul believed that (4) was true. But its truth does not follow from 1 Thessalonians 4:16, rather from elsewhere. (3) seems to be false since it seems to contradict what follows in the passage.

But the possibilities of deductive inference from single texts or sentences are strictly limited. Indeed the example just given is not actually a case of a deduction from a single text, for 1 Thessalonians 4:16 does not contain any reference to Paul and we must get the information that this was a belief of Paul's from elsewhere, from our knowledge of the authorship of 1 Thessalonians.

B. If we extend our inquiry to groups of sentences, then the following points need to be observed:

1. Some inferences from groups of sentences pass almost unnoticed. From John 1:11, "He came unto his own . . ." we naturally believe that the text tells us that *Jesus* came unto His own from information given elsewhere. The text does not *say* that *Jesus* came, it only says that *He* came. What is true of this one example is true of all the other occasions on which pronouns and other indexical expressions (expressions depending for their reference on the circumstances of the utterance which they form a part) are used. This point underlies a basic (Reformed and Lutheran) hermeneutical principle that the meaning of Scripture is Scripture.[10] The canon of Scripture is not constituted by words alone, or by sentences alone, but by words and sentences having a definite meaning in a natural language and in a particular linguistic context.

2. Another function of logic is the supplying of suppressed premises. There are many enthymemetic passages in Scripture. One of the most striking of these, frequently alluded to by both Reformed and Lutheran theologians in their treatment of the place of logic in theology, is in Mark 12:26 where Jesus proves the resurrection of the dead from the Lord describing Himself to Moses as the God of Abraham, Isaac and Jacob. Here Jesus supplies the missing premise, making explicit what had previously only been implicit.[11]

3. It must be borne in mind that the longer and more complex the groups of sentences from which we attempt to draw implications the harder that task may become. This can be illustrated from a classic case. One set of data in the New Testament implies, or seems to imply, that Jesus of Nazareth was a mere man: he had a human mother, grew up from infancy through adolescence to manhood, ate, spoke, learned, was angry, tired, prayed, and so on. Can we infer from this data

(a) Jesus was a man,
(b) No man is identical with God,
(c) Therefore, Jesus is not identical with God?

Blocking this inference is a line of data that implies that Jesus was more than a man, and is in fact God: he had a heavenly Father, he created the world, he had power to forgive sins, and so on. Can we infer from this second line of evidence

(d) Jesus is God,
(b) No man is identical with God,
(e) Therefore, Jesus is not a man?

One function of doctrinal formulae such as the Chalcedonian Definition of the person of Christ is to preserve both lines of biblical evidence from too hasty a logical treatment, to maintain that there is a sense in which an individual can be both God and man, namely in the case where two natures are united in one person without confusion, transmutation or division. The formula safeguards the mystery of the Incarnation from palpable self-contradiction.

One last point on this, one which frequently causes confusion. There is a difference between saying that a proposition p is consistent with q and that q follows logically from p. The relevance of this distinction can be illustrated as follows. It is sometimes said that the New Testament expresses different theologies, the theology of John, the theology of Paul, and so on, and this is said as though it reflects adversely upon the consistency and unity of the New Testament. But it only would reflect adversely on this unity if the theologies were mutually inconsistent.

C. Consideration of the Chalcedonian Definition leads naturally to consider a third use of logic in interpretation, the use of logic in theological construction, the formulation of a theological view of reality, of the nature of God, His creation, His plan, human hopes and destinies, from the text of Scripture. This involves generalizing from the data of Scripture regarding some particular matter and constructing a logically consistent account of that and its relation to other matters with which the Scriptures deal. One necessary condition for the success of such a procedure is the identifying of a class of basic or "axiomatic" texts or passages, texts whose meaning is clear or taken to be clear, and in terms of which other relevant texts are to be interpreted. The texts are axiomatic not in the strict geometrical sense according to which every conclusion must ultimately follow from them, but they are axiomatic in the sense that their meaning is taken to be basic and every other relevant text is understood in a way that is consistent with that basic meaning.

To illustrate, and keeping for the moment within evangelicalism, there are Calvinist and Arminian schemes of biblical interpretation, the logical elaboration of rival and incompatible theologies of grace. To be more specific, consider the respective attitudes of a Calvinist and an Arminian to those texts in which God is said to repent. A Calvinist will treat such texts, given the wisdom and immutability of God, as *facons de parler,* divine accommodations to human understanding, whereas an Arminian will typically regard them as changes in the divine will in the face of human autonomy.[12] For the Calvinist, texts regarding the divine sovereignty are *basic* texts. For the Arminian, since divine sovereignty is limited by human free will, texts which appear to teach the absolute dominion of God are interpreted differently.

In neither case is the interpretative procedure entirely *ad hoc*, but a purely logical consequence of accepting certain texts as clear and basic and others as not. To regard certain texts as basic is not purely arbitrary, since it depends upon what the texts *mean*, since both parties to this particular dispute wish to be faithful to what they take the Bible actually to teach.

Looking further afield into non-evangelical theology we find other positions. For example, axiomatic status may be given to Jesus' ethical teaching (at the expense of His ontological status) or (as with some modern Lutheran theologians) that status can be accorded to the principle of justification by faith alone, regarded not as a soteriological principle but as an epistemological axiom, cutting Christian faith off from any objective sources of knowledge.[13]

How to choose between rival axioms? We cannot go into this question in detail: suffice it to say that those ought to be chosen which will make most sense of the rest of the data, leaving fewest anomalies and loose ends.

D. For completeness one other way in which logic has been used, not so much in the interpretation of Scripture as in its apologetic underpinning, ought to be mentioned. This is the Anselmian program of showing the logical necessity of certain conditional propositions of the form "If *p* then *q*": "If there is to be an atonement for sin then God must become man and be the sinbearer."[14] Note that Anselm does not say that it is necessary, logically speaking, for there to be an atonement, but that it is logically necessary that *if* there is to be . . . *then*. . . .

Here logic is not being used to extrapolate from biblical data, as in A, B, and C just discussed, but to support the intelligibility and truth of the Christian faith by showing its internal consistency in a strict and formal way. Such a program goes beyond the ascertaining of the meaning of the text in proclaiming that logic requires that certain propositions be true if certain other propositions are true. While it cannot be doubted that all the divine decrees have an internal consistency, indeed that they are in effect one decree, nevertheless it is far from clear that the interpreter of Scripture is required to show that this consistency is as strong as logical entailment, certain acts of the divine will having to follow logically from certain others. It is possible to have a plan without it being the case that the means to the attaining the end of the plan are logically required by the end, for there may be more than one way of attaining the end. To suppose that one function of logic in theology is to show that what God has done He logically had to do comes dangerously close to the erection of an *a priori* theological requirement. But by the same token one cannot rule out the Anselmian program *a priori*. The point is that the program takes logic beyond the task of biblical interpretation and therefore beyond the scope of this paper.

II

We have outlined certain logical procedures in biblical interpretation. It is now necessary to consider the constraints within which such procedures must work. Three of these are quite general, constraints that apply to the use of logic in any discipline, one of them is peculiarly theological.

A. The constraint of literalness. The word "literal" can cause confusion. Here it is being used to refer not primarily to the intention(s) of an author, but to the meaning of the words and sentences uttered or recorded. "Literal" in this sense the *Concise Oxford Dictionary* defines as "Taking words in their usual or primary sense and applying the ordinary rules of grammar, without mysticism or allegory or metaphor." Augustine says, "For signs are either literal or figurative. They are called literal when they are used to designate those things on account of which they were instituted; thus we say *bos* (ox) when we mean an animal of a herd because all men using the Latin language call it by that name just as we do."[15]

Only if some propositions are literally true in this sense can there be logical deductions for only then is the meaning clear and only then do we have the resources to cope with metaphorical and other nonliteral expressions. A language in which all the predicates, say, were not literally meaningful would be logically intractable. Thus to describe someone as literally green is to be able to infer that the person is colored and that he is not blue. If on the other hand we know only that the person is nonliterally green we are not being told very much. But if we come to know that he is green in the sense of inexperienced, or green in the sense of being envious, then we can draw inferences, all of those inferences warranted by "(literally) inexperienced" or "(literally) envious."

This is important because of the large element of metaphorical, allegorical, parabolic and apocalyptic language in the Scriptures.

Such languages must be treated with extreme logical caution for it is only when such usages are fully understood that logical implications can be drawn from them. It may be a matter of legitimate debate which expressions are literal and which are metaphorical, and also a matter of legitimate debate what the literal equivalent of some non-literal expression is.[16]

It is necessary to go further. Even those parts of the Scripture which we wish to say are literal cannot be treated for the purposes of drawing inferences from them apart from a reference to the intention of their author or recorder or both. For there are degrees of literalness and it would be folly to base logical inferences on a degree of literalness that the author or recorder of the words did not intend. What A. A. Hodge said about the results of inspiration applies here:

> No one claims that inspiration secured the use of good Greek in Attic severity of taste, free from the exaggerations and looseness of current speech, but only that it secured the accurate expressions of truth, even (if you will) through the medium of the worst Greek a fisherman of Galilee could write and the most startling figure of speech a peasant could invent.[17]

Are the deductions drawn from the Scripture to be restricted to what deductions the original writer intended or foresaw, or might have intended or foreseen? No, for two reasons. The first is that it is impossible for us now to know what the writer intended or foresaw apart from the evidence of what he actually wrote. All else is pure guesswork and speculation. Second, the importance of referring to the intention of the writer lies in the help it gives in determining the meaning of what he wrote. What his writings imply is another matter, to be determined by logical reflection, but the logical reflection must take place upon the meaning of the sentences as decided according to the principles of grammatico-historical exegesis. And reference to the intention of the author is necessary for *that*.[18]

A word needs to be said here both about the legitimacy and utility of introducing into the interpretation of Scripture expressions which do not themselves occur in the Scriptures, words such as "trinity" and "inerrant" and phrases such as "of the same substance as." What is the warrant for doing so and what is the advantage? The only warrant for doing so is that the words newly-introduced express the sense of the Scriptures. This was the line of defense pursued by Athanasius in his *De Decretis* when he argued that the Nicene bishops, in using the phrase "one in essence" intended "to collect the sense of the Scriptures."[19] Such a phrase summarizes the biblical teaching (or has this intention) and brings out explicitly by a gloss on one scriptural phrase (e.g., the phrase "from the Father") what is implied in this and other relevant scriptural phrases.

There is the question of whether or not we can say that the concept of the Trinity, or the Son's being of the same essence as the Father, is in the Scriptures. There seem to be three possible views to take on this. To say that such concepts are not in, in the sense of entailed by, the biblical data, but that they represent a theological construction that best fits the facts, as far as we can tell. Second, to say that they do entail the concept, but that we cannot demonstrate this. Thirdly, to say that they do entail the concept and that this can be shown by showing how the relevant scriptural phrases entail the doctrine of the Trinity. Each non-scriptural expression will have to be judged on its merits. For my part it seems clear that the Scriptures do entail the doctrine of the Trinity and that this can be demonstrated.

The question of the advantage of introducing new terms now arises. There are two advantages. The first is purely pragmatic, for such phrases summarize what is presented in the Scriptures *in extenso*. More important, the explicitness of the new phrase blocks off false inferences that a less precise and therefore more ambiguous expression would allow. Athanasius said that the use of the phrase "one in essence" with the Father signified "that the Son was from the Father, and not merely like, but the same in likeness, and of shewing that the Son's likeness and unalterableness was different from such copy of the same as is ascribed to us; which we acquire from virtue on the ground of observance of the commandments."[20]

The introduction of such expressions is sometimes opposed on the grounds that Hellenic concepts have been introduced and have perverted the Hebraic teaching of Scripture. But as Hugo Meynell has recently insisted, "What was involved was not Hellenic *concepts*, but a Hellenic *technique:* that of clarifying by a linguistic rule what can and what cannot be said on any subject. The term *homousios* was not in fact current in philosophy before that time."[21]

In truth we ought not to make too much of the introduction of such terms. Compare the question, Does Descartes teach a body-mind dualism? Every student of Descartes would say that he did even though the term "dualism" does not occur in his writings.

In stressing the dependence of logical deduction upon the literal meaning of expressions I would not for one moment be taken to suppose that there is something inferior or second-best about the nonliteral expressions of the Scriptures. They are the product of divine wisdom, and no doubt part of the reason for conveying truth in such idioms is to secure an immediacy and vividness that a literal and exact form of words may not convey.

Nevertheless, literalness is essential to the *authority* of Scripture. Only if some texts are basically literal can other, nonliteral texts be interpreted in terms of them as having a confirmatory, illustrative and focussing role. How literal? It is impossible here to go into the problems raised by theological language, but we must say this much at least: that to use an expression literally of God is to mean at least as much as when that expression is used literally of a creature.[22]

Basic literalness must be stressed, for there must be passages of Scripture that have a theologically foundational role. For if there are no such foundationally literal passages then the authority of Scripture as a cognitive revelation vanishes. In this connection it is worth mentioning that in the eyes of some thinkers in the past and in the present (for example, occasionally John Locke and pervasively Immanuel Kant) Scripture is illustrative of sets of truths which can be known independently of the Scriptures, chiefly (in the case of Kant) propositions about the nature of moral duty.[23]

If we reject the Kantian position while still allowing that there is nonliteral language in Scripture (as we must) we must also maintain that this is cognitively parasitic upon the literal language of Scripture, which it illustrates and enforces.

B. The constraint of human finiteness. In considering the being and acts of God—His eternity, trinitarian character, government of all His creatures and all their actions, His incarnation in Jesus of Nazareth, and so on—all of us are faced with mystery, that is to say with dimensions of existence that our minds cannot fully grasp. The incapacity of the finite mind to grasp the infinite is not simply plain ignorance, though it entails ignorance. For there is a sense in which we are ignorant of even the most mundane object, say a pin. We could know more than we do about its history, its composition, its relation to other objects, what will happen to it in the future. Full knowledge of the pin will forever elude the most determined and competent investigator. When we turn our attention to God, however, we are faced not merely with our ignorance but with the fact that we do not fully grasp the concepts we are employing—and that He has given us to employ—to characterize Him. God is by definition *sui generis*, unique in His being and perfections.

How do such matters affect what we have been saying about the role of logic? We have been calling attention to facts about the limitations of human knowledge. It is important to recognize these, but it is equally important to insist that limited knowledge is not the same thing as total ignorance. God is not "something, I know not what." While our knowledge is limited, it is still knowledge. The Christian knows that God is three persons in one substance, that He is incarnate in Jesus of Nazareth, that He governs all the actions of His responsible creatures. What we do not know, and perhaps in the nature of things cannot know, is how these things are so.

As we noted earlier it would be a mistake to suppose that all our language about God was symbolic or analogical. Rather, when we say such things as "God knows that *p*" we mean "knows" in a literal and straightforward sense. It carries at least those logical implications that "Smith knows that *p*" carries when we contrast "know" with other epistemic terms such as "believe," "have the opinion that," "guess," and so forth. Where the qualifications arise in the case of God's knowledge is not over the meaning of "know" but over the manner and scope of the knowledge. For example, God knows but not by the use of His senses or by any process of learning, He knows what is future to us as well as what is past. These facts about the manner of God's knowledge do not in any way affect the fact that He knows any more than the fact that Smith gets his knowledge by means of his sense affects the fact that *he* knows. If it is said that God knows *infallibly* but Smith only fallibly, this can be granted. But we can *define* infallible knowledge solely in terms that are literally true of Smith, terms like "error" and "mistake." So that "knows" when applied literally both to God and to men is univocal, and similarly with other predicates applicable to God and men.

To stress that certain predicates are univocally applicable both to God and men made in the image of God[24] has one great advantage. We can conduct our theological thinking on the assumption that certain affirmative propositions about God are literally true of Him and are known or knowable by human beings to be literally true of Him. The limitations inherent in our knowledge of the Most High God, limitations that we have stressed, do not indicate a failure in logic or sanction nonsense or a complete suspension of our critical and rational faculties, for the following reason: what we know cannot be inconsistent with what is true but unknown to us or with what is true but unknowable to us. We know that God is sovereign and that human beings are responsible. If we know both of these propositions then both of them must be true, and if both of them are true both must be consistent with each other. Nothing that we do not as yet know, and nothing that is true but that we cannot know, can render these propositions inconsistent.

The important point of logic here is that the inability to demonstrate the logical coherence of a set of propositions is not equivalent to demonstrating the set's incoherence. Furthermore, proving the coherence of a set of propositions is a difficult undertaking for it requires a demonstration that the set of propositions in question is entailed by a proposition or set of propositions that is known to be coherent.[25]

The classical Christian christological and trinitarian affirmations provide illuminating illustrations of what is involved. They are not rationalistic explainings-away of divine mysteries nor do they sanction a peculiar theological logic or arithmetic. It is *not* an implication of the Chalcedonian Definition that something can be identical with something else distinct from itself, nor of the Constantinopolitan Creed that 1 plus 1 plus 1 equals 1. One of the functions of such formulae (whether carried out successfully or not is not a question here) is to lay down rules for consistent thought and speech about the divine mysteries.

C. The constraint of pride and prejudice, what earlier Reformed theologians called corrupt reason.[26] By this they did not mean that the reasoning powers of man were nullified by human sin, but that they were misdirected by unbelief and the corruption of the will. Many of the conclusions that the human reason would draw from the Scriptures are unwelcome, both truths about man and God, and human duties. This is a constraint that is not flattering but which must be recognized and striven against by prayer and spiritual discipline. Perhaps it concerns the application of the teaching of the Bible rather more than its understanding.

D. The constraint of the limitations of induction. Up to now we have concentrated our attention wholly on the place of deductive reasoning in the interpretation of Scripture. But it is important to remember that the Scriptures represent, at the most basic level, a body of empirically observed data, words and clauses, chapters and books. Any conclusion about what the Bible teaches or what that teaching logically implies is thus going to be grounded in the results of investigation that is essentially inductive.

The characteristic of inductive logic is that it is a form of argument in which the premises do not *entail* the conclusion but only render it probable to some degree. It follows that it is perfectly consistent (from the point of *de*ductive logic) to accept the premises of a valid *in*ductive argument but to deny that a certain conclusion follows from them. Thus the denial of the conclusion of a valid inductive argument is not a self-contradiction. It may be wildly improbable but it is not self-contradictory to suppose that the works attributed to Shakespeare are in fact the product of a school of blind monkeys learning to type. It is logically possible that the next piece of bread that I eat will fail to nourish me and poison me instead, despite the fact that all the bread that I have so far consumed has nourished me.

It is necessary to distinguish between two tasks that the Bible interpreter may set himself. The first is to determine the meaning of a single verse or definite class of verses or passages. The second, much more daunting task is to attempt to gain a fully scriptural position on some matter, to take into account *all* the relevant data. It is here that inductive procedures are vital, for it is necessary to make a judgment about what is relevant and what is not, and this judgment may have to be revised and as a consequence previous conclusions may have to be revised. What is not the result of induction (or deduction) is the formulation of the original questions, What is the biblical teaching on A?

That conclusions about what the Bible as a whole teaches do not follow as a matter of deductive logic from the data is not due to human fallibility or sin. The matter is a purely logical one. What effect should it have on the interpreter? It should make him cautious. Perhaps he has overlooked some datum or wrongly understood some datum that he has not overlooked. And this point of logic *still* holds even though it may be readily granted that there are no such things as "pure facts" and that the interpreter of any document comes to it with a preunderstanding of it. This is doubly true of the Christian interpreter of the Bible for whom Scripture has its authority solely in virtue of what he takes it, initially, to mean. But this is where the point about properly observing inductive procedures becomes important, for they preserve the interpreter against *a priori* dogmatism, and against an unwillingness to consider hitherto unnoticed or rejected evidence or new interpretations of texts whose meaning was thought to be clear and unchallengeable.

At the same time recognition of the inductive procedures that interpreting a document inevitably requires does not entail skepticism. Looked at from one point of view the hermeneutical principle that Scripture should be interpreted in accordance with the analogy of the faith represents the fruit of past inductive endeavors. We can agree with Augustine that "when investigation reveals an uncertainty as to how a locution should be pointed or construed, the rule of faith should be consulted as it is found in the more open places of the Scriptures and in the authority of the Church."[27] The "more open" places of the Scriptures are not necessarily those that are easiest in terms of grammar and vocabulary, but those parts that are more central to its message and in virtue of which Scripture has its authority. One use of the analogy of the faith is to prevent *ad hoc* and arbitrary resolving of apparent contradictions, special pleadings and the like. Not all possible reconcilings of apparently contradictory passages are satisfactory; some are *strained* when measured by the analogy of the faith.

But the existence of the principle of the analogy of the faith, important as it is, does not mean that the interpreter can throw caution to the winds. For since no set of data ever entails a particular hypothesis the wise interpreter proportions his belief to the evidence. This does not mean that no conclusions can ever be held with practical certainty but that there ought to be a range of strength of belief with respect to the varied data of Scripture based upon the kind of evidence available.[28]

NOTES

[1]What the corresponding condition is for non-cognitive language or for fiction is something that need not detain us here for obvious reasons. It is possible to entertain skeptical doubts as to whether translation in this sense ever succeeds, but we shall not treat such doubts seriously here. For each exposition we shall consider the case of sentences in the indicative mood. In the case of interrogatives one would have to substitute reply-conditions for truth conditions, in the case of imperatives compliance-conditions, and so forth. I shall assume that this can be done and that it raises no insurmountable complications.

[2]For accounts of the allegedly logically-odd character of religious discourse see for example D. Z. Phillips, *The Concept of Prayer* (London, 1965) and Ian T. Ramsey, *Religious Language* (London, 1957).

[3]Among theologians Augustine put the point long ago about the formal and hypothetical character of logic. "It is one thing to know the rules of valid inference, another thing to know the truth of propositions. Concerning inferences, one learns what is consequent, what is inconsequent, and what is incompatible. . . . Concerning the truth of propositions, however, the rules of inference are not relevant and the propositions are to be considered in themselves. But when true and certain propositions are joined by valid inferences to propositions we are not sure about, the latter, also, necessarily become certain." (*On Christian Doctrine* trans. D. W. Robinson [Indianapolis, 1958], p. 70).

[4]For recent discussion of the status of necessary truths see for example A. M. Quinton, "The *A Priori* and the Analytic," ed. P. R. Strawson, *Philosophical Logic* (Oxford, 1967); R. M. Chisholm, *Theory of Knowledge* (1966).

[5]See, for example, Rene Descartes, *Philosophical Letters*, ed. Anthony Kenny (Oxford, 1970), p. 11; T. F. Torrance, *Theological Science* (London, 1969), pp. 219-20.

[6]See the list given in J. I. Packer's *"Fundamentalism" and the Word of God* (London, 1958), p. 93n.

[7]As I try to show in chapter three of *Divine Revelation* (forthcoming).

[8]See G. W. H. Lampe, *God as Spirit* (Oxford, 1977), pp. 33, 139f.

[9]G. L. Bray, *One God in Trinity*, eds. Peter Toon and James D. Spiceland, (London, 1980), p. 45. Abraham Kuyper also defended a sharp distinction between Scripture and theology. See the discussion of his views in "Geerhardus Vos and the Interpretation of Paul" by Richard B. Gaffin, Jr., *Jerusalem and Athens*, ed. E. R. Geehan (Philadelphia, 1971).

[10]Heinrich Heppe, *Reformed Dogmatics* (London, 1950); Robert D. Preus, *The Theology of Post-Reformation Lutheranism* (St, Louis, 1970), Vol. 1, p. 336.

[11]F. Turretin, *Institute Theologiae Elencticae*, I.XII.IX; Robert D. Preus, *Post-Reformation Lutheranism*, Vol. 1, p. 152.

[12]John Calvin, *Institutes of the Christian Religion*, I.17.12-13.

[13]"Our radical attempt to demythologize the New Testament is in fact a perfect parallel to St. Paul's and Luther's doctrine of justification by faith alone apart from the works of the law. Or rather, it carries this doctrine to its logical conclusion in the field of epistemology. Like the doctrine of justification it destroys every false security and every false demand for it on the part of man, whether he seeks it in his good works or in his ascertainable knowledge." "Bultmann replies to his Critics," *Kerygma and Myth* (London, 1972), Vol. 1, p. 210f. The list of "hermeneutics" of Scripture could easily be extended. There is, for example, the ingenious "materialist hermeneutic" propounded by Thomas Hobbes in *Leviathan* (1651).

[14]Anselm, *Cur Deus Homo?* "If, then, it be necessary (as we have ascertained) that the celestial citizenship is to be completed from among men, and that this cannot be unless there be made that before-mentioned satisfaction, which God only can, and man only should, make, it is needful that it should be made by one who is both God and man."

[15]Augustine, *On Christian Doctrine*, p. 43.

[16]Cf. the contention of the Arians that "begotten" was used metaphorically of Christ. This seems to be the contention of Athanasius in *De Decretis*, trans. J. H. Newman, *A Select Library of Nicene and Post-Nicene Fathers of the Christian Church*, eds. Philip Schaff and Henry Wace (reissued, Grand Rapids, 1971), Vol. 4.

[17]*Inspiration*, ed. Nicole (Grand Rapids, 1979), p. 43.

[18]This is at least part of what Reformed theologians have meant by the *perfection* or *sufficiency* of Scripture, the fact that God reveals not only what is explicitly in Scripture but whatever else is logically entailed by that. This might be expressed formally as $(Kxp \& [p \rightarrow q]) \rightarrow Kxq$. This is clearly not true of the human authors of the Scriptures. What would be true of them would be $(Kxp \& Kx [p \rightarrow q]) \rightarrow Kxq$.

[19]Athanasius, *De Decretis*, Ch.V. 20 (*A Select Library* . . . Vol. 4, p. 163).

[20]Ibid., pp. 163-64.

[21]Hugo Meynell, "Lonergan on the Trinity," *One God in Trinity,* p. 98.

[22]See the interesting discussion of this point in Nelson Pike, "Omnipotence and God's Ability to Sin," reprinted in *Morality and Divine Commands,* ed. Paul Helm (Oxford, 1981). On the adequacy of language in general see J. I. Packer, "The Adequacy of Human Language," *Inerrancy,* ed. Norman L. Geisler (Grand Rapids, 1979).

[23]Immanuel Kant, *Religion Within the Limits of Reason Alone,* trans. T. M. Greene and Hoyt H. Hudson (New York, 1960); John Locke, *The Reasonableness of Christianity,* ed. I. T. Ramsey (London, 1958)

[24]Not all predicates. Only those that apply literally to both. Some are clearly applied to God in a non-literal fashion e.g., "a rock," while the status of others is indeterminate, "father." We cannot determine *a priori* which fall into which category. In the case of the intermediate group it would be wise to follow Basil Mitchell's advice, "A word should be presumed to carry with it as many of the original entailments as the new context allows, and this is determined by their compatibility with the other descriptions which there is reason to believe also apply to God," (*The Justification of Religious Belief* [London, 1973], p. 19. Historically, the univocity of predicates applied to both God and men has been stressed by, among others, Duns Scotus (see the selections reprinted in his *Philosophical Writings,* trans. Allan Wolter [Indianapolis, 1962]), and George Berkeley, *Alchiphron,* Dialogue IV.

[25]On issues raised by coherence in theology see Richard Swinburne, *The Coherence of Theism* (Oxford, 1977). For criticism, see the review by Peter Van Inwagen in the *Philosophical Review,* October 1979.

[26]Turretin, *Institutio Theologiae Elencticae,* I.IX.XIV.

[27]Augustine, *On Christian Doctrine,* p. 79.

[28]Some evangelical theologians and philosophers have recently proposed that the theologian's method in relation to the Scriptures is *abduction* or *adduction* (Arthur F. Holms, "Ordinary Language Analysis and Theological Method," *Bulletin of the Evangelical Theological Society,* 11 [Summer, 1968], pp. 131-38, and John Warwick Montgomery, "The Theologian's Craft: A Discussion of Theory Formation and Theory Testing in Theology," *The Suicide of Theology* [Minneapolis, 1970], pp. 267-313.) Two points on this proposal. Holms at least dismisses deduction for the wrong reasons. It does *not* follow from employing deduction that the historical narratives of Scripture will become only illustrative, or the events of redemptive history logically necessary. That would only follow if Scriptural theology could be reduced to a deductive system from a set of self-evidently true axioms. The narrative and history of Scripture are among the stock of propositions from which conclusions are deduced. Secondly, what of abduction or adduction? As far as I can see these are not names for a procedure that is distinct from both deduction and induction but which combines each together.

A Response to The Role of Logic in Biblical Interpretation

Mark M. Hanna
Associate Professor of
Philosophy of Religion
Talbot Theological
Seminary

A Response to The Role of Logic in Biblical Interpretation

Mark M. Hanna

What is the logic of an argument? What is the logic of the word "God"? What is the logic of physics? Questions like these call attention to three principal uses of the term "logic" in philosophical writings.

First, and most appropriately, it is used to refer to an ideal (i.e., nonempirical and nonpsychological) domain that consists of certain principles, rules, and relations that apply to propositions and arguments, and by extension, to thinking and reasoning. By the application of formal conditions, logic tests propositions for contradiction and it tests deductive arguments for validity—and by extension, it tests inductive arguments for acceptability. Secondly, the term "logic" is used by some to refer to patterned utilizations of locutions and their relationships in "language games." Thirdly, the term "logic" is used by some to refer to methods of inquiry used in various disciplines. It is important to keep in mind that it is the first usage of "logic" that primarily interests us in this discussion of the relation of logic to hermeneutics. Although logic, which is concerned with formal and consecutional generality, is distinguishable from hermeneutics, which deals with specific issues of cultural and historical particularity, the latter cannot proceed without the former.

Special revelation is essentially linguistic-semantic in character. A number of consequences stem from this, and Professor Helm has given us an excellent statement of some of them. I am particularly gratified that he has maintained the objectivity of logic against conventionalism. Logic, properly understood, is neither arbitrary nor merely human. And as Edmund Husserl demonstrated in his *Logical Investigations*[1], it cannot successfully be reduced to psychology. Helm has also rightly opposed the current, widespread error of cultural relativism. Specifically, it is ludicrous to claim that Hebrew and Greek thought are so different that the categories of logic do not apply to the former because they are the artificial constructs of the latter.[2]

Since I find myself in basic agreement with Helm's paper, I will not attempt to discuss all of his major points. My purpose in this paper is twofold: to reinforce his general perspective and to take issue with what I see as key ambiguities and inadequacies. To accomplish this, the following theses will form the outline of my essay.

1. Logic is primarily a formal discipline, and as such, it is not only an organon but also an ontologon, i.e., it is not only an instrument for arriving at truth but also an integral part of reality.
2. Logic is essentially the theory of warranted propositional inference.
3. Logic, which is a basic type of intelligibility, is essential for explicating the general perspicuity of Scripture, for interpreting individual biblical passages, and for drawing inferences from them.

I. LOGIC, WHICH IS PRIMARILY A FORMAL DISCIPLINE, IS BOTH AN ORGANON AND AN ONTOLOGON.

Helm's emphasis on the formal character of logic is excessive to the point of obscuring the content of logic. My first thesis states that logic is to be understood *primarily* as a formal discipline. It is not exclusively formal. In a way that is analogous to the universal-particular contrast, there is a relativity (not relativism) to the form-content contrast. For example, relative to the particular oak tree in my front yard, "oak tree" is a universal. But relative to the universal "tree," "oak tree" (as a species of tree) is a particular. And relative to the universal "plant," "tree" is a particular. It is a matter of class inclusion, a particular being a subclass of a class, or a member of a set.

When Helm says that "by 'logic' is meant certain basic, purely formal principles of thought and of deductive reasoning" (p. 842), four caveats are needed. First, the principles which constitute logic are "purely formal" only when contrasted with the empirical and the experiential. From the standpoint of ontology, they are part of the *content* of reality. Secondly, the principles of logic are not principles of "thought and deductive reasoning" in the sense that they are descriptive of our thinking or reasoning processes. All too often the latter proceed contrary to such principles. The basic principles of logic ("the truths of logic") are normative, i.e., if thinking and reasoning are to be done correctly, they must conform to these principles. The principles themselves are independent of thought and reasoning in the sense that they stand over against us and judge our inferential processes. They are insusceptible of creation, alteration, or destruction by us.

Thirdly, logic does not only consist of principles but it also includes *rules*. Such rules are based on principles, but the two categories are not the same. The normativity of logic finds explicit expression in the rules that are derived from the principles. The rules tell us what we ought and ought not to do if our reasoning is to be done correctly. Principles are propositions that are true or false (in the case of the basic principles of logic, they are true). Rules cannot be true or false. They are appropriate or inappropriate, but such propriety is determined by conformity with the principles and according to the conditions they specifiy.

Fourthly, logic should be distinguished from "principles of thought" when the latter are interpreted as reflections of language (a point carried to a self-defeating extreme by Benjamin Whorf and others) and in the sense of the distinctive constraints of a "language game" (a point overstated by Wittgenstein and some of his followers). Contrary to these special uses of the term, logic proper is universal, trans-cultural, and trans-linguistic. If I formulate a valid argument here and now, it will be valid in India tomorrow and in Japan in the year 2001.

II. LOGIC IS ESSENTIALLY THE THEORY OF WARRANTED PROPOSITIONAL INFERENCE

The term "theory" in this statement does not necessarily imply provisionality. Let us picture the domain of logic under the figure of concentric circles. All circles but the central one are characterized by tentativeness. Logic is a vast and complex discipline. Certain parts of it—the outer circles—are problematic and debatable. But at the core of logic there are both definitiveness and absoluteness. Indeed, without a nucleus of such principles and rules, neither the constituents of the problematic circles nor the debate about them would be possible. Logic is a theory in the sense that it is an explanation of the formal conditions of logical consecution.

Helm's statement that logic "is concerned *solely* with what follows from what" (p. 842, italics mine) is too restrictive. It is also concerned with the foundational principles of correct thinking and reasoning. It does not *merely* ask what other proposition(s) can be inferred from the presupposed truth of a proposition or propositions. Logic also asks what the formal principles are for all correct thinking.

It is at best misleading and at worst plainly false to say that "Logic does *not* provide an initial stock of true propositions. These must be quarried elsewhere" (p. 843, italics his). Of course, logic does not provide propositions about physics, biology, sociology, etc.—or about any of the states of affairs in our daily lives. Nevertheless, logic does provide an initial stock of true propositions, namely, the foundational principles that constitute the innermost circle at the core of its domain. Insofar as these principles are part of reality, logic is inseparable from ontology and epistemology. Distinguishable it is, but not separable. And it is especially at the point of logic's initial stock of true propositions that questions arise about the nature of a reality that includes such ideal structures and about the nature of human knowing that both apprehends them and invokes them as criteriologically normative.

Logic does not determine content, then, except in the one case of its own content. If logic were without content, logic would not be applicable to anything. Indeed, without content—formal and abstract as it may be—there would be nothing to apply.

Furthermore, I am puzzled by Helm's first paragraph in his discussion of "the constraint of the limitations of induction." He says that "the Scriptures represent, at the most basic level, a body of empirically observed data, words and clauses, chapters and books" (p. 854). What is meant by "represent" here? He seems to be saying that the Scriptures consist of these things. But who are the subjects who do the observing of empirical data? If he means that we today are the observers, then the statement is patently false. Scripture does not consist of *our* observations of empirical data.

If, on the other hand, the biblical writers are the observers, what is Helm referring to as the data? Are they historical events, theophanies, dreams, the audible voice of God? To be sure, the biblical writers do mention these things among the various means of divine communication. The Holy Spirit also imparted truths to their minds, however—in some instances without their own understanding of what was being communicated—and, accordingly, what they wrote down was not the result of empirical observation, i.e., in the sense of sensorily grasping a state of affairs. This is not to deny that certain statements of the Bible may have been arrived at inductively. But where such inductive conclusions are part of the divine teaching of Scripture, their truth is guaranteed by inspiration. Accordingly, they do not carry the epistemological liability that conditions inductively derived conclusions in general.

In view of Helm's contextual statements, however, I am inclined to think that he is not referring to the procedure by which biblical writers arrived at their statements but to the subsequent process of interpreting the Scriptures. It is a question of how we "attempt to gain a fully Scriptural position on some matter" (p. 855).

In at least two senses, induction is involved in the interpretation of Scripture. First, every translation relies on inductive judgments made with respect to linguistic and historical evidence. Even the collated text of the Hebrew Old Testament and of the Greek New Testament depends on an inductive procedure that takes into account the comparative merits and demerits of various manuscripts. So, in these senses, the work of interpretation rests on an inductively derived text. Secondly, the attempt to determine what a variety of biblical passages teach on some point or doctrine is an inductive procedure.

Nevertheless, this state of affairs does not entail skepticism about the basic teaching of Scripture. On this Helm and I are in agreement. However, since an interpreter may have "overlooked some datum or wrongly understood some datum that he has not overlooked" (p. 855), Helm sees only the possibility of practical certainty." Whatever "practical certainty" may mean, it is surely less than full certainty—or what I shall call epistemological certainty. Stopping at the point of "practical certainty" with respect to *every* interpretation is a mistake, in my judgment.

Let us consider an example to clarify this point. Suppose I find twenty-three passages of Scripture that teach that there is only one God, the Creator of all other beings and entities that exist. I make no claim that my findings are to be equated with the actual number of passages that are relevant to the question. There may be some passages that I have overlooked or others whose relevance to the question under consideration I have not seen. I do not need these other passages, however, in order to know that the Bible teaches that there is only one God, the Creator of all other beings and entities that exist. On the premise that the Bible is the word of God, who cannot lie or err, I must conclude that Scripture does teach this. For if God has inspired the totality of the sixty-six books that constitute the Scriptures, then there can be no teaching elsewhere in the Bible that contradicts the teaching of these twenty-three passages. For if there were such a contradiction, the Bible would teach nothing on this point—since to affirm and deny the same meaning (which is the nature of contradiction) is to assert nothing. Self-contradiction is self-annihilation.

My contention, then, is that although some interpretations of what the Scripture teaches may never rise above probability, there are other matters whose interpretation can be known with epistemological certainty. Two caveats are needed here, however. First, this contention is maintained on the basis of bracketing the more foundational procedures involved in arriving at a collated text, or a translation from the collated text.

Secondly, to return to our example, Scriptural passages other than the posited twenty-three may be germane to our attainment of a fuller understanding of God's oneness, transcendence, and relationship to his creation. The teaching of some passages will keep us from interpreting God's oneness in unitarian fashion. But—and this is the important point—epistemological certainty can be acquired because in order to know some things about an object one does not have to know everything about it. If this were not the case, then we would know nothing. This can be understood by the simple recognition that we know nothing exhaustively, for to do so we would have to know the ultimate constituents and the ultimate relations which characterize an object. Knowing with epistemological certainty is not to be equated with knowing exhaustively. *Additional data may be relevant to one's understanding of a certain object without pertaining to the truth or falsity of a particular proposition about that object.* Such data may enhance our understanding, but there can be no change in the truth-value of a proposition. The question is whether or not we can know, with epistemological certainty, the meaning of any statement in the Bible.

It is either true or false that the Bible teaches that there is one God, the Creator of all other beings and entities that exist. I do not have to know, when considering the truth-value of this proposition, all that was involved in his creation of heaven and earth. I do not have to know the number or all the kinds of beings and entities that God made. There is much to learn if my understanding of that great truth is to be extended and deepened. And some things I may never learn—in this life or the next. But that does not preclude my epistemological certainty with respect to the proposition whose referential meaning is explicitly circumscribed. This is a matter of logical relations. Given that the perspicuity of Scripture entails the logical consistency of its parts, the teaching of one passage cannot be contradicted by another passage. The point at issue, therefore, is whether it is possible to ascertain the teaching of any passage of the Bible.

In this regard, I find a serious ambiguity in Helm's paper. His phrase, "a fully Scriptural position on some matter," may mean a complete understanding of a topic in terms of both extensiveness and depth according to all of the biblical data. If it is to be construed this way, however, it would seem that he cannot avoid contradicting himself. For he apparently equates the meaning of the phrase with a conclusion drawn from various biblical passages.

If, on the other hand, the locution in question merely refers to a proposition that summarizes Scriptural teaching on a subject, then Helm is consistent—but it is an erroneous consistency. That is, in both instances he is referring to a single proposition ("a fully Scriptural position on some matter" on page 855 has the same referent as "conclusion(s)" on page 856). But since we may know, with epistemological certainty, that a proposition is true without knowing all there is to be known about the referent of the proposition, Helm faces a dilemma. To be both consistent and right, he should either give up the equation between the two locutions or he should abandon his denial that some propositions can be known with epistemological certainty. Logic dictates that he cannot have it both ways.

A gratuitous assumption seems to underlie his position, namely, that one can have epistemological certainty only with respect to a proposition that is a principle of logic or that states a valid deductive relation. But is not his own statement that the Bible is an empirical object, consisting of "words, and clauses, chapters and books," known with epistemological certainty even though it is not such a proposition?

Limited and simple as they may be, there are some texts whose meaning is "clear and unchallengeable," i.e., in terms of the truth of the referential meaning they express. If there are no unrevisable interpretations, in this sense, all the biblical injunctions about contending for *the* faith once for all delivered to the saints (Jude 3) would be undermined. It is indefensible to hold that the faith was once for all delivered to the saints but that the basic propositions that define that faith can never be known with epistemological certainty.

III. LOGIC IS ESSENTIAL FOR EXPLICATING THE GENERAL PERSPICUITY OF SCRIPTURE, FOR INTERPRETING INDIVIDUAL BIBLICAL PASSAGES, AND FOR DRAWING INFERENCES FROM THEM.

Whatever else may be involved in interpreting the Scriptures, it is a rational activity. That is, it is an attempt to understand the meaning expressed by the linguistic units that constitute the Bible. Without logical intelligibility, the very attempt to interpret is nullified. Helm correctly observes that "the choice is between intelligibility and babbling" (p. 843). His assessment of the arguments about the identity of Jesus, however, reflects confusion about logical intelligibility. From the data that characterize Jesus as human (e.g., he ate, spoke, slept, etc.), we are not entitled to deduce that he was merely human. But from passages that *state* that he was human (e.g., a univocal, straightforward use of the term "man" or some locution that denotes humanity, such as the synecdochic use of "flesh" in John 1:14), we are logically warranted in making a deductive inference that he was a man—and not a docetic apparition. We are not entitled, however, to deduce, on the basis of such passages, that Jesus is not God. Nor can other data or assertions that Jesus is God contradict the teaching of Scripture that he is human. The terms are not contradictory to one another.

For there to be such a contradiction, one of two conditions would have to be fulfilled. First, there must be a Scriptural statement clearly denying that Jesus is human or clearly denying that he is God. Such denials cannot be found. Secondly, Scripture must state the universal proposition that Helm supplies (but does not hold) in the two arguments on page 846. Scripture does teach that no mere human creature is divine in his nature, i.e., it teaches that there is an ontological discontinuity between God the Creator and man the creature. If Scripture taught that Jesus is in the category of "man the creature," then this would contradict other passages that teach that he is uncreated, eternal, and divine (John 1:1,14). The first premise of each of the arguments on page 846 can be inferred from the data Helm mentions. But the two propositions do not contradict one another.

Contrary to Helm's claim, it is not "logical treatment" (p. 847) that leads to the false conclusion of each of the arguments. The arguments are valid, but in each case the conclusion is false because one premise is false. The invocation of such a premise is not itself the result of "logical treatment." Rather, it is an ontological assumption, and if it means that "no one who has a human nature can also at the same time have the divine nature, in the sense that he is divine in his being," then that assumption is wrong. Logic does not determine the truth or falsity of such a presupposition. To be sure, whether one should or should not invoke that proposition is determined, for the Christian interpreter, by the relevant Scriptural teaching.

Helm's position on "axiomatic texts" is also unclear to me. First, he describes them as "texts whose meaning is clear or taken to be clear, and in terms of which other relevant texts are to be interpreted" (p. 847). He seems to revert to the same topic on page 856, where he refers to "the 'more open' places of the Scriptures." His statements about the latter evidently serve to equate them with "axiomatic texts." And yet he denies that they are distinguished by their clarity: they are "not necessarily those that are easiest in terms of grammar and vocabulary, but those parts that are more central . . ." (p. 856). I agree that some passages of the Bible are more central to its chief message than others, and some passages are more clear than others, but the two are not synonymous. Indeed, Helm contrasts them. Therefore, he is not entitled to appeal to clarity and centrality as though they are one criterion for determining which texts are basic and which are not.

I would like to suggest that a way out of this dilemma is the discrimination of biblical passages, for the purpose of interpretation, into two main categories: the clear and the difficult. Let it be acknowledged that there are degrees of clarity within the first category and degrees of difficulty in the second category. Next, within the category of the clear, let us differentiate two subclasses: the focal and the non-focal. That is, the focal consists of those passages that are central to the Bible's main message, and the non-focal consists of those that have no direct bearing on it. Such a procedure will direct us to what I shall call "touchstone texts." Among these are to be found those points of reference that "will make most sense of the rest of the data, leaving fewest anomalies and loose ends" (p. 848). But even these criteria should be supplemented by the importance that subsequent passages of Scripture give to earlier portions.

Helm leaves me wondering what he means when he writes of "the Christian interpreter of the Bible for whom Scripture has its authority solely in virtue of what he takes it, initially, to mean" (p. 855). The word "solely" in the sentence is particularly puzzling. If he had said that interpretation is inseparable from authority, I would not take exception to his assertion.

The authority of the Bible has its source in the authority of God. He is ultimate and sovereign. Man is answerable to him. It is because the Scriptures are inspired by God that they carry his authority. And that is the authority to provide answers to the basic questions of life, to be the arbiter of all debates on subjects about which the Bible speaks, and to lay down directives to man concerning what he ought to think, believe, and do. Clearly, the basic meaning of Scripture must be grasped for one to bring his life under its authority. Accordingly, the authority of the Bible and the experience of its authority should be distinguished.

The Bible does not have authority for a Christian solely in terms of what he takes it to mean. It would be better to say, "in terms of what he takes it to be." But even that would be misleading. Scripture has its authority in virtue of what it is, namely, the Word of God (cf. 1 Thess. 2:13; 2 Tim. 3:16, 17). Therefore, the whole Bible is authoritative for the Christian even if he has grasped only half of its meanings. To be sure, the proper application of Scripture to his life depends on a correct understanding of it. As A. C. Thiselton says in *The Two Horizons*, "To hear the Bible speak in its own right and with its due authority, the distinctive horizon of the text must be respected and differentiated in the first place from the horizon of the interpreter."[3] Since its authority is prior to, and distinguishable from, one's own reading of the text, the Bible, as the special revelatory deposit of the Holy Spirit, has the right and the function of correcting what the Christian interpreter takes it to mean.

Moreover, one should distinguish interpretation of an ancient document from application, in the sense of "making that meaning relevant to today's readers" (p. 481). Hermeneutics is essentially concerned with our apprehension of the author's intended meaning (which is generally singular), whereas application, if it is to be fully appropriate, shows the bearing that *that meaning* has on us and on our actions today (which is generally multifaceted). And logic is equally germane to both enterprises.

NOTES

[1]Edmund Husserl, *Logical Investigations*, translated by J. N. Findlay (New York: Humanities Press, 1970), 2 volumes.

[2]One of the most widely known examples of an exaggerated contrast between them is found in Thorleif Boman's *Hebrew Thought Compared with Greek*, translated by J. L. Moreau (New York: W. W. Norton, 1960).

[3]Anthony C. Thiselton, *The Two Horizons* (Grand Rapids: Wm. B. Eerdmans Pub. Co., 1980), p. XX.

A Response to The Role of Logic in Biblical Interpretation

John H. Gerstner
Professor at Large
Ligonier Valley Study Center

A Response to The Role of Logic in Biblical Interpretation

John H. Gerstner

This is certainly an excellent paper. Having said that with the deepest conviction, I shall devote the rest of this brief critique attempting to show that the paper may be slightly short of absolute perfection. I may well fail even in that attempt. Although we know from the inerrant Word that all the works of saints fall short of absolute perfection, it does not follow that this reviewer will be able to demonstrate that that is so in this particular paper. At least he has this consolation: he knows that he must be right though he should fail to prove it.

After convincingly asserting that logical principles are necessary for interpreting Scripture, Dr. Helm considers objections. The first one, that the logic of men is alien to the Word of God, is perhaps inadequately answered. The author's reply is that it cannot be alien because the only way to be intelligible is by the use of logic. The objector could well respond by granting that that is true of speech between man and man. But, what obligates God to conform to the laws necessary for human thought? If He clothes the Son of God in miracles to call attention to His divinity, why could He not clothe the speech of the Word of God in paradox and contradiction to call attention to its divinity? Helm would reply, no doubt: if that were so the fact would remain that, however, divine the Word was, it could not be understood by humans to whom it is addressed. But, have not some champions of the "alien" viewpoint being criticized said that contradiction could well be the hallmark of divine truth? Helm could and probably would say that even so the Word would then be denotatively indicated but not connotatively known. God has given us no intellectual apparatus for apprehending contradictions. Presumably, God wants us to know *what* He has said as well as *that* He has spoken. All of this I assume is latent in Helm's argument, but that is my point: it is only latent and not patent, which probably it ought to be.

The third objection is also dealt with soundly and well but not quite definitively. It should also be said in answer to the objection that logic is a "post-Enlightenment imposition upon the biblical text": it could not be imposed if logical power were not already constitutionally present. For, how could one understand eighteenth-century assertions about the necessity of logic if he were not by constitution the sort of being who would "see" that when imposed? If he saw it when imposed he must have known it all along.

Helm's answer to the fourth objection is inadequate. This is the argument for economy of interpretation. It would avoid drawing consequences from the interpretation as unnecessary. Helm's reply is essentially: Why not? Of course the answer would be: for economy's sake. Helm's earlier answer fattened up, (and not a mere rhetorical question) should be the final reply. He had said that the "implication" is what the Scripture *means*. If that is so then the objector, who refuses to draw necessary consequences, is not being economical but fradulent. He has ceased to be an interpreter. He has laid down his tools before the job is completed. That is not economy; that is a cop-out.

The answers to the first four objections are good, lacking only in sufficiency at points. But the reply to the fifth is, we think, failure. The objection is that logic involves treating Scripture as dogma which it is not. Unfortunately, Helm agrees that Scripture is not dogma. He then goes on to say that logic does not make it so. But "dogma" is usually defined as "a tenet or principle or system of principles" while "to dogmatize" is "to assert positively." If Scripture is not this and does not do this it must not be the sixty-six books of which I am thinking when I use that term. Scripture asserts facts, principles, tenets, systems and whatever it asserts it asserts most positively; in fact, absolutely. Logical interpretation does not make the Scripture dogmatic, it only shows what its dogmas are. We feel certain that Paul Helm thinks no differently, but, we do not know how to show it by his words here.

In the part dealing with the role of logic in interpretation, Helm is open to considerable criticism. First, the illustration of logic supplying suppressed premises in biblical enthymemes is something less than clear. Christ is cited as supplying such a premise in Mark 12:26-27 when He observes that the patriarchs Abraham, Isaac, and Jacob are living. Therefore, Christ reasons God is the God of the living and not of the dead. But Helm does not show how that proves the *bodily resurrection* in distinction from the continued life of the dead.

In Section 3 the explainer of the role of logic, Helm, is not logical himself. He begins by saying that "one set of data in the New Testament implies, or seems to imply, that Jesus of Nazareth was a mere man . . ." (p. 846). But the New Testament data neither imply nor even seem to imply that Jesus was a *mere* man. It simply says that he was a man. Making this initial slip by moving from the data to the illogical inference (Jesus was a man; therefore, he was *mere* man), Helm is caught in his own illogical web and presents this further illogical syllogism:

"(a) Jesus was a man,
(b) No man is identical with God,
(c) Therefore, Jesus is not identical with God?"

To make that syllogism sound, Helm must make (a) read: "Jesus was a mere man." The syllogism still does not necessarily follow as he has it. From this, further logical difficulties follow, as Helm proceeds:

"(d) Jesus is God,
(b) No man is identical with God,
(e) Therefore, Jesus is not a man?"

(b) to be cogent would have to be: No *mere* man (qua mere man) is identical with God. In that case (e) would read: "Therefore, Jesus is not a *mere* man?" Helm's moral is: "One function of doctrinal formulae such as the Chalcedonian Definition of the person of Christ is to preserve both lines of biblical evidence from too hasty a logical treatment . . ." But that is precisely *not* the point. What Chalcedon prevents is not "too hasty a logical treatment" but too hasty an *illogical* treatment (Again, perhaps that is what Helm means, but I fear, it is not what he writes).

Helm gets into even greater difficulties when he comes to consider the use of logic in theological construction. He says that theologizing must be done by determining that certain texts are clear and therefore determinative of the less clear. This is fair enough but when he gets down to cases, Calvinist and Arminian theologies, the water is muddied. Sovereignty texts are said to be basic for the Calvinist; free will texts are said to be basic for the Arminian. "In neither case is the interpretative procedure entirely *ad hoc*, but a purely logical consequence of accepting certain texts as clear and basic and others as not" (p. 848). Though Dr. Helm tries to avoid it, this presentation would make it appear that both Calvinist and Arminian are rather arbitrary in what texts they deem basic. From that arbitrary basis they proceed with logical necessity concerning other texts. Speaking as a Calvinist, I would say that all texts are basic and all texts are "Calvinistic." There simply are no such things as Arminian texts. A consistent evangelical Arminian would say exactly the same thing in reverse. All texts are basic and all are Arminian. There are no Calvinistic verses. If we are both to be true to Scripture we must resist strenuously any attempt on our part to bend Scripture to fit either system. If we do not let the Word of God have free course in us then we both must admit that we are not only not Calvinists or Arminians; we are not even Christians. Is that what Dr. Helm is so gently and so logically hinting? Probably not; but, if so, then he should make clear that the use of logic at this point is licit and leads to sound interpretation of Scripture and reveals unsound ones, rather than hinting that it could be legitimately used either way if arbitrary basics are first chosen.

After a brief allusion to other areas where logic is differently used neither Helm nor we choose to say anything further. But what is the general conclusion? "How to choose between rival axioms? We cannot go into this question in detail: suffice it to say that those ought to be chosen which will make most sense of the rest of the data, leaving fewest anomalies and loose ends" (p. 848). This does not show the relation of logic to theologizing which is the topic. Should Helm not say or would he say: Inasmuch as logic is a divinely given instrument for apprehending the interpretation of God's Word it will be a most certain test of the truth of an interpretation. That is, the analogy of faith and the analogy of logic are one and the same. If the interpretation is correct it will be logically consistent with other texts; if not, one or both interpretations are incorrect.

This issue is more particularly faced in the next topic where the Anselmian way of showing the logical coherence among divine decrees and actions is discussed. Helm goes part way with Anselm: "While it cannot be doubted that all the divine decrees have an internal consistence . . ." but not all the way: nevertheless it is far from clear that the interpreter of Scripture is required to show that this consistence is as strong as logical entailment . . . it is possible to have a plan without it being the case that the means to attaining the end of the plan are logically required by the end, for there may be more than one way of attaining the end . . ." (p. 849). Yes, there may be more than one way for finite and imperfect creatures to attain their end. There can be only one way for the all-wise and omnipotent God. He can choose only the best way and that way must be one. If there were another way it would, if not identical, be either worse (which God could never choose) or better (which God would most certainly choose). As Anselm has shown classically: if God would save He must save by the God-man. We may go a step further and say that if God chose to save it must have been better than His having chosen not to save. Therefore, His reason (not our importunity) constrained the all-wise God to save His elect by the God-man. Therefore, divine reason (as well as love, mercy, kindness, justice, power and all His attributes) compelled the act of mercy (which is unconstrained by us) and logic determined its form.

We will not comment on the generally excellent study of the "Constraints of Logic." Helm's discussion of the necessity of ultimate literalness even in metaphors, the reliability but limitations of human finitude, and the noetic influence of sin ("the constraint of pride and prejudice") leave very little to be desired and that mainly for some further amplification. (Helm can be exasperatingly cryptic in his masterful compression of a fifty-page paper into half that space.

We shall restrict our concluding criticism to "The constraint of the limitations of induction" (p. 854). Dr. Helm maintains that "the characteristic of inductive logic is that it is a form of argument in which the premises do not *entail* the conclusion but only render it probable to some degree" (p. 854). This is common thinking about induction. It is a well-nigh universal opinion that induction can never prove certainty but only suggest some degree of probability. We think, however, that this is dubious even in secular matters and virtually blasphemous in sacred things.

Take the secular example which Helm uses. Eating bread has always nourished him but that does not prove that the next bite will not poison him. It really does prevent *if* all things remain as they have been and are. That is, if the next bite is truly a bite of bread and if his body remains the same kind of body that it has always been the bread will nourish. Why not? The real reason for the skepticism is that we do not know certainly that the bread will remain the same and the body will remain the same. We assume that deductive reasoning is demonstrative because we assume that abstractions do not and cannot change. But what makes us so sure? If there were such a possibility deduction would be a probability argument also. If, on the other hand, things do not change the inductive would be as demonstrative as the deductive and if they do change deduction would be as nondemonstrative as the inductive.

When we come to God's Word, which, though heaven and earth pass away, will never change, induction must be as absolute as deduction and far more so. One word from God establishes the truth absolutely and forever of whatever that Word discloses. The proof is indisputable. Helm may respond: But this is a *deduction* from the text being God's Word. To be sure, but our point is that it is by induction that we *prove* the Bible to be the Word of God.

The analogy of faith is not to add more authority by a cumulative effect approaching certainty. That would make this great hermeneutical principle an insult to the deity. God does not have to repeat what He has once said, ever or forever. He cannot err and He cannot lie. Whatever He says is absolutely true for no other reason than that He has said it. The analogy of faith helps us to understand the meaning of the Word. It does not add an iota of authority to that which possesses infinite authority. "One little word shall slay him."

What a weak conclusion to a very strong paper: ". . . since no set of data ever entails a particular hypothesis the wise interpreter proportions his belief to the evidence. This does not mean that no conclusions can ever be held with practical certainty but that there ought to be a range of strength of belief with respect to the varied data of Scripture based upon the kind of evidence available" (p. 856). We believe that all that Dr. Helm means to say here refers to the difficulty of a certain interpretation of Scripture, though even that is overstated. There is no statement in this whole section that the inductive basis on which all logical consequences rest is ever anything more than a "practical certainty" at best. Scripture says "If you confess with your mouth Jesus as Lord and believe in your heart that God raised Him from the dead, *you shall be saved*." That is far more than a practical certainty though it is based on a limited induction indeed. We are sanctified by *truth* not by a practical certainty of the truth.

Appendixes

Appendix A

The Chicago Statement on Biblical Hermeneutics

Summit I of the International Council on Biblical Inerrancy took place in Chicago on October 26-28, 1978 for the purpose of affirming afresh the doctrine of the inerrancy of Scripture, making clear the understanding of it and warning against its denial. In the years that have passed since Summit I, God has blessed that effort in ways surpassing most anticipations. A gratifying flow of helpful literature on the doctrine of inerrancy as well as a growing commitment to its value give cause to pour forth praise to our great God.

The work of Summit I had hardly been completed when it became evident that there was yet another major task to be tackled. While we recognize that belief in the inerrancy of Scripture is basic to maintaining its authority, the values of that commitment are only as real as one's understanding of the meaning of Scripture. Thus, the need for Summit II. For two years plans were laid and papers were written on themes relating to hermeneutical principles and practices. The culmination of this effort has been a meeting in Chicago on November 10-13, 1982 at which we, the undersigned, have participated.

In similar fashion to the Chicago Statement of 1978, we herewith present these affirmations and denials as an expression of the results of our labors to clarify hermeneutical issues and principles. We do not claim completeness or systematic treatment of the entire subject, but these affirmations and denials represent a consensus of the approximately one hundred participants and observers gathered at this conference. It has been a broadening experience to engage in dialogue, and it is our prayer that God will use the product of our diligent efforts to enable us and others to more correctly handle the word of truth (2 Tim. 2:15).

Articles of Affirmation and Denial*

Article I.	WE AFFIRM that the normative authority of Holy Scripture is the authority of God Himself, and is attested by Jesus Christ, the Lord of the Church. WE DENY the legitimacy of separating the authority of Christ from the authority of Scripture, or of opposing the one to the other.
Article II.	WE AFFIRM that as Christ is God and Man in one Person, so Scripture is, indivisibly, God's Word in human language. WE DENY that the humble, human form of Scripture entails errancy any more than the humanity of Christ, even in His humiliation, entails sin.
Article III.	WE AFFIRM that the Person and work of Jesus Christ are the central focus of the entire Bible. WE DENY that any method of interpretation which rejects or obscures the Christ-centeredness of Scripture is correct.
Article IV.	WE AFFIRM that the Holy Spirit who inspired Scripture acts through it today to work faith in its message. WE DENY that the Holy Spirit ever teaches to any one anything which is contrary to the teaching of Scripture.
Article V.	WE AFFIRM that the Holy Spirit enables believers to appropriate and apply Scripture to their lives. WE DENY that the natural man is able to discern spiritually the biblical message apart from the Holy Spirit.
Article VI.	WE AFFIRM that the Bible expresses God's truth in propositional statements, and we declare that biblical truth is both objective and absolute. We

further affirm that a statement is true if it represents matters as they actually are, but is an error if it misrepresents the facts.

WE DENY that, while Scripture is able to make us wise unto salvation, biblical truth should be defined in terms of this function. We further deny that error should be defined as that which willfully deceives.

Article VII. WE AFFIRM that the meaning expressed in each biblical text is single, definite and fixed.

WE DENY that the recognition of this single meaning eliminates the variety of its application.

Article VIII. WE AFFIRM that the Bible contains teachings and mandates which apply to all cultural and situational contexts and other mandates which the Bible itself shows apply only to particular situations.

WE DENY that the distinction between the universal and particular mandates of Scripture can be determined by cultural and situational factors. We further deny that universal mandates may ever be treated as culturally or situationally relative.

Article IX. WE AFFIRM that the term hermeneutics, which historically signified the rules of exegesis, may properly be extended to cover all that is involved in the process of perceiving what the biblical revelation means and how it bears on our lives.

WE DENY that the message of Scripture derives from, or is dictated by, the interpreter's understanding. Thus we deny that the "horizons" of the biblical writer and the interpreter may rightly "fuse" in such a way that what the text communicates to the interpreter is not ultimately controlled by the expressed meaning of the Scripture.

Article X. WE AFFIRM that Scripture communicates God's truth to us verbally through a wide variety of literary forms.

WE DENY that any of the limits of human language render Scripture inadequate to convey God's message.

Article XI. WE AFFIRM that translations of the text of Scripture can communicate knowledge of God across all temporal and cultural boundaries.

WE DENY that the meaning of biblical texts is so tied to the culture out of which they came that understanding of the same meaning in other cultures is impossible.

Article XII. WE AFFIRM that in the task of translating the Bible and teaching it in the context of each culture, only those functional equivalents which are faithful to the content of biblical teaching should be employed.

WE DENY the legitimacy of methods which either are insensitive to the demands of cross-cultural communication or distort biblical meaning in the process.

Article XIII. WE AFFIRM that awareness of the literary categories, formal and stylistic, of the various parts of Scripture is essential for proper exegesis, and hence we value genre criticism as one of the many disciplines of biblical study.

WE DENY that generic categories which negate historicity may rightly be imposed on biblical narratives which present themselves as factual.

Article XIV. WE AFFIRM that the biblical record of events, discourses and sayings, though presented in a variety of appropriate literary forms, corresponds to historical fact.

WE DENY that any event, discourse or saying reported in Scripture was invented by the biblical writers or by the traditions they incorporated.

Article XV. WE AFFIRM the necessity of interpreting the Bible according to its literal, or normal, sense. The literal sense is the grammatical-historical sense, that is, the meaning which the writer expressed. Interpretation according to the literal sense will take account of all figures of speech and literary forms found in the text.

WE DENY the legitimacy of any approach to Scripture that attributes to it meaning which the literal sense does not support.

Article XVI. WE AFFIRM that legitimate critical techniques should be used in determining the canonical text and its meaning.

WE DENY the legitimacy of allowing any method of biblical criticism to question the truth or integrity of the writer's expressed meaning, or of any other scriptural teaching.

Article XVII. WE AFFIRM the unity, harmony and consistency of Scripture and declare that it is its own best interpreter.

WE DENY that Scripture may be interpreted in such a way as to suggest that one passage corrects or militates against another. We deny that later writers of Scripture misinterpreted earlier passages of Scripture when quoting from or referring to them.

Article XVIII. WE AFFIRM that the Bible's own interpretation of itself is always correct, never deviating from, but rather elucidating, the single meaning of the inspired text. The single meaning of a prophet's words includes, but is not restricted to, the understanding of those words by the prophet and necessarily involves the intention of God evidenced in the fulfillment of those words.

WE DENY that the writers of Scripture always understood the full implications of their own words.

Article XIX. WE AFFIRM that any preunderstandings which the interpreter brings to Scripture should be in harmony with scriptural teaching and subject to correction by it.

WE DENY that Scripture should be required to fit alien preunderstandings, inconsistent with itself, such as naturalism, evolutionism, scientism, secular humanism, and relativism.

Article XX. WE AFFIRM that since God is the author of all truth, all truths, biblical and extrabiblical, are consistent and cohere, and that the Bible speaks truth when it touches on matters pertaining to nature, history, or anything else. We further affirm that in some cases extrabiblical data have value for clarifying what Scripture teaches, and for prompting correction of faulty interpretations.

WE DENY that extrabiblical views ever disprove the teaching of Scripture or hold priority over it.

Article XXI. WE AFFIRM the harmony of special with general revelation and therefore of biblical teaching with the facts of nature.

WE DENY that any genuine scientific facts are inconsistent with the true meaning of any passage of Scripture.

Article XXII. WE AFFIRM that Genesis 1-11 is factual, as is the rest of the book.

WE DENY that the teachings of Genesis 1-11 are mythical and that scientific hypotheses about earth history or the origin of humanity may be invoked to overthrow what Scripture teaches about creation.

Article XXIII. WE AFFIRM the clarity of Scripture and specifically of its message about salvation from sin.

WE DENY that all passages of Scripture are equally clear or have equal bearing on the message of redemption.

Article XXIV. WE AFFIRM that a person is not dependent for understanding of Scripture on the expertise of biblical scholars.

WE DENY that a person should ignore the fruits of the technical study of Scripture by biblical scholars.

Article XXV. WE AFFIRM that the only type of preaching which sufficiently conveys the divine revelation and its proper application to life is that which faithfully expounds the text of Scripture as the Word of God.

WE DENY that the preacher has any message from God apart from the text of Scripture.

Appendix B

Explaining Hermeneutics: A Commentary on The Chicago Statement on Biblical Hermeneutics Articles of Affirmation and Denial

Norman L. Geisler

Article I. *WE AFFIRM that the normative authority of Holy Scripture is the authority of God Himself, and is attested by Jesus Christ, the Lord of the Church.*

WE DENY the legitimacy of separating the authority of Christ from the authority of Scripture, or of opposing the one to the other.

This first article affirms that the authority of Scripture cannot be separated from the authority of God. Whatever the Bible affirms, God affirms. And what the Bible affirms (or denies), it affirms (or denies) with the very authority of God. Such authority is normative for all believers; it is the canon or rule of God.

This divine authority of Old Testament Scripture was confirmed by Christ Himself on numerous occasions (cf. Matt. 5:17-18; Luke 24:44; John 10:34-35). And what our Lord confirmed as to the divine authority of the Old Testament, He promised also for the New Testament (John 14:16; 16:13).

The Denial points out that one cannot reject the divine authority of Scripture without thereby impugning the authority of Christ, who attested Scripture's divine authority. Thus it is wrong to claim one can accept the full authority of Christ without acknowledging the complete authority of Scripture.

Article II. *WE AFFIRM that as Christ is God and Man in*

one Person, so Scripture is, indivisibly, God's Word in human language.

WE DENY that the humble, human form of Scripture entails errancy any more than the humanity of Christ, even in His humiliation, entails sin.

Here an analogy is drawn between Christ and Scripture. Both Christ and Scripture have dual aspects of divinity and humanity, indivisibly united in one expression. Both Christ and Scripture were conceived by an act of the Holy Spirit. Both involve the use of fallible human agents. But both produced a theanthropic result; one a sinless person and the other an errorless book. However, like all analogies, there is a difference. Christ is one person uniting two natures whereas Scripture is one written expression uniting two authors (God and man). This difference notwithstanding, the strength of the likeness in the analogy points to the inseparable unity between divine and human dimensions of Scripture so that one aspect cannot be in error while the other is not.

The Denial is directed at a contemporary tendency to separate the human aspects of Scripture from the divine and allow for error in the former. By contrast the framers of this article believe that the human form of Scripture can no more be found in error than Christ could be found in sin. That is to say, the Word of God (i.e., the Bible) is as necessarily perfect in its human manifestation as was the Son of God in His human form.

Article III. *WE AFFIRM that the person and work of Jesus Christ are the central focus of the entire Bible.*

WE DENY that any method of interpretation which rejects or obscures the Christ-centeredness of Scripture is correct.

This Affirmation follows the teaching of Christ that He is the central theme of Scripture (Matt. 5:17; Luke 24:27, 44; John 5:39; Heb. 10:7). This is to say that focus on the person and work of Christ runs throughout the Bible from Genesis to Revelation. To be sure there are other and tangential topics, but the person and work of Jesus Christ are central.

In view of the focus of Scripture on Christ, the Denial stresses a hermeneutical obligation to make this Christo-centric message clear in the expounding of Scripture. As other articles (cf. Article XV) emphasize the "literal" interpretation of Scripture, this article is no license for allegorization and unwarranted typology which see Christ portrayed in every detail of Old Testament proclamation. The article simply points to the centrality of Christ's mission in the unfolding of God's revelation to man.

Neither is there any thought in this article of making the role of Christ more ultimate than that of the Father. What is in view here is the *focus* of Scripture and not the ultimate *source* or *object* of the whole plan of redemption.

Article IV. *WE AFFIRM that the Holy Spirit who inspired Scripture acts through it today to work faith in its message.*

WE DENY that the Holy Spirit ever teaches to any one anything which is contrary to the teaching of Scripture.

Here stress is laid on the fact that the Holy Spirit not only is the source of Scripture, but also works to produce faith in Scripture He has inspired. Without this ministry of the Holy Spirit, belief in the truth of Scripture would not occur.

The Denial is directed at those alleged "revelations" which some claim to have but which are contrary to Scripture. No matter how sincere or genuinely felt, no dream, vision, or supposed revelation which contradicts Scripture ever comes from the Holy Spirit. For the utterances of the Holy Spirt are all harmonious and noncontradictory (see Article XX).

Article V. *WE AFFIRM that the Holy Spirit enables believers to appropriate and apply Scripture to their lives.*

WE DENY that the natural man is able to discern spiritually the biblical message apart from the Holy Spirit.

The design of this article is to indicate that the ministry of the Holy Spirit extends beyond the inspiration of Scripture to its very application to the lives of the believer. Just as no one calls Jesus Lord except by the Holy Spirit (I Cor. 12:3), so no one can appropriate the message of Scripture to his life apart from the gracious work of the Holy Spirit.

The Denial stresses the truth that the natural man does not receive the spiritual message of Scripture. Apart from the work of the Holy Spirit there is no welcome for its truth in an unregenerate heart.

This does not imply that a non-Christian is unable to understand the meaning of any Scripture. It means that whatever he may perceive of the message of Scripture, that without the Holy Spirit's work he will not welcome the message in his heart.

Article VI. *WE AFFIRM that the Bible expresses God's truth in propositional statements, and we declare that biblical truth is both objective and absolute. We further affirm that a statement is true if it represents matters as they actually are, but is an error if it misrepresents the facts.*

WE DENY that, while Scripture is able to make us wise unto salvation, biblical truth should be defined in terms of this function. We further deny that error should be defined as that which willfully deceives.

Since hermeneutics is concerned with understanding the truth of Scripture, attention is directed here to the nature of truth. Several significant affirmations are made about the nature of truth.

First, in contrast to contemporary relativism it is declared that truth is absolute. Second, as opposed to subjectivism it is acknowledged that truth is objective. Finally, in opposition to existential and pragmatic views of truth, this article affirms that truth is what corresponds to reality. This same point was made in the "Chicago Statement on Inerrancy" (1978) in Article XIII and the commentary on it.

The Denial makes it evident that views which redefine an error to mean what "misleads," rather than what is a mistake, must be rejected. This redefinition of the word "error" is both contrary to Scripture and to common sense. In Scripture the word *error* is used of unintentional acts (Lev. 4:2) as well as intentional ones. Also, in common parlence a statement is in error if it is a factual mistake, even if there was no intention to mislead anyone by it. So to suggest that the Bible contains mistakes, but that these are not errors so long as they do not mislead, is contrary to both Scripture and ordinary usage.

By this subtle redefinition of error to mean only what misleads but not what misrepresents, some have tried to maintain that the Bible is wholly true (in that it never misleads) and yet that it may have some mistakes in it. This position is emphatically rejected by the confessors of this document.

Article VII. *WE AFFIRM that the meaning expressed in each biblical text is single, definite, and fixed.*

WE DENY that the recognition of this single meaning eliminates the variety of its application.

The Affirmation here is directed at those who claim a "double" or "deeper" meaning to Scripture than that expressed by the authors. It stresses the unity and fixity of meaning as opposed to those who find multiple and pliable meanings. What a passage means is fixed by the author and is not subject to change by readers. This does not imply that further revelation on the subject cannot help one come to a fuller understanding, but simply that the meaning given in a text is not changed because additional truth is revealed subsequently.

Meaning is also definite in that there are defined limits by virtue of the author's expressed meaning in the given linguistic form and cultural context. Meaning is *determined* by an author; it is *discovered* by the readers.

The Denial adds the clarification that simply because Scripture has one meaning does not imply that its messages cannot be applied to a variety of individuals or situations. While the interpretation is one, the applications can be many.

Article VIII. *WE AFFIRM that the Bible contains teachings and mandates which apply to all cultural and situational contexts and other mandates which the Bible itself shows apply only to particular situations.*

WE DENY that the distinction between the universal and particular mandates of Scripture can be determined by cultural and situational factors. We further deny that universal mandates may ever be treated as culturally or situationally relative.

In view of the tendency of many to relativize the message of the Bible by accommodating it to changing cultural situations, this Affirmation proclaims the universality of biblical teachings. There are commands which transcend all cultural barriers and are binding on all men everywhere. To be sure, some biblical injunctions are directed to specific situations, but even these are normative to the particular situation(s) to which they speak. However, there are commands in Scripture which speak universally to the human situation and are not bound to particular cultures or situations.

The Denial addresses the basis of the distinction between universal and particular situations. It denies that the grounds of this distinction are relative or purely cultural. It further denies the legitimacy of relativizing biblical absolutes by reducing them to purely cultural mandates.

The meaning of this article is that whatever the biblical text means is binding. And what is meant to be universally binding should not be relegated to particular situations any more than what is meant to apply only to particular circumstances should be promulgated as universally applicable.

There is an attempt here to strike a balance between command and culture by recognizing that a command transcends culture, even though it speaks to and is expressed in a particular culture. Thus while the situation (or circumstances) may help us to discover the right course of action, the situation never determines what is right. God's laws are not situationally determined.

Article IX. *WE AFFIRM that the term hermeneutics, which historically signified the rules of exegesis, may properly be extended to cover all that is involved in the process of perceiving what the biblical revelation means and how it bears on our lives.*

WE DENY that the message of Scripture derives from, or is dictated by, the interpreter's understanding. Thus we deny that the "horizons" of the biblical writer and the interpreter may rightly "fuse" in such a way that what the text communicates to the interpreter is not ultimately controlled by the expressed meaning of the Scripture.

The primary thrust of this Affirmation is definitional. It desires to clarify the meaning of the term *hermeneutics* by indicating that it includes not only perception of the declared meaning of a text but also an understanding of the implications that text has for one's life. Thus, hermeneutics is more than biblical exegesis. It is not only the science that leads forth the meaning of a passage but also that which enables one (by the Holy Spirit) to understand the spiritual implications the truth(s) of this passage has for Christian living.

The Denial notes that the meaning of a passage is not derived from or dictated by the interpreter. Rather, meaning comes from the author who wrote it. Thus the reader's understanding has no hermeneutically definitive role. Readers must listen to the meaning of a text and not attempt to legislate it. Of course, the meaning listened to should be applied to the reader's life. But the need or desire for specific application should not color the interpretation of a passage.

Article X. *WE AFFIRM that Scripture communicates God's truth to us verbally through a wide variety of literary forms.*

WE DENY that any of the limits of human language render Scripture inadequate to convey God's message.

This Affirmation is a logical literary extension of Article II which acknowledges the humanity of Scripture. The Bible is God's Word, but it is written in human words; thus, revelation is "verbal." Revelation is "propositional" (Article II) because it expresses certain propositional truth. Some prefer to call it "sentential" because the truth is expressed in sentences. Whatever the term—verbal, propositional, or sentential—the Bible is a human book which uses normal literary forms. These include parables, satire, irony, hyperbole, metaphor, simile, poetry, and even allegory (e.g., Ezek. 16-17).

As an expression in finite, human language, the Bible has certain limitations in a similar way that Christ as a man had certain limitations. This means that God adapted Himself through human language so that His eternal truth could be understood by man in a temporal world.

Despite the obvious fact of the limitations of any finite linguistic expression, the Denial is quick to point out that these limits do not render Scripture an inadequate means of communicating God's truth. For while there is a divine adaptation (via language) to human finitude there is no accommodation to human error. Error is not essential to human nature. Christ was human and yet He did not err. Adam was human before he erred. So simply because the Bible is written in human language does not mean it must err. In fact, when God uses human language there is a supernatural guarantee that it will not be in error.

Article XI. *WE AFFIRM that translations of the text of Scripture can communicate knowledge of God across all temporal and cultural boundaries.*

WE DENY that the meaning of biblical texts is so tied to the culture out of which they came that understanding of the same meaning in other cultures is impossible.

Simply because the truth of Scripture was conveyed by God in the original writings does not mean that it cannot be translated into another language. This article affirms the translatability of God's truth into other cultures. It affirms that since truth is transcendent (see Article XX) it is not culture-bound. Hence the truth of God expressed in a first-century culture is not limited to that culture. For the *nature* of truth is not limited to any particular *medium* through which it is expressed.

The Denial notes that since meaning is not inextricably tied to a given culture it can be adequately expressed in another culture. Thus the message of Scripture need not be relativized by translation. *What* is expressed can be the same even though *how* it is expressed differs.

Article XII. *WE AFFIRM that in the task of translating the Bible and teaching it in the context of each culture, only those functional equivalents that are faithful to the content of biblical teaching should be employed.*

WE DENY the legitimacy of methods which either are insensitive to the demands of cross-cultural communication or distort biblical meaning in the process.

Whereas the previous article treated the matter of the translatability of divine truth, this article speaks to the *adequacy* of translations. Obviously not every expression in another language will appropriately convey the meaning of Scripture. In view of this, caution is urged that the translators remain faithful to the truth of the Scripture being translated by the proper choice of the words used to translate it.

This article treats the matter of "functional" equivalence. Often there is no actual or literal equivalence between expressions in one language and a word-for-word translation into another language. *What* is expressed (meaning) is the same but *how* it is expressed (the words) is different. Hence a different construction can be used to convey the same meaning.

The Denial urges sensitivity to cultural matters so that the same truth may be conveyed, even though different terms are being used. Without this awareness missionary activity can be severely hampered.

Article XIII. *WE AFFIRM that awareness of the literary cate-*

gories, formal and stylistic, of the various parts of Scripture is essential for proper exegesis, and hence we value genre criticism as one of the many disciplines of biblical study.

WE DENY that generic categories which negate historicity may rightly be imposed on biblical narratives which present themselves as factual.

The awareness of what kind of literature one is interpreting is essential to a correct understanding of the text. A correct genre judgment should be made to ensure correct understanding. A parable, for example, should not be treated like a chronicle, nor should poetry be interpreted as though it were a straightforward narrative. Each passage has its own genre, and the interpreter should be cognizant of the specific kind of literature it is as he attempts to interpret it. Without genre recognition an interpreter can be misled in his understanding of the passage. For example, when the prophet speaks of "trees clapping their hands" (Isa. 55:12) one could assume a kind of animism unless he recognized that this is poetry and not prose.

The Denial is directed at an illegitimate use of genre criticism by some who deny the truth of passages which are presented as factual. Some, for instance, take Adam to be a myth, whereas in Scripture he is presented as a real person. Others take Jonah to be an allegory when he is presented as a historical person and so referred to by Christ (Matt. 12:40-42). This Denial is an appropriate and timely warning not to use genre criticism as a cloak for rejecting the truth of Scripture.

Article XIV. *WE AFFIRM that the biblical record of events, discourses and sayings, though presented in a variety of appropriate literary forms, corresponds to historical fact.*

WE DENY that any such event, discourse or saying reported in Scripture was invented by the biblical writers or by the traditions they incorporated.

This article combines the emphases of Articles VI and XIII. While acknowledging the legitimacy of literary forms, this article insists that any record of events presented in Scripture must correspond to historical fact. That is, no reported event, discourse, or saying should be considered imaginary.

The Denial is even more clear than the Affirmation. It stresses that any discourse, saying, or event reported in Scripture must actually have occurred. This means that any hermeneutic or form of biblical criticism which claims that something was invented by the author must be rejected. This does not mean that a parable must be understood to represent historical facts, since a parable does not (by its very genre) purport to report an event or saying but simply to illustrate a point.

Article XV. *WE AFFIRM the necessity of interpreting the Bible according to its literal, or normal, sense. The literal sense is the grammatical-historical sense, that is, the meaning which the writer expressed. Interpretation according to the literal sense will take account of all figures of speech and literary forms found in the text.*

WE DENY the legitimacy of any approach to Scripture that attributes to it meaning which the literal sense does not support.

The literal sense of Scripture is strongly affirmed here. To be sure the English word literal carries some problematic connotations with it. Hence the words *normal* and *grammatical-historical* are used to explain what is meant. The literal sense is also designated by the more descriptive title grammatical-historical sense. This means the correct interpretation is the one which discovers the meaning of the text in its grammatical forms and in the historical, cultural context in which the text is expressed.

The Denial warns against attributing to Scripture any meaning not based in a literal understanding, such as mythological or allegorical interpretations. This should not be understood as eliminating typology or designated allegory or other literary forms which include figures of speech (see Articles X, XIII, and XIV).

Article XVI. *WE AFFIRM that legitimate critical techniques should be used in determining the canonical text and its meaning.*

WE DENY the legitimacy of allowing any method of biblical criticism to question the truth or integrity of the writer's expressed meaning, or of any other scriptural teaching.

Implied here is an approval of legitimate techniques of "lower criticism" or "textual criticism." It is proper to use critical techniques in order to discover the true text of Scripture, that is, the one which represents the original one given by the biblical authors.

Whereas critical methodology can be used to establish *which* of the texts are copies of the inspired original, it is illegitimate to use critical methods to call into question *whether* something in the original text is true. In other words, proper "lower criticism" is valid but negative "higher criticism" which rejects truths of Scripture is invalid.

Article XVII. *WE AFFIRM the unity, harmony, and consistency of Scripture and declare that it is its own best interpreter.*

WE DENY that Scripture may be interpreted in such a way as to suggest that one passage corrects or militates against another. We deny that later writers of Scripture misinterpreted earlier passages of Scripture when quoting from or referring to them.

Two points are made in the Affirmation, the unity of Scripture and its self-interpreting ability. Since the former is treated elsewhere (Article XXI), we will comment on the latter here. Not only is the Bible always correct in interpreting itself (see Article XVIII), but it is the "best interpreter" of itself.

Another point made here is that comparing Scripture with Scripture is an excellent help to an interpreter. For one passage sheds light on another. Hence the first commentary the interpreter should consult on a passage is what the rest of Scripture may say on that text.

The Denial warns against the assumption that an understanding of one passage can lead the interpreter to reject the teaching of another passage. One passage may help him better comprehend another but it will never contradict another.

This last part of the Denial is particularly directed to those who believe the New Testament writers misinterpret the Old Testament, or that they attribute meaning to an Old Testament text not expressed by the author of that text. While it is acknowledged that there is sometimes a wide range of *application* for a text, this article affirms that the *interpretation* of a biblical text by another biblical writer is always within the confines of the meaning of the first text.

Article XVIII. *WE AFFIRM that the Bible's own interpretation of itself is always correct, never deviating from,*

> *but rather elucidating, the single meaning of the inspired text. The single meaning of a prophet's words includes, but is not restricted to, the understanding of those words by the prophet and necessarily involves the intention of God evidenced in the fulfillment of those words.*
>
> *WE DENY that the writers of Scripture always understood the full implications of their own words.*

This Affirmation was perhaps the most difficult to word. The first part of the Affirmation builds on Article VII which declared that Scripture has only one meaning, and simply adds that whenever the Bible comments on another passage of Scripture it does so correctly. That is, the Bible never misinterprets itself. It always correctly understands the meaning of the passage it comments on (see Article XVII). For example, that Paul misinterprets Moses is to say that Paul erred. This view is emphatically rejected in favor of the inerrancy of all Scripture.

The problem in the second statement of the Affirmation revolves around whether God intended more by a passage of Scripture than the human author did. Put in this way, evangelical scholars are divided on the issue, even though there is unity on the question of "single meaning." Some believe that this single meaning may be fuller than the purview of the human author, since God had far more in view than did the prophet when he wrote it. The wording here is an attempt to include reference to the fulfillment of a prophecy (of which God was obviously aware when He inspired it) as part of the single meaning which God and the prophet shared. However, the prophet may not have been conscious of the full implications of this meaning when he wrote it.

The way around the difficulty was to note that there is only one meaning to a passage which both God and the prophet affirmed, but that this meaning may not always be fully "evidenced" until the prophecy is fulfilled. Furthermore, God, and not necessarily the prophets, was fully aware of the fuller implications that would be manifested in the fulfillment of this single meaning.

It is important to preserve single meaning without denying that God had more in mind than the prophet did. A distinction needs to be made, then, between what God was *conscious* of concerning an affirmation (which, in view of His foreknowledge and omniscience, was far more) and what He and the prophet actually expressed in the passage. The Denial makes this point clear by noting that biblical authors were not always fully aware of the implications of their own affirmations.

Article XIX. *WE AFFIRM that any preunderstandings which the interpreter brings to Scripture should be in harmony with scriptural teaching and subject to correction by it.*

WE DENY that Scripture should be required to fit alien preunderstandings, inconsistent with itself, such as naturalism, evolutionism, scientism, secular humanism, and relativism.

The question of preunderstanding is a crucial one in contemporary hermeneutics. The careful wording of the Affirmation does not discuss the issue of *whether* one should approach Scripture with a particular preunderstanding, but simply *which* kinds of preunderstanding one has are legitimate. This question is answered by affirming that only those preunderstandings which are compatible with the teaching of Scripture are legitimate. In fact, the statement goes further and demands that all preunderstanding be subject to "correction" by the teaching of Scripture.

The point of this article is to avoid interpreting Scripture through an alien grid or filter which obscures or negates its true message. For it acknowledges that one's preunderstanding will affect his understanding of a text. Hence to avoid misinterpreting Scripture one must be careful to examine his own presuppositions in the light of Scripture.

Article XX. *WE AFFIRM that since God is the author of all truth, all truths, biblical and extrabiblical, are consistent and cohere, and that the Bible speaks truth when it touches on matters pertaining to nature, history, or anything else. We further affirm that in some cases extrabiblical data have value for clarifying what Scripture teaches, and for prompting correction of faulty interpretations.*

WE DENY that extrabiblical views ever disprove the teaching of Scripture or hold priority over it.

What is in view here is not so much the nature of truth (which is treated in Article VI), but the consistency and coherence of truth. This is directed at those views which consider truth paradoxical or contradictory. This article declares that a proper hermeneutics avoids contradictions, since God never affirms as true two propositions, one of which is logically the opposite of the other.

Further, this Affirmation recognizes that not all truth is in the Bible (though all that is affirmed in the Bible is true). God has revealed Himself in nature and history as well as in Scripture. However, since God is the ultimate Author of all truth, there can be no contradiction between truths of Scripture and the true teachings of science and history.

Although only the Bible is the normative and infallible rule for doctrine and practice, nevertheless what one learns from sources outside Scripture can occasion a reexamination and reinterpretation of Scripture. For example, some have taught the world to be square because the Bible refers to "the four corners of the earth" (Isa. 11:12). But scientific knowledge of the spherical nature of the globe leads to a correction of this faulty interpretation. Other clarifications of our understanding of the biblical text are possible through the study of the social sciences.

However, whatever prompting and clarifying of Scripture that extrabiblical studies may provide, the final authority for what the Bible teaches rests in the text of Scripture itself and not in anything outside it (except in God Himself). The Denial makes clear this priority of the teaching of God's scriptural revelation over anything outside it.

Article XXI. *WE AFFIRM the harmony of special with general revelation and therefore of biblical teaching with the facts of nature.*

WE DENY that any genuine scientific facts are inconsistent with the true meaning of any passage of Scripture.

This article continues the discussion of the previous article by noting the harmony of God's general revelation (outside Scripture) and His special revelation in Scripture. It is acknowledged by all that certain *interpretations* of Scripture and some *opinions* of scientists will contradict each other. However, it is insisted here that the *truth* of Scripture and the *facts* of science never contradict each other.

"Genuine" science will always be in accord with Scripture. Science, however, based on naturalistic presuppositions will inevitably come in conflict with the supernatural truths of Scripture.

Far from denying a healthy interchange between scientific theory and biblical interpretation, the framers of this statement welcome such. Indeed, it is acknowledged (in article XX) that the exegete can learn from the scientist. What is denied is that we should accept scientific views that contradict Scripture or that they should be given an authority above Scripture.

Article XXII. *WE AFFIRM that Genesis 1-11 is factual, as is the rest of the book.*

WE DENY that the teachings of Genesis 1-11 are mythical and that scientific hypotheses about earth history or the origin of humanity may be invoked to overthrow what Scripture teaches about creation.

Since the historicity and the scientific accuracy of the early chapters of the Bible have come under severe attack it is important to apply the "literal" hermeneutic espoused (Article XV) to this question. The result was a recognition of the factual nature of the account of the creation of the universe, all living things, the special creation of man, the Fall, and the Flood. These accounts are all factual, that is, they are about space-time events which actually happened as reported in the book of Genesis (see Article XIV).

The article left open the question of the age of the earth on which there is no unanimity among evangelicals and which was beyond the purview of this conference. There was, however, complete agreement on denying that Genesis is mythological or unhistorical. Likewise, the use of the term "creation" was meant to exclude the belief in macro-evolution, whether of the atheistic or theistic varieties.

Article XXIII. *WE AFFIRM the clarity of Scripture and specifically of its message about salvation from sin.*

WE DENY that all passages of Scripture are equally clear or have equal bearing on the message of redemption.

Traditionally this teaching is called the "perspicuity" of Scripture. By this is meant that the central message of Scripture is clear, especially what the Bible says about salvation from sin.

The Denial disassociates this claim from the belief that everything in Scripture is clear or that all teachings are equally clear or equally relevant to the Bible's central saving message. It is obvious to any honest interpreter that the meaning of some passages of Scripture is obscure. It is equally evident that the truth of some passages is not directly relevant to the overall plan of salvation.

Article XXIV. *WE AFFIRM that a person is not dependent for understanding of Scripture on the expertise of biblical scholars.*

WE DENY that a person should ignore the fruits of the technical study of Scripture by biblical scholars.

This article attempts to avoid two extremes. First, it affirms that one is not dependent on biblical "experts" for his understanding of the basic truths of Scripture. Were this not true, then a significant aspect of the priesthood of all believers would be destroyed. For if the understanding of the laity is contingent on the teaching of experts, then Protestant interpretive experts will have replaced the teaching magisterium of Catholic priests with a kind of teaching magisterium of Protestant scholars.

On the other hand, biblical scholars do play a significant role in the lay understanding of Scripture. Even the very tools (Bible, dictionaries, concordances, etc.) used by laypersons to interpret Scripture were produced by scholars. And when it comes to more technical and precise understanding of specific Scripture the work of experts is more than helpful. Hence the implied exhortation in the denial to avail oneself of the fruit of scholarship is well taken.

Article XXV. *WE AFFIRM that the only type of preaching which sufficiently conveys the divine revelation and its proper application to life is that which faithfully expounds the text of Scripture as the Word of God.*

WE DENY that the preacher has any message from God apart from the text of Scripture.

This final article declares that good preaching should be based in good hermeneutics. The exposition of Scripture is not to be treated in isolation from the proclamation of Scripture. In preaching the preacher should faithfully expound the Word of God. Anything short of a correct exposition of God's written Word is pronounced insufficient.

Indeed, the Denial declares that there is no message from God apart from Scripture. This was understood not to contradict the fact that there is a general revelation (affirmed in Article XXI) but simply to note that the only inspired and infallible writing from which the preacher can and must preach is the Bible.

Appendix C

Exposition on Biblical Hermeneutics

J. I. Packer

The following paragraphs outline the general theological understanding which the Chicago Statement on Biblical Hermeneutics reflects. They were first drafted as a stimulus toward that statement. They have now been revised in the light of it and of many specific suggestions received during the scholars' conference at which it was drawn up. Though the revision could not be completed in time to present to the conference, there is every reason to regard its substance as expressing with broad accuracy the common mind of the signatories of the statement.

STANDPOINT OF THE EXPOSITION

The living God, Creator and Redeemer, is a communicator, and the inspired and inerrant Scriptures which set before us his saving revelation in history are his means of communicating with us today. He who once spoke to the world through Jesus Christ his Son speaks to us still in and through his written Word. Publicly and privately, therefore, through preaching, personal study and meditation, with prayer and in the fellowship of the body of Christ, Christian people must continually labor to interpret the Scriptures so that their normative divine message to us may be properly understood. To have formulated the biblical concept of Scripture as authoritative revelation in writing, the God-given rule of faith and life, will be of no profit where the message of Scripture is not rightly grasped and applied. So it is of vital importance to detect and dismiss defective ways of interpreting what is written and to replace them with faithful interpretation of God's infallible Word.

That is the purpose this exposition seeks to serve. What it offers is basic perspectives on the hermeneutical task in the light of three convictions. First, Scripture, being God's own instruction to us, is abidingly true and utterly trustworthy. Second, hermeneutics is crucial to the battle for biblical authority in the contemporary church. Third, as knowledge of the inerrancy of Scripture must control interpretation, forbidding us to discount anything that Scripture proves to affirm, so interpretation must clarify the scope and significance of that inerrancy by determining what affirmations Scripture actually makes.

THE COMMUNION BETWEEN GOD AND MANKIND

God has made mankind in his own image, personal and rational, for eternal loving fellowship with himself in a communion that rests on two-way communication: God addressing to us words of revelation and we answering him in words of prayer and praise. God's gift of language was given us partly to make possible these interchanges and partly also that we might share our understanding of God with others.

In testifying to the historical process from Adam to Christ whereby God re-established fellowship with our fallen race, Scripture depicts him as constantly using his own gift of language to send men messages about what he would do and what they should do. The God of the Bible uses many forms of speech; he narrates, informs, instructs, warns, reasons, promises, commands, explains, exclaims, entreats and encourages. The God who saves is also the God who speaks in all these ways.

Biblical writers, historians, prophets, poets and teachers alike, cite Scripture as God's word of address to all its readers and hearers. To regard Scripture as the Creator's present personal invitation to fellowship, setting standards for faith and godliness not only for its own time but for all time, is integral to biblical faith.

Though God is revealed in the natural order, in the course of history and in the deliverances of conscience, sin makes mankind impervious and unresponsive to this general revelation. And general revelation is in any case only a disclosure of the Creator as the world's good Lord and just Judge; it does not tell of salvation through Jesus Christ. To know about the Christ of Scripture is thus a necessity for that knowledge of God and communion with him to which he calls sinners today. As the biblical message is heard, read, preached and taught, the Holy Spirit works with and through it to open the eyes of the spiritually blind and to instill this knowledge.

God has caused Scripture so to be written, and the Spirit so ministers with it, that all who read it, humbly seeking God's help, will be able to understand its saving message. The Spirit's ministry does not make needless the discipline of personal study but rather makes it effective.

To deny the rational, verbal, cognitive character of God's communication to us, to posit an antithesis as some do between revelation as personal and as propositional, and to doubt the adequacy of language as we have it to bring us God's authentic message are fundamental mistakes. The humble verbal form of biblical language no more invalidates it as revelation of God's mind than the humble servant-form of the Word made flesh invalidates the claim that Jesus truly reveals the Father.

To deny that God has made plain in Scripture as much as each human being needs to know for his or her spiritual welfare would be a further mistake. Any obscurities we find in Scripture are not intrinsic to it but reflect our own limitations of information and insight. Scripture is clear and sufficient both as a source of doctrine, binding the conscience, and as a guide to eternal life and godliness, shaping our worship and service of the God who creates, loves and saves.

THE AUTHORITY OF SCRIPTURE

Holy Scripture is the self-revelation of God in and through the words of men. It is both their witness to God and God's witness to himself. As the divine-human record and interpretation of God's redemptive work in history, it is cognitive revelation, truth addressed to our minds for understanding and response. God is its source, and Jesus Christ, the Savior, is its center of reference and main subject matter. Its absolute and abiding worth as an infallible directive for faith and living follows from its God-givenness (cf. 2 Tim. 3:15-17). Being as fully divine as it is human, it expresses God's wisdom in all its teaching and speaks reliably—that is, infallibly and inerrantly—in every informative assertion it makes. It is a set of occasional writings, each with its own specific character and content, which together constitute an organism of universally relevant truth: namely, bad news about universal human sin and need answered by good news about a particular first-century Jew who is shown to be the Son of God and the world's only Savior. The volume which these constituent books make is as broad as life and bears upon every human problem and aspect of behavior. In setting before us the history of redemption; the law and the gospel; God's commands, promises, threats, works and ways; and object-lessons concerning faith and obedience and their opposites, with their respective outcomes; Scripture shows us the entire panorama of human existence as God wills us to see it.

The authority of Holy Scripture is bound up with the authority of Jesus Christ, whose recorded words express the principle that the teaching of Israel's Scriptures (our Old Testament), together with his own teaching and the witness of the apostles (our New Testament), constitute his appointed rule of faith and conduct for his followers. He did not criticize his Bible, though he criticized misinterpretations of it; on the contrary, he affirmed its binding authority over him and all his disciples (cf. Matt. 5:17-19). To separate the authority of Christ from that of Scripture and to oppose the one to the other are thus mistakes. To oppose the authority of one apostle to that of another or the teaching of an apostle at one time to that of his teaching at another time are mistakes also.

THE HOLY SPIRIT AND THE SCRIPTURES

The Holy Spirit of God, who moved the human authors to produce the biblical books, now accompanies them with his power. He led the church to discern their inspiration in the canonizing process; he continually confirms this discernment to individuals through the unique impact which he causes Scripture to make upon them. He helps them as they study, pray, meditate and seek to learn in the church, to understand and commit themselves to those things which the Bible teaches, and to know the living triune God whom the Bible presents.

The Spirit's illumination can only be expected where the biblical text is diligently studied. Illumination does not yield new truth, over and above what the Bible says; rather, it enables us to see what Scripture was showing us all along. Illumination binds our consciences to Scripture as God's Word and brings joy and worship as we find the Word yielding up to us its meaning. By contrast, intellectual and emotional impulses to disregard or quarrel with the teaching of Scripture come not from the Spirit of God but from some other source. Demonstrable misunderstandings and misinterpretations of Scripture may not be ascribed to the Spirit's leading.

THE IDEA OF HERMENEUTICS

Biblical hermeneutics has traditionally been understood as the study of right principles for understanding the biblical text. "Understanding" may stop short at a theoretical and notional level, or it may advance via the assent and commitment of faith to become experiential through personal acquaintance with the God to whom the theories and notions refer. Theoretical understanding of Scripture requires of us no more than is called for to comprehend any ancient literature, that is, sufficient knowledge of the language and background and sufficient empathy with the different cultural context. But there is no experiential understanding of Scripture—no personal knowledge of the God to whom it points—without the Spirit's illumination. Biblical hermeneutics studies the way in which both levels of understanding are attained.

THE SCOPE OF BIBLICAL INTERPRETATION

The interpreter's task in broadest definition is to understand both what Scripture meant historically and what it means for us today, that is, how it bears on our lives. This task involves three constant activities.

First comes *exegesis*, the extracting from the text of what God by the human writer was expressing to the latter's envisaged readers.

Second comes *integration*, the correlating of what each exegetical venture has yielded with whatever other biblical teaching bears on the matter in hand and with the rest of biblical teaching as such. Only within this frame of reference can the full meaning of the exegeted teaching be determined.

Third comes *application* of the exegeted teaching, viewed explicitly as God's teaching, for the correcting and directing of thought and action. Application is based on the knowledge that God's character and will, man's nature and need, the saving ministry of Jesus Christ, the experiential aspects of godliness including the common life of the church and the many-sided relationship between God and his world including his plan for its history are realities which do not change with the passing years. It is with these matters that both testaments constantly deal.

Interpretation and application of Scripture take place most naturally in preaching, and all preaching should be based on this threefold procedure. Otherwise, biblical teaching will be misunderstood and misapplied, and confusion and ignorance regarding God and his ways will result.

FORMAL RULES OF BIBLICAL INTERPRETATION

The faithful use of reason in biblical interpretation is ministerial, not magisterial; the believing interpreter will use his mind not to impose or manufacture meaning but to grasp the meaning that is already there in the material itself. The work of scholars who, though not themselves Christians, have been able to understand biblical ideas accurately will be a valuable resource in the theoretical part of the interpreter's task.

a. Interpretation should adhere to the *literal* sense, that is, the single literary meaning which each passage carries. The initial quest is always for what God's penman meant by what he wrote. The discipline of interpretation excludes all attempts to go behind the text, just as it excludes all reading into passages of meanings which cannot be read out of them and all pursuit of ideas sparked off in us by the text which do not arise as part of the author's own expressed flow of thought. Symbols and figures of speech must be recognized for what they are, and arbitrary allegorizing (as distinct from the drawing out of typology which was demonstrably in the writer's mind) must be avoided.

b. The literal sense of each passage should be sought by *the grammatical-historical method,* that is, by asking what is the linguistically natural way to understand the text in its historical setting. Textual, historical, literary and theological study, aided by linguistic skills—philological, semantic, logical—is the way forward here. Passages should be exegeted in the context of the book of which they are part, and the quest for the writer's own meaning, as distinct from that of his known or supposed sources, must be constantly pursued. The legitimate use of the various critical disciplines is not to call into question the integrity or truth of the writer's meaning but simply to help us determine it.

c. Interpretation should adhere to the principle of *harmony* in the biblical material. Scripture exhibits a wide diversity of concepts and viewpoints within a common faith and an advancing disclosure of divine truth within the biblical period. These differences should not be minimized, but the unity which underlies the diversity should not be lost sight of at any point. We should look to Scripture to interpret Scripture and deny as a matter of method that particular texts, all of which have the one Holy Spirit as their source, can be genuinely discrepant with each other. Even when we cannot at present demonstrate their harmony in a convincing way, we should proceed on the basis that they are in fact harmonious and that fuller knowledge will show this.

d. Interpretation should be *canonical*: that is, the teaching of the Bible as a whole should always be viewed as providing the framework within which our understanding of each particular passage must finally be reached and into which it must finally be fitted.

Valuable as an aid in determining the literal meaning of biblical passages is the discipline of genre criticism, which seeks to identify in terms of style, form and content, the various literary categories to which the biblical books and particular passages within them belong. The literary genre in which each writer creates his text belongs in part at least to his own culture and will be clarified through knowledge of that culture. Since mistakes about genre lead to large-scale misunderstandings of biblical material, it is important that this particular discipline not be neglected.

THE CENTRALITY OF JESUS CHRIST IN THE BIBLICAL MESSAGE

Jesus Christ and the saving grace of God in him are the central themes of the Bible. Both Old and New Testaments bear witness to Christ, and the New Testament interpretation of the Old Testament points to him consistently. Types and prophecies in the Old Testament anticipated his coming, his atoning death, his resurrection, his reign and his return. The office and ministry of priests, prophets and kings, the divinely instituted ritual and sacrificial offerings, and the patterns of redemptive action in Old Testament history, all had typical significance as foreshadowings of Jesus. Old Testament believers looked forward to his coming and lived and were saved by faith which had Christ and his kingdom in view, just as Christians today are saved by faith in Christ, the Savior, who died for our sins and who now lives and reigns and will one day return. That the church and kingdom of Jesus Christ are central to the plan of God which Scripture reveals is not open to question, though opinions divide as to the precise way in which church and kingdom relate to each other. Any way of interpreting Scripture which misses its consistent Christ-centeredness must be judged erroneous.

BIBLICAL AND EXTRA-BIBLICAL KNOWLEDGE

Since all facts cohere, the truth about them must be coherent also, and since God, the author of all Scripture, is also the Lord of all facts, there can in principle be no contradiction between a right understanding of what Scripture says and a right account of any reality or event in the created order. Any appearance of contradiction here would argue misunderstanding or inadequate knowledge, either of what Scripture really affirms or of what the extra-biblical facts really are. Thus it would be a summons to reassessment and further scholarly enquiry.

BIBLICAL STATEMENTS AND NATURAL SCIENCE

What the Bible says about the facts of nature is as true and trustworthy as anything else it says. However, it speaks of natural phenomena as they are spoken of in ordinary language, not in the explanatory technical terms of modern science; it accounts for natural events in terms of the action of God, not in terms of causal links within the created order; and it often describes natural processes figuratively and poetically, not analytically and prosaically as modern science seeks to do. This being so, differences of opinion as to the correct scientific account to give of natural facts and events which Scripture celebrates can hardly be avoided.

It should be remembered, however, that Scripture was given to reveal God, not to address scientific issues in scientific terms, and that, as it does not use the language of modern science, so it does not require scientific knowledge about the internal processes of God's creation for the understanding of its essential message about God and ourselves. Scripture interprets scientific knowledge by relating it to the revealed purpose and work of God, thus establishing an ultimate context for the study and reform of scientific ideas. It is not for scientific theories to dictate what Scripture may and may not say, although extra-biblical information will sometimes helpfully expose a misinterpretation of Scripture.

In fact, interrogating biblical statements concerning nature in the light of scientific knowledge about their subject-matter may help toward attaining a more precise exegesis of them. For though exegesis must be controlled by the text itself, not shaped by extraneous considerations, the exegetical process is constantly stimulated by questioning the text as to whether it means this or that.

NORM AND CULTURE IN THE BIBLICAL REVELATION

As we find in Scripture unchanging truths about God and his will expressed in a variety of verbal forms, so we find them applied in a variety of cultural and situational contexts. Not all biblical teaching about conduct is normative for behavior today. Some applications of moral principles are restricted to a limited audience, the nature and extent of which Scripture itself specifies. One task of exegesis is to distinguish these absolute and normative truths from those aspects of their recorded application which are relative to changing situations. Only when this distinction is drawn can we hope to see how the same absolute truths apply to us in our own culture.

To fail to see how a particular application of an absolute principle has been culturally determined (for instance, as most would agree, Paul's command that Christians greet each other with a kiss) and to treat a revealed absolute as culturally relative (for instance, as again most would agree, God's prohibition in the Pentateuch of homosexual activity) would both be mistakes. Though cultural developments, including conventional values and latter-day social change, may legitimately challenge traditional ways of applying biblical principles, they may not be used either to modify those principles in themselves or to evade their application altogether.

In cross-cultural communication a further step must be taken: the Christian teacher must re-apply revealed absolutes to persons living in a culture that is not the teacher's own. The demands of this task highlight the importance of his being clear on what is absolute in the biblical presentation of the will and work of God and what is a culturally-relative application of it. Engaging in the task may help him toward clarity at this point by making him more alert than before to the presence in Scripture of culturally-conditioned applications of truth, which have to be adjusted according to the cultural variable.

ENCOUNTERING GOD THROUGH HIS WORD

The twentieth century has seen many attempts to assert the instrumentality of Scripture in bringing to us God's Word while yet denying that that Word has been set forth for all time in the words of the biblical text. These views regard the text as the fallible human witness by means of which God fashions and prompts those insights which he gives us through preaching and Bible study. But for the most part these views include a denial that the Word of God is cognitive communication, and thus they lapse inescapably into impressionistic mysticism. Also, their denial that Scripture is the objectively given Word of God makes the relation of that Word to the text indefinable and hence permanently problematical. This is true of all current forms of neo-orthodox and existentialist theology, including the so-called "new hermeneutic," which is an extreme and incoherent version of the approach described.

The need to appreciate the cultural differences between our world and that of the biblical writers and to be ready to find that God through his Word is challenging the presuppositions and limitations of our present outlook, are two emphases currently associated with the "new hermeneutic." But both really belong to the understanding of the interpretative task which this exposition has set out.

The same is true of the emphasis laid in theology of the existentialist type on the reality of a transforming encounter with God and his Son, Jesus Christ, through the Scriptures. Certainly, the crowning glory of the Scriptures is that they do in fact mediate life-giving fellowship with God incarnate, the living Christ of whom they testify, the divine Savior whose words "are spirit and . . . are life" (John 6:63). But there is no Christ save the Christ of the Bible, and only to the extent that the Bible's presentation of Jesus and of God's plan centering upon him is trusted can genuine spiritual encounter with Jesus Christ ever be expected to take place. It is by means of disciplined interpretation of a trusted Bible that the Father and Son, through the Spirit, make themselves known to sinful men. To such transforming encounters the hermeneutical principles and procedures stated here both mark and guard the road.

Appendix D

The Bible and the Conscience of Our Age

Carl F. H. Henry

This paper was the message delivered at the closing session of the Summit II: Hermeneutics Conference. It is included here because it summarizes the issues of the conference and affirms the role of the Bible in today's world.

At this stage of our gathering you have already survived more papers and presentations than the apostles may have endured in a lifetime. I am not suggesting that they would necessarily have been displeased with what we have been doing—or at any rate, with our authorial intention—although I do not think many of them would have stayed by for these closing remarks, I have been tempted to forgo them myself. But Dr. Radmacher, who by name is a wheel-maker, not being content with the wheels within wheels that your groups have provided, has added yet another wheel—not a big wheel, as you will soon realize—but a spare wheel, or a wheel that I wish he had spared, and perhaps you also.

You have heard the Scripture. It speaks of the unfettered Word of God, of the truth of God that we are to handle rightly. In the forefront Paul keeps the risen Jesus, who burst the bonds of the tomb, and he holds before us the resurrection to come, and assures us that the Lord knows which people are His. Paul also warns against needless disputes about words and godless chatter. He is passionately devoted to the truth and Word of God, and he is against semantics that sag out of this divine orbit and serve shoddy and earthly causes.

Ours is a mass media age and with the dawning computer age threatens to drown us in verbage. Will the truth of God be smothered by these torrents of modernity, by the words of man infallibly reproduced by computer systems?

No, says Paul; the Word of God cannot be fettered. Remember Jesus Christ risen from the dead. In God's great plan and purpose the Word in Scripture and the Word incarnate are indissolubly linked. They cannot be bound, but have the final say.

You have had two major working conferences. Against radical and mediating scholars who would bind the Bible by all manner of critical concession you have affirmed the inerrantly inspired Word of God; what God inspires is inerrant, and all Scripture—as Paul said—is God-breathed. Scripture must not be bound, you affirmed, by speculative theories that strip away its truth segment by segment until the reader is left with fragments of the comprehensive revelation of God.

Now the second working conference, on hermeneutical concerns, draws to a close. Against those who would frustrate the meaning and truth of scriptural revelation by interpretative artifices alien to the Christian heritage you have championed the literal sense of Scripture and insisted that neither the culture-rootedness of language nor the rise of science-oriented civilization nullifies the objective and universal authority of the Bible. You speak not from haughty pedestals of pride but from compassionate and anguished hearts. All of us lament the loss, by many theologians professing to speak for the Christian movement, of the objective reality of God and of the objective truth of His revelation. We see no sure outcome of this defection from the living God and His scriptural disclosure, other than looming skepticism and nihilism.

For two generations mediating theologies have been yielding to increasingly unstable alternatives; understanding of God collapses into self-understanding and the living God expires into the dying god—not the God Man who dies for sinners and rises to return in triumph, but rather the man-gods postulated by a generation fashioning divinity in its own likeness and image. The loss of absolutes—absolute truth, absolute right and wrong—follows from speculative efforts to vindicate truth and goodness independent of the living God who makes His nature and will known. The edifice of the Enlightenment, which charitably retained the supernatural, yet separated from the God of miraculous revelation and redemption the whole enterprise of nature, history, law, and every other discipline of study, is crumbling. All the intermediary godlings are disintegrating with it including religion itself carrying a universal validity claim, the special worth and dignity of man, a meaningful universe, and a patterned history. All are now buckling under to despairing hedonism.

Let God be God, we implore. Let us hear again the life-giving Word of the Lord who summons all humankind to divine truth and to the holy.

Some fifty-five years ago I first read a Bible. Though my mother was nominally Roman Catholic and my father nominally Lutheran our home had no Bible until I acquired a copy by removing it from the pew racks of the Episcopal Sunday School that I attended. I began reading the Gospel stories of Jesus' resurrection from the dead, cautiously maneuvering through the accounts much as a moth circles a flame.

Little did I realize that I was not the first to steal the Bible. The medieval church had kept the Book from the masses for whom it was intended and we evangelicals often keep it from nurturing our own lives. But in recent years a different type of theft has emerged as some fellow evangelicals, along with non-evangelicals, wrest from the Bible segments that they derogate as no longer Word of God. Some now even introduce authorial intention or the cultural context of language as specious rationalizations for this crime against the Bible, much as some rapist might assure me that he is assaulting my wife for my own or for her good. They misuse Scripture in order to champion as biblically true what in fact does violence to Scripture. It is one of the ironies of church history that even some professed evangelicals now speak concessively of divine revelation itself as culture-conditioned, and do so at the precise moment in Western history when the secular dogma of the cultural relativity of all truth and morality and religious belief needs fervent challenging.

In challenging the concessive mode of the day we must avoid certain temptations. One temptation is to overstate the strength of the critical camp and to under-represent the evangelical enterprise as but a corporal's guard or Gideon's band. Among teachers and clergy the defections from a fully authoritative Bible may be disconcertingly numerous. But the great masses of active churchgoers take the Bible at its word. There is no firm consensus or stability of outlook among those who hold a broken and inconsistent view of biblical authority.

A few years ago at the American Theological Society—which considers the survival of biblical inerrantists about as viable as that of dinosaurs—I proposed that those present list the five problematic passages constituting their main barrier to belief in biblical inerrancy and which, if resolved, would encourage commitment to a fully authoritative Scripture. I went on to say that such an exercise would demonstrate two things: first, the lack of unanimity concerning where the problem lies; and second, that the real objection to biblical inerrancy is philosophical and speculative, thus no amount of resolution of particular problems will serve to reinstate the evangelical view.

We are emerging into an age in which critical scholars increasingly claim the inspiration of the Spirit for their own production of novel critical theories. The Spirit of God is said to have inspired not only Moses and Isaiah and Matthew, but also editorial redactors who supposedly composed the biblical writings in their final stages (and who therefore ought to get credit for many noble passages that tradition ascribes to the prophets, apostles and Jesus). The Holy Spirit is alleged to inspire scriptural commentary also (not only midrash, but even commentaries by modern publishers). Divine inspiration, it is now sometimes said, extends to the special insights of biblical critics in their highly professional enterprise. Who indeed in a characteristically exuberant age would not want to share in such a universal outpouring of the Spirit? We hear scholars talking about God's inspiration not only of apocryphal but even of supposed pseudepigraphous writings, with Second Peter considered such.

In the early years of Fuller Seminary I was once driving through Pasadena with Dr. William F. Albright, who had come to give a lecture. We were talking about neo-orthodox emphasis on interpersonal divine encounter, that is a direct, inner, divine revelatory confrontation of individuals, incapable of being logically grasped by reason, yet in which God allegedly makes Himself known. A theology of encounter, said Albright, could open the door to a whole new era of demonism. We have yet to see the worst in an age that sunders the Spirit from the Scriptures.

I hope, too, that we have yet to see the *best* of a movement that holds Spirit and Scripture together as the risen Lord would have us do as He rules His Church through the Spirit by the Scriptures. May these days of fettering Scripture have brought us low before God, without Whose Word our cause is barren; before the risen Jesus, without Whose triumph over death the joy and power of Christian fulfillment would be gone; before the Holy Spirit, Who yearns to fill us daily with virtues that even now sample the age to come; and before the Bible, that we may be even more prone both to defend and to read it.

God said, "Let my people go," meaning free them from bondage and let them take the place in the world that I seek for them. "Let it go" seems now to say to us, "Let my Bible go": go beyond the limitations imposed by critics, beyond the walls of cloisters and

churches, beyond even evangelical reticence and timidity; g
and full scope in the world. *Let the earth hear my voice.*

In a nation in peril we need to address the conscien
people. We need to lift God's sure Word into the lively conf
of beggarly modern notions of the good life and the misguide
of money and sex and world image as life priorities. The fre
is superior to totalitarian societies that demolish freedom, th
icate both government and education on an atheistic view of
and that dismantle private property. Yet one can almost hear th
of Western civilization about to crumble into rubble and ruin th
the shameful erosion of its values by those who prize greed and
gratification above all else. A land with a million abortions wil
be spared by millions of Bibles whose moral imperatives go unhee

All around us a new concept of the good life is in the mak
one that perceives the biblical representation as a threat, even a
menace, to its realization. Some evangelists imply that if you co
to Christ, God will put you in financial clover, multiply sexual plea
ure, and cancel every need of hospitalization. But the worldli
senses that something is wrong. Even those who seldom read th
Bible suspect that God shows His people not how much they ca
aggrandize but how self-sufficient He can be for them. Let us no
reinforce uncritical aspirations that make for dissolution of a privileged nation, but speak instead to the sluggish conscience of America.

Presidents of the United States emphasize the superiority over totalitarian societies of our democratic nation, whose charter political documents affirm that God by creation has endowed mankind with inalienable rights; dictators, therefore, are not the final stipulators of right and wrong. Yet our public schools often give the impression that creation is a myth and that belief in divine creation has no legitimate place in the classroom. Are not we then encouraging young people to reduce to myth as well our insistence on divinely-endowed human rights?

We need to use the media to confront not only the public conscience but also the media mentality itself. For many writers, producers, and commercial sponsors the Nielsen ratings determine what is good and right to program; in the last analysis money (profit) transcends the conflict between good and evil. Have evangelical circles no far-sighted business leaders who will sponsor a television panel of courageous evangelical social and moral critics to speak to the moral dilemmas of the nation. Are not men like Chuck Colson, or Senator Hatfield, or Senator Armstrong, or Richard Ostling of

ive it free pect what "the Bible says" and are com-
e of the al deviations of humanists and behavior-
ontation the masses the Ten Commandments, the
pursuit d God Who is the Good and the Source of

world cal colleges and seminaries produce a "sun-
t pred- n course on the biblical world-and-life view?
eality, om New York University be allowed to preempt
e roar amming? Could not a cooperative venture enlist
rough r twelve evangelical schools to handle such great
self- g God of the Bible, the incomparable Book, the
not n, the messianic promise, the death and resurrection
ded. al judgment of people and nations, and the inevitable
ng, s Kingdom? A series of 15-minute presentations pre-
s a inute panel discussion could easily involve some 40
ne olars who survey the biblical view with dignity and
s- power.

g ow we must relate the witness of the inerrant Bible to the
e which God has intended it. Our concern to attest to an
n Bible must lead beyond our Essene community into the cul-
nstream, there to confront our contemporaries with the right
ns until they reach for the supreme answer.

s we leave Chicago we are aware that evangelicals have much
mmon, but also that some areas of debate exist that call for
rstanding and resolution. Institutions will of necessity maintain
cial emphases; the ever present danger exists, however, that even
gitimate differences may be promotionally and financially exploited
ways that increasingly fracture the evangelical community.

Nobody thought this hermeneutics conference would overcome the theological differences that distinguish the covenant and dispensational camps, for instance; yet who can deny the bearing of these perspectives on hermeneutics? We have probed and pooled our commonality in support of an authentic biblical understanding against those who would nullify it. While some differences need still to be addressed, our powerful impact upon a secular society and upon a confused theological scene can gain its full force only if we enlist every recruit where he or she is best able to serve and encourage every scholar to capture and preserve the terrain that needs to be retaken and held. But even more, we need bold, comprehensive, and imaginative engagement at the many frontiers of national life. We need to ask not only ourselves but also to ask God, Who says, "You have not because you ask not," what we can do togeth cannot do alone. Let us take God at His Word.

Remember Jesus Christ, risen from the dead. The Word is not bound.

ppendix D

. that we

of God